THE PALESTINIAN ENTITY, 1959–1974

Published in cooperation with
The Harry S. Truman Research Institute
for the Advancement of Peace
The Hebrew University, Jerusalem

THE
PALESTINIAN ENTITY
1959–1974

Arab Politics
and the
P L O

Second (Revised) Edition

MOSHE SHEMESH
*Ben-Gurion University of
the Negev*

FRANK CASS
LONDON • PORTLAND, OR

Second edition published 1996 in Great Britain by
FRANK CASS & CO. LTD.
Newbury House, 900 Eastern Avenue,
London IG2 7HH, England

and in the United States of America by
FRANK CASS
c/o ISBS, 5804 N.E. Hassalo Street, Portland, Oregon 97213-3644

Copyright © 1988, 1996 Moshe Shemesh
First published 1988
Second edition 1996

British Library Cataloguing in Publication Data

Shemesh, Moshe
 The Palestinian entity, 1959–1974 : Arab politics and the
 PLO. – 2nd rev. ed.
 1. Munazzamat al-Tahrir al-Filastiniyah 2. Israel–Arab
 conflicts 3. Palestinian Arabs – Politics and government
 4. Lebanon – History – 1946–1975
 I. Title
 956.9'4'052

Library of Congress Cataloging-in-Publication Data

A catalog record for this book is available from the Library of Congress

ISBN 0 7146 4253 3

Printed and bound in Great Britain by
Redwood Books, Trowbridge, Wilts

To the memory of my father, Yosef

Contents

Preface

The issue of Palestinian representation cannot be separated from the question of the Palestinian Entity. The new Palestinian national awakening which began in the late 1950s and early 1960s was directly related to developments in the Arab and Palestinian arenas over the course of the Arab–Israel conflict. Research on the question of the Palestinian Entity without a thorough investigation of the Arab background, and the Arab position regarding the conflict, is like a tree without roots. Scholars on the subject, Palestinian and non-Palestinian alike, tend to view the situation from an ethnocentric perspective which presents the Palestinian position and achievements regarding representation of the Palestinians and the Palestinian Entity in specific relation to Palestinian national awakening. This, they suggest, actively imposed itself upon the Arab world and consequently brought about changes in both Arab and international positions. This study attempts to examine the Palestinian Entity in an integrated fashion, investigating the complex mutual influences of the developments in the Arab arena, the Arab–Israel conflict and the idea of the Palestinian Entity. In this context it specifically examines the commitment of the Arab world to the Palestinian national movement in relation to the movement's dependence on the Arab position and on continued Arab support.

The Arabic word "kiyan" in its political context, corresponds to the word "entity" in English. The word "kiyan" appears in Arabic with the meaning of "existence", "being", or "nature". In spoken Arabic it is used as "state" or "status".

The term "Palestinian Entity" is relatively new in Arab–Palestinian politics and in the vocabulary of the Arab–Israel conflict. The term was first discussed in Arab institutions and inter-Arab forums as early as 1959. This term has had unique political meanings relating to the Palestinian cause, namely: the political organization of the Palestinian people, independent Palestinian political status, or the establishment of representative institutions of the Palestinian people. The Arab states did not need the term "Entity" in the process of their independence; thus no such term as the "Egyptian entity", the "Syrian entity" etc. was used. Nevertheless, I have borrowed the term "Jordanian entity" when I discuss the struggle for existence between the "Palestinian Entity" and the "Jordanian entity" to emphasize the essence of this struggle.

The term "Palestinian personality" arises in the discussion on the "Palestinian Entity" in the sense of preserving the elements of the Palestinian identity. The Palestinian National Charter, which was promulgated by Ahmad al-Shuqayri and approved by the Jerusalem Palestinian Congress of 1964, and revised in 1968, elucidates the term: "The Palestinian personality is an innate, persistent characteristic that does not disappear, and it is transferred from father to sons. The Palestinians are the Arab citizens who were living permanently in Palestine until 1947 whether they were expelled from there or remained. Whoever was born to a Palestinian father after this date within Palestine or outside is a Palestinian." This definition even applied to Palestinians who left Palestine for Jordan or those residents of the West Bank who accordingly remained Palestinian even though they were granted Jordanian citizenship.

Thus the term "Palestinian personality" is encompassed in the term "Palestinian Entity" and constitutes an integral part of it. The emphasis on the "Palestinian personality" was mainly a reaction to the efforts to assimilate the Palestinians in Jordan and grant them Jordanian citizenship, and to the suggestions or plans to settle them in the Arab countries.

There has not been an accurate definition of the term "Palestinian Entity". Different components and interpretations were given to it by various Arab states and the Palestinians themselves, in accordance to their perceptions and political views, the political situation in the Arab arena and the developments in the Arab–Israel conflict. During the inter-Arab discussions on the subject a number of notions were raised such as: elected institutions e.g. national congress and elected executive, Palestinian republic, government-in-exile, and Palestinian state. The establishment of these institutions was viewed as the realization or the revival of the "Palestinian Entity". In the beginning, Jordan strongly and effectively rejected the idea and its implementation. Today the acceptable interpretation of the term is: the creation of a Palestinian state in the West Bank and the Gaza Strip as an ultimate aim or as the first stage towards the establishment of a Palestinian state on all the territory of Palestine.

The need for the terms "Palestinian Entity" or the "revival of the

Palestinian Entity" derived from the political, social and demographic conditions of the Palestinians in the wake of the Arab–Israel war of 1948. Following this war the name "Palestine" or "Filastin" disappeared from the political and the geographical maps of the region. The eastern part of Palestine, which was conquered by the Arab Legion, was formally annexed to Jordan in April 1950 and became the West Bank of the Hashemite Kingdom of Jordan. The inhabitants of the West Bank and the Palestinian refugees who arrived in the Kingdom became Jordanian citizens.

The other part of Palestine which was occupied by the Egyptians was not annexed to Egypt and was described as the Gaza Strip. It was administered by a military government first headed by a Military Governor and after that by an Administrative Governor, a senior officer who until 5 June 1967 was appointed by the Minister of War and later, by the President. The military administration of the Gaza Strip was subordinate to the Ministry of War. The Palestinian residents of the Gaza Strip were granted a special identity card indicating their Palestinian origin. The Palestinians who went to other countries, e.g. Kuwait, Iraq, and Saudi Arabia, were granted the status of Palestinian refugees.

On 22 September 1948 the Arab Higher Committee headed by the Mufti Hajj Amin al-Husayni announced the setting up of the Government of All-Filastin. It was sponsored by the Arab League and particularly by Egypt. Ahmad Hilmi Abd al-Baqi was appointed as its Prime Minister. This Government pronounced the territory of Palestine, which was under the British Mandate, an "independent state" and Jerusalem its capital. Gaza was to be its seat of government. The main purpose behind the establishment of the Government of All-Filastin was to foil King Abdulla's intention to annex a part of Palestine territory to his kingdom. Despite recognition by the Arab states, with the exception of Jordan, this Government remained only on paper. It had no Palestinian territory and population to rule, no army, no budget nor even an administration. The Government of All-Filastin disappeared from the Palestinian and Arab scene within a short period and its members found other posts in Arab countries including Jordan. The Arab states were incapable of preventing the *fait accompli* created by King Abdulla while most of the Palestinian population and territories were under his jurisdiction.

What remained of this episode was Ahmad Hilmi who continued to be the representative of "Filastin" in the Arab League until his death in September 1963. A similar fate was shared by the Arab

Higher Committee. Husayni's role was confined to sending telegrams and petitions to Arab leaders claiming in vain that "the Arab
Higher Committee is the legitimate representative of the Palestinian people".

Chapter 1 deals with two major issues. First, it analyses the
background to the emergence in 1959 of the problem of the Palestinian Entity and representation, and the inter-Arab debates which
led to the establishment of the PLO. Second, it considers the
onset of "the struggle for existence" between the Palestinian and
Jordanian entities in relation to the various positions held on this
issue in the Arab world.

Chapter 2 is concerned with the rise of Shuqayri who, in May
1964, established the PLO. It examines his controversial character
and equally controversial activities, and the reasons for his eventual
fall from power. It considers the status of the PLO and its struggle
with Jordan, which at this stage was restricted to the political
sphere. In parallel, it examines the emergence, in 1965, of the
fidai organizations and their consequent struggle with both the
Palestinian establishment for the soul of the Palestinians, and the
Arab world for a recognized status.

Chapter 3 takes as its starting point the events which ensued as a
consequence of the Six Day War, after which the Arab–Israel
conflict became the cathartic force in Arab nationalism. It initially
examines Nasir's "phased strategy" towards a possible solution to
the conflict. It deals with the issue of the Palestinian Resistance as a
main factor in the Arab and Palestinian arenas, and in the Arab
struggle against Israel. It also deals with the 1968–9 takeover of the
PLO by the fidai organizations and proceeds to review the struggle
between the Palestinian Resistance and Jordan, which developed in
1970 into civil war. In this context it examines the impact of the
struggle on the relationship between Jordan and the West Bank. It
studies the process on the West Bank of national awakening, the rise
and fall of the traditional leadership, and the emergence of a
"young" nationalist leadership which had become the dominant
factor in West Bank politics.

Chapter 4 is divided into two sections. A central feature of the first
is the stabilization in the rule of Sadat, Asad and Saddam Husayn,
and the emergence of King Husayn as a "new" ruler. The key
positions are examined. First, Sadat's and Asad's concepts of a
solution to the Arab–Israel conflict are explored. Second, the
position of the PLO is discussed with respect to their achievements
regarding Palestinian representation; their deep internal crises, in

the wake of the termination of their activities in Jordan; the meaning of Husayn's plan (15 March 1972) to establish a United Arab Kingdom; the results of the municipal elections in the West Bank (March 1972); and the overall Arab position on all these factors. The second section examines developments after the Yom Kippur War, focusing on the changes which occurred in Arab strategy towards the Arab–Israel conflict. It analyses the significance of the PLO's "phased political programme" of June 1974, and the resolutions of the Rabat Arab summit which recognize the PLO as the "sole and legitimate representative of the Palestinian people".

Moshe Shemesh

Preface to the Second Edition

The Oslo Agreement between Israel and the PLO (September 1993) inaugurated a new era in the history of the Palestinian national movement, which would lead in the long run to Palestinian self-determination and the establishment of a Palestinian state in the West Bank and Gaza Strip. Moreover, this agreement and its repercussions – the peace agreement between Jordan and Israel, in particular, and the opening of the Arab world to Israel – all justified the claim that the Palestinian issue has been the core of the Arab–Israel conflict. Since June 1967 this conflict has been the focus of Arab nationalism.

Thus one cannot comprehend the process which led to the Oslo Agreement without a thorough study of the developments which occurred during the period surveyed in this volume and its aftermath. An Epilogue has been added to the second edition which outlines and analyses the developments and processes pertaining to the Palestinian national movement during the period 1975–93. It confirms the premise behind this study – namely, the mutual influences of the developments in the Arab arena, the Arab–Israel conflict and the Palestinian national movement. It also confirms the assessment given in the conclusion to this study.

The Epilogue deals with the following major issues:

1. The impact Egypt's strategy had on the process of solving the Palestinian national issue and its paramount influence on the decision-making of the Fatah/PLO institutions. The Peace Accords between Egypt and Israel (March 1979) were an indispensable step and vital impetus towards achieving the Oslo Agreement. In fact, the Oslo Agreement complemented the Camp David Accords. Although it seems that, notwithstanding the Sadat initiative (November 1977), Arafat would have agreed to participate in the political process on condition that its aim was either the establishment of a Palestinian state or Palestinian national rule.

2. The role of Fatah as the "backbone" of the PLO institutions, which continued to lead the PLO towards a political solution to the

Palestinian problem, as in June 1974 when the PLO endorsed the "phased programme". Fatah led another change in PLO strategy when the 19th PNC (November 1988) approved the principle of two states in Palestine and recognised UN Security Council Resolution 242. A further milestone was Arafat's declaration in Geneva (14 December 1988), which paved the way for the US Administration's official dialogue with the PLO, and later for the PLO participation in the Madrid conference – the climax of which was the signing of the Oslo Agreement by the Fatah/PLO.

3. The remarkable survival of the PLO establishment during the severe crises of the period 1975–83, namely: the Lebanon Civil War, 1975–76; the Syrian invasion of Lebanon in 1976; Sadat's peace initiative (1977) and its repercussions; Israel's invasion of Lebanon in June 1982; and Arafat's expulsion from Damascus (June 1983) and from Tripoli (December 1983). Paradoxically, as happened after the crisis in Jordan in 1970–71, the PLO status as the sole legitimate representative of the Palestinian people strengthened in both the Arab and international arenas. The Palestinians' national consciousness and identity also heightened.

4. The development of the West Bank and the Gaza Strip (*al-dakhil* – the inside) as the basis of the Palestinian National Movement and of the political and armed struggle against Israel. Thus radicalization of political activities intensified and was accompanied by a deterioration in security. The Intifada was an inevitable result of the deep political and social change that had occurred in the territories since June 1967. The "inside" political leadership gradually gained prominence in the decision-making of the PLO establishment (*al-kharij* – the outside).

5. Jordan gradually ceased to play a key role in solving the Palestinian national and territorial issues. Little was left of Jordan's position in determining the future of the West Bank. The Intifada proved to King Husayn that his influence in West Bank politics was almost negligible. Jordan's legal and administrative disengagement from the West Bank, declared by Husayn on 31 July 1988, was the last vestige of official connection with it. The Oslo Agreement was reached by secret negotiations with the Fatah/PLO delegation.

Although it would be reasonable to describe the status of Arafat's leadership as weaker today than in 1974, he still retains power and authority in the eyes of the Palestinians as the symbol of the Palestinian revolution and the veteran leader of the Fatah/PLO and the Palestinian national movement. There is no alternative to his leadership of the Palestinian National Authority, nor a substitute for his dominating presence in the quest for attaining a permanent agreement with Israel. Arafat will be recorded in the history of the Palestinian national movement as the right person, in the right role, at the right time.

Moshe Shemesh
March 1995

Acknowledgements

This book has grown out of my Ph.D. thesis which was written at the London School of Economics and Political Science. I would first and foremost like to thank my supervisor there, Professor Elie Kedourie who, by exemplifying an academic standard of the very highest order, creates an atmosphere imposing high demands on the work of his students. I am grateful for the privilege of being exposed to this atmosphere. I am also indebted to my teacher, the late Professor Jacob L. Talmon of the Hebrew University of Jerusalem, who encouraged me to undertake this research.

My deep gratitude goes to the Iraqi Jews Educational Development Fund in Israel, and to Mr and Mrs David Litman of Geneva, for their financial assistance which I received while working on my thesis. I also wish to thank Mr and Mrs Sidney Corob of London, the Anglo-Jewish Association and the B'nai B'rith Leo Baeck (London) Lodge for their aid. I would also like to thank the staff of the Israel State Archives, Jerusalem, for their help and guidance.

I am very grateful to The Harry S. Truman Research Institute for the Advancement of Peace, of The Hebrew University, Jerusalem, for their invaluable assistance in turning my Ph.D. thesis into this final book form. In particular I appreciate the contribution of Norma Schneider, the Institute's Director of Publications. My thanks also to Sarah Lemann for her dedicated work in typing the manuscript. And I owe thanks to David Hornik who spent many hours offering suggestions and advice for improving the language and style of the book. Whatever faults remain are solely the responsibility of the author.

The Ben-Gurion Research Center, Sde Boqer, of the Ben-Gurion University of the Negev, gave me invaluable support and encouragement, for which I am most grateful.

My sincere thanks go to my family, particularly my mother Noga, for their constant encouragement. Last, but not least, I am deeply indebted to my wife Racheli for the abundant patience and encouragement she has shown, as well as for her devotion and assistance throughout my work.

M.S.

List of Abbreviations

AC	Area Commander
ADC	Arab Defence Council
AHC	Arab Higher Committee for Filastin
AL(C)	Arab League (Council)
ALF	Arab Liberation Front
ANM	Arab Nationalists Movement
AOLP	Active Organization for the Liberation of Palestine
APO	Arab Palestine Organization
ASU	Arab Socialist Union
BG	Brigade Group
CC	Central Committee
CCD	Central Command
C-in-C	Commander-in-Chief
C-o-S	Chief of Staff
DC	District Commander
EC	Executive Committee
EGI	Egyptian General Investigation
ERC	Extraordinary Regional Congress
FAR	Federation of Arab Republics
GI(D)	General Intelligence (Department)
GM	Government Meeting
GS(D)	General Security (Department)
GUPS	General Union of Palestinian Students
HAGC	Heads of Arab Governments Conference
IDF(S)	Israel Defence Forces (Spokesman)
IMG	Israeli Military Government
INA	Iraqi News Agency
IS	Intelligence Service
JA	Jordanian Arab Army
JCP-WB	Jordanian Communist Party - West Bank
JDC	Joint Defence Council
JNA	Jordanian News Agency
JP	Jerusalem Post
MC	Muslim Council
MENA	Middle East News Agency
MER	Middle East Record
NC	National Congress
NF	National Front
NG	National Gathering
NUC	National Unity Committee
OTC	Occupied Territory Command

PA	Palestinian Army
PASC	Palestine Armed Struggle Command
PC	Preparatory Committee
PCR	Planning Centre
PCUPA	Preparatory Committee for United Palestinian Action
PDFLP	Popular Democratic Front for the Liberation of Palestine
PEC	Palestine Experts Committee
PFLP	Popular Front for the Liberation of Palestine
PFLP-GC	Popular Front for the Liberation of Palestine - General Command
PGE	Palestinian Government-in-Exile
PIC	Public Interests Committee
PJN(L)F	Palestinian-Jordanian National (Liberation) Front
PLA	Palestine Liberation Army
PLF	Palestine (Palestinian) Liberation Front
PLFS	Popular Liberation Forces
PLO	Palestine Liberation Organization
PLO-GOR	PLO - Gaza Office Record
PNC	Palestine National Congress
PNF	Palestinian National Front
PNLF	Palestinian National Liberation Front
PNU	Palestinian National Union
POLP	Popular Organization for the Liberation of Palestine
PPC	Palestinian Popular Congress
PPO	Palestinian Popular Organization
PPRC	Palestinian Preparatory Conference
PPSF	Palestine Popular Struggle Front
PR	Palestinian Resistance
PRFLP	Popular Revolutionary Front for the Liberation of Palestine
PRF-WB	Popular Resistance Front - West Bank
RC	Regional Congress
RCC	Revolutionary Command Council
RCL	Revolutionary Council
SA JISM	Israel State Archives Jordanian Records, General Investigations, General Security and Military Intelligence Departments
SANA	Syrian Arab News Agency
SCAF	Supreme Council of the Armed Forces
SEC	Supreme Executive Committee
SG	Secretary General
UAC	United Arab Command
UAK	United Arab Kingdom
UAR	United Arab Republic
UC	United Command
UNF	United National Front
UPO	United Palestinian Organization
WAFA	Palestinian News Agency
WPR	Weekly Political Report

Glossary

Fatah: Literally "conquest"; the term Fatah is an acronym drawn from the initial letters in reverse order of the Arabic name: Harakat al-Tahrir (al-Watani) al-Filastini (Palestinian National Liberation Movement) H.T.F. This was intended to give a special meaning to the name of the organization.

Fidai (plural fidaiyyun): "Self sacrificer(s)"; the term has been used by the Palestinian guerilla organizations e.g. Fatah, PFLP, PDFLP, Sa'iqa and ALF, to describe in a positive way their guerilla actions against Israel. The guerilla fighters are accordingly called "fidaiyyun" and their activity "fidai" actions.

Filastin: The term "Filastin" is used throughout the book in preference to "Palestine" when relating to Arab, and in particular, Palestinian attitudes or when giving quotations from Arab sources. The term "Filastin" rather than "Palestine" embodies the historical and emotional dimensions and is used when analysing the Palestinian problem and entity.

Iqlimiyya: Regionalism or provincialism; it indicates loyalty towards a part, namely one Arab country, rather than the whole Arab nation. Close to its meaning is the term "qutriyya" (territorialism).

Jabha, Jabhawi. "Front", "front-related"; the term "jabhawi" is specially used by the Palestinian organizations in the PLO. It means equal representation of the organizations in the PLO institutions regardless of their size.

Jordanization: Process initiated by the Hashemite regime aimed at assimilating the Palestinians, whether on the East Bank, or on the West Bank annexed to Jordan in 1950, or who have immigrated to Jordan since 1948. For this purpose the Jordanian government on 16 February 1954 granted citizenship with full rights to all Palestinians residing in the Kingdom provided they had Palestinian citizenship prior to May 1948. Moreover, on 2 February 1960 the regime extended the right to obtain citizenship to every Palestinian who so wished. Jordan utilized this process in its struggle against the plan for a Palestinian entity claiming that "Jordan is Filastin and Filastin is Jordan". It also argued that in view of the fact that the majority of its citizens were Palestinians, Jordan was the sole representative of the Palestinians.

Khawarij or *Kharijites* (singular *khariji*): From the verb "kharaja" meaning "to go out", "those who went out" – also used to denote secessionists, dissenters, or rebels. The Khawarij movement (which emerged in 658) was the earliest religious sect of Islam.

Kiyan: Literally "existence", "being" or "nature", but in its political context means "entity"; thus "Palestinian Entity" relates to the political organization of the Palestinian people, independent Palestinian political status, or the establishment of representative political institutions (see preface).

al-Ma'raka: The campaign, or the war against Israel.

al-Muqawama al-Filastiniyya: "The Palestinian resistance"; the term refers to the armed struggle of the Palestinian fidai organizations against Israel. Hence, the term "Palestinian resistance movement" refers to the Palestinian fidai organizations themselves. It is sometimes used to distinguish between them and the political Palestinian establishment – the PLO.

Palestinianization: Process of highlighting and strengthening Palestinian identity and characteristics among the Palestinians and in particular those of the West Bank, whether under Jordanian rule, until June 1967, or under the Israeli Government. This process has been an integral element of the Palestinian national awakening since the 1960s. This is also expressed in the politicization of all spheres of the social and cultural life of the Palestinians.

Qawmi: National; relates to pan-Arab ethnic nationalism.

Qawmiyya: Nationalism; denotes adherence, loyalty or allegiance of Arab people or individuals to the overall Arab nation or homeland, which is commonly defined geographically "from the (Atlantic) ocean to the Gulf". Hence, "al-Qawmiyya al-Arabiyya" refers to pan-Arab nationalism or pan-Arabism. Arab nationalists who advocate pan-Arab nationalism give it priority over "wataniyya" or "iqlimiyya". They perceive Arab unity as the ideal political incarnation of "qawmiyya".

Tazkiya: The process whereby prospective candidates for Parliament or municipalities are automatically elected because the number of candidates does not exceed that of seats assigned to the constituency.

Watani: National; in the sense of patriotism confined to a specific Arab country.

Wataniyya: Patriotism, refers to adherence to the "watan" (fatherland) in the sense of loyalty to a specific Arab country and its people. This in contradiction to "qawmiyya".

CHAPTER ONE

The Problem of the Palestinian Entity, 1959-1963

The issue of the Palestinian Entity (*al-kiyan al-filastini*) was brought up for the first time by the United Arab Republic (UAR), at the 31st session of the Arab League Council (ALC) on 29 March 1959. Once presented with the problem, the ALC decided on a high-level Arab conference to deal with "the stages of development of the Palestinian problem" and "the reorganization of the Palestinian people, highlighting its entity as a unified people rather than mere refugees, whose voice would be heard in the inter-Arab arena (*al-majal al-qawmi*) and in the international arena, through representatives elected by the Palestinian people."[1] By bringing up the idea of a Palestinian Entity, Egypt hoped to facilitate the establishment of independent political institutions which would represent the Palestinians as a people. It was no coincidence that this issue was raised in an inter-Arab forum by Egypt and in a "decisive period in Middle Eastern history", when "Arab nationalism was marching from victory to victory".[2]

The debates, discussions and decisions on this issue took place against a background of conflicting political developments and processes in the Arab world. This period represented both the climax and the nadir of the realization of the Arab national dream – the establishment of the United Arab Republic (UAR) (February 1958), and its disintegration in September 1961, which produced a "union crisis" that precluded the re-realization of this dream for many years. The foregoing events exacerbated the existing conflict between the concept of pan-Arab nationalism (*qawmiyya*) and that of regionalism (*iqlimiyya*): they created a polarity between "the revolutionary nationalistic" stream led by Nasir and the "moderate" stream, which advocated a federal unity (*ittihad*) that preserved the "independence and sovereignty" of the Arab states, led by Abd al-Karim Qasim.

This period witnessed the most serious inter-Arab conflicts since the Arab League was established in 1945. One cannot describe the Arab world at this time as one engaged in "cold war",[3] as it encompassed armed conflict between the Arab states. Nasir was the undisputed leader of the Arab world, and the "Arab public outside the UAR, especially in the Arab Mashriq, was largely enthusiastic towards Nasir and the union which he symbolized, a state of affairs that did not change even after the disintegration of the UAR".[4] Nonetheless, Egypt's stable regime was facing a fermenting and unstable Arab world. And, despite Nasir's decisive leadership and influence in the Arab world, he failed to implement such policies as the realization of "Arab unity", the overthrow of the Qasim and Husayn regimes or of the regime that arose in Syria after the disintegration of the UAR. Moreover, the *coups d'état* in Iraq (February 1963) and Syria (March 1963) came as a surprise to the Egyptians. Nasir's failures in these areas led to changes in the way he implemented Egyptian policy. Following the Sinai War of 1956 Nasir based his policies towards the Arab world on the principle of "united ranks" (*wahdat al-saff*), but after the UAR disintegrated his slogan became "unity of aim" (*wahdat al-hadaf*); and, following his call for an Arab summit conference in December 1963, his new slogan was "unity of action" (*wahdat al-'amal*).[5]

The years 1959–1963 witnessed a deterioration in the Arab–Israel conflict, due mainly to Israel's beginning work on the diversion of the Jordan River and declaring her determination to continue this project.

In late 1959 the UAR leadership assessed that 1963 or 1964 would be a decisive year in the Arab–Israel conflict as Israel would be completing its project to divert the Jordan. Apparently the UAR believed that completion of this project would strengthen Israel, and thereby pose a threat to the future of the Palestinian issue.[6]

Exactly how to prevent this project became an inter-Arab dilemma, as some of the solutions envisaged might lead to a war with Israel. Further, the Jordan River problem led to inter-Arab rivalry, as each Arab state tried to prove to the Arab public that it had the most extreme attitude towards the struggle against Israel. In fact, it sometimes seemed that opposing Arab states were trying to harm each other more than Israel. It was this rivalry that led to more activity on behalf of the Palestinian Entity.

The Egyptian Initiative

The Palestinian issue, in its widest sense, was one of Nasir's central concerns. The 1948 defeat and subsequent lessons were a starting point in the determination of Nasir's strategy in regard to the Arab–Israel conflict. He considered the war against Zionism as the second goal of Arab nationalism, comparable in importance to "the war against imperialism".[7] The Egyptian initiative (at the end of March 1959), aimed at reviving the Palestinian Entity, marked a historical turning point in Egypt's efforts to solve the Palestinian issue.

There were several reasons why Egypt made this move at this time. The UAR and the Arab world were militarily incapable of imposing a solution for the Palestinian issue or of preventing Israel from diverting the Jordan River. Thus the UAR felt the need to take political steps, in lieu of military ones, which would demonstrate its resolve to the Arab world. Nasir believed that his plan for a Palestinian Entity would show the Arab world that "the Egyptian-Syrian union, being a power in itself, is the way to obtain the rights of the Palestinian people", although he recognized his own growing ineffectuality.[8]

The basic policy behind Nasir's strategy in 1959 was not to become involved in a war with Israel as long as Arab victory was not assured, for "under no circumstances would war be initiated against Israel until we have completed building our military force to decisive superiority". Nasir believed that he should decide on a time and place for the war, only when "we are in a state of full preparation".[9] Nasir openly claimed that he had no plan for "the liberation of Filastin". The massive military intervention in Yemen, which began early in October 1962, involving sixty to seventy thousand soldiers by 1964, retarded Egypt's planned expansion of military power, thereby reinforcing a basic Egyptian assessment that she was unprepared for war with Israel. Egypt even feared that in the case of such a war, the other Arab states "would abandon her totally and see it as an opportunity to stab her in the back".[10]

Nasir also believed that Israel, with Western aid, was trying to liquidate the Palestinian issue by proving that the Arab–Israel conflict was between Israel and the Arab states rather than between Israel and the Palestinians. Nasir openly admitted that "the aim of the establishment of a Palestinian Entity was to frustrate Israel's effort to eliminate both the Palestinian problem and the rights of the Palestinian people". He averred that "the Palestinian Entity must be preserved because the extermination of this entity would mean the elimination of the Palestinian problem forever".[11]

Two events aroused Egypt's fear of the "conspiracy to eliminate the Palestinian problem". The first was an Egyptian envisaging, in

February 1959, of a massive immigration to Israel of three million Jews from the Eastern bloc. This immigration would mean "a doubling of Israeli manpower, a strengthening of its military power and the reinforcement of Israel's motivation for territorial expansion". The UAR predicted that such a wave of immigration would render impossible the implementation of the UN resolutions regarding the return of the Palestinian refugees to their land.[12]

The second event was the June 1959 report of Dag Hammarskjöld, the secretary-general of the UN, to the General Assembly, in which he recommended the absorption of Palestinian refugees by the Middle East states.[13] President Kennedy's despatch of 11 May 1961 to the heads of the Arab states, in which he emphasized his country's readiness to help solve the Palestinian refugee problem, only added salt to the wound. For Nasir the total picture was of a Western plan for "the elimination of the Palestinian problem by liquidation of the Palestinian refugee problem".[14]

Therefore, Egypt aimed to establish representative Palestinian institutions which would prove the existence of a Palestinian element with national aspirations. This Palestinian factor would bestow legitimacy on the Arab struggle against Israel, by authenticating the Egyptian claim that the basic conflict was between Zionism and the Palestinian people. The plan for the revival of the Palestinian Entity was thus designed to turn the Palestinians into a separate factor in the Arab–Israel conflict.

Nasir's intensive activity for the establishment of representative Palestinian institutions and for the approval of his plan in inter-Arab forums, was also designed to win over Arab public opinion, especially that of the Palestinians. It was also an attempt to enlist the Palestinians for the undermining of the Qasim regime in Iraq, the Ba'th regime in Syria and particularly the Husayn regime in Jordan where there was a large Palestinian population. This struggle for "the soul of the Palestinians" intensified when Nasir had to defend himself against propaganda attacks by Arab opponents who accused him of mishandling the Palestinian issue. Nasir believed that his strength lay in his ability to express "the will of all Arabs" within his political strategy. Therefore, he felt obliged to fulfil the expectations and desires of the masses "who became hysterically enthusiastic when he talked of the Palestinian problem". He even tried to portray the Egyptian military involvement in Yemen as a "step in the process of getting rid of Zionism which would lead to the liberation of Filastin".[15] Nasir was nonetheless aware that the Palestinians reposed great hope in his slogan "unity is the road to

Filastin". The Palestinian intelligentsia were very active in the pan-Arab parties, the Ba'th and the Arab Nationalists Movement (ANM).[16]

With the disintegration of the UAR, Nasir took care to serve notice to the Arab world that Egypt was still "the only Arab state which possessed influential political, economic and military clout which does not exist in the other parts of the Arab world". Egypt preached to the Palestinians that "unity is still the road to Filastin and this is why the Palestinians have an important role to play in the realization of unity".[17] In other words, they were to continue to support Nasir and his policies.

The Egyptian Conception of the Palestinian Entity

No clear conception of the Palestinian Entity emerged from Egypt's initial proposals in March 1959. Spurred by constant confrontation with Jordan over the matter, and by discussions in Arab League forums, Egypt was gradually able to develop such a conception. Egypt, having no direct control over the Palestinian population in Jordan, tried to implement the plan based on the principles of the Palestinian Entity in the Gaza Strip.

The first principle was *the establishment of elected representative political institutions*. The Egyptian plan discussed the election of a National Assembly by the Palestinians of the UAR, Jordan and Lebanon. This Assembly would elect an Executive, or a Palestinian Government, which would represent the Palestinians in the Arab and international arenas. "Filastin", in its new organizational framework, would join the Arab League. Thus in mid-1960 the Egyptians proposed, though not officially, to "secure the right of the Palestinian people to self-determination and national sovereignty".[18]

The Gaza Strip served as a good experimental laboratory. The starting point of the Egyptian political blueprint was the constitutional status of the Strip as a region "situated under the control of the Egyptian forces in Filastin".[19] Egypt determined that "the Gaza Strip was an integral part of the Filastin land" and destined to be a part of the future Palestinian state. The Constitution which was given to the Strip in March 1962 was described as temporary, until "the promulgation of the permanent Constitution of the Palestinian state". It was the first "Palestinian" document which defined Palestinians' rights and duties as citizens of a state.

The UAR was the only Arab state in this period to grant Palestinians any sort of representative institutions. The bodies of the Palestinian National Union (PNU) were first established in the Gaza Strip in 1959 through nomination, followed by elections in January 1961. In the Syrian Region the bodies of this organization were elected in July 1960. Egypt went so far as to include in the temporary Constitution of the Gaza Strip an article, albeit of no practical significance, according to which "the Palestinians in the Gaza Strip constituted a National Union which included all the Palestinians wherever they live". The Legislative Council of the Gaza Strip was referred to by the Egyptian media as "the representative of the Palestinian people".[20]

Egypt arranged "Palestinian representation" in international and inter-Arab forums by sending delegations on behalf of the Palestinians of the Gaza Strip to the ALC (August 1960), to African and Afro-Asiatic conferences, and also, in 1961–1963, to the UN General Assembly. Steps were also taken through the media, including such programmes as Sawt al-Arab's "Filastin Corner", which began on 29 October 1960 and was later called "Broadcasts of the Voice of Filastin"; and in March 1962 the newspaper *Akhbar al-Yawm* began to issue the weekly *Akhbar Filastin*, which from March 1963 was edited and printed in the Gaza Strip.

The highlight of this activity was the emergence of the idea, in 1962, of a Palestine Liberation Front (PLF). In August of that year the Egyptians contacted Palestinians in Jordan and Lebanon and suggested convening a conference to found the PLF. Especially active in this direction was Kamal Rif'at, a member of the Egyptian Presidential Council who had served in Egyptian intelligence and in the fifties had played a leading role in activating fidaiyyun and sabotage groups in Arab countries and Israel. It was suggested that the PLF would be composed of three bodies, political, military and financial, and that it would serve as a framework for all the existing Palestinian organizations, including the trade unions. The political organization of the PLF would be based on a General Assembly.[21] Egypt gave up this effort mainly because of decisions taken by the ALC in September 1963, including the nomination of Ahmad al-Shuqayri as "the representative of Filastin" in the ALC.

Egypt saw *the establishment of a Palestinian army* (PA) as another important element in the independent Palestinian Entity. This army was meant to complement the political organizations of the Entity in a subordinate posture. Although the Egyptians called for the formation of the PA from the Palestinian populations in all Arab states, they did not see the establishment of such an army as militarily significant; reliance on this kind of army meant that "the solution of the [Palestinian] issue would take hundreds of years". Instead, Egypt saw the formation of the PA only as a symbol of the Palestinians' will to use force towards "the liberation of Filastin".[22]

In fact, the Egyptians refrained in this period from declaring compulsory military service in the Gaza Strip; they had not been satisfied with the performance of the fidaiyyun and National Guard units they had established there in the fifties. These units had shown a lack of discipline and of independent initiative; also, the Egyptians had feared their involvement in political riots against Egyptian rule in the Strip such as those which broke out in late 1958 and again in late 1961, partly as a result of Jordanian subversive activity. Instead, the Egyptians contented themselves in this period with exhibiting the Palestinian Brigade, which was formed in 1957 as a Palestinian army. The Palestinians in the Brigade, who were graduates of the Egyptian Military College, were called "the officers of the PA".[23] Generally located in Sinai outside of the Gaza Strip, the Brigade was composed of regular army volunteers and about 2,500–3,000 soldiers; its function was mainly to guard and its actual activity was very limited. It engaged in propaganda and trained units of the Popular Resistance (al-Muqawama al-Sha'biyya) which was established in February 1960. By the end of 1960, 2,500 "volunteers" of the Popular Resistance had been trained in several courses; additional groups were trained in 1961.[24]

Also crucial to Egypt's conception was *the denial of Jordan's right to represent the Palestinians*. Egypt had never recognized Jordan's annexation of the West Bank – nor, indeed, the right to exist of the Jordanian Kingdom, which Nasir saw as an "artificial creation", a product of British foreign policy after the First World War. Egypt believed that coexistence between itself and the Hashemite regime was impossible; the gap separating their political outlooks was too deep to bridge. Nasir referred to Husayn as a "fifth column obstructing the road towards liberation of Filastin". Thus Nasir consistently attempted, by any and all means, to undermine and overthrow Husayn's regime.[25]

Nasir maintained that the unity of the two Banks under the Husayn regime was not only illegal, but also contradicted the principles of the Palestinian Entity. Egypt was aware that "the establishment of a Palestinian state in the West Bank might mean a shrinking of the Hashemite Kingdom to a Trans-Jordan amirate or, in short, the end of Jordan".[26] If the choice was between the integrity of Jordan and the realization of the Palestinian Entity, Nasir clearly preferred the latter. His argument that Husayn was an obstacle to the establishment of a Palestinian Entity was essentially correct, and was further used to justify the subversive activities against him.[27] The contacts which went on between Palestinian activists from the Gaza Strip, representatives of the Egyptian embassy in Amman and local politicians in the West Bank were designed to draw the latter into political activity (often clandestine) for the sake of the independent Palestinian Entity.[28]

Egypt emphasized that the annexation of the West Bank of Jordan was an illegal act, and that the West Bank was in fact a deposit in Jordan's safekeeping, much as the Gaza Strip was a pledge in Egypt's hands meant to be returned to its inhabitants immediately after the realization of the Palestinian Entity. Hence the conclusion: "the annexation of the West Bank means the elimination of the Palestinian Entity". This view was also expressed in formal secret despatches to other Arab states, in which Egypt talked of the West Bank as "a part of Filastin which was conquered by the Jordanian army".[29]

What was Nasir's long-range goal in his policy towards Jordan? Most likely, it was not only the fall of the Jordanian regime and the establishment of a nationalist regime that followed Egyptian policy, but more specifically the establishment of a Palestinian state which would replace Jordanian rule, and which would have a population that was two-thirds Palestinian. The Jordanian regime, however, was determined to survive, and the realization of this aim was postponed. Following the Six Day War when Jordan's territory became confined to the East Bank, the Palestinian organizations gained prominence in Jordan and the proposition became feasible once again.

Qasim's Reaction

Qasim reacted rather late to Nasir's initiative and his activity on behalf of a Palestinian Entity. Only in mid-December 1959 did Qasim come out with the idea of an "immortal Palestinian Republic" (*khalida*).[30] His plan was clearer than Nasir's as far as ultimate objective and geographical framework were concerned, but was obscure and without practical content with regard to implementation. The plan developed at the same time that the conflict between himself and Nasir was worsening.

Qasim's plan was a natural conclusion of his political outlook that, first, *Iraq was an independent political entity*, "immortal" and possessing internal unity. This was an expression of Iraq's characteristic isolation in the Arab arena. Qasim saw Iraq as "the Arab homeland", the "source of Arabism" and "a backbone of support for the liberation movements in Arab countries". Iraq would adhere, in her policy in the Arab arena, to the principles of "freedom, independence and sovereignty". Every country, to his mind, "must liberate itself through its own people". He claimed that "Iraq was part of the Arab nation but would by no means become part of another".[31]

Second, he believed in *Arab solidarity rather than unity*. Qasim claimed that, like Iraq, every Arab state had its own political identity and must be recognized. Their existence and particular national character must be preserved. Inter-Arab relations must be based on Arab solidarity, which itself should be founded on equality, freedom, independence and non-interference in internal matters of the Arab states. This solidarity would facilitate co-operation between the Arab states in all central problems such as Filastin and Algeria. These principles were in severe opposition to Nasir's concept of unity; Qasim favoured a form of union closer to a federation, rather than the form of unity between Egypt and Syria. Under Qasim the Iraqi leadership even aspired to become "the only Arab country worthy of winning the crown of leadership in the Arab world".[32]

Qasim was also concerned with *the manner of solving the Arab–Israel conflict*, though here he did not have a clear and definite strategy. His attitude was characterized by over-impulsiveness and over-confidence. The isolation of Iraq, her remoteness from the border of Israel and the lack of a large Palestinian population all contributed to his position on the Arab–Israel conflict. In his opinion, the Palestinian issue could be solved only through war. As he explained to an Arab diplomat: "In regard to Filastin, I understand it better [than anyone] because I fought there and I know how to exterminate Israel rapidly. The Arabs must decide on war and we will be the spearhead.... I am capable of destroying Israel in five days." In contrast to Nasir, Qasim interpreted his experience in the 1948 war positively, emphasizing that "the Iraqi army was not weaker [than Israel's] in the Filastin war. It taught Israel a lesson and bested [her]." However, the Arab–Israel conflict remained marginal for him, an aspect of his struggle with Nasir in the Arab arena.[33]

In addition, Qasim believed the Palestinians should follow *the Algerian example*; he saw the Algerians' struggle against the French as an instance of "the liberation of a people by its own hand". He pointed to his military and financial support of the Algerians as a fulfilment of his promise to further the "liberation of the Arab peoples". Qasim saw the West Bank after the future rise of the Palestinian Republic as a territory from which operations could be staged against Israel, like the territory from whence the Algerians operated against the French. He emphasized many times that the Palestinians, like the Algerians, "must assume the heavy burden [of struggle] for their independence and assert their [very] existence". He viewed the declaration of Algerian Independence (February 1962) as a corroboration of his outlook concerning the "liberation of Filastin".[34]

Finally, Qasim's political conception reflected the severity of the split between himself and Nasir, who was determined to prevent the consolidation of Arab regional nationalism in Iraq. Nasir feared the influence of such a nationalism in the entire Arab world, especially in Syria. Thus, in her struggle with Iraq, Egypt attempted to undermine Qasim's regime through conspiracies and vicious propaganda by pro-Nasir political circles in Iraq. The timing of the presentation of Qasim's idea of a Palestinian Republic must be seen in this context.

Already in October–November 1958, after the short "honeymoon" period between the UAR and Iraq, the Egyptians began trying to undermine the Qasim regime. Before the Shawwaf uprising (March 1959), Qasim's security service succeeded three times in uncovering conspiracies against him. The failure of the Shawwaf uprising only spurred Egypt to further activity; it attempted to unite the pro-Nasir opposition groups, which included army officers, and smuggled weapons to them. Qasim continued to see "the covetous" (*al-tami'un*), as he called the Egyptians, as the main opponents of Iraq. The weakness of the Iraqi regime in the second half of 1959 encouraged the Egyptians to call for Qasim's assassination.[35] They gave aid to two underground groups, one oriented towards terror against individuals, the other which favoured a *coup d'état* through military and civil revolt. On 7 October 1959, an attempt to assassinate Qasim by the first group failed. This group belonged to the pro-Nasir branch of the Iraqi Ba'th under the leadership of Fuad al-Rikabi.[36]

The UAR's attempts to undermine the Qasim regime did not cease during 1960, although in the middle of that year Nasir began to improve relations with Qasim. But Qasim's speech of 25 June 1961, in which he announced "the return of Kuwait to the Iraqi homeland",[37] caused the UAR to renew its propaganda campaign and its attempts to undermine Qasim. The September 1961 revolution in Syria, however, changed the inter-Arab constellation and weakened Nasir's ability to operate in Iraq, since his attention was now concentrated on Syria and Jordan.

Qasim's political plan of action, once he decided in October–November 1959 to change his tactics from defence to attack against Nasir, consisted of two main elements: the plan of the Fertile Crescent, and the plan of the Palestinian Republic.

In November 1959, Qasim called for the implementation of the Fertile Crescent plan, even though he had previously referred to it as "imperialistic". It was clear to him that this plan was damaging to Husayn's regime, which in his opinion was still "shackled by imperialism".[38] But Qasim really submitted this plan in order to support Syrian opponents of the Syrian–Egyptian union, thereby compelling the UAR to defend itself instead of attacking him. Although, to all appearances, this plan contradicted Qasim's advocacy of preserving "the independent identity" of Arab states, he had little intention of implementing it, his purpose being mainly one of propaganda. With the disintegration of the UAR this plan was abandoned and was even denounced again as "imperialistic".[39]

The Immortal Palestinian Republic

In presenting his plan for a Palestinian Republic, Qasim was trying to prove that anything Nasir could do, he could do better. Indeed, despite similarities between Qasim's plan and the Egyptian tactic, Iraq emphasized the differences with regard to the political and the geographical framework;[40] as noted above, Qasim's plan was more concrete in this respect, and less so with respect to practical implementation. We shall now focus on Qasim's conception of the actual emergence and the nature of the future Palestinian Republic.

1. *The representative-institutional element.* Qasim's call for the establishment of a Palestinian Republic was the first to be heard from the head of an Arab state. He called this Republic "immortal" after the "immortal Iraqi Republic"; for him it expressed the idea of a Palestinian Entity. However, regarding the representative political institutions of this Republic, Qasim made two obscure statements. On 11 August 1960 he announced the approaching establishment of the "National Arab Committees [Hayat Arabiya Wataniya] consisting of the Palestinians in the Arab countries"; on 16 August he announced that the "High Arab National Organiza-

tion for the Liberation of Filastin, as well as the national branches
and local committees representing every town and village in Filastin,
have come into being today". There was no follow-up, and it is not
clear what Qasim intended by these "representative institutions". At
any rate, he steered clear of every inter-Arab debate on this issue and
contented himself with stipulating that (1) the Palestinian people
would organize itself alone, and establish policies which would
be carried out by Palestinian representatives; (2) because they must
carry the burden of "struggling for the liberation of their homeland"
and off their own bat secure their rights, the Palestinians would have
to rely on themselves, uniting to establish their Palestinian Republic;
and (3) Arab states would aid them and guarantee the "political
and territorial sovereignty of the proposed Palestinian state".[41]

2. *The territorial element.* Qasim was clear in his outlook that the
Palestinian Republic must be established on "all of the Palestinian
lands" in two stages: first, on the West Bank and the Gaza Strip; and
second, "on all the territory of Filastin following its liberation". The
Palestinian state would be "a separate regional unit" encompassing
"the territories that were usurped by three thieves: one of them
hostile to Arab nationalism, Zionism, and the other two from within
the Arab camp: Egypt and Jordan." "This state must include all
three parts of Filastin, the eastern part [the West Bank], the western
part [the Gaza Strip] and the central part [Israel]. That is to say, all
the territories [from the Mediterranean] to the Jordan River and the
Dead Sea." The Palestinian Republic would, at the beginning,
embrace "all the territories except those in the hands of Israel" and
afterwards include "the territories conquered by Israel, Jordan and
the UAR". Like Nasir, Qasim tried to base his theory on the claim
that Jordan's annexation of the West Bank was illegal. He often
emphasized that "Jordan stole part of Filastin and annexed it to her
own territory after the Iraqi army withdrew [in 1949]". Qasim even
indirectly hinted that the Iraqi army handed the West Bank over to
Jordan as a "deposit", and in fact referred to the Gaza Strip in the
same way as "stolen and plundered by Egypt and annexed to it by
coercion".[42]

3. *The establishment of a Palestinian army.* Qasim promised
repeatedly that to help establish their Republic, he would aid the
Palestinians "with weapons, money, equipment and manpower" as
he had the Algerians. As proof, Qasim pointed to the establishment
of the Palestinian Liberation Regiment (Fawj al-Tahrir al-Filastini)

as the core of the Palestinian army. On 26 March 1960, the Iraqi government decided on "the preparation of armed forces for the Palestinian Republic".[43] The law concerning the establishment of the Palestinian Liberation Army was published in the official Iraqi gazette only on 29 August 1960, although its validity dated from 15 April 1960. According to this law the Palestinian Liberation Army would be established on a volunteer basis, attached to the Defence Ministry and subordinate to the commander-in-chief of the armed forces; graduates of the officer training course would be commissioned as lieutenants.[44]

The first training course for Palestinian officers began on 15 April 1960 within the framework of the Military College for Reserve Officers. In the first four months following its formation almost three hundred soldiers joined the Palestinian Regiment in addition to fifty Palestinian officers, the majority of the latter from the Gaza Strip. With the completion of their training in the north of Iraq (Mosul) and their return to Baghdad in November 1960, the establishment of the Palestinian Liberation Regiment was declared. In November 1960, the second Palestinian Officers Training Course opened. Four classes of Palestinian officers managed to complete the Military College for Reserve Officers before the end of Qasim's regime. The number of Palestinians who qualified as officers before 1963 reached 150 although the Fawj quota was only 32. The commander of the Regiment (Col. Abd al-Razaq al-Shaykh) as well as the senior officers were Iraqi; the Palestinian officers were only juniors and generally served as deputies to the platoon commanders.[45] This "army" was not a significant force, its achievements mostly limited to parades.

4. *Qasim's attitude to Jordan.* Like Nasir, Qasim denied the legitimacy of the Hashemite Kingdom on the assumption that the "Lausanne Agreement recognized the independence of Palestine, which had been torn away from the Ottoman Empire". He added that "Husayn, member of the treacherous dynasty, annexed half of Filastin to his false crown", emphasizing that "the Palestinians who inhabited Jordan had not been asked for their opinion concerning this union". Thus Qasim was aware that the establishment of the Republic of Filastin meant the disintegration and division of the Jordanian Hashemite Kingdom.[46]

The question arises how Qasim imagined the realization of the Palestinian Republic without interfering in the internal affairs of Jordan. The leaders of Iraq, however, did not contemplate undermining the Jordanian regime as Nasir did. They believed that "according to the logic of history, the situation in Jordan would develop so that Jordan would eventually accept one of the forms of democracy". In this new situation, "the rapprochement of Iraq and Jordan would be so natural and logical that it would probably lead to a federation or some other similar connection between the two states". And yet, although a change in the Jordanian regime was a necessary step towards establishing a Palestinian state on the West Bank, a change brought about by the Egyptians would probably mean the rise of a pro-Nasir regime, and the encircling of Iraq by regimes of that kind. It seems that even if the Qasim regime was aware of this dilemma, it had no solution for it. Qasim rejected every possibility of Iraqi military intervention in Jordan in the event of a deterioration of relations between Jordan and the UAR.[47] In the last analysis, Qasim's attitude towards Jordan was identical to his attitude towards Syria during the union with Egypt, that is, an expectation of "its liberation".

Characteristic of Qasim's plan was the big gap between his claim that soon "the Palestinian flag will be hoisted over the land of Filastin" – or his declaration to a congress of Iraqi students "I see Filastin independent even before you complete your studies"[48] – and any practical steps he envisaged, which were highly unrealistic at that point. It took another fifteen years and two wars before the PLO and the Arab summit adopted Qasim's phased conception for the establishment of a Palestinian state on the West Bank and the Gaza Strip as a step towards solving the Palestinian issue.[49]

The Ba'th: Inactivity[50]

The Ba'th party, as opposed to the ANM, was the only pan-Arab political movement to achieve any real power. It was the main Syrian actor during the era of the UAR and the ruling party in Iraq and Syria in 1963. However, although it eventually advanced a plan for a Palestinian Entity, it failed to implement its political ideas in general or those concerning the Palestinian Entity in particular. This was because the Ba'th party concentrated, precisely at the height of its achievement, on internal problems.

The Dilemma of the Ba'th

After signing the Union Agreement, Syrian president Shukri al-Quwwatli had said to Nasir: "You took a people every one of whom believes that he is a politician, 50 percent of whom believe they are leaders, 25 percent believe they are prophets and at least 10 percent believe they are God."[51]

The Ba'th party basically faced a dilemma, which was in fact also Syria's dilemma, between the pan-Arab aspiration (*qawmiyya*) and the tendency to regionalism (*iqlimiyya*) of its branches (especially the Iraqi branch, and at a later stage even the Syrian branch which controlled the National Command). Ba'th party leaders who were in the UAR government in 1958–1959 took great pains in dealing with this dilemma, especially after they had realized the "unity" principle of their doctrine. This dilemma was the context of their resignation from the UAR government, and in the last analysis was also the main cause of the disintegration of the UAR in September 1961. Hence the solution of the dilemma lay precisely in strengthening the separatist-regionalist tendency at the expense of the pan-Arab principle. The dilemma also loomed large when the Ba'th party rose to power in Iraq (February 1963) and in Syria (March 1963). At that point the party had the potential to realize the principle of Arab unity, and, according to Michel Aflaq, to "pioneer a new and daring road to Arab revolution for unity, freedom and socialism".[52]

Yet "the Ba'th party was always prone to two weaknesses: rule and regionalism", both of which amounted to "a preference for rule over party interest through involvement in regional matters and disobedience to the National Command".[53] In 1960 some of the leaders of the Ba'th in Lebanon even claimed that "in fact there exist several Ba'th parties and not just one, which coordinate their activities together". Already in the first weeks of the Ba'th party's rise to power in Iraq and Syria, "the leadership of the Regional Commands revolted against the authority of the National Command". The result in Iraq was "the loss of the revolution in less than ten months". And in Syria, after the revolution in March 1963, "the spirit of separatism grew within the party. Party considerations and regional issues were greater than national issues. The party became the party of the regime instead of the regime belonging to the party."[54]

Thus, regarding the Palestinian issue, it is no surprise that in April 1965 an official document of the 8th National Congress (NC) of the Ba'th party complained that "the National Command was not only conspicuous for its absence in the arena of Palestinian activity" but even "neglected the Palestinian issue in an abominable manner". Moreover, "the party had not succeeded [then] in reaching the

Palestinian masses to a sufficient extent to explain its positions" on the subject.[55]

The Ba'th and the Issue of the Palestinian Entity

The decisions of the Ba'th party tended to be of a theoretical cast.[56] This was true of the 6th Ba'th NC (October 1963) and also of the party's decisions on the Palestinian Entity in this period. The party's involvement with this issue was marginal; its attitude towards it developed in two main stages.

In the first stage, which lasted till August 1960, the party's stance was on the one hand to avoid any definite attitude relating to a Palestinian Entity, and on the other hand to stress that a Palestinian Entity must be based on the pan-Arab ideological principles of the party. In other words, the Palestinians had to act within the framework of the party and not within the framework of a separate Entity. The party's announcement on 16 February 1960 was a determined stand regarding the diversion of the Jordan River by Israel.[57] The evasion of the issue of the Palestinian Entity was interesting, since during this period (or at least until the end of 1959) the leaders of the Ba'th had been active participants in the discussions of the UAR government; obviously they were all well acquainted with Nasir's policies in this field. During the Ba'th Lebanese Regional Congress in December 1959, objections were raised to the political report submitted to the Congress by the leadership of the branch of the party censuring "its failure to relate to the Palestinian problem". The Lebanese Regional Command was required, according to the resolutions of the Congress in the wake of this criticism, "to pay greater attention to the problem of the Palestinians because of their influence in Lebanon generally and on the party apparatus in particular". The Congress called upon the party's newspaper *al-Sahafa* "to take an interest in the problems of the Palestinians and in information about their conditions".[58] Similar criticism was also levelled by the Ba'th Iraqi Regional Congress of August 1960, which called for the compilation of documents by the Ba'th 4th NC to explain the party's stand on the Palestinian issue.[59]

The National Command's declaration of 15 May 1960 was a criticism of the plans for a Palestinian Entity proposed by Egypt and Iraq. It emphasized that any Ba'th party position concerning these plans would have to accord with the correct pan-Arab national (*qawmiyya*) outlook which saw the Palestinian issue as "a pan-Arab national (*qawmiyya*) problem and not merely a regional one". It added that "the Arab states must cooperate in a serious and loyal manner to create an image of the *Nazihin* who were to emerge as the pioneers of the campaign" against Israel. The Ba'th party held that "the problem of Filastin would not be solved in any way other than a revolutionary pan-Arab national (*qawmi*) struggle".[60]

The declaration of the Regional Lebanese Party in June 1959 was an exceptional and unique one. A reaction to the Hammarskjöld Report on the refugee problem, it emphasized that the answer to this report must be "the establishment of a Popular Liberation Army recruited from Palestinian youth". Nevertheless, the declaration claimed "that the solution of the Palestinian problem must be a comprehensive and revolutionary one". At that time, the call for the establishment of a Popular Liberation Army was not adopted by the National Command. It seems that it was designed to attract the sympathy of the Palestinians in Lebanon for the good of the party. The announcement called upon the Palestinians "to choose a new, loyal leadership that would concern itself with their problems and express their determination to solve the Palestinian problem in a revolutionary way through action for unity, freedom and socialism."[61] It is possible that this call was initiated or influenced by Palestinian members of the party who were active in the Lebanese branch. It is clear, however, that there was no intention of choosing a separate Palestinian leadership, but rather of adherence to the Ba'th leadership itself.

The second stage, which lasted till October 1963, began with a change in the Ba'th position on the Palestinian Entity that occurred at the 4th NC (August 1960). This was the first NC after the Ba'th party's exit from the UAR government, and it was held whilst the issue of the Palestinian Entity was assuming centrality in inter-Arab discussion and propaganda. The Ba'th National Command could no longer delay adopting a stand, in view of the anticipated conference of the Arab foreign ministers in January 1961; nor could the National Command ignore the criticism of its policy in this area.

Two basic documents defined the party's stand on the issue of a Palestinian Entity at this stage: the resolutions of the 4th National Congress, and the January 1961 memorandum of the Ba'th National Command "concerning the problems of Filastin and Algeria", which was despatched to the Arab Foreign Ministers Conference (31.1.61).[62] These two documents stated, first, that "the correct way to establish the Entity of the Palestinian people is by the establishment of a Popular National Front for the Liberation of Filastin like the Algerian Liberation Front". Such a Front must represent the Palestinian people in its entirety, and must also "unite all the revolutionary elements among the Palestinians including popular organizations and rely on strong trade unions of workers, professionals and intellectuals". The Ba'th party demanded that the Arab states permit the Palestinians to organize themselves freely in the framework of this Front, and said that it should be regarded as "directly responsible for all matters concerned with the Palestinian problem". In other words, the Arab states were to view the Front as the representative body of the Palestinians. (It was during this period that the Ba'th party began to use the term "Palestinian Political Entity".) Second, this Front must be "independent in its organization, its work and its struggle and must remain detached from struggles between the Arab states". And third, in the context of its struggle against the Egyptian, Iraqi and Jordanian regimes, the Ba'th party opposed "all initiatives from any Arab state or a number of Arab states to establish Palestinian organisms connected to them and constituting a tool for their propaganda and their Arab regional policy". According to the party, these initiatives were "dangerous and would relegate the problem of the Arab Palestinian people to side issues in favour of this or that leader or regime, causing divisions between the Palestinians".

After the August 1960 4th NC, the Iraqi Ba'th party opposed the Qasim plan for the establishment of a Palestinian Republic. The party stated (September 1960) that "the establishment of the Palestinian Republic is the aspiration of the Arabs everywhere", but "its establishment is closely connected to the Arab Liberation Movement"; "it would not be realized by the improvisatory method of Qasim". The establishment of this Republic would demand "enormous material means", as would "a new state that would be capable of confronting a state which is supported by imperialism and world Zionism". Likewise great preparation would be required "in order that the idea [of the establishment of this state] be accepted in the international arena". "This plan would not be realized except through a unified Arab plan."[63]

The contribution of the Ba'th party during this period towards promoting a Palestinian Entity was insignificant. Its alternative plan of late 1960 did not create any reaction in the Arab world as did the plans of Nasir or Qasim. It does not even seem to have made an impression on the Palestinians themselves. The plan was essentially attached to the Ba'th doctrine which itself did not stand the test of fulfilment. Still, it was a necessary stage towards a more concrete stand when the issue of establishing the Palestinian Entity's institutions became actual and practical during 1964.

Jordan's Reaction

Husayn was clearly aware of the meaning of the Egyptian and Iraqi plans concerning the integrality of his kingdom, two-thirds of whose population were Palestinians.[64] He had to choose between two poor alternatives: either to adapt himself to Nasir's policy and agree to the plan of the Palestinian Entity with all its representative elements – which would entail the creation of a threat to the stability of a diminished Jordanian Kingdom on the East Bank – or to object to the plan of the Palestinian Entity with all his strength as long as he was capable of doing so, even if it were to mean continued subversive efforts to overthrow his regime. Husayn chose the latter as the lesser of the two evils, believing that he would be able to neutralize the risks involved. His ability to overcome the crisis of April 1957 encouraged his belief that he could successfully manoeuvre in the internal and inter-Arab arenas. Thus Husayn consistently and stubbornly objected to the establishment of every type of Palestinian independent representative institution, which he viewed as a threat to the very existence of his regime. He had to contend with three factors in his internal and inter-Arab policy.

First, Husayn had to deal with *incessant Egyptian and Syrian subversive activities*. These were aimed at shattering Jordan's internal stability and ultimately overthrowing Husayn's regime; they were his main concern in the fifties and sixties. Information concerning the subversive efforts of Egyptian and Syrian intelligence (often in cooperation) constantly reached the Jordanian intelligence and security services during these years.[65]

Husayn's "counter-revolution" in April 1957 put an end to Egypt's attempts to obtain gradual control over Jordan. Thereafter the leaders of Egypt/UAR resorted to such unrestrained subversive activities as inciting military revolution or popular rebellion, accompanied by wild accusations against the regime. After these methods failed, the Egyptians tried to assassinate the Jordanian leaders, in particular Husayn. This mission was conducted by the Egyptian General Intelligence attached to the Presidential Office and by the Syrian Deuxième Bureau under the direction of Colonel Abd al-Hamid al-Sarraj, who was afterwards appointed Chairman of the Executive Council of the Syrian Region.

In the second half of 1957, Egypt and Syria began to infiltrate terrorists into Jordan from Syria and the Gaza Strip. Preparations were made for a popular armed rebellion and large quantities of weapons, ammunition and explosives were smuggled from Syria to opponents of the regime. Details of the plot became known to the Jordanian security authorities, and opposition leaders were placed under house arrest and other participants imprisoned. An attempted military *coup d'état* of 17–19 July 1958 was frustrated through prior arrest of the heads of the conspiracy after the security authorities learned of the plan. On 14 March 1959 another *coup d'état*, planned for the night of 15–16 March, was forestalled; a few days later Sadiq al-Shar', deputy commander-in-chief of the armed forces, was arrested following his return to Jordan. The security authorities had known of this conspiracy in its earliest stages. Details of the thwarting of the efforts to murder Prime Minister Hazza' al-Majali and to overthrow the regime were published in March and July 1959.

The activities against the Husayn regime reached their climax on 29 August 1960, when Syrian intelligence cooperated with Jordanian exiles and their supporters in Jordan in an attempt to do away with Hashemite rule. This plan achieved partial success when Majali was killed by a time-bomb that was concealed in his office; but the conspirators had hoped also to harm Husayn himself, who was supposed to be chairing a government meeting.[66] They resumed their attempts in different ways, including the smuggling of a bomb into his palace. An attempt was also made to bomb the broadcasting station.

The resulting crisis in Jordan–UAR relations was one of the most severe to have occurred between the two states. After the murder of Majali, Husayn decided, under the pressure of the Bedouins and of members of Majali's family, to invade Syria; the Jordanian rulers now believed this would lead to an uprising against the UAR leaders.[67] Husayn also hoped, of course, to liberate himself from the nightmare of the Syrian subversion. Under the guise of manoeuvres under the command of Major General Akash al-Zibin, commander of the Armoured Forces, armour, infantry and artillery forces were concentrated at Mafraq. "D-day" was to be around 11–12 September 1960. However, under pressure from Britain and the United States and from non-Bedouin officers who opposed the venture, Husayn renounced the plan.[68] The UAR continued trying to undermine the Jordanian regime in 1960–1961, but less vigorously than the regime had expected on the basis of its intelligence from Syria and Lebanon.

The *coup d'état* in Syria on 28 September 1961 freed Jordan from fearing that the UAR would continue to act against it from

Damascus; the chances of a *coup d'état* in Jordan lessened. Egypt did continue trying, in 1962, to smuggle terrorists, weapons and explosives into Jordan from the Gaza Strip and Lebanon; the Jordanians were even afraid of fidaiyyun parachuting into the Aqaba area or some desert region of Jordan.[69] On 27 July 1962, the Moroccan security authorities frustrated an attempt by men in the service of the Egyptians to murder King Husayn during his visit to Morocco. With the massive Egyptian involvement in the war in Yemen, which began in October 1962, the Egyptian pressure on Jordan subsided.

The *coups d'état* in Iraq (February 1963) and Syria (March 1963) were a serious blow to Jordan, who feared their influence on her own internal stability. Indeed, the signing of the Tripartite Federation Covenant (17 April) between Egypt, Syria and Iraq caused a serious internal crisis, with demonstrations by high-school students in the West Bank and a vote of no-confidence in the government by the House of Deputies on 20 April 1963. This vote was without precedent in Jordanian history and considerably worsened the situation in the country. Significantly, the events of April 1963 in Jordan were not manipulated by Nasirist agents from outside; they were an internal and spontaneous expression of the deepest feelings of the Palestinians in Jordan towards the regime.[70] However, the opposition groups' opinion was that these events had erupted prematurely and that the army's loyalty to the regime could not be doubted. Moreover, the leaders of Syria and Iraq concluded that any change in Jordan's existing situation which was liable to lead to Egyptian control over Jordan and even military involvement with Israel, would not be to their advantage. In the light of this assessment the two states asked Egypt to stop her campaign against Jordan (a similar demand came from the Western powers). Although the regime was able to overcome this crisis, the attempts to undermine it continued and the calls for the removal of Husayn did not cease until the end of 1963.[71]

All this led to the second major condition within which Jordan had to function, *the transformation of Jordan into a police state.* Husayn's regime was not dependent on public opinion but on the loyalty of the army and the efficiency of the internal and counter-intelligence and security mechanisms. The regime thereby succeeded in preserving itself despite the hostility of the overwhelming majority of the Palestinians, whose sympathies were with Nasir and his policies. Indeed, the files of the Jordanian security and intelligence services list so many Jordanian secret agents that it seems as if almost every tenth person must have been employed in this capacity; even the mukhtars of the villages became informers. Up-to-date lists of fidaiyyun and agents who were trained by Syrian and Egyptian agents with the aim of penetrating Jordan, in which the names of members of the ANM were conspicuous, were distributed to all police stations in Jordan.[72] Still, this system was not completely hermetic as the Syrian intelligence did succeed in murdering Majali.

As a result of the information flooding the intelligence and security apparatus, the regime formed an exaggerated picture of the subversive activities, which were in fact far fewer than estimated. There was a policy of minute scrutiny of the prominent people of the West Bank, in particular those suspected of activity against the regime. Among these suspects were Hikmat al-Masri, Walid al-Shak'a, Ma'zuz al-Masri, Salah al-Anabtawi and Akram Zu'aytar. The regime applied severe censorship to postal communications and telephone conversations of political activists and sometimes even to the conversations of senior West Bank politicians. Publications damaging to the regime were confiscated before they reached their destination.[73]

Egyptian activities in Jordan escalated: the regime succeeded in destroying the majority of the opposition centres such as parties and trade unions, and also in purging unreliable officers. No strong opposition arose in Jordan after the elimination of these elements. Thus the regime was encouraged to oppose the Palestinian Entity proposal and the plans of Ahmad al-Shuqayri in the first half of the sixties, and, later, to take a strong stand against the Palestinian organizations in the late sixties.

The third factor was *Jordan's efforts to break out of her isolation*. In Husayn's struggle to maintain his position regarding the Palestinian Entity and to overcome the internal and inter-Arab pressure, it was imperative that he free himself from the state of isolation imposed on him by the UAR/Egypt and Iraq. He tried to persuade the Arab world that his opposition to the Palestinian Entity did not mean he was abandoning the Palestinian issue. Husayn's efforts to convince Nasir of the nationalist character of his regime without changing his internal and foreign policy were generally unsuccessful. It was clear to him that a reconciliation with Nasir also meant a dangerous granting of freedom of expression to Nasir sympathizers; therefore his approaches to him were basically disingenuous. Nasir understood this; as he said to a Lebanese diplomat: "Husayn advances one step forward but then quickly withdraws."[74]

Husayn's efforts to break out of his isolation were mainly in three areas. First, there were his efforts to convene an Arab summit, made unceasingly in 1959–1961 with the aim of discussing the Palestinian issue and inter-Arab relations. Husayn thought that if he succeeded in pressuring Nasir into participating in such a summit (and he knew that without Nasir's agreement there was no chance of convening one), this would pull Jordan out of its isolation and constitute a kind of approval by Nasir of Jordan's internal and foreign policy. In particular, it would oblige Nasir to cease undermining the Jordanian regime and alleviate the pressure on Husayn to change his position regarding the Palestinian Entity. To this end Jordan utilized the "Israeli card", emphasizing Israel's diversion of the Jordan River, increasing military strength and possible production of atomic weapons. Nasir, who understood the motivation behind these proposals, rejected them.[75]

Second, Jordan adopted an extreme stand against Israel, expressed during a series of inter-Arab conferences which discussed the Palestinian issue especially during 1961 (meetings of the Arab chiefs-of-staff, 20–22 April 1961, the Palestine Experts Committee, June 1961, the Joint Arab Defence Council, 10–18 June 1961), and compared to which Egypt's attitude was moderate. Jordan proposed a common Arab military plan to forcibly prevent Israel's diversion of the Jordan River; as well as provocative steps by Arab forces to make Israel change from a "defence" to an "attack" posture which the world would interpret as Israeli aggression. For this purpose Jordan offered to perpetrate artillery harassment as well as fidaiyyun activities by Palestinians. Simultaneously, Jordan demanded military aid, both weapons and money, to fortify her own border with Israel. The Egyptians rejected this proposal because it was clear to them that its outcome would be war with Israel. In contrast to this, the Egyptian proposals of a technical plan to divert the tributaries of the Jordan River and the establishment of a Joint Arab Military Command were accepted. Ultimately, Jordan reaped no benefits from this extremist policy.

Finally, Jordan made a direct initiative for reconciliation with Nasir. Husayn sent him two letters on 23 February and 2 April 1961; Nasir replied on 13 March and 7 May, respectively. Husayn's first letter was "a special surprise" for Nasir. This exchange of letters was designed to win over internal public opinion in Jordan so that the government could stand up to Arab pressure and the UAR would cease its subversive activities. This initiative also sprang from Western pressure which tried to convince Husayn that the best guarantee of his security lay in a reconciliation with Nasir.[76] Nasir, however, rejected Husayn's overtures. Sympathy demonstrations for Nasir broke out on 31 March and on 1 April 1961, an indication of his standing with the Palestinian population.[77] Apparently Husayn had no illusions about Nasir's reactions to his letters, but did gain breathing space for some months, during which he announced his engagement to an Englishwoman.

Jordan's Counter-Plan

Husayn believed that the aim of the Egyptian and Iraqi plans was "some kind of representation of the Palestinian people".[78] Therefore it was his task to persuade them that Jordan, in fact, was the sole representative of the Palestinians and also to justify its strong objection to the plan of the Palestinian Entity. Since the plan for a Palestinian Entity was part of a general plan for the solution of the Palestinian issue, Jordan needed to present a counter-plan that would be based on her own representation of the Palestinians and that would preserve the integrity of the Hashemite Kingdom. Thus Jordan presented several arguments against the plan of the Palestinian Entity.

The first was that Jordan was in actuality the representative of the Palestinians: "The Jordanian government is the sole legal representative of the Palestinians inhabiting Jordan, who possess the right to decide by legal means everything connected to their rights in Filastin", claimed Majali, the prime minister. Husayn claimed that "the Jordanian units of the National Guard constitute the Palestinian army. The armed forces located on the cease-fire line constitute the Palestinian army." As proof that the Jordanian government represented the Palestinians, Majali pointed to "the full participation of the Palestinian Arabs in the government of Jordan, in the legislative, executive and judiciary authorities and in all the political apparatus including the army. The great majority of Palestinians are Jordanian citizens. We are Filastin and its fate is ours." The Jordanian government pointed out that since "it speaks on behalf of Jordan's citizens and represents the overwhelming majority of the Arabs of Filastin, it could not, both for legal and institutional reasons, recognize the right of any body which would speak on their behalf or would want to represent any part of its inhabitants."[79]

Jordan's second argument was that the two Banks were united. Jordan's rulers claimed that the annexation of the West Bank to Jordan was a result of the free will of the inhabitants of the West

Bank to unite with Jordan "under one crown". Therefore "Jordan in its two Banks constitutes one unit". "Every plan for the solution of the Palestinian problem must recognize first of all the present status of Jordan and the legal and constitutional unity existing between the two Banks." In order to prove these claims and the claim that the West Bank Palestinians would not agree to any change in their situation by the establishment of a separate entity, Husayn proposed a referendum among the Palestinians in Jordan under Arab League auspices to determine their stand on this issue. He even expressed readiness to "bind himself" to any result of this referendum.[80]

Finally, Jordan maintained that the solution of the Palestinian problem must be comprehensive and not separate. Thus the problem of the Palestinian Entity could be discussed only in the framework of a comprehensive Arab plan. Contradicting Nasir, Jordan maintained that the Arab–Israel conflict "is not a struggle between the Palestinian people and Zionism, but a struggle between the Arab world and Zionism. Consequently, the responsibility for finding a solution to this struggle is imposed on all Arabs." Hence "every Arab state is forbidden to take any partial or independent step towards the solution of the Palestinian problem. The realization of the Palestinian Entity is nothing but a partial and insufficient step towards solving the Palestinian problem." Jordan understood that a comprehensive solution would mean its active participation in the inter-Arab planning, and the recognition of its status as representative of the Palestinians in its country. On the other hand, enlisting the Palestinians as a separate element in the Arab–Israel conflict would lead to establishing separate representative institutions for them. Thus Jordan vigorously opposed the plans of Nasir and Qasim to give "responsibility" to the Palestinians. "The conscription of the Palestinians must be done within the framework of total Arab mobilization for Filastin", because the problem would not be solved "by the distribution of rifles to some hundreds of Palestinians". Jordan suggested that solving the problem of the Palestinian Entity be postponed to a much later date, so that "the Palestinians would determine their political future only *after* Filastin was liberated".[81]

Realizing that these arguments were not enough, the Jordanian rulers presented plans for a comprehensive solution to the Palestinian issue in which they stressed the Palestinian character of Jordan. At the beginning of 1960 Jordan unofficially proposed to rename it the Palestinian Jordanian Hashemite Kingdom. Thus it would be recognized as the representative of the Palestinian people, and a Palestinian army would be established that would be attached to those Arab states containing a Palestinian population. However, the UAR rejected this plan and therefore Jordan did not dare to present it formally in inter-Arab forums.[82] The UAR even feared that the West, standing behind Jordan, might submit a plan to solve the Palestinian issue by establishing a Palestinian state in the West Bank that would be linked federally to Jordan.[83]

With the disintegration of the UAR and Jordan's improved situation in the Arab arena, it submitted another comprehensive solution for the Palestinian issue. Emphasis was again laid on the Palestinian character of the Jordanian Kingdom. According to this plan Jordan would become a base for initiating the "liberation of Filastin". Behind the plan stood the PM Wasfi al-Tall, who officially presented it to journalists as a White Book on 2 July 1962.[84] The basic idea was to transform Jordan into a centre of military power that would serve as an Arab security-belt-base surrounding Israel. It was claimed that "Jordan is the logical territory" to play this role because of its human reservoir, as well as military, geographical and psychological factors. Jordan emphasized that there were a million Palestinians "who are citizens of Jordan and who constitute two-thirds of her population". Moreover, Jordan controlled the longest border with Israel (650 kilometres) and "the West Bank constitutes the largest territory of the lands of Filastin". Finally, Jordan, with its accessible manpower and with the aid of Arab states, "is capable within a short period of becoming the centre of power within a complete defensive framework". The plan called for a united political, military, organizational and propaganda effort of all the Arab states in which the Palestinian issue would transcend all Arab differences of opinion. The plan also called for political, financial and military aid to Arab states in which there were refugees, particularly Jordan.

Jordan tried to gain a general Palestinian consensus for the plan, inviting prominent Palestinians to Jordan for consultation and holding talks with West Bank politicians. Shuqayri, invited to Jordan on 23 April 1962, was permitted to visit several places in the West Bank, mainly the Nablus area; but his contacts with local politicians were limited and his movements and discussions closely monitored. He generally won the sympathy of the inhabitants, and touched off debates among the local leaders about the Palestinian Entity and "the need to allow the Palestinians to decide on their fate following the example of the Algerians".[85] At the same time a delegation of the Arab Higher Committee for Filastin was summoned to Jordan despite the hostile relations between the two sides. Obviously, the reactions of Egypt and Iraq to the Jordanian plan were negative; it was labelled "the plan for the elimination of the Palestinian problem". One Iraqi newspaper even claimed that following this plan, "there is one likely possibility: the Jordanian Kingdom will turn into the Palestinian Kingdom to enable Husayn to demand the annexation of the Gaza Strip as part of [that] kingdom."[86] Nevertheless the regime persevered in this course for almost a year.

Throughout its struggle against the plans for a Palestinian Entity in 1959–1963, Jordan tried to prove that its policy was supported by the Palestinian population in its country. It organized the sending of telegrams expressing support, had members of the House of Deputies and the Senate pass decisions supporting Husayn's policy and denouncing Nasir's and Qasim's, and had letters sent to the Arab League conferences by West Bank politicians. Husayn toured the West Bank in order to enlist "spontaneous" support there. Although intelligence and political reports from the West Bank attributed such support to the populace,[87] it is also possible to discern in these reports a general feeling against the regime's stand and in favour of a separate Palestinian Entity and of Nasir's policy on this issue. This is no surprise in light of the open expressions of sympathy for Nasir which were made in March 1961 and April 1963. And in a meeting of West Bank politicians in Nablus, Hikmat al-Masri argued that the UAR was an essential partner to any discussion of the issue of the Palestinian Entity. A Jordanian intelligence report even emphasized that "most of the inhabitants in Jerusalem favoured the UAR", and that "seventy percent of the inhabitants of the West Bank support the idea of the Entity, in contrast to the expressions of support for the king and his policy". Another intelligence document reported that the issue of the Palestinian Entity "again aroused among the West Bank inhabitants the subject of discrimination against refugees as compared with the inhabitants of the East Bank"; the claim was made that "the establishment of a Palestinian Republic will safeguard our honour and rights in view of the still existing discrimination between the Jordanian and the Palestinian, in the field of jobs, in the army, in food distribution, in the Civil Service and in the distribution of business licences."[88]

This support for a Palestinian Entity remained basically passive and did not give rise to any real attempt towards organizing any kind of independent Palestinian representative institutions; there were only small-scale underground activities organized from outside Jordan. However, the support was an indispensable foundation for larger Palestinian organized activities in the future.

The Arab Higher Committee for Filastin

The Arab Higher Committee for Filastin (AHC), headed by the Mufti, Hajj Amin al-Husayni, demanded for itself the right to be the "legitimate representative of the Arab Palestinian people" and to speak on its behalf. As such, the AHC on 6 February 1958 asked for "the joining of Filastin, within its natural borders and as being the southern part of Syria, to the Union between Egypt and Syria".[89] It was apparent that the moment Egypt took a step towards new Palestinian representative institutions, it would strive to eliminate this anachronistic body. Egypt was right in assuming that the elimination of the moral influence of the Mufti meant the final burial of the AHC. And it indeed pursued this course relentlessly by means of Mamduh Rida, the political correspondent of the *Ruz al-Yusuf* weekly newspaper. Rida, who was probably instructed by Egyptian intelligence, launched in July 1959 an unbridled campaign of slander to destroy the past and public image of the Mufti. The aim was to remove him from the Palestinian political stage in general and Cairo in particular, so that he would not be identified with the Egyptian policy. The newspaper ended its campaign only after the Mufti settled in Lebanon, having left Cairo in mid-August 1959.[90]

Yet the Mufti refused to leave the political stage. Overestimating his influence on the Palestinians, he continued to fight for his position by seeking support among Palestinians in Lebanon, Kuwait and to some extent Jordan, which, along with his connections with Qasim, resulted in the prolongation of the campaign against him by the Egyptian press and the pro-Egyptian press in Lebanon.[91] But he did not gain any significant support from the Palestinian public, who absorbed the message of the *Ruz al-Yusuf* articles; and most of the Mufti's old supporters in Jordan either switched their allegiance to Husayn or ended their political activities.[92]

Thus the Mufti had only Qasim left, and Qasim used him as a tool for advancing his plans in the Palestinian Entity issue and for waging his struggle against Nasir. Qasim gave the Mufti financial aid to carry out propaganda including the AHC organ *Filastin*, and to conduct open and secret political activities among Palestinians mainly in Jordan and Lebanon. The Mufti also received aid from King Saud. Qasim's removal in February 1963 led to the closing of the AHC office in Iraq (opened in August 1961) and eventually to the termination of financial aid.[93]

Between Husayn and the Mufti lay a deep historical hostility. The remaining AHC activists and sympathizers in Jordan were under constant and thorough scrutiny. Propaganda material which was distributed by the AHC, especially *Filastin*, was banned by the security services. Jordan maintained that the Mufti's claim to represent the Palestinians was false and that "there no longer exists an AHC which could represent the Palestinian Arabs".[94] None of this prevented Jordan from initiating contact with the AHC when it was convenient for its struggle within the Arab arena; in March 1961, August 1962 and September 1963 there were visits by AHC delegations in Jordan. But none of these meetings was fruitful because of basic conflicts over Palestinian representation.

Still, the AHC made desperate efforts to promote its representation of the Palestinians, incessantly publishing declarations and sending letters to the Arab League and to the Arab governments. It used the Lebanese daily *al-Hayat*, which also enjoyed Saudi financial aid, as an AHC "organ" in which declarations were published almost every two or three days.[95]

The AHC had previously been able to claim representation of the Palestinians only at the UN General Assembly, to which it also sent delegations in 1960–1962. But this representation was snatched from the AHC with the election by the Arab League Council in September 1963 of Shuqayri as the head of the Palestinian delegation to the Assembly.

The Mufti had to join the bandwagon of the Palestinian Entity in order to foreclose any pretext of attack upon himself by the various opposing sides. He drafted his own plan for an Entity, derived from those of Egypt, Iraq and Jordan. Finalized in 1963, the plan determined *inter alia* that: (1) the right of self-determination of the Palestinian people should be realized after the liberation of Filastin, when its political destiny and the form of its regime would be established by a referendum; (2) the Palestinian Entity would be established by the formation of an organization which would represent the Palestinian people and which would be elected in general and free elections; and (3) the Entity was not intended to prejudice the *status quo* in the Gaza Strip and the West Bank; its objective was to be "the liberation of Filastin from Zionism and Imperialism".[96]

The Mufti's efforts to gain influence in the Arab and especially the Palestinian arena failed; in the end he was left with only Saudi assistance, and his final elimination was but a matter of time. The Egyptians put their trust in another Palestinian personality, Ahmad al-Shuqayri, whom they had raised to the Arab political stage despite his rejection by Saud. The Arab League's decisions of September 1963, followed by those of the first Arab summit, finally closed the Mufti's chapter in the history of the Palestinian movement, even if the process of fading away was to continue a little longer.

Prolonged Standstill in the Arab League Forums

For the most part, the Arab League proved an ineffectual means of resolving disputes and achieving consensus. It reflected the constellation of inter-Arab relations, but first and foremost Egypt's "revolutionary approach" to the implementation of foreign policy.[97] No Arab state negated the existence of the Arab League, but they all recognized its limitations and did not feel that they incurred any damage by boycotting its sessions. Nasir remarked that "a greater burden should not be put on the League than it is capable of carrying". That is, it was only a tool for furthering inter-Arab cooperation in economic, cultural and technical fields. He claimed that the League was a "framework which is designed for agreeing on what it is possible to agree on".[98] Still, Egypt tried to exploit this "tool" to realize its policy in regard to the Palestinian Entity. Iraq and Jordan objected to Egypt's predominance in the League and called for an equal status for all Arab states.

The Arab League Council's debate on the Palestinian Entity saw antagonism and polarization between Egypt (and Iraq) and Jordan. The UAR/Egypt pressed for operative decisions; yet Jordan obstructed a unanimous decision which would have committed all the Arab states in accordance with the Arab League Charter (Article 7). Jordan's main objective was to postpone any statements of principle on the Palestinian Entity, hoping that in time the circumstances in the Arab arena would change in its favour.

The balance of inter-Arab relations at this point did not permit a senior-level inter-Arab conference on the Palestinian issue. In September 1959, the ALC convened at the foreign-minister level with the Palestinian Entity on the agenda. Proposals on this subject were advanced by Saudi Arabia with the support of Egypt; but Egypt, because of Jordan's opposition and her own reluctance to provoke a crisis with Jordan which would ease Iraq's isolation in the Arab arena, agreed to postpone the debate on this issue till the next ALC session.

The February 1960 session, from which Iraq was absent, took place against the background of escalating Egyptian struggle against Israel, which since 1956 had reached considerable proportions. Egypt was seeking progress on the Palestinian Entity, and won Saudi Arabia's support. Majali remarked that "even the Jordanian government was amazed at the stubborn attitude" with which Egypt pressed its case.[99] Indeed, the UAR succeeded in isolating Jordan on this issue; the Jordanian foreign minister, the Palestinian Musa Nasir, had to oppose every formulation which could be interpreted as furthering the cause of the Entity. Nevertheless, operative decisions were not passed; instead, the ALC decided on "general principles" on the Palestinian Entity. The first principle determined that "it is the right of the Palestinian people to restore its homeland and decide on its self-determination";[100] the term "Palestinian Entity" was avoided.

The 33rd session of the ALC at Shtura in Lebanon, 22–28 August 1960, coincided with worsening relations between the UAR and Jordan as Nasir played the Palestinian card to maintain his leadership in the Arab arena. The participation of Iraq intensified Jordan's isolation. This time the UAR enlisted various Palestinian groups to exert pressure towards an operative resolution on the Palestinian Entity. Jordan understood that extreme opposition would only further its isolation; thus it tried to focus the discussion on its conflict with the UAR. But Jordan did not succeed; resolutions were passed on the Palestinian Entity which seemed to reconcile the stands of Egypt and Jordan. On the one hand, the Egyptian recommendations that had been accepted in March 1959 were re-endorsed, but now became operative decisions favouring "the reorganization of the Palestinian people and highlighting its entity as a unified people" and "the establishment of a Palestinian army in the Arab host countries". How all this was to be done was not determined. A new term was added to the articles of this declaration: "the preservation of the Palestinian personality", meaning the rejection of plans for the settlement of the Palestinians and/or granting them citizenship in Arab states, mainly Jordan. On the other hand, it was determined that "the Arab Palestinian people … would act to restore its homeland through the aid and participation of Arab states and peoples". The resolution urged the general secretary of the Arab League to establish a committee of experts, whose aim would be to "formulate a comprehensive plan for the restoration of Filastin".[101] These last two articles suited the basic Jordanian stand and indeed Jordan considered them an achievement.[102] However, this assessment was erroneous as the decision left ample room for pressuring Jordan, and at a later stage led to a more concrete decision.

The Arab Foreign Ministers Conference in Baghdad in January 1961, in which Iraq and Tunisia participated, occurred in the context of a reconciliation between the UAR and Iraq initiated by the former. The UAR expressed a willingness to compromise on certain points, including the Palestinian Entity; so that this conference did not take steps towards establishing the Entity. The Palestine Experts Committee met in June 1961 in the wake of deliberate obstruction by Jordan, but its recommendations, never discussed in the ALC, were anachronistic and peculiar; such a one was that "the Government of All-Filastin would represent Filastin in the Arab League" and "would represent the national aspirations of the Palestinian Arab people in all arenas including the international one". Jordan severely opposed this recommendation, which contradicted the principle of her "sole representation of Filastin", and stated that "the decisions of this committee were not binding".[103] Shuqayri, an "expert" present at that meeting, proposed two plans for the Palestinian Entity based on Egypt's March 1959 proposals. One plan, dealing with Palestinian representative institutions, envisaged a Palestinian National Council with 150 representatives that would convene once a year in Jerusalem, as well as military and financial organizations. To allay Jordan's fears, Shuqayri stressed that the Council would be independent and "would have no sovereignty over any part whatsoever of Filastin and above all would not harm the Jordanian entity or the West Bank". In his second plan Shuqayri suggested "the re-establishment of a genuine Palestinian Government" which would operate from Cairo within the Arab League framework; its members would be elected by a body to be agreed upon at some future date.[104] Jordan objected to these proposals in their entirety.

The disintegration of the UAR caused an escalation of inter-Arab struggle. The Palestinian issue was not enough to unite the Arab world and stayed in deep freeze for two years, during which time Egypt boycotted the ALC meetings in August 1962. The Yemen War then broke out in September 1962.

The 40th session of the ALC in September 1963 was a landmark in the issue of Palestinian representation. The need to appoint a substitute for Ahmad Hilmi, the head of the Government of All-Filastin who died on 29 June 1963, gave the Egyptians a pretext to abolish this institution once and for all and to move the issue of Palestinian representative institutions from the realm of words to deeds. For the first time the issue of the Entity was detached from that of representation, so that two "separate" resolutions were passed. Shuqayri was also invited to participate. During the discussions, two trends emerged. The first was towards separating the problem of Palestinian representation in the ALC, which was to be discussed immediately, from the "problem of the Entity" which was to be postponed until the next session. It was suggested that Filastin would be represented in the ALC by a three-member delegation: Shuqayri, a representative of the AHC and another from the Gaza Strip. This proposal was rejected. The second trend, however, was that the problem of the Entity could no longer brook postponement. Iraq spoke of a Palestinian National Council whose members would be elected by the Palestinians in Arab countries including Jordan. This Council would elect a Palestinian Government, which would be responsible for establishing a Palestinian Liberation Army. Jordan opposed; Shuqayri again stressed that "the Palestinian organization would possess executive sovereignty (*siyada tanfidhiyya*) but not territorial sovereignty (*siyada iqlimiyya*), that is, during this period it would not have sovereignty over the West Bank or the Gaza Strip. The organization would have territorial sovereignty over all Filastin only following its liberation. The Palestinian people would decide on its destiny only following the realization of its independence whether through the establishment of an independent state or through unity with an Arab state."[105]

This ALC session eventually passed two separate resolutions. On the issue of Palestinian representation, Shuqayri was appointed "the Representative of Filastin" in the ALC "until the Palestinian people would be able to elect its representatives". Thus the right of the Palestinian people to choose its own representatives was indirectly recognized, in opposition to Jordan's stand. Shuqayri would "form and head a Palestinian delegation" which he would take to the General Assembly of the UN; thus an important precedent was created, and the AHC representation in the UN was eliminated. Jordan, of course, registered her opposition and the Saudi Arabian representative expressed "disagreement with the principle upon which the decision was based" (meaning Shuqayri himself).

On the issue of the Palestinian Entity it was determined that "the right belongs to the Palestinian people to restore its homeland, to decide on its destiny and fully realize its national rights". The ALC also expressed support for Iraq's proposal for a Palestinian National Council and a Palestinian Government. Jordan, disagreeing, suggested instead that "the liberation of Filastin would be achieved through the aid and participation of the Arab states. Only after the completion of the liberation of Palestinian land from Israel would the Palestinians (*ahl Filastin*) decide on their political future in accordance with their wishes".[106]

The ALC, however, was not capable of passing binding operative decisions on such important issues; for that a senior-level meeting of the Arab heads of state would be required. But without the prolonged discussions of 1959–63, during which important new concepts relating to the Palestinian issue were clarified, the first Arab summit in January 1964 could not have passed those decisions that paved the way for the establishment of representative Palestinian institutions by Shuqayri.

Conclusion

UAR/Egypt was the main force in creating and pursuing the issues of the Palestinian Entity and Palestinian representation. Despite Jordan's opposition, Egypt's perseverance eventually led to the transition to operative decisions in this area by the two Arab summit conferences in 1964.

The year 1959 was the turning point for the Palestinian movement. It may even be called the Filastin year in that the problem of the Palestinian Entity came to be conceived in new terms. The Egyptian initiative would add to the Arab–Israel conflict a new and separate Palestinian dimension.

Qasim's 1959 plan for a Palestinian Republic was a reaction to the Egyptian initiative. Despite the plan's limitations, it acted as a stimulant to the Egyptian plan and added new elements to the inter-Arab discussions; it may even have inspired further ideas about the Palestinian Entity which grew up among the Palestinians themselves.

As for Jordan, Egypt's idea of the Palestinian Entity threatened its integrity and its very existence, not to mention Egypt's concomitant violent efforts to overthrow King Husayn in 1959. Moreover, it was precisely during this period that the regime was attempting to "Jordanize" the internal Palestinian population. Thus it is easy to understand Husayn's bitter and obstinate opposition to the

Palestinian Entity in all its representative components. This opposition was expressed in unrestrained repressive measures against the opponents who strove to overthrow him.

In the Palestinian arena itself, the year 1959 witnessed three important phenomena. In October, at a meeting of the Fatah founders, the Fatah organizational structure was finally established;[107] in November the General Union of the Palestinian Students was set up; and also in that year *Filastinuna*, the Fatah organ, made its appearance. It is symbolic that the process of the elimination of the AHC had also begun in that year.

Still, it was only towards the end of 1962 and especially in 1963 that additional, secret Palestinian organizations began to form in Lebanon, Kuwait and to a lesser extent the Gaza Strip. There were (1964–65) "some 40 organizations with memberships from 2 to 400".[108] They called for the establishment of such institutions as a Palestinian Government and National Assembly, for recognition of the West Bank as "a part of Filastin" and for the establishment of a Palestinian army. Among these Palestinian organizations were: Jabhat al-Tahrir al-Filastiniyya, Jabhat Thuwwar Filastin, Jabhat al-Tahrir al-Arabiyya al-Filastiniyya, al-Jabha al-Thawriyya li-Tahrir Filastin, Kataib al-Fidaiyyin, Jabhat al-Tahrir al-Watani al-Filastini and Talai' al-Fida li-Tahrir Filastin. A number of these organizations had secret contacts with West Bank inhabitants with the aim of organizing branches there, an activity that did not go unnoticed by the Jordanian security authorities.[109] In their meetings in the Arab states in this period, these Palestinian organizations demanded that the Palestinian Entity be elevated to the level of a top-priority issue.[110]

Nevertheless, any Egyptian initiative, Iraqi reaction or inter-Arab discussion stemmed merely from Egyptian and Iraqi considerations and not from pressures by a massive Palestinian popular movement. The reaction of the Palestinian population to such activities in 1959–1962 was generally one of passive sympathy or of activity inspired by the authorities rather than arising out of any independent initiative. In the years of the Egyptian–Syrian union there were no visible signs that the issue of the Palestinian Entity had led to any independent Palestinian political movement. Instead, the Palestinian intelligentsia showed a strong tendency to act within the pan-Arab framework (except for the founders of Fatah) and to support Nasir's dictum that "unity is the road to the liberation of Filastin". Even *Filastinuna* began to relate to the Palestinian Entity only at the end of 1960, when it called for the establishment of "a Palestinian revolutionary national rule on the Arab parts of Filastin",[111] that is, the West Bank and Gaza Strip. It seems, therefore, that Fatah was also influenced by Egypt's and Iraq's stand on that issue.

CHAPTER TWO

The Struggle over Palestinian Representation in the Arab and Palestinian Arenas, 1964–1967

At the first Arab summit, which took place on Nasir's initiative in Cairo 13–17 January 1964, it was decided that "Ahmad al-Shuqayri, the representative of Filastin in the Arab League, will continue his contacts with the member states [of the Arab League] and with the Palestinian people in order to establish the proper foundations for the organization of the Palestinian people, to enable it to fulfil its role in the liberation of its homeland and its self-determination."[1] This was the first practical resolution regarding a Palestinian Entity, since Egypt's initiative in March 1959, to be taken both unanimously and at the highest Arab level. It turned the issues of the Palestinian Entity and Palestinian representation from a subject for debate into a "fact",[2] and paved the way for Shuqayri to set up the Palestine Liberation Organization (PLO) in May 1964, at the end of the 1st Palestine National Congress (PNC) in East Jerusalem. The second Arab summit, held in Cairo 5–11 September 1964, "welcomed the establishment of the PLO as the basis of the Palestinian Entity and as a pioneer in the collective Arab struggle for the liberation of Filastin". Moreover, "the PLO's decision to establish the Palestine Liberation Army (PLA) was accepted". The second summit avoided any direct reference to the question how representative the PLO should be; but there was agreement over the general formulation that "the PLO represents the will of the Palestinian people in its struggle for the liberation of its homeland, Filastin".[3] In May 1965 the 2nd PNC met in Cairo, and in May 1966 the 3rd PNC met in Gaza.

This led to a conflict in the Arab and the Palestinian arenas over the PLO's representation of the Palestinian people, the components of that representation and how much recognition it would receive. The struggles were waged against a background of extensive changes in the Arab world, well described by Haykal to Nasir before his death: "Arab logic tends to retreat in the direction of instinct; our thought is dust while our emotions are fire; we were, and still are, tribes, raging at one moment, quiescent at another. We wave our weapon in front of one another, then later we clasp each other's hand and embrace as if nothing had happened."[4]

This period began with the Arab states cooperating in a plan regarding the Arab–Israel conflict, described as "the first [plan] in the history of the Arab peoples to be agreed upon by all the Arab leaders and peoples".[5] The character of the summit was set by Nasir's slogan "unity of action". But since "the problem of the Arabs is that of implementation [of action]",[6] this slogan turned out to have no logical basis "when matters were weighed in the balance of [Arab] reality and common sense".[7] Nasir, believing he could attain inter-Arab cooperation on a long-term plan for Israel's destruction, had not learned from his earlier experience. Two years later he realized that "the [Arab] reactionaries participated in the summit only in order to deceive" him and to undermine his standing by, among other things, setting up the "Islamic Pact". On 22 July 1966 he declared the collapse of the summit atmosphere, thereby failing to realize "unity of action", just as earlier he had failed with his slogan "unity is the way to Filastin". So this time he returned to his revolutionary path with the slogans "unity of the Arab struggle for the overthrow of the reactionary regimes", and "encounter of the Arab revolutionary forces ... for the liberation of Filastin".[8]

The result was a *rapprochement* between Nasirism and the Ba'th, and Egyptian recognition of the Ba'th regime in Syria. This "encounter of the revolutions" created a new polarization in the Arab world between the "progressive, revolutionary camp" of Egypt, Syria, Algeria and Iraq and the "reactionary, traditional camp" led by Jordan and Saudi Arabia. Only on the eve of the Six Day War (June 1967) did the Arab world, in a flush of enthusiasm, return to close military cooperation.

In this period a process began in which the Arab–Israel conflict became a rallying point for Arab nationalism. At the first summit the Arab states tried to confront the challenge of Israel's diversion of the Jordan waters without getting involved in a war. At the second summit (September 1964) they agreed on their own counter-diversionary scheme, gave the go-ahead for starting it and approved a military plan for defending it. At the third summit (September 1965), the Arab leaders faced a dilemma of how to continue diverting the sources of the Jordan and prevent Israel from destroying their work. Nasir responded with a new strategy for the Arab world, "the concept of stages", the principles of which had been approved at the second summit. This strategy "defined on paper, for the first time, the full formula for the campaign against Israel, the final goal of Arab collective action, the means and the stages of its realization".[9] The strategy marked a transition from a total solution for the Arab–Israel conflict to a two-stage solution.

The first stage would involve the diversion of the sources of the Jordan River and the establishment of an effective Arab defence force through the strengthening of the Arab armies, especially those of Jordan, Syria and Lebanon as well as that of Egypt. The building up of this force was to take two and a half to three years, until late 1967 to early 1968. A sum of 150 million Egyptian pounds was budgeted for that purpose. During this build-up period there would be no full-scale war with Israel; upon its completion, there would be a strong Arab deterrent force that would put Israel on the defensive.

The second stage would see the achievement of "the Arab national goal". As the second summit had decided, "the final aim in the military sphere is the liberation of Filastin from imperialism and Zionism". The commander-in-chief of the United Arab Command (UAC) was ordered to prepare a detailed military plan for Israel's destruction, which the third summit approved. This conference also authorized another 200 million Egyptian pounds for strengthening the Syrian, Jordanian and Lebanese armies; the aim was "to pass from the stage of defence to the stage of attack".[10] Nasir saw war with Israel as inevitable.[11] He consistently refrained from entering into war with Israel, the outcome and timing of which he could not be certain. Despite this, when he led the Arabs into war in June 1967, it was Israel that decided on its exact timing and form.

These developments in the Arab–Israel conflict, and especially the postponement of the "liberation" stage, obliged the Arab states to take more extensive measures regarding the Palestinian Entity and the PLO as its concrete expression. The PLO became the sole achievement of the summit. Meanwhile, the appearance of Fatah in early 1965, and later of other fidaiyyun organizations, intensified the competition over the allegiance of the Palestinians. On the whole, the Palestinian element of the Palestinian issue was gaining in importance alongside the Arab element. A survey of the developments in this period shows Shuqayri and his activities in a less negative light than in the period of his chairmanship of the PLO and subsequently.

Part One
The Founding of the PLO, 1964

SHUQAYRI'S CONCEPT OF REPRESENTATION

After his election as "the representative of Filastin" at the ALC (September 1963), Shuqayri admitted that the first problem he had to solve was exactly whom the Filastin delegation at the United Nations was representing. And after the first summit, Shuqayri had to try to determine what would be the representative composition of the first PNC.[12] His ideas on the question of Palestinian representation were mainly influenced by five factors.

First, Shuqayri was not elected by any Palestinian bodies as "representative of Filastin" in the Arab League, nor as the founder of the PLO; rather, he was imposed on the Palestinians by Arab states. More specifically, he was appointed by Egypt so that Jordan, which regarded him as the least of all evils, would agree to the establishment of the Palestinian Entity.[13]

Also, Shuqayri was traumatized by the fact that the PLO "was born in the bed of the summit conference" and was thus constrained by the conditions of the Arab arena. In his memoirs he admitted that "the biggest mistake in my forty years of public life lay in my joining up with the kings and presidents in the four years that ended with the Six Day War". In the election of the members of the Filastin delegation to the UN in 1963, he tried "to satisfy the wishes of the Arab governments ... and the groups of Palestinians", and in the composition of the PNC he put "most of his energy into gaining the support of the maximum number of Palestinians and Arab states" alike.[14]

Third, Shuqayri was umbilically connected to Nasir. Before attempting anything significant, such as the Palestinian Entity programme and the policy towards Jordan, he always sought Nasir's approval.[15] In essence he had no alternative, since aligning himself with Jordan's policies would mean the end of the PLO as representative of the Palestinians, and aligning himself with Ba'th policy would mean a standstill in the process of establishing the PLO. By harnessing himself to Nasir, however, he and the PLO gained strength in the Arab arena and among the Palestinians.

Fourth, Shuqayri worked in almost a total vacuum in the Palestinian arena; there were no popular Palestinian organizations or institutions from which the PLO could be built.

Finally, Shuqayri had strong personal motivation to succeed in his task and thereby improve the negative image which dogged him. He was prepared to use any means to succeed in establishing the PLO, even deceit, which became for him a "national obligation".[16] In the circumstances of 1964 he was the most suitable person for the job, but in the end his qualities militated against him.

As for the components of the PLO representative bodies, the decisions of the first Arab summit deliberately avoided stating how "the Palestinian people would be organized". The only way to reach a unanimous decision was to vote on the lowest common denominator; here Nasir adopted the right tactic by attempting to get Husayn's approval at any price, even if it meant acceding to Husayn's demand that the phrase "Palestinian Entity" not be mentioned. To the Arab heads of state, including Husayn, it was clear that what was meant was the establishment of Palestinian representative institutions. They left the details to deliberations between Shuqayri and Husayn.[17] The question whether or not the first Arab summit authorized Shuqayri to establish the institutions of the Palestinian Entity is irrelevant. Shuqayri's version that he had presented the heads of the Arab states with a *fait accompli* was intended to enhance his image.

A distinction must be made between, on the one hand, the way Shuqayri presented the composition of the 1st PNC and of the first Executive Committee (EC) of the PLO in the Arab and Palestinian arenas, and, on the other hand, the real composition that emerged. Shuqayri presented the principles of the PLO's representative institutions as follows.

1. *Total representation.* Shuqayri determined in the Palestine National Covenant and in the Constitution of the PLO that "all the Palestinians were natural members of the PLO and represented a single national front. The Palestinians will establish among themselves an organization called the PLO." The implication was that "the Entity is the entire Palestinian people".[18] This approach allayed Jordan's fears since it adopted the principle of "proportional representation" of the Palestinian population, that is, a majority in the PNC would be representatives of the "Jordanian" Palestinians.

2. *Geographical representation.* Shuqayri tried to prove that the members of the PNC and the EC represented the Palestinians "from the ocean to the Gulf". His report to the second Arab summit

included a special section classifying the PNC members according to their geographical representation, and pointedly including representatives from the East Bank of the Jordan.[19] According to this division, Jordan was allocated 216 places out of 396 (391 actually in attendance) or 54 percent, while the West Bank received 118 and the East Bank 98.

3. *Functional representation.* Shuqayri also tried to prove that the PLO represented all strata of Palestinian society, emphasizing in his report to the second summit the representation of women, workers and journalists and, further, pointing out that the members of the PNC also represented "members of the House of Deputies, ministers, mayors and local council leaders, chambers of commerce, unions of doctors, lawyers, engineers, students ... who were elected by the people".[20]

Since no Arab state except Egypt would allow elections to the PLO institutions on its own territory, Shuqayri chose the system of appointment as the procedure for composing the PNC. This system was particularly convenient to Jordan, and with its agreement Shuqayri appointed a Supreme Preparatory Committee which decided on the final list of members; the vast majority of PNC members, in fact, were appointed in close cooperation with Jordan and only with its agreement. The PNC represented interests and pressure groups which Shuqayri thought essential to achieving the Palestinian Entity. To this end, however, Shuqayri had to give way to Jordan's demand for complete control of the PNC.

Shuqayri's and Jordan's common desire to see the Jerusalem Congress succeed, together with Nasir's support for Shuqayri, ensured that the Congress would indeed succeed and that the aims of the three leading actors would be achieved. Close examination shows that Jordan was promised almost 65 percent of the total number of PNC representatives, and accounted, in all, for nearly 255 representatives. In fact, over 100 members of the PNC from Jordan (20 percent of the PNC members) served or had served the Jordanian government in an official capacity. Thus the PLO and the Jordanian establishment overlapped considerably, with the "Jordanians" representing Jordanian rather than Palestinian interests or at best having dual loyalties.[21] The 47 representatives from the Gaza Strip included at least 26 who served in some official capacity in the Strip;[22] in this way Shuqayri and Egypt ensured the loyalty of this contingent. Lebanon was supposed to have 22 representatives, but four were absent (one was forbidden entry into Jordan). Shuqayri and Jordan found this delegation problematic: it consisted of three representatives of the Palestine Liberation Front (PLF – Jabhat al-Tahrir al-Filastiniyya), two from the Palestine Liberation Movement (Harakat Tahrir Filastin), one from Arab Youth (al-Shabab al-Arabi), one from the Palestine-Arab Office in Washington and four women, as well as a number of Independents and supporters of the Mufti.[23] The Syrian delegation inclined towards the policies of the Syrian Ba'th party. The Fatah representatives participated as individuals and were put on the list of Kuwait and Qatar representatives; similarly, representatives of the Arab Nationalists Movement (ANM) were included in the Jordanian and Lebanese delegations.

In response to complaints by Palestinians about the pro-Jordanian composition of the PNC and his obvious pro-Jordanian bias, Shuqayri set up an Executive Committee with a "balanced" composition and showing an "independent" line, even though the majority in fact supported him. His attempts to co-opt Fatah representatives to this EC failed; academics and financiers resisted similar attempts. Shuqayri did succeed, however, in co-opting representatives of the ANM. On 9 August 1964 Shuqayri made public the names of the 14 members of the EC; the C-in-C of the PLA became the 15th member, but only after the second summit when the establishment of the PLA was approved. Apart from Shuqayri himself as chairman, the EC consisted of seven members known to support him (thus ensuring a majority for himself), four or five known for their independent line (including two from the ANM) and one from Syria. Shuqayri appointed seven people with higher academic degrees. Jordan was unhappy with the appointment of members of the Jordanian opposition, such as Bahjat Abu-Gharbiyya and Walid Qamhawi; among the Palestinians, however, there was general approval of the EC's composition.[24]

Shuqayri saw the PLA as a vital representative element in the Palestinian Entity, and wanted to set it up as an organization that would represent "the independence" of the Palestinians. For him the PLA was an expression of the fact that "the Palestinian Entity is not words alone"; he believed that by placing the PLA under the control of the PLO, the latter would be more readily accepted as a representative body of the Palestinians and would gain a military image. His desire to set up the PLA was influenced by the demands of young Palestinians during his visits to Arab countries – "Shuqayri brings us weapons, we want weapons". These young Palestinians, including those in the refugee camps, were then enthusiastic about joining the PLA the moment recruitment to its units was announced.[25]

ARAB AND PALESTINIAN ATTITUDES

The positions of the Arab states and the Palestinians on the establishment of the PLO and the composition of the PNC can be divided into three categories: *full support* – Egypt, Jordan and the north African Arab countries including Algeria and Morocco; *support with reservations* – Syria, the ANM and Fatah; *opposition* – Saudi Arabia, the AHC and small Palestinian organizations.

The Egyptian Position

The setting up of the PLO was the realization of Egypt's initiative in establishing the Palestinian Entity. Egypt gave Shuqayri full support, while simultaneously conducting a flexible policy in order to break, at any cost, the deadlock over this issue. To this end Egypt, together with Shuqayri, reassured Husayn about the purposes of the Entity in regard to his kingdom, suggesting it constituted "support for the Jordanian entity".[26] The Egyptian media embarked on an unprecedented campaign in support of Shuqayri and the Palestinian Entity, praising the results of the PNC and likening the Jerusalem Congress to the first Zionist Congress in Basel in 1897. It was emphasized that "the PLO saw itself as the sole representative of the Palestinians".[27] Egypt also advised senior West Bank politicians to support Shuqayri, assessing that this support was essential to his success in convening the PNC and establishing the PLO. These politicians gave Egypt's stand serious consideration. Egyptian newspapers redistributed in Jordan helped convey the Egyptian position to the West Bank Palestinians, who had harnessed themselves to Shuqayri's efforts.[28]

The Jordanian Position

Husayn made his first major error in the history of the struggle over the existence of the Palestinian Entity or the Jordanian entity when he signed the summit decision on the question of the former. Looking for short-term advantages, he underestimated the political repercussions within the Palestinian population in his own country, of setting up the Palestinian Entity. Upon agreeing to the summit decision, he was obliged to take the next step – namely, convening the PNC and setting up the PLO; in this way he unleashed a process which threatened (and still continues to threaten) the existence of his kingdom.

The considerations which moved him to agree to set up the Palestinian Entity at the first summit included, first, the support of all the Arab heads of state for its establishment. He was happy at being finally accepted into Nasir's "nationalist club" after seven lean years of isolation in the Arab world and constant attempts to overthrow him.[29] Second, he believed he would be able to turn the PLO into an organization of the regime, and so prevent it from becoming a threat to him, relying on his intelligence and security network. Finally, Husayn was satisfied with Nasir's and Shuqayri's promises that the Palestinian Entity would not harm "the unity of the kingdom" and his sovereignty over both Banks; in short, he believed he could handle someone like Shuqayri.[30]

Husayn left nothing to chance. In his talks with Shuqayri he made sure that the PNC's composition would guarantee the PLO's total subjection to Jordanian control and that the PNC's decisions would reflect Jordan's inclinations. In this he succeeded; Shuqayri accepted all his demands. To these ends Jordan took several steps.

First, apart from ensuring a "Jordanian" majority in the PNC, she intervened in the appointment of her own delegates. Husayn made sure that only a few days before the Congress convened (28 May 1964), the West Bank members of the Senate and House of Deputies joined the PNC. On 26 May 1964 another three delegates from Jordan were co-opted. To sustain his control over the PNC, Husayn ensured that the Jerusalem Congress was turned into a permanent National Congress and that Shuqayri was elected chairman of the Executive Committee, with the authority to appoint members to it. Husayn believed it would be easier to deal with one person rather than a group of leaders.[31]

Also, Husayn was the dominant person in the Congress; he personally made sure that its decisions were "flawless". Although opposition delegates managed to pass resolutions uncomfortable to Husayn in the subcommittees, these resolutions never passed the plenary sessions.[32]

Indeed, its final resolutions, including the items of the Palestinian Covenant and the Constitution of the PLO, were at one with Jordan's position and relieved her fears about the PLO. These two documents emphasized the following:[33] (1) "The PLO will not assert any territorial sovereignty over the West Bank, nor over the Gaza Strip, nor over the al-Hamma area." (2) "The Palestinian people will achieve self-determination after completing the

P.E.—C

liberation of its homeland." It was emphasized that the PLO would
not interfere with the internal affairs of the Arab states. (3) The
question of the PLO's representativeness of the Palestinians was not
mentioned at all in the Covenant or the Constitution; it was circumvented with the statement that one of the functions of the EC was
"representation of the Palestinian people". The decisions of the
PNC emphasized that "the PLO will represent *Filastin* (but not the
Palestinians) in the Arab League, in the United Nations and its
institutions. ... Only the PLO has the right to represent the Palestinians and to speak in their name." These last words were meant to
negate the AHC's claim concerning its "sole right to represent the
Palestinians".

In addition, Husayn did not accept the decision to set up the
Palestine Liberation Army. In his early talks with Shuqayri, he and
the senior officers of the Jordanian Arab Army (JA) had strongly
objected to the establishment of separate and independent Palestinian units in Jordan. Shuqayri displayed tactical flexibility in
this sensitive area, and in his talks with Husayn before the PNC
was convened, a formula was adopted whereby "the Palestinian
battalions would be set up with the agreement of the states concerned". Indeed, at the PNC meeting a resolution was accepted
calling on the Arab heads of state to instruct the UAC "to prepare a
plan for the opening of camps for the training of Palestinians in
the use of weapons and for the setting up of Palestinian military
battalions". The Constitution stated in its General Regulations that
"special Palestinian units will be set up in accordance with [both]
military necessities and the plan on which the UAC will decide, and
this will be by agreement and cooperation with the Arab states
concerned".[34]

Finally, the regime took strenuous security measures, which
succeeded beyond expectations, before and during the Jerusalem
Congress in order to prevent even the smallest disturbance. The
assessment of the Jordanian intelligence and security services
had been that "the existing divisions of opinion among the Palestinians in everything connected with the Congress and the subjects it will debate are likely to cause agitation and disturbances";
"demonstrations and violent clashes between demonstrating
groups are expected, including use of arms, [and these are] likely to
develop into activity against the kingdom". It was no wonder, then,
that during the Congress the West Bank was turned into a military
camp, and even Jerusalem was turned into a "detention camp"; the
responsibility for internal security was delegated to the army. Also,

the movements of the opposition parties' members, who were under surveillance, were limited. During the Congress entry into Jordan was forbidden for *personae non grata*, among them ten people from Lebanon including two leaders of the ANM, Ghassan Kanafani and Ahmad al-Yamani (the latter a PNC member).[35]

The "Reservations" Camp

Syria. Had it depended on the Syrian Ba'th party, the PLO would not have been established in 1964. The Ba'th proposals regarding the Palestinian Entity were rejected by Husayn. Rather than a programme like the Ba'th's, a maximalist one that envisaged a "Palestinian state" on the West Bank and the Gaza Strip, Nasir and Shuqayri needed a practical programme that considered the inter-Arab conditions of 1964. The Ba'th was strongly critical of Shuqayri, and of the way in which the PNC was constituted and the PLO established; it argued that "the PLO is the outcome of the compromise between the Arab heads of state", and that its establishment was meant "to suppress the Palestinian people's demands for the establishment of a revolutionary entity". The Ba'th also claimed that the Jerusalem Congress had not been democratically elected, but that "Jordanian tactics had dominated". "The Entity was born at the Jerusalem Congress without land and lacking autonomy in its activity." Still, the Ba'th was "not without hope that the PLO could be reformed" in a "revolutionary direction".[36] On the eve of the Congress, the Ba'th National Command realized that it was not enough to criticize Shuqayri and his plan but also necessary to present an alternative plan.

On 20 May 1964 the National Command published its own Plan for the Palestinian Entity. Its elements were, first, that the Entity must include the basic components of all entities – land, people and government (*sulta*). Second, "the Palestinian people has a legal right to its homeland within its borders which are not subject to partition and which include the conquered land of Filastin, the Gaza Strip, the West Bank of the Jordan River and the al-Hamma area of southern Syria. The Palestinian Entity is obliged to assert full sovereignty over all its homeland." Third, the Entity would have two ruling institutions: a National Assembly (Majlis Watani) and a Supreme Executive Committee. The National Assembly would be established through direct elections by the Palestinians of Filastin and in the other Arab countries; Jerusalem would be the capital of the Entity. The Supreme Executive Committee, which would be elected by the National Assembly, would represent the Entity and speak in its name in the Arab and international arenas.[37]

The Syrian plan was a synthesis of Qasim's plan and of Shuqayri's and Egypt's earlier plan. Its aim was clear: to upset Jordan's territorial integrity and to establish a "Palestinian state" – as a first stage, on the West Bank, the Gaza Strip and al-Hamma, and as a second stage, in all of Mandate Palestine. In principle this plan might have been acceptable to Nasir and Shuqayri, but for tactical reasons Shuqayri rejected it out of hand. With internal struggles and leadership changes in the Syrian Ba'th, the plan was pushed aside; the Ba'th's 8th National Congress (April 1965) did not consider it. Instead the Ba'th began to emphasize a new phenomenon in the Palestinian arena: Fatah and fidaiyyun activities.

Fatah. From the start Fatah had reservations about the way the PLO was set up, "directed by the Arab regimes". The Fatah leaders feared that Shuqayri's activity would undermine their attempts to recruit Palestinians and their aim of leading "the Palestinian national movement"; thus they decided to meet with Shuqayri in Cairo in early 1964. Abu Iyad told him that "an organization set up from above will be inoperable if it does not rest on an active [popular] base". He proposed a package deal according to which there would be secret coordination between the PLO's public activities and Fatah's secret activities. Accordingly, "the PLO would become a kind of Jewish agency, that is, the legal public body of the armed struggle which [Fatah] was waging". The link between the two organizations "would be made through the Fatah representatives, who would be appointed by Shuqayri as members of the PLO EC".[38] The Fatah leaders' purpose was clear: behind the scenes Fatah would be the dominant factor in the PLO. Shuqayri understood their intentions and rejected the proposal; he was still only beginning to make his way and enjoyed popularity, whereas Fatah was unknown.

The Jerusalem Congress presented a dilemma for Fatah; whereas its composition, Shuqayri's objectives and his "patronage" from Arab states all compelled them to boycott it, they could not afford not to exploit such a forum. Fatah decided to participate in the Congress but not in the institutions of the PLO. The seven Fatah representatives at the Congress used it to spread the idea of the "armed struggle" and of the existence of the organization itself. Two Fatah leaders, Khalid al-Hasan and Hani al-Qaddumi, rejected Shuqayri's offer to join the PLO EC.[39] Fatah's organ, *Filastinuna* (April 1964) called for the establishment of a "revolutionary

Palestinian Entity based on a military organization". Fatah was theoretically in favour of "making the Entity more prominent through the conduct of pure elections"; but it warned that "it is impossible to conduct free elections, because these would arouse [anew] hatred and blind factionalism".[40] In 1964, Fatah had not yet made its mark in the Palestinian arena.

The Arab Nationalists Movement (ANM). Throughout 1964 and 1965 the ANM was in close contact with Nasir.[41] Its organs identified with Nasir's new strategy regarding the Arab–Israel conflict; in its opinion the decisions of the first summit had opened up "for the first time, for the people of Filastin, the possibility of taking on responsibility for its problem by means of the proposed Palestinian Entity". Nevertheless the ANM criticized these decisions, since "they did not define at all the way in which the PLO would be set up". In its opinion this omission made Shuqayri's appointment possible.

Similarly, the ANM criticized the way Shuqayri established the PLO, the composition of its institutions and the appointment of the members of the Congress, who "were subject to the dictates of the Jordanian government and were distant from all revolutionary logic". The ANM advanced several demands regarding how the Palestinian Entity was to be established: (1) the Entity must be a "revolutionary organization" and must be established through free elections – or, if this was not possible, its composition must "represent the revolutionary forces in a true manner"; (2) it must be independent and not subject to any external influence; and (3) the aim of the Entity must be "mobilization of the youth of Filastin and their training in the framework of armed battalions under a single command linked to the UAC".[42]

> At the same time the Movement began to appreciate the growing challenge which some eight Palestinian organizations, including Fatah, posed to its long-established political position among the inhabitants of the refugee camps in Lebanon, Syria and Iraq. Consequently, [George] Habash and [Wadi'] Haddad formed a separate Regional Command for Palestine which was drawn from among the majority of the Palestinian members of the Movement.[43]

The ANM saw the establishment of the PLO as an opportunity to strengthen its hold on the Palestinians, and as "the beginning of a long and hard road to united Palestinian action. Therefore it [the ANM] is obliged to support and adopt it [the PLO] in order to push it

towards the establishment of a revolutionary Palestinian organization." Although Shuqayri rejected its demands, the ANM called on
its members to participate in activity directed at establishing the
PLO, with the aim of "moving revolutionary elements into the
[PLO] leadership" and "working with Shuqayri against inimical
groups such as the AHC". ANM leaders on the West Bank, like Dr
Walid Qamhawi and Dr Salah Anabtawi, cooperated with local
politicians such as Hikmat al-Masri and Walid al-Shak'a for the
benefit of the PLO. ANM representatives also took an active part in
the Jerusalem Congress; in the subcommittees they achieved a
number of objectives when working together with the Fatah
and Ba'th representatives. As a result of the 1st PNC, the ANM
reckoned that with a serious effort it could impel the PLO in a
"revolutionary" direction; thus it participated, during 1964–65, in
the management of PLO institutions including the EC, in which its
representative was Walid Qamhawi.[44] The organizational changes
within the ANM, as well as its decision to join the PLO establishment, were an expression of the "Palestinization" it was undergoing. This process took on a militant character with the appearance
of Fatah in 1965 and other fidaiyyun organizations in 1966–67.

The Opposition Camp

Saudi Arabia – from opposition to acceptance.   Saudi Arabia did
not oppose the Palestinian Entity in principle. But it continued to
have reservations about Shuqayri and the way in which he composed the Jerusalem Congress and founded the PLO, and instead
supported the Mufti. The Saudi authorities prevented Palestinians
from leaving to attend the Jerusalem Congress. They were afraid
that participation of Palestinians from their country in PLO activity
would lead to internal security problems for the regime.[45] Despite
this stand, Shuqayri held back from a confrontation with Saudi
Arabia through fear that it would disturb his efforts to set up the
PLO. Saudi Arabia's position, which came up at the second summit
as well, focused on the following points. First, the summit did not
authorize Shuqayri to set up the Palestinian Entity. Basing itself
on a literal interpretation of the summit's decisions, Saudi Arabia
argued that Shuqayri was merely asked "to establish contacts with
the Palestinians and to present a survey and a proposed plan on the
way in which the Palestinian Entity would be set up". Second,
"there are Palestinian groups which do not support the organization
set up [by Shuqayri]". Saudi Arabia meant, of course, the AHC.
Therefore, "the Jerusalem Congress does not represent the Pales-

tinians". Finally, Saudi Arabia demanded the establishment of a Palestinian Entity that would represent the Palestinians "in a democratic way, through elections".[46] It is hard to believe that Faysal, who was chairman of the second summit, really thought that these reservations would be accepted, especially after Husayn had supported the way in which the PLO had been set up. More likely, Faysal's stand stemmed from Saudi Arabia's obligations to the Mufti. Because of the unanimity of all the other Arab heads of state, Faysal was forced to give silent agreement; but Saudi Arabia retained its reservations about Shuqayri for a long time.

The AHC. The termination of the Qasim regime (November 1963) narrowed the Mufti's support and possibilities for action. After its offices in Cairo and Baghdad closed, the AHC had only five offices left: in Rabat, Jedda, Beirut, Damascus and New York. It was forced to be content with Saudi Arabia's material and political support and the Syrian Ba'th's passive and limited support. Thus the establishment of the Palestinian Entity led to a violent struggle between the Mufti and Shuqayri over the latter's plan. The Mufti was willing to try any means to topple Shuqayri. He boycotted the Jerusalem Congress, and, in an intensive propaganda campaign, derided the PLO's claim to represent Palestinians and attacked the way in which the organization was set up. He further claimed that "the AHC is the legitimate representative of the struggle of the Palestinian people", and that "Shuqayri has departed from the authority invested in him at the summit". In his opinion the summit decision was aimed at "the establishment of a political bureau whose function was limited to propaganda on the problem of Filastin and to speaking in the name of the Palestinians in the United Nations". The AHC called the Jerusalem Congress a "Zionist-imperialist plot aimed at eliminating the problem of Filastin".[47]

The AHC also worked within the Palestinian concentrations to counteract the efforts of Shuqayri and his supporters. After being forced to abandon its activity in the refugee camps in Lebanon, where it had met with hostile reactions, it focused on the West Bank and the Palestinian refugees in Syria. In the months of February, May and August 1964 the Mufti sent delegations to the West Bank in order to mobilize the support of the politicians. From Beirut he also sent by post his declarations against Shuqayri to tens of West Bank notables and politicians. In general the public reacted very negatively and the AHC activists were labelled "*khawarij*". Even the small group of veteran followers of the Mufti were deterred by Husayn's support for Shuqayri from supporting the Mufti actively.[48]

In addition, the Mufti engaged in subversive activities against Shuqayri, which reminded many Palestinians of his past activities. He distributed money in order to buy supporters; in Jerusalem he promoted the fictitious organization he had earlier set up called al-Haraka al-Wataniyya al-Filastiniyya. On the eve of the Congress (27 May 1964), one of his emissaries even fired at the home of Hikmat al-Masri in Nablus in an attempt to deter politicians from cooperating with Shuqayri and make the Congress fail.[49]

The crisis that broke out between Husayn and Shuqayri towards the end of 1965, and especially in mid-1966, led Jordan and the AHC to draw closer. An AHC office was opened in Jerusalem, and the Mufti began to praise Husayn for his policy regarding Shuqayri. The height of this *rapprochement* came on 1 March 1967 with the Mufti's visit to Jordan at the king's invitation, during which he came back to Jerusalem, which he had left thirty years earlier. A further expression of this *rapprochement* was the unopposed election to the House of Deputies (March 1967) of two AHC activists, Emil al-Ghuri and Muhi al-Din al-Husayni.[50] This episode had no effect whatsoever on the Palestinian arena.

The AHC had a strange relationship with the Ba'th regime in Syria. The latter permitted the Mufti to run an office in Damascus and to conduct activity among the refugees, but kept actual contacts with him at a low level. The aim was primarily to fight Shuqayri's plan and the Egyptian influence on the PLO. Even these relations were severely criticized by the "Filastin branch in Lebanon" of the Ba'th in its report to the 8th National Congress (April 1965), which expressed great disappointment "that the Syrian government has dealt with the subject of the AHC on matters of government and not on considerations of revolution". The Congress decided "on steps to eliminate the contradiction between the stand of the party and the stand of the government regarding the AHC".[51] Following this decision and the February 1966 overthrow of the government, the AHC's activities were banned in Syria and the propaganda mouth-pieces of the Ba'th began to attack the Mufti.

Egypt, for its part, continued to "hunt" and defame the Mufti. The Egyptians intensified their campaign against him after the outbreak of the crisis with Jordan and the Mufti's visit there. Shuqayri's resignation from his post and the rise of the fidaiyyun organizations after the Six Day War finally forced the Mufti to renounce all activity in the Palestinian arena and to concentrate on Islamic affairs. The AHC organ *Filastin* began to support the fidaiyyun organizations and their activities. The Mufti had no significant effect on the Palestinian arena during this period.[52]

Palestinian organizations. Shuqayri's activities in establishing the PLO brought about attempts among Palestinian organizations to set up a roof organization as an alternative to the PLO. At the end of January 1964 contacts were made aimed at uniting a number of secret Palestinian organizations under one leadership. Disputes arose regarding the organizational framework of cooperation, the form of unity, and the joint stance towards Shuqayri and the PLO. On 14 March 1964 a declaration was made on behalf of four Palestinian organizations calling for the establishment of the institutions of the Palestinian Entity on "revolutionary principles", free elections, the formation of regular army units and the election of a national congress which would, in turn, elect an executive committee to function as a collective leadership.[53] And in late May 1964 the more meaningful Political Bureau of the Palestinian Revolutionary Forces for United Action was established. It was composed of six representatives of six organizations for purposes of coordinating their activities, while preserving the organizational and ideological independence of each. Their joint platform called for the establishment of "an active, revolutionary Palestinian Entity" and for "unity of action" between all the organizations.[54]

CONCLUSION

The decisions of the first summit, Shuqayri's activities following it, the convening of the Jerusalem Congress, the establishment of the PLO and the decisions of the second summit all aroused enthusiasm among the Palestinians. Shuqayri was greeted sympathetically in all the Palestinian concentrations he visited, but especially among all strata of the West Bank, where support for him and the PLO reached 80 to 90 per cent of the population. The Palestinians followed with great interest the steps taken to set up the Entity, and saw in the establishment of the PLO's representative institutions the beginnings of self-determination. The fact that King Husayn, Nasir and Shuqayri were cooperating on this matter intensified their enthusiasm and saved political figures from being torn between dual loyalties.[55] This nationalistic arousal was, however, still passive and inspired "from above". Nevertheless, it impelled underground Palestinian organizations to surface in order to exploit the enthusiasm. The popularity of Shuqayri and the PLO during 1964 was a crucial factor in the Fatah leadership's decision to embark on their fidai activities in early 1965,[56] and was the background for the growth of the fidaiyyun organizations from 1965 to 1967.

Although the PLO was the formal representative of the Palestinians, in terms of its composition it was far from being representative. The period 1965-67 was now to see a struggle in the Palestinian and Arab arenas over the PLO's representative composition.

Part Two

The Struggle over PLO Representation of the Palestinians, 1965–1967

On the night of 31 December 1964 Fatah carried out its first act of sabotage in Israel.[57] With this, a new chapter was opened in the history of the Palestinian issue in general and of the question of the Palestinian Entity and representation in particular. At first Fatah was isolated in the Palestinian arena. It recruited Palestinians and mercenaries from among the veteran fidaiyyun who had worked for Egyptian and Syrian intelligence services in the 1950s. The Palestinian public "was content with silent, passive support. It did not show readiness to participate in fidai activity, although it did not hide its admiration for fidai actions undertaken by Fatah."[58] However, the Arab and Israeli media gave wide publicity to Fatah's sabotage activities, which aroused reactions far beyond the practical effectiveness or the number of activities carried out. In contrast to the PLO, Fatah showed the way for independent, militant Palestinian action. It appeared as an organization that had arisen from below; the wide support it gained among the Palestinians raised doubts as to how much the PLO represented the Palestinians, and caused dissension within the PLO. The emergence of Fatah also intensified the competition between Egypt and Syria. Egypt, which saw Fatah's activities as a threat to its strategy of stages, supported the PLO as the representative of the Palestinians. Syria, on the other hand, had reservations about the PLO and supported Fatah and the fidaiyyun organizations.

Fatah's activities put to the test the Arab readiness to fight Israel and highlighted the Arab states' military weakness in relation to Israel. The fidai actions contributed to the deterioration leading up to the Six Day War. With increasing discord in the summit and an intensified struggle between the PLO and Jordan over representation of the Palestinians, there was once again a question mark over the stability of the regime in Jordan. The Jordanian hold over the West Bank was now seen to be weakened, and Jordan's claim to represent the Palestinians was undermined.

EGYPT: SUPPORT FOR THE PLO

Until the Six Day War Egypt gave consistent support to the PLO as the representative of the Palestinians and to Shuqayri as its head. There were three main reasons for this policy.

1. *The PLO became the only achievement of the summit conferences.* On 23 December 1963 Nasir called for an Arab summit conference as a way out of the dilemma he then faced. He realized that he could not fulfil his 1959 promise that 1963 or 1964 would be the decisive year, when "the military preparations will be completed and our forces ready for action". Nasir needed pan-Arab legitimization for postponement of the decisive military action, and found it in the statement of the Syrian chief-of-staff, at a meeting of Arab chiefs-of-staff (7–9 December 1963), that "Syria will not be able to divert the waters of the Jordan in its territory because if it does so Israel will attack her and will conquer the sources of the Jordan, and we will not be able to do anything". Thus Egypt and Syria found themselves in a position of "lack of freedom of action in their territory".[59] Nasir called for the summit when he was certain that he could dictate his strategy to the Arab states. But he failed to realize two of its three essential components.

First, there was a stalemate in the Arab plan to divert the tributaries of the Jordan. The second Arab summit decided "to begin immediately to carry out the technical work for diverting the Jordan River". The commander-in-chief of the UAC, Ali Amir, calculated that Israel would carry out military action against the diversion works at or close to their completion. But Israel's attack proved surprising in its timing, coming at the beginning (March, May and August 1965) of the diversion works and without getting involved in a war. As a result, Amir declared to the third summit (September 1965) that "continuation of the technical work without military preparedness [for war] is not logical". The third summit decided to grant freedom of action in carrying out the diversion works to the Arab states directly concerned; Amir advised continuation of the diversion works in places far from the border. Lebanon, however, had ceased its diversion works even before the third summit; Syria transferred the works further from the border (about 10 km), but no significant progress was made until the Six Day War. Jordan carried out its plan for the Mukhayba Dam, which in itself did not damage Israel's water plans. Thus execution of this stage of Nasir's strategy failed some months after it began.

The paralysis of the UAC marked the second unrealized component. The UAC failed both to defend the diversion plan and to prepare the Arab armies for war with Israel. This resulted from the Arab states' lack of trust in each other and fear of interference in their internal affairs. The second summit did decide "to grant the C-in-C UAC full authority to move military forces, taking into account, when moving the forces from one state to another before the outbreak of hostilities, the constitutional laws of each state". Following the decision of the second summit to begin diversion works immediately, the UAC ordered (August 1964) the concentration of Arab forces near Israel's borders. Iraqi forces (more than an armoured brigade) indeed moved towards the Israeli border, but because of Jordan's objection to their entering its territory stayed at H3, while a Saudi brigade camped at Tabuk. Jordan agreed only to the entry of an Iraqi logistic unit, and then only in civilian dress; later, it also agreed to a Syrian radar station on its territory. Lebanon opposed the entry of forces into its territory, which prompted Amir to tell the third summit that "there is no advantage in having military forces stationed in the staging areas". Syria opposed the stationing of an Egyptian air force on its territory when the UAC proposed a Northern Air Command comprising Syria, Jordan and Lebanon under an Egyptian officer, demanding that they themselves should command this force.[60] After the summit atmosphere had been spoilt by Nasir, a number of Arab states including Saudi Arabia ceased funding the UAC. To conclude, the UAC was reduced to a coordination command for exchanging intelligence on the Israeli army and information on the Arab armies, financing arms deals, preparing training programmes, preparing plans for the PLA and arranging officers' visits to Arab countries. Eventually Amir proposed to the Arab Defence Council (January 1967) that the UAC disband or be suspended.[61] Thus Nasir failed to achieve "the formation of a central force" to wage war with Israel.[62]

2. Continuing to avoid war with Israel.   Nasir's point of departure remained non-involvement in war with Israel. This policy was strengthened following Syria's demand that the UAC (Egypt) respond to Israel's attacks on the diversion works in Syria. Amir told the third summit that in his view (actually Egypt's) Israel was determined to go to war if the diversion works continued; but at the second summit he had assessed the Arab forces to be weaker than

Israel's: "the UAC requires seven to ten days to repel a possible Israeli attack on any Arab state which begins to divert the Jordan's sources – and that means a certain Israeli victory".[63] Thus Nasir averred that "if Israel damages a tractor and I have to attack them the following day, that means that Israel has determined the timing of the war. I am the one who should determine the time and place of the campaign." Nasir emphasized that "there should be no going to war while the Arab states are not ready to defend themselves or to repel an attack".[64]

3. *Nasir, concerned about his image, attached great importance to Palestinian support for his policy.* He viewed the establishment of the PLO as the expression of the existence of the Palestinian issue. In his important speech to the 2nd PNC (31 May 1965), he portrayed the Palestinians and Egyptians as a united force for "revolutionary action for the return of Filastin".[65] He knew that the Palestinians pinned their hopes on him and supported his efforts to set up the PLO.[66]

As a result of all these developments Nasir faced a new dilemma. On the one hand, "the liberation of Filastin" had become "the pan-Arab national aim" (*al-hadaf al-Arabi al-qawmi*). Within a year of the first summit Nasir had succeeded in persuading the Arab world that he was at last on the way to the "liberation of Filastin", and that for the first time since the disintegration of the UAR, a practical and definite plan for the destruction of Israel had been decided upon, for which Egypt would bear the principal responsibility. On the other hand, following the failure of "unity of action" and the return to divisions in the Arab world, "a wave of despair began to flood Arab public opinion, especially Palestinian". Haykal's articles (July–August 1966) on "the crisis of Arab revolutionism" were in fact an expression of Nasir's own "crisis of revolutionism", and an apologetic attempt to excuse his strategic failure. To escape this dilemma, and to prove that he was making progress, Nasir pointed to the setting up of the PLO – the third element of his strategy – as "the turning point in the Arab action for the liberation of Filastin", "the positive and outstanding achievement of the summit conferences" and as an expression of "the failure of Zionism to eliminate the problem of Filastin".[67]

Expressions of Egypt's support. Egypt accepted in principle that *the PLO was the sole representative of the Palestinians.* Through its governmental institutions, it attempted to secure this status for the PLO, which in its view should handle any matter connected with the Palestinian Entity. Egypt considered the activities of Fatah (and the Palestinian organizations) as outside the PLO framework and a threat to its status, and directed both overt and covert actions against Fatah.

A campaign of suspicion against Fatah was waged through the pro-Egyptian press in Lebanon, pointing to "the connection between Fatah and the agents of CENTO and Israel". These newspapers emphasized that "Palestinian fidai activity on its own will not liberate Filastin".[68] Also, in inter-Arab forums Egypt tried to force Arab states to act against Fatah members and to refrain from facilitating Fatah's actions against Israel. In early 1965, following the Israelis' first pronouncement (12 January 1965) on Fatah's sabotage actions, the UAC several times ordered the chiefs-of-staff of Syria, Jordan and Lebanon to prevent fidaiyyun activities in Israel, requesting them "not to allow irresponsible people to carry out these actions at an inappropriate time". In the UAC's opinion "all activity, of any kind, that is not derived from the united military plan [of the UAC] is likely to lead to military campaigns against the enemy when the Arab states have not yet completed their preparations for these campaigns, and so only the enemy will benefit from them". These instructions remained in force until the Six Day War. In accordance with the recommendations of the UAC the Lebanese government prohibited (September 1965) the publication of information about Fatah in the Lebanese press, including Fatah's own pronouncements.[69]

In addition, the Egyptian intelligence and General Investigations departments were aware of Fatah's organization in the Gaza Strip and its preparations for sabotage acts in Israel at the end of December 1964. They kept a close watch; preventive detention of Fatah members stopped them from carrying out actions parallel to those executed from Jordan. Nevertheless, in February 1965 Fatah succeeded in carrying out three actions from the Gaza Strip. Through intensified control, increased detentions of heads of the organization and through capturing arms caches, the Egyptians prevented any further action from the Strip until the Six Day War. The detainees were released after signing an undertaking not to act "except with permiśion of the authorities". Attempts by Fatah leaders during 1965 to meet Egyptian officials failed.[70]

Finally, Nasir's dramatic and unexpected appearance at the 2nd PNC (31 May 1965) was intended to unite the ranks of the PLO and to renew confidence in Shuqayri. This appearance occurred against the background of his assessment that the PLO was facing a serious internal crisis following Fatah activities; signs that the atmosphere of the summit was deteriorating; the PLO's problems in Jordan, Saudi Arabia and Syria; and the strident criticism of Shuqayri. Nasir succeeded in his aim. In his speech he called for PLO unity and defended Shuqayri's policy towards Jordan. With a hint about Fatah, he told the participants of the Congress, "You represent the Palestinian people, Egypt stands by your side in heart and soul."[71]

Egypt also gave *aid in setting up the institutions of the PLO and the PLA*. It was only natural that Egypt should give Shuqayri all possible support to set up the institutions of the PLO. The Gaza Strip was, for Shuqayri, "Palestinian territory", even though in fact it was "under Egyptian sovereignty". On 5 June 1965 Nasir signed an order changing Article 2 of the Gaza Strip Constitutional Law of February 1962. The new article stated that

> the liberation of Filastin is the holy duty of all its sons and of every Arab. To this end the Palestinians in the Gaza Strip will act in conjunction with their brothers, the sons of Filastin, wherever they may be, to set up a national organization [*qawmi*] – the PLO – whose supreme aim is joint work for the return of the land stolen from Filastin, and for participation in the realization of the mission of Arab nationalism.[72]

In accordance with this order the governor of the Gaza Strip announced a decision (February 1965) to dismantle the Palestinian National Union and all its institutions in the Strip; all its property, buildings, offices, equipment and officials were transferred to the PLO. All the PLO offices in the Strip began to work under the PLO EC in Cairo and in coordination with the Egyptian government in the Strip. On 24 February 1965 Nasir approved a law imposing conscription to the PLA on all inhabitants of the Strip.

Nasir's declaration at the second Arab summit that "we agree to the formation of the PLA and put Sinai and the Gaza Strip at the disposal of the PLO to form the army" encouraged the summit to authorize the formation of the PLA. On 10 April 1965 the governor of the Gaza Strip promulgated the Liberation Tax Law, imposed on all economic and commercial activity in the Strip. The income from this tax went to the PLO.[73]

Finally, Egypt gave the PLO *aid in the field of information*, thereby strengthening the PLO's representative status. Egyptian radio broadcasts and especially Nasir's speeches were listened to throughout the Arab world. Egyptian newspapers, widely circulated in the West Bank, carried pro-PLO material. The PLO also gained the support of the pro-Egyptian press in Lebanon. On 1 March 1965 Cairo Radio began a "Voice of Filastin" corner, run by the PLO, and it almost became Shuqayri's personal radio station. Nevertheless, Shuqayri did not always gain Nasir's approval regarding the way he ran the PLO.[74]

Changes in Egypt's position on fidai actions.   The changes began to appear in mid-1966. The Egyptian media and the pro-Egyptian press in Lebanon began to show qualified support for these actions, which later became more enthusiastic. Egypt still expressed reservations about the timing of Fatah actions and the fact that they were not coordinated with pan-Arab or UAC policy; the PLO continued to be "the absolute realization of the Palestinian Entity".[75] The change in the Egyptian position stemmed essentially from two factors.

First, after Nasir's change of attitude about the summit atmosphere, the Palestinian issue became the main means for Egypt, Syria and the PLO to undermine the Jordanian regime. Second, Fatah actions in Israel aroused positive reactions from the Arab world and especially the Palestinians, as opposed to the perceived passivity of the PLO. Although Egypt was still opposed to fidai activities from the Gaza Strip, it became more flexible so that when Fatah leaders continued trying to meet with Egyptian leaders, this time the Egyptians were ready. In Cairo in mid-1966 Salah Nasr, head of general intelligence, met with Fatah leaders but without result. In another meeting in July 1966 between Fatah leaders and leaders of the ruling Egyptian Socialist Union, the Egyptians explained that "fidai actions must take place within the framework of and in coordination with overall Arab planning for the liberation of Filastin". Towards the end of 1966 Fatah offered to work with the Egyptians "in a defined and limited sphere". According to Abu Iyad, at a meeting with Shams Badran, the war minister, the Fatah leaders proposed "to form fidaiyyun squads in the Negev with the aim of weakening the Israeli army, in times of peace and war. Fatah would provide the personnel and the Egyptians, logistical support." Badran "mocked" this proposal and the meeting ended without results.[76]

Another change in the Egyptian position began in February 1967 and continued until the Six Day War. The Egyptians moved towards approval of fidai actions by Fatah or other organizations such as

Abtal al-Awda, which was connected with the PLO, but only to a limited extent and not from the Gaza Strip. Surveillance and preventive detention of Fatah members in the Strip continued in this period. This change came after two years' experience in which Egypt had learned that Israel was content with limited reprisals after fidai actions.[77] Thus the Egyptians did not want to fall behind the Syrians in supporting Fatah.

These changes in Egyptian policy unintentionally harmed both the PLO's and Shuqayri's status. From February 1967 it became clear Shuqayri could only maintain his position as PLO head by continually reminding Nasir of his moral obligations towards him, and by intensifying the struggle against Husayn and his regime. The Egyptians began to think about involving the fidaiyyun organizations in the PLO framework; the Six Day War delayed this plan, and also put an end to Egyptian support for Shuqayri. Egypt then decided to gamble on another horse – the fidaiyyun organizations and especially Fatah.

THE SYRIAN POSITION

Syrian policy on the Palestinian issue, and on the PLO in particular, moved, in this period, in a vicious circle. It wavered between the traditional Syrian tendency towards *qawmiyya* (pan-Arabism) and their adherence to *watanniyya* (patriotism); between extreme "revolutionary policy" and limited practical steps. Syria openly attacked Nasir's summit policy, but still signed the summit decisions. It was the first to begin diverting the tributaries of the Jordan – in the area most exposed to Israeli attack – and called for the use of force both to prevent Israel from diverting the Jordan and in reply to Israel's actions against diversion works in Syria; yet in practice it recognized that "Syria alone cannot effect the liberation of Filastin", and even tried to make the UAC fail. Syria supported unity and sought Nasir's recognition of the Ba'th regime, yet in Ba'th publications denigrated Nasir's regime.

At least until the end of 1966, Syria was isolated in the Arab arena. The Syrian Ba'th felt strong when the Arab world was split; solidarity meant that Nasir was the leader. These contradictions in Syrian policy stemmed in part from increasing struggles within the Syrian Ba'th. Aflaq emphasized (21 June 1964) that only "to the extent that the revolution in Syria succeeds in strengthening its position and realizing its aims, will it be able to implement the plan [of the Ba'th's Palestinian Entity]. There is a close connection" in the realization of both these goals.[78]

The Ba'th regime in Syria suffered two crises in this period: the "crisis of the party" and the "crisis of government". A struggle between the National Command and the Regional Command ended with the overthrow of the government in February 1966 and the transfer of Ba'th rule to the Regional Command. The struggle had begun with tension between the "young leaders" of the party, associated with the Regional Command, and the veteran leadership, which had sustained its power in the National Command. A group of young, left-wing officers managed, with the help of Alawite and Druze officers led by Salah Jadid, to instil its influence in the army and the party. In August 1965 the group called a Regional Congress which elected a new leadership under Dr Yusuf Zu'ayyin. President Hafiz drew closer to the veteran leadership, and with the help of his army contacts they all tried to thwart the group of young officers. In December 1965 the veteran leadership called a special National Congress which decided to disband the Regional Command and the left-wing government it had appointed. In the end the struggle was settled by the army in favour of the young guard of the party (February 1966). Once again the army had initiated a seizure of power.[79] Against this background the Syrian attitude towards "the problem of Filastin" and the Palestinian Entity can be divided into two phases.

1. *Up to the overthrow in February 1966.*   The basic Ba'th conception in this period was as follows. (1) "Syria cannot on its own execute a plan for the liberation of Filastin. It follows that any separate stand will be a theoretical stand without any practical value behind it." "The ideological division of opinion between Nasir's regime and the Ba'th has not been eliminated. The conflicts which exist between us and Israel are much more important than these divisions of opinion." (2) "There is no relying on the decisions of the summit conference." There must be "an offensive strategy in which the timing of the liberation and its form will be defined". To this end the Arab (read Egyptian) "preventive strategy" must be changed. Nevertheless, Syria supported the summit's decisions "without reservations, even though they represent only the minimum obligation by the Arab states regarding the problem of Filastin". The aim was "the liberation of Filastin from Zionism, the elimination of the state of Israel and the return of the Arab Palestinian people to its country and its homeland". (3) "There is a need to establish an Arab

deterrent force, always ready to respond to every Israeli attack regardless of where it took place, with the same or greater strength." (4) "The problem of Filastin must be seen as the most important Arab problem, and therefore the chief problem of the party, and the starting point of its programme of action."[80]

Syrian policy towards the PLO was ambivalent; that is, "the attitude of the party was different from the official Syrian position". The instructions of the National Command to party branches and their members regarding the PLO were not clear, at least until the end of 1965.[81] Officially, Syria remained critical of Shuqayri and of the PLO because of its "non-revolutionary" composition. It demanded both the reconstitution of the PNC and "the formulation of a new National Covenant". Hafiz even claimed that the PLO was "an organization for representation and not for liberation".[82] However, the "Filastin branch" of the Ba'th in Lebanon looked more favourably upon the PLO and its composition, stressing that although "there are conflicts within the organization, the PLO is an existing fact capable of advancing the Palestinian struggle by taking account of the strong forces operating within it". This branch proposed to the 8th National Congress reconsideration of its position on the PLO, recommending "the formation of a [Ba'th] Palestinian Command whose task would be to follow up developments, coordinate action and make day-to-day decisions. This Command would be directly linked on the one hand to the National Command and on the other to the various Palestinian organizations." This proposal was not accepted by the NC, which decided that "the Congress does not view the PLO as an instrument for struggle capable of bearing the burden of the campaign for the liberation of Filastin. This assessment demands that the party struggle for the establishment of a revolutionary entity capable of mobilizing the people of Filastin and leading it in the campaign for the return." Moreover, the Congress decided on "a gathering of Palestinians from all countries to debate the question of Filastin in a practical manner". In reality, however, the National Command concerned itself more with the struggle over its own rule and existence. During 1965 the party, in its decisions and publications, almost entirely ignored the plan of the Palestinian Entity which it had published in May 1964. It continued to support Fatah, and was strongly critical of the decisions of the 2nd PNC (May 1965) as well as of Shuqayri personally.[83] A few months later the Ba'th called for a "collective and democratic leadership in the PLO", and called on

Shuqayri to take steps "towards establishing Palestinian national unity of all the loyal Palestinian forces".[84]

The Syrian attitude towards Fatah during this phase was also ambivalent. Particularly obvious was the gap between Syria's official position and its real position, in which a number of the senior commissioned officers took a separate stand. Syria was the only Arab state openly to support Fatah's actions. Its media became the mouthpiece for Fatah pronouncements, which the other states avoided lest they be seen by Israel as responsible for Fatah actions. The Fatah organ *al-Asifa* was distributed in Syria and sent from there to Arab states.[85] And yet, during 1965, both the regime and the party in Syria lacked a clear policy on Fatah. As a centralized regime it regarded Fatah with mistrust, even referring to them as "separatists" (*infisaliyyun*).

Thus Syria tried to cultivate and control Fatah through ties with its "moderate" leaders and infiltration of Syrian supporters. Fatah, for its part, sought material, military and political aid from the regime while insisting on maintaining independence. When Fatah carried out its first action in Israel from the Syrian border (July 1965), it did so without the permission of the authorities; Syrian intelligence briefly detained the Fatah leaders who were in Syria at the time. In late 1965 a number of Fatah leaders, among them Arafat, were again detained when the organization was suspected of sabotaging the Tapline oil pipeline, but released when the charges were not proved.

In contrast, the "Filastin branch" in Lebanon tried to persuade the National Congress that Fatah was worth supporting. The Congress contented itself with a decision on "the establishment of a secret committee to discuss the question of Fatah and the party's stand towards it". And a group of young army officers helped Fatah despite official suspicion, among them Hafiz al-Asad, then commander of the air force, and Ahmad Suwydani, then head of military intelligence. With this group's help Fatah ran two training bases in Syria, one of them at al-Hame, and was also given an area for training with live ammunition in Syria's desert. Some Fatah members underwent training in the PLA, which Syria formed. Asad helped Fatah transfer arms, some from China, which the authorities had prohibited from being unloaded at Ladhiqiyya. Thus emerged the cooperation between Syrian intelligence and Fatah regarding reconnaissance and intelligence within Israel. Towards the end of the period Fatah was able to act against Israel from the Syrian border, and from Lebanon and Jordan where the fidaiyyun had penetrated from Syria.[86]

2. From 23 February 1966 to June 1967. In February 1966, with the rise to power of the young left-wing officers, Syrian strategy towards the Palestinian issue began to change to one based on the slogan "the popular liberation war as the sole way of liberating Filastin". Meant as an antithesis to Nasir's strategy, it emphasized "the armed struggle [against Israel] in which all the Arabs will participate, with the Palestinians at their head". Fidai activities became an integral part of Syria's strategy; it began to defend directly fidai actions in Israel from its territory, claiming that "Syria does not defend Israel's security". Syria also cooperated closely with Fatah, the PLO and Egypt in undermining the regime in Jordan, according to the slogan "today we will liberate Jordan, tomorrow Filastin". In Syrian official papers the West Bank was now designated "the Palestinian sector of Jordan".[87]

As for the PLO, with its new stand in favour of fidai activities, the Ba'th now called for cooperation between "the Palestinian revolutionary forces" in order to form a "national front" between the PLO, Fatah and the other Palestinian organizations. Shortly before the Six Day War, Syria recognized "the legitimacy of the PLO's representativeness of the Palestinian people". The Syrians went so far as to demand that the PLO "become a revolutionary fidai organization", and as such become the roof organization for all fidai groups. Another product of Syria's new approach was the Joint Struggle Agreement (2 December 1965) between Syria and Shuqayri, which involved subversive activities in Jordan.[88]

And as for Fatah, Syria now became the main coordinator behind the vast majority of fidai actions from Syria, Lebanon and Jordan. The Syrian army gave Fatah installations and military equipment, and helped it in training and exercises. This aid, and the entry of new Syrian operational units into Syrian fidai activity, led to increased Syrian control over Fatah actions; Fatah, because of its need for a stable base, was forced to cooperate while still trying to maintain its independence. Following the flight (May 1966) to Jordan of Muhammad Arake (director of the Palestinian Section of the Syrian intelligence, who was responsible for coordinating actions in Jordan and Israel and for contacts with Fatah), tension flared up between the regime and Fatah. The regime accused the Fatah leadership of involvement in the killing (May 1966) of two agents planted into Fatah by Syrian intelligence; the two had some connections with

Arake. In June 1966 a number of Fatah leaders, among them Arafat and Abu Jihad, were detained in Damascus, interrogated and later released. After a lull, however, the actions inside Israel were renewed, including the penetration of squads from Syria into Lebanon and from there into Israel with the full cooperation of Syrian intelligence.[89] A number of months before the Six Day War the regime set up Jabhat al-Tahrir al-Sha'biyya al-Filastiniyya for carrying out fidai actions inside Israel. The 68th Palestinian Commando Battalion, called the Jalal Ka'ush Unit, stood at the disposal of the Syrians for the same purpose.

JORDAN: CONFRONTATION WITH THE PALESTINIAN ENTITY

To establish himself as representative of the Palestinians, Husayn had to rule both the territory and the population of the West Bank. The PLO, on the other hand, needed only the political allegiance of the population. From this stemmed the inevitable bitter struggle between Jordan and the PLO for the soul of the West Bank Palestinians. As for the Palestinians in Jordan, they now faced a dilemma: was their allegiance to the Hashemite regime, which had annexed the West Bank, or to a Palestinian organization which had been set up to represent them? Both Husayn and Shuqayri used the phrase "Jordan is Filastin and Filastin is Jordan", but they meant diametrically opposite things.

Shuqayri's position. Shuqayri's short-term aim was "personal autonomy" for the *population* of the West Bank so long as the Hashemite regime controlled the *land*. The Palestinians would be permitted "to express freely their national activities, like the other Arab peoples, in the stages of their struggle". Thus independent political and military institutions were needed for the West Bank Palestinians, to be integrated with the political institutions of the PLO – for example, participation in elections to the PNC, in the Popular Organization and in the PLA. Shuqayri believed that, since the Palestinians were in the majority in Jordan and superior to the Jordanians in, for instance, education, this would lead in the long term to Jordan being taken over by the Palestinian Entity. This meant achieving "territorial sovereignty" after having achieved "personal autonomy". West Bank politicians understood Shuqayri's intentions and supported them. After the PLO began to adopt fidai activities and its confrontation with Jordan erupted, Shuqayri stated that the West Bank was "the launching area for the liberation of Filastin" and that "the way to Tel Aviv passes through Amman", that is, "the liberation of Filastin must begin with the liberation of Jordan from Husayn's regime through the establishment of a nationalist regime". There is no doubt that in his view the next step, after the overthrow of the monarchy, had to be "Palestinian self-determination" and the setting up of a Palestinian state in Jordan. He stated that "the East Bank is an integral part of Filastin", "Jordan has no right to exist as a state" and that "Jerusalem must be the capital of all Filastin".[90]

Shuqayri adopted Nasir's conception that these objectives could only be attained in stages while pacifying Jordanian leaders regarding the PLO's intentions. Only if these methods failed would it be necessary to resort to a popular uprising by the Palestinian population. But political circumstances in the Arab arena and his dependence on Nasir led Shuqayri to steer a zig-zag course.

Early in 1965, after setting up the PLO and getting the second summit's approval for forming the PLA, Shuqayri turned to the central problem: PLO activity in Jordan. He formulated several demands.

In the military sphere, Shuqayri demanded conscription for Palestinians in Jordan, and permission for the PLO to form, arm and train PLA battalions in Jordan subordinate to PLA command and in accordance with the UAC plan. The PLO also presented Jordan with a plan for strengthening the villages on the front line with Israel militarily, economically and socially. It also demanded permission to set up "popular training camps" for civil defence exercises for the West Bank population and to provide them with weapons for emergencies. Furthermore, the PLO asked to set up and run ideological military summer camps for youth and students, in cooperation with Jordanian officers.

Shuqayri also demanded free and general elections for the PNC among the Palestinians in Jordan in accordance with procedures approved by the EC of the PLO. The PLO would apply the Law on the Palestinian Popular Organization in Jordan. The PLO demanded that Jordan grant diplomatic immunity to the PLO centre in Jerusalem, members of the EC and PLO officials.

The PLO demanded permanent allocation of time on Jordanian radio for broadcasting of "nationalist" programmes and permission to conduct propaganda campaigns in both print and speech.

Finally, Shuqayri demanded the imposition of a 3 per cent tax on the salaries of Palestinians in Jordan for the PLO, and permission to conduct popular fund-raising campaigns. He also demanded that the Jordanian government put into effect the Protocol prepared by the Arab League regarding freedom of movement, place of residence and work for the Palestinians.[91]

These demands implied duality in the government, and the creation of a kind of a state within the state. The PLO would become an additional executive authority in Jordan, responsible for the "Palestinian section". Since this section comprised two-thirds of the population, it seemed clear that Jordan would have to turn into a "Palestinian state" with the Jordanians in a minority or at least a confederal state.

The Jordanian conception. The starting point of the Jordanian conception continued to be the White Paper of 1962. Wasfi al-Tall's view was that in this programme "the subject of the Palestinian Entity was included, and the principles and implications of the Palestinian personality thereby defined as essentially one with the Jordanian entity. These principles were accepted by the participants in the summit conferences, as a result of which the Palestinian Entity was set up with the support of King Husayn and the government."[92] Tall now attempted to put this plan, devised under his inspiration, into practice. The principles of the Jordanian conception regarding the PLO, as Tall conceived and executed them, can be summarized as follows.

First of all, the PLO must be "the prop of the Jordanian entity, all of whose activity is directed at becoming a centre of power for the campaign for Filastin". In other words, "the concentration of Palestinian potential by the PLO complements the role embodied in the Jordanian entity in all its constituent elements and complements the activity of the state and the people since Jordan was established". In this capacity the PLO is "the Arab arm of Jordan and Filastin".

Second, "the state is responsible ... for directing [its] citizens, organizing and training them in accordance with the laws. All activities, in whatever framework, connected with the citizens, must be directed by the state apparatus or with its permission." Thus every action connected with PLO activity must be based on the following principles: "wholeness of the Entity, of the Kingdom of Jordan, its interests and internal unity, the laws of the kingdom, its sovereignty and security considerations, the foreign and internal policy of the state."

Third, since the majority of its citizens are Palestinians, Jordan is the sole representative of the Palestinians. Therefore, there is no need to establish separate "Palestinian bodies" in Jordan. "Jordan, both its Banks, is Filastin, and represents the launching point for its liberation"; the Palestinians in Jordan are "Jordanians of Palestinian origin".

Finally, the Palestinian Entity is a diplomatic necessity whose aim, first and foremost, is to further Arab efforts in the international arena. "The setting up of the PLO is meant to keep the Palestinian problem in existence and to help organize and mobilize the Palestinian potential outside of Jordan."[93]

These policy principles left no doubt about Jordan's position regarding Shuqayri's demands. The Jordanian regime, however, tried to show that it was actually satisfying these demands by its own methods. Of course, Jordan's attempt to identify the Hashemite state with Filastin stood in contrast to its actual policy of "Jordanization" of the Hashemite Kingdom with special emphasis on the East Bank.

The following, then, were Jordan's reactions to the demands put forward by Shuqayri and the PLO. In the military sphere, Jordan refused to cooperate, repeatedly asserting that 60 per cent of the soldiers in the Jordanian army were Palestinians and that all Palestinians in Jordan received Jordanian citizenship. Conscription would hurt many workers in Jordan and beyond, as well as their families in Jordan. Instead Jordan preferred a volunteer army: "Jordan is forming new battalions whose number is four times what the PLO demands and these are deployed on the front lines."[94] The government passed the Law on Defence of Front-Line Towns and Villages, and army headquarters issued a special order for its implementation. Training and distribution of arms to the villages began on 16 June 1965. Jordan claimed that it was implementing a plan for "popular training" of all its inhabitants, and as proof pointed to exercises by the Civil Defence and summer camps for military training of students and youth (20,000 were trained in 1965).[95]

As for PLO institutions, Jordan agreed in principle to holding elections to the PLO institutions so long as this was done through the Jordanian Interior Ministry. It argued that all Jordanian citizens already participated in "popular organizations", such as the House of Deputies, the Senate, the government, the army, town councils, trade bureaux, professional and labour unions, schools and educational institutions. It agreed to grant diplomatic immunity to the PLO offices and officials.

Jordan did agree to cooperate with the PLO in the sphere of

media and information, in accordance with Jordan's own national guidance plan.

Also, Jordan agreed in principle to the demand for a "liberation tax", but this was conditional on its being imposed on all Jordanian citizens and not only "on those of Palestinian origin".[96]

The confrontation. Disputes between the PLO and Jordan were inevitable once the summit deliberately avoided defining the role of the PLO in Jordan. As a result each party acted according to its own conception. The second summit made the location of units of the PLA conditional on "the agreement of the state concerned". Shuqayri failed to obtain from the third summit a pan-Arab seal of approval for his demands on Jordan, in view of Husayn's resistance to these demands. Furthermore, Husayn opposed Shuqayri's referring to the West Bank during the summit debates as "Palestinian territory". Husayn demanded that the PLO's role in Jordan be defined, but the summit refrained from this, and contented itself with a decision regarding the Popular Organization and "general, direct elections to the PNC", and a statement that "the PLO will maintain contact with the member states concerned in order to achieve understanding regarding the steps necessary" for such elections.[97] No decision was taken on the question of conscription.

Thus no agreement between Husayn and Shuqayri was possible. In this period the relationship between the PLO and Jordan went through a number of stages.

In the period until 30 September 1965, the relationship developed against the background of Nasir's desire to sustain the summit's atmosphere. Husayn, aware of this policy, rejected Shuqayri's demands, but was also aware of the mood on the West Bank and so avoided an open split with Shuqayri. On 19 June 1965 the PLO and Jordan approved in principle a draft agreement prepared and presented by Amir Khammash, the Jordanian chief-of-staff, involving fortification of the front lines and the formation of guard units of 15,000 to 20,000. This force, which would be armed with light weapons only, would be subordinate to the Jordanian army exclusively; its formation would be financed by the PLO. The agreement did not deal with the question of forming the PLA in Jordan.

Other demands of Shuqayri were settled according to the Jordanian conception, since Shuqayri was under pressure from Nasir, who wanted an agreement which would alleviate Jordan's misgivings about the PLO's intentions in Jordan so that the PLO could gain a foothold there. In this context two Jordanian officials were appointed in June 1965 to key positions in the PLO – Ali Khiyari as head of the Military Department, and Najib Rsheydat as a member of the EC. The June 1965 agreement was never put into effect because of Jordanian obstruction, and especially because of strident opposition within the PLA HQ, which insisted that the Palestinian commando and fidai units in Jordan be under PLA command, and which even threatened to censure the plan openly "as treacherous". Faced with this pressure Shuqayri withdrew from the agreement, and returned to the third summit with his earlier demands.[98]

In the period from October 1965 to June 1966, Nasir, hoping to pressure Husayn into carrying out the summit's decisions, hinted to Shuqayri about embarking on a limited propaganda campaign against the king. Shuqayri did this in his speech on PLO Radio on 1 October 1965. Jordan counter-attacked; Husayn appealed to Nasir to restrain Shuqayri. Nasir advised Husayn and Shuqayri to reach an agreement between themselves.[99] On 24 December 1965 an agreement was reached between Shuqayri and the Jordanian ambassador to Cairo, Anwar al-Khatib, who was pro-Egyptian. According to this agreement the PLO would conduct a popular fund-raising campaign in Jordan; summer camps would be set up for training youth and students, by Jordanian teachers and officers chosen by agreement between Jordan and the PLO; elections to the PNC would be conducted by the PLO under Jordanian supervision; Jordan would allocate a "corner" for the PLO on Amman Radio under control of the Jordanian Information Ministry; Jordan would put into effect the Arab League Protocol concerning the Palestinians; both sides agreed that the UAC would consider the question of the formation of PLA battalions in Jordan; the problem of the "popular organization" and "the popular training" would be reconsidered as soon as possible between the two sides. However, within the Jordanian government there was serious dispute regarding stipulations that entailed Jordanian concessions, and Husayn refused to approve the agreement. Khatib seems to have erred in assessing flexibility on his government's part.[100] The mutual propaganda attacks now became even more bitter. Through the mediation of the secretary-general of the Arab League, representatives of the PLO and Jordan reached a temporary agreement (10 January 1966) on cessation of the propaganda attacks and postponement of the PNC convention; they also agreed that the two delegations would meet on 21 February 1966 to continue the negotiations – on the basis of both the Khatib–Shuqayri accord and the Jordanian Foreign Ministry announcement (6 December 1965) on Jordanian policy.[101]

Jordan, not wanting to be attacked during a forthcoming meeting of Arab heads of government (expected for mid-March 1966), and especially in view of Nasir's support for Shuqayri's demands, concluded the discussions with the PLO by signing an agreement on 1 March 1966. Its terms can be divided into three categories. (1) On some matters Jordan did not compromise and its stand was accepted: conscription, arming of the front-line villages, and the form of a "popular fund-raising campaign" for the PLO and a "liberation tax" imposed on the entire Jordanian population. (The "liberation tax" caused much resentment among officials and army officers, which Jordanian authorities directed towards the PLO.) A decision on the formation of PLA units was transferred to the UAC. (2) On some matters Jordan had already made concessions – PLO information, summer camps for the training of youth and students, freedom of movement for the Palestinians. (3) There were also important matters on which Jordan made new concessions – "full freedom for the PLO to implement the law on elections to the PNC as approved by the EC". The PLO was permitted to set up centres of the Popular Organization in Jordanian districts. Significantly, the agreement said nothing that could be interpreted as showing any special attitude towards the inhabitants of the West Bank; the words "Palestinian" and "West Bank" were not mentioned, not even in the section on "freedom of movement and work".[102]

Jordan signed the agreement without any intention of implementing it, desiring simply to obtain peace within and without. In a secret memorandum (5 March 1966) to his ministers and the directors of the General Security and General Intelligence, Tall gave clear directives about exactly what PLO activity would actually be allowed in Jordan. All avenues for penetration into the PLO by "opportunists, destroyers, saboteurs who serve party and opportunist interests" must be closed. "All contact between the PLO and citizens, for whatever purpose, without permission of the State or its special offices and not in accordance with its laws, must be prevented." "The PLO must be warned against employing party members or saboteurs. The War Laws regarding communism and parties must be carried out immediately and literally." "Any printed or photographed material must be prohibited." Tall also warned that "the moment it is proved that the doors of this cooperation [between the PLO and Jordan] lead to confusion and sabotage, the State will reconsider" this cooperation.[103] This document speaks for itself. All that was left to Shuqayri if he wanted to be active in Jordan was to turn the PLO into a Jordanian organization.

A few weeks after the agreement was signed, first steps were taken to carry out the spirit and letter of the prime minister's directives. In early April 1966 a wave of arrests began which involved about 300 activists of the Ba'th, the Communist Party and the ANM. This was a crackdown on PLO or pro-PLO activists, and also included leaders of the Popular Organization which the PLO had begun to set up in Jordan, and which the Jordanian authorities feared would turn into an insurgent nationalist movement on the West Bank. The authorities also wished to prevent demonstrations being organized for Filastin Day on 15 May 1966.[104]

Jordan failed, however, in its attempt to make the 3rd PNC in May 1966 collapse by trying to "persuade" most Jordanian representatives to boycott the gathering. Although 80 delegates from Jordan did absent themselves, those that were present failed to influence the proceedings and were even drawn into the stands of the various blocs within the PNC; some even returned to Jordan with positive views on the PLO. The Jordanian delegates proposed that in the next PNC two-thirds of the delegates would be allocated to Jordan, but this was rejected; Shuqayri proposed that the Palestinians in Jordan should get 60 out of 150 PNC members.[105] All in all, an open split was imminent between the PLO and Jordan. Shuqayri prepared for it by attempting to transform the PLO in Jordan into an underground organization.

In the period from June 1966 to May 1967, the Jordanian leadership began by assessing the situation confronting them. Their conclusions were to break off contact with the PLO; to eliminate completely PLO activities in Jordan while undermining its representativeness of the Palestinians; and to cast aspersions on Shuqayri's leadership. Husayn first openly expressed this decision in a speech in Ajlun on 14 June 1966. In a message to Nasir on 14 July 1966, Husayn stated that "in view of the PLO's deviation from the purpose for which it was established, it was not possible for us to cooperate with it".[106]

Husayn had correctly assessed that Nasir intended finally to end the atmosphere of the summit, which would mean a worsening of relations between Egypt (and Syria) and Jordan, and a renewal of

Egypt's campaign to undermine the Jordanian regime, signs of which were already apparent. The Jordanian leadership considered Nasir's speech of 22 June 1966 a turning point in his attitude towards Jordan.[107] The regime received decisive information regarding subversive activity by the PLO and Syria in Jordan, in addition to PLO attempts to penetrate the army. In May 1966 Jordanian intelligence warned of an increase in PLO activity on the West Bank; the Popular Organization, whose activity increased after the March 1966 agreement, began to take on a secret character and became inimical to the regime. Election committees set up by the PLO throughout the West Bank drew up the electoral rolls independently and made direct contact with the inhabitants. It was clear to the regime that, in the PNC about to be elected, Jordan would lose its absolute majority and thus the basis on which Jordan had agreed to the setting up of the PLO would collapse. The deliberations and decisions of the 3rd PNC (20–24 May 1966), which concentrated on attacking Jordan, left no doubt in the regime's mind about the PLO's future goals in Jordan.

In the light of all this Jordan concluded that the PLO intended to set up a "Palestinian state" stage by stage in the West Bank and the Gaza Strip. It judged that in the first stage the PNC (to be elected) would elect a government which would demand authority over internal matters of the West Bank and the Strip; in the second stage this government would attempt to have Jordan's annexation of the West Bank revoked and would then declare an independent "Palestinian state".[108] Husayn once again had to choose the lesser of two evils: he could reorient Jordan's policies and join the "revolutionary camp", which meant submitting to Nasir's and Shuqayri's dictates regarding the Palestinian Entity with all the danger that entailed for his regime; or he could wipe out the PLO entirely from Jordan in the full knowledge that this would lead to increasing attempts to undermine and eventually overthrow him. He chose the latter, believing that he could rely on the loyalty of his army, security forces and intelligence. Shuqayri, with Nasir's support, embarked on a vitriolic propaganda campaign which questioned the kingdom's unity and its very right to exist. Jordan replied with a massive personal counterattack on Shuqayri. After Nasir's decision not to participate in the summit, Shuqayri stepped up his campaign against the Jordanian regime; Fatah activities from the Syrian and Jordanian borders, which received considerable support from the West Bank population, gave the campaign impetus.

The Israeli attack on Samoa' (13 November 1966) precipitated a further deterioration in relations with Jordan, as well as with the PLO, Fatah and Egypt. It led to intense agitation among the West Bank population, which in Nablus became so severe that for the first time (21 November 1966) the army had to intervene. The demonstrations were fuelled by inflammatory broadcasts by the PLO, Damascus and Cairo, aimed at encouraging a civil uprising involving the army. It should be emphasized, however, that most of the demonstrators were high-school students, sometimes joined by inhabitants of the refugee camps; most of the populace supported the demonstrators but only passively. The agitation on the West Bank continued until early December 1966.[109]

The Egyptians and the PLO set themselves three possible goals during this crisis: elimination of the Jordanian Kingdom and its replacement by a pro-Egyptian republic; leaving the kingdom intact but replacing the Wasfi al-Tall government with a pro-Egyptian one; or leaving the kingdom and the government intact on condition that they remain neutral in the Egypt–Saudi Arabia conflict. Until the Samoa' attack, Egypt was ready to accept the third possibility; after the attack, it strove towards the second option and did not rule out the first.[110]

It emerged once again that demonstrations, propaganda attacks and acts of sabotage could not in themselves bring down the Hashemite regime, at least so long as it could rely on the army's loyalty. And the agitation did not spread to the East Bank. On 29 January 1967 Jordan sent a message to the secretary-general of the Arab League saying that Jordan "does not see Shuqayri as a suitable person to represent the Palestinian Entity".[111] With this, the circle begun in January 1964 was temporarily closed.

The Palestinian awakening in the West Bank. Jordan's initial joining of the summit atmosphere, and the relatively sustained internal calm in the country, did not win support for Husayn from the Palestinians in his kingdom. Nasir's star was rising and his picture once again appeared in Jordanian cities; Egyptian newspapers also reappeared and sold briskly, while Cairo Radio broadcasts were listened to avidly. Under the influence of the UAC commander-in-chief, who visited Jordan in July 1964, Husayn dismissed some one hundred of his most long-serving and faithful officers from key command posts.[112] This policy of drawing closer to Egypt, internal liberalization and demonstration of a nationalist foreign policy raised fear among Husayn's long-standing supporters regarding the future of the regime and of their own positions in it, and led to political upheaval. On 6 July 1964 Sharif Husayn bin-Nasir was replaced as prime minister by Bahjat al-Talhuni, who devoted much effort to improving relations with Egypt; but Husayn replaced Talhuni upon his return from the second summit. With the appointment of Wasfi al-Tall as prime minister on 14 February 1965, a new phase emerged of withdrawal from a nationalist foreign policy and a tightening of internal security. Tall, anti-Egyptian and anti-PLO, was the right person at the right time to execute this policy. He had to meet three challenges: PLO activity, which had put in question the regime's claim to represent the Palestinians in its country; Fatah activity in Israel, which had led to Israeli reprisal raids and a deterioration of the situation on the border; and Syrian attempts to undermine the regime. The team working with Tall, well chosen by Husayn, included Muhammad Rasul al-Kaylani (director of general intelligence, appointed April 1964), Radi Abdulla al-Khasawna (director of general security, appointed 16 March 1965 and a close colleague of Tall) and Amir Khammash, chief-of-staff, Jordanian army. This team must be given the credit for the regime's ability to handle the internal crisis. The Jordanian intelligence, as in the earlier period, was able to penetrate the PLO institutions, the Fatah organization as well as Syrian intelligence, thereby managing in time to prevent them from executing their plans.

The establishment of the PLO was greeted with satisfaction by the Palestinians in Jordan, who closely followed anything connected with the organization. The PLO and Shuqayri received their greatest support after Samoa'; during the riots of November 1966 chants were heard against Husayn and other Jordanian leaders. Leaflets were distributed calling for the declaration of a Palestinian Republic. The higher echelons of the local leadership discussed the issue of the separation of the West and East Banks. The hatred reached the point where "the inhabitants of Qalqilya were ready to open fire on soldiers if the army opened fire on the demonstrators and killed even one of them". Once again feelings of discrimination were aroused among the West Bank inhabitants; two members of the Tulkarem Council dared to resign (1 August 1966) partly on grounds of "discrimination between the citizens".[113]

At the same time support was growing for Fatah and its actions, which were described as "acts of heroism". This support included influential Jordanian politicians, even members of the House of Deputies such as Muhammad Hajja. In Jerusalem a secret society of Fatah supporters was set up, including notables from Jericho,

Hebron and Jerusalem; three members, Rasim al-Khalidi, Is-haq al-Dazdar and Subhi al-Tamimi, were detained in late December 1965 following the arrest of another member who was transporting ammunition for Fatah from Hebron to Jerusalem. In view of their status, however, they were released.[114]

The political leaders of the West Bank decided to hold a convention in Jerusalem on 15 December 1966; it was to declare a "national covenant" which would express their opposition to the regime and their support for the PLO and Fatah. The authorities, aware of this intention, banned the convention, but the "preparatory committee" managed to publicize the text of the "national covenant", which called for the repeal of Jordan's emergency legislation, support for Egypt and "for the armed Arab struggle as the only way to eradicate Zionism". It also expressed "support for the PLO as the only representative of the will of the people of Filastin", stating that "the convention recognizes the importance of fidai activities as part of the campaign for the liberation of Filastin".[115]

As in the earlier period the regime was receiving constant warnings from intelligence about subversive activity, especially in the period between the PLO–Jordan split and the Six Day War. These warnings included information on the training of about 200 Syrian saboteurs and fidaiyyun, Fatah members and PLO agents in Syria, for purposes of sabotage in Jordan and Israel. There were also reports of fidaiyyun being sent by Egyptian intelligence from the Gaza Strip, through Israel or Syria, to Jordan. The targets of this sabotage were to be government buildings, electricity and water installations, bridges and public installations; the country's leaders, including the king and Tall, were to be assassinated. Owing to "reliable information ninety percent of the actions delegated [by Syrian intelligence to] the members of the Palestinian Ba'th were discovered in time"; most of the saboteurs who penetrated Jordan were arrested.[116] Nevertheless, as a result of cooperation between Shuqayri and the Syrians, saboteurs succeeded in carrying out a number of actions in Amman, Jerusalem and Nablus in December 1966 and January 1967.

Thus Jordan took extensive security measures during this period. Party members were kept under surveillance, and telephones of local leaders such as Anwar Nusayba, Aziz Shahada, Walid Shak'a, Hikmat al-Masri and Akram Zu'aytar were tapped; from the middle of May 1965 intelligence began to monitor closely the activities of trade unions and social clubs. Heavy security and preventive measures were taken on historic days, such as 15 May in 1965 and 1966; the king ordered Tall to prevent demonstrations "and to strike with force anybody that does evil to the state". Shuqayri and the PLO were also a main focus of attention; an order of January 1966 from the director of general intelligence put the PLO at the top of the list for gathering information, and a directive of 25 August 1966 included Palestinian activities, parties and organizations along with them, specifying the ANM and Fatah. And in June 1966 the Jordanian authorities embarked on total elimination of PLO activity in Jordan, prohibiting any contact with it. On 16 June 1966 the work of the Elections Committee to the PNC was stopped; on 14 July 1966 the prime minister forbade the diplomatic corps and Jordanian representatives abroad to join the PLO or the PLA, or participate in their activities. On 31 January 1967 recognition of the Union of Palestinian Women was withdrawn and all its activities banned; its activists were placed under surveillance. And on 5 January 1967 the PLO offices in Jerusalem were closed and its leaders and officials detained, among them the secretary of its Military Committee.[117]

As for Fatah, the policy during 1965 was cautious; no special effort was made to suppress it so as to avoid opening a second front of confrontation (in addition to the PLO) with the Palestinians. Fatah activities in this year were confined to cross-border actions, so that they represented a smaller danger to Jordan's internal security than the PLO. On 28 November 1965 Tall said regarding Fatah that "personally, I appreciate these youngsters and I have friendly connections with some of them, I'm impressed by their heroism, but their deeds are not enough to liberate Filastin".[118] This undefined policy encouraged soldiers at the lower ranks to help Fatah infiltrate into Israel; on occasion Fatah members were assisted by influential politicians in Jordan (such as Muhammad Hajja) and were released from detention through their intervention. At the same time clear and detailed instructions were given to the army and police units to prevent cross-border infiltration and to detain Fatah members, with emphasis on this being done on the orders of the UAC. In the course of 1966, however, the regime intensified its steps against Fatah, both on the border and inside Jordan. This followed a deterioration of the border situation with Israel and subversive actions by Fatah against the regime. In an extensive campaign, dozens of known or suspected Fatah members were detained. Large quantities of arms and explosives were discovered, and orders to prevent border crossings by fidaiyyun were made more stringent, while guard over the Syrian border was reinforced. Still, the regime did not bring to trial the fidaiyyun or PLO activists detained during this period. But when Jordanian soldiers for the first time killed a fidai, a Fatah member returning from action inside Israel (4 January 1965), the incident became a symbol of the violent struggle between the Palestinian Entity and the Hashemite regime.[119]

THE STRUGGLE FOR REPRESENTATION IN THE PALESTINIAN ARENA, 1965–1967

Shuqayri's declaration that "the PLO is the only legal authority representing the will of the Palestinian people"[120] did not stand up to reality. The appearance of Fatah was an expression of the struggle between two political generations, each with its own political conceptions. In view of the unbridgeable gap between them, one had to depart from the political scene. The reasons for Shuqayri's downfall lay in the way he directed the PLO and in his failure in the very spheres in which he wanted to base the PLO's representation of the Palestinians.

First of all, Shuqayri's assertion that "the PLO represents the will of the Palestinians" contradicted his actual policy; in essence he was far more concerned with maintaining his own leadership position than with the correct representative composition of the PLO or even with his personal popularity. Shuqayri attacked Fatah and its activities even as these were gaining wide support among the Palestinians; already on 3 January 1965 the PLO office in Beirut denied any connections between the PLO and Fatah actions inside Israel. Shuqayri and PLO spokesmen claimed that "the limited actions of individuals which Fatah is carrying out are of no advantage to the problem of Filastin", and that "these actions will involve the Arabs in war [but] not at the [most] convenient time for them".[121] In his meetings with Fatah leaders in 1965 and 1966, Shuqayri tried to persuade them to cease their sabotage activities and instead join the political and military framework of the PLO. Fatah rejected this; it expressed readiness to cooperate in fidai actions with the PLO through delegating different sectors of activity to each of them and through fidaiyyun from Fatah joining PLO squads. The Fatah leaders already saw themselves as the alternative to the PLO in the event of the latter's demise, and they campaigned for the leadership of the Palestinians.[122] To this end, Fatah sent a memorandum to the 2nd PNC which was widely distributed, and which attacked the PLO's composition and emphasized fidai activity. And in a message to the third Arab summit, it stressed that the meeting of the PLO and Fatah must take place "on the battlefield and not in offices or in congresses"; in other words, the PLO must become a fidai organization. Fatah, in contrast to the PLO, emphasized "its independence and freedom of action" in the Palestinian arena. In a memorandum sent to the 2nd PNC it discussed the PLO composition and proposed that the PNC should comprise 50 members, of whom at least two-thirds would come from the leadership of "popular organizations". Its message to the third Arab summit claimed that Fatah's approach to the PLO had been positive at first, but "time has proved that the PLO has inherited the contradictions which exist in the Arab arena". Fatah would modify its attitude only if the PLO would adopt the military struggle as its strategy. In a message to the Heads of Arab Governments Conference (March 1966) it appealed to be allowed "to act from all Arab territories", to be given arms and to have the ban (operative in most Arab states) on publication of its communiqués lifted.[123]

Second, Shuqayri acted not only "like a prime minister and foreign minister" but even as a president of a state in whose hands executive authority is concentrated. In justifying the dictatorial way he ran the PLO, he claimed that "the imposition of dictatorship on the Palestinian people" was not only "the only way" open to him but "it would be acceptable to the Arab masses and the Palestinians alike".[124] He took important decisions without consulting the EC. He ran the PLO as his own organization, and emphasized such marginal showpiece achievements as the opening of PLO offices in various countries and the despatch of delegations to them.[125] As a result, the PLO was labouring under a very heavy bureaucratic structure.

Finally, Shuqayri failed in his attempts to set up bodies which would give the PLO a wide popular base and which would justify his assertion that the PLO represented the Palestinians.

The *Palestinian Popular Organization* (PPO – al-Tanzim al-Sha'bi al-Filastini) was the organizational framework of the PLO. The Popular Organization Law, approved by the 2nd PNC, stated that its aim was to "make the Palestinian Entity prominent in the widest sense of the term by building up the popular Palestinian base". In the framework of the PPO, Palestinian trade unions and organizations for social groups and students would be set up. The PPO was to be based on the active members of the PLO; it would be established through elections at local and regional level, a "national conference" and a "supreme popular conference".[126] In Jordan, preparations for setting up the PPO were already under way in February 1965, before agreement had been reached between the PLO and Jordan on the PLO's mode of activity in Jordan. The heads of the PLO's Department for the Popular Organization conducted a propaganda campaign in the West Bank towns and refugee camps to spread the idea of the PLO and its activities and enlist activists; at the head of this campaign stood Faysal al-Husayni. Preparatory committees were set up in the towns and refugee camps for establishing the PPO. Following the crisis between the PLO and Jordan in October 1965 this activity was halted, but Husayni had already begun to enlist activists for setting up a secret PLO organization on the West Bank. Jordanian intelligence was well aware of all this activity, having watched it from close quarters. Renewed action for establishing the PPO began after the agreement of 1 March 1966 but, as mentioned, was stopped in June 1966. Lebanon and the Ba'th regime in Syria did not permit any activity for setting up the PPO.[127]

Thus the Gaza Strip was the only area in which the PLO could set up the PPO without interference. Attempts to do so, however, proceeded slowly and without enthusiasm among the inhabitants. The Gaza Strip Palestinians were less politically conscious and less involved with the PLO than the West Bank Palestinians; they viewed the PLO as yet another organization like the Palestine National Union. Those that did join the PLO were mainly party activists from among the ANM, Communists and Ba'thists who desired positions of influence in the PPO. Registration for "active membership" in the PLO was opened in the Gaza Strip on 20 February 1965; Shuqayri reported to the 3rd PNC (June 1966) that 15,000 male members and 2,000 female members had registered out of a total of approximately 400,000 inhabitants. Elections to the institutions of the PPO in the Gaza Strip were held in April 1966, and on 30 September 1966 the PPO National Bureau (of the Gaza Strip) met for the first time. Yet the PPO never managed to engage in popular activity. Disputes over authority broke out among the heads of the organizations themselves, and between the secretary of the PPO and the director of the PLO office in Gaza. A particularly bitter dispute erupted at the first convention of the National Bureau as a result of strident criticism by Dr Haydar Abd al-Shafi, secretary-general of the PPO, concerning the presence of representatives of the Investigations Department of the police at PPO meetings. As a result the head of the PPO Department of the PLO dismissed the Bureau and appointed another in its place. Thus the work of the PPO was in fact frozen before it even got under way.[128]

Shuqayri failed in his attempt to involve the General Union of Palestinian Students (GUPS) and the Palestinian Workers Union in the activities of the PPO, because these organizations were dominated by the ANM and Fatah activists. It should be emphasized that the Palestinian students, including those in the USA and Canada, generally inclined towards Fatah and the fidai organizations, with whom they maintained contact and for whom they collected money. Fatah dominated the GUPS branch in West Germany.[129]

Also significant was *the failure to conduct elections to the PNC*. At the 2nd PNC Shuqayri promised that the 3rd PNC would be an elected one. But he made no special effort to conduct elections. It is true that these were dependent on the agreement of Jordan, which was not in any case enthusiastic about them. Shuqayri feared that the composition of an elected PNC would not be to his advantage. On 18 July 1965 he publicized the first draft of the Election Law, according to which the PNC would comprise 217 representatives elected according to the following distribution: Jordan 100 (46%), the Gaza Strip 40, Lebanon 14, Syria 13, Kuwait 10, Egypt 5, Iraq 2, Saudi Arabia 5, Qatar 3, Algeria 2, Libya 2, the Palestinian diaspora 15, the PLA 5. Clearly this would eliminate the absolute majority Jordan had held in the 1st and 2nd PNCs. The proposal, however, came in for severe criticism from Palestinian circles and also from the Syrians, and changes were made. On 18 December 1965 the EC of the PLO approved the final version, of which the Arab states had been informed. The agreement of 1 March 1966 between Jordan and the PLO allowed the EC to decide (21 March 1966) on implementation of the law for 26 March 1966, including Jordan.

According to the new law the PNC was to comprise 150 representatives, divided up as follows: Jordan 60 (40%), Gaza Strip 35, Syria 12, Kuwait 7, Egypt 3, Saudi Arabia 3, Iraq 2, Qatar 2, Algeria 2, Libya 2, the diaspora 5, the PLA 5. The elections were to be held within six months, before August 1966. The elections in Jordan were to take place under Arab League supervision. This time Jordan strongly complained about its limited representation and demanded two-thirds of the seats. The crisis that broke out between Jordan and the PLO in June 1966, and the cessation of the work of the Elections Committee in Jordan (17 June 1966) brought the elections process to an end.[130] To this day elections to the PNC have never been held.

Another factor was the *failure to make the PLA subordinate to the PLO*. In early September 1964 Shuqayri presented a detailed plan to the UAC on the establishment of the PLA. It proposed the setting up of five infantry brigade groups and six fidaiyyun battalions, to be allocated among the Gaza Strip and Syria. Units would be formed in Iraq according to military circumstances. Shuqayri proposed that these forces be set up through conscription and be subordinate to the UAC in times of both peace and war. However, the PLA would be subordinate to the PLO in all administrative, logistical and personnel matters. The PLO also proposed the establishment of 35 bases for "popular training" of 56,000 Palestinians each year. The proposed budget was 5.9 million dinars.

The UAC commander-in-chief had reservations about most elements of the plan. He argued that "it is not possible that he should be responsible for a Palestinian army liable to act in opposition to the plans of the UAC or [of] the Arab states" in which it was located. He was not opposed to the arming and financing of the PLA with the PLO's authority; but in his opinion the appointment of officers by the PLO and the introduction of conscription would raise legal problems in view of the citizenship of these officers and of the status of the Palestinians in the Arab countries. He therefore suggested that an agreement be worked out in the Arab League. He believed that the status of the PLA should be identical with that of Arab armies, that is, operational subordination to the commanders of the fronts in which the PLA force operated, or subordination to the UAC when it was in general reserve.

The second summit approved this stand, including the issue of operational subordination. It decided that "the formation of PLA forces, their training and arming, will be in accordance with the plan formulated by the UAC in cooperation with the PLO". The location of these forces would be "with the agreement of the state concerned". The summit authorized a budget of 5.5 million dinars. Lebanon was opposed to the formation of PLA units on its territory. After the summit, Shuqayri appointed Wajih al-Madani as PLA commander-in-chief. The PLO and the UAC drew up a plan in November 1964 according to which the PLA would comprise six infantry BGs and a further ten commando battalions, allocated among Egypt, the Gaza Strip, Sinai and Iraq.

The third summit once again considered the structure and purpose of the PLA. There was general agreement that the aim of the commando units was to disrupt the disposition of the enemy behind the front lines before the start of the war, while the regular units of the PLA would be deployed alongside the Arab armies. The third summit rejected Shuqayri's demand to impose conscription on the

Palestinians and the granting of authority to the PLA HQ. Owing to lack of finances it decided upon only a limited continuation of the plan, meant to be carried out from 1 October 1965 to 30 September 1966. However, Shuqayri's report to the 3rd PNC regarding progress in forming the PLA was very dismal. The first stage had been fully completed. The PLA's HQ was located in Egypt, but only ten percent of the personnel establishment was filled. There were also personnel shortages in Sinai, the Gaza Strip, Syria and Iraq. Thus the plan for the second stage was not carried out at all, since the UAC made no grant for this purpose to the PLO. Until the Six Day War the Arab states were content with completing establishments and carrying out routine training of the first-stage units.

In practice the PLA HQ had no operational or command authority over the PLA units formed in these countries. Its authority was confined to making financial grants and to logistical coordination. The Egyptian chief-of-staff demanded that the PLA units in Gaza be formed by him without any involvement by the PLA HQ. In late December 1966 the Egyptian army HQ issued an order defining the status of the Ayn Jalut Force HQ, which was to be subordinate to the commander of the Egyptian Eastern Military Region in everything connected with operations, training and preparations for war. In Syria the situation was essentially the same. The transfer of the 68th Commando Battalion to the PLA on 3 May 1965, and Shuqayri's declaration regarding return of the command over PLA units to the Syrian army HQ in May 1966, had ceremonial and propaganda value only. The PLA commander-in-chief's role was confined to granting money for the forming of the Hittin Force there and to participating in show parades and exercises. In his memoirs Shuqayri admitted that he failed to create an "independent and autonomous" PLA, even though he had devoted "ninety percent of his work schedule" to it.[131]

Thus the PLO was deprived of one of the foundations on which Shuqayri thought he could rely – the military one. The greater the expectations, the greater the disappointment. The PLA commander-in-chief had no choice but to become involved in political matters. As a result the PLA became a burden to the PLO rather than an asset.

Finally, during this period *strong opposition to Shuqayri crystallized within the PLO*. Representatives of the ANM formed the nucleus of this opposition; the Ba'th, Fatah and other Palestinian organizations were also involved. This opposition was very active during the 2nd PNC; in addition to Fatah's memorandum which

strongly attacked the PLO, the ANM distributed a pamphlet containing a "survey of the principles of the revolutionary Palestinian
action" and including a proposal to change "the basic organization"
of the PLO. Within the PNC a "revolutionary wing" emerged,
influenced by Fatah and its activities, which called for "adoption of
the armed struggle as the way to the liberation of Filastin" and for
"collective leadership" of the PLO. It referred to the appointment
of Jordanians to key positions in the PLO as the "Jordanization" of
the PLO, and accused Shuqayri of one-man leadership.

This opposition gained strength in the months preceding the Six
Day War. Shuqayri was then also criticized for "dealing less with
problems of liberation and more with bloating an administrative
apparatus, and for his frequent trips abroad and those of PLO
officials as well as [his] numerous speeches". Among the heads of
the "revolutionary wing" should be noted Bahjat Abu Gharbiyya,
Dr Walid Qamhawi, Niqola al-Dirr, Is-haq al-Dazdar, Burhan al-
Dajani and Walid al-Khalidi. Some of them demanded Shuqayri's
replacement and a change in the Constitution so that the EC would
be elected directly by the PNC. All believed that it was necessary to
change the PLO's outlook in a "revolutionary" direction and to
adopt the path of "revolutionary action". Under their influence the
PNC made "an unwritten decision, in which Shuqayri was requested
to maintain contact with Palestinian organizations, including secret
ones, with the aim of coordinating Palestinian action". In the face of
this opposition Shuqayri, after the 2nd PNC, began to dismiss
opponents from key positions in the PLO and especially the EC. He
did not co-opt ANM representatives to the second EC, which he
appointed (20 June 1965) after the 2nd PNC. Furthermore, he
transferred their representatives from key positions to secondary
posts in the PLO. As a result the ANM decided (August 1965) that
its representatives would resign from PLO institutions, including
the director of the National Fund, Mundhir Anabtawi, all the
while promoting an anti-Shuqayri campaign. Shuqayri claimed
that his intention was to rid key positions in the PLO of "party
apparatchiks".[132]

Shuqayri's initiatives. Shuqayri's inevitable decline meant that
the PLO, in the form in which he had set it up, had in fact ceased to
represent the Palestinians. Yet for several reasons he stayed in his
post a long time. First, there was no alternative; the opposition was
not sufficiently strong and could not agree on a candidate to replace
him. Moreover, Nasir left no doubt in his speech to the 2nd PNC that
he supported Shuqayri. Jordan, which had a majority in the PNC,

saw him as the least of all evils. Without these considerations Shuqayri would not have succeeded in his "exercise" at the opening of the 2nd PNC, when he offered to resign from his chairmanship of the PLO on the grounds that his demand to expel Tunisia from the Arab League was rejected at the Heads of Arab Governments Conference (May 1965). His aim was to show his critics that there was no replacement for him. His re-election and renewed self-confidence allowed him to renege on the promises he had made to his opponents to change over to a collective leadership in the PLO's management and regarding the appointment of members to the EC, the composition of which he announced on 20 June 1965 (ten members; among them one Jordanian).[133]

To neutralize opposition within the PLO Shuqayri initiated (in January 1966) meetings with Palestinian organizations with the declared aim of reaching an agreed formulation on "unity of action". A Preparatory Committee for United Palestinian Action (PCUPA) was set up; the PLO and five other organizations were represented in it, among them the Palestinian Organization of the Ba'th and of the ANM. Fatah refused to participate so as not to be identified with ideological organizations or those loyal to a particular Arab state. The deliberations of the PCUPA highlighted the various approaches of its participants, none of which coincided with that of Shuqayri. But Shuqayri deliberately protracted the discussions in order to prove to the 3rd PNC that he was acting for the benefit of "collective leadership" and "the unity of Palestinian action". In mid-April 1966 the PCUPA drafted principles for further cooperation between the PLO and these organizations; they lacked any operational significance. The Report of the PCUPA summarized its activities and decisions to the 3rd PNC; it emphasized that "the EC of the PLO made progress towards realization of the decisions of the 2nd PNC". This report also allowed Shuqayri to declare to the PNC that "we are in the stage of united action for the liberation of Filastin. The PLO has acted for the unity of the [Palestinian] organizations." Thus from Shuqayri's point of view the PCUPA had completed its task; but the principles on which it had agreed remained as "an epitaph on the grave".[134]

The 3rd PNC (June 1966) was a test for Shuqayri which he passed with flying colours to receive a further extension in his post. At this PNC it was hoped that he would change his course, based on his new favourable stand towards fidai activities and his extremist position towards Jordan. He again promised to act in the framework of a "collective, revolutionary leadership and to direct his efforts towards unification of the revolutionary forces". The PNC's decisions were marked by extremism towards Jordan and included a secret decision according to which "secret movements will be set up in every country which prevents the establishment of PLA units". The new EC, which Shuqayri announced on 15 July 1966, comprised twelve members, among them potential opponents like Shafiq al-Hut and Ahmad Sidqi al-Dajani.[135]

The PLO had now begun to change in favour of fidai activity. Up to the Six Day War, this change went through two stages. First, in May 1966 Shuqayri and his propaganda mouthpieces began to praise fidai actions inside Israel. The PLO was even presented as a "fidai organization".[136] This was influenced by similar Egyptian changes but especially by the stepping up of Fatah activities, Fatah's popularity among the Palestinians, the appearance of additional Palestinian organizations and the resulting competition over "the soul of the Palestinians". Also significant was criticism of Shuqayri by the "revolutionary wing" of the PLO, and the PLO's crisis with Jordan. Second, in October 1966 the PLO began to provide finances, training and arms for fidai actions and to participate in them in Israel and Jordan. The PLO had close connections with two fidai organizations set up in October 1966, the Abtal al-Awda organization based in Lebanon and eventually active in Israel and Jordan, and the Abd al-Qadir al-Husayni Unit, which was the military arm of Jabhat Tahrir Filastin, active in Jordan. When the first organization began to act in Israel in October 1966, the PLO radio was the first to publicize its announcements. The Abtal was connected to the ANM, whose members underwent sabotage training in Egypt. Shafiq al-Hut (director of the PLO office in Beirut) was responsible on behalf of the PLO for the operational side of its actions, including training and the enlistment of fidaiyyun. Ahmad al-Yamani, who underwent military training in Egypt, was responsible for operations on behalf of the ANM.[137]

Meanwhile Shuqayri continued his talks with the Fatah leaders. At some of these meetings, representatives of the Palestinian Organization of the Ba'th and of the ANM also participated. Shuqayri assessed that Fatah's joining the PLO would pave the way for the other organizations to join, and proposed coordination between the PLO and Fatah as well as material aid. He urged the Fatah leaders to join the PLO and its leadership, which would then take care of all fidaiyyun needs. But Fatah took a more intransigent stance, claiming that Shuqayri was dismantling the PLO. Fatah had to be the prominent factor in any unification; fidai actions had to be left mainly in their hands, and they were to be called al-Asifa, while the PLO would be the means of publicizing Fatah's communiqués. The last meeting before the war took place on 27 April 1967. The talks reached no conclusion apart from an agreement to cooperate against the Jordanian regime.[138] It appeared that Fatah was not so much interested in cooperation as in dominating the PLO.

This period also saw a declaration on setting up a "Revolutionary Council". Shuqayri's changed stand on fidai actions and the results of the Samoa' attack helped improve his image, but EC members still criticized his management of the PLO and his failure to consult with them. Shuqayri exploited the disturbances in Jordan after the Samoa' raid by persuading the EC to decide (14 December 1966) to authorize him "to reconstitute the EC". Thus on 27 December 1966 Shuqayri surprised everyone by announcing the establishment of a "Revolutionary Council" (RCL, Majlis Thawra) for the PLO. Shuqayri shrouded the RCL in secrecy; only on 10 February 1967 did he announce three decisions it had made, among them the setting up of a "Political Bureau" and of a "Liberation Council" which would change the PLA into a "revolutionary army". Shuqayri described his steps as intended to "unite fidai activity and to topple Husayn's regime".[139] In fact, this "Revolutionary Council" never existed. It was yet another of Shuqayri's devices to prove that the PLO had become a "revolutionary fidai organization" and to get rid of his opponents in the EC; whose members, at any rate, had justified suspicions about the RCL.

Once again opposition to Shuqayri was crystallizing inside the PLO, this time led by Shafiq al-Hut, whose close connections with Nasir led to speculation about Nasir's support for Shuqayri being shaken. The ANM joined the opposition, as did EC members Dajani, Ahmad Sa'di and Raji Sahyun as well as senior PLO officials like Salah al-Dabbagh, Haydar Abd al-Shafi and Rif'at Awda, and eventually also the PLA commander-in-chief. A number of senior PLO officials even resigned in protest against his methods of action.[140]

Shuqayri let his opponents understand that Nasir still supported him. Furthermore, on 26 February 1967, he announced a newly constituted EC with eight members – excluding his opponents from the previous EC. He ensured the support of the PLA commander-in-chief by co-opting him to the EC. This step only outraged his opponents even more and they stepped up their campaign against him. On 12 May 1967 Shuqayri succeeded in getting the EC to transfer Hut from Beirut to Delhi; Hut refused, and protested to the Egyptians. Hut's transfer was cancelled following the Six Day War.[141]

Shuqayri's resignation. The Six Day War changed the attitude of the Arab world to the PLO and to Shuqayri as its head. The Khartoum summit (29 August 1967 – 1 September 1967) witnessed his declining position in the Arab and Palestinian arenas. Several factors contributed to this. First, the period of reconciliation in inter-Arab relations had begun, with King Husayn becoming a "nationalist leader". Second, doubts were arising as to the PLO's ability to absorb within its framework the Palestinian organizations, and even its right to exist. Shuqayri became an anachronism. Not only the fidai organizations called for his resignation but also the ANM and even Palestinian intellectuals like Walid al-Khalidi. At the Khartoum summit he was pushed into a corner, losing his senior status; Nasir displayed a hard attitude towards him. The PLO was not even mentioned in the Khartoum summit's final communiqué. Third, the fidai organizations became undisputed rulers in the Palestinian arena. The trend was now towards "Palestinization" of "the Palestinian movement" and of the PLO. Finally, the shock-waves passing through the Arab world did not bypass the PLO. The Six Day War strengthened the need for fundamental change in its representative composition; some EC members also demanded radical change in the PLO's *modus operandi* and plans. The PLO's institutions came to a virtual standstill while awaiting the results of the Khartoum summit, and after it, Shuqayri's departure – without which change in the PLO's institutions was not possible. Despite this, Shafiq al-Hut came out against "talks on the disbanding of the PLO since it was a symbol of the existence of the Palestinians and a framework capable of absorbing all the Palestinian forces who believe in the armed struggle".[142]

Shuqayri did not draw the necessary conclusions. He wanted to be remembered positively in Palestinian history; but once again his actions led him in the opposite direction. While he indeed proclaimed "abandonment of political activity and concentration on revolutionary action", he did not have the means for this. All he had was the EC – which no longer obeyed him. He walked out of the Khartoum summit on the final day after the rejection of his demand that "no stand will be taken regarding the future of Filastin and the outcome of aggression [the Six Day War] without the participation of the PLO" and that "no Arab state will sign a separate agreement resolving the problem of Filastin". But this time the "exercise" made no impression. Shuqayri continued to defend the PLO as "the sole representative of the Palestinian people", and called for the realization of the Palestinians' right to self-determination.[143]

Under pressure from the Arab arena and the Palestinians, Shuqayri tried once again to justify the PLO's existence as the roof organization of all the Palestinian organizations and to display his connection with fidai actions, which had been renewed on the West Bank. On 7 December 1967 he declared the establishment of the "Revolutionary Command for the Liberation of Filastin" (Majlis Qiyadat al-Thawra li-Tahrir Filastin). He claimed that a "military conference had met within the homeland, which included the fidaiyyun leaders and had decided on the establishment of a Revolutionary Council". This was a fictitious body, just like the earlier "Revolutionary Council" of the PLO. Shuqayri made an announcement (9 December 1967) of sabotage actions by the "Revolutionary Command Council", and claimed responsibility for sabotage actions carried out in fact by Fatah. An announcement of 11 December 1967 claimed "Council" responsibility for an action carried out by fidaiyyun from the 421st Battalion of the Iraqi PLA. Furthermore, Shuqayri claimed that the "Council" was a roof organization of all fidai organizations and was "standing at the head of the armed resistance in conquered Filastin". He exploited the assistance provided by the 421st Battalion in Jordan to Fatah in order to demonstrate that there was cooperation on the ground between the PLO and Fatah, on the assumption that the PLA was subordinate to the PLO.[144]

Shuqayri renewed his contacts with Fatah but without success. Fatah, which had renewed its fidai actions on the West Bank on 27 August 1967, rejected his proposal that the PLO be responsible for the "propaganda side" and the fidai organizations for the "operational side"; instead it intensified its struggle against him. On 14 November 1967 Fatah called for PLO finances to be handed over to it and for PLA soldiers and Headquarters to join Fatah, since "Shuqayri's organization is declining and no longer serves as representative of the Palestinian people. The PLO's time has passed." Iraqi PLA soldiers in Jordan and Syrian PLA soldiers were already defecting to Fatah. On 9 December 1967 Fatah made an announcement denying the existence of Shuqayri's "Revolutionary Council"; on 14 December 1967 it sent a memorandum to Arab foreign ministers condemning "Shuqayri's false announcements". Fatah also stated that "unity of action" among the organizations was possible only between those engaging in fidai activities. With this slogan it intended to claim for itself the decisive position in any future organizational framework.

In late September 1967, Fatah launched a propaganda campaign in the Beirut press intended to create an image as an independent organization and an alternative to the PLO.[145] The Egyptian media ignored Shuqayri; they enthusiastically supported the fidai organizations and called for their unification. Shuqayri reached a new low when, on 14 December 1967, seven EC members accused him of promoting a fictitious "Revolutionary Council in the Conquered Homeland" and demanded that he resign. On 18 December 1967 the Popular Front for the Liberation of Palestine (PFLP) announced its support for this demand, as did the GUPS and the Palestine Workers Union, followed by other Palestinian organizations.[146] Shuqayri's response was to announce (19 December 1967) a reduction in the membership of the EC to seven. When the chairman of the National Fund (who was a member of the EC) joined the anti-Shuqayri group, the former EC had eight members, a majority, demanding his resignation. On 23 December 1967 Shuqayri met Nasir's deputy, Zakariyya Muhi al-Din, apparently to determine finally Egypt's position on his possible resignation. On 24 December 1967 Shuqayri tendered his resignation to the EC and, in addition, to the secretary-general of the Arab League as "representative of Filastin". Yahia Hammuda was appointed acting chairman of the EC. On 24 December 1967 Hammuda announced that "the PLO is not a party but an instrument for representing the Palestinian people". On 24 December 1967 the EC decided to initiate consultation "for gathering a national assembly which would express the will of the people and from which a collective leadership would be composed".[147]

CONCLUSION

"No great Arab statesman ever bowed his head and admitted to the incipience of a new era (or the rise of a new generation) and as a result went out of the door of politics before being thrown out the window."[148] Shuqayri was no exception, even if he was not a great statesman. His problem was the huge gap between his verbiage and his actions – a gap filled, for a time, by Egyptian support for him. If until mid-1965 he still enjoyed support in the Palestinian arena, from then until the Six Day War he relied mainly on Egyptian support and the changing political circumstances of the Arab arena.

The termination of Egyptian support after the Six Day War ended his political career. In his memoirs Shuqayri tried to attribute his failure to inter-Arab conditions, but in fact his own role was crucial; during his chairmanship the PLO bore his personal stamp. Still, he made an important contribution to getting the PLO off the ground; it is hard to point to any other Palestinian politician who could have done so at this time. The fidaiyyun organizations were capable only after the Six Day War; in this sense they inherited a ready-made framework.

Egypt continued in this period to advocate the Palestinian Entity and to support the PLO, especially after the deterioration of the summit atmosphere. The PLO, which displayed an ability to survive beyond the expectations of its leaders, benefited both from the atmosphere of the summit and from the polarization in the Arab world. As for Egypt, activity on behalf of the Palestinian Entity and PLO provided Nasir with a temporary way out of the dead end in the conflict with Israel, which he had entered as a result of his inability to fulfil the promises he had made since 1959 regarding the "liberation of Filastin". He had twice drawn up a timetable and failed to stand by it; he had trapped himself with his promises and had entered the Six Day War in order to escape from this dead end once and for all. The Egyptian army entered the Six Day War when its long-term buildup, begun in 1960–61, was almost complete; "the secret of Egypt's downfall in the war lay in the weakness of the human component."[149]

In this period the Palestinian Entity lacked land and population with which to establish itself. All the Arab states involved realized this. The Ba'th expressed this openly and specifically in its plan of May 1964. The moment Shuqayri began to cultivate the allegiance of the Palestinian population for the PLO, Husayn correctly saw it as a threat to his throne and his kingdom, and he began to fight the PLO as hard as he could. As long as the West Bank was under Jordanian rule, the regime's chances of winning were good. As in the earlier round, Wasfi al-Tall was the conductor. His method was to display a positive attitude to the PLO in order to gain time, making concessions the moment a serious crisis between Jordan and the PLO emerged; then, following these concessions, he waged "war" in order to efface the PLO's gains and return to the starting point. But this was only a temporary solution; it prepared the ground for a more bitter round.

The Syrian role in this period was relatively mild and indirect. It supported Fatah, at first in propaganda and later also in material aid; from 1966, after Jordan and Lebanon had intensified their actions against the organization, Syria became the most stable base for Fatah actions inside Israel. In this it influenced Egypt and the PLO in favour of fidaiyyun activity.

With the establishment of the PLO and the appearance of the fidaiyyun organizations headed by Fatah, the Palestinian issue took a major turn. A new "political generation" of Palestinians arose, destined to lead the Palestinian movement. This was a generation which grew up on Arab nationalism as Nasir was designing it, and on the disappointment of the Arab world at the breakup of the Egypt–Syria union. It criticized the veteran Palestinian leadership, of whom Shuqayri was the Last Mohican. Only three years after its appearance, Fatah managed to establish itself as the leader among all the Palestinian organizations. By early January 1967 it had committed seventy acts of sabotage in Israel. The process of "Palestinization" of the Palestinian issue accelerated in this period, while the process of "Jordanization" of the West Bank was on the decline; the Six Day War put an end to the latter process. "Palestinization" expressed itself in an intensified consciousness of the Palestinian identity, aimed clearly at reducing the connection, which Shuqayri symbolized, with the Arab summit and with inter-Arab conditions. The Palestinians became a component of the totality of the Palestinian issue. The outcome of the Six Day War accelerated this process.

After Shuqayri's fate was sealed, the leaders of the organizations had second thoughts about disbanding the PLO. Fatah and other fidaiyyun organizations began to see advantages in preserving a framework which already had an established machinery and was recognized in the Arab arena. So the framework was indeed preserved, but its representative composition was changed.

CHAPTER THREE

The "Palestinian Resistance": Representation and Confrontation, 1968–1971

The Six Day War marked the completion of the process in which the Arab–Israel conflict became the sole focus of Arab nationalism, governing virtually all fundamental issues of regime, economy and foreign policy in the Arab world. This conflict had now evolved into "a struggle between the Arab nation as a whole with all its resources; and Zionism as a whole, with all its resources".[1] Nasir called for mobilization of the entire Arab political, economic and military potential for war on Israel.[2] The conflict was moreover transformed into what was to be known as the "Middle East crisis";[3] and both the Soviet Union and the United States intensified their role in the region. Although Nasir still led the Arab world in planning strategy for resolution of the conflict, he had difficulty dictating tactical moves because military defeat had dimmed his image as leader. At the Khartoum summit (29 August 1967 – 1 September 1967), convened when the Arab world was reeling under the impact of defeat, Nasir succeeded "beyond his expectations" in persuading the leaders of the Arab states (other than Syria, which boycotted the meeting) to agree to a new stage-by-stage strategy.

The first stage would be "the elimination of the traces of aggression", or the solution of the "1967 problem" through "liberation of the Arab lands occupied by Israel" in the war. Nasir believed, and allowed the Arab world to believe, in the feasibility of realizing this stage. The Khartoum summit resolved on "the unification of efforts [in the sphere of] *political* action, in the international and diplomatic arena, for the elimination of the traces of aggression" and the securing of an Israeli withdrawal "to the boundaries of 5 June 1967", all "within the frame of the basic principles that are binding upon the Arab states, namely no peace (*sulh*) with Israel, no recognition of her, no negotiations with her and adherence to the right of the Palestinian people in its homeland". The summit resolved that Saudi Arabia, Libya and Kuwait would annually pay 135 million dinars to Egypt (90 million), Jordan (40 million) and Syria (5 million) and thereby help them all to hold on until the "elimination of the traces of aggression" was accomplished.

The second stage would see the achievement of the long-term strategic goal: the "liberation of Filastin" or the solution of the "1948 problem". The war had created doubts in the Arab world, particularly among the Egyptian leadership, as to whether this goal could be realized. A cautious Egyptian assessment admitted that "the elimination of the aggression of 1948 is an abstract aim", but elimination of the results of 1967 would mark a turning-point toward solving the "1948 problem".[4]

The new status of the West Bank and the Gaza Strip meant that the Arab territorial issue and the Palestinian national issue were closely linked; that is, solution of the Palestinian issue was divided into the "liberation of the occupied Palestinian territories" and the "liberation of Filastin". Thus Egypt, Jordan and the Palestinians were forced to determine their position on the future of the West Bank and Gaza after Israel's withdrawal. Yet the crucial question as to who would represent the Palestinians in deliberations over the future of the West Bank led to renewed struggle between the Jordanian entity and the Palestinian Entity; once more, Husayn had to fight to preserve his regime.

As for Nasir, to obtain the political and military cooperation of the major Arab states, he had to create a "new order" in inter-Arab relationships. This meant the erasure of any distinction between "progressive" and "reactionary" Arab states, "non-support for the creation of Arab axes, non-interference in the internal affairs of the Arab states and opposition to any personal, factional or ideological struggle". After the Khartoum summit Nasir ordered Egyptian intelligence to cease subversive activities in the Arab states and ended Egyptian military intervention in Yemen.[5] But Nasir's acceptance of Security Council Resolution 242 (22 November 1967) and his insistence on continued political action led to opposition. The first "refusal camp" of the Arab arena was formed, incorporating Saudi Arabia, Syria, Iraq (after the Ba'th revolution of July 1968) and Algeria. Husayn became Nasir's most "faithful" ally almost until the death of the Ra'is. Nasir's initiative in November 1967 for the convening of another Arab summit was stubbornly resisted by Saudi Arabia and Syria. Faysal rejected a political solution to the conflict, the 242 resolution and the Jarring mission; in his view "the armed struggle and *jihad* were the only means to ensure victory". It was only after the Arab Defence Council had concluded (in November 1969) that the "solution by peaceful means" had failed that another summit became possible. But the Rabat summit of December 1969 was a failure. Egypt's War of Attrition against Israel did not help Nasir in his demand that a plan for Arab mobilization be drawn up. Faysal demanded that the summit opt for war, whereas Nasir claimed that "one could not set a time for war". Nasir's efforts in early 1968 to found an Eastern Front (Command) also proved fruitless; meetings of the heads of the "confrontation states" (September 1969, February 1970) did nothing to promote this plan. Nasir's consent to the Rogers initiative (July 1970) only exacerbated the divisions in the Arab world. "Coordination on the pan-Arab plane did not exist. Coordination among states of identical political and social orientation was scant", and "a chasm yawned between the rich states and the poor states".[6]

Against this backdrop and with the deteriorating situation on the Israeli borders with Egypt, Jordan, and to a lesser extent, Syria, the issue of the Palestinian Entity took on deeper significance. The PLO institutions were transformed in February 1969, with the fidai organizations or "Palestinian resistance" (PR) (*al-muqawama al-filastiniyya*) becoming the main component of the PNC and the EC. Support for the PR was the sole point of consensus at the Rabat summit. However, "in default of an (Arab) strategy outlined at pan-Arab level, relations between the fidai organizations and the Arab governments or parties became both bilateral and clandestine".[7] The Arab states began to compete for influence within the PLO; paradoxically, this also led to conflict between the PR and the "confrontation states", especially Jordan and Lebanon where armed clashes took place.

EGYPT

In this period the core of political and military support for the fidai organizations shifted from Syria to Egypt. For the leaders of Fatah, Egypt now became "the first, the strongest and the chief support" and Nasir their "greatest ally in the region".[8]

Nasir worked to consolidate recognition of the PR and the PLO as representing the Palestinians in the Arab, the Palestinian and even the international arenas. Being on good terms with Husayn, Nasir refrained from overtly defining the goals of the Palestinian Entity, although the use of the terms "people" and "homeland" spoke for itself.

Egypt's Strategy for "Elimination of the Traces of Aggression"

The first component was *combined political and military struggle.* Nasir told senior army officers (25 November 1967) that a military solution would be possible only after five years. He realized, however, that meanwhile the "occupied land could become Israeli", and thus advocated combined political and military struggle. He did not negate the political solution provided it did not overstep the Khartoum limitations. But in the prevailing international constellation he saw no chance of an imposed solution "as similar as possible to that of 1957". For him the purpose of political action was to gain time for a military build-up, while striving to induce the United States to change its position. Nasir accepted Resolution 242 and construed it as "laying down the need for an Israeli withdrawal from the Arab lands occupied in the war of June 1967". Thus the PR was within its rights to oppose this resolution, since a precondition for a "just and lasting peace" was the "realization of the legitimate [or just] rights of the Palestinian people", namely, the solution to the "1948 problem". He sometimes hinted that this meant implementation of UN resolutions, including the Partition Resolution of 1947.[9]

Nasir was defeated by Israel three times, twice as leader. He opposed any concession to Israel as a result of her military victory, and he now prepared for the military option as though the political option were doomed to failure. Nasir believed – and transmitted this belief to his army – that "what was taken by force will not be recovered except by force". He thought that Egypt could exert enough military pressure on Israel to be able to conduct political talks from a position of strength, forcing Israel into making concessions and the United States into pressuring Israel to do so.[10] Thus, Nasir accelerated military expansion, urged the Soviet Union towards greater involvement on the Egyptian front, repeatedly attempted to found an Eastern Front and supported the PR against Israel. His War of Attrition embodied his concept of the "combined struggle".

The second component of Egypt's strategy was the *comprehensive solution.* Nasir absolutely rejected any separate Egyptian–Israeli settlement; Israeli withdrawal from *all* the occupied territories was for him "a basic point which is not open to discussion and cannot become a subject of negotiation". He made it clear that he was referring to Sinai, the Gaza Strip, the West Bank including (East) Jerusalem, and the Golan Heights. He thereby reinforced the linkage between the territorial component and the Palestinian national issue, and was finally obliged to define his own position on the latter. Nasir regarded the comprehensive solution as an expression of his pan-Arab nationalist (*qawmiyya*) commitment, and himself as the standard-bearer of Arab nationalism.[11]

The third component was Nasir's *support for the PR as an expression of a nationalist stance*. Nasir regarded the PR "as one of the justest and most honourable manifestations of the contemporary Arab struggle", and asserted that "the loyalty of any Arab party towards the national [*qawmi*] struggle is unequivocally predicated on its attitude towards the PR". He further described the PR as "one of the noblest manifestations engendered by the defeat of June 1967. All the Arab forces should conduct themselves on this basis."[12]

The PR as part of the military struggle. Nasir regarded fidai activities as integral to the military struggle against Israel. He classified Egyptian military activity on the Canal front into different stages of escalation.

The first was the *defence stage*, lasting from June 1967 to March 1968. This was subdivided into two periods: (1) The "pure and simple defence" (*al-difa' al-baht*), June–November 1967, commenced with the rebuilding of his forces. On 23 November 1967 Nasir declared that "we have arrived at the completion of our defence capacity". (2) Re-establishment of Egyptian military strength to its prewar level. In February 1968 the minister of war gauged that "the Egyptian forces have reached 70 percent of their strength of before 5 June". On 30 March 1968 Nasir announced the completion of the stage of military build-up, but claimed that the army was still not ready for offensive action in Sinai.[13]

Second came the *steadfastness (al-sumud) stage*, April 1968 – August 1968. Egyptian military activity was confined to cross-Canal sabotage operations in Sinai; military expansion continued. In April 1968 a first official meeting took place between Nasir and the Fatah leadership, agreement being reached on aid and co-ordination; on 10 April 1968 he for the first time emphatically declared his support for, and intention of aiding, the PR. Nasir saw fidai activities in the occupied territories as an important way of harassing Israel.[14]

Next came the *active deterrence (al rad' al-fi'li) stage*, September

1968 – June 1969. On 8 September 1968 Egyptian artillery bombarded Israeli forces on the east bank of the Canal; on 14 September 1968 Nasir declared the "completion of the steadfastness stage". On 12 November 1968 Nasir decided that within the month harassment activities deep in Sinai should begin. On 30 December 1968 he said that "a switch should be made from a negative to a positive defence posture", by "graduated execution of military actions". In February 1969 he stated that "the military situation [of Israel] should now be aggravated by the intensification of fidaiyyun actions in Sinai – in view of their importance for the constant attrition of the enemy's forces". On 16 December 1968 the existence of the Arab Sinai Organization, which was perpetrating fidai actions in Sinai as a cover for operations by Egyptian army units, was made known in order to prove that Egypt was actively involved in fidai actions and to prompt Syria and Lebanon to open their borders to such activity. This policy was, in both political and military terms, a clear expression of the Egyptian approach to the PR, as first indicated in Nasir's speech of 20 January 1969 and again, in greater detail, on 1 February 1969.[15]

The fourth stage was the *War of Attrition (harb al-istinzaf)*, July 1969 – August 1970. The War of Attrition began in July 1969, but the decision to escalate operations was taken in April 1969. At a cabinet meeting on 15 April 1969 Nasir reported that he had "approved military measures on the front, which would commence during the next few weeks". Nasir hoped that escalation of hostilities in the Canal Zone, as well as on the Jordanian, Syrian and Lebanese frontiers, due to fidai actions supported by the armies of those states, would result in pressure on Israel by the superpowers for political concessions.[16] Accordingly, Nasir redoubled his efforts for the founding of the Eastern Front. The military situation did not, however, develop according to plan.

On 20 June 1970 a "verbal message to the foreign minister – 19 June 1970" was delivered to the Egyptian foreign minister from the US secretary of state (the Rogers initiative). Simultaneously delivered to Jordan and Israel, it proposed a three-month cease-fire between Egypt and Israel. The US explained that meanwhile the military *status quo* west and east of the Canal would be preserved: anti-aircraft missiles would not be moved and no new military installations would be set up. Sadat and the Egyptian foreign minister believed that "there was nothing new in it" (the initiative); Nasir commented on learning (21 June 1970) the wording of the note while in Libya that the initiative was "in line with his overall strategy", and announced his consent to it in a speech on 23 July 1970.

His main considerations were (1) priority to military rather than political objectives. He thought that "its chances of succeeding were no more than one-half percent". Nasir "accepted the initiative because he found that the scale of military escalation on the Egyptian front was reaching a level at which it was necessary to call a halt, so as to re-equip [his forces] for an electronic war – at a time when, day by day, over a period of weeks, an average of one thousand tons of bombs were being dropped", and when the Egyptian pilots were "fighting as blind men fight". (2) He recognized that because of Israeli air supremacy, he could not complete construction of the SAM missile system in the Canal Zone. He admitted that "to continue the War of Attrition while Israel has full air supremacy means that we will simply exhaust ourselves". (3) His hopes of setting up an Eastern Front were progressively shaken during 1970. He was disillusioned as to the willingness of the "confrontation states" to cooperate with him and the preparedness of the Arab world for a general mobilization. (4) He sought to create a "big propaganda surprise". Having already decided while still in Libya to support the initiative, Nasir planned that during the cease-fire period he would move the Egyptian–Russian missile complex east-wards to within 30 kilometres of the Canal, and bring the forward wall of missiles up to its western bank. With the Russians' help, this commenced on the very first night of the cease-fire and was com-pleted in August 1970. The missile complex now covered an area that reached up to 20 kilometres inside Sinai. Nasir reported at a cabinet meeting on 7 September 1970 that "our military situation is good. Israel can neither attack us nor cross the Canal".[17]

The fidai organizations as the sole combatant element in the Eastern Front. The setting up of an Eastern Front was "one of Nasir's fondest hopes". It would be responsible for the "liberation of Jerusalem, the West Bank and the Golan Heights". Having learned from the failure of the UAC, Nasir sought to set up two coordinated front-line commands: the Western Front (Egypt) and the Eastern Front incorporating Jordan, Syria and Iraq.

Nasir believed – rightly, as events proved – that "basically this is a political issue". Arif's Iraq had good relations with Syria and still better ones with Egypt, and a resolution was passed in May 1968 regarding the "founding of the framework of the Eastern Front that conformed to agreements signed between Syria, Egypt and Iraq on the one hand, and between Egypt, Jordan and Iraq on the other". Syria's objections to cooperating with Jordan were thus circumvented. To facilitate coordination, the command of the Eastern Front was given to Iraq. But in practice the hostility between Syria and Jordan was such that this HQ commanded the Iraqi forces only, and occupied itself in coordination with the Western Command (Egypt). At the same time an Iraqi armoured division was encamped in Jordan. The accession to power of the Ba'th in Iraq (17 July 1968) exacerbated Iraq's relations with Syria and Egypt; it now became virtually impossible to activate the Eastern Front.

Yet Nasir was not to be denied. On the eve of the four-party summit (Husayn, Nasir, Atasi and Iraqi vice-president Ammash) of 1 September 1969 he made a gesture towards Syria by consenting to sign an agreement with Atasi whereby "a political leadership for the campaign would forthwith be founded". "This leadership will appoint a military commander who will be in charge of the military planning of the war, while precedence in planning will be accorded to the air and air defence forces."[18] But the conference did not fulfil Nasir's expectations. Ammash would not commit himself. The meeting passed some insignificant resolutions and agreed to the appointment of Fawzi, Egypt's minister of war, as commander-in-chief. The same fate met the second Conference of the Heads of the Confrontation States in Tripoli (21–22 June). Here Nasir told Iraqi president Bakr "I have no faith in you" in answer to Bakr's suggestion that the Egyptian army should fight on two fronts.

Eventually, Black September and Syria's abortive invasion of Jordan spelled the demise of the Eastern Front idea. Iraq's attitude did not prevent her from building up her forces in Jordan so as to exert political influence in that country. The buildup of the Iraq expeditionary force (Salah al-Din Forces) in Jordan continued throughout 1969–1970 until Iraq had three armoured, one mechanized and two infantry brigades, five artillery battalions and division HQ – about 20,000 soldiers and 265 tanks (the HQ of the Eastern Front and one Iraqi infantry brigade were located at Dar'a). After September 1970, however, Iraq decided to withdraw from Jordan and did so by March 1971. The Eastern Front thus remained a "[mere] hope that never became a palpable fact", and the PR became the only factor integrated into the Egyptian "military struggle". Sadat commented (28 February 1971) that "the confrontation with the enemy in recent years has been limited to Egypt on her front and the PR on the Eastern Front".[19]

Egypt's Attitude towards the Issue of the Palestinian Entity

Concerning the PR as representative of the Palestinians, Nasir viewed the PR under Fatah's leadership as "a Palestinian national leadership possessing national [*qawmiyya*] loyalty and representing the will of the Palestinian people and its hope, and speaking in its name". He saw this as the fulfilment of his own hope that "in the Arab arena there would be someone more radical than himself ... something akin to the Stern or the Begin group, namely, our own irresponsible arms". He therefore backed Fatah with full vigour.

In 1968 Egypt faced two dilemmas. First, she continued to regard the PLO (after the dismissal of Shuqayri) as the institutional framework representing the Palestinians. Nasir therefore pressured the leadership of the fidai organizations, especially Fatah, to integrate within the PLO, and encouraged the PLO leadership (the EC) to facilitate this integration. Fatah's decision to join the PLO solved this problem. Second was the enhanced image of the fidai organizations in the Arab and Palestinian arenas – the antithesis of the regular armies that had been defeated in war; Israeli propaganda and reprisals boosted this image. Thus Haykal, with the aid of the Egyptian media, was to prove that "the fidaiyyun organizations alone cannot precipitate a decisive outcome in the Arab–Israeli struggle nor even reach the stage of the elimination of the traces of aggression". The Egyptian propaganda campaign of 1968–1970 claimed that: (1) "The Palestinian problem is first and foremost a pan-Arab problem. This means that Egypt bears the brunt of the burden"; "the aim of liberation is beyond the capacity of the PR." (2) "The PR is one of the forces operating in the campaign [against Israel]"; "its true basis is the entire Arab potential." (3) "The PR is not capable of realizing what the Algerian Resistance realized."

Nasir believed that the most the PR could do in the military sphere was "to trouble the enemy's rest"; in the political sphere it could "revive the Palestinian personality and crystallize the political existence of the Palestinian people". In 1968 Nasir judged that "the Jews are greatly troubled by these [fidai] actions which inflict fifteen fatal casualties every week, [a loss which is] most painful to the Jews".[20]

As for Fatah as leader of the PLO, Nasir did not permit himself to leave the arena of the PR shorn of his influence. He came to realize that "the parties operating in the Arab arena [Ba'th and ANM] were relocating their activity, including their disagreements, into the circle of the PR", and concluded that Fatah was the most capable of all the Palestinian organizations of undertaking the official leadership of the PLO. He was most impressed by Fatah's "independence" and lack of a social ideology. He correctly gauged its popularity among the Palestinians, especially after the "Karama operation" (March 1968), and its ability to lead the PLO. Following his "historic" meeting with the Fatah leadership in April 1968, at which time he enquired into Fatah's history, ideology, sources of finance and the personality of Arafat, Nasir wanted Fatah to serve as an axis for inter-organizational unity. At this meeting he decided to set up contact with Fatah at senior political level and not through general intelligence, which had been the pipeline so far. He appointed Haykal as liaison officer with Fatah on all political matters, and the head of military intelligence on all military affairs; he promised the Fatah leaders military aid. Fatah could hardly have found more effective backing for its ambition to lead the PLO, as planned since Shuqayri's time; and Nasir's support undoubtedly influenced Fatah's decision to integrate into the PLO. Moreover, on the eve of the 5th PNC (February 1969), Nasir agreed to help Fatah achieve leadership of the PLO with a view to ensuring a majority in the PNC.[21] All in all, Nasir's encouragement gave Fatah an impetus no other Arab state could have delivered during this period.

Another important development was a *return to the components of the "Palestinian state"*. The altered status of the West Bank helped Nasir further define his official position regarding the Palestinian Entity; in his speech to the 5th PNC (1 February 1969) he asserted that the problem of the Palestinians was "the problem of a people that has a homeland". He implied that in the wake of the Israeli withdrawal, Palestinian rule would be established in the West Bank and the Gaza Strip. He stressed two components.

The *national component* meant that "no one can relegate the problem of the Palestinians to its previous status as a refugee problem". Nasir spoke of the basic national and legal rights of a people "driven off its land". He depicted the PR as a national liberation movement, and stressed "the right of the Palestinian people to fight for freedom and for the restoration of its land from which it was expelled in 1948".[22]

Nasir viewed the *territorial component* as the key to the solution of the "1967 problem" and as important for the solution to the "Palestinian national problem". He argued explicitly that "the Gaza Strip is an integral part of the Palestinian territories" and that "its fate must be determined in accordance with the free will of the Palestinians"; Egypt maintained its position that the Strip must be part of any future Palestinian state. As for the West Bank, however, Nasir avoided any specific reference to its future after Israeli withdrawal, although his views on this can perhaps be inferred from his views on the Strip. This probably stemmed from Husayn's having been entrusted by Nasir with the political negotiations over the "liberation of the West Bank". For Nasir, Husayn was the only means of negotiation with the US (and indirectly with Israel) over Israeli withdrawal from the West Bank. Nasir never backtracked on his fundamental refusal to recognize the annexation of the West Bank to Jordan.[23]

In this period, Nasir undoubtedly continued to view the founding of a "Palestinian state" as the aim of the Palestinian Entity, but for tactical and political reasons he and official Egyptian spokesmen avoided saying so explicitly. In August 1970, when relations with the PLO were strained (due to his accepting the Rogers initiative), Nasir, in a talk with Fatah leaders, decried the PLO's unrealistic policy and argued that a "mini-state on the West Bank and in the Gaza Strip would be better than nothing". He expressly rejected, however, Palestinian self-government or a "Palestinian state" arising from agreement between the Palestinians (inhabitants of the West Bank) and Israel. His approach to the "Palestinian state" can be understood from his position on the 1947 Partition Resolution, which Egypt sometimes invoked through diplomatic channels as, for example, when Jarring enquired about "secure and recognized borders". Egypt's reply (27 March 1969) was that "when the Palestine problem was raised in the UN in 1947, the General Assembly passed Resolution 181 dated 29 November on the partition of Palestine and defining the Israeli borders".[24]

Highly significant was the publication (13 October 1967) by Ahmad Baha al-Din, then editor of the Egyptian *al-Musawwar* weekly, of a "Draft for the Founding of the State of Filastin" which "will incorporate Jordan – the West Bank and the East Bank – and the Gaza Strip ... namely, all that remains of Filastin in addition to what is called the East of Jordan which was annexed in the past to Filastin". In his opinion the founding of the "state of Filastin" was an integral part of the "elimination of the traces of aggression", and was "a step to be taken once this aim had been achieved". Because of Baha al-Din's status, and because it was assumed that his plan was inspired by the authorities, there was considerable response especially from Palestinian and Egyptian intellectuals. Significantly, the Palestinians did not reject the idea in principle. Some supported it fully, such as Mustafa al-Hussayni, Ghassan Kanafani and also Shafiq al-Hut who wrote that "to call Jordan by the name of Filastin will solve the problem of the existing dual loyalties [of the Palestinians] in Jordan". Others had reservations only about the timing of the proposal, such as Walid al-Khalidi. Burhan al-Dajani claimed that the draft was too vague; Anis Sayigh voiced partial reservations. Jordan, of course, reacted to the plan with indignation since it would obviously mean the "Palestinization" of Jordan.[25] This proposal was actually a reformulation of an idea that had circulated in Egyptian ruling circles and in Shuqayri's mind even before the Six Day War. Baha al-Din's draft reflected a basic, although unofficial, Egyptian position as to the future of the West Bank and Gaza.

Egyptian aid to the PR. In the political sphere, the turning point in Nasir's policy *vis-à-vis* the PR was his speech of 10 April 1968, delivered after he had crystallized his attitude towards Fatah. He declared that the PR was "legitimate" and that Egypt was "fully prepared to support and arm the Palestinian Resistance movement". He told the PNC (1 February 1969) that "Egypt is extending to the PR all material and moral support – unstintingly, unreservedly and unconditionally". This was an accurate description of the situation, except that in financial matters he referred the Fatah leaders to Faysal. Nasir reiterated this position even more vehemently at the Rabat summit, and soon had the Arab states vying with one another to support and gain influence in the fidai organizations. Egypt saw to it that official political contacts took place, as in the past, through the PLO, its authorized institutions and its official representatives. In talks with leaders of the Third World and the Eastern bloc, Nasir tried to gain recognition for the PLO and the "legitimate rights of the Palestinian people".[26] He also "secretly" attached Arafat to his entourage in his visit to the Soviet Union in July 1968, and arranged Arafat's first meeting with the Soviet leadership (3 July 1968). There is no doubt that Nasir's support for the PR, and especially its right to represent the Palestinians, was decisive in influencing the Soviet attitude towards the PR.[27]

No Arab political support came anywhere near Nasir's in benefiting the PR in general and Fatah in particular. The entire Arab world eagerly awaited Nasir's speeches, which were universally headlined by the Arab media. In almost every speech he praised the PR and stressed that it represented the Palestinians. In addition, Haykal's articles were fully reproduced in many Arab media, including *al-Quds* (published in East Jerusalem), the Cairo broadcasting stations with their wide audience in the Arab world and the pro-Egyptian press in Lebanon. Nasir, very sensitive to his nationalist image in the Arab world in general and among the Palestinians in particular, admitted (15 May 1968) that he had officially come out on the side of the PR "at the demand of the Palestinians themselves". In 1969 he supported the fidai organizations during their crises in Lebanon and procured the Cairo Agreement of November 1969. In September 1970 he tried to halt the slaughter in Jordan even though he had been unable to prevent it, and effected the Cairo Agreement of 27 September 1970. His death the day after the signing of the agreement – which was his last political act – became symbolic; it was said that he "went to his death in order that the Palestinian Entity and the Palestinian struggle would remain".[28]

Anyone examining the Egyptian media of this period must be astounded at the tremendous publicity and hyperbole given to the fidai organizations and especially Fatah. PLO transmissions over Cairo Radio continued to be broadcast daily. It was hard to tell whether Palestinian organizations or "a unit of the Egyptian army", as Haykal described Nasir's attitude towards them, were being referred to. But the gap between image and reality was so wide that Haykal had to tone down these highly coloured accounts. And criticism was voiced regarding the organizations' lack of unity and the true representativeness of the PLO when organizations continued to exist outside of its framework.[29]

It was clear that when Nasir spoke of the PR he mainly meant Fatah. It was he who suggested to Fatah setting up a special broadcasting station, *Sawt al-Asifa*, which began transmitting over Cairo Radio on 11 May 1968; he also encouraged them to publish their own organ. The Egyptian media, in fact, became a mouthpiece for the organization, evidently at the authorities' behest. And once Arafat's name had been publicized as the spokesman of Fatah (15 April 1968), his image began to be cultivated.[30]

As for the military sphere, aid to the fidai organizations, including Fatah, commenced in late 1967 but gained momentum in early 1968, and was institutionalized after Nasir's meeting with the Fatah leaders. In furtherance of her traditional ties with the ANM, Egypt also extended military aid to the PFLP (founded in late 1967). This continued during 1968, but the PFLP's conversion to Marxism–Leninism, and its criticism of Nasir's efforts for a political solution, drove a wedge between it and Egypt; "the result was a complete divorce from Nasirism", and Egyptian aid to the PFLP ceased in June–July 1969. Two other small pro-Egyptian fidai organizations received Egyptian aid: the Arab Palestine Organization (APO) led by Ahmad Za'rur, and the Active Organization for the Liberation of Palestine (AOLP) led by Isam Sartawi.

But the bulk of the military aid went, of course, to Fatah. Apparently a group of Fatah personnel underwent basic military training at Egyptian bases, as early as the end of 1967 and the beginning of 1968. The training of Fatah personnel was stepped up after April 1968; there were intelligence, commando and marine sabotage courses, and advanced officer training courses at Egyptian military academies. Egypt also flew weapons, including small arms, and sabotage materials to Fatah in Jordan (1968) without first coordinating with Jordan; the Jordanian authorities protested about this aid more than once. In fact, operational cooperation between Egypt and Fatah was particularly conspicuous in Jordan, at a time (the beginning of 1968) when Egypt was eager for fidai actions against Israel from some border other than her own. From late 1967 to early 1968 fidaiyyun belonging to the Egyptian 141st Palestinian battalion, which had been at the disposal of the Egyptian headquarters in the Gaza Strip before the war, were sent by Egypt to Jordan, partially to execute sabotage acts against Israel from the Jordanian border. Fidaiyyun of this battalion, in cooperation with Fatah members, attacked the oil storage reservoir at Eilat on 13–14 January 1968. It seems not unlikely that in other actions against ships at the port of Eilat (15–16 November 1969, 5–6 February 1970, 15 May 1970) Egyptian and Fatah members participated.[31]

The PLO chiefs, and especially the Fatah leaders, had cannily assessed the importance of Nasir's total support for the PR and for the PLO, and of Egypt's position as the "centre of gravity of the Arab region in both peace and war". They had almost absolute confidence in Nasir; they admitted that he had helped them "in time of defeat" and "in time of trouble". He was "father, pioneer and commander ... as no Arab leader before him had been".[32] Even so, when Nasir's actions appeared to the PLO leaders as contradictory to "the armed struggle as the sole means" of achieving their objective they did not balk from a confrontation with him, at least for a while.

The First Confrontation: The Rogers Initiative

Nasir's support for the Rogers initiative surprised the fidai organizations, especially Fatah. Their immediate reaction was hysterical.

Their publications, including Fatah's, condemned Egypt and even Nasir himself. *Sawt al-Asifa*, on Cairo Radio, threatened to "use bullets to quash any attempt to impose a political solution". These Fatah broadcasts created consternation in Egypt; on the night of 28 July 1970 Egyptian intelligence picked up orders being transmitted by Fatah leadership to their officer in charge of broadcasts in Cairo: "Say everything firmly and directly". Finally Nasir decided to call a temporary halt to the transmissions of *al-Asifa* and of the PLO. Egypt expelled the activists of the PFLP and the Popular Democratic Front for the Liberation of Palestine (PDFLP), which uncompromisingly rejected the Egyptian position. On the other hand, the two pro-Egyptian organizations, APO and AOLP, supported Nasir's "tactical position", although once the cease-fire came into effect on 7–8 August 1970 this support became qualified.

After the initial shock, however, Fatah leaders appeared to have second thoughts, and Nasir and Haykal explained to them Nasir's military reasons for his decision. Although Fatah knew the implications for themselves of his acceptance of the initiative, they judged: (1) that they could not afford to sever relations with Egypt; (2) that a conflict between the PR and Nasir would mean "a rift among the Palestinian masses and an upset of the balance of forces in Jordan", which at the time seemed to favour the organizations. In their view, the Palestinians had been "connected with Nasir for eighteen years" and "it was impossible to convince them that [Fatah] was right and Nasir was wrong". Finally, any confrontation with Egypt would make it easier for Jordan "to strike out at the organizations" – and this would mean fighting on two fronts. Abu Iyad later summed up Fatah's attitude as follows: "To attack the Ra'is was suicidal on our part at a time when we are in danger of being knifed in the back by Husayn".[33]

Nasir, for his part, emphasized to Fatah's leaders the following points, in addition to the military considerations: (1) Egypt recognized their right to oppose the Rogers initiative and the political settlement. (2) His consent to a cease-fire was in no way binding upon the fidai organizations. (3) Egypt adhered to two principles for a peaceful settlement: "complete liberation of the lands occupied in June 1967, and securing the rights of the Palestinian people". (4) If the PR rejected having its activity restricted, it must not do the same to any other group. Nasir underlined the importance of Egyptian support in view of the danger of confrontation with the regime in Jordan. On the eve of the PNC convention he reported to Arafat on his talks with Husayn of 21 August 1970 (the contents of which were deliberately leaked to *al-Ahram*, 24 August 1970), in the course of which he had acquainted Husayn with "the pan-Arab [*qawmi*] interest that dictated using all means to preserve the PR movement".[34]

However, because the cease-fire was taking effect on the night of 7–8 August 1970, because they had been persuaded by Nasir and because of events in Jordan, the Fatah leadership decided on an out-and-out rejection of the Rogers initiative; no political attack on Egypt or Nasir; and mobilization for "defence of the Palestinian revolution against the opposing forces in Jordan". Arafat dictated this position to the PNC, which convened in Amman on 27–29 August 1970.[35]

This crisis proved that, however close the two parties were, a clash was inevitable when Egyptian tactical–political moves to achieve the interim aim (of the "elimination of the traces of aggression") were assessed by the PLO as frustrating its own strategic objectives. Nasir's declaration that support for the PR was an expression by an Arab state of its nationalism now boomeranged.

SYRIA

The Syrian Ba'th acted as though the war had not created new circumstances in the region, and remained unaffected by the post-war era and its events. Any modification of the Ba'th's concept of the conflict would imply admitting the failure of the strategy of the group in control since February 1966, which in turn would open the way for its ousting. The Syrian Ba'th not only clung to its strategic concept of the "popular liberation war" but added another element, the "armed struggle". Hence the opposition to Nasir's strategy, the boycotting of the Khartoum summit and the low-echelon representation at the Rabat summit. Syria felt far more comfortable leading the "refusal camp" than being drawn into Nasir's policy.

The Syrian Ba'th's attempt to extricate itself from a deadlocked policy and from growing domestic struggles, as well as to strengthen its position in the Arab arena, led to the abortive military invasion of Jordan (September 1970). This in turn led to the downfall of Jadid's regime and Asad's accession to power (16 November 1970). The regime's weakness was also partly due to the leadership's being retained by a group of officers belonging to the Alawite minority. This regime tried to base its rule on two deeply rooted characteristics of Syrian politics, Arab nationalism and the cultivation of Syrian nationalism. A separate strategy in the conflict would show Syrian independence and distinctiveness. "The revolutionary strategy ... was forging the [Syrian] nation for a single fate", and transforming "Arab Syria into a stout fortress in the liberation campaign".[36] Thus Syria's internal political struggles remained bound up with her position in the conflict, including her attitude to the issue of the Palestinian Entity.

The domestic struggles in this period were between two wings of the Syrian Ba'th. One was the "civilian wing" headed by the Ba'th deputy secretary-general, Major-General Salah Jadid, with the participation of Prime Minister Zu'ayyin and Foreign Minister Makhus; this wing dominated the civilian apparatus of the party. It favoured a radical separatist line in inter-Arab policy, thus refraining from cooperating with such "reactionary conservative" regimes as Jordan and Saudi Arabia. The other was the "military wing" led by Hafiz al-Asad, minister of defence and commander of the air force. Asad emphasized the "pan-Arab nationalism [*qawmiyya*] of the campaign" against Israel; the strategic point of departure was the "armed struggle", and military coordination between the confrontation states, regardless of differences in their regimes. This wing supported military cooperation with Egypt and intensification of efforts to found the Eastern Front. "Escalation of fidai action and its continuation is connected with the defensive capability of the Arab fronts."[37]

The struggle between the two wings intensified, and Asad, during the Regional Congress and the National Congress of the Syrian Ba'th (September–October 1968), overran the general headquarters and the radio and television stations with the help of units commanded by his brother Rif'at al-Asad; this enhanced his control of the army and caused the downfall of the government. President Atasi formed a government under his premiership from which Zu'ayyin and Makhus were excluded (28 October 1968). Asad replaced Jadid's followers with loyal army officers; by late 1968 he had achieved total control of the army. After the 4th RC (20–31 March 1969), which did not settle the internal struggle, the "civilian wing" converted the Ba'th fidai organization, al-Sa'iqa, into an arm of the party. IDF reprisals on 2 April 1970 and 24–26 June 1970, the Egyptian and Jordanian acceptance of the Rogers initiative, Syria's abortive invasion of Jordan and Nasir's death all helped catalyse the confrontation. When Atasi resigned (18 October 1970) as president and prime minister, Jadid tried to gain support in the National Congress which convened from 30 October to 12 November 1970, and adopted (12 November 1970) a number of resolutions in his favour. Asad countered promptly: on 13 November 1970 army units overran governmental and party institutions, and the leaders of the "civilian wing" were arrested. A new provisional Regional Command was set up, manned by Asad's supporters.[38] Asad, as president, became the new ruler of Syria, and one more chapter in the history of the Syrian Ba'th came to an end.

Syria's Strategy towards the Conflict

The Ba'th strategy was anchored in bombastic nationalistic slogans such as "historic responsibility" and the "fateful and sacred campaign". Its principles were, first, *a comprehensive and total solution.* This meant "the annihilation of Zionism in Filastin as personified by the state of Israel", after which would be founded an "Arab Palestinian state within the framework of pan-Arab liberation [*qawmi*] and inclusive of Arab unity". The Ba'th stressed the "Arab character of Filastin" (*urubat Filastin*) and dissociated itself from the Fatah/PLO notion of a "democratic Palestinian state", or from any setting up of a "Palestinian state" other than by means of the "armed struggle". The Ba'th did not find it necessary to determine the future of the territories after the "elimination of the traces of aggression". "The solution of the Palestinian problem is contingent on the victory of the Arab revolution, the struggle against imperialism including Israel, the national [*watani*] and the pan-Arab [*qawmi*] struggle and the social struggle within Arab society." Thus the Fatah slogan of "non-interference in the internal affairs of the Arab states" or "the independence of the Palestinian revolution" was impracticable.[39]

The second principle was *armed struggle*, which included "the comprehensive popular liberation war" (*al-shamila*). Syria rejected Resolution 242 in its entirety on the grounds that it "disregarded the rights of the Arabs in Filastin" and established "a permanent peace between the Arabs and the artificial Zionist entity".[40]

The *establishment of a forum of the progressive forces* was the third principle. As a substitute for the Arab summit, Syria proposed a "forum of the progressive forces" in the Arab world, which would "unite the military, political and economic resources of Syria, Egypt, Algeria and Iraq and place them at the service of the common campaign" against Israel. Syria's participation in the "confrontation conferences" was in line with this concept.[41]

Syria's Position on the Issue of the Palestinian Entity

Syria continued to be what the Fatah leaders had defined as "the land of sanctuary" (*ard al-himaya*). Abu Iyad claimed that "for us, Syria was, from the beginning of our activities, the heart and the lung".[42] It was no coincidence that such designations stressed the practical aspect of Syria's support rather than the political-leadership aspect as with Egypt.

The Palestinian Resistance was the ideal expression of the Syrian strategy. The Syrian Ba'th had no doubts about the PR's capacity to represent the Palestinians, though it might have questioned the organizational framework and representational composition of the PLO. The Ba'th conceived the "fidai action" as the "pioneer of the armed struggle", and "as proof that the armed struggle is the sole means of liberation and that the popular war of liberation is no mere slogan"; "every fidai is a part of the strategy of the popular liberation war".[43] The Ba'th did in fact agree that "the resistance movement cannot be a complete substitute for the regular military force", but claimed it was the vanguard of the regular force. "The PR, in bringing about reprisals [by Israel], serves as a catalyst forcing the Arab states to increase their military strength." The charge was made, however, that the PR's development had not been of a quality or rate "equivalent to those of the regular armies. The targets of attacks by the Resistance, the scope and depth of operations had not changed from the Karama operation" (March 1968) up to the end of 1970. The Ba'th called for fidai activity "to the point of general uprising"; otherwise the PR would become "a force of secondary importance" and a "mere routine manifestation in the eyes of the enemy soldiers".[44] To set a goal of such magnitude for the PR was unrealistic, and indeed it became "a mere routine manifestation".

The "Organization of the Vanguards of the Popular Liberation War: al-Sa'iqa Forces" came into existence in December 1968 through a merger of three fidai organizations linked to the Syrian Ba'th: the Palestinian Popular Liberation Front, the Vanguards of the Popular Liberation War and the Popular Upper Galilee Organization. The decision to found this body was adopted at the Regional Congress of the Palestinian Section (al-Tanzim al-Filastini) of the Ba'th Party (Damascus, May 1968), designated the Palestinian Preparatory Conference (PPRC), in which repre-sentatives of the "Palestinian branches" of the Ba'th party in the

Gaza Strip, the West Bank, the East Bank, Syria and Kuwait participated and which also founded the United Palestinian Organization
(UPO) (al-Tanzim al-Filastini al-Muwahhad) of the party. It was
resolved that this "organization" would "constitute the backbone
of the Sa'iqa organization". It was also resolved that the Sa'iqa
command would serve as Regional Command of the UPO.

Sa'iqa was founded because, first, the Syrian Ba'th wanted more
influence over fidai activity, especially in light of Fatah's increasing
strength and closeness with Egypt, as well as the PFLP's debut. The
fight for influence in the PLO during 1968 obliged the Ba'th to
set up one "big" organization which would facilitate greater Syrian
influence in the PNC and the EC. Second, the Ba'th sought to
validate the doctrine of "popular liberation war" more convincingly
than it had before the war. Finally, the "civilian wing" aspired to
found a military force as a political bulwark. The party chiefs were
aware of the decline of the three organizations and their failures in
fidai activities. They wanted to halt the drift of fidaiyyun from these
organizations towards Fatah.[45]

As soon as the Ba'th proclaimed the founding of Sa'iqa in
December 1968, in fact, the two wings of the party began to battle
for influence over it. At the 10th NC (October 1968) Jadid had
influenced a decision that the party would be responsible for recruitment, administration and ideology, while the army would handle
military matters. But at the 4th Extraordinary Regional Congress
(March 1969) Asad demanded that all Sa'iqa fidai activity be
supervised by the army. The ERC approved his motion in principle
but nothing was actually done about it; control of the UPO Regional
Command, which was responsible for Sa'iqa, remained in the hands
of Jadid. In February 1970 a compromise was apparently reached
between the two wings: the Ministry of Defence would continue to
be responsible for Sa'iqa's military activity, while a Fidai Action
Bureau (Maktab al-'Amal al-Fidai al-Qawmi) was set up at the
National Command, which was under the control of the "civilian
wing". Meanwhile, Sa'iqa continued to expand in both size and
operations in Jordan, Lebanon and the West Bank. Many party
activists were required to serve in it for a time, so that it became
more a Syrian than a Palestinian organization. The struggle for
control of it ended when the battle for power was won in November
1970. The leading commanders of the organization were arrested by
the new regime and ousted from their positions.[46]

Sa'iqa was founded at a relatively late stage. Because it was
backed by Syria, it did not live up to expectations regarding fidai

activity, this because, *inter alia*, of its involvement in Syria's internal struggles. Its association with the Syrian Ba'th made it difficult to recruit Palestinians into its ranks.

As for Syria's position on the representative composition of the PLO, the starting point for Sa'iqa (or the Syrian Ba'th) was the need for overlap between the political framework of the PLO and of the fidai organizations. "The PLO must incorporate first of all the chief combatant forces"; the PNC was to be "a revolutionary body serving as the leadership of the Palestinian people" that must encompass "all the combatant organizations that believe in popular liberation war". The structure and composition of the PLO must be altered "radically", so that it would become a "coherent national front [*mutamasika*] which could serve as the sole leadership of all the Palestinians". Sa'iqa proposed that this "front" be founded by direct talks, outside the official framework of the PLO, between the fidai organizations until they agreed to operate within the institutions of the PLO "as a single bloc and not as factions".

The Ba'th, however, faced a dilemma. To make this concept a condition for its participation in the PLO institutions meant isolating Sa'iqa in an important arena of activity and narrowing its ability to influence that arena. This would allow Fatah unlimited control over the PLO institutions, since it was clear (after the 4th PNC) that the PFLP was becoming factionalized. Thus Sa'iqa developed the concept of stages, which would ideologically legitimize its active participation in the PLO institutions with hardly any previous conditions. The "coherent front" would be founded in stages, "until it could develop to the level of general leadership"; this was because "no fidai organization can pretend to be capable of assuming the general leadership of the Palestinian people". Accordingly, Sa'iqa propounded a number of principles regarding its participation in the PLO institutions: (1) "A minimal prerequisite as a basis for cooperation between the organizations" within the framework of the PLO. This meant consent to any form of inter-organizational cooperation, on the assumption that it would eventually be possible to develop this "minimal prerequisite" into wider cooperation "while raising the level of fidai activity". (2) Initiating a "*jabhawi* forum" outside the PLO, by promoting more cooperation between Sa'iqa and other organizations with which it might find "deeper understanding of basic problems". The success of such a consummation would promote the evolution of a "coherent front". On this basis Sa'iqa participated in the 4th PNC (July 1968), and on the eve of the 5th PNC (February 1969) it in fact posed minimal conditions for attending which were acceptable to the other organizations taking part in the PNC, especially Fatah. Another reason Sa'iqa gave for participating in the PNC was "to prevent any organization from overrunning the PNC, the leadership and institutions of PLO", an obvious reference to Fatah.[47]

Unlike Egypt, which regarded Fatah as the leader of the PLO, Syria saw both Fatah and Sa'iqa in this role. It considered that the most important result of the 5th PNC was that Fatah and Sa'iqa "were for the first time given responsibility for the leadership of the PLO". Fatah, of course, did not agree to be represented on an equal footing with Sa'iqa; and Syria eventually recognized the unique status of Fatah within the PLO. At the Rabat summit (December 1969) the Syrian delegation supported Fatah as the foremost Palestinian organization, and Arafat (as its leader) as leader of the PLO. The entry into the PLO institutions of the PDFLP at the 6th PNC (September 1969) further weakened Sa'iqa; and Fatah never met the Ba'th's expectations about establishing a "*jabhawi*" forum. The PDFLP, which Syria also viewed as a potential partner in this "forum", was not prepared for this. By and by, Sa'iqa was drawn in the wake of Fatah which, together with the PDFLP, formed a coalition to lead the organization. Such influence as Sa'iqa had was derived from being a Syrian organization and not a "Palestinian" fidai organization; Syria, however, exploited its membership in the PLO to influence indirectly the EC and PNC deliberations.[48]

Because of the changes which had taken place in the PLO, at the beginning of this period Syria also needed to retain its patronage of the PLA. Shuqayri, who aspired to establish the PLA at all costs, waived the direct command of the EC over these forces. During his term of office bilateral agreements were signed between the EC and the states that had set up the PLA units (Egypt, Syria and Iraq), providing *inter alia* that the PLA units would not be transferred from one country to another without the consent of the army headquarters of the countries concerned. Each Arab state was adamant about having its own PLA units subordinated to the commander-in-chief of its own army. After the war, the Hittin Forces (Syrian PLA units) emerged as the chief component of the PLA, and their headquarters were relocated to Damascus. The Ayn Jalut Forces (Egyptian PLA) had fared very badly in the fighting and had to be reorganized. After the war the Iraqi 421st PLA Battalion (Qadisiyya Forces) was located in Jordan under command of the HQ of the Iraqi expeditionary force stationed there. Syria viewed the PLA forces and HQ as a Syrian rather than a Palestinian force, and one which had the right to veto any change in its status or command. Under these circumstances the 4th PNC amended Article 22 of the PLO Constitution: henceforth the PLA HQ "would be independent and would operate under supervision of the Executive Committee; would implement its directives and decisions, both extraordinary and general". With a view to making this clause effective and ridding itself of Syrian tutelage, the EC decided on 29 July 1968 to appoint Abd al-Razaq Yahya as PLA chief of staff, in place of Subhi al-Jabi, and made some personnel changes in the PLA HQ. (On 29 January 1968 the post of C-in-C PLA was abolished.) The EC's reshuffles in the PLA HQ included the appointment of Musbah al-Budayri to the position of commander of the Hittin Forces in place of Uthman Haddad, and the appointment of a new commander for the Popular Liberation Forces in Jordan. This hasty step by the EC indicated a misunderstanding of the Syrian approach to this matter. Obviously the Syrians, who were well aware of the significance of this decision, would do their best to prevent its execution. For them, this issue became a test case of their claim that the PLA and its HQ in Syria constituted "extraterritorial terrain", and that any modifications relevant to them must be made with Syria's consent. The Syrian authorities incited the PLA HQ and the senior officers of the Hittin Forces and of the PLA fidai organization, the Popular Liberation Force (PLFS), to "rebel" against the changes. When Razaq arrived in Damascus to take up his duties he was placed under house arrest by the PLA forces; he had to resign and a replacement acceptable to the Syrians was appointed instead. Jabi then also agreed to resign (20 October 1968). On 19 December 1968 the media published the appointment by the EC of Musbah al-Budayri as PLA chief of staff;[49] this finally determined who made important decisions regarding the PLA.

Syrian aid to the PR. Because she was ruled by the Ba'th and isolated in the Arab arena, Syria's political support for the PR carried far less weight than Egypt's. Syrian support was important chiefly in the broad military sphere. The Syrian political support for the fidai organizations was especially conspicuous during the crises in Jordan and in Lebanon. "Filastin Corner" on Damascus Radio relayed the regime's policies to the Palestinians. Because of its geographical location both as a "confrontation state" and as the centre of the "fertile crescent", Syria served as a base for the activities of the organizations (especially Fatah and Sa'iqa) in

Israel, Lebanon and Jordan, and helped them become established in the latter two. Syria wielded decisive influence over the organizations' activities in those countries, and from there against Israel; and it gave them significant aid during the crises in Jordan and Lebanon. Its political weight was vital for the PLO, inasmuch as that body had adopted a "refusal" position towards Egypt's mode of solving the conflict. Syria now became its most important ally.

As previously, the regime gave military aid mainly to Fatah, which it described as "a basic factor for the Ba'th". Syria placed at its disposal various training bases such as al-Hame and Maysaloun; hundreds of fidaiyyun who had joined Fatah after the "Karama operation" were trained there. Syria also served for Fatah as a logistics base and as an arsenal for the weapons and military equipment arriving for Fatah from the Arab states (such as Algeria), or from China and the Soviet Union. Fatah had a central office in Damascus and published its organ there. Syria also gave limited military aid to the PDFLP. The Syrians tried to draw the PFLP-General Command into their orbit, the leader, Ahmed Jibril, being a former officer of the Syrian army; but it did not succeed. A number of joint fidai actions were mounted by Sa'iqa with other organizations such as Fatah, the PLFS and the PDFLP.[50]

The question of how much freedom Syria would grant the fidai organizations for actions inside Israel over the Syrian border was a problematic one; the concept of the "popular liberation war" was being tested. The Syrian policy on this issue falls into three stages.

From June 1967 to January 1969, the regime prevented fidai actions from the Golan Heights so as to prevent border tensions. The Syrian army was then reorganizing and expanding. The regime, seeking an activist image, published fictitious announcements of border activity in the name of Sa'iqa. There were, however, 105 actual operations during this period, most of them waged in the southern Golan by fidaiyyun, often from the PFLP, who had infiltrated from Jordan. Syria's inactivity was commented on by the Arab and especially Lebanese press; the regime averred that "the resistance movement has not spread to the Golan Heights because of the small number of inhabitants" remaining there, the majority "having been uprooted by Israel". Fatah aided Syria with some further inept explanations such as "the [Israeli] targets are situated far from the border" or the "concentration of Israeli forces on the short Syrian frontier makes it a difficult border to cross".[51]

At the start of the second period, February 1969 to the end of 1969, the regime permitted fidai actions from the border and actually encouraged Fatah and Sa'iqa in that direction. This change was attributable to the army's completion of its reorganization, and the growing military activity in the Suez Canal Zone. In this period large-scale operations were mounted by groups of 15 to 25 men. The Israeli air force's attack on Fatah bases (24 February 1969) led to some reduction of operations, but their number increased each month (five in March, 13 in April, 21 in May, 36 in July, 43 in August). The Syrian army also activated the artillery and the air force so as to point to a "hot border".[52]

The period from January 1970 to September 1970 began with stepped-up activity on the Syrian border; fidai actions reached a peak at the end of March 1970. In the Israeli "day of battle" of 2 April 1970, three Syrian MiG-21s were shot down. The Syrian army responded with massive artillery bombardment (8 June 1970) and raids on military positions (24 June 1970). Following a sharp Israeli retaliation (24–26 June 1970) in which several hundred Syrian soldiers were injured and killed, 38 taken prisoner and four aircraft shot down, border activity came to a virtual standstill but then resumed again. After Asad's accession in September 1970, the number of actions decreased sharply. During January–August 1970 the fidai actions reached 50–70 a month; then they declined from 52 in August to eight in October and 12 in December.

The activity in this period resulted from Egyptian pressure and from the resolution of the Heads of the Confrontation States Conference (7–9 February 1970) to escalate border activity.[53]

Restrictions on fidai activity. The Ba'th regime continued to keep fidai activity under tight surveillance in this period, inside Syria as well as on the border, mainly for purposes of domestic security and to enable Sa'iqa to establish itself in Syria particularly among the Palestinians. Since it valued Syrian support for its activity, Fatah did not confront the regime over these restrictions. During the period until April 1969, the two "wings" both favoured surveillance of the organizations in Syria, but the conflict between them prevented a systematic approach. Some steps were taken to limit Fatah's and the PFLP's activities so as to prevent infiltration into Syria of subversive elements. Certain limitations were imposed on Fatah members as regards leaving and entering Syria. The Fatah leadership had to obtain prior approval for fidai actions (from Syrian territory) from a special military commission. To prevent fidaiyyun from the three organizations connected with the Ba'th from switching to Fatah, and to facilitate Sa'iqa's recruitment and expansion, Fatah was prohibited from recruiting "Syrians" to its ranks; further, its activity in the Yarmuk refugee camp near Damascus was curtailed.

While these measures were undertaken "quietly", no such precaution was deemed necessary in regard to the PFLP, because of the historic rivalry between the Ba'th and the ANM. On 19 March 1968 three PFLP leaders then in Damascus were arrested: George Habash, Faiz Qaddura and Ali Bushnaq. The reasons for this were, first, that the regime suspected that their presence in Damascus was connected with the activity of the ANM leaders, and had to do with the founding of a Progressive National Front in opposition to the Ba'th regime. Second, the authorities had seized a quantity of weapons illicitly smuggled in from Jordan to Syria for the PFLP. Finally, the PFLP had, without permission, successfully perpetrated fidai actions inside Israeli terrtory via the southern part of the Syrian border close to Jordan. The PFLP was unable to get the three leaders released by diplomatic means, but on 3 November 1968 smuggled them from the prison and out of Syria. At the same time the PFLP was forbidden to propagandize in Syria and its membership cards were not recognized at the frontier stations.[54]

After the Ba'th RC (March 1969), Asad as defence minister issued a special order in early May 1969 regulating the organizations' activity and especially the modes of surveillance of this activity. This order, which took effect on 1 June 1969, also listed the organizations that would be permitted to operate in Syria: Fatah, Sa'iqa, PLFS and PFLP – apparently meaning the PDFLP and PFLP–GC. The Syrian intelligence (Branch 235) was to be responsible for liaison and coordination with these organizations. The order made the following provisions: (1) The fidai personnel would be subject in the main to the same regulations as Syrian army personnel regarding registration, movements in and out of Syria and reports on new recruitments. (2) The collection of contributions in any form whatsoever was prohibited; military uniforms could be worn and weapons carried outside the camp only during a mission and with permission from intelligence; the arrest or interrogation of civilians was prohibited; distributing information or holding meetings or parades required permission. (3) Border-crossing for operations in the occupied territories was forbidden without written authorization from the minister of defence. (4) Syrian intelligence was entitled to examine the offices and branches of the organizations and their camps. Asad carried out this order to the letter, and Fatah held its peace so as to cover up for the regime. Under the order, following the deterioration of relations between Iraq and Syria, the activity of the Arab Liberation Front (ALF) (a fidai organization under the auspices of the Iraqi Ba'th) was abruptly terminated in July 1969. Around 20–21 July the authorities arrested and interrogated dozens of ALF activists and its offices were closed; through PLO (in fact Fatah) mediation the detainees were released except for the ALF representative in Syria.[55]

This two-faced Syrian policy towards the PR was a constant feature of relations between the sides. Both had to live with it because of their respective needs: the strategic-political needs of Syria and the military needs of the PR.

IRAQ[56]

The Ba'th regime which returned to power in the *coup d'état* of 17 July 1968 was determined to remain in power by whatever means. Violence became part of its ideology, as the execution of "spies" was elevated to the status of "a revolutionary act that the regime had accomplished". The struggle against Israel also became a means for keeping the party in power; the Iraqi Ba'th presented itself as more Nasirist and nationalist (*qawmi*) than Nasir and more Ba'thist than the Syrian Ba'th. It dreamed of leading the Arab world when, in its eyes, Nasir's leadership was teetering following his acceptance of the Rogers initiative. The regime displayed even more militant attitudes towards the Arab–Israel conflict than the Syrian Ba'th,[57] and its declarations were even more vastly out of proportion to its performance. Iraq actually lacked the basic prerequisites for leading the Arab world, and its particularism cast it into forced isolation.

The Ba'th's Strategy towards the Conflict

The starting point of Iraq's declared policy on the Arab–Israel conflict was pan-Arab nationalism (*qawmiyya*). "The war for the liberation of Filastin is a war of Arab character and Arab import, and its destiny is Arab. It is a war between the Arab liberation movement on the one hand and imperialism, Zionism and reaction on the other hand." The only path was that of "popular, armed struggle developing into a popular war of liberation". "The road to liberation as well as the road of [Arab] unity are connected one with the other." In the Ba'th's view "the basic responsibility for the liberation of Filastin devolved upon the Arab liberation movement; the Palestinian people must bear the responsibility, the initiative and the sacrifice". After the "liberation of the occupied lands ...

there would arise the Democratic Socialist Unity State in Filastin, where the Jew would live as an Arab citizen". The Ba'th coined the slogan "All Arabs are Palestinians until Filastin is liberated". It viewed the fidai organizations as "an expression of the revival of the Palestinian Entity". The 10th Iraqi Ba'th National Congress (Baghdad, 1–10 March 1970) went so far as to call upon the Iraqi regime "to make Iraq become, in relation to fidai activity, as Hanoi in relation to Vietnam".[58]

The Ba'th's Position on the Issue of Palestinian Entity

The Iraqi Ba'th's position on this issue evolved in two stages. The first, lasting till June 1969, was the *negation of the existence and composition of the PLO*. The Ba'th severely criticized both the way the PLO was founded and its representative composition, claiming that "the PLO which was founded by the Arab summit is another Arab regime, the purpose of whose founding was to prevent the evolution of the Palestinian struggle towards armed resistance". "The PLO's representation of the Palestinian people was a geographical representation", hence "a large number of people operating in the sphere of the struggle were prohibited from participating in the PLO because they were born several dozen miles from the border of Mandatory Filastin". The PNC was described as "a council of a political entity and not a revolutionary council. It was open to the Palestinian who was not fulfilling any function in the revolution and was closed to the Arab who was fulfilling such a function." The Ba'th demanded "changing the structure and composition of the PLO to a revolutionary one". The fact that the fidai organizations joined the 4th PNC (July 1968) did nothing to alter these reservations. The Ba'th also criticized the representative composition of the 5th PNC (February 1969) and the 6th (September 1969), which "did not provide the minimal ... conditions required for the realization of a national entity", even though the fidai organizations now controlled the PLO institutions.[59]

The most conspicuous expression of its objection to the PLO composition was the formation of the Arab Liberation Front (ALF), which Iraq first announced on 11 April 1969, although the end of 1968 was cited as the date of its formation. It was the last fidai organization to be founded by means other than by splintering from a parent organization. It did not have a constituent assembly until September 1972.

There is no doubt that the founding of Sa'iqa by the Syrian Ba'th in September 1968 impelled the Iraqi Ba'th to form its own "unique" organization. The ALF was to fill the vacuum that had arisen "in the absence of the pan-Arab [*qawmi*] dimension in fidai activity", through promoting the "Arabization" (*ta'rib*) of the "Palestinian resistance": in other words, to reverse the "Palestinization" process which had been occurring. The ALF was purposely designated "Arab" rather than "Palestinian", and its members were citizens of various Arab states (the Palestinians accounted for 30 percent, Lebanese 35 percent, Iraqis about 30 percent as well as some Syrians and Eritreans). The leadership was mainly Iraqi; the Ba'th assistant secretary-general, Shibli al-Aythami, was responsible for political organization, while the Minister of War, Hardan al-Tikriti, controlled military activities. In December 1969 the General Command of the Arab Liberation Front resolved to form a Supreme Military Command of the Combatant Forces. Abu Jabara was appointed commander of combatant forces. In a lecture to the General Command of the ALF, which became a central part of the Political Report of the 10th National Congress, Aflaq outlined what should be the Ba'th's goals in founding the ALF: (1) "Renovation of the entire party through the Filastin campaign and the popular armed struggle." (2) To attract the youth to join the party; "the appeal for a liberation campaign would heighten the bond between the party and the masses. In this way the party would be rebuilt by new pioneering elements." (3) "The aim that must be attained is that the ALF command should become the supreme command of the party." The 10th NC ratified a number of decisions in line with Aflaq's points. It affirmed that the party was the backbone of the ALF; the ALF's ideology was that of the party including the Palestinian issue. Also, the ALF was not the "military arm of the party in Filastin and the occupied lands, but is the party's formulation of the national struggle". "The entire party must fight within ALF; every party member must at least have some role in the ALF." Thus the ALF became an Iraqi rather than a Palestinian organization. The Palestinian issue was claimed to be the tool for reviving and strengthening the Ba'th party "after the deadlock and ailments that had beset it for ten years" – as Aflaq had put it some years before, "the crisis of the party" and "the crisis of the government".[60] However, in his present proposals he in fact gave impetus to those very crises.

The second stage saw the *participation of the ALF in the PLO institutions*. In July 1969, several months after its creation, the Ba'th (or the ALF) made a policy change. At first it agreed to selective participation in the PLO institutions (until February 1971) and later to full participation. Aware of the contradiction, the ALF continued at the same time to criticize the composition and structure of the PLO. A number of factors contributed to these developments. First, the ALF was isolated in the Palestinian arena. The slogan of pan-Arab nationalism had failed to arouse enthusiasm among the Palestinian or even the Arab masses since the dissolution of the UAR. The trend among the Palestinians was, on the contrary, towards greater "Palestinization". Second, Iraq's traditional isolation in the Arab world deterred Arabs from joining the ALF, which therefore could not contribute significantly to fidai activity. The Iraqi Ba'th had no active cadre outside Iraq except in Lebanon. Third, the situation in Jordan was deteriorating, and other organizations, particularly the PFLP, were gradually joining the PLO institutions. The ALF, rather than have Sa'iqa be the only Ba'th organization to participate substantially in the PLO, concluded that it was "not sufficient to fight from the outside" and that it must participate "through its Palestinian elements" in PLO institutions "with a view to transforming the PLO into a revolutionary institution and overhauling its structure".[61] This valiant attempt, of course, had no chance of success.

At first the ALF's participation was limited. On 27 September 1969 it joined the Palestine Armed Struggle Command (PASC) "with a status equivalent to that of the other organizations". The PASC had been founded by the EC in February 1969 to coordinate inter-organizational military activity. The ALF claimed that "to have joined the PASC did not entail adhering to the political line of the PLO". The ALF attended the 6th PNC (September 1969) and also the 7th (May–June 1970) in the status of "observer". Together with the other organizations, the ALF took part in the United Command, formed by the fidai organizations in February 1970 to handle their conflict with the Jordanian regime. The ALF also proposed replacing the PNC with a "National Congress" (the epithet "Palestinian" being omitted) which would consist of "representatives of the fidai organizations regardless of nationality ... of representatives of the trade unions and of independent Palestinian and Arab personalities connected with the Palestinian revolution". Representatives of the Palestinian organizations would number not less than 75 per cent but with no organization gaining full control. The ALF also took part in the Central Committee that was set up by the PNC in August 1970.[62]

After the "September massacre" of 1970 and the PFLP's decision to participate fully in the PLO institutions, the ALF also joined them, at first by being fully represented at the 8th PNC (February 1971). At the 9th PNC (July 1971) the ALF was also fully represented in the EC. Thus the ALF was transformed into a "Palestinian" organization, though in structure and concept it remained pan-Arab. It continued to criticize the structure of the PLO, and to submit alternative plans for its reconstruction and for "national unity".[63]

Iraqi aid to the organizations. In early 1968 the Arif regime, following Egypt's example, extended military aid to Fatah and PFLP. Iraqi army units encamped in Jordan rendered logistic aid to Fatah. The 421st Iraqi PLA battalion took part in fidai actions from Jordan, and helped transfer military equipment from Syria to Jordan and the West Bank.

Under the Ba'th regime, the Iraqi forces in Jordan continued to aid the organizations.[64] The regime sought to take Fatah under its wing, thereby neutralizing Egypt's influence over it and driving a wedge between Fatah and Sa'iqa in the PLO. As early as August–September 1968 the regime proposed to Fatah that it set up a Palestinian ministry to be headed by a Fatah member. Fatah rejected this proposal. But with Fatah's strengthening of relations with Egypt and the Ba'th decision to create the ALF the relations between Ba'th and Fatah cooled, though military and financial aid to Fatah continued (except for periods of tension in 1969). Fatah was permitted to set up bases in Iraq for basic and advanced training for its members.

In early 1969 the regime began to improve its relations with the radical organizations, especially the PFLP (which remained outside the PLO), to which it gave arms and other military equipment. Members of the PFLP trained in Iraq, via which they also received arms and *matériel* from Communist China. Iraq supported PFLP financially; eventually this became a regular monthly allowance. It seems plausible that PFLP may have had recourse to the good offices of Iraq (such as the diplomatic mailbag and passports) for its activity in the Arab states and Europe. Iraq also supplied money, arms and training to the AOLP. Cooperation with the PDFLP began after its relations with Asad's regime had cooled. Following PDFLP leader Hawatma's visit to Iraq in March 1971, this organization, like PFLP, became a recipient of Iraqi military and monthly financial aid. Still another organization that received Iraqi financial support was the Palestine Popular Struggle Front (PPSF).

A *rapprochement* also took place between Iraq and the PFLP–GC, which received military and monetary aid and with which Iraq coordinated political positions.

Encouraged by this progress, Iraq tried in late 1969 and 1970 to form a roof organization for the radical fidai bodies; but the ALF suspended this plan by joining the PLO institutions. In 1971 Iraq tried again to create what Saddam Husayn meant to be a "rejectionist front" composed of the organizations that opposed a political solution. These efforts proved fruitless.[65]

As for propaganda, the Iraqi media were not to be outdone by their Egyptian and Syrian counterparts in their support for fidai action. In May 1968 (during the Arif regime), a special broadcast was introduced over Baghdad Radio called "The Sacred March" ("al-Zahf al-Muqaddas"), intended to promote the organizations and especially Fatah. It was cancelled during the Ba'th era, but replaced in 1970 by "The Voice of the [PLO] Central Committee from Baghdad". At first the content of these broadcasts was co-ordinated with the PLO, but after the September 1970 crisis the PLO Central Committee dissociated itself from the programme (27 September 1970). The Ba'th, of course, opposed any policy for a "Palestinian state" on the West Bank and Gaza, which in its opinion would be designed "finally to eliminate fidai activity and the Palestinian problem".[66]

The Iraqi Ba'th's attitude towards Jordan's struggle with the PLO over the right of representation was fully expressed during the crisis of September 1970. Like Qasim, the Ba'th questioned the *raison d'être* of the regime and of Jordan as an independent entity; in its opinion "Filastin in the full sense is just one country, there is nothing dividing the east of the Jordan and the west". "It is quite impossible to progress in the direction of the liberation of Filastin without first setting up a unified revolutionary authority east of the Jordan." Iraq viewed the West Bank and Gaza as part of "the unified democratic state" that would arise after the "liberation of Filastin".[67]

Like the Ba'th in Syria, Iraq imposed *restrictions on fidai activity* out of internal security considerations and insisted on coordination of the activities with the authorities. The restrictions were no less stringent than those in Syria, even though Iraq had no common border with Israel. Around March 1969 most of the Fatah offices in Iraq were closed down; Fatah was prohibited from hanging posters in the streets of Baghdad and from having contact with any institutions whatsoever in Iraq "except for the officer in charge of this in military intelligence". A harsher measure was taken in April

1969 when the Revolutionary Command Council sent a "secret note" to seven fidai organizations then operating in Iraq, PLO, Fatah, PFLP, ALF, PFLP–GC, AOLP and PPSF, pointing to their "offences" and enumerating conditions they must fulfil "because otherwise, cooperation between Iraq and the organization[s] will cease". The conditions included: appointment of a liaison officer from each organization; limitation of bases to one per organization, to be located far from the principal towns, and detailed arrangements in all matters pertaining to finance, arms and passports. They were also forbidden to have contact with political organizations in Iraq, and could not conduct any other political activity, including propaganda, without permission of the authorities. In line with this, the authorities confiscated a shipment of Chinese weapons that arrived for Fatah at Basra; they gave the arms to Fatah only after the latter guaranteed that they would be removed from Iraqi soil. While the PDFLP severely criticized these orders, Fatah was compliant; it "did not want a rift with Iraq" any more than with Syria, and "tried to resolve difference through dialogue, in an attempt to get Iraq to change her position step by step".[68]

In early 1970 the Ba'th founded the National Bureau for Filastin (al-Maktab al-Qawmi li-Filastin) which was subordinate to the Ba'th National Command. The organizations were to maintain contact with the authorities solely through this Bureau. "This step led to the curtailment of their activity"; in June 1971, further such steps were taken following the deterioration in Syrian–Iraqi relations and the huge influx of Iraqi youths into the organizations following the crisis in Jordan. Intelligence and security personnel conducted surprise searches of the organizations' offices in Baghdad. The Bureau, now renamed the Filastin and Armed Struggle Bureau, sent them a number of "secret notes" containing further "security" orders such as: prior permission to be obtained before circulating any political announcement; the Bureau to be supplied with the names of Iraqi citizens wishing to join the organizations for purposes of security screening; and prohibition of trade in arms, contraband or unlawful goods.[69]

The Iraqi Ba'th party's policy did not meet the test of Arab and Palestinian reality during this period. Iraq did not become another "Hanoi" and the ALF remained a marginal organization. The Ba'th party did not "renew itself"; instead the power struggle continued, and some months after the ALF's creation an opposition group formed within it calling itself the Arab Democratic Front. In order to survive, the ALF had to undergo a process of "Palestinization", even though it had been set up to achieve the precise opposite, namely "Arabization".

JORDAN

Jordanian Strategy

The postwar regime in Jordan was in a state of shock at the kingdom's having shrunk back to its 1948 size. For Husayn, the issue of Palestinian representation (Entity) had become most acute; the West Bank problem became the central factor in his postwar policy.

Husayn aimed, first, for *recovery of the West Bank as a strategic goal.* At one stroke, the war had stripped Husayn of two of the most important justifications for his claim that Jordan represented the Palestinians: the West Bank as part of Filastin, and the largest concentration of Palestinian population. The West Bank inhabitants now had a new option for resolving the dilemma of their political allegiance. The West Bank's relationship with Jordan became a subject for negotiation in the Arab, Palestinian and international arenas, while its future was becoming inextricably bound up with the solution of the Palestinian issue. Husayn viewed the restoration of the West Bank to Jordan as his primary goal, responsibility for which meant that he continued to represent the Palestinians and that the West Bank was still part of Jordan. Indeed, with Nasir's help, he was empowered by the Khartoum summit "to do everything for the restoration of the West Bank and Jerusalem" – within, of course, the four limits imposed by the summit. Husayn correctly assessed that time was working against him on the West Bank, and that unless he could recover it soon (one to two years) after the war, its very restoration might undermine his regime because of the Israeli influence and the prolonged severance from Jordan. The fidai organizations' increasing strength in 1968 reinforced his opinion. Nasir shared his view that "every day that passes with the West Bank under Israeli occupation, binds it more strongly to Israel".[70]

Second, Husayn recognized the necessity of *alliance with Nasir.* The two leaders had become mutually dependent in their interim aims, especially the "liberation of the West Bank". Nasir's support was vital to Husayn as proof of his nationalism and to make possible political negotiations with the United States and also indirectly with Israel. Not since 1952 had Jordan enjoyed such a sustained period of cordial relations with Egypt. To preserve his "alliance" Husayn adopted nationalistic domestic and foreign policies which in fact jeopardized his regime. He aspired to a separate agreement with Israel but only on condition that it was acceptable to Nasir, or at least appeared to meet Nasir's condition of Israeli withdrawal from the West Bank and a solution for the problem of Jerusalem. In secret talks between Husayn and Israeli statesmen (such as Allon and Eban), he rejected the very components of the Allon Plan.

Aware of Husayn's ambitions, Nasir obliquely warned him against direct talks or a separate agreement with Israel, stressing the "internal difficulties" he could expect in consequence. In Nasir's view (March 1968), "Husayn will not be able to sign a separate agreement with Israel for many reasons and his situation is therefore difficult". In the wake of his talks with the Israelis, Husayn realized that a separate agreement with Israel would entail significant concessions which he could not afford. He therefore concluded that the restoration of the West Bank would be feasible only under the terms of a "comprehensive agreement" which could be achieved only through Egypt. Like Nasir, Husayn recognized that it was easier to reach an agreement over Sinai than over the West Bank. In taking part in the War of Attrition, supporting the fidaiyyun and consenting to the Rogers initiative, Husayn strove for collaboration with Nasir.[71]

Husayn also provided *support for the PR*. For freedom of manoeuvre over a political solution for the West Bank, he had to support the fidai organizations as proof of his nationalism. His dilemma was how to continue claiming to represent the Palestinians while simultaneously supporting the PR, thereby promoting a process whereby the West Bank population's political loyalty would switch to the PR (PLO). He decided to take a calculated risk. Husayn saw fidai activity in his country as a trump-card for achieving a settlement with Israel, and believed that once an agreement acceptable to Nasir was reached, Nasir would support him in imposing it on the organizations.[72]

Finally, there was *the Israeli factor*. Israel intensified the contest between Jordan and the PR over the right to represent the Palestinians by in effect supporting Husayn. A community of interest had developed between Husayn and Israel, which became deeper the stronger the fidai organizations became. Husayn was concerned that the Israeli position remain unchanged, and that the bonds between the two Banks should continue. It seems that his talks with Israel were intended not only to put out feelers concerning a settlement, but also to convince Israel that the "Jordanian option" was in fact open and that she ought therefore to refrain from any measures affecting the status of the West Bank.

In his talks with Israeli leaders – Eban, Allon or Ya'acov Herzog, or with all three together (May and September 1968, February 1969, October 1970) – as well as in additional messages exchanged through the Americans between 1968 and 1970, Husayn emphatically stated that any agreement should be based on UN resolution no. 242, adding that Israel must declare officially that she was prepared to implement it before entering any negotiations. He did not hide, in these talks, that he was seeking a settlement which would be acceptable to Nasir and the Arab world, and that he must coordinate his steps with Nasir and get his green light for starting negotiations with Israel. Husayn was prepared not to deploy the Jordanian army in the West Bank after IDF withdrawal; instead he insisted on Jordanian civil administration and police jurisdiction. Concerning Jerusalem, he said that it was not enough to hoist an Arab flag; Jerusalem (East) must be Arab. It seems that through these talks he sought to bring about flexibility in Israel's stand.

The regime made every effort to prove that the West Bank was still "an integral part of the Hashemite Kingdom and its inhabitants Jordanian citizens". Husayn persuaded the Khartoum summit to acknowledge, even if not explicitly, that "Jordan is the party chiefly responsible for what is done on the West Bank". The West Bank local leaders were given to understand that the severance of the West Bank was only temporary, and Husayn maintained the Senate and House of Deputies to show "the integrity of the kingdom". The Jordanian government continued to treat the West Bank local authorities as if they were Jordanian by giving them operational directives, paying salaries and extending them financial aid. It opposed any form of "self-rule", "civil administration" as proposed by Israel or any idea of a "Palestinian state".

The issue became more acute after "September 1970" when Bourguiba, encouraged by the US, proposed a "Palestinian state" in the West Bank and Gaza. When similar demands were voiced on the West Bank and "an Arab state proposed the forming of a Palestinian government-in-exile", Husayn retorted that "the Palestinian problem is a pan-Arab national [*qawmiyya*] problem and no Arab state is entitled separately to propose any solution or settlement whatsoever to it". In November 1970 Husayn demanded a discussion on the "Palestinian state" at an Arab summit, rightly believing that the idea would be officially rejected, even though a number of Arab states were inclined to accept it as an interim solution and then only after an Israeli withdrawal from the West Bank.[73]

With a political solution nowhere in sight, Husayn concluded that the "unity of the two Banks" ought to be consolidated on new foundations, and embarked on decentralization of the government. The notion of West Bank autonomy was raised by Husayn and some of his advisers following the events in the West Bank after the Israeli raid on Samoa' (13 November 1966); a draft for an autonomy plan was even prepared in mid-1968, a year after the Six Day War. But the king first publicly expressed the idea in the British newspaper, the *Observer* (15 December 1968), saying he would be prepared for the West Bank to become a "new state" called "Palestine" "if that is what the people want"; "if it came to the pinch, he would be content to remain ruler of the East Bank of the Jordan." He admitted that "even before the June war he had been exploring ways of granting more self-government for the West Bankers". Husayn, whose spokesman amended this version of his statement, did not voice it again once he realized what damage it had done him. He later formulated his position along more moderate lines: (1) "Awarding the right of self-determination to the Palestinians *after* liberation of the West Bank." (2) After Israeli withdrawal from the West Bank and restored Jordanian sovereignty, "greater decentralization would be instituted in the government." (3) "After the liberation", Jordan would accept "the [Palestinian] people's choice as to the character of the government and the degree of its affinity for Jordan". In other words, they could "choose between the founding of a state of their own and remaining part of Jordan."[74] Husayn deliberately avoided raising the issue of representation at inter-Arab forums, in his meetings with PR leaders or even in his public statements. At the Rabat summit (December 1969) he remained silent on this issue. After he had liquidated the PR's footholds in Jordan, the struggle between him and the PLO for the right of representation became overt and intense.

Position of the "Palestinian Resistance": Violent Coexistence

From the outset the fidai organizations, especially Fatah, fundamentally mistrusted Husayn because of his approach to the Palestinian Entity. Even when Fatah was founded, it determined that "Gaza and Jordan are the basis" for fidai activity and that "there is no avoiding a change of the situation in Jordan", *inter alia* "by a *coup d'état* which will shift matters into our hands, if there is no other way". In 1964 Naji Alush had already asserted that "the road to Filastin" lay "through the liberation of Jordan from the reactionary junta".[75] Thus the temporary coexistence between the PR and the regime was tactical only. The PR's position, of course, was basically that of Fatah, as dictated to the PLO institutions.

First, emphasis was put on *Jordan as a "safe base"* (*qa'idat irtikaz* or *al-qa'ida al-amina*). Fatah leaders described the Resistance as "a revolution on a flying carpet" which "would remain such until reaching safe ground – namely Jordan". Jordan was "the surest base on which to rely" and the best – it had the longest border with the occupied territory, and one that made for direct contact with the West Bank population, and a Palestinian majority that could be leaned on while the organizations were building up. From 1968 to 1970 the organizations contrived to transform the East Bank into the "base of support of the revolution". Indeed, from June 1967 to September 1970 fidai actions from the Jordanian border accounted for 55–70 percent of all such actions. Fidai activities after the war reached a climax in December 1969, which saw close to 530 actions in all sectors. From January to September 1970, actions stabilized at about 450 a month, except for two months of crisis, February and June 1970 (285 actions from the Jordanian border in January 1970, 170 in February, 285 in May, 215 in June).[76]

Second, the PR saw *the "armed struggle" as "the sole path to the liberation of Filastin"*. "It is therefore strategy rather than tactics." During this period the organizations rejected any compromise on the "armed struggle" as the means of achieving the "liquidation of the Zionist existence" and the establishment of "an independent democratic Palestinian state on the entire Palestinian area". Indeed there were times when the "armed struggle" appeared to be an end in itself.[77]

What resulted was *dual rule or the "state within a state" in Jordan* (*izdiwajiyyat al-sulta*). To maintain their "safe base" the organizations became *de facto* partners of the Jordanian regime. The regime, the organizations, Nasir and the other Arab leaders acquiesced in "dual rule" and "state within a state" as a description. Between 1968 and 1970 the organizations set up autonomous governmental institutions of their own in all spheres – military, political and social. The Wahadat refugee camp near Amman was dubbed the "Republic of Filastin" and at its entrance flew the Filastin flag. The fidaiyyun shared "almost equally [with the regime] in the execution of laws"; "the Palestinians felt themselves superior" to the Jordanians "who feared that the Palestinians would overrun the state and seize power". Arafat boasted in August 1970 that "the Palestinian Revolution has 36,000–38,000 rifles" in Jordan. The commander of the military arm of Fatah, Abu Jihad (Khalil al-Wazir), described the situation thus: "We were mini-states and institutions [of states]. Every sector commander considered himself God, the intelligence resembled a state, the political organization – a state, the militia – a state, everyone set up a state for himself and did whatever he pleased." The PR had become the predominant political organization in Jordan, filling a vacuum that had existed there since 1957. The organizations thus became not only partners in power, but also the opposition to the government.[78]

Relations between the Regime and the "Resistance"

Relations between the regime and the fidai organizations up to September 1970 developed along two diametrically opposed lines. The organizations tried to maintain and even expand their political and military freedom in Jordan, and to prevent the regime from asserting itself as the representative of the Palestinians; the regime tried to impose its sovereignty on the East Bank by curtailing fidai activities and retaining its freedom of manoeuvre regarding a political solution. Three clashes, each more intense than the last, stemmed from those opposing policies. There was a build-up in stages towards the September 1970 confrontation. From the regime's point of view, the decision to resolve the conflict in this way was political and not military.

1. *June 1967 – March 1968.* Husayn's political activity aimed at regaining the West Bank proved fruitless. He also sought without success the endorsement of the Khartoum summit regarding "the danger of the fidai activity which Syria encouraged"; he continued to emphasize the uselessness of fidai actions, since they supplied Israel with an excuse for reprisals – and created a need to prevent these actions by force. But the regime did not curtail the actions of the fidaiyyun, who were based in the Jordan Valley, especially the Karama area; in fact, Jordanian army units on the Israeli border cooperated with them in launching their actions despite orders to prevent fidai action.

The day after an IDF retaliatory strike on 15 February 1968, which confirmed the regime's fears of a large-scale Israeli military action, the king threatened to "act with force and determination" against the fidaiyyun. The minister of the interior declared (17 February) that the government "would strike down with an iron fist all who harmed security". But this policy was opposed by the prime minister, Talhuni – the first time since the Nabulsi government of 1957 that a prime minister was openly opposing the king. On 21 February 1968 a popular assembly was held in Amman, and there for the first time since the 1950s public appeals were voiced in support of the fidaiyyun. The IDF operation at Karama (21 March 1968) caused Husayn to change his policy regarding fidai actions.[79]

2. 21 March 1968 – November 1968. In Cairo on 6 April 1968 Husayn met with Nasir; Talhuni, Rifa'i and the chief of staff Khammash also participated. Nasir plainly stated that there could be no question of a separate or a political settlement with Israel; he himself would continue his preparations for war. Talhuni expressed fears over a possible Israeli operation to occupy part of the East Bank "after which she would force the king to consent to a Palestinian government on the West Bank". Khammash tried to obtain Nasir's approval for restricting fidaiyyun actions from the Jordanian border, but Nasir suggested that the "activities be coordinated with Fatah". The upshot was that Husayn's freedom of action was reduced, reinforcing the process whereby, since the Karama operation, his policies had begun to fall in line with those of Talhuni, who believed in conforming to the Egyptian line. Husayn began publicly to express his solidarity with the fidai actions; two days after the Karama operation he said that "we may well arrive at a stage when we shall all be fidaiyyun". Although he warned against "an intensification of their activities unless some indications of a settlement are seen", at the same time he called for "full coordination of fidai action".[80]

The Jordanian press, which was heavily influenced by the regime and indicative of the mood on the East Bank, in the months immediately following the war almost ignored the fidai actions. But in early 1968, and especially after the Karama operation, obituaries mourning the death of "heroic combatants" and a plethora of information on fidai actions (although usually attributed to the IDF spokesman) began to appear. In August 1968 the weekly magazines *Amman al-Masa* and *Akhbar al-Usbu'* began to give extensive coverage to the organizations, especially Fatah. A new stage commenced in September 1968 when the daily *al-Difa'* began publishing the military communiqués of Fatah, and *al-Dustur*, considered a government mouthpiece, followed suit.[81]

The fidai organizations thus established themselves in Jordan; the Jordan Valley became their "autonomous area" after having been emptied of its inhabitants. The regime worked towards a *modus vivendi* with the organizations, especially after some sharp Israeli reprisals and complaints issued during talks at senior level, such as a meeting between Chief-of-Staff Bar-Lev and Chief-of-Staff Khammash in May 1968, and between Bar-Lev and Husayn and Khammash in October 1968, both in London. Following the shelling of Irbid by the IDF (4 June 1968), the regime and Fatah reached an agreement whereby Fatah consented, among other things, to coordinate its activities on the border with JA units; but Fatah did not keep its commitments. Another agreement was reached in September 1968 after the Salt Operation of 4 August 1968, and after the shelling of Beit Shean for the first time from the East Bank (16–17 September 1968); under the terms of this (unsigned) agreement, the organizations, including the PFLP, were to coordinate their activities with the JA, and fire from the East Bank was prohibited although the fidaiyyun were permitted to infiltrate into the West Bank. But the organizations did not keep to this arrangement either, and the JA did not attempt to impose it by force.[82]

When, however, the regime took steps on 10 October 1968 to enforce this agreement, a crisis broke out. The organizations associated these steps with reports of secret contacts between Jordan and Israel over a political settlement; Fatah issued a condemnatory statement on 13 October. The crisis was aggravated by clashes between the security forces and the fidaiyyun; a demonstration on 2 November 1968 during which a slogan was voiced about a "fidaiyyun republic"; and also the firing of a rocket-launcher (2–3 November 1968) by Fatah from Aqaba on Eilat. On 5 November 1968 Jordanian armoured forces shelled bases of Fatah and the PFLP in Amman and Zarqa. On 6 November the crisis ended; the regime emerged with the upper hand. A 14-point agreement was signed on 16 November; its essentials were: (1) The fidaiyyun were prohibited from bearing arms and wearing uniform in the towns; they were not to impound cars or arrest any person; persons subject to the draft or having deserted from service were not to be recruited to the organizations. (2) Several clauses, not officially published, dealt with operational activity. No Israeli targets were to be shelled from the East Bank; no fidai action was to be mounted from the Aqaba area; fidai actions in the southern region (south of Dead Sea) were to be executed at a depth of not less than 10 km "within the occupied Palestinian lands"; any infiltration would be coordinated with the local JA commander. (3) An arrangement would be made regarding the passage of fidaiyyun over the Jordanian frontiers. Thus for the first time an official document recognized their presence and activity in Jordan, and their very right to exist there. Still, the terms of the agreement favoured the regime; the organizations never intended to honour it. Several days after signing it they proceeded to breach it, such as by firing from the East Bank.[83]

3. *December 1968 – January 1970.* This period marked the culmination of the "dual rule" process in Jordan. The regime's main problem was internal stability and the undermining of its authority in the country; of lesser concern was the situation on the border with Israel. Husayn and Nasir agreed that "the political activity for the elimination of the traces of aggression has yielded no positive results". However, in early 1969 Husayn suspected that Nasir might be working towards a separate agreement; Talhuni therefore stated that "we will not pursue separate political activity. Withdrawal must be complete and must take place from all the occupied territories." During this period Husayn talked a good deal about the "inevitable war"; the War of Attrition in the Canal Zone and Nasir's pressure on Husayn led the Jordanians to "heat up" the Jordan–Israel border in March–June 1969 and again, more markedly, in August–October 1969. Husayn even agreed to the reinforcement of the Iraqi forces in Jordan. As a result, Nasir supported Husayn's regime "unreservedly and unconditionally". The declared position of the regime in support of the fidaiyyun was further reinforced. In March 1969 Husayn publicly and for the first time admitted the aid of JA units to the fidaiyyun in their border operations. The Jordanian press began regularly reporting the organizations' military communiqués, and publishing articles about them including the PFLP. No such coverage was given by Amman radio or any official publication.[84]

The organizations and the regime avoided an armed confrontation. The regime reluctantly tolerated breaches of the November 1968 agreement, although relations did become temporarily strained when Eilat came under rocket fire (8 April 1969) from Fatah fidaiyyun. The regime was worried by changes made in the representational composition of the PLO at the 5th PNC (February 1969), by Arafat's having been elected chairman of the EC and by Nasir's reference to "a people which has a homeland". Husayn feared that the EC might be converted into a kind of "Palestinian government". As early as 16 February 1969 Husayn met with EC members, and acceded to Arafat's request that he renew Jordan's financial aid to the PLO, stopped in June 1966; but he rejected a request to permit PLA units to enter Jordan.

Another point of tension was the reshuffles in the Jordanian government, and the reorganization of the intelligence and general security services towards strengthening domestic security surveillance and control over the army and security forces in case of confrontation with the organizations. On 26 December 1968 Kaylani was again appointed director of general security, a post he had held until his dismissal in April 1968 at Talhuni's demand. On 24 March a new government was formed under Rifa'i. On 30 June 1969 the Chief-of-Staff Amir Khammash was "relieved" of his duties and appointed minister of defence. He was replaced by Nasir Bin Jamil who thus became commander-in-chief of the JA. Ali Khiyari was appointed chief-of-staff, Kaylani minister of the interior and Izat Qandur director of general security. These steps were in preparation for a possible curtailing of the organizations' activity, and restoring domestic order. *Sawt al-Asifa* claimed that the changes presaged "the execution of a conspiracy for the suppression of the fidaiyyun". On 12 August 1969 the Rifa'i government resigned; Talhuni was reappointed prime minister, while Kaylani remained minister of the interior. Talhuni favoured co-ordination of functions between the regime and the fidaiyyun within the framework of the War of Attrition, believing that only in this way could the regime regain its authority.[85] A meeting between Chief-of-Staff Bar-Lev and Jordanian C-in-C Bin Jamil took place in late September 1969 in London to discuss the situation on the border, in which Bar-Lev received a promise regarding JA steps to be taken against the organizations.

4. *February 1970 – September 1970.* This period was described by the Fatah leaders as "the coexistence of the strong" or "the coexistence of two opposites". Both sides had stumbled into traps of their own making: the organizations into the trap of belief in their power and the regime into the trap of helplessness. Only a decisive outcome would resolve the situation. Abu Iyad admitted that "we were sovereigns, masters of the situation". The Rogers Plan (1 December 1969) underlined the organizations' fears that the regime might reach a political agreement over the West Bank. Husayn believed that if the United States was to pressure Israel to make concessions, he must demonstrate his control over domestic affairs; he evidently decided that it would suffice to show, at least for the present, that he could prevent fidai action from the East Bank.

The crisis of February 1970 began when, on 10 February, the Jordanian government published a 12-point communiqué which dealt with the enforcement of the legal authority within the state. Its prohibitions were more stringent than those of the November 1968 agreement. The immediate background to these orders was the Rabat summit, at which the Resistance was recognized (unofficially at least) as representing the Palestinians. Husayn feared the organizations might now declare the establishment of "governmental institutions" such as a Palestinian government-in-exile, and then claim for themselves full or partial "responsibility" for the West Bank.[86] The organizations were surprised by these orders and their severity; they resolved not to comply with them even if it meant resistance by force.

On 11–12 February, after security forces began enforcing the orders, the two sides clashed in the areas of Amman and Salt. Egypt took an even-handed stance; Iraq, with its forces stationed in Jordan, pressured the regime to abrogate the steps. On 12 February 1970 the Jordanian government announced its shelving of the orders and expressed support for the fidai activity. The understanding that was reached between the regime and the organizations on 22 February 1970 was based on the directives of the organizations' United Command, dated 19 February 1970, which laid down rules for conduct of the fidaiyyun in the towns without touching on the question of the regime's authority. Thus the maintenance of order in Jordan had come to depend on the will of the organizations; the regime thereby gave its official stamp to the "dual rule".

The regime's retreat was not due to any disadvantageous balance of forces. Husayn, in a message to the Israeli foreign minister (transmitted 17 February 1970), asked Israel not to take advantage of the opportunity offered whilst he was obliged to thin his forces on the border; Israel agreed. Also the possibility of a clash with the Iraqi forces was undoubtedly taken into account. Most likely Husayn's initiative was influenced by some of his inner circle, chiefly Kaylani, who favoured restricting the fidaiyyun. Husayn estimated that a show of force would suffice to deter the organizations, but faced with the prospect of internal schisms and civil war, and when a group within the cabinet, of which Talhuni was one, steered in the direction of a peaceful solution, the king retreated. This is the background to Kaylani's resignation as minister of the interior (23 February 1970). Encouraged, the fidaiyyun organizations succeeded, by dint of demonstrations held

14–17 April 1970, in preventing the scheduled 17 April visit of the US assistant secretary of state, Joseph Sisco. On 16 April 1970 King Husayn made a militant speech in which for the first time he declared that there was no longer any chance of a political solution.[87]

On 19 April 1970 the Jordanian cabinet and the JA command were reshuffled. The JA chief-of-staff was appointed minister of defence; his military post was filled by Mashhur Haditha, known to be acceptable to the fidai organizations. A new director of general security was appointed; the interior portfolio went to Najib Rshaydat who as early as 1966 had called for support for the fidaiyyun. Of the group that had been appointed on 30 June 1969 to ensure the gradual restoration of authority to the regime, there now remained only Commander-in-Chief Bin Jamil. These appointments reflected the regime's and Talhuni's policy – to motivate the organizations to cooperate in maintaining law and order.

The crisis of June 1970 erupted when a further attempt to impose authority was made early that month, after incidents between fidaiyyun and JA forces that climaxed on 9 June with the fiercest collisions to date. On 11 June 1970 the PLO Central Committee demanded the dismissal of Bin Jamil and Zayd Bin Shakir (OC 3rd Armour Division). On 11 June, for reasons similar to those of February 1970, the regime backed down, assessing that to dislodge the fidaiyyun from their strongholds in Amman was impossible without all-out confrontation. The king, in his greatest concession yet, announced the resignation of Bin Jamil and Bin Shakir. Husayn spoke on 17 June 1970 of a formula for cooperation "which would ensure to honourable [*sharifa*] fidai activity greater capacity for action". The status of Haditha, who took a balanced position between the king and Arafat and avoided using force against the organizations, was considerably augmented.[88]

On 27 June 1970 Talhuni resigned; the king saw him as pressing for retreat by the regime. A new government was formed under Rifa'i, a nationalist coalition among whom fidai supporters were prominent; no cabinet since Nabulsi's in 1956 had had such a radical composition. Aid to the fidaiyyun was stepped up. The Confrontation States Conference in Libya (21–22 June) resolved to despatch a "committee of four" to settle the crisis in Jordan. This committee by 10 July 1970 had negotiated an agreement whereby "the freedom of action of the fidaiyyun would be preserved and ensured on condition that it did not injure the sovereignty of the state". The organizations undertook to conform to the agreement of November

1968. PFLP, PDFLP, ALF and Sa'iqa dissociated themselves from the agreement; like its forerunners, it was simply not implemented. Yet another crisis broke out following Nasir's agreeing to the Rogers initiative (23 July 1970), with the organizations attempting to dissuade Husayn from following suit. But after persuasion by Nasir's emissaries, Fatah permitted the nationalist ministers in the Jordanian cabinet to vote (26 July 1970) in favour of the "initiative". The government stressed to the United States that Jordan was not responsible for the fidai action that might be launched from her territory during the cease-fire.[89]

The Crisis of September 1970

Husayn's initiative on 16 September 1970 for liquidating the fidaiyyun footholds in Jordan, a process which ended in July 1971, was not prompted by a desire for a political settlement with Israel, as Palestinian writers and fidai leaders have since been trying to prove. The prospects for a political solution in September 1970, after the Rogers initiative, were no brighter than before. Nasir's agreement, indeed, surprised Husayn; in his letter of appointment of the Rifa'i government (27 June 1970), characterized by unprecedented militancy, Husayn indirectly negated the Rogers initiative (which Jordan received on 20 June 1970). Only later did Husayn become aware of Nasir's military motives for consenting to the initiative. The liquidation of fidai activity in Jordan was the result of a struggle for survival between the regime on the one hand, and the PLO and the fidai organizations on the other. Sure enough, Husayn realized (late September 1970), apparently from the organizations' documents which the general security acquired during the September massacre, that his initiative had indeed thwarted a *coup d'état* planned by the organizations to begin 18 September 1970 with a call for a general strike throughout the country.

After the crisis of June 1970 Husayn once more had to choose between the lesser of the two evils: either Jordan would become a "Palestinian state", or he could keep his throne – but at the cost of isolation and subversion from without. His decision to impose his sovereignty must have been taken in June 1970, after his second defeat. He accurately assessed that he could not afford a third defeat, and began making preparations.

To begin with, as the JA was virtually his only source of power, Husayn ensured that in case of crisis it would balk at nothing to suppress the fidaiyyun. Most to be feared were the junior officers who were sympathetic to fidai activity. Along with the two deposed officers, Bin Jamil and Bin Shakir, he toured army units in late June 1970 to determine how much support there would be for a massive strike against the fidaiyyun. At the beginning of August 1970, to strengthen his control and curtail the chief-of-staff, he made extensive changes in the senior officer ranks; a new commander was appointed for the 2nd Division, and Bin Shakir was appointed deputy chief-of-staff for operations. The king retained supreme command of the army and also of the armour. During August 1970 the Amman area and the areas close to the Iraqi forces were reinforced with armour and infantry units transferred from the Jordan Valley. At the "confrontation summit" (June 1970) and at the meeting of the Defence Council (August 1970) Husayn requested that the Iraqi forces be subordinated to the JA HQ, but this was refused. On 21 August 1970 he sought Nasir's agreement to the evacuation of the Iraqi army from Jordan, but Nasir refused.

A special effort was also made to infiltrate the organizations. The Jordanian IS managed to recruit agents in key positions in the organizations, including the PFLP and Fatah, and the regime was thus privy to attempts by the organizations to recruit senior JA officers. On the whole, Jordanian IS reaped considerable success during the crisis of September 1970–July 1971. Correspondingly, the regime waged an intensified anti-fidaiyyun propaganda campaign in the army; and in the course of the fighting the JA proved not only cohesive but enthusiastic, beyond what Husayn had hoped. In contrast to the chief-of-staff, senior officers called for firm measures against the fidaiyyun. On 9 September 1970 a few armoured units decided to move towards Amman for an operation against the fidaiyyun, against orders from above. The chief-of-staff was bypassed and the chain of command went from the king directly to the division commanders; and on 15 September 1970 Haditha resigned. Habis al-Majali was appointed commander-in-chief and military governor; actual command was retained by Bin Shakir.

On 16 September the army began moving into Amman, and also into towns in the north that were under the organizations' control. Desertions from the JA during the September crisis were not significant (2,200–2,400, including 70–90 officers), but these included a few senior officers, including the OC Engineering Battalion and the OC 4th Infantry Brigade, Sa'd Sail.[90]

Another important factor was the consolidation of the leadership. Wasfi al-Tall coordinated (from behind the scenes) the military operation under the king's supervision. He began his preparations in June 1970. During September 1970 the leadership rallied solidly around the king; along with Tall the group included Zayd Rifa'i (secretary to the king), Ahmad al-Tarawna, Salah Abu Zayd and Bin Shakir. Tall's appointment to the premiership on 28 October 1970 was a natural step. The king also, seeking to consolidate the "Jordanian family", held meetings of tribal chiefs, beginning on 21 August 1970, in which he warned Jordanian and Bedouin elements of the dangers of the fidai organizations with their ambition to establish a "Palestinian state from the remainder of the land of Filastin and the Jordanian homeland".[91]

As for the Husayn–Nasir meeting, 21 August 1970, there can be no doubt that Husayn's visit to Cairo was mainly designed to gauge Nasir's feelings about a military sweep against the organizations. Husayn stressed to Nasir that "there is a limit to [my] patience". Nasir asked Husayn "not to act against them" but at the same time did not exclude action against "evil or opportunistic elements". Husayn's impression was that Nasir had given him licence to act only against the radical organizations (PFLP, PDFLP). This may explain Husayn's decision of 1 September 1970 to take over control of the organizations' strongholds, evidently the same day that an attempt was made on his life by the PDFLP. Husayn, at any rate, was not deterred by the meeting. Nasir's death merely made things easier for him.[92]

The organizations' efforts to overthrow the regime. After the crisis of June 1970, the organizations were confident of their power and their ability to "establish a democratic national rule" – in other words, overthrow the monarchy. They disagreed only as to the means and the timing; there were two schools of thought, represented by the PDFLP and Fatah, respectively.

As early as September 1969 the PDFLP had coined the slogan "there is no rule higher than the rule of the Resistance". They saw the results of February 1970 as marking "a decisive change in the balance of forces ... in favour of the rule of the Resistance". Once Jordan had consented to the Rogers initiative, various slogans were coined like "all rule to the Resistance" and "an Arab Hanoi in Amman on behalf of revolutionary national rule resting on the will of the Resistance". But judging these extremist slogans to be impracticable, the PDFLP replaced them with "the rule of the Resistance, the soldiers and the armed people".[93]

As for Fatah, in theory it refrained until September 1970 from declaring in favour of overthrowing the regime. The slogan by which it was guided, not without Nasir's influence, was "coexistence". But in practice it was working towards the same goal as the PDFLP. Alush defined it neatly, saying that

Fatah had acted strategically for the liquidation of the regime by military, organizational and mass expansion, and [at the same time] declared a defensive posture. This meant that Fatah had realized the slogan, 'all rule to the Resistance', whereas the PFLP and PDFLP were merely mouthing slogans. To the extent that the behaviour of the PFLP and PDFLP provoked the regime, the behaviour of Fatah intimidated and frightened it.

Fatah aspired to the Palestinization of Jordan no less than did the PFLP and PDFLP, but preferred to do things by stages. Fatah's conception was that "when the revolution enters into confrontation with the regime, it [the Resistance] will be capable of forcing an outcome in its favour".[94]

The organizations viewed the JA as the key to overthrowing the regime; they tried, but failed, to recruit senior officers to their cause. In fact, the conduct of the JA "exceeded their worst expectations". The organizations had predicted that the army would split from within. In August 1970, the PDFLP decided to stage or at least prepare for an "uprising" (*intifada*); the PFLP emphasized preparations for a military putsch. To this end, contacts were maintained with the OC 2nd Infantry Division. The Jordanian IS evidently got wind of the affair and the OC was dismissed.

The "scope and cruelty" of the army's action of 16 September 1970 came as a complete surprise. But the resolutions of the extraordinary meeting of the PNC (27–28 August 1970) had left no doubt as to which way the PLO/Fatah was headed, and spurred the king to resolve the conflict once and for all. The PNC resolved that the PR, "represented by the PLO and the Central Committee, is the sole representative of the people of Filastin", and "viewed the Jordanian–Palestinian arena as one arena of struggle". This implied the conversion of Jordan into a "Palestinian–Jordanian" state. On 9 September the Central Committee of the PLO went even further than the PNC statements had, calling for a "direct struggle for realization of the national government [in Jordan] and the over-throw of the [Hashemite] rule".[95]

The reaction of the Arab world. The king's initiative was a calculated risk on the assumption that the situation could hardly get any worse. He managed to withstand the pressure of the Arab arena, and stopped his military campaign once he had gained sufficient time to execute the first and most important stage of his plan. Iraq did not honour her promises that the Iraqi army in Jordan would come to the organizations' aid, nor did she make good her threat to Husayn (1–2 September 1970) that "unless he stopped firing on the fidaiyyun ... the Iraqi forces would intervene in [their] favour". During the September 1970 crisis the Iraqi army "stayed in its place", no doubt on orders of the Iraqi defence minister. The Salah al-Din Forces contented themselves with providing military and other supplies to the organizations. This enabled the JA to turn its attention to the Syrian invasion.[96]

On 19 September 1970 Syrian forces invaded Jordan, intending to render massive aid to the fidaiyyun. This unprecedented move expressed the Syrian Ba'th's basic stand against "the reactionary regime" in Jordan and its desire to overthrow it. The Syrian Ba'th adopted Jadid's policy of pressing for military intervention (on 17 September 1970, following the king's moves of 16 September 1970); Asad demurred. Jadid hoped such a move would fortify his own status in Syria, as it was feared that the king might gain total victory over the fidaiyyun. In the invasion, the Syrian army for the first time deployed an armoured force of 250 to 260 tanks and also heavy artillery. The aim was limited to occupying the northern region of Jordan and establishing a "liberated area". In the fighting with the JA, and especially the well-trained 40th Armoured Brigade, Jordanian supremacy was evident. The Syrian forces began to retreat, completing their evacuation on 23 September 1970.[97]

Nasir's reaction was delayed for several days since he underestimated the severity of the crisis. When he realized what Husayn's intentions were, he attempted, by exerting maximum diplomatic pressure on Husayn, to halt the hostilities as quickly as possible. He rejected, however, any direct Egyptian military intervention. He did order three PLA battalions to be despatched from Egypt (the Ayn Jalut Forces) as immediate aid to the organizations, but they actually remained in Syria, and afterwards (August 1971) returned to Egypt after Jordan refused them entry. On 21 September he sent Husayn a sharply worded note demanding a cease-fire, emphasizing that Egypt "would not permit the liquidation of the Resistance". At Nasir's invitation, meetings were held, on 22 September, of a number of Arab leaders in Cairo, to resolve the crisis and terminate the massacre of the fidaiyyun. Nasir opposed Qadhafi's suggestion of sending Arab forces to Jordan, arguing that "in Yemen we lost ten thousand dead, I am not prepared for a single Egyptian soldier to lose his life on Jordanian soil". Nasir wanted to prevent American – or Israeli – military intervention; the Soviet Union called on him to exercise restraint. He summoned Husayn to Cairo so as to impose a cease-fire on him; Husayn arrived in Cairo on 27 September, and on that very evening the Cairo Agreement was signed by Husayn, Arafat and leaders of the Arab states.[98]

Its 14 articles were couched in general and "balanced" terms. It provided that "the guarding of security is the province of the internal security authorities" and that the "inter-Arab commission" should draw up an agreement between the protagonists, "ensuring the continuation of fidai activity, and respect for the sovereignty of the state in the framework of the law other than those exceptions necessary for fidai activity". More important as regards the right of representation was the Amman Agreement of 13 October 1970, which regulated the relationship between the regime and the organizations, the nature of fidai activity and the location of their bases. Here too an attempt was made to strike a balance, which gave rise to a certain contradiction. The first article provided that: *"Jordan on both her Banks, land and people* is *a unit single and indivisible"* – which left no doubt as to Jordan's right to represent the Palestinians at least of the two Banks, and was antithetical to Nasir's position regarding the "people which has a homeland" and to the PNC resolution of August 1970. The convoluted Article 4, on the other hand, stated: "The Palestinian people alone, represented in the Palestinian revolution, has the right to self-determination". This wording betrays the debate that raged behind the article. It was not by chance that the word "alone" was positioned before the word "represented" and after "the Palestinian people". Hence the privilege of "sole representation" is taken away from the "Palestinian revolution". The word "alone" has no connection with the representative rights of the "Palestinian revolution", so that the actual meaning of this clause is "The Palestinian people alone – has the right of self-determination". Notwithstanding the constructions placed on it by Palestinian writers, this does not expressly establish that "the Palestinian revolution alone represents the Palestinian people". The PLO, not unintentionally, is not mentioned in the agreement in the context of the right of representation, but only when reference is made to "the Central Committee of the PLO as being responsible for the Palestinian revolution". The Amman Agreement reiterated the article of the Cairo Agreement whereby "fidaiyyun freedom of action … will be ensured on condition that it does not prejudice the sovereignty of the state and the framework of the law, consideration being accorded to exceptions necessary for fidai action".[99]

The Regime's Policy after September 1970

Husayn signed the Cairo and the Amman agreements with the intention of not implementing them. For him they were like an intermission, after which he meant to exact further concessions from the fidai organizations and gradually eliminate their activity in Jordan. In this sense he rightly viewed the Cairo Agreement as his achievement. In his talk with Allon (early October 1970) he promised to do his best to prevent fidai actions against Israel. The process of eliminating the fidai bases was to consist of three stages: (1) October 1970–March 1971 – liquidation of their bases in the Irbid and Salt regions, and the weakening of their positions in Amman; (2) April 1971 – evacuation of the fidaiyyun from Amman; (3) mid-July 1971 – liquidation of their main and last stronghold in the region of Jarash-Ajlun.

It seems the regime had planned this long-term strategy vis-à-vis the organizations in late December 1970 and early January 1971. The first indication of this policy came in Husayn's speech of 23 September 1970, in which he specified the conditions under which fidai action would be permitted in Jordan. From this it is obvious that his assent to the Cairo and Amman agreements was a mere tactical move. The principles of his strategy were (1) that the sovereignty of the state was above any other consideration; (2) that security, stability, internal law and order were the basis of all political and military action; and (3) that he and the Jordanian government were the representatives of the Palestinians on both Banks. The Resistance could function in this framework only.[100] In practical terms these principles translated as follows.

1. *Fidai activity* must be under the complete control of the regime, which would recognize only "true or honourable [*sharif*] fidai action". Organizations "having contacts with political and party organizations" would not be permitted to operate (i.e., Sa'iqa, ALF, PFLP and PDFLP); the regime was prepared to recognize only Fatah and the PLA (including the PLFS) as "honourable". The number of fidaiyyun permitted in Jordan would range from 600 to 1,000. The fidaiyyun, including the PLA, would have two bases, as designated by the JA HQ. All their military, administrative and logistic activity would be conducted inside these bases only, through full coordination with the JA and under its supervision. Every fidai

would be issued with identification papers by the JA. In sum, the fidaiyyun were actually to become "commandos of the JA". After July 1971 the regime tried to implement this policy. It gave the PLA one base (at Khaw, near Salt) where the PLA battalion was set up under Nuhad Nusayba, with not more than 600 men. This battalion was coordinated by the JA, and operated under its orders. The regime also provided money, weapons and training to a group of defectors from Fatah headed by Muhammad Abd al-Hadi, known as Abu al-Abd, who had been one of the chiefs of the Western Sector, responsible for operations in the occupied territories. This group set up (August–September 1971) a fidai organization under the regime's auspices, called the Fatah-Salah al-Din Forces; it numbered a few dozen members and was based near Karama. In coordination with the JA, it mounted a few operations within the occupied territories (e.g., in the Gaza Strip on 6 October 1971). This organization was disbanded (January 1972) after the murder of Tall on 28 November 1971.

2. *In the operational sphere*, fidai actions were to be executed only "deep inside the occupied territories", "in coordination with the Operations Branch of the JA". Fire from the East Bank would be prohibited; operations would also have to comply with the pan-Arab operational plan.[101] The regime followed these guidelines throughout the Saudi–Egyptian mediation efforts which commenced in July 1971 and ended abruptly with the murder of Tall. Through such steps the regime reduced the Cairo and Amman agreements to a dead letter.

As for *Jordan as representative of the Palestinians*, one of Husayn's main aims in phasing out fidaiyyun activity in Jordan was to be able once again legitimately to claim to represent the Palestinians of both Banks. Thus the immediate result of the September 1970 crisis was that the issue of Palestinian representation became central to the struggle between the regime and the PR. As Husayn put it officially, "the Hashemite Kingdom of Jordan comprises one people in one state; all subjects are represented by the king, by the lawful state authorities and by its representative institutions. It serves as the main base for the liberation of Filastin." The regime was aware, however, that merely claiming the right to represent the Palestinians was not enough; doubts must also be cast on the representativeness of the PLO as newly composed. Here the regime argued, first, that neither the PLO nor the fidai organizations were representative of the Palestinians, including the inhabitants of the West Bank. Second, special emphasis was placed on "the right of the West Bank inhabitants to decide on their future free of terrorization" and on "their right ... to speak in the name of the Palestinian people more authentically than the gentlemen meeting in Damascus, Beirut and Cairo". The regime summed up its position with the statement: "The PLO cannot represent all the forces of the Palestinian people. It can only represent the fidai organizations." It is noteworthy that Husayn, in his meeting with Allon (October 1970), did not rule out the idea raised by Allon of establishing a Palestinian political framework in the West Bank as an alternative to the organizations' leadership. However, neither did he indicate acceptance of such an idea.[102]

Reaction of the Organizations: Liquidation of the Regime

"The events of September inflicted a deeper wound in the heart [of the Palestinian people] than did the events of 1948." The year 1971 was depicted as a year of "to be or not to be". Fatah leaders emphasized that "the entire Arab world took part in the slaughter of the Palestinian revolution ... in order to reach a political solution". The organizations' struggle against the regime now became total and uncompromising; yet they were plunged in confusion, and dissension surfaced within Fatah regarding the regime. The standpoint of the PLO/Fatah from October 1970 to July 1971 had been influenced by the following major factors. First, the Arab arena was in a transitional phase. Egypt, Syria and Iraq were suffering from their own domestic crises (the latter recalled its forces from Jordan), leaving Jordan free to execute its plan with hardly any interference. The organizations preferred to avoid conflict with the "confrontation states" because "they did not want to lose any more Arab political, moral or material support". Second, the organizations were undergoing a crisis and a collapse of morale. The JA's military campaign had seriously weakened them all, including Fatah; the confidence of the rank-and-file in the Fatah leadership broke down. Third, Saudi Arabia played an important role as Faysal attempted to reconcile the regime and the Resistance on the basis of the Cairo and Amman agreements. The Saudis expressly threatened to cut off monetary aid to Fatah (and also to Jordan) unless it consented to participate in the mediation talks Faysal had initiated together with Sadat. Fatah was now sorely in need of Saudi financial support; in addition to its own expenses it had to take care of several thousand deserters from the JA and set up military frameworks for them (such as the Yarmuk Brigade).[103]

This explains the complicated position adopted by Fatah, which in cooperation with Sa'iqa led the PLO during this critical period. Fatah now pursued two lines of policy: one of overt mediation talks, the other of covert subversive activities. To rob the regime of any pretext for action against the fidaiyyun, Fatah leaders repeatedly declared that they did not aspire to rule the East Bank but sought only "freedom of action in Jordan for the realization of their aims in the occupied land". Fatah believed that by giving its "not to be published" consent to the evacuation of the fidaiyyun from Amman (April 1971) it would "prevent further slaughter", and in return the regime would permit the fidaiyyun to concentrate in the area of Jarash-Ajlun. But the regime went ahead with its campaign, and on the pretext of "protecting tourist sites" liquidated their bases in this area in mid-July 1971. Under pressure from Faysal and Sadat, Fatah/PLO consented to negotiate with the regime for a settlement based on the Cairo and Amman agreements. Its very consent was due to "the wish not to forfeit the friendship of the Arab states" and to "the need to reorganize".[104]

At the same time, in early 1971, Fatah began to organize itself clandestinely in Jordan. In March 1971 Fatah was sabotaging vital installations and governmental institutions in Jordan; at this stage Fatah did not take official responsibility for these acts. Sabotage was also perpetrated by other organizations, including the PFLP–GC. The Fatah leadership decided (March 1971) to set up "a secret apparatus in Jordan which would be responsible for preparations for toppling the regime"; heading the apparatus was Abu Iyad. Plans included the assassination of leading Jordanians and Palestinians serving in the Jordanian establishment. The Jordanian internal security got wind of the full details of this plan, and this, along with the sabotage activities, hastened the regime's decision to wipe out the fidai strongholds in Jordan (13 July 1971).[105]

Despite its declaration of limited objectives, Fatah was forced by the September massacre to adopt a position acceptable both to its own extremists and to the radical organizations. Fatah did this by appealing for the "establishing of national rule" in Jordan and by giving "unity of the two Banks" a meaning different from that of the regime. The 8th PNC (February–March 1971) resolved that "the unity of Filastin and East Jordan is a national [*qawmiyya*] unity" expressed in a national Jordanian Front. "There is no agreed basis for the creation of a political entity in the east of Jordan and another [entity] in Filastin." Contradicting itself, this resolution emphasized, on the one hand, the existence of the Jordanian national element, and, on the other, its absorption in the Palestinian Entity – in other words, the Palestinization of Jordan, in the sense that Filastin and the East Bank were to constitute "national unity [of a people] and territorial unity". This approach was ratified by the 9th PNC (July 1971). In March 1971 the CC PLO approved a secret resolution to topple the regime, averring that "there is no place for coexistence with Husayn's regime". During this period Fatah organs refrained from making any explicit appeal for the overthrow of the regime.[106]

The position of the radical PFLP and PDFLP, on the other hand, was clearly defined. Their basic attitude – that coexistence between the regime and the Resistance was impossible – had been proved correct. PDFLP leader Hawatma called for

> the liberation of East Jordan and the founding of a national republic on this territory to which will be annexed such areas as Israel withdraws from. From and through this republic the Palestinian people will continue its campaign for the liberation of the rest of the occupied lands and the liquidation of the political existence of Israel.

Habash called for "the overthrow of the regime by revolutionary violence". The two organizations therefore refused to participate in the mediation talks between the PLO and Jordan.[107]

Change in the Position of PLO/Fatah after July 1971

The elimination of fidaiyyun activity in Jordan led Fatah – and, as a result, the PLO – to change its declared and actual attitudes towards the regime. Fatah now followed the line of the radical organizations. Its policy was hammered out in two meetings of its leadership: at the Central Committee (September 1971) and its 3rd General Congress in Damascus (September–October 1971) with some 300 representatives. With respect to the Jordanian regime, the Congress laid down the following principles: (1) "The interim goal is the overthrow of the Jordanian regime" with the aim of "converting Jordan into a major base" for fidai activity. "The conflict between the organizations and the regime is [now] a major one" similar to the conflict with the "Israeli enemy". (2) The Congress resolved on three main arenas of action: the Arena of the Occupied Land (Kamal Udwan as its head); the Arena of Jordan, where "all force" was to be used against the regime; and the international arena, that of "special operations", whose aim was "to attack the imperialist, in particular American interests, as well as the Jordanian interests and leaders outside Jordan". For the Fatah leadership "the most suitable way of liquidating the regime is through the murder of its leaders", since there was seen to be no possibility of perpetrating a military *coup d'état*. Abu Iyad was "responsible" for the "Jordan Arena" and for "special operations", for example, the murder of the Israeli athletes in Munich (5 September 1972). Fatah adopted "Black September" as a cover name to avoid political complications in the Arab and international arenas. Its first spectacular act was the murder of Tall on 28 November 1971; further strikes against Jordanian and Western targets followed. Fatah stepped up its sabotage against the regime, this time claiming responsibility. From July to September 1971 attacks averaged 15–20 a month; they peaked in October with 30–35 actions (some from Syria). These attacks had a nuisance value. The security authorities discovered many Fatah arms caches, and the regime executed some saboteurs in order to deter others. Abu Iyad was the first of Fatah leaders to call (26 July 1971) for the "liquidation of the Hashemite family"; others followed suit.[108]

The PLO as representative of the Palestinians. Having lost the military campaign, the PLO in July 1971 began to wage a political campaign over its right to represent the Palestinians. The PLO/Fatah leaders feared that the crisis in Jordan, and Jordan's attitude towards the right of representation, would stimulate tendencies to establish an independent Entity on the West Bank and the Gaza Strip. Jordan's isolation in the Arab arena after its July 1971 move helped them in this regard. On 29 July 1971 the PLO sent the Arab heads of state a note demanding that they "confirm by official document that the Palestinian people is represented solely by the Palestinian revolution, through its leadership, being the EC of the PLO, and the PNC"; and that they "confirm the right of the Palestinian revolution to build up the unity of the two Banks". Algeria supported this fully. The 9th PNC (July 1971) emphasized in its resolutions "the right of the Palestinian revolution to represent the Palestinian people". Fatah's 3rd Congress resolved that "the Palestinian people possesses the right of self-determination and has absolute sovereignty over its land". At the same time the organizations used every available means to prevent independent activity on the West Bank which might negate their right to represent the Palestinians. Fatah deliberately refrained in its propaganda from pointing to any connection between the political activity on the

West Bank after September 1970 and Jordan, lest it suggest that Husayn had any influence on the West Bank.[109]

This round of the struggle between the Jordanian regime and the PR ended in victory for the former. The murder of Tall "symbolized the crisis within the Palestinian revolution itself, more than its victory over one of its enemies".[110] Although Jordan still did not gain the right of representation even of the West Bank Palestinians, the stability of its rule was ensured. The regime had once more evinced extraordinary viability, with the army, the intelligence and security services and the Jordanian element of the population remaining its chief prop. The "armed struggle" of the organizations was now directed towards two goals instead of one: "the liberation of Jordan" and "the liberation of Filastin". The struggle for the fidaiyyun's freedom of action passed to Lebanon, which now became a target for the establishment of the "safe base", and the outcome was no different from that in Jordan: civil war. Thus military and operational dependence on Syria increased.

THE PALESTINIAN ARENA

The Representative Composition of the PLO Institutions

From the day Shuqayri resigned until the present day, a key problem in relations between the organizations has been their representation in the PLO institutions (the PNC, the EC), which is seen as a yardstick of political influence in the PLO. This issue was expressed in the notion of "national unity", which was described by the leaders of the organizations as "a basic condition for victory in the struggle for the liberation of Filastin", and as a panacea, the lack of which has been responsible for all the PR's difficulties. Arafat admitted that "the number of fidai organizations reached 33, but 23 of them either voluntarily disbanded or joined other organizations".[111]

The organizations still surviving in this period were: Fatah; PFLP (led by Dr Habash), formed in late November 1967; PDFLP (led by Hawatma), the "left-wing faction" that seceded from the PFLP in February 1969; PFLP–GC (led by Ahmad Jibril), one of the components of the PFLP which seceded in October 1968; Sa'iqa; ALF; AOLP (led by Sartawi), which merged with Fatah in July 1971; APO (led by Za'rur), which seceded from PFLP–GC in August 1969, merging with Fatah in July 1971; POLP (Popular Organization for the Liberation of Palestine), whose central faction merged with the PDFLP in June 1969; PPSF, founded in late 1967; and PLA (PLFS as its fidai arm).

The multiplicity of the organizations and their divisions had a number of causes. First, there was the heritage of the past. The characteristic features of Palestinian society have been defined as "individualism, tribalism and alienation". It is a society "devoid of frameworks since it is devoid of the relatively stable connections that would ensure its internal cohesion". The leadership stratum of the Palestinians in the 1950s and 1960s felt alienated from Arab society, as may be seen in Halim Barakat's research (1969) on alienation in Arab society; hence the intelligentsia's search for different frameworks of political affiliation (such as Ba'th and ANM). Being dispersed, the Palestinians came under a wide range of political influences. The result was the politicization of almost all social activity; thus "the relations inside the Resistance movement are closer to the tribal and personal form than to the revolutionary-party form".[112]

Another cause was organizational fanaticism (*ta'assub tanzimi*). "The Resistance Movement is in a state of ideological and organizational seclusion. Every organization is trying to justify its historic existence in the Palestinian arena, and to seek special qualities that will differentiate it from the others, rather than seeking points in common." Fatah in particular typified this tendency. Every "national unity" plan submitted by any of the organizations stressed the preservation of the organizations' "ideological, organizational and political independence". Abu Iyad admitted that "even in historic and fateful resolutions the leaders of the organizations put the interest of the organization above the general interest". Unified frameworks were established under pressure of crises and not out of conviction. A group of about 35 Palestinian and Arab academics and writers submitted to the 8th PNC a research report on "national unity", and concluded that a true formula of unity must allow every organization to preserve its ideological and party independence and also its political and party activity.[113]

Third, the ideological controversy had its effect. There was no disagreement over the final strategic goal: the liquidation of the state of Israel. Differences centred on the means. These differences were an important factor in how much popularity among the Palestinians and support from Arab states an organization achieved; in the final analysis they even influenced the representative composition of the PLO. Apart from Sa'iqa and the ALF, it is necessary to outline the aims of three additional major organizations.

Fatah "has no defined policy. It determines its policy in accordance with [changing] reality, but rejects all patronage of the Arab states." Fatah emphasized "Filastinism" or the "Palestinian character" and the "national struggle" (*watani, qutri*). "The Palestinian revolution is Palestinian as to its origin, Arab as to its depth, pan-Arab national [*qawmiyya*] as to its aims and results." Its slogan was "non-intervention in the internal affairs of the Arab states" and "concentration of efforts on the liberation campaign in which secondary conflicts vanish for the sake of the major conflict, which is the liquidation of the Zionist entity". Fatah thinking had an Islamic motif. Fatah postponed dealing with social problems until "after the liberation". It stressed maximum support from the Arab and Palestinian circles; the FLN served as an example.[114]

The *PFLP* was the opposite of Fatah in its thinking. This is an example of a pan-Arab movement (ANM) turned into a militant Palestinian organization. It described itself as "a Marxist–Leninist revolutionary party ... based on a political and organizational strategy". In its outlook "the enemy was not just Israel, but the Zionist movement, world imperialism and the forces of reaction in the Arab world". It advocated "pan-Arab nationalism" (*qawmiyya*). "The campaign against Israel is Arab to the same extent as it is Palestinian." "At the same time it is also a class war." PFLP "is part of the world revolutionary movement, hence any damage to the interests of imperialism anywhere is an integral part of fidai activity." "In order for the Palestinians to be able to wage a lengthy war, there must be a 'Hanoi' in the Arab homeland."[115]

The *PDFLP*, like the PFLP, was "Marxist–Leninist", but its conclusions were different. Central to its outlook was the "integration of theory and practice [*al-nazariyya wa al-mumarasa*] even though the practice may not be consonant with the theory, but providing that the deed constitutes a step in the direction of realization of the theory". It believed in "pan-Arab nationalism"; the PR must interfere in "all matters having to do with the Palestinian problem, which are dealt with by the Arab states". It was the first to emphasize a "Palestinian–Jordanian national front" and "the unity of the struggle on both Banks".[116]

A fourth cause of the organizations' multiplicity was the Arab arena itself. Although the Arab states spoke of the need for "national unity", in practice they routinely acted to preserve their divisions. Each state fostered the fidai organization that supported its interests and outlook. Egypt and Saudi Arabia enthusiastically supported Fatah and Iraq the radicals; Syria and Iraq both had organizations operating under their auspices. "Axes" thus developed among the organizations matching those in the Arab arena. Qadhafi did in fact threaten to halt financial aid to the organizations unless they set up a united command, but in practice he worked against the "bunch of Marxist theoreticians" (the PFLP). Faysal proclaimed at the Rabat summit (December 1969) that he recognized Fatah as representing the Palestinians and had reservations about the PLO as representative. At Rabat the Syrians favoured Fatah as the most important Palestinian element and Arafat as the leader of the PLO, while Algeria supported the PLO as representative of the fidai organizations. Financial and military aid or providing bases were the levers with which the Arab states influenced PLO decisions.[117]

The transition period: January 1968 – January 1969. During this period the organizations were undecided as to whether to preserve the framework of the PLO as an umbrella organization, or to regard it as a separate one. Three organizations took part in the negotiations over the status and composition of the PLO.

The first was the *EC–PLO.* The PLO leadership was limited to the EC members from Shuqayri's time, under the leadership of Hammuda, after all its institutions had ceased to be. The EC members tried to free themselves of the shackles of the Shuqayri era. They wanted mainly to set up a new PNC, but knew this could not be done without the fidai organizations and especially Fatah. The EC's positions as summed up in its deliberations of January–March 1968 were: (1) The PLO is "the official representative of the whole Palestinian people in the Arab and the international arenas", and was to be retained as a framework "that has been approved and recognized by the Arab states". (2) The PLO "is the mother organization with which all the fidai organizations will merge"; in this they enjoyed full Egyptian support. (3) The PLO would adhere to the National Covenant and "to the right of the Palestinian people to self-determination". The EC members tried to embrace Fatah's outlook by promoting its slogans and presenting the PLO as a fidai organization. (4) The EC proposed to set up a 100-member PNC out of which "a collective leadership would be elected".[118]

During the first half of 1968 the *PFLP* was still crystallizing. Its position, expressed in a "note from the Political Bureau to the EC" (early January 1968), was that the PLO must continue to exist as "official representative of the Palestinian people in the Arab and international arenas". It must not be the sole Palestinian organization, but "a broad framework" for all the organizations. The call for "total representation of the Palestinian people is unrealistic"; the PNC should have 50 to 75 members, most of them from Palestinian organizations such as students', workers' and women's associations, as well as Fatah and the PFLP. The PNC would elect an Executive Committee.[119]

As to *Fatah*, its leadership viewed Shuqayri's departure and Fatah's enhanced status as preparation for its assuming leadership of fidai action and of the PLO. Unlike the PFLP, Fatah presented the PLO as a separate organization. At this stage Fatah stressed cooperation between the fidai organizations, with a view to creating a "front" that would contend for the leadership against the PFLP and the EC. On 5 January 1968 it called upon twelve Palestinian organizations to meet to prepare a "national conference"; the EC and PFLP did not accept. In the meeting, held on 17 January 1968 in Cairo, seven organizations in addition to Fatah participated, including three connected with the Syrian Ba'th, three allied to Fatah and another allied to Egypt. The meeting resolved to form a Permanent Bureau of the Palestinian Organizations,[120] but its main purpose was to enable Fatah to make a show of strength.

In negotiations between the EC, PFLP and Fatah on the PNC's composition, which lasted several months, a Fatah proposal was finally adopted: to set up a Preparatory Committee (PC) which would decide the composition of the PNC and approve the list of candidates. The PC was made up of 21 members: six from Fatah, six from the PLO, two from the PFLP, one from the PLA, one from the National Fund (NF) and five "independents" who actually supported the PFLP and Fatah (meaning that those two had a majority). The consensus within the PC was that the PNC should consist of 100 members; the debate now focused on the distribution of mandates in the PNC. Fatah proposed 50 for the organizations (45 for the Permanent Bureau and five for the PFLP), 20 for the PLA and 30 for the PLO. The PFLP objected and its allocation was increased to ten, that of the Permanent Bureau being reduced to 38 with the remaining two classified as "independents" (although actually they were Fatah sympathizers). This "officially" prevented 50% of the seats from being reserved for the Permanent Bureau and PFLP together. The final makeup of the PNC was as follows: 38 out of the total membership of 100 went to the Permanent Bureau, five of them representing Sa'iqa and another four representing the four Bureau organizations. When several of the latter joined Fatah, this meant that Fatah actually controlled 30–32 seats.

The remaining 62 seats were divided as follows: 10 to the PFLP, 20 to the PLA and PLFS, 30 to the "independents" (including 9 members of the EC) and 2 to women's organizations and labour unions (who supported the line of the Permanent Bureau). The list of 30 "independents" was drawn up jointly by Fatah and the PFLP, in such a way that the PLO representatives remained in the minority; the "independents" included a number of Fatah sympathizers. The list of the PLA and PLFS members was finalized through agreement with the EC. Representatives of the "combatant organizations" amounted formally to 68% (in fact 70%). The list of members of the organizations was not published; two names missing from it were the Fatah leaders Arafat and Abu Jihad. The composition of the PNC reflected the then prevailing balance of political forces in the Palestinian arena. Having achieved this, Fatah now prepared itself for the struggle for control of the EC.[121]

The 4th PNC session convened in Cairo (10–17 July 1968). At Fatah's suggestion it ratified a number of amendments to the Covenant stressing its Palestinian character; for instance, its name was changed from the Pan-Arab National (*qawmi*) Covenant to the National (*watani*) Covenant. "The Palestinian masses ... organizations or individuals, will set up a single national front." It was also established that "the PLO represents the forces of the Palestinian revolution", meaning it was not totally representative of the entire Palestinian people. The Constitution was amended to provide that all EC members would be elected by the PNC, and would in turn elect a chairman. Heartened by its popularity following the Karama operation, Fatah demanded a majority of six seats at the EC. But Sa'iqa representatives called for a "collective leadership"; the PFLP delegation, already showing signs of a split between the Jibril group and the ANM, was also opposed. The PLA representatives feared for their own standing if control were retained by Fatah, and secured the PLO representatives' support for their objection. The result was a deadlock. To prevent a crisis, the PNC resolved (17 July 1968), with Fatah's consent, to instruct the EC to proceed with its work, which included composing a new PNC within six months. Without having achieved its goal, Fatah had nevertheless demonstrated its strength. It began preparing to achieve its target in the next PNC, exploiting its enhanced status, the changes that had occurred in the "map" of the organizations in the second half of 1968 (once the "interim period" was over) and the stabilization of the number of organizations.[122]

composed of "the combatant nationalist organizations" and of independent members with "revolutionary qualifications". These proposals were not adopted by the PNC. Thus this attempt by the PDFLP to combine theory and practice ended up instead by dividing them.[125]

The composition of the PNCs and the ECs. Not since the founding of the PLO had democratic elections been held for the PNC. Representation in this period was not on a "geographical" basis. From the 5th PNC, the PLO was a political and military movement that claimed to express "the will of the Palestinian people". As there was no viable alternative to this movement, the fidai organizations imposed themselves on the Palestinians, with the help of the Arab states. Thus their struggle focused on gaining legitimacy as representatives of the Palestinian people, and PNC members questioned the PLO's representative status. The PLO was indeed disunited and unrepresentative, especially while some organizations, including the PFLP, continued to act independently. Research on the organizations' social structure conducted in 1971 showed them to be undifferentiated as to members' occupations and social status. Skilled and unskilled labourers accounted for 45.1 percent (23.8 percent unskilled), students 23.5 percent and inhabitants of the refugee camps 80 percent.[126]

Since no elections were held, and each organization kept its membership secret, the principal yardstick of any organization's strength and scope was its fidai actions. Therefore small organizations who could mount only few operations resorted to more spectacular actions such as hijacking aeroplanes, or actions designed to result in heavy loss of life. The organizations also vied with one another in giving highly coloured and overblown accounts, to the point of absurdity, of the number of attacks they mounted and the extent of losses inflicted on Israel. Fatah, for example, claimed that in October 1968 it had killed or wounded 600 Israeli soldiers; the PLFS boasted of causing 230 Israeli casualties in the same month. In fact, the total losses inflicted by *all* the organizations that month amounted to seven dead (of whom five were soldiers) and 73 wounded (of whom 27 were soldiers). This hyperbole came in for sharp criticism from Palestinian and Arab writers. In reporting to the 7th PNC, the deputy chairman of the EC, Ibrahim Bakr remarked: "The overrating of fidai actions imbues the masses with the feeling that they will realize victory." Yet the fidai actions generated high expectations, as can be seen from a public opinion poll taken in June 1969 among 200 "educated Palestinian youths" in Lebanon, aged 18 to 22. Ninety-seven percent affirmed that military action was the only road to "return"; 85 percent replied that the solution of the Palestinian issue was in the hands of the Palestinians. The organizations also began to compete for the "credit" for large-scale actions. The eventual outcome, according to Bakr, was "that doubt came to be cast on the reliability of the military communiqués of the organizations".[127]

Fatah maintained its status as the leading organization. As Abu Iyad said in March 1975, "the decision of Fatah is the Palestinian decision. Any decision unacceptable to Fatah will not see the light." Fatah had given the PLO direction ever since its decision to join it in February 1969. In fidai activity, Fatah could lay claim to having been the first in the field. It had been the pioneer of the new "Palestinian national movement" – indeed, to a large extent, its founder. It had proved itself the stablest and most cohesive of the organizations, although it had undergone temporary upheavals even in its own leadership (the most serious one would come from the Abu Musa faction in 1983 with the aid of the Syrians). As mentioned, it gained the Arab states' recognition as leader of the PLO; its political concept was the highest common denominator of the attitudes of the major Arab states (Egypt, Syria, Saudi Arabia, Algeria) and some other states. (Qadhafi admitted to having proposed that the PFLP–GC merge with Fatah.) As for its popularity with the Palestinian public, "in 1965 the number of Fatah members did not exceed several dozen combatants", whereas "two weeks after the Karama operation Fatah membership increased from 722 to 3,000 persons". The scope of its activity is shown by the fact that 73.1 percent of all fatalities suffered by the organizations were from Fatah (1 January 1965–30 October 1971). It controlled the "popular organizations" such as the General Union of Palestinian Students; most PLO representatives in various states were Fatah members. Fatah was indeed the "backbone" of the PLO.[128]

Fatah preferred to lead the PLO through an EC built on coalitions and on condition that it retain power of final decision. Sa'iqa and the PDFLP were the principal partners. Joining these three organizations in the EC were some independents who on the whole leaned towards this or that organization. The PDFLP did not find "any great conflict between its aims and those of Fatah and Sa'iqa, in the short term". Most likely this coalition helped keep the PFLP outside of the PLO for a long time, since it rightly assessed that its influence would be slight. Through this coalition Fatah succeeded in reducing

PLA representation from 20 at the 4th PNC to a minimal number with no meaningful influence.[129] These trends are illustrated by the various PNC sessions.

In the 5th PNC (1–4 February 1969), membership was set at 105; but only 87 were present – 12 PFLP and the six PLA representatives were absent, because the PLA HQ was protesting over its small allocation. The official distribution was: Fatah, 33 seats; 11 members of the EC from Shuqayri's time; Sa'iqa, 12; 28 independents; three trade union representatives. If one includes its ten sympathizers among the "independents", the total of Fatah members and sympathizers accounted for 50 percent (in the absence of the PFLP and the PLA) – more than at the 4th PNC. The dominant status of Fatah was also assured in the EC elected on 3 February 1969, which had 11 members. Officially the distribution was: Fatah, four (including the chairman and the head of the Political Department); Sa'iqa, two; and five "independents" (three of them Fatah sympathizers, one a Sa'iqa sympathizer), and also the chairman of the National Fund. Fatah was thus assured, in practice, of seven seats.[130]

At the 6th PNC session (1–6 September 1969), PNC membership was increased to 112, but 102 actually took part since the PFLP, allocated ten seats, boycotted the session. Fatah still retained 33 places and Sa'iqa 12. The PDFLP for the first time joined in with eight places. The number of "workers' union" representatives went from one to five, students from one to three, women from one to two; also the writers now had one representative. There were four more "independent" representatives (two of whom leaned towards Sa'iqa) so that they now numbered 32; the PLA HQ had one delegate; PFLP–GC, three; APO, one; PPSF, one. The mandates of Fatah and its sympathizers increased from among the trade union representatives so that, overall, percentages remained unchanged. The coalition within the EC remained, with a membership of 12 after the inclusion of a PDFLP representative. The number of Sa'iqa sympathizers among the independents increased from one to two, so that Sa'iqa now totalled four while Fatah still had seven.[131]

At the 7th PNC session (30 May–4 June 1970), membership increased to 115. This was the first PNC in which all 11 organizations participated, PFLP with a token presence of one representative. The balance of forces remained unchanged. Three organizations joined in for the first time, each with a single delegate: POLP, ALF and AOLP. The EC composition remained unchanged.[132]

Membership at the 8th PNC session (28 February–5 March 1971) increased to 123, the balance of forces remaining the same. There were three additional "representatives" of the Arabs of Israel; PLA representation increased from one to six. Fatah still had an official total of 33, plus 15 to 20 sympathizers from among the independents and trade union delegates and thus, altogether, nearly 40 percent of the seats. It was resolved (5 March 1971) to leave the EC composition unchanged, and to charge it with deciding on the composition of a new 150-member PNC.[133]

The 9th PNC session (7–13 July 1971) convened with a "new" composition, the previous PNC (of February 1969) having completed its term of office in March 1971. Membership stood at 155, four new members having joined at the first session (one from the trade unions and three "independents") in addition to the 151 fixed by the EC. An effort was made to broaden the PNC's public basis by increasing the representatives of the "popular organizations". The fidai organizations were allocated 85 mandates, a large majority: the trade unions had 26, while the number of "independents" rose to 44. The official totals of the organizations were as follows: Fatah, 33; Sa'iqa, 12; PLA, six; PFLP, 12 (fully represented for the first time); PDFLP, eight; ALF, eight; PFLP–GC, three; the rest were divided among the three small organizations. During the PNC session, the APO and AOLP declared that they were merging with Fatah. The official percentage of Fatah representatives seemed to have decreased from that of the 8th PNC; but if we add the sympathizers and actual Fatah members from among the "independents" and trade union representatives, who represented political positions rather than professional interests, Fatah representation approached, once again, 40 percent. There were a number of changes in the EC's composition; the final totals were: Fatah, four (including the chairman and the head of the Political Department); Sa'iqa, two; one each – PDFLP, ALF, PFLP (the latter two organizations newly added); independents, four (two leaning to Fatah, one to PFLP and one in fact a representative of PPSF). Fatah thus retained six out of 13 (40%).[134]

Criticism of the PLO institutions. "The PNC, by reason of its character and composition, cannot formulate any plan whatsoever; all it can do is debate a plan submitted to it, and amend or ratify it." All the important resolutions adopted by the PNC were achieved behind the scenes; the PNC only gave formal approval. The deliberations of the PNC were described as *suq ukkaz.* "Only ten percent of its members take part in its activity, while the role of the other ninety percent is confined to sleeping in hotels, raising hands and acting like the delegate of Yemen" (at the meetings of the Arab League). Review of PNC resolutions reveals a surprisingly large number of resolutions for "coordination" or "unity" and that nothing was being done about them. The situation at the EC was no better; Husam al-Khatib, a member, stated: "All topics were summed up outside. Generally the EC gave formal approval to matters already decided. ... Arafat as leader of the PLO sometimes took various measures without having first consulted the EC, which would then ratify them retroactively."[135]

Sharp criticism of the representative composition of the PNC was voiced by the PFLP, the PLA and a group of independents, groups not included in the "coalition" that led the PLO. In June 1970 the PFLP claimed that "the Palestinian revolution does not need a parasitical creature such as [the PNC]. It is not a legitimate representative of the Palestinian people, deriving its authority therefrom by means of free elections." The PFLP voiced such criticism even after joining the PNC, although not so acidly.[136] The PLA HQ criticized the PNC's composition at almost all its meetings, especially the 8th PNC (after the September 1970 crisis) and the 9th. When after September 1970 the PLA remained unharmed, all its units concentrating in Syria, it felt encouraged and its commander-in-chief demanded at the 8th PNC that it be given representation of the Palestinian people and of other elements outside the fidai organizations. He also demanded a collective political leadership "which would not be controlled by any organization". On the eve of the 9th PNC, conciliation was achieved when the PLA was promised a relatively large number of representatives.[137]

At the 7th PNC a small group of independents left over from the Shuqayri era, led by three members of the EC of his time, Yahya Hammuda, Nimr al-Masri and Abd al-Khaliq Yaghmur, demanded a change in composition of the PLO institutions so as to deal with "difficulties and conflicts within fidai activity". After September 1970 they stepped up their activity in cooperation with the C-in-C PLA, forming a bloc called the Palestinian National Gathering at the 8th PNC. They demanded *inter alia* that the PNC be made up of a majority of independents. The three group leaders and also Abd al-Muhsin Qatan boycotted the deliberations of the 9th PNC to protest over its new composition. In December 1971 the Shuqayri-era independents held a meeting in Shuqayri's house to discuss "the correction of fidai activity" while preserving the PLO framework. Even though they were not influential, this group damaged the PLO's image among the Palestinians. An Egyptian newspaper claimed (November 1970) that "the PNC does not represent the entire combatant and non-combatant Palestinian arena". And a Palestinian journalist queried (March 1971), "Who will represent the Palestinians at the next stage?" – that is, in the wake of Black September.[138]

The forming of ad hoc *representative bodies.* The failure to achieve "national unity", the boycotting of the PLO institutions by a number of organizations and the successive crises in Jordan all encouraged the formation of *ad hoc* bodies, especially military ones, outside the official framework of the PLO. Hence the phenomenon of intensifying efforts towards national unity in times of crisis, and the heightening of controversy between crises. On 20 October 1968 the Bureau of Military Coordination was set up with representatives from the PLO, Fatah and Saʻiqa. But instead of coordinating activity, it became "coordinator of relations between the organizations for the solution of the problems arising among them". On 17 February 1969 the new EC decided to create the Palestine Armed Struggle Command (PASC) with the participation of Fatah, Saʻiqa and PLFS; PDFLP joined on 25 March 1969. As a "military command" it was joined by organizations that had been outside the establishment (except for PFLP) – ALF, APO, PPSF and PFLP–GC, on 15 July 1969, 29 July, 30 September and 15 October, respectively. Theoretically, relations within the PASC were grounded in equality; but in practice "it became a rostrum for inter-organizational quarrels over the responsibility for actions". The PDFLP seceded from it on 18 December 1969; in the end, the PASC became "a military force for maintaining order and discipline" in Jordan, and afterwards in Lebanon.[139]

On 11 February 1970, immediately on the outbreak of the crisis in Jordan, the United Command for Fidai and Popular Activity in Jordan was formed at a meeting of representatives of "all the fidai organizations, the Jordanian trade unions, political parties and a number of leaders of public opinion [in Jordan]". The UC aimed to ward off "the liquidation that threatened the organizations" after the publication of the regime's twelve points on 10 February 1970, and to be a substitute for the PASC. All ten organizations, including PFLP, joined it on the principle of equal representation; the PFLP gauged that this would be an *ad hoc* framework outside of the PLO. This very aspect aroused arguments in the Palestinian arena, since it underlined the PLO institutions' incapacity for handling crises and just how unrepresentative of the Palestinians they really were.

Shafiq al-Hut, the PLO representative in Beirut, believed that those who negated the PASC and favoured the UC "did so because the former believed in the PLO and its institutions as an arena of encounter, while the UC imposes no [such] obligation ... and persists in regarding it [PLO] as one among the existing organizations". In his opinion "recognition should not be extended to the UC as a substitute for the PLO".[140]

The organizations also produced a communiqué (6 May 1970) agreeing to the setting up of a Central Committee (CC) "with the participation of all the Resistance organizations so as to lead the Resistance movement; it will derive from the PNC and will replace the UC". The 7th PNC ratified the founding of the CC, and provided that "the EC will implement [its] resolutions". Its composition was: the chairman of the PNC, EC members, the PLA commander-in-chief, three independents from among the PNC and a representative of the leadership of each organization signing the communiqué. Nonetheless, Khatib was right in claiming that its creation was a blow to the status of the PNC, and even to the Covenant. He cited three reasons for this: (1) The communiqué of 6 May 1970 was approved by a body whose composition was "combatant and popular, Palestinian and Jordanian", and very different from that of the PNC; (2) the CC had not been elected by the PNC nor was any proviso made for having its members approved by the PNC (on the model of the EC); and (3) its members, unlike those of the EC, were not obliged to be members of the PNC – in other words, they need not be Palestinians. The founding of the CC gave rise to confusion, conflicts and overlap of authority. On a practical level, the CC stripped the EC of its *raison d'être*; the 8th PNC in fact received no report from either body on the most critical period of September 1970, and the CC deliberations were sharply criticized; Abu Iyad claimed that "impotence, individualism, and, finally, frivolous resolutions" prevailed. The CC operated with no internal regulations and its membership was frequently changed; matters were settled by two or three of the organizations' leaders reaching an understanding. The PFLP's membership in the CC was suspended on 12 September 1970 because it infringed the CC's resolution of 10 September 1970 not to blow up hijacked aeroplanes and to release hostages. Yet it returned to the CC because of the crisis of 16 September 1970. At the 8th PNC the EC was instructed to compose a new PNC while ignoring the CC; although the latter was not officially disbanded, it in fact ceased to exist with the convening of the 9th PNC and the election of a new EC.[141]

In this period the PLO was dominated by Fatah, both in its failures (the continuing divisions and the elimination of fidai bases and activity in Jordan) and in its achievements (such as the increased status of the PR in the Arab and Palestinian arenas). Fatah tried to lead the PLO democratically. Because factionalism was rampant in the PLO and Palestinian society, and because of the conditions obtaining in the Arab arena, it appears in retrospect that Fatah was indeed best suited to lead the PLO, as Shuqayri had been in his time; leadership by radical organizations would have meant greater internal disunity and isolation. Nasir's choice was once more vindicated.

The West Bank: The Rise and Decline of the Traditional Leadership[142]

Central to political developments on the West Bank during this period were two important and parallel processes: the rise and decline of the traditional leadership and the emergence of a "young" and nationalist leadership. The question was – who properly represented the population *vis-à-vis* the Israeli Military Government (IMG).

The traditional leadership refers to those functionaries from the Jordanian era, most of whom continued in office after the Six Day War – mayors and members of municipal councils (other than the mayors of al-Bira and Ramalla), members of the House of Deputies and the Senate, the heads and members of the Chambers of Commerce, district governors and former cabinet ministers. The term "traditional leadership" appropriately describes them, even if strictly speaking this was not an authoritative, traditional leadership (except perhaps for Ja'bari, mayor of Hebron) and the term "notables" is in a sense more accurate. Their status derived primarily from being part of the Jordanian establishment, when they represented the regime to the inhabitants and not vice versa.[143] After the war they took on the role of representatives of the inhabitants to the IMG, which regarded them as the *de facto* leadership of the West Bank. Thus they found themselves to be *ex officio* leaders, as a result of which they moved from nominal to active leadership.

The nationalist radical leadership centred on the intelligentsia and were mostly aged 30 to 40. They were led by activists of opposition parties that had been suppressed for ten years under the Jordanian regime (Ba'th, ANM and Communist). The Israeli occupation gave them renewed impetus. Unlike the traditional leadership they enjoyed public backing and controlled front organizations; they were of course anti-Hashemite. The process of "Palestinization" which overtook the ANM, and very slightly the Ba'th, was more pronounced on the West Bank. The radical leadership pressured the traditional leadership to adopt a nationalist stance *vis-à-vis* the IMG. They considered themselves the "true" representatives of the population, and aspired to replace the traditional leadership. Two generations thus began to vie with one another, along the lines of the earlier struggle between the PLO leadership of the Shuqayri era and the PR leadership.

Founding of representative bodies. In the immediate postwar period, the traditional leadership tried to establish itself as a recognized political leadership with representative status *vis-à-vis* the IMG. Similar attempts were made by the nationalist leadership, but at a later stage. All such attempts were thwarted by the IMG.

The Muslim Council (al-Hay'a al-Islamiyya) (MC) was the first "official" representative body to be founded after the war. It was formed in Jerusalem on 24 July 1967 by 22 local leaders. In a protest against the Israeli government's decision to unify the two parts of Jerusalem and annex East Jerusalem to Israel, they proclaimed themselves "representatives of the Muslim inhabitants of the West Bank, including Jerusalem", responsible for conducting their affairs "until the termination of the occupation". This body was composed of political rather than religious figures, and contained five clergymen including the chairman, Abd al-Hamid al-Saih and three leaders of the Ba'th, the ANM and the Communist parties. Most of them had held official positions under the Jordanian regime; all were from the Jerusalem and Ramalla areas. The MC conducted radical nationalist activities against the IMG; but it could not, because of its narrow geographical composition, serve as a representative body for the whole of the West Bank. Its influence, which was strong until the end of 1967, waned progressively after the expulsion of six of its members to Jordan (including the chairman, on 21 December 1967) and the death of some others. The MC continued to operate as an "official" Jerusalem body in the political–religious field, but less intensively.[144]

A further attempt to form an all-West Bank leadership, which would draw up guiding political principles for relations with the

IMG, was made during September–December 1967 by a joint effort of the traditional and the nationalist leadership. Most prominent were Hamdi Kan'an, Hikmat al-Masri, Salah al-Anabtawi and Hilmi Hanun. At the end of December 1967, the National Charter of the Arabs of the West Bank (signed by 142 prominent persons) was finally ratified. Its main points were: (1) "Unity of the two Banks" through "avoidance of a repetition of the mistakes of the Jordanian regime and also the founding of a democratic constitutional regime." (2) "The Palestinian problem is a pan-Arab problem. Neither the Palestinian people on its own nor any Arab state on its own has the right to handle it separately." Support "for collective Arab action is required for the elimination of the traces of aggression". (3) "Firm rejection of all suspicious appeals for the founding of a Palestinian state ... which means the final liquidation of the Palestinian problem." Although this *ad hoc* gathering did not become a political organization for the entire West Bank, the principles of the Charter continued to guide the West Bank leaders in their contacts with the IMG. Adherence to these principles became proof of the nationalism of the traditional leaders in the Arab and Palestinian arenas.[145]

Regional bodies were also formed in Jerusalem, Nablus and Hebron. The Higher Committee for National Guidance (al-Lajna al-'Ulya lil-Tawjih al-Watani) was set up in Jerusalem in August–September 1967. It was a coalition of representatives of the parties and of the traditional leadership in Jerusalem (and Ramalla). The Committee fostered resistance against the IMG, including strikes, demonstrations and petitions. Its activity declined following the expulsion of its chairmen, Ruhi al-Khatib (3 March 1968) and Kamal al-Dajani (6 September 1969, along with Daud al-Husayni); in the course of 1968–69 other activists were expelled. Attempts to renew its activity proved fruitless.[146]

Nablus retained its traditional role as the centre of political activity on the West Bank, becoming as well the centre of the nationalist leadership. Thus the rivalry between the traditional and the nationalist leadership became fiercest there. Kan'an, mayor until his resignation in March 1969, refused to cooperate with the nationalists, but local leaders such as Hikmat al-Masri, Qadri Tuqan and Ma'zuz al-Masri formed an unofficial forum to consider the policy towards the IMG which was sometimes attended by nationalist leaders. In November–December 1968 the nationalist leaders founded the Committee for National Solidarity (Lajnat al-Tadamun al-Qawmi), which was to represent the town, dictate an extremist policy towards the IMG and undermine the status of the traditional leadership. Later, similar committees were to be set up throughout the West Bank, leading eventually to a representative leadership for the entire West Bank. Yet no sooner had the Committee been secretly founded than the IMG dissolved it. On 6 January 1969 two of its leaders were expelled from the West Bank; during 1969 further activity by its members led to additional measures against its activists, including deportation (June and September). Thus the Committee's activity was suspended. Still, during 1968–69 there were two leaderships in Nablus, a traditional one whose authority was being shaken, and a nationalist one working to strengthen its influence.[147]

Hebron was an exception; because of Ja'bari's leadership there, no nationalist political activity which might undermine his authority ever got under way. Ja'bari did, however, find it necessary to set up (December 1969) the Public Interests Committee (PIC) (Lajnat al-Masalih al-'Amma), of which he was head. Its membership at first consisted of 50 notables, but eventually increased to some 150 to 300 of Ja'bari's immediate circle. It met at Ja'bari's initiative during 1970–71. The PIC was formed in order to strengthen Ja'bari's status as leader of the Hebron region, after other West Bank leaders had done their best to isolate him, Jordan and the fidai organizations had attacked him and nationalists had been active in Hebron against the IMG. The PIC generally concentrated on practical responses to IMG actions such as arrests and demolition of houses. Ja'bari did, it is true, table such subjects as the Palestinian Entity and fidai activity, but the PIC in its resolutions did not touch directly on these matters, trying to strike a balance between the fidai organizations and the IMG. In an attempt to enhance his image outside of Hebron, in April 1970 Ja'bari applied for permission to call a meeting of all West Bank mayors, but the IMG refused.[148] Yet the activity of the nationalists in Hebron was significant, even encompassing Bethlehem. In April–May 1968 a National Committee was formed with the participation of Ba'thists; its activists included Husam Badr (inspector of education), the pharmacist Hikmat al-Hamuri, Dr Yahya Shawir, Dr Muhammad al-Natsha and Yasir Amru. They instigated civil disobedience and some of them maintained links with the fidai organizations – as did even traditional Hebron notables such as the senator, Rashad al-Khatib, and the mufti of Hebron, Sheykh Abd al-Hay Arafa. The activity of the National Committee waned after the deportation of its activists in the latter half of 1969.[149]

Crisis of the traditional leadership. The PLO and the PR leadership had achieved such prominence in the Arab and Palestinian arenas that the status of the West Bank traditional leadership was dwarfed in comparison. With the West Bank nationalists also strengthening their position, the traditional leadership found itself in a prolonged crisis. Since it could not conduct an independent policy it attempted to preserve the West Bank *status quo*, and to balance conflicting pressures: the IMG, Jordan and the Arab arena, the fidai organizations and the West Bank nationalist leadership.

This period saw a *nationalist reawakening on the West Bank.* This reawakening commenced in early 1968 (after the period of shock was over) although there were already signs of it in late 1967. The nationalist opposition circles operated not only in the National Committees but also through front organizations such as the West Bank Students Union (based in Nablus), the Teachers Association (Ramalla, at Bir Zayt University) and also various trade unions and women's organizations. The process went, inevitably, from political organizations to civil disobedience, and from there to fidai groups and activity. As early as the beginning of 1968 the intelligentsia and the white-collar class participated in the fidai groupings and activities of the PFLP and Sa'iqa, and later also of Fatah. The political fidai group within the PFLP, which was exposed in February 1969, included some 200 to 300 activists and extended to a number of towns, chiefly Ramalla and Jerusalem, branching out even into the Gaza Strip; its leaders included the lawyer Bashir al-Khayri, the priest Elya Khuri, Dr Nabih Mu'ammar and several women. Similarly structured groupings among the Ba'th and the ANM were discovered in 1968–69. During 1970–71 fidai activity sharply declined as a result of the IMG's efforts and the crises in Jordan.[150]

Nationalist arousal in the West Bank could also be seen in increased passive resistance, the younger generation's readiness for fidai activity and the population's increasing sympathy for that activity. During 1968–70 passive resistance intensified, reaching a peak in 1969 when 42 prominent persons were deported from the West Bank, including Jerusalem, for passive resistance or for involvement in fidai activity. In Ramalla, for example, there were 15 commercial and school strikes during 1968, 30 in 1969, about 15 in 1970 and none at all in 1971. During 1969 there was a record number of demonstrations with slogans chanted supporting the fidaiyyun. In 1968, 69 fidai actions were perpetrated on the West Bank including Jerusalem (26 of them in Jerusalem); in 1969, 169 (34 in

Jerusalem); in 1970, 132 (13 in Jerusalem); and in 1971, 46 (eight in Jerusalem), a decline due to the crisis in Jordan. Large numbers of people were detained in connection with such activity and many sabotage units were exposed by the Israeli security forces: in 1969 over 1,600 suspects were arrested (1970 – 1,350; 1971 – 1,300) and some 45 (over 60% belonging to Fatah) small fidaiyyun units detected (1970 – 70; 1971 – 98). Demolition of houses on the West Bank – a punitive measure for participation in fidai activities – serves as another indicator. During 1967, 115 houses were destroyed, 64 of them in East Jerusalem (1968 – 125, 66), (1969 – 287, 73), (1970 – 191, 94), (1971 – 231, 127). Clearly, among the population both sympathy and assistance for the fidaiyyun were growing. Involved in this activity were prominent personalities including some in municipal office (such as the treasurer and the secretary of the Nablus municipality), some of whom simultaneously collaborated with the IMG. The improvement in the West Bank's economic situation in those years did not, it transpires, prevent these trends.[151]

Since the leaders of the organizations were mainly interested in intensifying the "armed struggle" and civil disobedience, they disdained political organization or unification of forces. They seemed to fear the emergence of a cohesive, radical, political leadership which might upset the PR's claims to represent the West Bank and Gaza Palestinians. They did their utmost to prevent any independent political initiative by the traditional leadership or its cooperation with the IMG in the political or indeed any other sphere, beyond essential, day-to-day matters. They therefore ruthlessly persecuted those who collaborated with the IMG including "traditional statesmen and leaders", threatening them over *Sawt al-Asifa* broadcasts and by mail, with particularly severe warnings against collaboration with Israeli intelligence. This method proved remarkably effective. For example, as a result of being threatened by *Sawt al-Asifa* all 12 candidates approved (1 February 1970) by the Jerusalem Municipal Council for membership in its subcommittees refused, in February 1970, to accept the appointment; all 12 published refusals in *al-Quds*. No data are available on the murder or attempted murder of collaborators with the IMG; material published by the organizations indicates that from the Six Day War to late 1971, some 50 to 60 such murders were perpetrated or attempted on the West Bank.[152]

Because of its weakness and the pressures on it, the traditional leadership opted for *adherence to Nasir's strategy*. This position was outlined in the Charter of December 1967. The Palestinian population remained basically pro-Nasirist, even after military defeat; both the traditional and nationalist leaders believed that "Nasir had the right to speak in their name". Coordination between Nasir and Husayn strengthened them in their view that the West Bank's fate must be determined by means of pan-Arab agreement in which "the Palestinians should have the decisive position". Representatives of the traditional leadership, some of whose members such as Hikmat al-Masri and Rashid al-Nimr had for years been connected with Egypt, were frequently in touch with Nasir either through letters or in person, reporting *inter alia* on their talks with Israeli statesmen; the first meeting between Nasir and a delegation of this leadership, headed by Masri, took place in May 1968. It was made clear to them that they must not attempt any independent initiative nor deviate from the Arab and Egyptian line. Nasir's death was deeply mourned on the West Bank.[153]

The leadership's attitude towards the Jordanian regime still reflected the era of Jordanian rule. However, up to September 1970 the local leaders stressed that restoration of the West Bank to the Hashemite Kingdom would have to be on entirely different terms from those before the war. But their disseverance from Jordan, as well as developments regarding the Palestinian Entity including Nasir's position, reinforced their consciousness of the Palestinian identity; and the growing role of the fidai organizations in Jordan made them ponder the "Palestinization" of Jordan. The September massacre marked a turning-point; pent-up resentments towards Husayn's regime that had long been accumulating erupted bitterly. The September massacre directly or indirectly affected every fourth or fifth family on the West Bank. For the first time since the war almost the entire population was now united in its condemnation of Jordan and in its support for the Palestinian Entity, for Palestinian self-determination and the view of the West Bank as Palestinian territory separate from Jordan. Qadri Tuqan (December 1970) stated: "Jordan is Filastin. Eighty percent of the inhabitants of the East Bank are Palestinians. The king is not Jordan, but Jordan's king". Anwar Nusayba referred to Husayn's routing of the fidaiyyun as a "traumatic event almost comparable to the Six Day War". The September massacre and the elimination of fidai activity in July 1971 further pushed the West Bank inhabitants towards viewing the Palestinian establishment as representative of the Palestinian Entity;[154] the status of the traditional leadership further declined.

P.E.—G

As a result of these developments, *attitudes towards the PLO and the PR over the issue of representation crystallized.* The fidai organizations now figured in the traditional leadership's attitude to the IMG, the conflict and the issue of the Palestinian Entity. They came to support the PR as an expression of their nationalism (in accordance with Nasir's approach), sometimes to the point of risking the deterrent force of the IMG. There was a significant difference between the vague, publicly declared attitudes towards the PR and their true ones, privately expressed. As a substitute for publicly declaring sympathy, the leaders contacted the fidai organizations outside the West Bank and also met with PLO/Fatah leaders. Qadri Tuqan described (March 1968) the Resistance as "an acceptable movement. I will not act to its detriment." And in late 1968 the mayor of Tulkarm, Hilmi Hanun, dared to declare:

> I see no use in holding talks with the Palestinians of the West Bank independently, unless the Israeli authorities agree on negotiations with a deputation which will represent the PLO, the fidai organizations and the municipal councils on the West Bank. This is because these circles alone constitute the true representation of the will of our people.

In his visit to Amman in November 1968 Kan'an tried to meet Fatah/PLO leaders but they refused; his request for a meeting with Nasir was rejected by the Egyptians on Talhuni's recommendation. He finally secured a meeting with a PLO representative in Beirut, hoping to improve his image which had been tarnished by his close contacts with the then Israeli defence minister, Dayan. While in Beirut he declared (1 December 1968) that the origin of the PR "is in the right of the Palestinians to oppose occupation". In Nablus (December 1968) he justified the activity of Fatah and added: "Israel is deceiving herself if she believes that not all the Palestinians support the fidaiyyun both inside and outside the occupied territories."

The achievements of the fidai organizations in 1969 served to reinforce these trends. The crisis of September 1970–July 1971, the PNC resolutions of 1970–71 and the intensified struggle between Jordan and the PLO over the right of representation left the leadership no choice but to admit that the PLO represented the Palestinians. Contacts now increased between members of the leadership, who visited Jordan and Lebanon, and the heads of PLO/Fatah.[155]

Proposals for a "Palestinian state". Plans for founding an independent Palestinian Entity on the West Bank and Gaza were mooted after the war by three individuals acting independently.

Azis Shahada, a Christian lawyer from Ramalla, believed that Husayn could not save the Palestinians and therefore they themselves must take the initiative. He published in September 1967 a plan calling for a settlement with Israel, based on the following points: (1) The Palestinians possessed the right of self-determination "prior to the liberation" by the founding of a Palestinian state which would also incorporate the Gaza Strip, based on the UN resolutions including the Partition Resolution. (2) A Palestinian Congress should be held, with representatives from all concentrations of Palestinian population; this would form a Palestinian National Assembly (*qawmiyya*) which would in turn elect a "national body" (*hay'a qawmiyya*) to speak for the Palestinians. (3) Jerusalem should be the capital of the state. Jordan attacked his proposal and demanded that Shahada cease his activity; Shahada therefore suggested that the future Palestinian state should federate with Jordan. After threats on his life by the fidai organizations, he stopped promoting his plan in early 1968; in the course of 1969–70 he also stopped publicly expressing his opinions because the threats against his life continued. After September 1970, however, Shahada plucked up enough courage to restate his views in *al-Quds* (November 1970), but drew no meaningful response.[156]

Dr Hamdi al-Taji al-Faruqi was a Ba'th member who was persecuted by the Jordanian regime. In November 1967 he published a pamphlet entitled "Proposal for the Palestinian State" which proposed: (1) Implementation of the Partition Resolution, after its approval in a Palestinian referendum. (2) The state thus established would be under the practical supervision of the United Nations, and the nominal supervision of the Arab League, for five years. (3) Jerusalem as the capital. Following an attempt on his life (28 December 1967) in Ramalla and threatening letters, he amended his plan; in July 1969 he suggested that the future Palestinian state be united with Jordan. Then in May 1970 he expressed agreement with the fidai organizations' plan for "a unified state in the whole of Filastin". He claimed that "during three years of talks in the West Bank he had learned that ninety percent of the Palestinians opposed [the idea of] a Palestinian state on the West Bank". In September 1970 he admitted that it was no longer possible to consider his plan.[157]

Shaykh Muhammad Ali al-Ja'bari announced his plan during August–September 1967. Ja'bari was not deterred by being called "traitor" by Jordan, nor by the fidai organizations' threats. In his opinion the Palestinian people were entitled to self-determination, in accordance with the following principles: withdrawal by Israel from the West Bank and Gaza; these areas to be under UN rule for five years, followed by a referendum in these areas to establish an independent Palestinian state within Partition Resolution borders. Ja'bari called on the Palestinians to be realistic and to learn the lessons of the past. He proposed holding a Palestinian Congress of some 1,000 persons who would elect a body to speak in their name. In his opinion, it was Israel that rejected this proposal.[158]

Another voice was the *al-Quds* daily newspaper, which began to appear in Jerusalem (East) in November 1968, and was both owned and edited by Mahmud Abu al-Zuluf. The Arab press accused him of being close to the Israeli Ministry of Defence and enjoying its support. The newspaper served as an open forum for all those who advocated an independent Palestinian Entity on the West Bank and the Gaza Strip. The leader writers included Yusuf al-Najjar (Abu Marwan), Sani al-Bitar, Muhammad Abu Shalbaya and sometimes also Shahada and Anwar al-Khatib. *Al-Quds* advocated the following: (1) Self-determination for the Palestinians, to be realized by referendum under neutral supervision. (2) An end to the Israeli occupation; UN resolutions, including the Partition Resolution, should be implemented. (3) Calls for permission to hold public, political activity, including the forming of political bodies. In the wake of Black September the newspaper served as a forum for condemnation of the Jordanian regime. The newspaper began to stress "the PLO's being the representative of the Palestinians". Its editorials neither denounced nor supported the fidai activities explicitly.[159] Over the years the newspaper undoubtedly strengthened Palestinian identity among the West Bank inhabitants, although not in accordance with the PLO's or the organizations' conceptions during this period. It created public opinion favourable to a Palestinian state on the West Bank and Gaza, a position which became the interim objective of the PLO after the war of October 1973.

As for *Israeli proposals*, the IMG, while encouraging the advocates of the Palestinian Entity on the West Bank, did not propose anything that would mean the forming of an independent Palestinian Entity or the granting of autonomy. Officials like Moshe Sasson (then adviser to the prime minister), in talks with local leaders, proposed setting up a "civilian administration" (*idara madaniyya*) to be run by the local population, or creating independent "regions" such as the "Hebron region" – but not more. Abba Eban, then foreign minister, proposed (14 May 1970, in an Arabic-language broadcast over the Voice of Israel) giving "civilian independence" (*istiqlal madani*) to the West Bank and Gaza. It was obvious that the local leadership would reject any such proposals; for example, Anwar al-Khatib characterized the Eban proposal as calling for "a Quisling-style ... independence, or independence of the Vichy government – and under an occupation resembling it". Moshe Sasson concluded from his talks with the West Bank leaders (July 1969) that "the public in the territories is not independent and fears to take any step that might be construed as betrayal by the Arab states". Both the traditional and the nationalist leadership, out of adherence to the Charter, rejected immediately any notion of a Palestinian state in the West Bank and Gaza.[160]

Turning to *the attitude of the organizations*, in this period they, as well as Jordan and Israel, were all opposed to the establishment of a Palestinian state on the West Bank and the Gaza Strip. The organizations prevented the emergence of any body on the West Bank that could claim to represent the Palestinians; no sooner was the idea of a Palestinian state mooted after the war than they threatened its advocates with murder. Sure enough, during 1968–1969 dissemination of the idea on the West Bank declined sharply. Members of the traditional leadership such as Masri, Nimr and Kan'an received threats. The subject of the Palestinian state came up once more after September 1970; the organizations now gauged that the possibility "was realistic at a time when the Resistance Movement was not capable, concretely and objectively, of proposing a short-term substitute". Thus, to make the deterrent factor even more potent, the CC PLO decided (23 October 1970) on a Revolutionary Tribunal to judge "anyone acting in the name of the Palestinian people outside the framework of the Revolution". In a meeting with West Bank leaders (November 1970) Arafat threatened: "If anybody raises his head and demands an abortive state, we shall behead him." West Bank leaders received similar threats from the fidai organizations.[161]

The fidai organizations opposed the "Palestinian state" principally for the following reasons. First, the aim of the plan was "the Balkanization of the Palestinian problem in part of Filastin" and the creation of a "Palestinian mini-state" (Filastinistan) that would be "feeble, devoid of economic, political and military foundations" and led by the traditional leadership. Second, the state would recognize Israel, in other words, "the liquidation of the Palestinian problem" and the PR. Third, "the Palestinian people have no right to agree to Partition or to Resolution 242". "The right of self-determination will be achieved only by the elimination of the state of Israel through armed struggle." The PFLP was prepared to agree to a Palestinian state "in liberated parts of the West Bank or elsewhere which will be imposed by force of the armed struggle". Finally, Fatah was obliged to respond to proposals submitted to the PLO/ Fatah leadership by Soviet and Tunisian officials, and even Palestinians, concerning the founding of a Palestinian state as an interim objective. Fatah's answer was that the Palestinian state "would not lead to the attainment of the final aim" and that "our struggle is not divisible into stages". In its opinion, "a policy of demand and take does not apply in respect of the Palestinian revolution".[162]

The *resignation of Hamdi Kan'an*, mayor of Nablus, is a good example of the leadership crisis on the West Bank. He drew his conclusions in good time, departing from the political arena before being ejected from it. In the summer of 1968 he suggested holding elections for the municipal councils, but subsequently resigned three times from his job on 12 September 1968, 30 December and 12 March 1969. The first time he retracted under pressure from the local Nablus leadership and after a "referendum" which called for his reinstatement; on the second occasion he succumbed to pressure by the town leaders and withdrew his resignation. The immediate reasons for these resignations were, first, his helplessness in administering the affairs of the town. Kan'an admitted his inability "to bear any longer the pressures being exerted on him in his handling of public affairs". Second was his bitter dispute with Talhuni in late 1968 regarding his proposal for elections, and the submission of a memorandum to the king accusing the Talhuni government of "helplessness in handling the affairs of the West Bank in general and Nablus in particular". Finally, he wished to be independent in running the town's affairs, refusing to surrender to the radicals' pressures or even to those of the local traditional leadership, who therefore did not side with him during his crisis with Talhuni or the IMG. He attempted to maintain evenly balanced relations with all pressure groups, but failed. On 1 August 1971 he again appealed for municipal elections, this time more insistently in an article in *al-Quds* entitled "How to Get Rid of the Deadlock".

Underlying these difficulties was the central issue of the representativeness of the municipal councils and their heads, or, in other words, of the traditional leadership. Kan'an adduced a number of reasons why elections should be held: (1) The need for "a true leadership [or true representatives] has become primary". The municipal councils had "ceased to represent the people in the proper manner". "This leadership is a fanatical one which recognizes only its own personal interests." (2) Already by the end of 1968 he was stressing that "there is a general claim on the part of West Bankers that there is a vacuum in true popular representation". He believed that "there is no solution to this complaint except the holding of elections to new councils for the municipalities and to the Chambers of Commerce". (3) "A long period has elapsed, double that provided by law" for the councils' terms of office. "The members of the councils should return their mandate to the people so that the people may realize its right." Kan'an correctly assessed that the function of the municipal councils included "the political sphere" which was, however, "not within their authority"; in other words, they could not adequately represent the population. The IMG responded to this appeal with an order (26 November 1971) to hold municipal elections.[163]

CONCLUSION

History is cruel. It judges leaders not by their intentions but by their deeds. Although Nasir had intentions regarding ways of solving the Arab–Israel conflict, he will be remembered more for his military defeats. Even so, Nasir will go down in history as the leader who laid the foundations for the establishment of the Palestinian Entity and for its consolidation in the Arab and Palestinian arenas. The Palestinian issue in its broader sense served as the "emotional, political and strategic justification for the spread of Nasirism in the Arab world". The Palestinians saw Nasir as "the only leader capable of galvanizing the Arabs into action even when he himself was defeated".[164] Nasir resolved Egypt's historical dilemma – choosing between Egyptianism and Arabism – by linking Egypt to the Palestinian issue, which had become the essence of Arab nationalism. He viewed the new "Palestinian national movement" as a product of and a tool for the realization of Nasirism; the Fatah leaders identified with him deeply and even emotionally, and felt closer to Egypt than to any other Arab state. This mutual relationship also generated crises when the parties' expectations of each other were not fulfilled.

Had the fidai organizations not existed, Syria would have

invented them, and not only to justify her concept of the "popular liberation war". The organizations served the Syrian Ba'th during this period as the Palestinians had served Nasirism during the 1950s in the struggle against Israel and the Arab "reactionary" regimes; for Syria the PR expressed the principle of *qawmiyya*. Syria complemented Egyptian support for the Resistance, but could not replace it. The development of the Palestinian movement during this and even the succeeding period would have been inconceivable without the support of Egypt and Syria. This has created a fundamental problem for Fatah/PLO in their relations with these two countries, especially when the two have been in conflict.

Retrospectively, the Six Day War may be said to have saved Husayn's regime from a threat to its existence, even if developments in Jordan during 1968–70 seem to belie this assessment. The West Bank would have seriously threatened to undermine the regime. It was no coincidence that after the Cairo Agreement (27 September 1970) Nasir mused: "Were it not for the '67 defeat, what happened in Amman and Jordan would not have happened and thousands of innocent people and children would not have been killed." His regaining of authority within the state allowed Husayn to decide (early 1971) that if the war on the Egyptian front was renewed, he would not join.[165] Undoubtedly, changes in the PLO's composition, and recognition of it and of the Resistance as representative of the Palestinian people, were a second decisive factor in the elimination of the fidai activity in Jordan. Husayn realized that his efforts to integrate the two Banks had failed. In the crisis of September 1970–July 1971, however, Husayn lost the moral right to claim that he represented the Palestinians. The Arab world, which failed to meet the test of its pan-Arab nationalism (*qawmiyya*) when it proved unable to prevent either the September massacre or the routing of the fidai activity, tried to compensate by publicly supporting the PLO's right to represent the Palestinians. To cope with this development, Husayn had to propose a different structure for his kingdom "on both Banks".

For the PR in this period the Karama operation (March 1968) was the high point, and the September massacre the low point. Palestinian action passed from "aspiration to Palestinian activity in an Arab framework to Arab activity in a Palestinian framework";[166] the Resistance became an Arab problem more than an Israeli problem. During 1970–71 the organizations fought for their right to exist. The Arab world derived scant satisfaction from their fidai activity; they did not fulfil expectations after the defeat of the regular armies.

Paradoxically, Nasir's advocacy of a political solution to the conflict, despite the organizations' protests, aggravated the struggle for the right to represent the Palestinians in the Palestinian and Jordanian arenas, and finally led the Arab world to settle the matter in the PLO's favour at the Rabat summit (October 1974). Precisely because the Resistance was the pan-Arab (*qawmi*) expression of the conflict, it clashed with almost all the Arab states when the latter tried to guard their separate (*watani*) interests. Khalid al-Hasan, a Fatah leader, described (September 1971) this clash:

> Palestinian action is based on a pan-Arab national [*qawmiyya*] security policy which does not distinguish between the Lebanese, Syrian, Jordanian or Egyptian borders. This policy conflicts with the regionalism [*iqlimiyya*] and the local thinking of the Arab states. Hence the collision between the fidai freedom of action and the sovereignty of the state and the saying: "fidai freedom of action within the limits of the sovereignty of the state".[167]

In this period there was still some doubt in the Arab and Palestinian arenas as to how much the PLO did actually represent the Palestinians. The Resistance sometimes used terrorization in the Palestinian arena to impose its claim of representation. On the West Bank there was still a generation gap between the traditional leadership and the PLO leadership; it was to be bridged only later after the "changing of the guard" that followed two rounds of elections to the municipal councils, in 1972 and 1976; between those years there was yet another Arab–Israeli war. It was ironical that two bloody confrontations, one inter-Arab (September 1970) and the other Arab–Israeli (October 1973), paved the way for the Arab states, including Jordan, to recognize the PLO as the "sole legitimate representative of the Palestinian people".

CHAPTER FOUR

The PLO: Crises and Achievements, 1972–1974

Part One
The Crises, 1972 – September 1973

The year 1971 was a turning point in the modern history of the Middle East. In Egypt and Syria, new regimes were established; in Jordan, the sovereignty of the regime was unquestionably reasserted and a period of stability began such as the country had not known since the annexation of the West Bank in 1950; in Iraq, Saddam Husayn became the unquestioned leader of his regime. These changes contributed to the chain of processes which led to the Yom Kippur War (the October 1973 War).

At this juncture the Arab world had two main characteristics. The first was *the crisis of leadership* brought about by Nasir's death. Sadat and Asad had to struggle to assert the legitimacy of their regimes; although there was no alternative to Egypt's leadership and to its centrality in the conflict, Sadat could not dictate his political moves to the Arab world. He conducted a policy of "openness to all the forces in the Arab world, without any inhibitions or sensitivity, and without any consideration of the social make-up" of the Arab regimes. Against the background of "the total dismantling of the Arab front" he postponed the idea of an Arab summit, preferring to reformulate Arab cooperation regarding the conflict through bilateral contacts. The end of the "decisive year" (1971) came without any decision; and this gave rise in 1972 to a crisis of confidence in Sadat's leadership, both in Egypt and in the Arab world at large. His attempts to mobilize the Arab world bore fruit only in 1973 when the Arab states were persuaded that he had indeed intended war. Sadat correctly assessed that with the outbreak of war "the Arab divisiveness would be ended", and the Arab states "would give the maximum".[1]

The second characteristic was *the campaign (al-ma'raka)*. True leadership is not based on force or on referenda, but on deeds. This was clear to both Sadat and Asad. It meant that achievements in the midst of the conflict became a test of the legitimacy of Sadat's leadership of Egypt and of the Arab world, and of Asad's leadership in Syria. As early as November 1971, Haykal declared that "the stage after the taking of the decision" of the inevitability of war would "turn Sadat into a historic leader of his people and his nation". The conflict became the focus and goal of local patriotism (*wataniyya*), as well as of pan-Arab nationalism (*qawmiyya*). Thus Sadat raised Egyptian nationalism to the same level of importance as pan-Arab nationalism; so that in a situation of political deadlock and of "no war and no peace", war became inevitable. As Sadat declared: "The problem of Filastin has become the conscience of the Arab world, an integral part of the struggle of every people … and as regards the Egyptian people, a part of its life." "War is the solution to all problems … above everything."[2]

Likewise for Asad, "the campaign" represented the prime goal. What resulted was the longest period of closeness between Egypt and Syria since the dismantling of the UAR in September 1961. Because both states represented – since the rise of the Ba'th to power in 1963 – extreme approaches to resolving the conflict, their cooperation on strategy now meant that they could dictate to the Arab world, while a rift between them would mean divisions in that world. Sadat saw in his alliance with Syria a guarantee of success against Israel, which would be forced to fight on two fronts. The military alliance was strengthened in early 1973 when operational plans for war were begun. Sadat called Syria "the heart of the Arab national movement"; Asad described Sadat as "the fighter who stands for noble deeds".[3]

Although remaining faithful to the strategy which Nasir had dictated at the Khartoum summit, the means which Sadat and to a lesser extent Asad used were more pragmatic and realistic. In this way Sadat managed to close the huge gap with which the Arabs were left after 1948 between their goals and their ability to achieve them. The region indeed entered a new era of progress in stages towards achieving the first goal of "eliminating the traces of aggression". This change strengthened the linkage between the territorial question and the Palestinian national question. Sadat's stand on the latter question was clearer and more concrete than Nasir's; as for Syria, her support of Palestinian claims was a key source of her strength in the Arab world.

In Sadat's view the Arab world was divided into two areas of action: the Federation of Arab Republics (FAR), set up on 17 April 1971 between Egypt, Syria and Libya to express "unity of rank", and the rest of the Arab world, in which he should endeavour to achieve "unity of action" that was essential for the impending war. The latter was attained only in the first half of 1973, and reached its climax with the outbreak of the War. The setting up of the FAR was intended more to strengthen Sadat and Asad and to align their positions than as "a huge step towards great Arab unity" (Sadat). Once its practical aims were achieved its usefulness ceased, and even Qadhafi became an obstacle rather than a help.[4]

Jordan, during most of this period, was isolated in the Arab arena; internally it was stable, allowing Husayn significant freedom of movement, leading to publication of his plan for the United Arab Kingdom (UAK; 15 March 1972). This plan was indicative of his continued efforts to regain the West Bank. Publication of the plan forced the Arab states, especially Egypt, to take a clear position on the Jordan–PLO struggle over representation. In view of the enmity towards him over his wiping out of the fidaiyyun bases, his negative approach to a military solution of the conflict and his efforts to achieve a political settlement with Israel, it was clear that Husayn's claim to representation would not prevail – indeed, just the opposite. Thus the struggle over representation in fact became a struggle between Jordan and the Arab states, with Sadat setting the tone.

In early 1972 the fidai organizations asked themselves: "Whither the Palestinian Resistance?" The PR continued to be more an Arab than an Israeli problem in relation to fidai activity, though not in relation to the Palestinian Entity. The stand of Golda Meir, the Israeli prime minister – no recognition of the Palestinian Entity, refusal to accept a Palestinian state on the West Bank or anywhere "between the Mediterranean and the Iraqi border" and her viewing Jordan as the framework for "the national expression of the Palestinians" – helped to exacerbate the struggle over representation and to strengthen the Arab commitment to solving the "Palestinian national problem". In this period the Arab states (except for Jordan) and the PLO began acting in the international arena to transform the Palestinian issue from a refugee problem to "a national liberation movement".[5]

SADAT'S POLICY

Like Nasir, Sadat stated openly most of what he said in diplomatic discussions or in official Egyptian forums. He declared his loyalty to Nasirism, but in building his own leadership he slowly distanced himself from Nasir's conceptions, culminating in the peace agreement with Israel. Sadat had accompanied Nasir since the revolution and was familiar with all aspects of the conflict, regarding which, according to him, he sometimes disputed Nasir's policies. He assessed that if he maintained Nasir's strategy, the situation would remain unchanged for many years. He was free of all the complexes, sensitivities and obligations which beset Nasir during the 18 years of his rule, and determined to avoid his predecessor's mistakes. In contrast to Nasir, who was impulsive, the artist of doctrine and strategy, Sadat was characterized by "patience and silence" of almost religious proportions and by a calculated pragmatism that was not without its cunning. He was the artist of political tactics, initiative and movement. He strove at all times to sustain "momentum", seeking limited, stage-by-stage achievements which would eventually lead to his strategic goals. He was, in fact, so concerned with tactical steps that at times it seemed there was an overlap between them and the strategy, or even that they were a substitute for it. One gains the impression that Sadat sought war as a tactical step towards achieving his larger goals.[6]

The Elements of Sadat's Stand on the Conflict

Sadat adhered to the two essential principles of Nasir's plan for the "elimination of the traces of aggression": (1) "No concession over any piece of Arab land", that is, "Israeli withdrawal from all occupied lands, i.e., Arab Jerusalem, the West Bank of the Jordan, the Gaza Strip, Sinai and the Golan Heights"; (2) "Securing the legal (and natural) rights of the Palestinian people ... and a solution to the problem of the Palestinian homeland."

Sadat accepted the UN Assembly resolution of 4 November 1970 to extend the cease-fire for another three months. On 4 February 1971 he announced his new political initiative while accepting a further cease-fire extension of 30 days, until 7 March 1971. On 7 March he announced that "we do not feel ourselves bound by the cease-fire, nor to hold back from opening fire", although "this does not mean a cessation of political activity".[7] The cease-fire on the

Egyptian front was maintained by Egypt until the outbreak of war on 6 October 1973.

Sadat's initiative. In October 1970 Dayan publicly raised the idea of a "partial solution", namely, Israeli partial or gradual withdrawal from the Suez Canal accompanied by partial political agreements. Golda Meir discussed (25 October 1970) this proposal with Henry Kissinger. In December 1970 Egypt discussed with the US an "interim agreement", and especially the idea of opening the Canal to shipping in exchange for the withdrawal of Israeli forces some yet unspecified distance. On 4 February 1971 Sadat announced for the first time details of his initiative to settle the conflict in stages: (1) Partial Israeli withdrawal from the eastern bank of the Canal, by which he meant as far as the Mitla and Jiddi passes. (2) Egyptian agreement to a six-month cease-fire allowing "Jarring to set a timetable for carrying out the articles of Security Council Resolution 242", "the first of which would be complete withdrawal from all Arab territories". (3) If this were agreed, Egypt would "begin immediately to clear the Canal and to reopen it to international navigation", that is, in exchange for partial withdrawal. Israeli shipping would not pass through the Canal until a comprehensive agreement had been reached. (4) This initiative would be "only a step in return for a step, towards a comprehensive solution"; "a clear connection must be established between the first step and the comprehensive solution in accordance with the Security Council resolution". The Israeli withdrawal was imperative "not only from Egyptian lands, but from all Arab lands occupied on 6 June 1967". (5) After the Israeli withdrawal, "Egyptian forces must cross to the east bank of the Canal as a realization of Egyptian sovereignty over Egyptian land". "Egypt is ready for practical arrangements for the disengagement of the combatant forces during the period of the cease-fire." Egypt rejected any discussion of an Israeli presence at Sharm al-Sheikh or of the demilitarization of Sinai; Sadat emphasized that "our border is the international border".

After Egypt–US and Israel–US discussions, Sadat judged, with some justification, that the US was trying to turn his initiative into a partial or separate solution with Israel, which would lead to similar agreements between Syria and Jordan and Israel. Against this background, and following negative reactions from the Arab world, he emphasized the following intentions underlying his initiative: (1) "The Rogers initiative has failed." (2) "The initiative is only an administrative move organically linked to a comprehensive solution on the basis of the Security Council resolution in all its articles. First among these is Israeli withdrawal from all Arab lands occupied on 6 June 1967." Its aim was "to move the problem towards a solution and as a test of [Israeli] intentions [for peace]." (3) "There is no such thing as an Egyptian, Palestinian, Syrian or Jordanian solution. There is only an Arab solution." Sadat was well aware that Israel sought a prior, separate agreement with Egypt.[8] With this initiative Sadat broke down the stage of "elimination of the traces of aggression" into intermediate steps in order to prevent stalemate. In fact, his proposal was a "military agreement", which included "disengagement of forces" and an "interim agreement", without his making significant political concessions from Israel's point of view; and the initiative did not bear fruit. Its principles were realized only after the War, with the "disengagement agreement" (January 1974) and the "interim agreement" (September 1975).

Readiness for a peace agreement with Israel.   The starting point for Sadat's approach – and where he differed from Nasir – was that it was unrealistic to exterminate Israel, *inter alia* because of America's commitment to it, and because the previous Arab–Israeli wars had proved that military means were not enough. Sadat believed that the Arabs could aspire at most to obtaining an Israeli withdrawal to the pre-1967 borders. This approach was expressed in Egypt's "surprising" answer to Jarring's questions of 8 February 1971, put simultaneously to Egypt and Israel following Sadat's initiative of 4 February 1971. Jarring requested that Egypt "would give a commitment to enter into a peace agreement with Israel on a reciprocal basis ... covering the following subjects: (1) termination of all claims or states of belligerency; (2) respect for and acknowledgement of each other's sovereignty, territorial integrity and political independence." Egypt responded that she was ready to give this commitment, but added some reservations: "Israel should [first] give a commitment to implement all the provisions of Resolution 242 including withdrawal of its armed forces from Sinai and the Gaza Strip, [and] a just settlement of the refugee problem in accordance with United Nations resolutions." Thus Sadat, to his credit, was openly and officially prepared for a peace agreement with Israel; Egypt also made this clear in her diplomatic contacts with Arab states, though emphasizing what her basic conditions were and that she had in mind a "peace agreement" rather than a "peace treaty" (which would mean diplomatic relations). "Full peace" would come for Egypt only with a comprehensive agreement that included Jordan, Syria and the Palestinians. Thus, in May 1973, Sadat raised the idea of a "peace conference" for a solution to the conflict.[9]

Political deliberations in this period hinged around the Sadat initiative; the Khartoum resolutions were by now anachronistic. Support for the Palestinian cause became essential to Sadat so as to prove his loyalty to pan-Arab nationalism and his determination to achieve a comprehensive solution. The Sadat initiative and his readiness for a "peace agreement" can be seen as complementary. Retrospectively it is reasonable to see them as the start of the process which led to his 1977 peace initiative; the results of the War accelerated this process.

1971 – "The year of decision". Sadat's success in wiping out the "centres of power" opposed to him on 15 May 1971, and the subsequent internal stabilization of his regime, allowed him to concentrate on the conflict. It appears that during June 1971 he made an estimate of the situation concerning his February 1971 political initiative in view of Israeli and American reactions to it. He concluded that the political process was in crisis and needed impetus. On 22 June 1971 he announced for the first time that "1971 is the year of decision" (*hasm*), "whether [in the direction of] war or peace". On 23 July 1971 he emphasized that "we will not accept a state of no war and no peace", since this meant permanent Israeli retention of occupied Arab lands. It appears that, in about October 1971, Sadat concluded that "there is no longer such a thing as a political solution", and "we need to think of the military option and to prepare for it seriously, without neglecting political efforts". He believed that the February 1971 initiative was no longer valid, and that war was now inevitable. At the end of 1971 he concluded, however, that the Egyptian forces were not yet ready for war. That "the year of decision" ended without a decision was a letdown for Arab and Egyptian public opinion; and by early 1972 Sadat's status had reached its nadir. He now saw his support for the PR as an important means of demonstrating his militancy and improving his national image. His intent was to embark in March 1972 on a campaign of support for the PR; the release of Tall's assassins on 29 February 1972 can be understood in this context. Publication of King Husayn's plan was a convenient opportunity for him.[10]

Limited war. Sadat's point of departure was the year 1967, in contrast to that of Syria and the PLO for whom it was 1948; therefore his focus was "elimination of the traces of aggression". Political developments in 1972 strengthened his assessment that only war could give momentum to the political process. Continuation of the stalemate, he believed, meant also "a crumbling of the internal front". It appears that his final decision regarding an Egyptian(–Syrian) military initiative was taken in about August 1972. This was, first of all, his personal decision. The question was how to ensure a high degree of success without having to undergo lengthy preparations lasting several years. In the discussions (September 1972) of the Egyptian National Security Council, and also later (October 1972) of the GHQ of the armed forces, three options were presented: (1) To continue political talks. This was rejected since it meant "surrender" to Israeli dictates. (2) To adopt Nasir's approach, namely, continuing to build up militarily with the aim of a total war to reconquer Sinai. The war minister, Muhammad Sadiq, and some senior GHQ officers supported this approach; Sadat rejected it on the ground that it only meant continuation of the stalemate. (3) The chosen strategy was a limited military initiative, using Egypt's full strength, in which the chances of success were high and which would "break the cease-fire situation" and give the political process momentum. Sadat argued (as he claimed he had told Nasir) that "crossing the Canal and seizing even ten centimetres of Sinai will change the political situation from the international and Arab aspects". On 26 October 1972 he dismissed the war minister and some of his supporters in the GHQ, replacing him with Ahmad Isma'il, chief of military intelligence, who shared Sadat's thinking. Preparations for war now went into the operational stage in conjunction with the Syrians.

The master plan was ready by early 1973 when tentative dates for the attack were presented by the then chief of operations, Jamasi. The plan was approved by Asad and Sadat who met in April 1973. In December 1972 even the Egyptian economy was put on a war footing. In a "political–military order" to the war minister (1 October 1973), Sadat declared that "the strategic goal is ... challenging the Israeli conception of security by means of a military action in accordance with the capabilities of the armed forces". In a "strategic order" to the war minister (5 October 1973), Sadat ordered the armed forces to achieve, among other things: (1) "Elimination of the present military stalemate through breaking of the cease-fire beginning 6 October 1973." (2) "Action to liberate the occupied land in graduated stages in accordance with the possible developments and the capability of the armed forces." The "operation order" to the armed forces established the operational objective as occupation of the line of the western mountain passes in Sinai and, at least, of the east bank of the Gulf of Suez, to be achieved in three operational phases. For Sadat, successful achievement of even the first phase – crossing the Canal and establishing a continuous bridgehead ten to 15 kilometres deep – would be a notable victory.

Having decided on war, Sadat in his contacts with the Americans in early 1973 once again emphasized a comprehensive settlement, meaning Israeli withdrawal from the territories and a solution to the Palestinian issue. Egypt even set a time – September 1973, by no means coincidental – by which at least the "fundamental principles" of a settlement must be agreed upon. In August–September 1973 Sadat, apparently to deflect the criticisms of some of his tactical moves, told the PLO leaders several times of his intention to go to war "before the end of the year", but they did not believe him.[11]

Stalemate on the Eastern Front. Sadat saw the Eastern Front as being composed of Jordan, Iraq and the PR. Following the elimination of fidai activity in Jordan, withdrawal of Iraqi forces, and Jordan's decision not to participate in another war, Sadat concluded (August 1971) that there was no hope of reviving the Eastern Front. In late 1972, after the decision to go to war, discussions with Jordan on establishing such a Front were held, and were later continued also by Syria until the eve of the War. Experience had taught Husayn that under no circumstances should he participate in such a Front, since it meant turning the clock back. His position hardened even more when he learned, in May 1973, of concrete preparations for war by Egypt and Syria. Jordan would consider serving as an Eastern Front in the framework of a joint Arab military command, but only under the following conditions: (1) Agreement on a coordinated, long-term plan against Israel, to be decided upon by the heads of the Arab confrontation states, which would determine the policies of the United Arab Command (UAC) including the plans of action of the three Fronts. (2) War would be decided upon *only* by common agreement and *only* after it was clear that there could be no political settlement without it. (3) No foreign (apart from Saudi) forces would enter Jordan before she had completed strengthening her own forces, so as not to give Israel a pretext to attack. Any foreign force entering Jordan would be subject to, and its strength determined by, the Jordanian GHQ. (4) Arab aid to Jordan, which had been agreed upon at the Khartoum summit but had since been suspended, was now demanded to give the Jordanian army the strength to withstand Israeli attack. This condition had to be met *before* any Arab forces entered Jordanian territory. These conditions speak for themselves. They emptied the Eastern Front of any content; in fact, Husayn made the renewal of hostilities contingent upon agreement by *all* the Arab states and upon the UAC not being made operational without his agreement.[12] Thus the only remaining option was for Iraq to send reinforcements to the Northern Front (Syria) – which meant that these would come under Syrian command. Iraq, realizing this, gave two reasons for not sending a force to Syria: the border controversy with Iran, and the Kurdish revolt in the north. Iraq did, however, express willingness to despatch troops when a war broke out – and in fact did so.[13]

Towards the end of 1972 Egypt renewed her efforts towards inter-Arab military cooperation. Talks on the subject were conducted at the following conferences: the Arab League Council (9–13 September 1972), the Arab Defence Council (ADC; 27–29 November 1972, 27–30 January 1973) and Arab Chiefs-of-Staff (12 December 1972, 21–22 April 1973). The January 1973 ADC reconfirmed the policies from the Nasir period, namely, that "united Arab action to liberate the occupied territories" would be executed in three stages: steadfastness, attrition and liberation. The ADC concluded that Jordan and Syria had not yet reached the "steadfastness stage", hence no concrete discussions on the liberation stage could take place. Also, the ADC decided on the establishment of three "fronts", each with its own command, and appointed the Egyptian war minister as their commander-in-chief. Under Egypt's influence the ADC postulated that the aim of Arab action was the "elimination of the traces of aggression and avoidance of damaging the Palestinian cause and the rights of the Palestinian people". The Egyptian position was accepted, namely that the "political action will take place parallel to military preparation and action. The military plan will serve as a prop to the political plan." They rejected "partial solutions [as] damaging to the Palestinian problem".[14]

The Egyptian Attitude towards Jordan

Sadat did not have a moral commitment towards Husayn, as Nasir had, and Jordan ceased to be Egypt's ally. Sadat saw his stands towards Jordan and towards the Palestinian Entity as closely connected. This linkage was clearly expressed in Sadat's speech of 6

April 1972, responding to Husayn's United Arab Kingdom plan, in which two issues determined Egypt's policy towards Jordan: the regime's position regarding PR freedom of action in Jordan; and the extent of its participation in preparations for the War.

Egypt's relationship with Jordan developed in four stages. In the period *October 1970 – 13 July 1971*, Egypt argued that "Jordan is the principal base for the PR". Sadat, however, was unable to help the fidaiyyun in Jordan since he was opposed to military intervention; instead he called for the implementation of the Cairo and Amman agreements, and avoided attacking Husayn in his speeches. Sadat even condemned the radical fidai organizations and called for freedom of Fatah activity in Jordan. Despite a PLO request (March 1971) to Egypt for assistance in removing the regime, Egypt concluded that such a step was not in her interest. Jordanian–Egyptian relations were further clouded by the appointment of Wasfi al-Tall as PM, and by Sadat's belief that meetings between Husayn and Israeli leaders had taken place despite Husayn's denials.[15]

In the period *14 July – December 1971*, the elimination of the fidai bases in Jordan called for a change in Sadat's tactics towards the regime. He made cautious attacks within the context of his declaration of the "year of decision", but he did not wish to undermine the possibilities of mediation, for which Saudi Arabia was pressing. During the mini-summit meeting called by Qadhafi (Cairo, 17 July 1971), Sadat rejected Qadhafi's proposal for military intervention in Jordan. Instead the summit emphasized that "the Palestinian revolution represents the Palestinian people and expresses their will and aspirations". For the first time (23 July 1971) Sadat personally attacked Husayn in a way reminiscent of Nasir's attacks on him prior to the Six Day War. Husayn's success, and his firm stand during the mediation talks, added another layer to Sadat's lack of faith in him. The degree of his abhorrence of Husayn was expressed in his support of the PR, and was echoed by the Egyptian media. No wonder, therefore, that the murder of Tall was seen by an Egyptian newspaper as predictable and inevitable.[16]

Next came the stage marked by *Husayn's plan (1972)*. Sadat's condition – that his attitude towards Husayn would depend on the latter's stand regarding the PR – was again tested when Husayn announced his plan (15 March 1972). It was clear to Sadat that the challenge presented by this plan was: who represents the Palestinians? Details of this plan were made known to Sadat, Asad and Qadhafi prior to its announcement at the FAR summit in Cairo which ended 14 March 1972; the official Egyptian reaction was published only on 18 March 1972 as an official condemnation on behalf of the FAR's presidents. Sadat first condemned the plan in his speech of 30 March 1972, and Haykal attacked it in his 17 March 1972 column. Sadat assessed the implications of the plan as follows: (1) It provided a solution to the Palestinian national issue within the framework of the UAK, with Jordan (*both* Banks) as a "homeland" for the Palestinian people. (2) It meant "emptying the Palestinian problem of its content" and "reducing the Arab–Israel conflict to a dispute over borders alone". (3) It would result in "the elimination of the Palestinian identity" and the undermining of any Palestinian representation by the PLO or the PR. (4) It showed that details of the plan had been coordinated with the US, and that it was deliberately announced shortly before the West Bank municipal elections (28 March 1972). (5) It was yet another sign of Husayn's openness to a separate agreement with Israel, particularly against the background of ongoing contacts between Husayn and Israeli leaders (e.g., his meeting with Golda Meir). Thus Sadat, desiring to improve his image in the Arab world and by now bitter towards Husayn, retaliated against him at his most sensitive point: he robbed Husayn of his right to represent the Palestinians and did so fully aware of the implications for the West Bank's future. It seems as if he purposely delayed announcing his stand until the convening of the PNC (6 April 1972) in order to maximize Palestinian support. Sadat broke off relations with Jordan and declared the PR "the sole, legitimate representative" of the Palestinians. He thus deprived Husayn of the mandate he had received, supported by Nasir, at the Khartoum summit "to do all to liberate the West Bank", and at the same time denied Husayn's claim of sovereignty over the West Bank – consistent with the Egyptian policy of not recognizing the Jordanian annexation. Egypt, despite this and aware of the Israeli attitude towards the PLO, displayed to the US (February 1973) flexibility in its tactical stand regarding negotiations over the West Bank. Egypt's starting point was that, whereas Israeli withdrawal on the Egyptian and Syrian fronts should be to the international borders, regarding Jordan the border had never been established. It followed that talks about the West Bank would be conducted between Israeli and Jordanian representatives, or with an Arab delegation (presumably with Palestinian participation in either case). In this instance Husayn would serve only as an instrument to "liberate" the territories. Clearly the intention was that the West Bank would be governed by the Palestinians through the PLO.[17]

By the final stage in *1973, leading up to the War*, all Sadat's actions served "the campaign". In his tactical artistry Sadat acted according to the priorities he had set for each stage, side-stepping positions of principle when necessary. He was prepared to ignore Husayn's plan and settle for a Jordanian undertaking that "it will be executed [only] following the liberation of the land". The king indeed promised Sadat (early December 1972) that "no Arab ruler or king is able to hand over Jerusalem to the Jews and [that] Jordan will not seek a separate solution". Of course, Jordan was not really conceding anything. Sadat also accepted a formula according to which fidai activity, including that from Jordan, would fall within the overall planning of the UAC. This attitude was confirmed by the ADC (January 1973) when it agreed that "Jordan's role will centre primarily on holding down the bulk of the enemy's forces to the Israeli border". Despite Egyptian flexibility, Husayn held to his principle of non-participation in the war "which might end in the occupation of the East Bank"; the question of the PR's return to Jordan was set aside.

The talks among Egypt, Syria and Jordan continued without result. Since the war was fast approaching, and in order to prevent Husayn seeking a pretext for not participating in it, Sadat and Asad agreed, although Husayn had not changed his policy, to accept his proposal to hold a tripartite summit. This took place on 10 September 1973. The significant outcome, as far as Jordan was concerned, was the renewal of diplomatic relations between the two countries and Jordan. Husayn wanted the meeting to secure his freedom of manoeuvre once war broke out, and at least to help him regain his nationalist image. Sadat's assessment that with the outbreak of war "Husayn would be unable to rule his people or [control] his army", so that they would force him to participate, proved grossly exaggerated.[18]

Sadat and the Question of the Palestinian Entity

Sadat, more than any other Arab leader of his period, provided a concrete definition of the Palestinian Entity, including its tenets, territory and aims; hence his influence on the internal Palestinian arena and on discussions within the PLO institutions. His stand became the cornerstone of the pan-Arab position after the War and contributed to the change in the PLO's position in the direction of Egypt's strategy of stages. There is no doubt that his conception forced him to think of practical ways to solve the "Palestinian national problem". Thus the linkage between the "territorial problem" and the "Palestinian national problem" became more defined.

During 1971 Sadat maintained Nasir's policy on the Palestinian Entity, avoiding his phraseology but promoting his conception of "a nation which has a homeland". This policy had two main elements. One was *"the national rights of the Palestinian people"*, without defining how these would be achieved. Sadat emphasized that the Palestinian issue should be resolved "not on the basis of a [humanitarian] solution to the refugee problem, but on the basis of a solution to the question of the Palestinian homeland", which would include the right to self-determination. He repeated Nasir's stand that the Palestinians had the right to reject Resolution 242. The second element was *Fatah as the leader of the PLO and the PR*. In this respect Sadat maintained Nasir's policy and sustained close contacts with the Fatah/PLO leaders; on the other hand, he was hostile to the PFLP and the PDFLP. The Egyptian security authorities kept a close watch on Palestinian students in Cairo who were members of these two organizations, arresting some of them in 1972 and early 1973 for participating in the student riots.

Against the background of the organizations' internal crises there was, in late 1971, criticism of the Fatah/PLO stand in the Egyptian press, not without authorization from above. This came especially from the Palestinian writer Faysal Hurani, deploring the negative attitude of the Palestinian movement "which did not lead to any achievements or successful results". Hurani called on the Palestinians "to be active in the search for an accepted and reasonable formula which will define the fate of the Palestinian people within the realm of the possible".[19]

The fact that 1971 ended without "decision", in addition to the political stalemate, drove Sadat to concentrate on the Palestinian Entity. The announcement of Husayn's plan also helped crystallize his position. His policy was made up of three components which, together, add up to one conception.

1. *The PLO as the sole representative of the Palestinians.* Sadat's speech (6 April 1972) at the Palestinian Popular Congress (PPC, also the 10th PNC) was a turning point in his declared policy on the Palestinian Entity. In a concise and carefully phrased speech he explained the two considerations which guided his policy. The first was *historical and present rights*. Within the "rights of the Palestinian people" there were two aspects to which Egypt adhered: (1) "the *historical* rights of the Palestinian people which underscore

the legitimate rights of this people to self-determination"; and (2) "the *present* political rights [*al-rahina*] of the Palestinian people which demand an end to the enemy occupation of the lands taken in 1967, namely the West Bank, Jerusalem and the Gaza Strip." This distinction was made in order to orient perceptions in the direction of his step-by-step approach. It was clear that achieving "present rights" had priority; the "historical" component was to be further postponed. It could be assumed that Sadat purposely coupled "self-determination" with "historical rights" in order to pre-empt criticism from the Palestinians. In fact, his purpose was to include "self-determination" in "present rights". And in a clearer formulation the rights of self-determination of the Palestinians were to be attained on the West Bank, Jerusalem and the Gaza Strip once these had been "liberated".

His second basic consideration was *the PLO as the sole representative*. "The sole legitimate representative of the Palestinian people which Egypt recognizes, is the legitimate [Palestinian] resistance, namely, you [the PNC] .... The Palestinian people will not be represented by anyone from the political slave market" (i.e., Husayn). A clear statement. Here he linked both the "national Palestinian" and the "territorial" elements. The meaning of his speech – and he left no room for doubt – was that the West Bank and Gaza (including East Jerusalem) were to be handed over to PLO rule once Israel withdrew from them. Sadat's distinction between these two types of rights was clearly understood by the organizations. They strongly criticized his views, but only in internal publications and meetings so as not to upset their relationship with him. Fatah, for example, believed that the aim of such a distinction was "to drive the Palestinian revolution ... to a peaceful solution and to force it to abandon in practice its strategic aim, which is to liberate the whole Palestinian land and to establish a national democratic Palestinian state". Fatah held that the "resolutions of the PPC thwarted the attempt at such a distinction".[20]

2. A Palestinian government-in-exile (PGE).   As early as the third Arab summit (September 1965) the king of Morocco proposed to Shuqayri to set up a Palestinian government-in-exile (similar to the Algerian one); Shuqayri declined. Sadat, prior to his speech in the PPC (6 April 1972), suggested a PGE for the first time during a special meeting with the Fatah leadership and soon afterwards in a meeting with the EC PLO members. This proves that the idea of a PGE complemented his concept expressed in his speech to the PPC.

At this stage he did not publish his proposal, possibly because the PLO leaders' immediate reaction was unfavourable. On 28 September 1972 Sadat openly proposed a PGE, this time without prior consultation with Fatah, presumably because they had already heard about it from him. He intended to influence their decisions in his favour, especially as a number of Fatah leaders supported his proposal. The announcement of his proposal was preceded by a "softening up" by two leading Egyptian journalists who were close to the regime. Ihsan Abd al-Qudus called (1 July 1972) for a distinction between "the [political] entity of the Palestinian people" ("which will remain intact whilst all the Arab states share their responsibility towards it",) and "the fidai activity which should be based upon secret organizations". Ahmad Baha al-Din called (2 July 1972) on the PR "to go underground and to concentrate its activity within the occupied territories".

Sadat's declaration had several aims: (1) To express the existence of the "Palestinian national problem" and "to realize the Palestinian Entity", as a response to Golda Meir's declaration that "there is no such thing as the Palestinian people or the Palestinian Entity". (2) To strengthen the Palestinian element, thus depriving Jordan of any legitimacy in conducting separate West Bank negotiations and preventing her from entering into a separate agreement. (3) To set up a purely political Palestinian establishment which, upon assuming formal political responsibility, would presumably adopt a more realistic approach to the Palestinian issue. This idea was diametrically opposed to the one Nasir had expressed early in 1968. (4) To win international recognition for the PGE, which would make political contacts with it easier than with the PLO or the PR. Later on a further explanation was presented, namely, that such a government would represent a "national liberation movement" around which the Palestinians of the occupied territories would gather, unlike the PLO which served as an umbrella organization for independent bodies. Sadat assessed that Egypt could gain recognition for the PGE from the Eastern bloc and from the "non-aligned" states, thereby isolating Israel in the international arena. It was clear to Sadat that such a government would not only claim "personal representation" of the Palestinians but also sovereignty over "Palestinian territory", that is, the West Bank and Gaza; thus this suggestion accorded with the concept of "present rights". It is reasonable to assume that Sadat's proposal was related to his idea that Palestinian representatives should participate in the political negotiations for settling the conflict. During 1973, and as part of his planned moves for the postwar period, he raised the possibility (including before Fatah leaders in August and September 1973) of a "peace conference" in which Palestinian representatives would take part.[21]

3. *Return to the Partition Resolution.* The 1947 partition borders had already been discussed by Egyptian diplomats during Nasir's time as a possible interpretation of the concept "secure and recognized borders" and as a basis for solving the Palestinian issue. Sadat's regime now proposed this formally and within the international forum. As early as February 1971 Sadat had argued that a just solution "could rest only on UN resolutions on this issue from 1947 to the present day". This allusion to the Partition Resolution shows that soon after becoming president Sadat had made a special study of the various plans and proposals to date regarding the Palestinian Entity. These included proposals based on the Partition Resolution by Bourguiba and by supporters of an independent Palestinian Entity in the West Bank and Gaza. As part of Sadat's efforts to prepare international opinion for his planned military initiative, and to prove Egypt's willingness for a peace settlement with Israel, thereby isolating Israel, Dr Hasan al-Zayyat demanded in the Security Council, as part of its debate (6–15 June 1973) on the Middle East crisis, that the Council "decide to respect the rights and aspirations of the Palestinian *nation* [emphasis added] ... to live in peace within safe and recognized borders in their homeland, Filastin ... in accordance with the Partition Resolution of 1947". Whereas he defined the international borders of Egypt and Syria as the ones to which Israel must withdraw, the question of "how the border [partition] should be decided and who will define it so that it will be secure and recognized and agreed upon, is up to the Palestinians, and they will, if they so desire, recognize this border with Israel on condition that they too will have a secure, recognized and agreed-upon border". For the first time a senior Egyptian politician had expressed formally, and in an international forum, readiness to recognize the existence of Israel within any borders. In doing so Zayyat legitimized Bourguiba's proposals of 1965. Therefore Bourguiba was interviewed (4 September 1973) in the Egyptian newspaper, *al-Akhbar*, wherein he reiterated his views concerning the acceptance of the Partition Resolution, emphasizing that "his proposal grants a firm judicial basis" for recognition of an independent Palestinian Entity. It should be noted that Zayyat stressed the legal aspect of his demands based upon UN resolutions,

hence his use of the concept "nation", which is accepted in international law, rather than the concept "people". Egypt did not disguise the meaning of her demand, namely the establishment of a "Palestinian state" in "half of Filastin". In order to soften the PLO's reaction, *al-Ahram* (10 June 1973) posed the question as to "who should represent the Palestinians from a legal point of view". Its answer was that "the PLO alone, until the right conditions arise for a referendum ... is able to transform the idea of a Palestinian state into a palpable fact". Egypt, in explaining to Syria and to the Fatah leaders why she had raised the Partition Plan in the Security Council, emphasized the legal aspect.[22]

The Fatah/PLO's reaction to Zayyat's suggestion was ambivalent, whereas the radical organizations rejected it instantly. Generally, the PLO tried to prevent a crisis with Egypt by avoiding direct criticism. On the one hand Fatah/PLO regarded positively the Security Council debate itself during which the Western governments expressed support for the "legitimate aspirations of the Palestinians"; on the other hand they cautiously criticized Zayyat's proposal which "opposed the concept of the armed struggle for the liberation of the Palestinian homeland". Still, Fatah did not reject the "legal basis for the right of the Palestinian people to self-determination".[23]

Support while demanding strategic coordination. Sadat rose to office when the PR, which was entering a grave crisis, was in need of Egyptian military and particularly political support. Indeed such support was "full, unlimited and unconditional". Sadat's position on Palestinian representation and his overt support for it was the best propaganda the PLO had in the Arab and Palestinian arenas. Realizing this, the Fatah/PLO leaders avoided a crisis with Sadat even when they disagreed with his tactics or with his policy towards Jordan during 1973. The relationship between the two sides was guided by considerations not basically dissimilar from those in previous periods. Sadat reiterated Nasir's position that "we will measure the attitude of every Arab country according to its relation to the PR". The Egyptian media praised the fidai activities, though not the "operations abroad" of Fatah/Black September.

From the organizations' point of view there was no substitute in the Arab world for Sadat's support. Military aid, mainly for Fatah, continued, including instruction and training in Eygpt. Sadat permitted the renewal of Fatah broadcasts from Cairo on 15 January 1971. The Egyptian media continued to cover extensively the organizations' military and political activities, especially Fatah's, and to be the organ of the PR. Egypt gave the PLO and the other organizations full backing in their activities in the West Bank and Gaza; Egypt and the PLO/Fatah coordinated their stands on the 1972 West Bank municipal elections. Egypt continued to express its special connection with the Gaza Strip, and its rejection of any "Palestinian state" in the form proposed by the supporters of the independent Palestinian Entity in the West Bank. It condemned all cooperation with the Israeli Military Government (IMG) or with the Jordanian regime.[24]

Yet this was only one side of the coin in the Egypt–PR relationship. Sadat was firm when he presented (28 February 1971) the PLO with his conditions for cooperation: "It is not in our interest to impose custodianship on anyone, and at the same time we will not accept custodianship from anyone." "We have no right to speak in the name of the Palestinian people." Sadat led the organizations to understand that he would not tolerate a crisis similar to the one caused by the Rogers initiative. It was important to Sadat to achieve "strategic coordination" with the PLO/Fatah in order to justify both his actions and his inaction. He even seemed to threaten them when he said, in his important speech (6 April 1972) to the PPC, that the PLO's responsibility was "the greatest coordination with united Arab action. Without [this] cooperation … you are in danger of isolation."

In August 1972 Fatah believed that following the expulsion of the Soviet advisers the "Egyptian regime preferred the partial solution … which means the concentration of pressure on the PR to abandon the policy of armed struggle". Sadat's dilemma, between large-scale support for the PLO and wanting to subordinate fidai activity to his strategic considerations, worsened from the end of 1972, when he began to prepare for war and, together with Syria, wished "to avoid marginal campaigns" which might entangle Egypt and Syria in an inopportune confrontation with Israel. Therefore he tried, together with Asad, to end the May 1973 crisis between the organizations and the Lebanese regime by pressuring the organizations to suspend their actions on that border; this same group also pressured President Franjiyya to curtail the Lebanese army's actions against the organizations.

Egypt used all her influence to get the inter-Arab conferences of late 1972 and early 1973 to accept resolutions, with Syria's consent, on the coordination of fidai action. First, the ADC decided (November 1972) that "all obstacles should be cleared from the

PR's path in a way which will not clash with the national sovereignty" of the states within which it was active (reminiscent of the Cairo Agreement between the PLO and Jordan). This was rejected by the Fatah/PLO leaders, who argued that they were not bound by the cease-fire and that "fidai activity has spread outside the Arab arena because of the limitations imposed on it in this arena". Second, the conference of the Arab Chiefs-of-Staff (December 1972) recommended, *inter alia*, that fidai activity should be part of an overall Arab plan which required the approval of the commander-in-chief of the Arab Fronts. Finally, the ADC of January 1973 adopted the recommendations of the chiefs-of-staff. Aimed among other things towards easing Jordan's integration into the Eastern Command, these resolutions did not achieve their aims owing to Jordan's uncompromising stand. The fidai activity from Syria was in any case under the supervision of the regime, whereas from Lebanon the organizations agreed, under pressure, to suspend their actions.[25]

The Fatah leaders reacted with unprecedented vigour against all such attempts to subordinate their activities to the Arab strategy, especially when the resolutions were accompanied by Egyptian and Syrian steps to improve relations with Jordan without requiring Jordan to change its policy on fidaiyyun freedom of action from its territory. Until the outbreak of the War the organizations continued to attack attempts to draw closer to Jordan, demanding that Jordan undertake "the return of the organizations [to its territory]".[26]

SYRIA: ASAD'S POLICY

A Fatah leader described Syria's relations with the PR as "a sort of Catholic marriage – although there are differences of opinion between the couple, they must live together forever". The PR saw in Syria "a strategic base for which there is no substitute". Their complicated relationship was one of both alliance and struggle. Asad reiterated Fatah's slogan that "Syria is the lung through which Palestinian activity breathes", adding that "she will continue to be so".[27]

There are a number of reasons for the increasing importance of Syria to the PR. First, following the liquidation of the fidaiyyun bases in Jordan (July 1971), Syria and Lebanon remained the only "bases for support" (*qawa'id irtikaz*). The organizations realized that the liquidation of one of the two meant they would "be under the total influence of the regime in the other base", subject to its demands. Thus they had to maintain freedom of movement within Syria and Lebanon, and between the two. Syria, in addition to being a logistical rear and operational base for their activity, also became a "shelter" for the Fatah and PLA forces evacuated from Jordan. During the first half of 1972 there were in Syria (apart from three Sa'iqa battalions) most of the Fatah regular and semi-regular forces (including the Karama and Yarmuk brigades), as well as fidaiyyun units, Fatah headquarters, the training and administrative network, Syrian PLA units (Hittin Brigade) and Iraqi PLA units (Qadisiyya Brigade), totalling 8,000–9,000.

Second, Syria provided the rear for activity in Lebanon; the latter became both the "safe base" and the "last base in which the PR enjoyed relative freedom of movement". A number of factors contributed to this situation: the refugee camps became an extra-territorial area for the organizations; they were "a secure and stable" source for mobilizing manpower and for establishing the organizations in Lebanon; South Lebanon (especially "Fatah-land") and the Lebanese coast were more convenient than the Syrian border for launching activities against Israel (including via the sea) and for contact with the Israeli Arabs, the West Bank and the Gaza Strip. Furthermore, the weakness of the regime, and the existence of a sympathetic "left bloc" as well as of the "communal balance" in Lebanon assisted their consolidation. The organiza-tions, as in Jordan, had a militia and clandestine organizations in the cities, especially Beirut. Against the background of fidai actions from the border and Israeli reprisals, clashes began between the fidaiyyun and the Lebanese army which reached a climax in May 1973. This contributed to the civil war of 1975. The organizations lived under constant fear of an attack by the regime similar to the September 1970 crisis in Jordan. President Franjiyya complained that there were "two authorities, the Lebanese and the Palestinian" in his country, creating a problem of "dual sovereignty", and feared the organizations would drag Lebanon into a battle with Israel. Extremist Christians even spoke of the "division of Lebanon". Abu Iyad averred in May 1976 that "the road to Filastin passes via Junya ... in order to avoid the division" of Lebanon.

Given the decisive Syrian influence on Lebanese politics, the organizations felt dependent on Syrian backing for their activities both in Lebanon and against Israel from Lebanon. Indeed, during the crises between the organizations and the authorities, Asad promised Arafat that "we are with you, beginning with political pressure, including closure of the border [with Lebanon], and ending with fighting alongside you".[28]

A third reason for Syria's importance was common opposition to a political solution. The PLO Planning Centre (PCR) emphasized (January 1973) that "causing the political solution to fail as a tactical aim calls for the Resistance to deepen its ties with the forces rejecting the [political] solution". The PCR recommended, among other things, "strengthening Syria's tendency toward war and acting to reduce Saudi Arabia's negative influence on the situation in Syria". Syria and the PLO both opposed a possible separate or partial agreement on the Egyptian front; indeed, during 1972 there were signs of a coordination of stands between Fatah/PLO and Syria, with Asad's participation, and also between Fatah and Sa'iqa. Following the May 1973 crisis in Lebanon Fatah claimed that "the pan-Arab [*qawmi*] and the national [*watani*] character of the Syrian regime ... ensures preservation of close ties between Syria and the PR. Syria is the chief active partner in the Arab struggle against the Zionist enemy."[29]

Asad's Strategy Regarding the Conflict

Asad's regime is the most stable, consolidated and long-lasting of the Syrian regimes since the first revolution by Husni al-Za'im (30 March 1949). It has notably narrowed the gap between declared policies and deeds which had characterized the Ba'th regime since February 1963. Asad achieved this through tactical flexibility in the conflict, in internal politics and in the Arab world. An author close to the regime stated: "If the strategic principles in Asad's thinking are permanent ... his political talent, indeed, lies fully in the tactic he employs, which is distinguished by its great flexibility and influenced by events and developments which match international, regional and local changes." "Asad's way is apparent when he steps towards the brink, which allows him progress towards the fulfilment of his aims." That is to say, he is a past master in brinkmanship. The regime's conception was that "the interim aim of a serious political movement should be capable of realization and should serve the strategy, otherwise it will be romantic and unrealistic". At the same time "one should beware lest in this way the tactics become strategy or its substitute".

It seems that the secret of Asad's success lies in the "balance" which he tried to create between pan-Arab nationalism (*qawmiyya*) and Syrian patriotism (*wataniyya*); he has satisfied strong Syrian aspirations in both directions instead of swaying uncertainly between them. This "balance" was also expressed pragmatically in implementing Ba'th doctrine internally and in the inter-Arab arena, to the point of distancing himself from Ba'th doctrine itself. Having experienced the Ba'th's internal struggles from February 1963, Asad concluded that the Ba'th doctrine could not be implemented in existing Arab and internal Syrian conditions. The attempt to do so by using "narrow socialistic slogans" created a long-term stalemate in Syrian political life, caused struggles and internal instability and was liable to "burn the bridges between Syria and every other Arab state". Asad described his regime as a "rectification movement" (*tas-hih*). His regime has been marked by a transition from "party rule" to a personality cult of the "leader"; Asad has held the highest posts: president, supreme commander of the army and secretary-general of the Ba'th party. He has also tried to give his regime a "democratic" image in order to blur its sectarian (Alawite) and military character. In short, Asad has tried "to be a socialist without resorting to socialist dogmatism", "to be democratic without his personal rule being pulled from under his feet".[30]

Asad tried to realize these principles in his conflict with the Jadid wing. His strategic aim did not differ from that of his predecessor, namely, "the liberation of Filastin and the Arab occupied territories and the establishment of a single Arab state". This aim was to be realized in three stages: "the complete liberation of the territories occupied in June 1967, liquidation of the Zionist entity [in Israel] and establishment of a progressive, secular, democratic Palestinian state on her ruins and the realization of Arab unity". This entailed the "restoration of the full rights of the Palestinian people, above all its right to self-determination, and realization of total sovereignty on all of its national land".

Unlike the previous regime, Asad adopted Nasir's concept of stages and the resolutions of the Khartoum summit. The distinction between the stage of "liberation of the occupied territories" and that of "the liberation of Filastin" gave Syria flexibility and opened a door for a settlement in stages, provided it did not go against the strategic goal. For Asad "Israel's withdrawal from Sinai and the Golan will only settle the problem of the June '67 aggression, but the essence of the problem remains – the Palestinian people; therefore we shall continue to fight alongside them whether Israel withdraws from the Golan or not". "There is no difference between the Golan, Sinai or the West Bank." Syria was against any partial or separate settlement with Israel on any of the three fronts. "We have no hope in political action; the basic and concrete solution lies in military action."[31]

The principles of Syrian policy were, first, the *"armed struggle"* as the only way of settling the conflict. This became the essence of Syrian Ba'th ideology and the regime's *raison d'être*. The slogan "the popular liberation war" was pushed aside. The regime presented "the armed struggle as the strategic point of departure for the strategy of action in the areas of internal, including economic, Arab and international policy". The existing stage of the conflict was characterized as "the stage of national liberation". Asad followed Nasir's view that victory in the war required "mobilizing all the states and resources of the Arab nation ... to prepare [their] military and economic strength which will be capable of deciding the struggle in the best way for us".[32]

The second Syrian principle was *political action as a supportive factor*. Asad did not rule out "political action", as distinct from a "political solution", which he totally rejected. Already in March 1971 he declared his support for Sadat's political activity, arguing that "political activity is an important aspect in the confrontation with Israel, its aim being the isolation of Israel in the international arena in order to facilitate the activation of the military option". At the same time he stressed that "we have no hope in political activity" and that one should regard it "in the right proportion". Syria claimed that it was behind Resolution 242 in an interpretation congruent with its own. The defence minister, Mustafa Tlas, maintained that regarding 242 "the Syrian position following 16.11.70 is no longer as in the past an uncompromising stand which rejects the resolution for the sake of rejection alone". Asad's rejection of 242 was conditional "since it does not include two essential requirements, recognition of the rights of the Palestinian people to return to its homeland and total and unconditional Israeli withdrawal from all the occupied Arab territories". In other words, for Asad the "interpretation" of the resolution and its meaning were most important.[33]

Third, Syria stressed *the Arab arena*. Asad's pan-Arab policy was that "all differences of opinion between the Arab states should be secondary ... confrontation with the enemy calls for broad Arab action". Contrary to the previous regime, he acted "to improve the atmosphere between Syria and the other Arab states as an essential prerequisite for the campaign", and "without taking into account the nature of their internal regimes". Syria's relations with the Arab states, especially Egypt and Jordan, "were based on the extent of their contribution to the campaign". He viewed Arab unity "as a revolutionary dream which is not realistic", and strove instead to achieve "Arab solidarity". Since the "armed struggle" was the top priority, "Arab solidarity should be put before the struggle for the realization of socialism". This is the background to Syria's joining the Federation of Arab Republics, its military alliance with Egypt and its attempts to improve relations with Jordan.[34]

The Regime's Position Regarding the Palestinian Entity

The Syrian approach to the question of the Palestinian Entity was territorial-nationalist. This expressed Syria's concept of the close link between "the 1967 problem" and "the 1948 problem". Its position on the Palestinian Entity was integral to its position on the conflict and rested on the following principles.

1. *Filastin as part of the "Syrian region".* Asad stated that "Filastin is not only a part of the Arab homeland", but "is also the basic part of southern Syria" and "part of the Syrian state". Hence, the "liberation" of Filastin was integral to the "liberation" of Syrian territory. Asad thought in terms of "the Syrian region" or "greater Syria" encompassing Syria, Jordan, Lebanon and Filastin in one political framework centred on Damascus. Within this framework one could solve the problem of the economic viability of a "Palestinian state", including the refugee problem, and also the differences between the PLO and Jordan, while maintaining the regime in Jordan. Asad saw in this "region" a single defence unit against either Israel or Iraq under the rule of the Ba'th. This unit would also guarantee the security of the southern and eastern flanks; Lebanon was considered part of Syria's defence belt in the west and Jordan in the south, since "it is difficult to distinguish between Lebanon's security, in the widest sense [of the term], and Syria's security". In 1976 Fatah (and the other organizations) described the Syrian invasion of Lebanon as "the fulfilment of the Syrian regime's dream to control Lebanon, Jordan and part of Filastin and to establish a confederation". Regarding the conflict, Damascus in this Syrian perception is seen as "a centre of power" of radical nationalism, as against the political and military strength of Egypt.[35]

2. *The place of the Palestinian issue.* As far as Syria was concerned, "the Arab liberation movement would remain during this period largely Palestinian in its content. Its primary interest is the

struggle against Zionism. The outcome of this struggle is the key to the political and social liberation of the entire area and to unity, freedom and socialism." In other words, the struggle was the national and pan-Arab goal of the regime and would bring about the fulfilment of the Ba'th slogans. Asad declared that "the Palestinian issue is our problem, and the Palestinian people is part of our people". Therefore "the Palestinian issue is not the problem of the Palestinians alone, it is an Arab problem, and first and foremost a Syrian problem". In this sphere "there is no difference between a Syrian citizen and a Filastin citizen". Against this background the regime demanded "true cooperation between it and the Palestinian Resistance in determining decisive and fateful stands". Syria maintained that "a Palestinian patriot must be pro-Syria", and argued that "the PLO is no more a representative of Filastin than we are". This Syrian outlook clashed with one of the fundamental principles of the organizations, and of Fatah in particular – "independent Palestinian decision making [and action] and resistance to all attempts at influence or imposition [of decisions]". The most extreme expression of these opposing positions was Syria's invasion of Lebanon in 1976. No wonder, therefore, that relations between Syria and the PLO were tense, unlike those between the PLO and Egypt.[36]

3. *The future of the "Palestinian territories"*. During this period the regime rejected any discussion over the future of the "Palestinian territories" following their "liberation", maintaining that any debate on such matters at present would be based "on the possibility of a political solution and the possibility of the Palestinians joining in such a solution". "If it is possible for the Arabs to realize a military victory over Israel and to regain the Palestinian territory – then the slogans [being proclaimed now] will become meaningless ... [therefore] one should not regard Palestinian-Entity slogans as sacred in themselves." "One should debate and decide the political and constitutional future of the Palestinian territories after [the withdrawal or liberation] and within an Arab framework alone."[37]

The regime's dilemma over the Jordanian–Palestinian issue. The regime faced a dilemma in its policy towards Jordan. On the one hand, after the abortive invasion of Jordan (September 1970) they were determined not only to avoid a similar move but to improve relations with Jordan in order to mobilize it for "the campaign" and to secure Syria's southern flank against an Israeli outflanking via north Jordan. Asad was thus more interested in establishing an Eastern Front than Sadat; he therefore emphasized the need for cooperation between Jordan and the PLO. On the other hand, improving relations with Jordan without any change in Jordan's stand towards fidai activity meant favouring the regime at the expense of the PR. Asad, who was free of the Black September complex, tried to persuade the organizations to free themselves too, claiming that the needs of "the campaign" required improved relations with Jordan. He held that "responsibility for the events of September 1970 is divided between King Husayn, the PR and the Arab states". Asad thought that Jordan must not be pushed towards a separate agreement with Israel. At the same time it was necessary to prevent exploitation (by Israel) of PLO–Jordan enmity in order to influence the West Bank leaders to accept self-rule; or to put pressure on Jordan to accept the Allon plan; or to advance the proposition of a "substitute homeland" (i.e., a Palestinian state on the East Bank).[38] The position of the Syrian regime in this controversy went through a number of stages.

From November 1970 to late 1971, the regime avoided military pressure on Jordan, except for allowing minor raids against Jordan from Syrian territory. Until 13 July 1971 Syrian activity was concentrated on abortive attempts to mediate between Jordan and the PLO. However, Syria reacted to the repression of fidaiyyun activity in Jordan on 13 July 1971 by closing its border with Jordan on 25 July 1971. Following a further unsuccessful attempt at mediation, Syria broke off relations with Jordan (12 August 1971). The regime made the "return of the organizations to act against Israel from the Jordanian arena" a condition for the renewal of relations. At the same time the regime criticized the PLO/Fatah on two counts. The first was that the PLO/Fatah "makes the question of who represents the Palestinian people the major problem, rather than the question of forcing Jordan to agree to the return of the fidaiyyun…. This means concentrating the struggle around the question of who will sit with the enemy at the negotiating table." Second, it criticized the way the PR handled its relations with the Jordanian regime, blaming the PR for being "shortsighted" and for "its tribalism, demagogy and improvisation". "One [PR] faction supports toppling the [Jordanian] regime without having the means to do so, [while] the other wants to fight it in order to prevent the return of the West Bank to its previous status should the enemy withdraw as a result of a peace settlement." The regime also criticized the slogan "the road to Filastin passes through Amman".[39]

The 1972 stage began with Syria rejecting the UAK plan immediately after it was announced. Generally, Syria's reaction was moderate. (1) "Should Husayn's plan be executed it will officially exclude Jordan from the Arab struggle against Israel." "The West Bank cannot be the Filastin region, since it is only part of the Palestinian land and not the entire land." The plan's "aim is to divide the internal front of the Palestinian people and to engage it in a struggle about marginal and deferred questions instead of concentrating on the struggle against the occupation." (2) The plan "in fact was meant to deprive the PR of the absolute right to represent the will of the Palestinian people and to deprive the PLO of the right to embody the Palestinian personality and the Palestinian Entity, but this does not oblige part of the revolutionary leadership to behave as though they were a party competing with the king's party" over control of the West Bank and the Gaza Strip. "The question of the Entity and of the regime to be established [in the territories] should be debated [only] after the liberation." (3) "Palestinian effort should be concentrated on decisive and continued rejection of any formula aimed at a peaceful solution, and on continuing the strategy of armed struggle."[40]

The 1973 stage saw changes in policy. On 1 December 1972 Syria decided to reopen its border with Jordan. After Egypt's and Syria's decision to go to war, Syria had concluded that keeping the border closed did not constitute a means of pressuring Jordan. At the same time Syria (and Egypt) saw a possible change in Jordan's position on the Eastern Front. In talks at the beginning of 1973, Asad presented a number of conditions for renewing cooperation: opposition to any partial or separate solution with Israel; Jordan would have to join a United Arab Command of the armies of the confrontation states, whose commander-in-chief (clearly Egyptian) would have full authority over these armies; Jordan would allow fidai activity in and from its territory according to a plan to be laid down by the commander-in-chief of the UAC (this meant Jordanian readiness to accept the compromise confirmed by the ADC in January 1973). Asad was prepared to view Husayn's plan as an internal Jordanian issue, but to realize it Jordan would have to reach an agreement with the Palestinians. It therefore seems that Syria was prepared to ignore Husayn's plan in exchange for Jordanian readiness to cooperate militarily against Israel.

Yet Jordan, as mentioned, remained steadfastly opposed to the Eastern Front. At the same time Husayn accepted Syria's demand to prevent Israel from outflanking the Syrian front via north Jordan in time of war. Husayn repeated this promise in the tripartite summit of 10 September 1973 – the only practical result. Relations between Syria and Jordan were renewed, and on 14 September 1973 Syria closed the Fatah broadcasting station in Dar'a as a gesture towards Jordan. Syria's reply to severe criticism from the organizations was that "if the war was to break out, it would justify every step", and that "the struggle between the PR and Jordan is secondary to the campaign" against Israel. To prove that it still supported the PR, Syria pointed out that fidaiyyun actions along the Syrian–Israeli border had escalated. The organizations, especially Fatah, remained sceptical about Husayn but did not want to generate a crisis with Syria.[41]

The composition of the PLO institutions. Asad's regime, like its predecessor, continued trying to influence the PLO's institutions through Sa'iqa. Sa'iqa remained in the coalition leadership of the PLO; but its proposals to change the PLO institutions according to the new regime's concepts were rejected. However, the regime assessed that the existing structure of the PLO met the needs of the Palestinian issue and the Palestinian representation. The regime purged Sa'iqa's leadership to remove Jadid-regime supporters and to nominate its own supporters. On 23 November 1970 the Ba'th leadership decided to appoint Mahmud al-Mu'ayta, of the Jordanian Ba'th, as Sa'iqa's secretary-general. In June 1971 further purges occurred including the arrest of three Sa'iqa leaders in Jordan, Dafi Jami'ani, Yusuf al-Burj and Hasan al-Khatib. The Ba'th leadership in Jordan was accused of maintaining contacts with the Jadid wing, which now operated in Lebanon, and of secret contacts with and financial support from Iraq. It seems they also initiated contacts to cooperate with the Fatah leadership without coordination with Damascus. The regime argued that during the crisis in Jordan the Ba'th leaders there adopted policies opposed to those of the new Ba'th regime. Zuhayr Muhsin, who had served as Sa'iqa's branch secretary-general in Lebanon during 1970–1971, was appointed secretary-general of Sa'iqa.[42]

Sa'iqa now began calling for a *United National Front (UNF).* Sa'iqa distinguished "between the special character of the fidaiyyun resistance which should unite within the framework of a UNF, and the PLO which is the framework of the Entity of all the Palestinian people". The PLO "was set up as the political-entity framework of the Palestinian people, to give prominence to Palestinian feelings of affiliation following their dispersion in various countries and to stress the Palestinian personality as a way of continually keeping the problem alive in the eyes of the world". "According to the PLO Covenant and its Constitution every Palestinian who subscribes to the Covenant naturally becomes a member of the PLO." The PLO as such "keeps a seat in the Arab League, conducts official political talks with Arab and foreign states and signs agreements".

As for the UNF, in Sa'iqa's view it did not differ in content from the "coherent national front" except for the term "united". The UNF would be set up outside "the framework and complications of the PLO, its Covenant and Constitution", from among the fidai organizations on the basis of "the widening of the common denominator between them up to the very limit". The fidai organizations "will unite in one front, and as such will participate together with the trade unions and the independent nationalist individuals in the PLO leadership". In fact the UNF would represent "the supreme leadership of the Palestinian people". Sa'iqa was aware that its plan would not be accepted by the PNC, but it held that "development of the fidai organizations' participation in the leadership of the PLO institutions will bring about an overlapping between the [political] Entity and the Revolution, or a narrowing of the gap between them until the realization of a true organizational unity". Hence, and considering the concept of the "armed struggle", Syria stressed that the PR "expressed the will of the Palestinian people" more than the PLO as a political-entity framework, claiming that the PR "had become a complete national Palestinian movement [*mutakamila*] and a national political leadership of the entire Palestinian people".[43]

These principles facilitated Sa'iqa's participation, as it had in the earlier period, in every kind of coalition in the PLO leadership, as long as it could influence the decisions taken. At the same time, it criticized Fatah's and the other organizations' efforts to further national unity, doubting the possibility of its realization. It characterized the debate on national unity in the PPC and in the 10th PNC as a "public auction". Sa'iqa maintained that the PR "has no need for the researches of institutes and planning centres to teach it how to set up a United National Front". Sa'iqa rejected the proposal to enlarge the PNC with "talented independents", fearing that this would strengthen Fatah in the PNC.

In the plan it presented to the 11th PNC Sa'iqa called for setting up a "comprehensive national front" (*shamila*). It demanded, among other things, formation of "a clear organizational structure for the PLO and its internal constitution, the realization of national unity within the framework of the PLO's institutions, absorption of all the organized sectors of the Palestinian people and strengthening of the PLA as the primary force for liberation". Fatah rejected these proposals. The Syrian Ba'th leadership's mood was expressed (June 1972) by Hanna Bat-hish, secretary-general of Sa'iqa in Lebanon, who concluded that in view of the inability to realize "national unity" there were two ways open to the PR leadership: "a decision on true national unity based on a united national programme, or to resign from its position so that a new leadership will take its place, with new blood, who will possibly be able to realize unity". Bat-hish called for "a radical change in the leadership of the factions of the Resistance". His meaning was clear to the Fatah leaders. A strong call for a change in the PLO leadership was also voiced following the Syrian invasion of Lebanon in 1976, but there was no possibility of achieving it.[44]

Another point of contention was *a "Palestinian state" and a Palestinian government-in-exile (PGE).* The regime continued to oppose a Palestinian state in the West Bank and Gaza in the context of a political solution with Israel. However, they stressed that "there is nothing to prevent the setting up of a state upon part of the liberated Palestinian land". The regime, like its predecessor, advocated "a democratic Palestinian state which will be established on all Filastin territory". The regime joined the organizations' campaign against collaborators with the IMG in the occupied territories. The West Bank municipal elections (March 1972) were described as "part of Jordanian–Israeli planning in order to create an authority which will claim to represent the Palestinian people". Sa'iqa called, early in 1973, for the establishment of secret trade unions in the West Bank and Gaza which would oppose the IMG.[45]

As early as March 1972, the regime objected to the idea of a PGE when it was raised among the organizations as a response to Husayn's plan. After Sadat publicly adumbrated the idea in September 1972, the Syrian regime reacted even more strongly, insisting that the PLO was the representative of the Palestinians. Sa'iqa rejected the proposal on the following grounds: (1) The PLO "fully meets the aim of expressing the Palestinian Entity and the Palestinian personality." "It is recognized by all the Arab states, except Saudi Arabia, as well as by a large number of friendly states." Setting up a PGE required "recognition by a sufficient number of states. These states will demand, as a condition [for recognition], definition of the borders of the state for which the PGE will be set up." Furthermore, "who will recognize her if we say that it will include all of Filastin?" (2) The declaration of a PGE "means granting priority to diplomatic activity rather than to military activity". (3) Within the PLO "all the national forces are in an alliance and are representing all the groups of the Palestinian people". A PGE will "eventually become a name without content similar to the All-Filastin Government set up in 1949".[46]

The regime's support for the PR. This period witnessed continuous tension between the two allies. Each party had high expectations of the other, and particularly the organizations of Syria. Their strategies over the conflict were almost identical, but for this reason each party was sensitive about the other's moves. Abu Iyad aptly described (December 1975) the relationship as one between a "state" and a "revolution". "For us, as a revolution, the decisive factors are different from those of Syria the state." The relations between the two therefore developed along two axes: on the one hand "the strategic alliance", and on the other "the struggle" in the tactical sphere. In 1972 the organizations became disappointed with Asad "since his considerations have become regional and personal". Asad's dilemma regarding the PR was in essence no different from that of the Jadid regime; it worsened because of his open policy in the Arab arena and the preparations for war. The regime saw fidai activity as an expression of "armed struggle", yet granting freedom of action to fidai activity clashed with Syria's national security interests, particularly since such activity led to Israeli reprisals.

In giving political support, the regime described the PR as "representing both the Palestinian personality and the Arab rejection of the Zionist entity", as "a part of the Arab liberation movement" and as "a historical national need". At the same time Asad stressed that "one should not put the burden of liberating the occupied territories on the PR alone; that is the task of the regular forces". He held that the PR should adjust its activity to Syrian strategy. When the organizations intensified their criticism of the Egyptian–Syrian contacts with Jordan (as of late 1972) and of the decisions on coordination of the organizations' activities with the UAC, the regime decided to reorganize its information system directed at the Palestinians. As of 1 January 1973 broadcasts of "The Voice of Filastin from Damascus", under the direct control of the broadcasting authority, were placed under the National Fidai Action Bureau headed by Sami al-Attari, who was a member of the Ba'th National Command, secretary of Sa'iqa's General Command and secretary of the EC PLO. A "central information committee" was appointed to direct this broadcast daily, headed by the Chairman of Regional Command of the United Palestine Organization. The reorganization was justified by "the need to organize our masses, on the basis of the correct theoretical starting points while giving attention to the needs of our masses in the occupied land".[47]

As for military aid, Asad's regime continued the tradition of giving various kinds of military aid to the organizations, particularly Fatah and those with a pro-regime orientation. It had severed relations with the PFLP, while those with the PDFLP and the PFLP–GC were limited. The acid test of the regime's support was the extent to which it allowed an organization freedom of action from the Syrian border, and the logistic-operational support it gave for activity against Israel in and from Lebanon. The regime's dilemma was further complicated when Israel held Syria responsible, though indirectly, for fidai actions against Israeli targets outside the region, whose perpetrators left from Syria or were trained there (e.g., the murder of the Israeli athletes in Munich, 5 September 1972), and also when, during 1973, there was a need to suspend fidai activity from both the Syrian and Lebanese borders. The regime's policy towards fidai actions from its territory went through the following stages.

1. *January–December 1971.* Activity from all the borders was reduced as of July 1971. During January–March 1971 there were 18–20 actions from the Syrian border per month. From April to mid-July 47 actions took place (May – 16, June – 14) out of a total of 116 from Jordan, Syria and Lebanon. From mid-July to the end of 1971 only 35 actions were carried out (August – 2, September – 10, October – 9, November – 12, December – 2), out of a total of 53 from Lebanon, Syria and Jordan. The regime prohibited an increase in activity. During this period a number of joint actions – by Fatah, PDFLP and PFLP–GC, or by PFLP–GC and PDFLP – were carried out.

2. *January–March 1972.* Following IDF reprisals against fidaiyyun bases in south Lebanon (as a result of increased activity from there in December 1971), the regime permitted an escalation. There were 51 actions in January–February 1972, and 13 more mainly in the first half of March as a direct reaction to IDF reprisals in Syria and south Lebanon (25–28 February 1972).

3. *April–August 1972.* With activity from the Lebanese border suspended as of February 1972, Syria became the only staging

ground; yet the regime kept the number of actions limited. In all about 40 were carried out from the Syrian border (compared with none from Jordan and few from Lebanon) (April – 9, May – 6, June – 8, July – 7, August – 10). The PDFLP and PFLP–GC participated.

4. *September 1972–January 1973.* During this period, the IDF struck deep in Syrian territory after fidai actions on the border and outside the region (e.g., Munich, 5 September 1972). The Syrians responded to the IDF operation on 8 September 1972 by intensifying their activity on the border, and the number of actions reached about 25 (October – 6, November – 7, December – 5, January – 7). Syrian soldiers and members of Fatah and other organizations (except the PFLP) participated. Israel reacted on 3 October 1972 by attacking Tal-Kalah, a fidaiyyun camp; on 15 October 1972 it attacked by air fidaiyyun bases in Syria and Lebanon, and again on 30 October 1972 fidaiyyun targets near Damascus. Following further fidai actions on the Golan Heights, Israel's air force attacked Syrian army targets on 9 November 1972, and also on 21 November 1972 when seven Syrian planes were shot down; on 25 November 1972 the Syrians reacted with artillery fire on the Golan Heights. On 8 January 1973 Israel's air force attacked military and civilian/economic targets deep in Syria in the areas of Ladaqiyya and Tartus, in addition to fidaiyyun targets. Some 400 Syrian civilians and army personnel were hit, as well as anti-aircraft batteries, an army camp near Ladaqiyya and a radar post deep in Syria. The Syrians presented this as a "war of attrition".

5. *February–6 October 1973.* The number of actions averaged only one to two per month, similar to the situation on the Lebanese border. Abu Iyad admitted (January 1973) that "friendly states ask us to cease our fighting from south Lebanon, and even in Syria we are required to coordinate with the authorities and to consider its circumstances ... and we are forced to stop [our] actions".[48]

The period also saw criticism and limitations placed upon the PR. Among the "progressive-nationalist" Arab regimes only a centralized one like Asad's, whose strategic aims in the conflict were almost identical to those of the organizations, could permit itself to criticize bitterly the PR, to restrict its activities in Syria (and Lebanon) and eventually to conduct a war against it in 1976 in Lebanon. The regime did not tolerate criticism from the organizations, treating them as an extension of itself. As early as January 1971 the new regime had warned the organizations not to attack its policy. "The leadership of fidai activity should not ... repeat its mistake when it attacked Nasir and Egypt when they agreed to the

Rogers initiative." "The PR should clearly distinguish between the present and future aims of fidai activity and those of Arab activity." The murder of Tall was bitterly criticized as an "adventurist step". And Fatah's "actions abroad" were a source of concern to the regime, particularly in view of Israel's retaliations against Syria. Such activity, the regime claimed, "does not achieve any objective and is not part of the armed struggle". In early 1973 the regime concluded that Fatah should cease this mode of action. From 18 March to 1 April 1973 Damascus radio, in its Sawt Filastin corner, broadcast about nine commentaries on this topic. They called on the organizations "to abstain from marginal wars" and "from carrying out futile suicidal acts". "What is important is not the headlines but the actual results of the actions abroad"; "such considerations demand not only an end to such actions but, where they are carried out, to avoid declaring responsibility at all." In their efforts to coordinate fidai activity Syria admonished the PR (April 1973) to beware "lest they undergo in Lebanon what had happened to them in September 1970".[49]

Asad, who as defence minister signed the May 1969 decree limiting fidaiyyun activities in Syria, as president implemented it more strictly than had the previous regime. In line with this, in late May 1971 the authorities confiscated some BTR armoured troop carriers which had arrived at Ladaqiyya for Fatah's Yarmuk Brigade, then deployed in the Dar'a area. Fatah had not obtained permission to bring in this equipment, and the regime further suspected that Fatah wanted to strengthen its regular units in competition with the PLA – possibly leading to Fatah–PLA clashes in Syria. Some of the BTR carriers were released after the Jordanian anti-fidaiyyun campaign in July 1971 and some more after the later crisis with the Lebanese authorities.

Following the cessation of fidai activity in Jordan the regime stressed once more to the organizations its rules concerning actions from the Syrian border. Following the border tension from September 1972 to January 1973, the regime ordered the organizations to transfer their bases to a point 15 kilometres away from the border and to avoid movement of fidaiyyun in uniform or bearing arms in these areas. Even during the period under review Fatah tried to overlook these limitations, to deny any tension between the two sides and to proclaim "Syria's noble stand regarding the PR generally and fidai activity in particular".[50]

JORDAN

This period saw the restoration of "stability, security and the sovereignty of law and order" to Jordan. Since the mid-1950s the Hashemite regime had not enjoyed such a period of stability as that from 1972 to the present day. In this sense the consequences of the Six Day War were felt only from early 1972. The leadership of the regime remained united and decisive; Tall's assassination did not cause internal turmoil or a change in policy. The king continued to rely on the army, the security and intelligence services, the Bedouin and the Transjordanian families. Zayd Bin Shakir was appointed chief-of-staff on 4 March 1972 and became the king's right-hand man.

As a result of the crisis, the Jordanian consciousness of the Transjordanian population was strengthened, as was their support for the regime's steps to suppress any hostile Palestinian action or any strengthening of the Palestinian element of the population. Husayn's self-confidence and ability to withstand Arab pressures were evident. Jordan's position in the Arab world was one of splendid isolation, with increased freedom of manoeuvre regarding the conflict.

The leadership pondered the future of the West Bank. There were two points of view, both relating to the preservation of the kingdom. One view, which developed within a group headed by Crown Prince Hasan, argued for Transjordanian "isolation" from the West Bank; they thought it best for Jordan to divest itself of the Palestinian issue and accept the loss of the West Bank. Hasan argued that in 1967 Jordan did not lose any of its own territory since the West Bank belonged to the Palestinians. This hard-line group included Ahmad Tarawna, Salah Abu Zayd, Mraywud al-Tall (the brother of Wasfi al-Tall), Riyad al-Muflih and Abd al-Wahab al-Majali; they enjoyed the support of the Queen Mother Zayn and Sharif Nasir. They believed that any Palestinian state set up on the West Bank would inevitably be connected with and influenced by Jordan; this would also help improve Jordan's relations with the Palestinians and the Arab states. Mraywud al-Tall expressed this view (January 1972) when he said that "we like the way we are – a Transjordanian state". He saw "the setting up of a Palestinian Entity or state as an historical necessity". Hasan later asserted that a Palestinian state on the West Bank, even under PLO leadership, was the lesser of the two evils, since the Palestinians would migrate from the East to the West Bank and thus the traditional friction between the Transjordanians and the Palestinians would lessen. The new state would direct its attention towards Israel. The second view was held by the king together with such Transjordanian personalities as Ahmad al-Lawzi and the Talhuni–Rifa'i group. They considered that without the West Bank, Jordan would lose its special position in the Arab world. Husayn argued that Jordan could not abandon the Palestinian issue "which had become an integral part of her and which, for Jordan, is a question of life or death". Husayn apparently believed that, through struggling to retain the West Bank, he would divert debate away from the subject of the existence of the Hashemite regime itself – which would not be the case if he gave up the West Bank. So long as Israel saw him as part of any future West Bank negotiations, he would gain bargaining power and freedom of manoeuvre. Therefore Husayn persisted in his efforts to recover the West Bank albeit in a different political framework, even though he was aware of West Bank political developments which were not in his favour.[51]

Husayn's Strategy towards the Conflict

Apart from the internal stability of his kingdom, Husayn's attitude to the conflict was also influenced by the accession of new rulers in Egypt and Syria and their ideas on the conflict in general and the Palestinian Entity in particular. First of all, Husayn was freed from his commitments to Nasir concerning the pan-Arab position approved at the Khartoum summit. After the liquidation of fidai activity in Jordan, he was released from the need to prove his nationalism in the Arab arena. There was deep distrust between Sadat and Husayn; the regime even allowed itself to reciprocate Egyptian propaganda with similar intensity. Husayn even dared claim that the Khartoum "Nos" had weakened the Arab position. Second, Sadat's initiative and his readiness to reach a "peace agreement" with Israel meant Husayn, legitimately, could go even further than he did in Nasir's time in expressing his own readiness for a peace agreement. Husayn feared a partial or separate agreement on the Egyptian front following US activity in this direction; Jordan wanted to link any settlement between itself and Israel with one between Egypt and Israel so as not to be in a weak bargaining position towards Israel.

Third, Husayn was very conscious that Jordan's claim to represent the Palestinians was losing legitimacy. With the intensified Jordan–PLO struggle over representation and its development into an Arab problem, Husayn concluded that his regime should enhance its claims to representation, including strengthening ties with the traditional West Bank and, if possible, Gaza Strip leadership.

Finally, despite Husayn's moderation regarding the conflict, he was very much aware of his historic mission as representative of the Hashemite dynasty with its ties to the Palestinian issue. Husayn is an Arab nationalist, but in his own way; hence his commitment to the return of Jerusalem. He did not want to go down in history as a "traitor" to the foremost problem both of his regime and of the Arab world. He reiterated his claim that "the problem of Filastin for this country is a problem of life or death and a problem of to be or not to be".[52]

The tenets of Husayn's strategy were as follows.

Rejection of the military option. During this period Husayn openly rejected war as a solution. He believed it would result in "a catastrophe and further loss of lands"; "it is not my right to drag someone else into war and not anyone's [right] to drag us into one." Following Jordanian contacts during inter-Arab meetings (late 1972–early 1973) on establishing the UAC and apparently through intelligence information, Husayn, towards late April and early May 1973, concluded that "the Arab nation [Egypt and Syria] is preparing for a new war". "This will be a premature war. ... As long as there are no data to prove that indeed the chances of victory over Israel are two to one, and as long as our faith in them [Egypt], which we lost through their fault, is not revived, we will not naively participate in the war ... the inevitable outcome of which will be catastrophic."[53]

The elements of the political solution. During this period Husayn's activities aimed at a settlement with Israel were the fruit of independent initiative, without coordination with Egypt or Syria and against the policy acceptable to them. He had talks with the US and secret talks with Israeli leaders (among others, meetings – with Golda Meir – in autumn 1971 and in summer 1972) or through emissaries (e.g., Anwar Nusayba, late 1971–early 1972). In contrast to the previous period he declared (3 February 1973) before departing to the US that "I shall not speak officially in the name of any Arab leader; officially I shall speak for myself, in the name of Jordan and in the name of the family in occupied Filastin" (i.e., the West Bank Palestinians). Indeed, in the US he presented details of a proposed agreement with Israel. In principle he was ready to sign a peace treaty with Israel with all that it entailed; his conception as to the components was as follows.

First of all, he saw Resolution 242 as the key. He believed it guaranteed Jordan "the right to regain the West Bank as part of its land" – thus "Jordan is a responsible party to the negotiations regarding the West Bank"; and it also guaranteed the integration of "the problem of the people and the problem of the land in the direction of a comprehensive solution". The basis for a settlement must be the return of the West Bank to Jordanian sovereignty – while being prepared for small and mutual border adjustments.

As for Jerusalem, any solution must be based on the "return of Jordanian sovereignty to the Arab quarters of the city including the holy Moslem places". Husayn was prepared to discuss Jordanian–Israeli cooperation in administering the city – with West Jerusalem as capital of Israel and East Jerusalem as capital of the Filastin Region. It seems that he was prepared, within some kind of compromise, to grant Israel sovereignty over the Jewish holy places and some part of the Old City; he spoke of Jerusalem being turned into "an open city". The Jerusalem problem had great symbolic and religious importance for him.

Husayn preferred a comprehensive territorial solution to the conflict (since the Palestinian national problem did not exist as far as he was concerned). But he did not reject a separate settlement between Jordan and Israel, even before one with Egypt, if his territorial demands were met and the problem of Jerusalem resolved. He did not reject the principle of direct, official negotiations with Israel, provided that there were *prior* agreement over the principles of the settlement and that Israel's territorial concessions, and those over Jerusalem, were clearly known *in advance*. His secret contacts with Israel were aimed, among other things, at exploring such concessions. To the Israelis he said that after such prior agreement on principles had been reached, he would be ready to start negotiations on the ways to implement it including reciprocal territorial changes. In his talk with Golda Meir (1972), Husayn emphasized his difficulties in making any change in his basic attitudes, in order to meet Israel's policy demand for "territorial compromise". Husayn was ready for a comprehensive agreement based on total Israeli withdrawal from the West Bank in stages, in the framework of which he was prepared to allow Israeli military outposts along the Jordan River to remain *temporarily*. In return for a total Israeli withdrawal he was prepared to allow, under Jordanian sovereignty, of course, a number of civilian settlements on the West

Bank. In his secret talks with the Israeli leaders he continued to reject the Allon plan or the permanent presence of military outposts along the Jordan River. However, he was prepared to discuss possible demilitarization of part of the West Bank such as those areas near the Jordan River. In the course of 1973 he concluded that, in view of Israel's stand on his conditions, the chances for a separate settlement with that country were slim, and so he began to emphasize a comprehensive solution. Husayn judged, however, that open pursuit of a settlement might impel both Sadat and Asad to improve their relations with him to prevent his reaching a separate agreement. He also sought in this way to demonstrate Jordanian responsibility for the Palestinian issue and to present Jordan to the Muslim world as responsible for the holy places and for Jerusalem. He wanted to present Jordan as a reliable factor for negotiating the settlement, even if the US preferred at the first stage to concentrate on the Egyptian front.[54]

Jordan and the Palestinian Entity

The position on the PR. Events in Jordan during 1968–70 were traumatic for the regime. It held steadfastly to the principles laid down in 1971 concerning fidaiyyun presence and activity in Jordan. Husayn declared (February 1973) that "we are unable ... to agree to turn the clock back, to a hellish situation which ceased and which will never return". He added (May 1973) that "we will never allow the PR to reappear in our country". Husayn succeeded in preventing fidai activity from Jordanian territory, either by clandestine local organizations or fidaiyyun units penetrating Jordan from Syria. From mid-July 1971 to the end of that year only two actions were carried out from the Jordanian border against Israel, in 1972 only eight and in 1973 only two until October. Feeling confident, the regime hardened its policy on the conditions under which organizations in Jordan could act.

The regime continued to permit the PLA's 600-soldier, 423rd Battalion to be based in Khaw, naturally under full JA supervision. In December 1972 the battalion's commander, Nuhad Nusayba, was ordered to withdraw from Jordan a group of Egyptian PLA soldiers (Ayn Jalut) called the Abu Hani Group (*Majmu'at Abu Hani*), because of "doubts about their loyalty" after apparent contact between their head and the Egyptian army (possibly Egyptian intelligence). The group (consisting of 67 soldiers, among them three officers) began to arrive at Dar'a on 16 December 1972.

In Arab Defence Council debates (January 1973), Jordan claimed that allowing fidai activity from its border would only lead to an Israeli attack against Jordan. Therefore it demanded that the fidai activity be within the prospective plan of the commander-in-chief of the armed forces of the confrontation states, that is, within an agreed Arab strategy.

Husayn stressed that the "true PR" is the one "which stems from our people" on both Banks. "It should be directed against the enemy on the occupied land and not against Jordanian towns." The regime was well aware of the fidai organizations' efforts to undermine it and particularly to assassinate the king, the royal family or the regime's leadership. But the few attempts which were made failed, and no opposition group managed to organize itself during this period. The regime also knew of clandestine fidai organizations in Jordan, including those of Fatah, PFLP and PDFLP. But these failed to undermine security, apart from minor attacks. The regime conducted a bitter propaganda campaign against the organizations; among other things the PR was labelled the "Hashashin movement" or "rotting carcass".[55]

The United Arab Kingdom (UAK) plan. On 15 March 1972 Husayn presented, to a gathering of dignitaries in his palace, a new plan for a United Arab Kingdom. It would "convey the country into a new phase of reorganization of the Jordanian–Palestinian home ... which will basically concentrate on liberation". This phase would be based "on absolute adherence to the legitimate rights of the Palestinian people" in accordance "with the pact [in which] we undertook to grant [them] the right to self-determination", "and without in any way harming the rights achieved [al-muktasaba] by every citizen of Palestinian origin in the Jordanian regime or [every citizen] of Jordanian origin in the Palestinian region". Husayn purposely avoided any explicit reference to timing, so as to suggest that the plan was tangible and its implementation near. Later he indirectly clarified that it would be implemented "after the Israeli withdrawal and after the implementation of Resolution 242".

The plan proposed turning the kingdom into a federation between the two Banks, each with local autonomy within the UAK framework. The principles of the plan were: (1) The state would comprise two regions: the Jordanian Region (*Qutr al-Urdun*) consisting of the East Bank, with Amman as its capital; and the Filastin Region (*Qutr Filastin*) consisting of the West Bank and "other Palestinian territories to be liberated and whose inhabitants wish to join it", with Jerusalem as its capital. (2) The king would be the head of the state and of the central executive authority. A central government would be appointed. The legislature would comprise the king and an Assembly (*Majlis al-Umma*) with an equal number of members from both regions. A central judiciary would also be established. The UAK would have one army, with the king as supreme commander. (3) In each region an executive would be established consisting of a governor-general and a government whose members came from the region. The legislature in each region would be in the hands of a People's Assembly (*Majlis al-Sha'b*), which would elect the governor-general. Each region would have its own judiciary.

The plan was worked out, according to the king's guidelines, by a special committee which included Ahmad Tuqan, Ahmad Tarawna, Mudar Badran, Salah Abu Zayd, Adnan Abu Awda, Sa'id al-Tall (brother of Wasfi al-Tall and lecturer in education) and Ibrahim al-Habashna (interior minister). In the days before its announcement the regime conducted an extensive campaign of persuasion. Among other things, it was presented (13 March 1972) to a group of 13 Palestinian personalities, some of them close to the fidai organizations (among them Ibrahim Bakr, Bahjat Abu Gharbiyya, Yahya Hamuda and Daud al-Husayni). In view of the occasion, their immediate reaction was qualified support. The plan was also presented (14 March 1972) to dignitaries in Jordan, to nationalist personalities remote from the leadership such as Nabulsi and to West Bank leaders who were in Jordan or had been invited there for this purpose. Some notables in the West Bank itself were also informed of the plan. The US was informed of it before its announcement and supported it.

For the first time the king himself had undertaken to grant unconditional autonomy to the West Bank. Yet it seems that were the plan to be implemented, he had little intention of going as far as granting real autonomy. In Jordanian public life under the king, members of the government and the legislative institutions have little real importance, and this would hold for the future government of the "Filastin Region".

Some of the king's main reasons for preparing and announcing the plan can be pointed out. First, there was the desire to stop the accelerating detachment, since September 1970, of the West Bank from Jordan. The plan was meant to solve the king's dilemma: how to preserve the "unity of the two Banks", and at the same time prevent endangering the regime if and when the West Bank was returned. The plan was also meant to give West Bank inhabitants a hope of being integrated into Jordan, while at the same time fulfilling their national aspirations, since in the past Husayn's promises had not been treated seriously.

As for the East Bank, the plan was intended to serve as a compromise between the Palestinians, who saw themselves as second-class citizens, and the Transjordanians who were uncertain as to the government's intentions towards the West Bank in view of demands by some Jordanian politicians for separation. The regime strove to demonstrate its determination not to give up the West Bank, while at the same time satisfying those who sought to rid themselves of this burden and to meet the Palestinians' aspirations.

In addition, the regime wanted to block all claims against Jordan as representative of the Palestinians. It re-emphasized that "Filastin is Jordan and Jordan is Filastin". Husayn sought through his plan to prevent any developments in the Arab arena in favour of PLO representation; he feared that Egypt and other Arab states would recognize a separate Palestinian Entity such as a PGE, deliberations on which were then being held among the Fatah leadership. Later (February 1973) Husayn argued that the plan was proposed "in order to abolish the idea of setting up a substitute homeland [*watan badil*] for the Palestinians on the ruins of East Jordan", and to emphasize that when Israel claimed that "there is no Palestinian people", "the problem is that of the right of the Palestinians to Palestinian land and not to any other land". Undoubtedly, the timing of the plan's announcement was connected with the West Bank municipal elections (28 March 1972) and was intended to "obstruct any attempt to change the local leadership in order to establish a self-rule [by Israel]".

Finally, in preparation for his departure in late March 1972 to the US, Husayn tried, through his plan, to pursue a Jordanian–Israeli settlement by inviting the US to pressure Israel to make concessions. From both his direct and indirect contacts with Israel, Husayn concluded that her position on the West Bank was still inflexible, and feared that Egypt would go ahead with a separate and partial settlement. He assessed that the plan would enhance his claim as spokesman of the West Bank Palestinians.[56]

The regime exploited the political momentum following the plan's announcement to expand its conception of "the unity of the two Banks" and bolster up its claims to represent the Palestinians. It reiterated that "the Palestinian identity is in fact anchored in the unity of the two Banks and in the plan for the united kingdom", which "is the path to solving the Palestinian issue". Husayn did not leave any room for doubt that he was referring to the Gaza Strip when he spoke of "other Palestinian territories". In return for favours obtained for the Gaza Strip inhabitants during his visits to Jordan, Gaza Mayor Rashad al-Shawwa declared that the plan "is worthy of consideration and contains good possibilities".[57]

Reactions of Palestinian leaders in Jordan were not "positive" as the regime tried to claim. On 3 April 1972 12 Palestinian personalities (among them seven of the group of 13, and also Sulayman al-Nabulsi, who is not a Palestinian but is identified as such, Ruhi al-Khatib and Rif'at Awda) sent a message to the Palestinian Popular Congress (PPC; which convened on 6 April 1972) condemning the UAK plan "as denying the right of the Palestinian people to self-determination on its land". This was the first time since September 1970 that a Palestinian group in Jordan had made a public declaration against the regime. All this was made known to the authorities, according to one version by Nadim Zaru who attended the meeting but did not sign the message. Fearing that the message would be seen as expressing the reservations of *all* the Palestinians in Jordan towards the plan, the regime conducted a campaign denouncing both the signatories and the message itself. Ruhi al-Khatib was detained for interrogation (8 April 1972); likewise the regime prohibited dozens of Palestinian dignitaries from leaving for the PPC in Cairo. The media called for boycotting the PPC, and warned that participation in it would "mean estrangement from Jordan and disloyalty to her sovereignty".[58]

Reactions to plans for a Palestinian Entity.   After the political storm aroused by the UAK plan, the regime had to withstand further tribulations. Jordan strongly objected to Sadat's proposal for a PGE (28 September 1972), connecting it to "Sadat's aim of arriving at a separate solution" and stressing that "Sadat has no right to speak on behalf of the Palestinians of the East Bank, the West Bank or the Gaza Strip". As for Zayyat's proposal at the Security Council, Jordan saw a number of dangers in it: the granting of political independence to the Palestinians outside the Jordanian framework; an independent state west of the Jordan that would claim sovereignty over the East Bank as well. This could mean a separate settlement between Egypt and Israel involving the negation of 242, the exclusion of Jordan and the rejection of her "responsibility for the West Bank".[59]

In March–April 1965 Bourguiba called on the Arab states to give up their "everything or nothing" policy and to negotiate with Israel on the basis of the Partition Resolution and the establishment of an

Arab–Palestinian state. On 6 July 1973 he went further and proposed a Palestinian state to replace Husayn's regime. He reiterated
Nasir's doubts (pre-June 1967) as to the Hashemite regime's right to
exist in Jordan.

> Jordan's problem can be solved at an Arab summit which will
> discuss the establishment of a Palestinian state. ... Husayn
> should yield to the people's decision under a democratic
> regime which will decide the fate of the state, instead of
> experiencing the fate which befell his grandfather and his
> cousin King Faysal.

Jordan viewed Bourguiba's statements with grave concern, particularly as they followed Zayyat's proposal, and even more so since the
statements had not drawn objections from the Arab countries.
Indeed, on 17 July 1973 Jordan decided to sever diplomatic relations
with Tunisia, an unprecedented step in Jordan's relations with the
Arab states.[60] The period June–July 1973 was a political low point
for the Hashemite regime in everything connected with the Palestinian Entity, its right to represent the Palestinians and its aspiration
to regain the West Bank.

Action Taken by the PLO and the Organizations

The massacre of September 1970 was a traumatic event for the
new "Palestinian national movement". It emphasized the need for
"Palestinian territory" under Palestinian rule, and as a stable and
safe base from which the organizations could wage their struggle
against Israel. They still saw the East Bank as "Palestinian territory"
as much as Jordanian territory, and considered the regime the
source of all their disasters and internal crises in the Arab and
Palestinian arenas.

In this period the organizations began to implement a policy
towards Jordan whose lines were determined during the second half
of 1971. The starting points were: (1) "We must again secure the
fundamental support [*irtikaz*] base in Jordan", in order to turn the
PR "from an Arab problem to an Israeli one". (2) A total rejection
of any compromise or peaceful coexistence with the regime. The
return to Jordan could take place "only by means of guns". In the
final analysis, the struggle between the regime and the organizations over representation became a struggle for the soul of the West
Bank and Gaza Palestinians, with Israel as a third party to that
struggle.[61]

Overthrow of the regime. The organizations now made explicit, public and official decisions regarding the overthrow of the regime as an interim aim, and its replacement by a "democratic national regime". Their dedication to this aim was such that they lost sight of whether it was at all feasible, and whether the results would necessarily be to their advantage (e.g., attitude of the Transjordanian population, the JA, Israel's possible intervention). They admitted that "conditions in the region do not encourage a change of the regime ... but this problem should not deter us from our struggle against it".[62]

The various organizations had somewhat different views. The PDFLP's position was summed up in the 1st General National Congress (October 1971), which called for "a united Palestinian–Jordanian national front" that would "overthrow the reactionary royal regime and establish a democratic national regime". "The interim link, in the events following September, will be to turn the East Bank into an arena for clandestine, armed and mass resistance."[63]

The PFLP's position crystallized at its 3rd Congress (March 1972), which resolved that the PR had two tasks: "the liberation of Filastin and the overthrow of the regime in Jordan", the latter through "revolutionary violence". It called for a "Jordanian Revolutionary Party" and a "Palestinian–Jordanian national front which includes the Jordanian national and revolutionary forces and also the PR forces who see the toppling of the regime as their central aim" (i.e., without Sa'iqa).[64]

Fatah/PLO's position was expressed in the resolutions of the PPC/10th PNC (April 1972) and the 11th PNC (January 1973). The PPC's decisions were based, except for minor alterations, on the Plan for a Palestinian–Jordanian National Liberation Front (PJNLF) which had been prepared by the PLO Planning Centre (23 March 1972). These decisions stated that "the struggle for toppling the regime in Jordan is a need equal in its urgency to that of the struggle against the Zionist occupation". "The struggle of the Palestinian and the Jordanian peoples should be integrated within [the framework of] a Jordanian–Palestinian national liberation front" which will "direct the struggle of both peoples to toppling the regime ... and to granting the Palestinian revolution freedom of political action in Jordan and [freedom to] establish its military lunching bases [there]." The 11th PNC (January 1973) reiterated these decisions. Abu Iyad called (March 1973) for "turning Jordan into an Arab Hanoi. She cannot be such as long as the king exists."

On 17 March 1972 Fatah's Revolutionary Council resolved that "the toppling of the regime in Jordan is an interim aim" of the organization.[65]

The pretensions of the organizations, including Fatah, could not meet the test of actual execution. Their leaders admitted their failure in internal forums, though the efforts to assassinate the king continued during and after this period. In 1972 the organizations estimated that the regime could be overthrown either by encouraging dissension within the army or by assassinating the king. In August 1972 Abu al-Walid (Sa'd Sail), commander of Fatah's Yarmuk Forces, opined that "with joint efforts of the revolution [and officers] from within, it is possible to bring about a revolt in the army, in spite of the difficulties". In December 1972 the PFLP tried to convince its members of "strife within the military establishment … which will inevitably lead … to an upheaval in the regime and to a weakening of its strength".

There were two "serious" but abortive attempts in this direction. In the Major Rafi' al-Hindawi affair (October 1972), this Jordanian officer made contacts in Cairo, during a visit in 1971, with Abu Iyad and Libyan representatives. He reported to them a purported network of tens of officers, for which he received money through the Bank al-Urdun. He was caught when a courier who passed his letters to Fatah took them to the Jordanian general intelligence. It emerged after his arrest that he had acted alone, and had fabricated the entire claim to extract money from Fatah and Libya.

Then on 15 February 1972 Jordan announced the arrests of Abu Daud, a member of Fatah's Revolutionary Council, and his group (16 people) after they had infiltrated from Syria. The group's main aim was to occupy the American embassy and the office of the Jordanian prime minister and in both cases take hostages in exchange for the release of detained members of the organizations in Jordan. Abu Daud acted according to Abu Iyad's directions. He was arrested during his reconnaissance of Amman after one of his assistants in Jordan disclosed the operation to Jordanian intelligence. On 4 March 1972 the king signed the death sentence against Abu Daud and 15 members of his group; on 14 March 1973, after Husayn had extracted all possible propaganda advantage from the affair and from Abu Daud's confessions, their sentence was reduced to life imprisonment. The group was released during the general amnesty of September 1973.

After these two incidents, and considering that the group's plan was revealed only a short time before its execution and that

Hindawi's contacts with Fatah had continued for quite a while before discovery by the authorities, the regime decided to reorganize the intelligence and security services. Furthermore, in this period the intelligence received much information on planned actions by the organizations against the regime and apparently also against the royal family. On 5 March 1973 Kaylani was appointed director of general intelligence (in place of Nadir Rashid) and as the king's adviser for national security.[66]

Sabotage against the regime. These actions, which were decided upon in 1971, continued throughout the period. The organizations grossly exaggerated their effectiveness. They were carried out mainly by Fatah, and a few by the PFLP and PDFLP. They were of three types: inside Jordan, from the Syrian border and "special operations" which were undertaken jointly by Fatah's "Jordanian arena" and the "arena of special operations" under Abu Iyad, under the name of Black September or the Jordanian National Front. The actions declined towards late 1971 but were renewed with added vigour after announcement of the king's plan (15 March 1972). Against this background the EC PLO decided in May 1972 to abolish the organizations' open presence in Jordan since they had earlier gone over to a system of clandestine local organizations. During 17–31 March 1972 some 15–17 sabotage actions took place, about seven from the Syrian border and the rest in northern Jordan. Two or three were carried out by the PFLP in Jordan. In April 1972 there were 28–30, 16 of them from Syrian territory; there were also some actions in Amman and Irbid. By May 1972 and especially towards the end of the year the actions declined due to intensified Jordanian security measures (arrests, mining and fencing of the Syrian border) and the restrictions imposed by Syria on actions from her territory. The number of actions in May–June was approximately 16 per month, mainly in the towns.

The organizations started to smuggle arms and explosives in cars and caches while using forged documents, with help from Iraq. In September 1972 Fatah, under the name of Black September, also began to send letter bombs to Jordanian notables such as Adnan Abu Awda, Mustafa Dudin and the ambassador in Oman, but these were defused in time. Within "the arena of special operations", an attempt was made (5 October 1972) on the Jordanian ambassador in Beirut; under the name Black September, there was another attempt (15 December 1972) on the life of Zayd Rifa'i, the ambassador in London; and, under the name of the Jordanian

National Liberation Movement, an attempt was made (16 December 1972) to attack the Jordanian embassy in Geneva. Under the same name an attempt was made to hijack a Jordanian plane en route from Cairo to Amman (19 December 1972). The attacks ceased in 1973.[67]

Change in the conception of "unity of the two Banks". As a lesson from the Jordanian crisis, the organizations began to emphasize "Jordanian nationalism" as the equal of "Palestinian nationalism". The PLO Planning Centre stated in a working paper in March 1972 that "relationships within the PJNF are those of a democratic alliance and not of absorption, hence the necessity for preserving the independent existence [of both nationalisms]". The PDFLP stated in the decisions of the 1st Congress (October 1971) that Jordanian–Palestinian relationships must be within the framework of "the United JPNF on the basis of full regional and democratic equality within a national democratic state on both Banks". It distinguished between "the national and democratic rights of the [non-Palestinian] inhabitants of the East Bank" and those of the East Bank Palestinians.

The PFLP did not give a clear-cut answer to this question. It asserted that the establishment of the PJNF assumed from the start "that the PR would not see itself as a substitute for the Jordanian revolutionary movement". "The unity of the two Banks must be built on a democratic national basis and on the basis of the historic unity between the Palestinian and the Jordanian peoples and [their] common kinship with the Arab nation."

The position of Fatah/PLO, however, was decisive. The PLO–PCR, in its report on the PJNLF, proposed the following objectives for the latter in clear order of preference:

> the removal of the regime in Jordan, liberation of Filastin from the Zionist occupation and the establishment of a federal state [*ittihadiyya*] on the land of Filastin and Jordan, which would ensure the preservation of sovereignty of the two peoples and strengthening of the relationship of brotherhood and equality [between them] by means of equal rights in the constitutional, legal, cultural and economic aspects.

This formula was not accepted by Fatah/PLO at the 10th PNC, but is a key to Fatah's view of the relationship between the Palestinian Entity, if set up in the West Bank and Gaza, and Jordan – namely, the possibility of a federation on the basis of equality between the two regions. At the 10th PNC, the proposed political manifesto stated that the PJNF's aims were "toppling the regime in Jordan and liberation of Filastin from the Zionist occupation and establishment of a democratic state on the land of Filastin and Jordan which will ensure the national sovereignty of the two peoples ... and strengthening of the bonds of brotherhood and equality [between them]". The final PNC declaration (10 April 1972) spoke of "revising the attitude to the unity of the two Banks and its renewal within the framework of a national democratic regime, based on full equality in rights and obligations". The 11th PNC approved a version which combined the PCR's and the 10th PNC's proposals while omitting the words "the establishment of a federal state".[68]

The organizations' approach to this subject was marked by a kind of paternally superior attitude towards the Transjordanians, a "magnanimity" in acknowledging the existence of "Jordanian nationalism".

The UAK plan. The organizations' total rejection of this plan was out of all proportion to its prospects of implementation. Only Sa'iqa's attitude, since it reflected Syria's, was exceptional. The organizations clearly understood the import of its announcement: that is, a decisive stage in the struggle between themselves and Jordan over Palestinian representation, and the plan's implementation as a threat to their very existence and to the chances of establishing an independent Palestinian Entity. Hence, they focused on the Arab and Palestinian arenas in order to block Husayn's aims and achieve full recognition of the PLO as sole representative. The PLO leadership learned of the plan (from their people in Jordan) on the eve of its announcement after it had been presented to the group of 13; on 14 March 1972 the EC debated it and the first public reaction came from Fatah on 15 March 1972. Fatah rejected it and stressed that "the PR is the sole, legitimate representative of the Palestinian people on the land of Filastin and wherever this people may be". During the first EC debate three groups emerged: those who kept silent (presumably the Sa'iqa delegates), those who asked to study the matter and not to make a hasty decision so as to reduce the plan's importance and those who demanded a clear and immediate response in order to avoid confusion among the Palestinians about the PLO's attitude. Official statements were made by some of the organizations on 15 March 1972, whereas the PLO's statement was only issued late on the night of 16 March 1972. On 17 March 1972 Fatah's Revolutionary Council announced its reaction.

The organizations' analysis of the plan's consequences was as follows. (1) The plan aimed "to liquidate the PR and the Palestinian problem once and forever". "The king has confined the problem of the Palestinian people to the West Bank ... whereas the Palestinian homeland is the entire land of Filastin." (2) Husayn was seeking a separate solution "and to co-opt the Palestinians in direct or indirect negotiations" with Israel, "for implementation of the resolution of the Security Council whose aim was to recognize the legitimacy of Israel's existence". This would ensure the realization of the Allon plan, thereby turning Egypt's and Syria's relationships with Israel into a question of borders alone. (3) "Husayn is trying to prove that he is the official spokesman of the Palestinian people"; that the issue of representation "has become more urgent and immediate than ever." "The plan aims at creating a substitute for the PLO ... in the form of a provisional government for the Filastin Region." (4) "The king appoints himself guardian of the Palestinian people while ignoring its right to self-determination through its legitimate institutions." "The right to self-determination will not be realized by a royal decree but on the liberated Palestinian land." The organizations connected the timing of the plan's announcement to the IMG's ordering of the municipal elections; the plan and the elections were the focus of debate at the PPC/10th PNC. The PPC decided that "the PLO is the sole legitimate representative of the Palestinian people and that no one else has the right to decide on the question of Filastin". The 11th PNC declared that "the Palestinian revolution will continue to be the legitimate political leadership of the Palestinian people and it alone will be its spokesman". These statements were directed at the Palestinians to prevent any possible cooperation with the regime regarding the king's plan, or, following the elections, with the IMG, in order to form a "substitute leadership".[69]

Finally, Isam Sakhnini of the PLO's Palestinian Research Centre expressed an interesting approach to Jordan's future in September 1975. It reflected the impasse in attempts to overthrow the regime, and the correct assessment that a "change in the East Jordan regime, or its fall" could not "make East Jordan a stable base of the revolution, unless there is also a change in the entity structure of East Jordan itself; otherwise it means [merely] replacing one regime with another". The aim, that is, should be creation of a "Palestinian East Jordan" as a "substitute entity which embodies the present and historical characteristics of the Palestinians and the East Jordanians", that is, to view "East Jordan as the homeland of both the East Jordanians and the Palestinians". This would be "a step in the direction of Greater Filastin, and will enable the Palestinians to expand, from there, west of the river as in the example of North Vietnam and its relations to its south". This concept fitted in with his view of the West Bank as "middle Filastin" (*al-wusta*) and clearly denied the existence of "Jordanian nationalism".[70]

THE PALESTINIAN ARENA: THE CRISIS

The PLO: Efforts at "National Unity"

The organizations' crisis was accompanied by self-criticism both in internal forums and in publications. Rarely in modern Arab history has a political movement dealt so openly with its failures, almost as "group therapy", even though the conclusions drawn were not always implemented. To this end, Fatah developed the PLO's Planning Centre in order to prepare surveys and reports, sometimes with the help of leading Palestinian researchers. The "strategic distress" in which they found themselves, particularly in 1972, was expressed in a number of ways.

A *lack of action* (*in'idam al-fi'l*) or "vacuum" was created in fidai activity. After their crisis in Jordan, the organizations concentrated their activities against Israel from Lebanese territory. But as a result of Syrian and Egyptian pressure as well as IDF actions against their bases in Lebanon and Syria, they had to restrict their activity from the Syrian border and suspend it from the Lebanese border. Then there were the crises with the Lebanese authorities, particularly in September 1972 and May 1973. The organizations sought to limit these; they suspended their actions following IDF attacks on their bases in Lebanon in February, June and September 1972, and following arrangements with the Lebanese authorities agreed upon in June and September 1972. The May 1973 crisis broke out after the IDF raid in Beirut on 10 April 1973. In 1972 a total of 28 to 30 actions took place (January–February – 7 each month; March – 2; April–August – 1 each month; September – 4; October–December – 6). From January to October 1973, there were only 9 actions. This, combined with their inability to carry out actions in the West Bank and Gaza, added up to a "lack of action": an inability to wage the "armed struggle".

Thus they turned to "operations abroad"; from May 1972 to

November 1973 Fatah was the leader in this area. The PLO–PCR warned (August 1972) that continued "lack of action" might "cause increased unrest among the rank and file", and proposed such activities as "intensive training and political and ideological indoctrination". But it was the state of continued alert following the IDF attacks, and the crises with the Lebanese government, which helped relieve the "lack of action" and the crisis of morale among the fidaiyyun.[71]

The leadership crisis was expressed in the weakening of the organizational frameworks and of the rank and file's confidence in the leadership, and in the lack of discipline among the leaders themselves and the cadres. As Abu Jihad described it (August 1972): "the majority of the young think of refuge and flight [from the organizations] as though the revolution is almost in the last phase of its liquidation".

In the case of Fatah, for example, a severe crisis developed in 1972 in its branch in Lebanon, which "saw itself as having equal status to the Central Committee", between "the military and the civilian wings while the dispute spread to the refugee camps in Lebanon". Another severe crisis broke out in October 1972 when Abu Yusuf al-Kayid, commander of a Fatah base in al-Biqa' in Lebanon, refused to obey orders of the Fatah chief of operations, Abu-Za'im. His camp was besieged; so as to avoid armed confrontation with his unit, he was allowed to leave for Algeria without a trial. Following these crises changes were made in the leadership personnel of the Lebanese branch. In general, it seems that the tensions in the Fatah leadership resulted from the rise to power of the "military wing" under the leadership of field commanders, which in turn stemmed from the setting up of regular Fatah units and the entry of a number of senior officers into the central institutions of Fatah. As a result of "the lack of a clear definition of [Fatah's] policy on many issues, members of the leadership were beginning to express their personal views". For the first time there emerged, in the 11th PNC and in the debates behind the scenes, two "currents" in the Fatah leadership. One, whose spokesman was Khalid al-Hasan (an EC member), presented "the concept of realism". Hasan claimed that the PR "is undergoing a crisis of strategy and not of tactics". He added that "we are in an era of international peace ... and solution to international problems by peaceful means". "The danger is that this [peaceful] way will be imposed on the PR." Hence he called for "definition of an interim goal and not only a strategic goal"; but he did not present any plan of action of his own. His position was negatively received within the Fatah ranks, and in the gathering of Fatah cadres (August 1972) an activist from Yugoslavia called him "a Saudi agent who wants to remove Arafat". Arafat himself (and with him Abu Iyad and Naji Alush, backed by members of the second rank), who represented the dominant radical current in Fatah, countered that "this era is not characterized by peaceful solutions but is the era of revolutions". Khalid al-Hasan was not re-elected to the EC. However, the leadership remained united around the policy endorsed by the majority of the Fatah leadership.[72]

As another example, on 7 March 1972 a small group calling itself "the left wing" of the PFLP announced its secession from the organization, and set up the Popular Revolutionary Front for the Liberation of Palestine (PRFLP). The secessionists included three members of the PFLP leadership and cadres from its Lebanese branch. The PRFLP leaders were only of the second and third ranks of PFLP leadership. This new organization had no significant influence; Fatah, in cooperation with the PFLP, prevented it from joining the PNC, and Egypt prohibited its leaders from entering Cairo during the 11th PNC there.[73]

As for *the Arab arena*, Abu Mazin, a Fatah leader, clearly summed up (August 1972) the situation of the PR within it:

> the Palestinian revolution is in a state of fundamental contradiction to the Arab regimes.... The moment we declare this, these regimes will see it as a pretext to strike at the revolution without argument. The PR should distinguish, not between progressive or reactionary [Arab] regimes, and not between right and left regimes, but between a Jordanian regime on the one hand, and other Arab regimes on the other. All the Arab states are strategically against the revolution. ... Nevertheless our relations with all of them should be good.

The organizations could not escape being an Arab problem. A Fatah leader defined the interim goal as "release from the guardianship of, and [our] affinity towards, the Arab regimes". Except for Lebanon, the organizations could not function freely and openly in the Arab states. The establishment (November 1972) of the "Arab Front Participating in the Palestinian Revolution" (*musharika*) in place of Fatah's slogan (in its early days) of a "Supporting Arab Front" (*musanida*) did not succeed because it did not enjoy support from the Arab regimes. Abu Iyad's outburst (21 January 1973) against the Arab states generally and the oil-producing states in particular was unprecedented, and indicative of the organizations' crises and the heavy pressure on them to coordinate their activities with the confrontation states.[74]

"National unity". The causes of the divisions between the organizations remained, even though the general crisis and Fatah's radicalization contributed to cooperation between them and widened their representation in the PLO leadership (the EC). "National unity" was presented as a way to extricate them from crisis; the Arab states continued to call for it. The gulf between plans and their execution remained huge, yet each body steadfastly held to its organizational and ideological independence.

On the question of "national unity", the PFLP limited itself to laying down general principles. The PLO should be maintained as a representational framework, even if its composition did not express its own aspirations. It suggested the "minimal border plan" (on the basis of which it participated in the 9th PNC, July 1971) "as a limited possibility for gradually increased cooperation towards establishing a Broad National Front". This Front "would gather all the forces of the left around a revolutionary ... plan which defines the relations between the organizations on *jabhawiyya* foundations while maintaining their organizational and ideological independence".[75]

In April 1972, the PDFLP proposed setting up the United National Front (UNF) outside the PLO. It would operate within the PLO as a "united bloc" "until a full overlapping between the PLO and the UNF is achieved". The UNF would act for the total "unity of the functional institutions such as the military forces and the trade unions while each party [in it] has the right to maintain its internal ideological and organizational independence". The PDFLP presented a detailed plan to the 10th PNC but agreed that, as long as it was impossible to establish the UNF outside the PLO, the principles of establishing the UNF would be applied within the PLO.[76]

The ALF, in a programme presented to the 10th PNC, proposed a Palestinian National Liberation Front (PNLF) which would include all the PR parties and popular organizations. The political institutions would be composed on a *jabhawi* basis, the functional institutions amalgamated. Political representation would be restricted to the PNLF alone. The name of the PLO did not appear in its programme; in its memorandum to the 11th PNC it called for "a National Liberation Front ... which would give direction to the PLO's leadership and institutions". In its view, the PLO "still inherits many of the negative aspects in its composition and relations with the Arab regimes". The PLO should be "the official political and executive instrument of the PNLF leadership". Despite its view of the PLO, the ALF continued to participate in the EC.[77]

Fatah's position was crucial to the acceptance of any plan for unity by the PNC. Fatah's institutions decided early in 1972 that "realization of national unity is one of the main tasks of the next stage". A radical element was prominent within the leadership; its spokesman, Kamal Udwan, demanded "imposing unity, even by force". Arafat countered that "the principle of liquidation [of groups] is very dangerous"; he supported "unity by means of democratic relations", and his approach was approved by the Fatah institutions. Fatah did not present a plan for unity to the 10th PNC; it supported the general formula of "national unity within the PLO without conditions or limitations", and immediately. Instead, with Fatah's approval, the PLO–PCR presented a plan whose principles were to be applied to the PLO framework. This was a pretentious plan, regarding which a Fatah leader correctly claimed that "the seeds of its failure are sown in its wording".

In the 10th PNC debate on the National Unity Plan each organization tried to prove that it was more interested in unity than the others, but without considering whether in fact the plan could be implemented. Critical arrows were directed at Fatah to make it abandon its dominant position, and instead favour *jabhawi* representation; Fatah reacted with extreme proposals for "full amalgamated unity" – for example, Abu Iyad's absurd proposal to implement unity within one month. The 10th PNC eventually ratified a compromise resolution which contained internal contradictions: on the one hand it included the PCR plan with its emphasis on the organizations' "independence", while on the other it included Fatah's proposal which sought "national unity on the basis of *jabhawi* composition of the PLO's leadership institutions, unity [amalgamation] of the armed forces of the organizations in one military establishment, complete unity of the financial sources ... information machinery and all foreign relations offices of the organizations". The resolution declared that the groundwork for the plan would be laid "within three months"; the PNC endorsed the establishment of a 22-member committee to follow up the fulfilment of unity. Plainly, this plan was never meant to be carried out. The PDFLP accused Fatah of striving "to assimilate within it the rest of the organizations"; the PFLP rejected the principle of amalgamation, declaring that "it would be a dangerous illusion to imagine the implementation of real steps, particularly concerning military and financial unity".[78]

Change in the approach to unity. Unity between organizations is not simply an administrative move nor a matter of momentous decisions meant to impress the public. It is a matter of principle that requires compromise on dogma and independence. The organizations played the game, but not for long. Fatah was never optimistic about the efficacy of the Follow-up Committee, and the organizations were contemptuous of it. At the committee's first meeting on 5 May 1972 with 16 members present, Arafat reported on the EC decisions on "national unity", including publication of a "united" weekly called *al-Thawra al-Filastiniyya;* "unity" of broadcasts, to be called *Sawt Filastin;* setting up a "Palestinian News Agency" (WAFA); unity over information to be implemented on 5 June 1972 and "a united military establishment under one command" within three months. The Follow-up Committee was a failure. In its last meeting, meant to sum up its work for the 11th PNC, nine members were present (not even a quorum). The chairman, Khalid al-Fahum, had no choice but to present a personal report admitting the committee's failure and emphasizing that "fidai activity has failed until now to realize the first serious step on the road to national unity. Foundations have not been laid for a practical interim plan which can be implemented." "The PNCs have approved broad guidelines [for unity] which are closer to emotional aspirations left hanging in the air." Already in August 1972 the PFLP had admitted the total failure of efforts at unity; "it is a big mistake to expect more than is possible".

In view of Fahum's criticism, the leaders of the organizations had to start again by outlining a realistic, feasible plan for unity. The EC decided (1 December 1972) to set up a subcommittee called the National Unity Committee (NUC) from among its members, to debate the "practical steps for unity which can be implemented through taking into account the conditions and needs of reality". The NUC drew up some lines of action which were a total retreat from both the PDFLP's and Fatah's original plans: (1) Limiting *jabhawi* composition to the EC only, which would serve as the "supreme political leadership"; institutional amalgamation would only be done "gradually", which in fact meant postponement of its implementation. (2) The EC would be empowered with the authority of the United Information Council "in directing united information" with "commitment to the political programme and the Covenant". All activities would be announced in the name of "the HQ of the Revolution". (3) In the military sphere they confined themselves to the setting up of the Supreme Military Council by the

EC. It would comprise the chairman of the EC Military Department and one representative from each organization; its chairman would be the EC chairman. "All the armed forces will be under its command." Completely ignored was the issue of amalgamation of forces. (4) Concerning the PLA, Fatah argued in the NUC's deliberations that it "is a hurdle towards unity as it does not obey the ... political leadership [i.e., the EC] and is not disciplined". The rest of the organizations, apart from Sa'iqa, supported Fatah's demand that the PLA be subordinated to the political leadership. The NUC recommended that it be co-opted to the Supreme Military Council, and that it should act only "as a military institution". Furthermore, its "legal" and inter-Arab basis would come under review. (5) "Financial unity will be considered at a later stage." (6) The NUC recommended that the PNC set up a permanent follow-up committee, composed of three times the number of EC members, "to meet every three months and follow up implementation of PNC decisions between [PNC] sessions". The only important outcome, therefore, of the NUC's deliberations was Fatah's concession on an almost *jabhawi* composition of the EC. With that, all the hullabaloo around the unity plan of 1972 ended.

The NUC also recommended, without the EC reporting it to the PNC, reducing the number of EC members to 9: three to the independents, two to Fatah and one each to the PFLP, PDFLP, Sa'iqa and ALF. The NUC agreed that this recommendation serve as a guideline, but the Fatah and Sa'iqa representatives asked for time to consult their respective leaderships. During the 11th PNC the *jabhawi* principle was endorsed, although it was not fully implemented. Fatah indeed conceded the principle of the "backbone" but maintained its dominant position on the EC.[79]

Another important outcome of the change in Fatah's concept of "unity" and the radicalization of its positions was a Fatah–PFLP *rapprochement*, from which both benefited. However, this led to tension between Fatah and Sa'iqa, exacerbated by the argument over the PLA's status and by Syria's relationship with Jordan. The Fatah–PFLP cooperation was particularly noticeable in operational matters, though it was not spelled out in any official document. It included cooperation in the military sphere in South Lebanon, in the refugee camps and to some extent also in "actions abroad". This "alliance" was decided upon in the PFLP leadership as a central plank of its policy. Cooperation also extended to the institutions of the General Union of Palestinian Students, with representatives of both organizations forming a coalition which helped the PFLP obtain additional votes in the union's branch elections in various countries. Fatah's policy of cooperating with the PFLP helped it to neutralize every possibility of the other organizations forming a coalition opposed to Fatah.[80]

The representative composition of the PLO's institutions. In order to demonstrate the PLO's right to represent the Palestinians, the organizations called a Palestinian Popular Congress (PPC) which took place 6–10 April 1972. The 10th PNC met with the sole purpose of formally endorsing the PPC's resolutions; the PPC was in fact an enlarged assembly of the 10th PNC. The main aims the organizations delegated to the PPC were: confirmation of the PLO as sole representative of the Palestinians (a reaction to the municipal elections and Husayn's plan); presenting "a united front among the Palestinian people, whether in the territories or in Jordan"; reconfirmation of the "continued armed struggle as the only way to liberate Filastin"; and re-emphasizing that "the right to self-determination means complete liberation and the establishment of a Palestinian national state on the entire land of Filastin". Therefore, an attempt was made to have the PPC appear widely representative of "all strata of the Palestinian people including popular organizations, trade unions and the armed organizations". But the PPC's composition did not meet these expectations. In its first memorandum to the EC on preparations for the PPC, the PLO–PCR made two recommendations as to its composition: "to elect its members through popular regional assemblies in the main Palestinian concentrations"; and to elect members from the occupied territories "on the basis of group, regional and organizational representation, not on the basis of notables and invitations to some nationalist personalities". Neither of these two proposals was implemented.

Instead, there was an absence of delegates from the East and West Banks. The Preparatory Committee sent (via Belgrade) some 100 invitations to various West Bank personalities and some 30 to Gaza Strip figures, without taking into account the distribution recommended by the PCR. It is difficult to detect any clear pattern to the invitations. The number of people invited from each area was not commensurate with the number of its inhabitants. There were first- and second-rank traditional leaders including mayors, religious leaders and also some nationalists. The regional distribution was as follows: from the Hebron area some 20, not including Ja'bari, were invited, many of them nationalists; from the Bethlehem area about eight, including a member of the previous Jordanian establishment and his wife, and a Ba'thist, but with no mayors invited; from Jericho three, among them Musa al-Alami and a Communist; from Jerusalem ten, among them Anwar al-Khatib, religious leaders (Hilmi al-Muhtasib and Sa'd al-Din al-Alami) and the Ba'thist Abd al-Muhsin Abu Mayzar; from Ramalla about 20, among them mayors (such as Karim Khalaf), a member of the Jordanian Parliament and some nationalists; from Nablus more than 20, including some traditional leaders (such as Ma'zuz al-Masri, Hamdi Kan'an and Walid al-Shak'a) and the nationalists Walid Qamhawi, Hatim Abu Ghazala and Bassam al-Shak'a, with Hikmat al-Masri not invited; from Tulkarem five, among them Mayor Hanun and also nationalists; from Qalqiliya three, among them the mayor and a member of Parliament; from Jenin five including the mayor.

After an IMG warning that whoever left for the PPC would not be permitted re-entry, the invitees did not leave. Nevertheless, some 36 nationalists sent the PPC a message expressing support for the PLO as representative of the Palestinians. Nabil Sha'ath, head of the PCR, stated that "until it is possible to create a revolutionary organization of iron among the West Bank and Gaza inhabitants, the 'inside' [i.e., the West Bank and Gaza] will remain represented by fewer [delegates] than ... the 'outside' and will be less influential". Indeed, in its personnel and organizational composition, the PLO has not represented in due proportion the West Bank and Gaza inhabitants. It is not clear how many invitations were sent to Jordan, though one source reported 147; in any event there were more than 100, including Palestinian personalities (such as Yasir Amru and Ibrahim Bakr, and members of Parliament) and Jordanians such as former prime ministers Rifa'i and Talhuni. The Jordanian authorities also prohibited the exit of those invited to the PPC.[81]

If we ignore the origin of the PNC members, the PPC could not pretend genuinely to represent the majority of the Palestinians, since some 200–250 of the invited West Bank, Gaza and East Bank delegates did not participate and had not, in any case, been elected.

Regarding the composition of the PPC, the PLO leadership invited a large number of participants – some 700–750 – so as to increase the impression of its representativeness. From Egypt alone 80 people were invited to represent a population of 10,000 Palestinians. According to the PDFLP the number who "registered" (apparently a reference to those who accepted the invitation) reached 540. Four hundred actually arrived in Cairo to participate in the PPC, including the PNC members; but no more than 250 actually participated in the deliberations and important votes. This low percentage stemmed from, among other things, scepticism about the PPC's ability, in its existing composition, to achieve much. The PPC included delegates from different strata of the Palestinian population including the traditional leadership, among them heads of clans in the refugee camps in Syria and Lebanon, and professionals such as senior officials, contractors, doctors, engineers and lawyers, particularly from the Persian Gulf countries, Saudi Arabia and Lebanon. Also prominent were intellectuals, writers and academics especially from Palestinian research institutes. The popular organizations and workers' associations, most of whom were affiliated to the PLO, had 50–60 places in the PPC, in addition to non-PNC, fidai organization activists.

With such a composition the number designated as "independents" was, not surprisingly, relatively high. The radical organizations criticized the PPC's composition, the PDFLP claiming that "its class composition leaned towards Fatah, so that proposals of a progressive nature failed while those which increased Fatah's influence were accepted". During the PPC and afterwards in the PNC, Fatah and the independents proposed increasing the number of PNC members so as to increase the delegates from among the independents, professionals and academics in the PLO's institutions; this was against the background of criticism over the PNC's composition. The radicals (PFLP, PDFLP) argued against "flooding the PNC with independents", judging that this would weaken their influence, "upset the existing equilibrium between the organizations in the PNC and turn the alliance between Fatah and the independents into a large majority". Dr Sha'ath warned against exaggerated use of the term "independents". The proposal to enlarge the PNC passed 200–100, with the rest not voting. During the 10th PNC the proposal was passed (11 April 1972) 40–32 with 8 abstentions; most of the Sa'iqa, PLA and ALF delegates absented themselves. The resolution stated that "the PNC agrees to enlargement of the PNC. Implementation of the resolution will be passed to the EC with the participation of the PNC chairman. Half of the additional members will be from the popular organizations and the trade unions." Because of expectations regarding "national unity", it was decided to leave the EC's composition unchanged.[82]

Shortly before the 11th PNC (6–12 January 1973), early in December 1972, the EC decided, with general agreement by the organizations, to increase the PNC members by 16. Eight would be elected by the trade unions, the other eight nominated from among the "independents". However, because of demands by the trade unions on the eve of the PNC meeting to enlarge their representation, the 11th PNC decided to increase its members by 26. The total number of PNC members, therefore, was meant to be 181 (in the 9th and 10th PNCs there were 155), although PLO sources reported only 180. These additional nominations were clearly part of the game of distributing mandates among the organizations while the tendencies of the "independents" were known. Among those co-opted were the writers Naji Alush, Dr Sidqi al-Dajani and Dr Sa'id Hamud, and also Fuad Nassar, secretary-general of the JCP. The co-option of Khidir Shahada, a PFLP member (from the students union), was ratified despite his being detained in Egypt. The PNC assembled with about 18 members missing because the Jordanian authorities had prohibited their exit.

During this PNC the Sa'iqa reopened the debate over the PNC's composition. Refuting the EC's previous recommendations as to how the membership should be allotted, it demanded two official mandates, claiming that it was the largest organization after Fatah. There was a proposal for a smaller EC of nine members, and another for a larger EC with 12 members. The compromise was to add an additional independent member sympathetic to Sa'iqa. The EC therefore now comprised 10 members, with the following formal distribution and on the basis of *jabhawi* representation: Fatah 2 (including the chairman); Sa'iqa 1; PFLP 1; PDFLP 1; ALF 1; independents 3; PLO spokesman 1 (independent). A categorization according to political tendencies would read: Fatah 4–5 (including 1–2 of the independents and the PLO spokesman), Sa'iqa 2 (including 1 of the independents). The PDFLP's proposal to co-opt to the EC Salah Rafat, a member of its leadership (who was a prisoner in Jordan) was rejected. The PFLP–GC refused to participate so as not to commit itself to the EC's decisions.

The PNC decided to renew the institution of the Central Committee (CC), but unlike its predecessor it was elected with the PNC's approval and from among its members. It was decided that it would number 19–21 members elected by the EC, and would serve as the link between the PNC and the EC between PNC sessions. Its composition was to be as follows: the EC members, in addition to 9–12 members drawn from among representatives of the popular organizations and independents. The CC under the PNC chairman included: Fatah 4; Sa'iqa 2; PFLP 2; PDFLP 2; ALF 2; Palestinian unions 6; independents 5 (total of 23).[83] One should not, therefore, view the PLO institutions as in fact having *jabhawi* composition in the full sense of the word. It should more accurately be called an "organizational alignment"; but in this too was a certain amount of progress on the long road towards "national unity", a goal not achieved to date and seemingly unlikely to be in the foreseeable future. On the contrary, against the background of the PLO adopting the strategy of an interim goal after the War, and the fierce debate between the organizations over that strategy, even this "alignment" fell apart.

The status of the PLA. The dispute about the PLA's status intensified. Kamal Udwan defined it by saying (August 1972) that "the PLA is not a Palestinian instrument, its HQ has no connection with the PR and its location in Jordan is a breach of orders". The question was again one of the subordination of the PLA to the PLO political leadership (the EC) as laid down in the PLO's Constitution. The problem intensified because, first, the organizations (excluding Sa'iqa) saw both the PLA battalion's presence in Jordan and the cooperation between its commander, Nuhad Nusayba, and the regime as an absurd situation and one which served the regime's interests; they correctly saw it, too, as a bitter contradiction of the PLO's decision to overthrow the regime. Budayri, the PLA chief-of-staff, supported (not without Syrian backing) the battalion remaining in Jordan; in his opinion, as long as the PLO's decision to overthrow the regime remained on paper "one should create a cease-fire atmosphere with the ... regime to facilitate infiltration into the Jordanian-Palestinian masses and their mobilization in preparation for the overthrow of the regime".

Second, the question of the PLA's status in the framework of national unity was linked to the essence of the problem, which was the PLA's subordination to the EC and whether its political affinity was to the PLO/Fatah or to preserving its "independence" (in effect, subordination to Syria). The PLA HQ had strong reservations about the unity plan the PPC had endorsed. The PLA's integration within this plan would mean its assimilation in a military framework under Fatah, which is what the other organizations understood. Budayri argued that any change in status required the consent of the Arab states to whom the PLA units belonged. The PLA HQ made far-reaching accusations against Fatah (June 1972) such as that it was "trying to engulf the fidai organizations". It proposed that instead "the fidai organizations [should] be amalgamated in the

PLA institutions", through which the PLA would become "the basic power and the alternative to the PR units and to the various organizations".

It is clear that the PLA HQ's arguments on these two subjects were formal only. Abu Iyad's declaration (November 1971) is the key to Fatah/PLO's position: "the struggle is about the PLA's affinity to one country or another.... The PLA is under a command which is not its own" (a hint about Syria); "the PR has two options: total confrontation with the PLA or giving it up ... If we cannot decide in favour of the PR in this campaign ... we should say to the Arab states that either we rule the PLA or – you can take it [from us]." Fatah, with the help of the other organizations (excluding Sa'iqa), tried and failed to impose on the PLA subordination to the EC. In July 1972 the EC decided to transfer the 423rd PLA Battalion from Jordan to Syria or Iraq. To force the PLA's HQ to obey, the EC decided to cease, as of June 1972, paying salaries to the PLA (which came from the National Fund). The PLA HQ in Syria and the battalion's commander in Jordan refused to obey; the Jordanian regime promised Nusayba financial aid to maintain his battalion. Against this background, and possibly owing to Syrian pressure, payment of PLA salaries was renewed.

In the 11th PNC the question of the PLA's status was again raised with reference to the recommendations of the EC's National Unity Committee. Again Fatah leaders criticized the PLA, demanding its exit from Jordan and the cessation of financial allocations. The PNC made no practical decision, and the situation remained unchanged. On 7 August 1973 the EC again decided that the PLA battalion must move from Jordan to Syria. This time the decision was meant to disrupt Jordan's steps to improve relations with Egypt and Syria, and to present the PLA battalion's presence as proof of its readiness to station a "fidai" force on her territory. At the same time *Sawt Filastin* (Fatah) in Cairo explained the decision, arguing that the commander of the battalion, Nusayba, "is an agent and collaborates with Jordanian intelligence". This decision too was not implemented.[84]

In sum, the struggle to influence the PLA was waged between Fatah/PLO on the one hand and Sa'iqa/Syria on the other. Syria aimed to maintain its control over the PLA HQ as a powerful instrument in the Palestinian arena, and succeeded. In its favour was that most of the PLA forces were deployed in Syria, namely the "Hittin Forces" (brigade) and most of the Iraqi PLA (Qadisiyya Brigade); the Egyptian PLA (Ayn Jalut Forces) were then in Egypt as part of the Egyptian army. The location of the battalion in Jordan fitted in with Syria's basic policy towards Jordan. Indeed, in the future (1976) the PLA would serve as an instrument in Syria's conflict with Fatah and the other organizations during her invasion of Lebanon.

Palestinian government-in-exile (PGE). The idea of a PGE was raised as early as the late 1960s in response to the crises faced by the organizations and to Jordanian steps regarding Palestinian representation. The matter was raised by senior politicians from the Eastern bloc and Africa in their discussions with PLO leaders, with the Algerian government-in-exile as the model. Leaders of the organizations deliberated on the subject in early 1972, when announcement of King Husayn's plan made it more pressing. The Fatah leadership decided in March 1972 that the Planning Centre should prepare a research report on the idea before a decision was made. This was presented on 23 March 1972. The Fatah Central Committee discussed the matter but was not persuaded by the advantages, so the matter was passed to the Revolutionary Council, which was also not convinced even though some Fatah leaders supported the PGE as a way of frustrating Husayn's plan. In Fatah camps the motion was met with the response: "You are trying to sell the [Palestinian] problem." Sadat, it seems, was aware of these discussions and attempted (as he did later in September 1972) to influence their outcome when he met with Fatah leaders (6 April 1972). However, Fatah decided not to make a decision on this matter.

The other organizations decided to reject the April 1972 proposal, but so as not to damage relations with Sadat they did not disclose his proposal to the Fatah leaders and the EC members. Sadat's proposal of 28 September 1972 created a new situation. For the first time an Arab leader had publicly raised such a proposal; the PLO leaders had to make a formal response. Their considerations in rejecting it remained valid. They were faced with a dilemma: while they very much needed Sadat's political support, openly rejecting his proposal would possibly harm him personally and their relationship with him. Because of the lesson they had learned from the crisis with Nasir over the Rogers initiative, the organizations decided to deal with the issue sensibly and quietly. The EC met from 29 September to 1 October 1972 and decided on these lines: (1) Rejection would be indirect and unofficial, stressing that "the EC has decided on the need to emphasize the Palestinian personality represented by the PLO as the sole representative of the Palestinian people". (2) To explain to Sadat the reasons for not accepting his proposal through a PLO delegation. The delegation met Sadat on 7 October 1972. Even after the meeting their official position was that "the establishment of a PGE is a decision to be taken by the Palestinian leadership when it judges that there is a need for it to be established", that is, the option should be left open so that the hands of the Fatah/PLO would not be tied.

Fatah's reasons for rejecting the proposal were based on the Planning Centre's research report. The PFLP adopted this report in its internal publications; the other organizations generally took the same position. The reasons for rejection were as follows:

(1) Assuming the PGE adopted a revolutionary strategic line and, further, was recognized by the Arab states, it would be forced into confrontations with these states to resist pressure to accept their policies. As a public and therefore vulnerable body, the PGE would be unable to withstand such confrontations. The PLO's position was preferable; if conflict arose with the Arab states, the organizations could go underground. If the PLO fell, the dangers were not as great as if a PGE fell.

(2) The PGE would have to campaign for recognition. But conditions in the Arab world did not guarantee this; even if some Arab states did recognize it, its position would be weaker than the PLO's with its relatively wide recognition. Furthermore, Eastern-bloc countries would not recognize it unless the Arab countries did so. The Arab states would certainly demand significant political concessions from the PGE in return for their recognition, for example, acceptance of a strategy for "elimination of the traces of aggression" in accordance with Resolution 242 or the acceptance of partial solutions. The Arab states would also demand that individuals supporting their own policies join the PGE and thus would inject the PGE with the conflicts pervading the Arab world. The PLO could cope with this as long as it continued with its revolutionary line.

(3) Establishment of a PGE would create a rift between the organizations themselves and within the Palestinian masses at a time when national unity was still a distant goal. A PGE might repeat the failure of the Government of All-Filastin.

(4) Establishment of a PGE would be the answer to Husayn's plan,

but would not deal with the common strategic interests of the Palestinian and Jordanian peoples.

(5) There was no comparison between the situation of the PLO and the organizations and that of the Cambodian National Front Government. A PGE required liberated land on which to set up a revolutionary regime. The main forces of the organizations were outside the land and almost besieged by the "host" Arab countries. Therefore, the proposed PGE would not be able to address the needs of the inhabitants of the occupied territories, nor of the Palestinians outside the refugee camps, since the Arab states considered them subject to their laws and sovereignty. So, according to the Planning Centre, in the final analysis "the PR does not have the independent and objective power" to sustain a PGE.[85]

Policy Turnabout in the PDFLP

In the first half of August 1973 a significant change occurred in PDFLP policy. This was a consequence of its ideological starting point, namely, "planning the tasks of the struggle through closely interconnected links, with definition of the central link in each stage, in addition to definition of the strategic goal". The PDFLP's new position distinguished between "present national rights" (*al-rahina*) and "historic national rights", reminiscent of Sadat's speech of April 1972. The fourth session of the PDFLP Central Committee (August 1973) endorsed "the general line of the interim plan [*marhali*] in the occupied areas and Jordan". "The Palestinian revolution must concentrate its efforts on the present stages for the struggle to liberate the Palestinian areas occupied in 1967 ... and on guaranteeing freedom of self-determination of the Palestinian people in these areas, i.e. [guaranteeing] its rights to national independence and getting rid of the Hashemite annexation [of the West Bank] and its guardianship ... . Achievement of this interim goal will facilitate establishment of a support base [*irtikaz*] for the mobilization of the potential of the Palestinian and Jordanian peoples. This is for the continuation of the struggle against Zionism for a free, democratic and united Filastin." The PDFLP's starting point was that "realization of the historic solution [or goal] is not realistic in terms of the present balance of forces". It spoke of "different interim tasks and plans of action for each area [i.e., concentration of Palestinians], so that all of them flow together to serve the strategic aim", and stressed that "most of the [Palestinian] people live in the occupied areas and in eastern Jordan". Achievement of the interim goal "will accelerate establishment of the united, democratic, national movement for the Palestinian and Jordanian peoples on the East Bank and will facilitate its success in establishing a democratic, national regime" in Jordan.[86] Although this interim plan (*marhali*) departed from the all-organization consensus, it was adopted after the War by the PLO.

DECELERATION ON THE WEST BANK[87]

The process reviewed in the last chapter – namely, a decline in the status of the traditional leadership, and a rise in the strength of the nationalist leadership – slowed down in this period, on account of the crises now facing the fidai organizations. At the same time, the process of political detachment of the West Bank from the East Bank continued, while consciousness of the Palestinian identity grew. The "aging" of the traditional leadership became evident. It maintained a low political profile, while the nationalist leadership was weakened by the expulsion of its leaders, the dismantling of its political frameworks and the decline of the organizations' contacts with the West Bank. This together with the cessation of fidai actions and of passive resistance forced a change in the organizations' modes of action towards the West Bank and Gaza, leading to greater freedom of manoeuvre for the IMG, which, in turn, facilitated the holding of municipal elections.

This period saw the appearance in (East) Jerusalem of two new newspapers – from mid-April 1972 *al-Fajr* (weekly) and from 17 July 1972 *al-Sha'b* (daily). These two, and particularly *al-Sha'b's* editor Ali al-Khatib (Abu Ghassan), took an extreme nationalist position in contrast to *al-Quds's* more moderate stance. They emphasized: (1) A strong anti-Israeli and anti-IMG line, with total rejection of any local political initiative, such as elections, which implied co-operation with the IMG. (2) Support for the fidai organizations with publicity and justification for their activities, and publicity for the PLO's and the organizations' announcements. They called for "restoration of all the legal and historic rights of the Palestinian people" and "its right to self-determination", and support for the PLO's right to representation. (3) Both newspapers conducted a campaign against the traditional leadership, "which do not even represent themselves". (4) An extreme position against Husayn's regime. It is reasonable to assume that at some stage both these newspapers began to receive material aid from the PLO, either directly or indirectly. The question whether they created or only reflected public opinion is irrelevant, since the outcome was the same in either case: they became a substitute for the expressions of protest (against the IMG) which had almost died out during this period. They seriously competed with *al-Quds*, which continued (together with, to some extent, *al-Anba*) to back an independent Palestinian Entity on the West Bank and the Gaza Strip.[88]

The Municipal Elections

In October 1971 the Israeli government decided to hold municipal elections, according to Jordanian law; elections had last been held in 1963. The articles of this law, dating from 1955, ensured the councils' loyalty to the regime. The elections were personal, direct and secret. Voting rights were extended only to males above age 21 who had paid taxes (such as property tax or any municipal rates) of at least one dinar during the preceding year. The interior minister was allowed, with government consent, to appoint two additional members to each municipal council. The chairman of the council was appointed from among the council members by the government, on the minister's recommendation. Each council had a four-year period of office, but on 2 August 1967 the IDF commander on the West Bank issued an order (No. 82) extending the councils' period of office until further notice. On 26 November 1971, an order was published on the holding of elections on the West Bank. They were conducted in two stages. On 28 March 1972 elections (the order to hold these was made on 19 December 1971) were held in the Nablus, Jenin, Tulkarem, Qalqiliya and Jericho areas (the Samaria region), and on 2 May 1972 in Ramalla, Bethlehem and Hebron (Judea). Candidates could register from 13 to 15 March 1972.

The PLO position. On publication of the first order (26 November 1971) the organizations called on the West Bank population to boycott the elections. Their alarm reflected the feeling of crisis within the organizations. Arafat described (January 1971) the elections' possible success as "a real historical and shameful defeat". Abu Lutuf said the danger was "the creation of a stratum of Palestinian leadership which would lay claim to representing the West Bank inhabitants, and thus to the right to negotiate over the West Bank's future with the IMG". For Arafat this meant "establishment of an autonomous rule or a Palestinian state on the lines of a Bantustan". The success of the elections "will lead to a split between the Palestinians on the West Bank and Gaza and those outside it, to the rise of a leadership leaning towards the Israeli or Jordanian regimes and working towards establishment of an independent government or integration with Husayn's plan", and eventually to "a Palestinian Entity which would be a substitute for the PLO".

The PLO connected the elections with the announcement of Husayn's plan. The Central Committee of Fatah decided to obstruct the elections, assigning the task to Kamal Udwan who had been elected by Fatah's 3rd Congress (November 1971) as a member of the Central Committee and appointed as the person "responsible for action in the occupied land". The elections were his first serious test in this position; the extent to which the organizations could undermine them became a test of their strength and influence on the West Bank. For the IMG, the elections were also a test of its ability to effectively govern the West Bank. Thus the elections became a struggle between the PLO and the IMG over the "soul" of the West Bank Palestinians, with Jordan as a secondary factor.

The organizations, mainly Fatah, were confident of their ability to obstruct the elections. The Fatah leadership rejected out of hand suggestions by Nablus nationalists such as Dr Hatim Abu Ghazala that "it is possible that the elections will not fail. What is your attitude to us, the young nationalists, entering the lists [as candidates]?" These nationalists asked the organizations not to oppose the elections; in retrospect their assessment was correct. The organizations and the IMG both rightly viewed the attitude of the Nablus leadership as the key to the success or failure of the elections.

PLO activity developed in two main stages, according to developments on the ground. In the first, 19 December 1971–9 February 1972, the organizations conducted a comprehensive propaganda campaign on the West Bank through the media and through distribution of leaflets. In late December 1971 Arafat personally warned a number of West Bank leaders against running for election: "Do not allow the dialogue between us to become a dialogue of blood." The Jordanian Communist Party – West Bank (JCP–WB) participated in this campaign by distributing leaflets (mid-January 1972) under the name "Popular Resistance Front West Bank" (PRF–WB), and through its organ *al-Watan*. In the second stage, 10 February 1972–28 March 1972, after individuals from Nablus began to enter the lists and Hamdi Kan'an began to draw up his own list of candidates, the EC PLO decided (8–10 February 1972) to issue warnings and active threats of attack against candidates or anyone who supported the elections, and to label them as "traitors and collaborators". Anwar Nusayba (who had been an intermediary between Jordan and Israel) was labelled "chief of the king's agents and one of the planners of the municipal elections". The JCP–WB called on the West Bank inhabitants "to punish those who present their candidature". In March 1972 threatening letters were sent to candidates in Nablus and other towns, while Fatah broadcasts made direct threats to named individuals. The EC made secret decisions as to how to carry out these threats if necessary. As the elections approached some attacks were made, but only three succeeded.[89]

The election campaign. The nationalist and traditional leaderships rejected Kan'an's proposal of 1 August 1971, although not through formal resolutions. Only a small group of intellectuals supported it in the hope that the traditional leadership would be replaced by a younger leadership; Ja'bari was among the opponents. These opponents saw in the elections a change in the *status quo.* The order of 19 December 1971 created a new situation, and all declared attitudes took on a concrete political significance as the elections became a reality. Because of the importance of Nablus we shall concentrate on events in that town, which developed in a number of stages.

Stage 1: 19 December 1971–15 March 1972. Immediately after the order was published, the municipal council condemned the elections as "an Israeli plot to reach a political solution by granting self-rule to the inhabitants of the occupied territories". Jordan's official position was one of outright condemnation. But in early January 1972 information began reaching the West Bank that whatever its public declarations, Jordan's opposition was waning, apparently through fear that if its own preferred candidates did not stand, Israel's would be elected. So personalities generally considered pro-Jordanian were given the go-ahead to stand for election. At this stage a number of people with no special status also expressed willingness to stand as candidates.

In mid-January 1972 the town's leaders looked for a way to cope with this complicated situation, by electing the municipal council through *tazkiya* (without elections – with the number of candidates not exceeding the number of seats on the council). The plan failed because of Hamdi Kan'an's refusal to cooperate. But most activity revolved around Kan'an. Early in January 1972, he began to draw up a list of ten candidates (the same number as on the council) without including himself. He sought to enlist candidates well known for their nationalist views, preferably younger and academic people. He would thereby achieve his aim of replacing the town's (and possibly the West Bank's) leadership with younger forces, and in so doing circumvent criticism by the Arab states, the PLO, and, inevitably, West Bank nationalists. Kan'an, believing his list would enjoy huge support, turned to personalities like Dr Shawkat Kaylani (Communist), Dr Samih Taqtaq, the pharmacist Yasir Kamal (formerly of the ANM and from the start supporting Kan'an's approach) and Dr Ghazi al-Qasim. Most refused, except for the last two, who made their agreement conditional upon Kan'an entering his own name on the list.

Because of such pressure Kan'an agreed to do so on 12 March 1972, but his attempts to find nine other candidates with the qualifications he demanded failed. At the last moment (15 March 1972) he presented a list of eight men who, apart from him, included the pharmacist Yasir Kamal (age 37), Bashir Khanfar (Communist, teacher, 28), Dr Ghazi al-Qasim (34), Radwan Nabulsi (merchant, 60), Ruhi Shakhashir (merchant, 55, both of whose daughters had been detained for fidai activity), Mahmud al-Aqqad (merchant, 54) and Ahmad Jamusi (contractor, 54). His manifesto stated that opposition by the Arab states and the organizations "prevented the good elements... from presenting their candidacy". It contained three short sections: (a) non-involvement in political matters (to prevent criticism); (b) "attention to the interests of prisoners and deportees"; and (c) extension of municipal services. This manifesto was intended to make the very fact that he was running easier for himself, and to attract nationalists to his list. At the time the list was entered, none of the candidates had been threatened.

Meanwhile, Hikmat al-Masri went to Amman on 8 March 1972 for consultations, and presumably also to learn about the organizations' and Egypt's position on the elections. With the closing date for entry, 20 candidates had presented themselves including eight from the Kan'an list; the other 12 were mostly over 50, without any standing in the town and mostly of limited or even no formal education. They included two members of the municipal council (one of whom withdrew on 18 March 1972; the other was a 70-year-old merchant); two drunkards; one mentally unstable person; a postal clerk; and the youngest, a 36-year-old owner of a photographic studio.

Stage 2: 16–21 March 1972. The organizations' threats influenced the candidates. The IMG wanted to hold the elections on the basis of the candidates competing among themselves. Events moved fast. On 19 March 1972 an attempt was made to set the car of candidate Bashir Jardana alight; on the same day he announced the withdrawal of his candidature in *al-Quds*. On 19 March 1972 six members of the Kan'an list informed Kan'an of their intention to withdraw after receiving threatening letters. Because of this, and of himself receiving such a letter, he too decided to withdraw. The commander of Judea and Samaria and the defence minister met him personally that very day to persuade him not to withdraw, but they failed. Hikmat al-Masri had by now returned from Amman and Beirut where he had met members of the organizations who gave him a severe warning to pass on to Kan'an. On 20 March 1972 Kan'an's entire list formally withdrew – an important achievement for the organizations.

Stage 3: 21–27 March 1972. A crisis had arisen in Nablus. The IMG was now faced with a question as to who ruled Nablus – itself or the organizations. The only candidates remaining were insignificant, and even their candidature was doubtful. The IMG attempted to neutralize the organizations' influence and to force the town's leadership to participate in the elections. It indeed succeeded in this, but not without taking deterrent steps. The town leaders were warned that, unless the elections were held, an Israeli officer would be appointed in place of the town council, and in fact an officer was appointed on 21 March 1972 in preparation for this. Economic sanctions were imposed on the town; and its notables were advised that the lists of names under the "family reunion" scheme were being re-examined. Also, the military presence in the town was strengthened. Hikmat al-Masri was detained for interrogation on 23 March on suspicion of contacts with the organizations; he was released the next day. The town's leadership now held extensive discussions on the crisis. On 25 March the IMG announced a new timetable, beginning 26 March, for candidates to register, while continuing to warn against surrender to the organizations. On 25 March the leadership agreed on seven candidates, but the next day they all withdrew after one candidate's photographic studio was set on fire. On 26 March the town's leaders agreed to al-Masri's proposal that the council enter itself *in its entirety* for the elections – with all other candidates withdrawing. In this way they would all be elected in *tazkiya*. The IMG opposed this, and the leadership reversed its decision. On 27 March the entire council entered their names; the final number of candidates was 23 (including the 10 council members). Among the ten elected, eight were from the outgoing council. The two newcomers did not affect the political or social structure of the council (one was a graduate of al-Azhar, the other a contractor). The elections in Judea were held on 2 May 1972 without disturbance.

In all, the number of electors on the West Bank (excluding Jerusalem) was 31,746, of whom 24,649 (85 per cent) voted. A total of 311 candidates contested 192 places. If we take into account that two councils were elected by *tazkiya* (Salfit seven, Hebron ten), then the elections were contested for 175 places (see Table 1).

TABLE 1
RESULTS OF THE MUNICIPAL ELECTIONS 1972

Area	Number of seats	Number of candidates	No. of candidates on outgoing councils	No. re-elected	New members
Samaria	83	137	52	40	43
Judea	109	174	63	44	65
Total	192	311	115	84	108

Most significant in the elections was not the behaviour of the electors but the nature of the candidates. The voter was not asked to choose between "traditional" and "nationalist" candidates. The candidates were very similar to the outgoing members, and so the *status quo* was preserved. Not all the outgoing council members sought re-election; among those who did 74 per cent were re-elected. They were distributed as follows: just under 20 per cent (30–33) had nationalist leanings; 3 per cent were under age 30, 50 per cent over 51; 10 per cent had at least some higher education, 25 per cent had secondary school education, 65 per cent had limited or no formal education; 75 per cent were involved in agriculture or commerce, 12.5 per cent were white-collar workers.

Despite changes in the councils' composition, the public in fact accepted the principle of consensus upon which the notables had agreed in Nablus (26 March 1972), namely, preservation of the *status quo*. The higher proportion of voting in the election can be attributed, *inter alia*, to a fear of losing benefits from the IMG (since their identity cards would not have been stamped if they had not voted), and to the fact that the Nablus leadership (and others) had been a party to the decision to participate. Therefore, no conclusions should be drawn about the political attitude of the West

Bank inhabitants towards Jordan, the PLO or the IMG. From this point of view the assessments of IMG personnel and various academics should be seen as over-optimistic: that "the elections led to a shake-up in representation in the councils"; or demonstrated "an independent stance, as opposed to the stance of Jordan and the fidai organizations"; or that the population "prefers advancing local interests, within the framework of the reality of the IMG, over taking a political-ideological stand according to external directives". Yet had the elections been conducted without the PLO's opposition, and with the participation of nationalist candidates, the results would undoubtedly have been very different. We should note that a large proportion of younger voters (those in their twenties), who went through their formative years under the influence of the PLO's violent nationalism, did not vote. It seems that the Nablus traditional leadership, because of its weakness, could not cope with the two pressures (the IMG and the organizations) on it, and so succumbed to the stronger of the two.

The local leadership did not attribute the same political importance to the elections as did the organizations. Since Jordan played no significant role in the elections, the formal commitment of the leadership to the regime in Jordan was reduced. Jordan was left with no choice except to recognize the elections and those elected as mayors.[90] The Fatah/PLO had to admit that their "decision to boycott the elections was not wise"; they minimized the impact of their results. They correctly calculated that once the elections had taken place in Samaria there was no point campaigning against them in Judea, and admitted that "the efforts [we made] in Nablus did not achieve the outcome we dreamed of", and that "a number of insignificant actions were carried out, such as the burning of motorcars". In contrast, the JCP–WB viewed the results as "a success".

The elections highlighted the complexity of relations between the West Bank leaderships and the PLO. The PLO leaders, with an uncompromising fervour resulting from the crisis they were then undergoing, were cut off from the day-to-day interests of the inhabitants and especially from the pressures of the IMG, which were, however, important for the West Bank leaders and were not connected with their attitude towards the PLO. The PLO did not present any practical alternative to the leadership, apart from total resistance to the elections.[91]

The Traditional Leadership

Husayn's plan and the municipal elections were the only tests faced by the leadership during this period. Although the elections gave their leadership legitimacy, they did not contribute to a change in their political or representational status. Nor did this leadership have any pretensions to a political role; the elections were the last "blood transfusion" in their political decline. Hamdi Kan'an disappeared almost completely from the scene. Because of the lack of fidai activity and of passive resistance on the West Bank, there were no conflicts between the IMG and the traditional leadership (or even the nationalist leadership) which demanded a clear political stance. The leadership remained largely pro-Egyptian regarding both the conflict and the PLO; local leaders continued to visit Cairo for consultation. They believed Egypt "would never accept a partial agreement which was not linked to a comprehensive agreement". They continued to oppose any Israeli proposal for changes in the military government, for example, a "self-administration" or a "civilian administration". *Al-Fajr* and *al-Sha'b*'s unrelenting campaign against this leadership damaged its status considerably.[92]

The traditional leadership's freedom of manoeuvre *vis-à-vis* Jordan increased compared to the period of the Husayn–Nasir alliance. The gap which had been created between the regime and the West Bank in September 1970 continued to widen. The leadership ceased speaking of "the unity of the two Banks", since the king's plan proved that such unity was impracticable. They even desisted from any clear public expression of support for Husayn. As with their approach to the IMG, they distinguished between the official attitude towards the regime and their daily connections with it, although the regime tried (unsuccessfully) to link the two.

Their approach to the regime was reflected in three cases. One was Anwar al-Khatib's three articles in *al-Quds* (March 1972), under the pseudonym "A Well-Known Palestinian Politician", in response to publication of the UAK plan. Khatib was well aware of this plan's background, its timing and aims. He doubted it would work because of the position of the interested parties, including "the will of the Arab nation" (i.e. the PLO and Egypt). In his view the plan meant "dismantling the unity" of the two Banks, to be replaced by a "weak federation" which would be an anachronism. Khatib stressed "preservation of the national uniqueness and the historical heritage of the [Palestinian] people". Therefore, "it would have been preferable if the plan were presented in a free referendum [for approval]." His articles implied that Husayn had no right to speak for the West Bank inhabitants or to determine their future. In other words, they should be allowed to decide their future after the "liberation" of the West Bank (apparently it was because of this implication that he wrote anonymously). No doubt Khatib voiced the dominant viewpoint of the traditional leadership – more moderately expressed. At the heart of the matter was separation from Jordan and an "independent Palestinian Entity" which would determine its future relations with Jordan. This attitude was strengthened following Egypt's plans for the Palestinian Entity. Khatib believed that the Palestinians – by which he meant those in the occupied territories and in the Arab countries as well as the fidai organizations – should be party to any possible solution.

The second case was the rejection of Jordan's proposal for a Palestinian congress in Amman on 15 May 1972, in response to the PPC's gathering in Cairo to demonstrate Palestinian support both for the regime and Husayn's plan. The king's emissaries went to the West Bank in early May 1972 to talk with its leaders; among those invited to the proposed conference were Hikmat al-Masri, Husni al-Suqi, Hamdi Kan'an, Hilmi Hanun, Abd al-Rauf al-Faris and even Ja'bari. All refused, and the regime abandoned the idea.

Third was the protest to the Jordanian government by the mayors, the Muslim Council and the local leaders over the steps it took against the 13 people who signed a petition to the PPC. They rejected the king's plan and demanded an end to all actions against the 13. Here there was coordination between the traditional and nationalist leaders.[93]

No leadership can survive in a vacuum regarding its political conceptions, especially in a society with a rapidly crystallizing national identity. In view of the traditional leadership's identification with the pan-Arab consensus, developments in the Palestinian and Arab arenas and the process of detachment from the regime in Jordan, the leadership's political affiliations pushed towards the PLO. Since there were no internal or external pressures on it, its approach towards the PLO did not need to be clearly or openly articulated during this period. But a number of indirect factors are significant, such as the pride and enthusiasm with which invitations to the PPC were received; had the IMG permitted it, large numbers would most likely have attended. Then there was the deep mourning throughout the West Bank, which went on for two weeks with the municipal councils participating, over the assassination of two

Fatah leaders and the PLO spokesman in Beirut (10 April 1973). There was also the protest against the death sentence imposed on Abu Daud and the petitions against the demolition or sealing up of houses by the IMG for involvement in fidai activities.[94]

Thus the traditional and nationalist leaderships' approaches converged. This was reflected in the political activity on the West Bank which followed the Security Council debate (June 1973) on Zayyat's proposal and Bourguiba's declaration and in memoranda, one to the chairman of the Security Council (23 July 1973) and one to the UN secretary-general (30 August 1973). The first was signed by 108 prominent persons (including five from Gaza) representing the entire West Bank political spectrum. The signatories demanded, *inter alia*, "the right to self-determination and to sovereignty on their own land for the inhabitants of the West Bank and Gaza Strip". The second memorandum was even more important since it showed a new consensus between the traditional and nationalist leaderships, which replaced the National Charter of late 1967; it was signed by 155 prominent personalities (including 15 from Gaza). The signatories of the second memorandum included mayors, members of the Muslim Council, of Chambers of Commerce and of the free professions, leaders of women's organizations, supporters of the independent Palestinian Entity (except Ja'bari), trade union leaders and heads of charitable organizations. The composition of the signatories pointed to the changes in the personal political map of the West Bank following the expulsions of leaders since June 1967, and to the rise of young nationalist forces. The end of the memorandum emphasized: "Our people on the West Bank [including Jerusalem] and in the Gaza Strip, is an integral part of the entire Palestinian people"; "peace and stability in the area will not come about except through ensuring the legitimate rights of our Arab Palestinian people, chief among them the right to self-determination in absolute freedom on its land and to return to its home in accordance with the Declaration of Human Rights and the United Nations Charter." Taking the cautious wording into account, they clearly wanted to come as close as possible to the Arab and the PLO positions – and this without provoking a strong IMG response. In contrast to the National Charter (late 1967), there was no mention of any link with Jordan; the West Bank was defined as Palestinian territory and as the territory for self-determination. It is no surprise, therefore, that this document was welcomed by the organizations.[95]

The position of the independent Palestinian Entity supporters.
Faruqi and Shahada had ceased almost entirely to declare publicly
their positions. *Al-Quds*, *al-Anba* and *al-Bashir*   continued to
be a platform for the supporters of an independent Palestinian
Entity, chief among them Abu Shalbaya, Ahmad Barham and
Ibrahim D'aybis. Encouraged by Sadat's initiative and the PLO's
strengthened position, the supporters of an independent Entity
proposed (February 1972) "the establishment of a delegation which
will contact the Palestinians overseas and in the Arab states in
order to reach agreement over setting up a temporary Palestinian
committee recognized as the legal representative of the Palestinian
people". This group naturally rejected the UAK plan and criticized
the contacts between Jordan and Israel, with Anwar Nusayba as
intermediary; and they logically enough accepted Zayyat's proposals, since those of Shahada, Faruqi, Ja'bari and the *al-Quds*
group were already based on the Partition Resolution. It also called
on Israel "to come to terms with the existence of a Palestinian
nation [and people] on its land as a neighbour". "The concept of
nationalism and [of] the holiness of the national land should not be
treated with contempt." It praised the policy of Egypt, which
"regards the PLO as the political and diplomatic representative",
and its call for "the establishment of a Palestinian state".[96]

Ja'bari, however, stubbornly clung to his own principles. He
claimed that at this stage "it is impossible to set up a Palestinian
state, because we have no economic resources ... . Where will its
capital be, in Jericho, or in Ramalla?" After his re-election as mayor
he called on the IMG to grant the mayors the authority of *muhafiz*,
that is, of a district governor. He justified the annexation of the West
Bank to Jordan on the grounds that "if the regime treated us
like second- or third-class citizens, we would not live with it one
moment". But Zayyat's proposals led him to change his mind.
"After deep consideration" he altered his position on annexation of
the West Bank to Jordan; in an interview in *al-Anba* (late July 1973),
which Abu Shalbaya called "a historic declaration", he argued that
"Filastin was never part of Jordan, the Palestinian was never a
Jordanian, just as the Jordanian was never a Palestinian". After
1948 "the Palestinian people gathered on the West Bank and
decided to join with East Jordan in order to defend itself against
destruction and annihilation ... . Because of this the Palestinian
people swore loyalty to the king of Jordan on condition that this oath
would not detract in any way from [its] rights in its homeland or its
citizenship or its right to self-determination ... . The Palestinian

people has never abandoned its aspiration to establish its own Arab Palestinian state." "The most effective solution ... is to set up a Palestinian state on the West Bank and Gaza Strip according to the Partition Resolution of 1947, the basis of its [the state's] existence being no less than that of Lebanon or Jordan." He thus negated any legal claim by Husayn that the West Bank should be returned to his rule.[97]

Changes in PLO Tactics

The organizations' assessment of their situation on the West Bank (and Gaza) in the first half of 1972, and especially after the municipal elections, was very pessimistic. The main points in this assessment were: (1) The organizations were "isolated from the occupied lands and without any direct line of contact with the West Bank". (2) Their severe defeat in Jordan had had a "negative influence on the inhabitants of the occupied territories". "The masses in the territories live in a state of despair and apathy." (3) The IMG "has managed to realize its political, economic, agricultural and cultural plans", as a result of the "strengthening of coexistence" between it and the inhabitants. (4) "The stalemate [in the fighting] in the region has considerably affected the organizations' ability to act inside [the territories]." (5) Their failure to undermine the election campaign, and the liquidation of the local fidai organizations by the Israeli security authorities, showed the lack of "a broad political foundation". They concluded that their "concentration on military activity led to [their] neglecting political activity", which proved to the traditional leadership's advantage. The organizations saw three possible courses of action.

1. *Fidai activity.* The importance of fidai actions on the West Bank and Gaza was exaggerated by both Fatah and PFLP leaders. As early as November 1971 the Fatah Congress had designated "the occupied land" as one of the three arenas of action. According to Kamal Udwan, who was responsible for this arena, "the shift in focus from Beirut and Damascus to Nablus and Gaza will lead to a huge change in Fatah['s situation]. An intensification of internal actions [on the West Bank and Gaza] will reduce the importance of actions abroad." Fatah even laid down new foundations for its organization in the territories "based on local commanders" and "resting on cadres of [politically] conscious and educated people". Fatah viewed this activity as a means of restoring faith in the

leadership and of strengthening the self-confidence of the organization's members.

In September 1972 the PFLP, too, set itself over-ambitious goals for fidai activity in the territories. It laid down that in anti-Israeli activity "there is no difference between civilians and military personnel". Among the goals were "attacks on the enemy's political and military cadres, on new settlements and on concentrations of Zionist immigrants, continuation of clandestine resistance, especially in the area of 1948 and in the towns, suicide missions with political significance, burning down of factories and poisoning of water for agriculture and grazing". The PFLP decided that their leaders in the territories should be co-opted to the PFLP leadership at all levels; it also attempted to enlist students from the territories travelling to study abroad.[98]

There was a huge gap between aspirations and achievements. Fidai activity in the territories during this period was in fact at a low point. In 1972 there were only 40 actions on the West Bank (of which three were in Jerusalem) – an average of three to four each month. There was some recovery in 1973, with 68 actions (in addition to 15 in Jerusalem), an increase of 84 per cent. Forty of these actions took place from October to December, that is, after the War. Most of the actions were not serious: only 13 involved handgrenades and firing of bazookas, the rest (55) consisting of insignificant sabotage. In contrast to higher totals in previous years, in 1972 only 27 local units were exposed by the security authorities in the West Bank (including Jerusalem); 220 persons were arrested in this action, and with 440 other arrests there was a total of 660 in that year. In 1973 there was an increase in terrorist activities, with 37 local units being detected (12 during October–December) and 270 arrested, in addition to 370 other persons, totalling 640 (110 were detained during October–December). The local units generally consisted of seven to eight people, the biggest being a 24-member PFLP unit exposed in Nablus in November 1973. Fatah was prominent: in 1973 22 units from Fatah, five PFLP, four PLFS, and six unaffiliated ones were exposed. The decline was also evident in the number of houses demolished as punishment for involvement in fidai activity: in 1972, 34 were demolished (ten in Jerusalem) and in 1973, 35 (22 in Jerusalem). The situation in the Gaza Strip was similar.

Against this background one can understand the organizations' emphasis on "actions abroad". The PLO leaders' concern over the situation can be seen from Habash's unprecedented message of encouragement broadcast by Fatah Radio from Cairo (12 March

1973) to the West Bank and Gaza, following the assassination of three PFLP leaders in Gaza on 9 March 1973. There was also little passive resistance, apart from historical anniversaries such as 5 June (1972, 1973), on which anti-IMG leaflets were distributed and the flag of Filastin raised. The JCP–WB was active in this connection. The mayors of Ramalla (Karim Khalaf) and al-Bira (Abd al-Jawad Salih) were outstanding in their nationalist activity and their incitement of the population to resist. They did not hide their sympathies for the fidai organizations and for the PLO as representative of the Palestinians.[99]

2. *Collaborators.* The organizations feared that their weakness would encourage the supporters of an independent Palestinian Entity just when they most needed to strengthen the PLO's representative status. Kamal Udwan defined the problem as "how to wipe out the [collaborationist] elements in order to arouse and activate the nationalist elements". Therefore, they attempted to impress upon the inhabitants and leadership of the territories that "the supreme political leadership of the Palestinian people is in the hands of the PLO".

After the elections there were no new political initiatives on the West Bank which necessitated a campaign of threats and warnings; most efforts were now directed against cooperation with Husayn regarding his plan. On this issue the organizations linked, unjustifiably, Hikmat al-Masri with Ja'bari and Gaza mayor Rashad al-Shawwa. Shawwa received the bulk of the threats because of his visits to Amman and his declarations, which sounded as if he was supporting the king's plan. They threatened al-Masri that "his fate will be no better than Shawwa's". Ja'bari was again called "a traitor", and written threats were sent to him by the PFLP. The PFLP made two assassination attempts on Shawwa during this period, leading to his temporary resignation. Fatah leaders rejected attacks on Shawwa (or any other leaders) outside the territory of the Gaza Strip, since this would demonstrate, in their opinion, their weakness inside the Strip. Shawwa's request to meet a Fatah leader in Beirut in the first half of 1972 was rejected, but when he arrived there that July, specifically to meet a leader of the organizations, the Fatah leadership decided that one of them should indeed meet him. During the meeting Fatah demanded his resignation and threatened his life; his request for a further meeting was rejected.

In this sphere too, however, the organizations did not realize their expectations. Kamal Udwan admitted (August 1972) that "we drew up a list [of collaborators] but in the course of seven months we carried out only two or three attacks, and these were valueless". Apart from a few PFLP successes in the Gaza Strip, the organizations failed in this area.[100]

3. *Establishment of the Palestinian National Front (PNF).* Estimating that "liberation of the West Bank is not a matter of two or three years", the organizations planned a long-term policy for the territories. They agreed that creation of a broad political foundation, based on active cadres which would serve as a political prop for the PLO in its struggle against the IMG in the territories, would thwart any local efforts to collaborate with the IMG and would also strengthen the PLO's claim to represent the Palestinians. All this required the creation of a crystallized political leadership for the entire West Bank which would encompass all the nationalist groups and individuals. Once the goal had been determined, the problem was how to achieve it.

The PFLP's stand was clear:

> A national front must be established which would include all the nationalist forces in the Gaza Strip and the West Bank and the Arabs of the 1948 area in a clear political framework; account would have to be taken of divisions of opinion between the PFLP and the JCP–WB [regarding] the peace solution and other problems.

Fatah's stand was hesitant in light of the problems of survival in which it found itself in 1972. It was unsure what the Front's composition would be, or its relationship to the "national unity" plan which the PLO was debating. Fatah was not prepared to cooperate with the JCP–WB; furthermore, the West Bank nationalist leaders who were expected to lead the Front did not in the main lean towards Fatah. So, when established, the Front would be led by the JCP–WB and the radical organizations, namely the ANM (PFLP, PDFLP) or the Ba'th; and a situation could arise in which the Palestinian establishment was led by Fatah, while the Front, intended to be its arm in the territories, was led by the radicals.

Consequently, Fatah suspended as far as possible any decisions by the PLO's institutions on this question. The first of these was the EC decision of 6 September 1972 calling for a "national united front on the West Bank and Gaza Strip for resistance to the occupation and against all activity and plots to liquidate the Palestinian problem". *Al-Fajr* responded quickly and positively (9 September

1972), calling on the inhabitants to establish a "committee for national unity". But this resolution remained a paper decision for some time yet. The JCP on the West Bank and Gaza saw this decision as an opportunity to widen its influence and to gain recognition from the PLO, thereby participating in its institutions. Its organ, *al-Watan*, argued (late September 1972) that "a front such as this exists in practice and is constantly active against the occupation and for [Israeli] withdrawal, in accordance with Resolution 242". *Al-Watan* was referring to the front organizations of the party, namely the Front for Popular Struggle on the West Bank and the United National Front in Gaza. Early in November 1972 the party distributed leaflets in the name of both these organizations, calling for "unification of all the nationalist elements in the territories and beyond in one national front based on a minimal plan – Israeli withdrawal according to Resolution 242". It was clear that the PLO would not accept this as a basis. To facilitate these efforts and to build for itself a "fidai" image, the party in early 1973 began to set up armed units in the territories, and during that year its members joined the Fatah and PFLP local organizations. The JCP-WB saw the establishment of a National Front as its supreme task. It tried to penetrate existing popular organizations on the West Bank and even made preparations to set up new ones such as the West Bank Teachers Union.

The EC's decision was endorsed by the 11th PNC (January 1973). The PNC decided on "the need to initiate the necessary contacts for the establishment of a united national front inside [the territories]". Among the organizations themselves and their representatives in the territories the deliberations on setting up the Front lasted more than six months. Fatah tried to coordinate its position with the PFLP, relying on their increased closeness during this period, which was important to Fatah in view of the PFLP's status on the West Bank and especially in Gaza. Against this background the PFLP rejected a proposal by the PLA HQ to establish a National Front without Fatah's participation. The JCP–WB conducted the activity in the territories for setting up the Front by coordinating with the PFLP and the PDFLP; it also helped formulate the Front's manifesto. And it tried to mobilize the support of the heads of the trade unions and of popular organizations.

On 15 August 1973 the establishment of the Palestinian National Front on the Occupied Land (PNF) was announced. The decision on its establishment was taken on 11 August 1973. The composition of the forum that decided on this is not clear, but nationalist leaders, chief among them the Communists, undoubtedly participated, including Abd al-Muhsin Abu Mayzar, Abd al-Jawad Salih, Dr Walid Qamhawi and Arabi Awad. The JCP–WB undertook to distribute the manifesto throughout the territories. Its main points were: (1) "The PNF is an integral part of the Palestinian national movement represented by the PLO." (2) "Guarantee of the legitimate rights of the Arab Palestinian people, chief among them ... self-determination on its land and the return to its home". (3) "Rejection of the plan for a Palestinian Entity [in the territories], civilian administration, self-rule and the Allon–Husayn plan." The emphasis on the PNF being part of the PLO was intended to persuade Fatah to support the PNF. Indeed Fatah did not create obstacles to setting up the PNF, as long as it desired cooperation with the other organizations within the PLO institutions. Furthermore, it was important to Fatah that, while Jordan's status in the Arab arena was improving, it could point to a representative body in the territories as an arm of the PLO. The EC PLO welcomed the setting up of the PNF. But the problems for Fatah remained: What should be the PNF's composition? Who controlled it? Was it an alternative to the PLO in the territories or an arm of it? Fatah wanted the balance of power within the PNF to reflect that within the PLO institutions. When it did not succeed in this, it later turned towards establishment of another representative body, the Committee for National Guidance.[101]

CONCLUSION

In this period the Arab world moved towards a new phase in the Arab–Israel conflict, to begin after the War. The basic lines were laid down for an active Arab stand on the question of the Palestinian Entity in general and of representation in particular. Achievements were determined more by Arab political considerations than by the PLO's ability to impose its representation of the Palestinians on the Arab arena and, to some extent, on the Palestinian arena. The Arab states, Egypt and Syria in particular, had some success in gaining international recognition for the PR as a "national liberation movement". On the eve of the War, agreement was reached among the Arabs, except Jordan, regarding the PLO as the legitimate representative of the Palestinians.

Egypt, under Sadat, continued to be the leader in advancing the notion of the Palestinian Entity. While Nasir had laid the conceptual foundations for its establishment, Sadat laid the practical foundations for an independent Palestinian Entity. In this way Sadat, more than any other Arab leader, influenced the PLO's concept of stages, already emerging at the end of this period. On the eve of the War, Egypt's conception of the Palestinian Entity could be summarized as follows: the Palestinian issue is one of a "national liberation movement" which needs to be solved through self-determination for the Palestinians in the form of a Palestinian state on the West Bank (including Jerusalem) and the Gaza Strip; Egypt's task was to bring about the return of these territories for the Palestinians and anything beyond that was up to the Palestinians themselves; the PLO was the sole legitimate representative of the Palestinian people; Fatah was the leading Palestinian organization; Palestinian representatives would have to participate in the peace negotiations which would take place after the War.

Asad's regime played a secondary role during this period. It was towed behind Egypt once Sadat had decided on war. It took a passive position on the Palestinian Entity, reacting rather than initiating. Unlike Egypt, whose contribution was mainly political, Syria contributed mainly to the organizations' "armed struggle" against Israel. The organizations' dependence on Syria in this regard increased during this period of their crisis, at a time when fidai activity was their *raison d'être*. Syria did not attach the same importance to the Palestinian Entity and representation as did Egypt; it viewed the PR from the perspective of the "armed struggle" rather than from that of the political solution, as Sadat saw the PLO. There was almost complete identification between the PR's and Syria's approaches to the "armed struggle" strategy. Because Egypt and Syria were aligned on the subjects of the War, fidai activity and its subordination to Arab strategy, the PLO's and organizations' freedom of manoeuvre was limited. However, the "strategic alliance" continued between the two parties, as did their "struggle" over the degree of Palestinian independence in decision-making and action.

Leaders or heads of states do not necessarily propose long-term political plans with the complete certainty, or even complete conviction, that they will be implemented according to their spirit and letter. They may also be intended to gain time, to slow down undesirable political processes or give impetus to desirable ones. Husayn announced his plan for the UAK in order to halt the process of the detachment of the West Bank from his kingdom; and also to retain some bargaining power in prospective West Bank negotiations – despite his reliance on Israel's principles of not recognizing a Palestinian Entity, and her viewing the Jordanian Kingdom as both the "Palestinian homeland" and the only legitimate party in negotiations regarding the Jordanian front.

Husayn's plan was the maximum he could suggest; anything more would have been tantamount to waiving Jordan's right to the West Bank and to represent the Palestinians. But the plan was now much less comprehensive than what the Palestinians aspired to, considering that they had support from Egypt, Syria and the Arab world. Announcement of the plan served the PLO by leading to some recovery from its crisis and by impelling the Arab decision in the Jordan–PLO struggle over representation of the Palestinians and the future of the West Bank. Husayn's plan was an antithesis to King Abdulla's formal annexation of the West Bank in 1950. Ironically, it was the grandson who renamed the West Bank "Filastin" after his grandfather had attempted to erase that name from the political lexicon of the Middle East – final proof of the failure to integrate the two Banks. Husayn in fact recognized the existence of an autonomous Palestinian Entity, although not yet an independent one. When his plan was announced it was already as anachronistic as his proposal of late 1968 had been.

Towards the end of this period the problem of Palestinian representation became more a function of political struggles in the Arab and Palestinian arenas than of the extent of fidai activities. In 1973, preparations for war pushed fidai activity into a corner and both Egypt and Syria attached little importance to it. The organizations' leaders became more and more aware that the PR could not exist without "Palestinian land" under its control, or at least land which would serve as a substitute for Jordan as a "safe base". Their options were very limited. At this stage the only substitute for Jordan was Lebanon, where the organizations, in order to obviate a possible "Lebanese Black September", prepared a clandestine military network which would be even stronger than the one they had had in Jordan. The weakness of the Lebanese regime indeed prevented a "Lebanese Black September", but with the collapse of legitimate government nothing could prevent the civil war (1975), the armed conflict with the Syrians (1976) and eventually the armed confrontation with Israel (June 1982).

The search for "Palestinian land" led the organizations, at the same time, to change their concept as to how to realize their strategic goal. The PDFLP was the pioneer in this direction since the strategic goal of establishing a "secular Palestinian state on the entire land of Filastin" seemed to it unattainable in the short run. Paradoxically, the organizations' crises and conflicts increased the consciousness of Palestinian identity among the Palestinian population, which now felt the need for a channel to express its political affiliation with a Palestinian establishment. The only one which existed was the PLO. The overlap between the PR and the PLO abetted this. The composition of the PLO institutions did not even give minimal representation to the majority of the total Palestinian population (on the West Bank, the East Bank and the Gaza Strip). But this did not halt the growing recognition of the PLO as representative of the Palestinians. The successful candidates in the West Bank municipal elections, who were mainly from the traditional leadership, did not have the power to compete with the PLO's claim to representation; on the contrary, they recognized this claim. This leadership was in the last stages of decline.

Part Two
Achievements, October 1973 – November 1974

Two climactic events in the Arab world since 1948 have contributed to the realization of the Arab national goals: the establishment of the UAR in 1958, and the military initiative and strategic victory of October 1973. In both cases the result was a return to division in the Arab world: the dismantling of the UAR in September 1961, the decline of Arab solidarity that followed the Interim Agreement between Egypt and Israel (September 1975) and the division of the Arab world into two camps after Sadat's peace initiative and visit to Jerusalem (19 November 1977), particularly after the signing of the Camp David Accords (September 1978). The military initiative of October 1973 was the strongest expression of the turnabout in modern Arab history which began in 1971. It transformed Sadat and Asad into charismatic leaders, and gave legitimacy to Sadat's leadership of Egypt and the Arab world and Asad's leadership of Syria. The direct appeal to the Arab peoples which characterized Nasir's rule and era gave way to "personal diplomacy" from which all Arab leaders have benefited. "Pride of victory" swept the Arab world, which Sadat described as the "sixth [super]power". Arab solidarity, which replaced the concept of "Arab unity" and which encompassed radical as well as conservative states, reflected the process of depolarization in the Arab world which had started in 1971. The distinction was between the confrontation (i.e., fighting) states and the assisting states, or financial sponsors of the War. Thus the oil states, headed by Saudi Arabia, gained political and economic importance. Arab solidarity in this period was the point of departure for every Arab move concerning the conflict. The agreement between Egypt and Syria on a way of solving the conflict continued to be the basis for Arab solidarity, whereas disagreements between them were the cause of its decline.[102]

After the War Egypt regained its leadership of the Arab world in regard to the conflict. Egypt had generated every move and initiative related to the War (including the cease-fire), convening the Geneva Conference on 21 December 1973, signing the disengagement agreements in January 1974 and May 1974, removing the oil embargo (18 March 1974) and coordinating between Jordan and the PLO. But its status impaled Egypt on the horns of a dilemma. On the one hand, it wished to keep leading the Arab world and playing a central role in the conflict, thereby enjoying Arab political and financial support. On the other hand, it wished to retain the freedom to conduct an independent policy in the process of resolving the conflict. In this period Egypt generally tended to adhere to preserving Arab solidarity. This solidarity facilitated the emergence of a central Arab leadership consisting of four leaders: Sadat and Asad, who held the military power as well as the power to make political and military decisions regarding the conflict; Faysal, who controlled the oil weapon and wealth and was the epitome of the "sixth [super]power"; and Boumedienne, the strong man of the Arab Maghrib, who, with a bias towards Sadat, held the balance of power in this period. The radical camp, which included Iraq and Libya, was relatively weak.

For the new Palestinian national movement, 1974 was a very important year in terms of political achievements in the Arab arena, beginning with the Algiers summit (November 1973) and ending with the Rabat summit (October 1974). Behind these achievements was Egypt. The question of a Palestinian Entity or Palestinian representation became central to inter-Arab discussions on the political solution, its resolution being the condition for a solution to the conflict. Paradoxically, progress towards a political solution made the fundamental problems of the conflict, primarily the Palestinian issue, more pressing. Hence the need to make parallel progress regarding the Palestinian Entity – a situation which brought increased likelihood of stalemate in the political process and of disagreement in the Arab world. Commitment to securing "the national rights of the Palestinians" became a nationalist criterion for Arab regimes, and a condition for the legitimacy of any agreement with Israel. Whereas progress on the Egyptian or Syrian fronts was fundamentally an Egyptian or a Syrian problem, any settlement on the Jordanian front was an Arab problem requiring the participation of the PLO and Jordan, that is, a settlement between them against the background of Israel's positions, which ruled out negotiation with the PLO and regarded Jordan as the "Palestinian homeland". An Arab decision was therefore required in the Jordan–PLO struggle for representation. This development, and the subsequent recognition of the PLO as the "sole representative of the Palestinians" and as a party to the conflict, increased

Arab competition to influence Palestinian decision-making in all aspects of the political process.

The resolutions of Arab summits are never rescinded; they are confirmed by the following summit and/or, parallel with them, new resolutions are made. Such was the case when the Algiers summit (26–28 November 1973) practically abolished the Khartoum "Nos" and gave the go-ahead to negotiations with Israel. Sadat as the "hero of the crossing" (of the Canal) dictated his strategic concept of a solution to the conflict and to the question of Palestinian representation. In a speech on 16 October 1973 he defined the principles of his "peace plan", which had been conceived and crystallized before the War. Central to his plan was "an international peace conference" which would include the confrontation states and the PLO. The "top secret" resolutions of the Algiers summit marked a change in the Arab position by determining an "interim aim" (*hadaf marhali*). This is a development of an earlier Nasir strategy after the Six Day War regarding a solution of the conflict in stages. The summit decided on a number of "immediate aims of the Arab struggle".

First, in the territorial sphere: (1) "Full liberation of all the Arab territories which were occupied in the aggression of June 1967." (2) "The liberation of Arab Jerusalem and rejection of any situation which might prejudice the full sovereignty of the Arabs over the Holy City." The summit's declaration maintained that "to realize peace, there must be an Israeli withdrawal from all the occupied territories and in particular from Jerusalem; and also a restoration of the inalienable national rights of the Palestinian people". This was the first time an Arab summit had defined an "interim aim" – in essence, a strategic aim for whose achievement the Arab states are willing to conduct negotiations for a permanent peace in the area. The Lebanese foreign minister defined "interim aims" as "resolutions which can be implemented in the present, rather than in the long run … i.e. withdrawal from the territories which were occupied after the 5th of June". The summit did not take a formal decision regarding the Geneva Conference, nor set up conditions for conducting the negotiations after Egypt and Syria had expressed their willingness, in principle, to participate in it. There was an agreement to allow Egypt and Syria "freedom to decide on political and military matters".

Second, in the Palestinian sphere: "Adherence [*iltizam*] to restoring the national rights of the Palestinian people in accordance with resolutions of the PLO, which is the *sole* representative of the Palestinian people" (emphasis added). Jordan, consistent with its position, had objected to this article. It is noteworthy that the summit had recognized the PLO as "sole" but not "legitimate" representative. Also, because of Arab disagreement on the issue, it avoided a definition of "national rights", leaving it to the PLO. Sadat was determined to bring about endorsement of the PLO's representative status, in order to help him dictate his phased strategy, including an agreement to participate in a "peace conference". On this issue he was supported by Asad, Boumedienne, Bourguiba and Faysal. Bourguiba claimed that "Jordan could remain within the East Bank" and his foreign minister argued that "it is just that Palestinian land which was deposited in Jordanian hands should be returned to the Palestinian people". Boumedienne declared that "the West Bank was part of Filastin and therefore to have a referendum on this issue was like having a referendum on Sinai, to determine whether it was part of Egypt". Saudi Arabia supported the resolution only after it had become apparent that all the other leaders supported the PLO, and after failing to obtain assurances that the Fatah/PLO leadership would exclude leftist organizations from its ranks in exchange for Saudi support.[103]

Knowing the position of the Arab leaders following the discussions of the Arab Foreign Ministers Conference (which had decided on the agenda of the Arab summit), King Husayn preferred not to attend; he was represented instead by Bahjat al-Talhuni, the chief of the Royal Cabinet. By so doing Husayn appeared to show his determination to continue opposing the proposed resolution both during the summit and after its adoption. A compromise motion calling for substitution of the word "sole" by "legitimate" was rejected. To soften the impact of this resolution on Jordan, it was decided to adopt a Saudi–Moroccan suggestion not to make public the resolution on the representative status of the PLO. This secret resolution was released to the press by the secretary-general of the Arab League and by the PLO. There is no doubt that Jordan's non-participation in the war on its border contributed to the Arab states' adoption of this resolution. Husayn's part in the war was limited to sending about one armoured division (two armoured brigades plus artillery, support and service units) to Syria, where it fought on the Golan Heights. The first brigade reached the battle area in Syria on 14 October 1973 and began to take part in the fighting only on 16 October 1973. On 1 January 1974 the force was withdrawn from Syria. Husayn took every possible step to prevent the outbreak of fighting on the Jordanian border, including sending messages to Israel via Kissinger to explain his policies and the reasons behind the despatch of his troops to Syria. He also strenuously refused to allow fidai actions from the Jordanian border.[104]

EGYPT'S POLICY

In its tactical political moves in 1974 towards a solution to the conflict, Egypt was guided by a number of principles.

1. *"Translating the military victory into a new political reality".* Sadat was afraid to lose the impact of the "scale of the victory", which led him to race against time. He strove towards political achievements as long as the momentum of "victory" "was capable of generating sufficient pressure" to achieve the war aims.

2. *Maintenance of the political momentum.* This meant keeping the initiative in Egyptian hands; the slogan was "he who does not advance goes backwards". Fahmi, the foreign minister, claimed that "there is a great difference between steadfastness and a stalemate which may deny us the translation of the victory into new facts". Sadat tried to avoid a return to a state of "neither peace nor war". It was clear to him and to the rest of the Arab world that another war might jeopardize the achievements of the October War. The tactical flexibility of the Egyptian policy often caused "astonishment" in the Arab arena, though Egypt maintained that "each step is well calculated and does not prejudice the basic goals".

3. *Freedom of manoeuvre* within the framework of Arab solidarity. Sadat described Arab solidarity as "one of the greatest achievements of the October War"; he praised "the fraternity of arms and blood" with Syria. He reiterated that "there will be no separate peace". He described the disengagement of forces on the Egyptian front as a "purely military move"; for him "the Golan Heights, Jerusalem and Hebron are as important as Sinai". Nevertheless Sadat did not regard Arab solidarity as a "holy" goal; "it is our right to maintain freedom of action", "as long as we act within our agreed strategy". Sadat adhered to "steadfastness" up to the point where solidarity tended to create a long stalemate in the political process.

In his view deviation from Arab solidarity did not mean relinquishing strategic goals, but, on the contrary, was a way of achieving them.[105]

The Palestinian Entity

Sadat successfully persuaded the PLO/Fatah leaders to apply the "phased conception" in their realization of the PLO's strategic goals. In the context of his efforts to convene the Geneva Conference and of the political discussions on the conflict, he had to define (for himself) the interim goal to which the Palestinians should aspire. For the establishment of a Palestinian Entity, he defined the following aims: (1) "The establishment of a Palestinian homeland is inevitable." He reiterated that "the problem of Filastin is the political problem of a people". (2) The Palestinian Entity or "Palestinian national rule" must be established "on every centimetre of the liberated land of Filastin". (3) The goal is "the establishment of a Palestinian state on the West Bank and the Gaza Strip, with a linking corridor". This state should decide on the nature of its relationship with Jordan, assuming there must be some kind of link between the two states.[106] It seems as if Sadat, like Nasir, had his doubts even about the right of the Jordanian Royal Regime to exist in a territory where the majority of the population was Palestinian, that is, the East Bank. Sadat assumed that in the long run there would be a "Filastinization" of the East Bank government.

Egyptian policy had now for the first time reached an operative stage in the implementation of Nasir's 1959 initiative on a Palestinian Entity.

Sadat's Efforts to Convene a Geneva Conference

During 1974 Sadat tried relentlessly to convene the Geneva Conference. To achieve this and keep the political momentum going, he conducted a zig-zag policy which baffled the Arab world and sometimes seemed to deviate from his basic policy on the Palestinian issue. He affirmed that the Geneva Conference's aim was "to discuss the final solution and lasting peace, in order to carry out UN resolutions which are linked to one another, i.e. a return to the 1967 borders and the establishment of a Palestinian Entity, and beyond it the establishment of a Palestinian state". To secure a successful outcome of the Conference, Sadat stipulated certain conditions.

1. Stabilization of the cease-fire on the Egyptian and Syrian fronts.
Sadat strove for a "balance" between the two fronts to demonstrate

parallel progress. Hence he sought vigorously, after the disengagement on the Egyptian front (January 1974), a like agreement on the Syrian front; to speed up its signing he personally pressured Kissinger and Asad. Sadat presented the disengagement agreement on the Syrian front (31 May 1974) as an essential step towards the Geneva Conference; "it is impossible to go to Geneva without Syria".

2. *The representation of Egypt, Syria, Jordan and the PLO.* These elements should go to Geneva as "one bloc" to avoid making the conference a "stage for declarations". According to Fahmi, the Egyptian foreign minister, "it is impossible to go to Geneva unless we are certain that full solidarity exists between all sides, which Israel cannot break". To achieve such solidarity, Sadat saw the need to overcome two obstacles. The first was the opposing positions of Jordan and the PLO, which Sadat saw as the deepest single breach in the Arab front. It had to be overcome because, on the one hand, of the Arab commitment (particularly his own) to the resolutions of the Algiers summit calling for the sole representation of the Palestinians by the PLO, which meant the PLO's participation in the peace talks, and on the other hand because of Israel's objection to PLO participation in the Conference. The second obstacle was the differing approaches of the US and USSR as guarantors of Resolution 242 and as hosts of the Conference: the US advocated a step-by-step policy, giving priority to progress on the Egyptian front, whereas the USSR, fully supporting Syria and the PLO, advocated a Geneva Conference with the participation of all parties towards a comprehensive solution. Sadat assumed that without US–USSR agreement the Conference would result in polarization, with the USSR defending the Arab position and the US backing Israel. This would lead to stalemate, a state of neither peace nor war so that "another war would be inevitable". At this stage Sadat ignored the basic opposition between Egypt and Syria on the nature of a solution to the conflict. He believed that the two states' understanding on the "interim aim" as agreed upon in the Algiers summit was sufficient for coordination towards the convening of the Conference.[107]

To ensure success at the Geneva Conference, or at least its first stage, Sadat had to solve the problem of Palestinian representation. This he did in two stages. In the first (October 1973–May 1974), he urged the PLO/Fatah to adopt an "interim aim" which would correspond with the "interim aim" of the Algiers summit. Sadat pressured Fatah for PLO consent to participate in the Conference.

In the second stage (July 1974 – September 1974), he needed to find a formula acceptable to both Jordan and the PLO for representation of the Palestinians or their case at Geneva. The emphasis in his policy shifted towards Jordan or Jordan–PLO coordination.

SYRIA

Syria entered the October War as a senior partner to Egypt, but its perception of the war's aims remained fundamentally different from Egypt's. Ever since the dismantling of the UAR (September 1961) these two countries had seen eye to eye only on matters relating to war with Israel, but had disagreed during any lull in the conflict. Since the 1950s the Syrian Ba'th was haunted by an "Egyptian complex"; it oscillated between the conviction that Syria could not achieve its goals in the conflict without Egypt, and a reluctance to follow Egypt's lead and lose its freedom to act independently. After the war the two countries moved in different directions with short-lived tactical agreements on specific issues. It seemed as if all the elements shaping the status and leadership of Egypt (as part of the Nile Valley, separated from Israel by a desert), compared with those of Syria (the centre of the Fertile Crescent and the Arab Mashriq, separated from Israel's Green Line border by the thin strip of the Golan Heights), found expression in this period and after, influencing relationships between the two central states involved in the conflict. This rivalry was part of an ever-deepening Syrian suspicion that Egypt was moving towards partial or separate agreements with Israel. American versus Soviet orientation also contributed to the tensions between the two countries, as did different interpretations of the Arab "interim aim".

Syrian Strategy after the War

The results of the war reinforced the regime in its original strategy, which had been set forth after Asad's rise to power, despite Syria's lack of any territorial gains. Asad interpreted the Arab "interim aim", in letter and spirit, as a stage towards his strategic goals.

> The October War brought the Arab nation for the first time to the stage where it is capable of setting up a timetable, deciding upon clear interim aims achievable within the existing framework without giving up the overall strategic aim which was the liquidation of the Zionist aggression and full liberation of the Arab Palestinian land.

(Egypt, on the other hand, strove to achieve the Arab "interim aim" as a strategic aim in itself.) Syria was therefore opposed to "partial or separate solutions and settlements" which were, in its view, a "liquidation of the Palestinian problem". What was required was a comprehensive solution or a parallel solution on all fronts, on the premise that "Arab land is one complex". Egypt interpreted Arab solidarity in a liberal fashion; Syria did so in rigid accordance with the resolutions of the Algiers summit.

Syria accepted (24 October 1973) Resolution 338 calling for a cease-fire "on the basis that it meant a complete Israeli withdrawal from all Arab land occupied in June 1967, and securing the rights of Arab Palestinian people". Whereas Egypt saw the disengagement agreement in Sinai (January 1974) as a step towards the Geneva Conference, Syria regarded the Golan disengagement agreement as an "important step towards achieving the interim aims of the Arab struggle ... and as a solid basis for continuing the struggle on all levels". Syria refused to take part in the first session of the Geneva Conference (21 December 1973), claiming that the aim of the conference was "to dissolve the fundamental problem" and that "the first condition for convening the Conference must be an Arab–Palestinian agreement which would define the Arab and Palestinian interim demands". But following the Golan disengagement agreement, Syria agreed to participate in the Conference "if it proved an efficient means to achieving a just peace ... [i.e.] complete [Israeli] withdrawal and securing the rights of the Palestinian people". Asad made Syrian participation conditional on the "Palestinian delegation sitting next to Syria ... . Filastin is the essence". At a later stage Syria demanded "the participation of a united Arab delegation".

Contrary to Sadat's "political action", Asad adhered to "political struggle" with the same determination with which he had conducted the "armed struggle"; he wanted to prove thereby that he did not follow Egypt. He acted as if the political process was imposed upon him, a position manifested in a war of attrition against Israel which he conducted (from 11 March 1974), while the Kissinger talks on Golan disengagement were in progress, up until the signing of the agreement on 31 May 1974. Given these views, Asad was not optimistic about the outcome of the political talks; he was, therefore, simultaneously preparing a military option.[108] In fact, one might say that Asad's strategic conception represented a continuation of Nasir's conception.

The Palestinian Entity

When practical discussions on the Palestinian Entity began, as part of the political negotiations after the War, Asad had to fulfil his obligation towards Filastin as the "southern part of Syria". Sadat's efforts to gain recognition for the PLO as "sole representative of the Palestinians", the PLO resolutions on this subject before the War, and Sa'iqa's being part of the Palestinian leadership – all these led Syria to interpret the Algiers summit resolution on the PLO as "sole representative" as strictly as it had interpreted the Arab "interim aim". At the same time, the Syrian regime believed that the problem facing the Palestinians was twofold: their presence at the Geneva Conference, and the future of "Palestinian territories" from which Israel would withdraw after a solution. The regime decided on the following priorities concerning the Palestinian issue, in accordance with its overall view of the conflict and with the fundamentals of the Arab "interim aim". (1) *The end of occupation*, which was "the most urgent demand at present ... towards which one must concentrate all activities ... in the Arab and Palestinian arena". The aim was to "resolve the fundamental opposition with the enemy [Israel]." (2) "Preservation of the national character of the Palestinian people and insistence on its national rights." (3) "The struggle against the restoration of Hashemite sovereignty over the West Bank, and the transformation of the liberated Palestinian territories into an independent national Palestinian Entity ... which is the historical antithesis of the Zionist existence." The regime reiterated that "first and foremost one must secure a withdrawal of the enemy from the Palestinian territories and only later discuss their future. This should be done not only with the Hashemite regime, but within an Arab context, such as an Arab summit and in accordance with previous resolutions of the Arab League and Arab summits on the prominence of the Palestinian Entity and the PLO status as the sole legitimate representative of the Palestinian people."

As in the previous period, Syria attributed much less importance to Jordan's refusal to accept PLO representation, or to the basic tenets of the Palestinian Entity, than did Egypt and the PLO. Syria regarded Jordan as part of the "Syrian Region" and of a "centre of gravity" against Egypt, and also as the protector of Syria's southern flank in a state of war. In Sa'iqa's view a Jordan–PLO struggle over the future of the West Bank before Israel's withdrawal "would force the Palestinians to make major concessions on the essence of

the [Palestinian] problem itself". "It will not be difficult for the
Palestinian people to choose [after a solution] a legal or political
framework, even if the Jordanian regime continues to oppose it." If
Jordan refused to hand the West Bank over to Palestinian rule "the
entire Arab nation would stand by the Palestinian people, to take it
out of Jordanian hands, in accordance with the summit's resolution
making the PLO ... sole legitimate representative of the Palestinian
people and confirming its right to self-determination". Sa'iqa
rejected the "Jordanian complex" of the other Palestinian organizations. "The road to the West Bank is potentially via two gates, the
Tel Aviv gate or the Amman gate." Syria preferred the "Amman
gate" because "Jordan is an Arab country and as such its right to
exist is recognized [by the Arab states], whereas Israel's existence is
illegal. Closing the gates to Jordan would mean pushing the Palestinian people into a corner, which would force them to open
the gates to Israel." According to Zuhayr Muhsin (July 1974),
"the Palestinians cannot avoid reconciliation with Jordan because
current circumstances require concentration of effort to end the
Israeli occupation." "If Israel withdraws from the West Bank,
these territories should be handed over to an Arab administration
agreed upon by the Arab League. This administration, which would
exclude Jordan, would be a stage towards the transfer of rule over
these territories to the Palestinian people."

Sa'iqa reiterated that "the PLO as a political organization would
not remain the appropriate body after a political solution had been
reached". Until then "the national character of the Palestinian
people as manifested by the PLO, which embodies the theoretical
political entity, should be preserved". Sa'iqa had its doubts as to
"whether the present leadership of the PLO is authorized to discuss
[the nature of] self-determination of the Palestinian people" after
"the liberation". "The PNC and the present [PLO] leadership
should [only] confirm the inherent right to self-determination."
Sa'iqa continued to be part of the coalition which led the PLO
(recognizing Fatah's senior position in the leadership), as long as it
could influence the leadership's resolutions by virtue of its Syrian
backing. Sa'iqa took an active part, together with Fatah and the
PDFLP, in formulating the PLO's "phased programme" which was
approved by the 12th PNC (June 1974).[109]

JORDAN

Objection to the Algiers Summit Resolution

Jordan continued to raise reasons for objecting to the Algiers summit resolution on Palestinian representation, both to Arab states and in diplomatic talks. Since its argument with Shuqayri, Jordan's position had been in principle remarkably consistent. It realized, however, that after the Algiers resolution it faced a much more serious challenge, and so used all the cards at its disposal. Its main arguments were as follows.

Jordan's basic thesis was that "the most important concern is the liberation of the West Bank. It is better to agree on the need to liberate it, rather than argue about its future ... or the question of representation before liberation." In so arguing, Jordan clearly capitalized on the Syrian position. Jordan repeated its claim that according to Resolution 242 "Jordan is responsible for the liberation of the West Bank, since it is a Jordanian territory occupied by Israel". Therefore "Jordan should fully represent the West Bank at a Geneva Conference intended to implement Resolution 242".

Second, Jordan claimed that it "is not willing to put up with PLO representation of all Palestinian residents in the Kingdom of Jordan. Some of them have become naturalized citizens and constitute a large part of its people on both Banks of the Jordan River. They hold Jordanian identity cards and are integrated into all institutions and establishments both in government and in the army. It is difficult to distinguish between a Palestinian and a Jordanian in the East Bank." Moreover, "there are Palestinians in the West Bank who have leaders who declare that we [Husayn] represent the Palestinians more than anyone else". Jordan admitted that "we alone do not represent the entire Palestinian people, likewise nobody else should claim to ... especially if this body [the PLO] was imposed [upon the Palestinians] by the Arab camp". Regarding Palestinian representation Jordan suggested a "division of roles" and a "timetable". It agreed to the presence of a PLO delegation at the Geneva Conference, but only "in order to discuss the rights of the Palestinian people beyond the 5th of June [1967] borders ... which were [the rights] agreed upon in UN resolutions on the Palestinian problem", and "only at the appropriate time". Husayn reiterated his position, dating from Shuqayri's era, that "Jordan had recognized the PLO in the September 1964 Alexandria summit as a representative of the Palestinian people, [only] in order to voice its defence of the Palestinian problem in both the Arab and the international arenas". "The PLO should represent the Palestinians outside Jordan, the West Bank and the Gaza Strip." Husayn would recognize the PLO "as the legitimate but not sole representative of the Palestinian people".

Third, regarding the right to self-determination, Husayn intentionally refrained in this period from making direct reference to the UAK plan. He and other leaders stressed that "following the restoration of the West Bank to Jordan in a final settlement", Jordan would be willing "to grant the West Bank inhabitants the right to determine their future in a referendum in complete freedom and under international and neutral supervision". In this referendum the inhabitants would choose between: a separate Palestinian government; unification with Jordan in accordance with the UAK plan; or a return to being part of the Jordanian Kingdom. Zayd Rifaʻi, the Jordanian PM, opposed a referendum after disengagement of forces on the Jordanian front or "as long as the Israeli occupation continues".

Fourth, Husayn played the Israeli card as it was virtually his only practical means of obstructing the implementation of the Algiers resolutions and to prevent their re-endorsement at the Rabat summit. Husayn exploited both Israel's attitude towards the PLO and the Arab states' fear of a vacuum in the West Bank should Jordan decide to dissociate itself from this territory and its future. Indeed, Zayd Rifaʻi stressed that recognition of the PLO as the voice of the Palestinians would "strengthen Israel's occupation of the Palestinian land". Husayn and Rifaʻi threatened a number of times, particularly at the Rabat summit, that should the Arab states "place *sole* responsibility with the PLO for strategy and consequent action leading to a restoration of the occupied Palestinian land including the West Bank and Jerusalem, and of Palestinian rights ... we [Jordan] should free ourselves from our present basic responsibility", since with this "Jordan's right to negotiate on behalf of the Palestinians is in fact being forfeited". Thus "Jordan would not participate in the Geneva Conference or in any diplomatic or international initiative in accordance with Resolutions 242 and 338, since it will have no occupied land to claim back".

Finally, Jordan attached great importance to its "shadow" presence in the West Bank. Faced with Arab and PLO resistance to the restoration of Jordanian administration to the West Bank (including by disengagement of forces) or to any part of it from which Israel might withdraw, Husayn pointed out (notably at Rabat) that "Jordanian administration in the West Bank exists *de facto*".

> The administrative machinery in the West Bank is linked to the central machinery in Amman, so that the governors, clerks, municipalities, various trade unions, passports, education, culture and many more aspects of civic life are linked to the central government in Amman. Jordan pays for these administrative institutions including wages and loans. The only element separating the West Bank from the East Bank is the Israeli occupation.

In this period Jordan tried to prove these claims by continuing to pay wages to clerks and by demonstrating a greater openness to the demands of West Bank mayors. But Husayn also attempted to act in a more persuasive and tangible way by seeking a disengagement of forces on the Jordanian front.[110]

Jordan's Efforts to Sign a Disengagement Agreement

Whereas after the Six Day War Husayn had concentrated his diplomatic efforts on the restoration of the West Bank as part of a comprehensive settlement, his main goal after the 1973 War was an agreement on disengagement of forces on the Jordanian front, despite the fact that Jordan had not participated in the War on its border. After the Algiers summit, Husayn rightly assessed that time was running short for any future bid for the West Bank. He thought that if he could regain even one kilometre of it (according to Sadat's slogan on the Sinai), it would reinforce his claim to responsibility for the "liberation of the West Bank". This would also buttress his opposition to the PLO's representative status, and prove that he was an important party to the Geneva Conference.

All this would only be relevant in the light of Israel's attitude to the PLO. From his talks with Israeli leaders Husayn became aware of the difficulties involved in achieving a West Bank settlement. He was as afraid as Asad was of a partial or separate settlement on the Egyptian front, and therefore declared his adherence to the Arab position on the terms of a comprehensive settlement. He tried to exploit both Sadat's flexibility and enthusiasm for convening the Geneva Conference, and Asad's set of priorities. He therefore closely coordinated his steps with Sadat and at the same time kept Asad informed of the details of his contacts with the US, including those relating to a disengagement on the Jordanian front. This was done to prevent action to frustrate his political efforts, and to ensure Arab endorsement of his moves. Husayn was fully aware that, given his position in the Arab arena, he could not afford to take any separate steps. He strove to obtain an Arab mandate, or at least a mandate from Sadat, to conduct talks on disengagement on the Jordanian front. He was keen to present such a disengagement as the "beginning of the implementation of the principle of full Israeli withdrawal from the occupied land". "None can dispute that any piece of land which we may recover from the occupier is pure gain to all Arabs."

Even back on 15 December 1973, during a meeting in Amman between Kissinger, Husayn, his brother Hasan and Rifaʻi, Rifaʻi had urged Kissinger "to suggest that Israel undertake a modest pullback so as to turn over to Jordan the city of Jericho". During the first session of the Geneva Conference, Rifaʻi demanded (22 December 1973) in the Military Committee that the "disengagement of forces should include the Jordanian front". No objection was raised, nor was the issue discussed. According to Kissinger, in another meeting with him (19 January 1974)

> the Jordanians [Husayn, Hasan, Rifaʻi and Bin Shakir] put forward a disengagement plan in which Jordan and Israel would each pull back eight kilometres [Rabin's version was 12 km] from the River to the foothills of the mountain ranges that mark the Jordan Valley. Jordanian civil administration would be established in the area vacated by Israel, especially in the town of Jericho. No Jordanian forces would cross the river or come closer than eight kilometres. A working group should be formed as rapidly as possible to ensure Jordan's claim to represent the Palestinians.

Husayn proposed a disengagement agreement along these lines when he met with Golda Meir in March 1974, but Meir rejected this proposal, suggesting instead that a corridor (later known as the Jericho Corridor) be set up to give Jordan a direct link to the Ramallah area. Husayn and Rifaʻi did not hide their proposals from Arab heads of state; they even announced them openly. Husayn emphasized that he sought "an Israeli withdrawal from the river line, from the north to the Dead Sea, to an agreed distance, as a test of Israeli readiness for a complete withdrawal". What he had in mind was a "military agreement" similar to that drawn up with Egypt, without having to pay a political price, as had been the case with the Sinai and Golan disengagement agreements. To leave the door open for future negotiations, Israeli leaders reintroduced the Allon plan to Kissinger and Husayn. According to Husayn it involved "Israeli withdrawal from large parts of the West Bank, restoring civil administration to all vacated areas, on condition that Jordan agree that Israel would maintain a line of military outposts along the Jordan River and ... that the discussion on the issue of Jerusalem would be postponed to a later stage". In the Rabat summit Husayn claimed that "Israel offered us corridors between the [Israeli] settlements along the Jordan River". Naturally Husayn rejected this proposal, as he had done before the War. He argued (and reiterated at Rabat) that "Israel should not be allowed to set up military outposts or civilian settlements in any part of the West Bank. Jerusalem is not negotiable and Arab sovereignty must be restored over the entire Arab part of Jerusalem." After the signing of the Golan disengagement agreement, Husayn tried to focus attention on a similar agreement on the Jordanian front, which Jordan presented as "an essential condition for [its] participation in the efforts to achieve a just and lasting peace". Husayn called for a "balance" between the three fronts.[111]

PLO: THE "PHASED PROGRAMME" *(al-Barnamij al-Marhali)*

Egyptian Pressure, October 1973 – May 1974

Sadat believed that a united Arab stand at the Geneva Conference was necessary for its success. He therefore strove for a definition of a Palestinian "interim aim", and to get the PLO to participate in the Conference. He thus made the PLO decision the key to convening the Conference. Sadat used all his weight and prestige in pressuring the Fatah leadership, rightly convinced that the Fatah position was synonymous with the PLO position. In this context, the Palestinian Entity became an issue in the Arab arena, and ultimately in the international arena. Paradoxically, Arab decisions on this issue contributed to a stalemate in the political process. Sadat spoke in vague terms about Palestinian representation at Geneva rather than PLO representation. Sadat stressed that "everything should begin and end with Filastin". In his very personal way, he strove for political achievements for the Palestinians; his tactical steps were sometimes seen to be at odds with his basic position. With astute understanding of the character of the PLO leaders, Sadat did not attempt to impose his policy on them but did his best to persuade them. Here he found fertile soil, because the PLO leaders were aware of the need to set up an "interim aim". Furthermore, even before the War, the PDFLP was the first to change its views.

On 26 October 1973 Sadat summoned a number of Fatah leaders and suggested that they participate in a "peace conference" "while ignoring Resolution 242". The Fatah leadership discussed his proposal early in November 1973; on 12 November 1973 Arafat informed Sadat of their resolution "not to decide either positively or negatively before receiving an official invitation" to the Geneva Conference. However, Egyptian pressure persisted up to the 12th PNC session (1 June 1974) in order to bring the PLO institutions, and later the PNC, to adopt the "phased concept" and a resolution calling for participation in the Conference. Sadat, aided by the Foreign Minister, Ismail Fahmi, and the Egyptian media, was personally involved in this persuasion campaign which included meetings with Fatah leaders. Sadat employed the following tactics.

On the one hand, he tried to demonstrate Egypt's commitment to the Palestinian issue by complying with PLO demands on the consolidation of its status and representation; on the other, he played upon their sense of moral obligation towards him on account of this commitment by demanding a change in their position. Apart from his activities in the Arab arena, he also tried to alter the US position on the PLO but without much success (e.g., his failed attempt to arrange a meeting between Kissinger and Arafat). He sought, in the international arena, recognition for the PLO as "legitimate representative", and "support for the national rights of the Palestinian people". A considerable part of his talks with Nixon in Egypt (June 1974) was devoted to the Palestinian issue.

Second, Sadat argued that PLO participation in the Geneva Conference was unlikely as long as its strategic aim was "a democratic state in the entire land of Filastin", which meant the liquidation of Israel. He reiterated that "the Palestinians have the right to reject Resolutions 242 and 338". Egypt was opposed to any change in 242, as had been demanded by the PLO. In his talks with Fatah leaders, Sadat argued that the mere invitation of the PLO to Geneva and its participation there would automatically mean a change in 242 and recognition of the PLO.

Third, in his talks with Fatah leaders (and later in Rabat) Sadat also reiterated his concept, which had been applied in the War, that "a Palestinian Entity should be established even on a single square centimetre of the liberated Arab land".

Finally, as the 12th PNC approached, Egypt's efforts to persuade and expressions of commitment to the PLO and the Palestinian issue were conveyed extensively through the media. Egypt wanted to help the Fatah leaders persuade the PNC to adopt the change in Fatah's attitude. Sadat's letter to the PNC (1 June 1974) was a final effort in the Egyptian marathon. In an uncharacteristic move Sadat did not deliver a speech at the opening of the PNC so as not to be seen to apply pressure. His letter stated, among other things: "A historic responsibility is placed on you"; "the decision should be purely Palestinian"; "we are still committed to the view that you alone have the right to speak on behalf of the Palestinians"; "we are still committed to the view that the legitimate right of the Palestinian people as defined by its representatives should not be disregarded"; "we have committed ourselves, together with our Arab brethren, in the Algiers summit, to the resolution recognizing the PLO as the sole legitimate representative of the Palestinian people, and we are still committed to this view." The media used these arguments, calling on the PNC "to reach a brave and wise decision which would take into account realities ... " such as "the three million Jews who live on the land of Filastin, and the existence of the state of Israel, which is recognized by almost the entire world". Ahmad Baha al-Din stressed (31 May 1974) that "the establishment of a national rule on Palestinian soil would mean the realization of the Palestinian Entity by adding the element of land ... and by restoring the title of Palestinian citizenship, which is not held by any Palestinian". He was hinting, with a certain degree of satisfaction, at the proposal he had first made in October 1967, which he still considered to be practical. On 8 June 1974 he mentioned the Jordanian "threat", averring that "there is information about a disengagement of forces on the Jordanian front ... . Jordan is expecting to regain the town of Jericho. In such a situation the Palestinians and the Jordanians are bound to clash."[112]

The 12th PNC Session: Approval of the "Phased Programme"

One of the ultimate tests in the history of a national movement, or of a political leader, is when the time comes to take a decision which requires a radical change and reappraisal of aims previously fought for. In this situation a decision may become a "historic decision"; or lack of decision a "historic failure". The Fatah leaders made it clear to the Palestinians that they had reached such a stage. Of course, the fidai organizations who carried the flag of violent Palestinian nationalism had not schooled their members on the merits of achieving their strategic aims in stages. The Palestinian National

Covenant posits only one strategic aim: "the liberation of all Filastin and the liquidation of the Zionist imperialist presence" in it. It further claims that "the armed struggle is the only way to liberate Filastin and is therefore a strategy and not a tactic".

Yet the Algiers summit resolutions, the continuation of the process to solve the conflict by peaceful means, the agreement between the USSR and the US on this process and the need to discuss the future of the Palestinian territories after an Israeli withdrawal (which seemed likely at the time), all presented the PLO and the Palestinians with a new situation. Abu Iyad admitted that "we face a new reality which requires realistic solutions". "We should know our precise size and ... influence ..., without exaggeration which misleads both us and the masses." The dilemma facing the PLO/Fatah leaders was how to compromise between the "historic rights" and "present rights" without relinquishing the former. Furthermore, not joining the Arab "phased concept" would mean, according to Abu Iyad, "a confrontation with the two central states which conducted the October War", as well as with the USSR. In order to respond to the immediate political developments after the War (and before Fatah or the PNC could take a decision in principle), the PLO Central Committee took a number of decisions (5–7 November 1974) which represented a temporary consensus among the organizations. It called for: "adherence to the historic right of the Palestinian people to liberate Filastin"; "not to return the West Bank and the Gaza Strip to King Husayn"; "the right to self-determination of the Palestinian people."[113]

The turn in Fatah's position.   In December 1973, the Fatah leadership made a decision in principle to adopt a "phased concept". The "interim aim" was defined as "the establishment of a national rule over the Palestinian territories from which Israel would withdraw". This was a return to the point of departure of its early days, when in November 1960 its organ *Filastinuna* had called for the "establishment of a revolutionary Palestinian national rule in the Arab parts of Filastin". Fatah apparently returned to Qaddumi's suggestion to its CC of July 1967, calling for the "establishment of a mini-state in the West Bank and Gaza" after Israeli withdrawal from them. Abu Iyad claimed that after the War this idea "met with fierce opposition, despite its realistic nature".

Fatah's resolution was presented to the CC PLO for approval (20–21 December 1973). The CC took a number of secret decisions on this issue which were a compromise between Fatah's positions and those of the radical organizations which refused to join the political process (PFLP, ALF and PFLP–GC). These resolutions were: (1) "to act to prevent the return of the Palestinian territories to Jordan"; (2) "use of struggle to achieve *by force* the right to self-determination and the establishment of a national rule in these territories" (emphasis added); (3) "to allow the political leadership of the PLO [EC] freedom to take any necessary political steps to achieve this aim"; (4) "adherence to the National Covenant and the political manifesto of the PLO and the rest of the 11th PNC resolutions"; (5) "to guard against confrontation with the Arab regimes"; (6) "to intensify political activity in order to implement the Algiers summit resolution stating that the PLO is the sole legitimate representative of the Palestinian people." Naturally, the PDFLP and Sa'iqa supported Fatah's position.[114]

As soon as these principles were approved, the organizations launched a campaign among the Palestinians prior to discussion of the issue in the PNC. On the one hand, Fatah (and the PDFLP) tried to convince the other organizations of the need for an "interim aim", for example, the establishment of "national rule" and conditional rejection of Resolution 242 and PLO participation in the Geneva Conference. This campaign was headed by Abu Iyad, who had contributed much to the approval of this line in the Fatah and PLO institutions. The PFLP, on the other hand, was bitterly opposed, insisting that "national rule" should only be achieved by "armed struggle". There was no argument about the aim, only the means. Fatah ultimately prevailed but not without considerable difficulties, including opposition from within Fatah and from its leadership. It is striking that arguments advanced before the War against a "Palestinian state" in the West Bank and Gaza, which had often led to threats on the lives of people who advocated such a state, now disappeared. The catch-phrase was: "Liberation will only be completed in stages". Fatah raised the following central considerations.

1. *The need for "Palestinian territory".* Abu Iyad claimed that "until we achieve the strategic aim we need a safe base, whose fate should not be similar to the one in Jordan." "Gaining even ... twenty-three percent of Filastin is an interim achievement."

2. *The historical lesson.* The Fatah leadership had instinctively rejected positions "which had characterized the traditional Palestinian leadership for fifty years". Fatah now attacked that sort of "negative rejection" by the PFLP. Abu Iyad even claimed that the

situation was one of "to be or not to be ... the rejection path will lead the revolution to a dead end".

3. *The struggle with Husayn.* To argue against the return of the West Bank to Palestinian rule would appear to imply its return to Jordanian rule. "Leaving the future of the West Bank to a settlement between Jordan and Israel would mean ... PLO denial of responsibility for the West Bank and of their representation of the Palestinian people." "Absence from the discussions would mean leaving the political arena to Husayn."

4. *Adherence to the strategic aim.* Abu Iyad promised that "present achievements will not come at the expense of historic rights; the aim of the establishment of national rule is to complete the full liberation of the land of Filastin and the establishment of a Palestinian democratic state, and the liquidation of the Zionist entity"; "it does not mean the abolition of the National Covenant."

5. *The USSR's position.* Fatah attached great importance to this. On a visit to the USSR (November 1973), a PLO delegation found that the Soviets encouraged Palestinian representation at Geneva and rapid PLO integration in the political process. They left the form of representation to an Arab decision. They also encouraged the PLO to adopt an "interim aim". As a possible solution to the problem of Palestinian representation in Geneva the Soviets suggested that a delegation from the West Bank and Gaza participate there on behalf of the PLO. It is noteworthy that in his book Abu Iyad claimed that in early 1974 Habash suggested to Fatah "to nominate Palestinians from the occupied territories to participate in the discussions of a political solution while limiting our role to guiding them secretly". Fatah rejected this suggestion. During this period the USSR refrained from recognizing the PLO as sole representative of the Palestinians, as long as the issue was still being debated in the Arab arena. It did, however, express its support for "securing the legitimate national rights of the Palestinian people".

6. *The Israeli factor.* Fatah presented "Palestinian national rule" as the answer to Israel's position which "is against a withdrawal or a real peace", and as a means "of undermining her policy of breaking up the Resistance within two or three years". As a proof of their claim, they quoted Israeli prime minister Rabin who reiterated Golda Meir's position when he presented his new cabinet (3 June

1974), emphasizing that "Israel rules out the establishment of an additional Arab state between herself and Jordan. The political identity of the Palestinian and Jordanian Arabs can find expression in the neighbouring Jordanian–Palestinian state."

In January 1974, Arafat summed up the options open to the Palestinians should Israel withdraw from the occupied territories: the territories would be returned to Jordan as part of the UAK plan; they would be under international control; they would be transferred to Arab control, Syrian, Egyptian or Saudi; establishment of self-rule as part of the "Allon plan"; or establishment of Palestinian national rule. By presenting these options, Arafat made the choice a rather obvious one.[115]

The PDFLP position. In principle the PDFLP's reasons for supporting the "phased concept" were not fundamentally different from Fatah's; after all, the PDFLP had spoken before Fatah on this issue, in August 1973. Unlike Fatah, the PDFLP simultaneously stressed another consideration: "the independent Palestinian national rule would become the support [*irtikaz*] base for the struggle to topple the Jordanian regime, and for the unity of both peoples [Jordanian and Palestinian] and ... regions based on national democratic foundations ... which would transform them into the base of the Palestinian and the Arab revolution for the continued struggle to liquidate the Zionist entity in Filastin." The PDFLP did not rule out a "struggle on the diplomatic front" to achieve the aim of "national rule".[116]

The PFLP position. The PFLP remained committed to its prewar position. "The main lesson of the ... seventy-six months from June 1967 to October 1973 and of the War itself was the vindication of the logic of the Palestinian revolution. Only an armed struggle using armed force is capable of bringing about victory." The second lesson "is the futility and collapse of the logic [use] of concessions and the search for peaceful solutions". The PFLP categorically rejected Resolution 242 because it recognized Israel within secure and recognized borders, which meant "giving up seventy-seven per cent of ... Filastin to the Zionist movement". "Taking the PR to Geneva would mean that the PR would sign its own document of liquidation." The PFLP rejected the distinction between "present rights" and "historic rights". Yet it emphasized that it "would continue to operate within the PLO in order to get its position accepted". It threatened the PLO with a split, however, "should it decide that the revolutionary road passes through the Geneva Conference".[117]

Fatah initiated discussion in the PLO EC and CC to formulate a new political manifesto acceptable to all the organizations, in order to ensure the success of the PNC. Discussions in February and March 1974 centred around two working papers: one submitted by the coalition of Fatah, Sa'iqa and the PDFLP, the other by the PFLP. The two papers agreed that the strategic aim was opposition to the return of Jordanian rule to the West Bank or any part from which Israel would withdraw and the "continuation of the struggle to topple the 'hireling' Hashemite regime". Fatah added "the renewal of Palestinian–Jordanian unity on national democratic foundations"; the PFLP added "the establishment of national democratic rule which would facilitate the continuation of the fight to liberate Filastin". However, whereas the PFLP rejected 242 outright, Fatah's rejection was qualified, because "it ignores the presence of the Palestinian people and their political [legitimate] rights". Fatah continued to avoid taking a position on the Geneva Conference, arguing that "an invitation has not yet been received". Fatah agreed to conduct "a military and political struggle as part of the tactical steps" but kept stressing that the aim was the "expulsion of the occupying forces from the West Bank and the Gaza Strip unconditionally and without making any political concessions".

Another difference was that while Fatah advocated establishment of national rule through a "political and military struggle", the PFLP called for a "struggle against the plans to establish a Palestinian state or Palestinian rule in part of the Palestinian land" on the basis of Resolution 242 or the Geneva Conference. In relation to these discussions, the PNC was postponed several times and was finally set for 1 June 1974. Also contributing to this delay was the Fatah leadership's anticipation of the Golan disengagement; Fatah rightly assessed that the signing of such an agreement would help it get its plan approved in the PNC. Through a growing awareness of the importance of the "Palestinian decision", Fatah attempted to achieve a consensus between all the organizations. To formulate a new manifesto, a "seven-man committee" was set up (six leaders of the organizations and a PLF representative who was expelled from the West Bank). It managed to produce a ten-point manifesto defining the "aims of the struggle in the next stage", a version of which was included in the Political Report submitted to the PNC by the EC.[118]

The "phased political programme" (al-barnamij al-siyasi al-marhali). The argument in the 12th PNC session (1–8 June 1974) centred around two problems, the Geneva Conference and Resolution 242; "absolute refusal" and "positive refusal"; between a clear position on the Conference and a vague one which would leave the PLO leadership considerable freedom of political and diplomatic manoeuvre. In spite of strict discipline imposed on Fatah members to avoid criticism of the "ten points", the writer Naji Alush sharply criticized the leadership's position and by this associated himself with the PFLP. The Political Bureau of the PFLP set out the guidelines of its position at the PNC on the eve of its convention, stating that it would aim at a precise and unambiguous position on the Conference and, should the PNC adopt a fluid position, it would not participate in a new EC. It would remain a member of the PNC "until zero hour", that is, the point at which a PLO delegation participated in a Geneva Conference. The PFLP regarded the "ten points" as the absolute minimum. It seems as if the Fatah leaders had managed to persuade the PFLP to accept the manifesto, arguing, among other things, that a political solution was not realistic at this stage, so that the problem of PLO participation in Geneva was irrelevant. Furthermore, to appease the PFLP and the radicals, Abu Iyad suggested an addition to the "ten points" according to which "should a fateful situation arise which concerns the future of the Palestinian people, a special session of the PNC would be called for in order to discuss it". This was intended to anticipate a possible invitation to the PLO to participate at Geneva; the suggestion was accepted.

At the end of the discussion the "phased political programme" ("ten-point plan") was endorsed as suggested by the EC. Only four delegates voted against it: Dr Sa'id Hamud (PFLP), Yusuf al-Khatib (Sa'iqa), Naji Alush (Fatah, who resigned and joined the "rejection front") and Rif'at al-Nimir. The PFLP and ALF demanded that their reservations be recorded in the minutes. The PFLP reiterated its position in principle and in so doing gave its interpretation to the "ten-point plan". The ALF registered its motion to change the "ten points" to include the "rejection of the principle of direct or indirect negotiations with the enemy", "a clear position on the UAK plan" and an "emphasis on previous PNC resolutions on the regime in Jordan [i.e., its removal]".

The approval of the "phased programme" was an achievement for Fatah. The "ten points" it contained covered the following issues.

1. *The political settlement.* The first PNC point stressed "the PLO's previous position on Resolution 242, which obliterated the national [*wataniyya*] and pan-Arab [*qawmiyya*] rights of our people, and regards our people's cause as a refugee problem"; "therefore the PNC rejects cooperation with this resolution on this basis, at any Arab or international forum including the Geneva Conference." This version included a qualified negation of 242. The impression is that Fatah (and with it the PDFLP and Sa'iqa) was willing to accept 242 on the basis of "recognition of the legitimate national rights of the Palestinian people", and to participate in the Conference on condition that the invitation recognize the PLO as "sole representative of the Palestinians".

2. *The interim aim.* The second point stressed that "the PLO would struggle with *all possible means* at its disposal, the foremost of which is armed struggle, in order to liberate Palestinian territory and establish the people's independent national authority [*sulta*] over any part of the Palestinian territory which was liberated" (emphasis added). This meant approving political activity alongside the "armed struggle". The notion of "national authority" was later replaced by that of a "Palestinian state". By this the PLO brought itself into line with the Arab "interim aim". It is nonetheless noteworthy that Point 4 indicated that "any step towards liberation constitutes a continuing implementation of the PLO strategy of establishing a democratic Palestinian state" ("on their [the Palestinians'] entire national territory" – as mentioned in the introduction to the programme). Point 3 stated that the "PLO will fight any plan for a Palestinian Entity whose price is the recognition of Israel, peace, secure borders, relinquishment of the national right of our people and deprivation of our people's right to return and our right to self-determination within our national land". This did not rule out the establishment of a Palestinian Entity through political negotiations, on "part of the Palestinian territory" after its "liberation", on condition of the non-recognition of Israel.

3. *Jordan* (Point 5). "The PLO will struggle together with the National Jordanian Forces for the establishment of a Jordanian–Palestinian national front aimed at establishing a democratic national rule in Jordan which would merge with the Palestinian Entity to be established as a result of the struggle." This phrasing reflected a certain change in the Fatah and PFLP working papers, though even this version indicated the eventual liquidation of the

Hashemite regime. The description "what is nationally possible" (*al-mumkin al-watani*), given to this plan by EC member Abu Mayzar, was singularly appropriate.

The composition of the PNC. The official number of members in the 12th PNC session was 187; in practice, about 160–165 participated. In its first session the PNC approved the joining of two new Fatah members (who replaced Kamal Udwan and Yusuf al-Najjar), Abu Salih (Ahmad Salih) and Abu Mazin (Mahmud Abbas), both members of Fatah's central committee. It also approved the replacement of three Fatah members, two PDFLP, one ALF and one PFLP–GC. The significant change, however, was the addition of eight leaders of the Palestinian National Front who had been expelled from the West Bank, supported by 90–120 of the 120–130 members who voted on their inclusion. A motion calling for inclusion in the PNC of the secretary of the PPSF, Dr Samir Ghosha, was rejected (Fatah did not support it). The balance of power between the various organizations and their supporters was unchanged compared to the 11th PNC.

The composition of the EC. The PFLP suggested leaving the present EC in office (nine members after the death in April 1973 of Kamal Nasir who was not replaced) and adding nine members: six representatives of organizations and three independents. Fatah and PDFLP opposed the renomination of Dr Yusuf Sayigh (who had sharply criticized the "ten-point plan") and Zahdi al-Nashashibi (Sa'iqa). Sa'iqa supported the re-election of Sayigh, and also, naturally, Nashashibi's election. Finally a 14-member EC was agreed upon, seven of whom were from the previous EC (two were killed and Sayigh was not elected). Six new members joined: three representing the PNF (Salih, Abu Mayzar and Qamhawi), Talal Naji (PFLP–GC), the priest Elya Khuri ("independent") and Abd al-Aziz al-Wajih ("independent", formerly a PLA colonel). The official composition was: Fatah two (chairman and head of Political Department), PFLP one, Sa'iqa one, PDFLP one, ALF one, PFLP–GC one, PNF three, independents four. Given the political inclination of the PNF representatives and the "independents", the real result was: Fatah four to five, Sa'iqa two, PFLP two. Thus the coalition Fatah–PDFLP–Sa'iqa, which unreservedly supported the "phased programme", was sure of an eight to nine majority, whereas the radical line (PFLP, ALF and PFLP–GC) had no more than five members. The PFLP–GC joined the EC for the first time to reinforce the radical line, a move probably influenced by Libya and Iraq who supported this organization. In view of the criticism of the insufficient representation of the West Bank and Gaza inhabitants in the PNC and the EC, the joining of the eight leaders expelled from the West Bank, three of whom became EC members, reflected the "increase" in representation of these territories in the PLO leadership. This step indicated the central place of the territories in PLO policy, particularly in relation to the discussions on their future.[119]

SADAT: COORDINATION BETWEEN JORDAN AND THE PLO, JUNE–SEPTEMBER 1974

The PLO's "phased programme" did not live up to Sadat's expectations of the PNC to show "historic responsibility". The PNC did not take a positive decision on the Geneva Conference, and its acceptance of Resolution 242 was conditional. In this respect, it created obstacles to the Conference rather than paved the road for it. Nonetheless, Sadat had to keep the political momentum going in one of two directions: convening the Conference, or getting another settlement on the Egyptian front. After the 12th PNC, he began stage two of his efforts to convene the Conference, that is, "removing the opposition between Jordan and the PLO". This move required a temporary deviation from the Algiers resolutions and his promises to the PLO leadership on the eve of the PNC convention. Sadat planned two stages in his effort to achieve Jordan–PLO coordination: a meeting between himself and Husayn, and later one between Egypt, Syria, Jordan and the PLO. Taking Israel's position into account, the problem facing him centred on who would represent the Palestinians at Geneva and the timing of their participation; and to what extent a "division of roles" between the PLO and Jordan, or a "timetable" for their participation, was possible. Thus, Sadat switched his activities to Jordan; attaching great importance to the mission, he undertook it personally, and had two rounds of talks with Husayn.

1. *Sadat–Husayn talks 4–6 April 1974.* In early April 1974, Sadat summoned Husayn for talks aimed at ascertaining Husayn's position. Sadat wondered whether he could "extort" some concessions which might be useful in his persuasion campaign with Fatah and the PLO. His achievements were limited. The official communiqué after the talks intentionally emphasized Sadat's sole achievement, which was in favour of the Palestinian position. The

communiqué was not phrased as an agreement or mutual commitment but simply referred to the talks only. It stated that they "included the legitimate rights of the Palestinian people and its right to self-determination, to defend its cause in international forums and to participate independently at the Geneva Conference". Husayn did not give up his basic position on the PLO's role (not mentioned in the communiqué), which was "defending the [Palestinian] problem in international forums". According to the Jordanian version, this meant a Jordan–PLO division of roles.

The communiqué presented two "concessions" by Husayn. The first was his agreement to an independent Palestinian delegation at Geneva, contrary to his previous insistence on a Jordanian delegation with Palestinian representatives. However, the timing of its participation was not mentioned so as not to overshadow this "achievement". It was nonetheless clear that this delegation would not participate in the first stage of the Conference. The second "concession" was Husayn's agreement to recognize the Palestinians' "legitimate rights", but not their "national rights" (which were not mentioned in the communiqué). It is likely that a prospective disengagement agreement on the Jordanian front was also discussed, but a conclusion postponed to a later date. Sadat and the Egyptian media exploited Husayn's two "concessions" (particularly his willingness to accept "independent representation"), to demonstrate Egypt's determination to obtain PLO representation at the Conference and to point out Husayn's "wise" position.[120]

2. *Sadat–Husayn talks 16–18 July 1974.*   After the Golan disengagement agreement and the PNC convention, Sadat began another stage of his effort for Jordan–PLO coordination, this time with a bias towards Jordan. He invited Husayn to Alexandria, where talks were held 16–18 July 1974. Their official communiqué set out a number of principles: (1) Both sides agreed that the "PLO is the legitimate representative of the Palestinians except for those who reside in the Hashemite Kingdom" – a clear deviation from the Algiers resolutions and a significant concession to Husayn. On the other hand, Husayn recognized the PLO as the "legitimate representative" of the Palestinians, but this in practice was insignificant. Furthermore, "both sides see eye to eye on the need to include the PLO at an *appropriate time*, as an independent delegation in the ... Geneva Conference, in order to stress the [Palestinians'] right to self-determination" (emphasis added). Here too Sadat accepted Husayn's position on the "division of roles" and a "timetable",

which in fact meant that the PLO would participate at a later stage and would not negotiate on Israeli withdrawal from the West Bank. (2) Both sides "agreed on the need for a disengagement agreement on the Jordanian front, as a first step towards a just and peaceful solution". This paragraph complemented the previous one in recognizing Jordan's right to conduct negotiations on Israel's withdrawal from the West Bank. Sadat thereby gave the Egyptian seal of approval to Husayn's demand to reach a disengagement agreement with Israel. (3) "Both sides agreed on the need to set up permanent and regular coordination between Syria, Egypt, Jordan and the PLO ... to ensure early Arab mutual understanding before resuming the working of the Geneva Conference."

What had caused Sadat's compliance with Husayn's demands, to the extent that the content of their communiqué stood in the way of any possible reconciliation between the Jordanian and PLO positions? Did Sadat, by taking this line, give up his stand in principle on the PLO's representative status, for which he had fought before and after the War?

First of all, at that time Sadat started to envisage a further "military agreement" on the Egyptian front without making any political concessions. He called it a further disengagement agreement. In his talks in Washington (mid-August 1974) Fahmi raised this possibility, expressing the hope that the principles of such an agreement could be set down before September 1974, that is, before the forthcoming Arab summit. Fahmi was fully aware of the difficulties which might arise after the summit. In this context, Egypt's demonstration of its wish to create a "balance" between the three fronts by striving for a disengagement agreement on the Jordanian front, was aimed at covering up its efforts to obtain such a settlement on its own border, and escaping Syrian criticism for signing a "partial and separate" agreement. This assessment is reinforced by the fact that Sadat did not show any enthusiasm for seeking a disengagement agreement on the Jordanian front, and did not make it a condition for convening the Geneva Conference or for progress on further settlements on the Egyptian or Syrian front. He was, however, aware of the difficulties involved.

Second, Husayn had made a disengagement agreement on the Jordanian front a condition of his participation in the Geneva Conference. Sadat hoped that by his consent to such a clause in the communiqué he would be depriving Husayn of any pretext for refusing to participate at Geneva. Sadat left the initiative in Husayn's hands. He believed that Jordan was very important to any solution concerning the West Bank and Israeli withdrawal from it. Sadat, taking into account Israel's attitude to the PLO, recognized that granting the PLO the role of negotiation would mean a prolonged stalemate.[121]

Arab reactions to the Alexandria Communiqué were very sharp, far beyond Sadat's expectations. Besides the PLO, there was broad opposition to the communiqué from Syria, Algeria, Iraq and Libya. Fatah supported Sadat's efforts to coordinate between Jordan and the PLO, as long as they were not at their expense. The EC had even decided before Husayn's visit to Egypt to show willingness "to coordinate with the Jordanian regime on condition that it recognize the PLO as the sole legitimate representative of the Palestinian people and recognize the Cairo Agreement [September 1970]". Furthermore, as early as 17 July 1974, *al-Ahram* wrote that the Sadat–Husayn talks would result in an important announcement after which Jordan would withdraw its reservations concerning the Algiers resolutions. Fatah/PLO tried to prevent a crisis, hoping that Egypt would ultimately change her position. It interpreted the communiqué as "undermining the right of the Palestinians to full sovereignty over the land of Filastin", "an attempt to split the Palestinian people, divide its homeland, blur its national identity and help carry out the UAK plan", "contradicting the resolutions of the Algiers summit and the Islamic summit in Lahore". It also argued that the "disengagement would prevent the realization of an independent Palestinian national rule in any liberated territory". Syrian opposition stemmed chiefly from fear that the communiqué paved the way for a separate or partial Egyptian agreement with Israel. Syria interpreted the communiqué as a unilateral Egyptian move against her, aimed at obstructing Jordanian–Syrian co-operation.[122]

In response, Egypt embarked on a propaganda campaign personally headed by Sadat and Fahmi, intended to soften Fatah/PLO opposition and explain the communiqué's tactical motives; it was conducted through diplomatic channels and personal talks. Egypt's explanations attempted to separate the problem of representation from the territorial problem. They did not deny the communiqué's content, but tried to take advantage of its omissions and vague wording – which itself reflected Egypt's difficulty in formulating it.

Sadat claimed that "when Palestinians serve in King Husayn's armed forces, government and other official posts, I cannot tell him that the PLO represents them, if he so begs to differ". In Sadat's view the PLO, in keeping with his interpretation of the Algiers resolutions, was "the sole and legitimate representative of all the Palestinians in the West Bank, the Gaza Strip, Lebanon, Syria, Kuwait and so on". Sadat and Fahmi tried to play down the word "sole", though they were fully aware of the difference between it and "legitimate". Jordan's recognition of the PLO as legitimate representative, they claimed, was an Egyptian achievement for the PLO.

Concerning the status of the West Bank, Egypt adhered to its official position of not recognizing its annexation to Jordan in 1950. Sadat did not go back on his agreement to enable Jordan to seek a disengagement agreement with Israel. Sadat and Fahmi stressed that "the Jordanian government accepted the Egyptian argument that the West Bank is a pledge in Jordan's hands just as the Gaza Strip was a pledge in Egypt's hands". They led the PLO to understand that Jordan would only be "instrumental" in obtaining the territory, which would be transferred to the PLO after Israeli withdrawal. In this, Egypt remained consistent with its proposals to Kissinger in February 1973.

And as for disengagement of forces, Egypt informed the Fatah leadership that it

> opposed the return of the West Bank to the Jordanian civil or military authorities, because it considered the land as the territory of the Palestinian people. Their legitimate representatives should determine when a disengagement agreement on the Jordanian front would come into effect – their national, pan-Arab and international responsibility through cooperation with the confrontation states, the Arab League and the UN.

The communiqué amounted to "total [Egyptian] support for ... independent Palestinian national rule, on any territory evacuated by Israel either through the Geneva Conference or by force". Egypt reiterated its opposition to the UAK plan. Fahmi even claimed to have received "a written assurance" from Husayn that he would not bring Jordanian troops to the West Bank as part of any disengagement agreement (a condition he accepted in his talks with Kissinger in January 1974). Husayn also accepted that the West Bank was under a Jordanian mandate.

Egypt communicated these details, and its consent to Jordan's efforts for a disengagement of forces, to the US (late July–early August 1974), in order to avoid misunderstandings about the Alexandria Communiqué. The subject was likely to be raised in the

Fahmi talks in Washington (mid-August 1974). Jordan acted with restraint, even though she must have realized the erosion of Egypt's position; her main aim was a disengagement agreement. Husayn played for time, believing it was on his side. In view of the disagreement of Syria and the PLO with Egypt, a four-party meeting was obviously impossible. Syria and the PLO even rejected a tripartite meeting without Jordan, demanding that Egypt withdraw the communiqué. In order to keep the disengagement idea going, Jordan asked (20 July 1974), no doubt with Egyptian support, to postpone the Arab summit due to begin 3 September 1974. Egypt considered, correctly, that convening the summit amid Arab division on the Palestinian issue would not be in its interest. In spite of Syrian opposition, Egypt managed to mobilize the necessary majority to postpone the summit.[123]

Like the UAK plan before it, the Alexandria Communiqué stirred bitter Arab debate on the Jordan–PLO struggle for representation and the future of the West Bank. Once again it was apparent how difficult it was, in dealing with the West Bank's future, to separate the territorial aspect from the Palestinian national aspect. This time a clear decision on the Jordan–PLO dispute was inevitable, and the decision went in favour of the PLO. Husayn's achievement was short-lived, and ultimately backfired on him.

EGYPT: A RETURN TO THE BASIC POSITIONS

August 1974 was an important month for political developments towards a solution of the conflict. It was a month when all states directly involved in the conflict had to reappraise their next steps: Nixon resigned and Ford became president (8 August 1974); a new cabinet had been established in Israel (June 1974) and FM Allon had visited Washington (late July 1974), where he discussed possible directions for political negotiations; FM Rifa'i arrived in Washington (9 August 1974) followed by Husayn (18 August 1974); FM Fahmi arrived in Washington (11 August) where he met (among others) President Ford (14 August); Syrian FM Khaddam also arrived in Washington that very month. Following this flurry of activity and Arab developments towards the end of the month, Egypt reassessed its position. The conclusion was: its policy should return to the basic principles preceding the Alexandria Communiqué. The first manifestation of this change was an *official* Egyptian invitation (26 August 1974) to Syria and the PLO for a "tripartite conference" in Cairo, to coordinate Arab views on the convening of the Arab summit. This step was taken only after contacts with the Fatah leaders, when Egypt had indicated the anticipated change in its position, and after it had been convinced that such a conference was feasible. It seems that Egypt's estimate of the situation was based on the following considerations.

1. Egypt concluded that in view of the new political conditions, mainly in the US, it could no longer expect a further substantial settlement ("a second disengagement of forces") in Sinai in autumn 1974. Following Fahmi's talks with Kissinger, Egypt considered that there could be no discussion before late 1974 or early 1975. Fahmi indicated to Kissinger that Egypt would prefer the next stage of the settlement to be on the Egyptian front, in order to maintain the political momentum (and indeed, during Kissinger's October 1974 visit to the area on the eve of the Rabat summit – a visit aimed at maintaining the momentum, but little more – Egypt suggested an Israeli withdrawal to the al-Arish-Ras Muhammad line without paying any significant political price). Mahmud Riyad, Secretary General of the Arab League, writes in his *Diaries* that in early March 1975, Jordanian PM Zayd Rifa'i complained to him that Egyptian FM Fahmi, thinking that an agreement could be reached between Israel and the PLO, had advised Kissinger not to attempt to achieve a disengagement agreement between Jordan and Israel.

2. The usefulness of the Egyptian–Jordanian move seems to have been exhausted far too quickly. Egypt found out through its con-tacts with the US (among others) that in view of Israel's position, a Jordanian–Israeli disengagement agreement was highly unlikely in the long term, let alone in the near future. Therefore, making a Jordanian–Israeli move a condition for convening the Geneva Conference meant a long stalemate and an eventual dead end. Egypt could still argue that it had fulfilled its duty towards Jordan and that it continued to regard Jordan as an important partner to the Conference.

In view of these observations, Egypt regarded the division in the Arab world following the Sadat–Husayn communiqué as counter-productive. Contrary to common belief among Palestinian and other writers, the negative Arab response to the communiqué was not responsible for the shift in Sadat's policy; that was of secondary importance in his assessment. Sadat proved that negative Arab reactions to tactical and even strategic steps did not deter him if he believed that they would lead to his strategic aims. It seemed as if Sadat assumed that the convening of the Arab summit, which was expected to endorse the Algiers resolutions and which, with Syrian pressure, would prevent him from pursuing a "separate political settlement", would not interfere with his planned moves for 1975, that is, the convening of the Conference or a further "disengagement agreement" in Sinai. On the contrary, adherence to a pan-Arab position would help him in these moves. Sadat decided to retain the political initiative in the Arab arena, correctly assuming that drawing up principles for understanding and coordination between Egypt, Syria and the PLO would mean dictating these principles to the Arab summit and thereby ensuring its success.[124]

Egypt now took an active part in ratifying the PLO request to the Arab League Council to include the "Palestinian problem" as a separate issue on the agenda of the UN General Assembly. Until then this issue was discussed as part of the "situation in the Middle East". The PLO's aim was to present it as "a problem of national liberation". This move marked a shift in PLO policy; in the wake of the "phased programme" it had decided to turn to the UN in order to strengthen its representative status and establish itself as a party to a solution of the conflict. On 2 September 1974 the ALC adopted a resolution calling for: (1) "The ratification of the PLO request to include the 'Palestinian problem' as a separate motion on the agenda of the 29th General Assembly." (2) Any motion tabled in the General Assembly on this issue should emphasize the following principles: "the inalienable human rights of the Palestinian people"; "its rights to self-determination without outside interference, and guarantees for its national independence and its right of return"; "the right of the Palestinian people to act with all the means at their disposal, to achieve their basic rights in accordance with the aims and principles of the UN Charter." (3) "The Arab delegations to the UN will strive to get the PLO invited to the General Assembly to present the views of the Palestinian people during the debate on the problem." Jordan opposed this resolution. These principles were indeed endorsed in the 29th General Assembly. The ALC decided to convene the Arab summit in Rabat on 26 October 1974, after a meeting of the Arab foreign ministers on 22 October 1974 to set up an agenda. The Egyptian media again referred to the PLO as the "sole legitimate representative of the Palestinian people", a title which they had not used after the Alexandria Communiqué.[125]

The Tripartite Meeting

This meeting took place on 20–21 September 1974 between Fahmi, Khaddam and Qaddumi. It practically set up the principles of the Arab strategy which was later ratified at Rabat. After the talks a joint declaration was issued, mainly outlining agreement on the following points: (1) "Rejection of any attempt to realize any partial political solution because the problem is regarded as a whole." (2) "Emphasis on the establishment of an independent Palestinian national rule over the Palestinian territory which would be liberated by political or military means." (3) "Continuation of aid to the PLO as the sole legitimate representative of the Palestinian people, and assistance in securing its entrenchment within the occupied territories." (4) "Action aimed at achieving a resolution by the UN General Assembly, as part of the Palestinian motion on its agenda, and in accordance with the principles of the [ALC] resolutions in Cairo in September 1974."[126]

It was clear from the composition of the meeting, and from Egypt's wish to reach a positive conclusion, that the three parties would decide in favour of the PLO on the Palestinian issue, by adopting the resolutions of the 12th PNC, and in favour of Syria, against concluding any "partial or separate settlement". The result was a *formal* Egyptian withdrawal from the Alexandria Communiqué. The wording did not take away Egypt's right to reach a further "disengagement agreement" in the Sinai. It was, no doubt, an achievement for Syria and the PLO. From a Jordanian viewpoint, the declaration turned the wheel back. In order to maintain Jordan's role in the Geneva Conference the three avoided referring to disengagement on the Jordanian front, to which Syria did not object in principle.

Jordan's Reaction

Jordan was fully aware of the severe impact of the tripartite declaration on its position. Khaddam rushed to Amman to explain Syria's support for the PLO, stressing the long-term Syrian strategy to establish a "regional federal framework between the future Palestinian state in the West Bank and the Gaza Strip and Jordan, as a first stage, and later with Syria". Sadat reassured Husayn that the tripartite declaration did not contradict the Alexandria Communiqué and that "there is no Geneva without Jordan". Nonetheless, on 22 September 1974 the Jordanian government reacted sharply by announcing "the freezing of all activities or Jordanian political moves which stem from Jordan's consent to participate in the ... Geneva Conference ... and of any activity which results from Jordanian acceptance of Resolutions 242 and 338 and the invitation to it by the US and the USSR to participate in the Geneva Conference as a state whose territories were partially occupied during the June 1967 war". Jordan added that "this freeze was only temporary, until the ... forthcoming Arab summit. The adoption of the tripartite declaration by the summit would mean that Jordan was relieved of any political responsibility and of its special direct link to the [Palestinian] problem. All Arab states would bear responsibility for this resolution and its consequences." By this statement, Jordan placed the initiative back in Egyptian hands, hoping that the underlying threat would persuade Egypt to return to the "Alexandria spirit". It is likely that Jordan also intended to put pressure on the US and Israel towards Israeli flexibility on a possible settlement with Jordan. This was also Jordan's political aim until the Arab summit.[127]

Husayn now focused on Israel. He believed that, if he could present the summit with a territorial achievement, he could prevent its endorsement of the tripartite declaration. His efforts, however, were in vain. In his talks in the US, and through the Rifa'i talks (August 1974), Husayn was under the impression that the "Jordanian option" was still open, though it became clear to him that there was no chance of achieving a disengagement along the Jordan River as he had proposed. Rifa'i was certainly informed about FM Allon's talks with Kissinger at Camp David early in August 1974, in which Allon again raised the idea of an "interim settlement" based on the "Jericho corridor" as a stage in the implementation of the Allon plan. This proposal was unacceptable to Jordan. On 29 August 1974, Husayn met Rabin, Peres and Allon in the Tel Aviv area; they turned down his proposal for a disengagement of forces. Once more, after the tripartite declaration and before the Arab summit, Husayn met the three Israeli leaders (19 October 1974) near Tel Aviv; again they rejected his disengagement proposal. According to Rabin, Husayn was offered four alternatives relating to "a comprehensive political settlement" based on territorial compromise. Husayn rejected all these proposals.[128]

THE RABAT SUMMIT, 26–29 OCTOBER 1974

The Arab Foreign Ministers' Conference

The conference took place on 22–25 October 1974, to prepare the agenda of the summit. Three working papers were submitted: one Egyptian, one Syrian and one on the Palestinian issue by the PLO, based on the resolutions of the 12th PNC. The conference finally ratified the same articles which had been approved in the tripartite meeting. A bitter argument between Jordan and the PLO preceded the endorsement of those articles relating to the Palestinian issue. Zayd Rifaʻi opposed discussing the PLO working paper, reiterating Jordan's basic position on this issue. Mediation attempts by Saudi Arabia and Morocco which lasted for two days failed. Qaddumi rejected "any form of conciliation". When the Palestinian articles were tabled for a vote, Rifaʻi suggested avoiding any decision on the subject and leaving it to the summit to decide. This was rejected. Jordan assumed that a decision at the conference would make it harder for Husayn to tackle the problem, or to change or withdraw it in the summit. Rifaʻi was forced to register his reservation on a paragraph of the resolution stating that "any Palestinian territory which would be liberated through various forms of the struggle, should be returned to its owner – the Palestinian people [PLO motion adding "under PLO leadership" was accepted], stressing the right [of this people] to establish its independent national rule over the liberated territory". The foreign ministers recommended that the summit endorse the principles of the "interim aim" which had been adopted by the Algiers summit, including the paragraph on Palestinian representation to which Jordan was strongly opposed.[129]

Summit Deliberations

The discussions of the summit centred around the Jordan–PLO dispute on Palestinian representation. The debate was crucial and "historic" for the two sides, who each presented rigid and uncompromising positions which required a clear decision either way.

Sadat's position.   Egypt went to this summit with the clear aim of making it a "Filastin summit". In Fahmi's briefcase was a document which contained "the wording of a historic announcement on the establishment of the State of Filastin" (i.e., of a Palestinian government-in-exile). However, such an aim required Husayn's presence, and therefore Sadat continued trying to persuade him to participate in the summit until the eve of its convening. Sadat communicated to Husayn (among other things) that the Alexandria Communiqué did not stipulate "an *immediate* establishment of Palestinian national rule" (emphasis added), indicating that, as previously agreed, Husayn had a role to play. Egypt even hinted to Jordan that she still maintained that the PLO could not be described as the representative of "those who are in the Jordanian army or ... government". Sadat went to the summit with the idea of some sort of federal link between Jordan and the future Palestinian state on the West Bank and Gaza. He considered this possible and probably the only way out of the Jordan–PLO entanglement, and a "guarantee for the rights of the Palestinian people and its legitimate representatives, and a means to prevent Israel from exploiting the division between them". "Both sides would agree on the conditions and means of implementing the federal or confederate link after a specific period of time, reserving the right of each side to decide whether or not to remain within the framework." Egypt would not consider it wrong "should two organizations leave the PLO as a result" of such a move.

Sadat reiterated his proposals on a Palestinian government-in-exile, claiming that the "summit can overcome Israel's declared opposition to cooperation with any party other than Jordan". He also reiterated his argument that "the Palestinians should take every centimetre of land which could be achieved for them, even by Kissinger". He wanted to separate the pan-Arab nature of the political solution from his freedom to achieve a further "military agreement" in Sinai. He therefore decided to try focusing the summit's attention on the Palestinian issue, and to do everything to avoid discussion on political settlements. These had already been discussed with Syria in the tripartite meeting. Sadat was successful in his efforts.[130]

Asad's position. Asad's point of departure was not a positive one. He did not seek conditions for a further settlement on the Golan Heights, but he did try to prevent Sadat from reaching a further settlement in Sinai, correctly assuming that the US preferred a further Israeli withdrawal there. For Syria the possibility of an Egyptian–Israeli political settlement, which would effectively take Egypt out of the cycle of war, was traumatic. Khaddam described the summit's aim as being to "lay down principles which would oblige all to prevent concessions and complications by those who are in a position to make them" (i.e., Egypt). On the eve of the summit Asad was convinced that Sadat had reached an agreement with Kissinger on Israeli withdrawal to the al-Arish-Ras Muhammad line. Asad proposed to Kissinger in Damascus in October 1974 the convening of a Geneva Conference in which one Arab delegation including PLO representatives would appear, and in which the discussions would centre on issues rather than on separate (geographical) fronts. In this respect Asad's decision in favour of the PLO was aimed more against the Egyptian scenario than against Jordan. This decision would, in Syria's view, prevent a separate political settlement on the Jordanian front, which would take Jordan out of the cycle of war. In the summit, Asad opposed renewed US efforts for another partial agreement in Sinai and called for "Arab solidarity as a basic and prime weapon of the campaign [against Israel]".

At the heart of his speech to the closed session of the summit, Asad stressed the "urgent need to bridge the gulf between Jordan and the PLO", which he regarded as "the Achilles heel" of the Arab stand. He called for "getting rid of the September complex". "The US and Israel wish to limit negotiations on the West Bank to Jordan in order to transform the problem into a border problem. The situation would be different if the problem were to be presented as one of a people who should return to their homeland, and who have a right to an independent state." Asad thought the rift could be healed by "unity between Jordan and other states", that is, a federal unity which would include the "Syrian Region" together with the PLO as an independent political entity. The Syrian regime considered an interim solution to the Jordan–PLO crisis (though it was never raised in the summit): on the one hand, Jordan should recognize the PLO as the "sole legitimate representative of the Palestinian people and its right to establish national rule over any liberated territory"; on the other, the "PLO should give up the idea of establishing a substitute homeland" (*al-watan al-badil*) in the East Bank.

Asad argued against some Arab leaders' attitudes in the debate "as if the West Bank is in our hands and Israel's decision to give up the West Bank depends only on our decision to whom to give it. Thus we are discussing whether to give it to the PLO or to Jordan." He added that the US adhered to leaving the West Bank to Husayn, which was why Israel and the US were doing their utmost to prevent recognition of the PLO. Therefore we "must stick to the representation of the Palestinian people by the PLO; this would not reduce at all the role of any Arab country" (i.e., Jordan).[131]

Husayn's position. There is no doubt that Husayn was the star of the summit. He presented an uncompromising position; any concession on his part would mean that he would not regain any territory from which Israel would withdraw, even if he were to negotiate for the return of the West Bank. It is likely that Sadat's promise on the eve of the summit and the hope that Faysal would stand by him gave Husayn reason for optimism.

Husayn struggled at the summit for the East Bank no less, and perhaps even more, than for the West Bank. He played the only card he had – the Israeli card. He mobilized all possible arguments to prevent a final decision on Palestinian representation in favour of the PLO. In his central strategic speech he tried to persuade the summit that only he could bring about the "liberation" of the West Bank. He outlined his kingdom's contribution to the Palestinian issue and its position on the conflict. He suggested a separation between "the problem of the territories which were occupied in 1967" and "the Palestinian [national] problem". As Salim al-Lawzi described it: "One should view the current struggle as one for borders." Husayn reiterated his known views on Palestinian representation, disengagement of forces and freedom of choice for the West Bank inhabitants after Israel's withdrawal. Among other proposals, he suggested that the Arabs be represented at Geneva by one delegation. He stressed that "Jordanian administration exists in the West Bank *de facto*", and emphasized his willingness to recognize the PLO as the "legitimate" but not "sole" representative. He repeated his threat of the consequences should the summit recognize the PLO as "sole representative". He nonetheless added that "Jordan would finally accept any resolution of the summit, and would not withdraw from it". Husayn reiterated that the dispute over the West Bank's future was useless before its "liberation". He emphasized that in such a crucial issue of representation there cannot be compromise resolutions: "if I am a party in a political discussion to regain the land, I will not move unless I have the maximum support of my brothers."

The other leaders knew that Husayn's position was crucial and that any unanimous decision depended on his consent. The Arab consensus was once again to his detriment and Husayn understood this very well.[132]

Arafat. Standing on the threshold of the Palestinian movement's greatest political victory in the Arab arena, and encouraged by the tripartite declaration and the recommendations of the Arab foreign ministers, Arafat naturally rejected any compromise or "interim solution" of the problem of Palestinian representation. Any concession on *his* part would mean that Jordan would negotiate the future of the West Bank, even if Arafat were promised that this territory would eventually revert to the PLO. Arafat's position should be understood in light of the fact that the attempts on Husayn's life had not ceased at that period. (On the eve of the summit an assassination attempt in Rabat, by a squad belonging to the Special Operations Arena of Fatah directed by Abu Iyad, was foiled by the Moroccan security authorities. In defending this attempt, Abu Iyad argued on 19 November 1974 that "the Jordanian question is a matter of life or death".) Arafat demanded endorsement of the Algiers resolutions on Palestinian representation and the recommendations of the foreign ministers. In response to Husayn's threats, he claimed that "Jordan's resignation from Arab political activities is likely to enhance Palestinian and other Arab political activities". He declared in the summit that "the Arab League did not officially recognize the decision to annex the West Bank to Jordan".[133] In other words, unlike Husayn, Arafat wanted "to create a new reality" which regarded the struggle against Jordan as a "struggle for survival".[134]

Boumedienne. Boumedienne took an unambiguous stand supporting the PLO as "sole representative". He sharply reacted to Husayn's speech, saying:

> After the historical lecture of the king of Jordan on the history of the Hashemite family, I ask: What is the problem today? The resolutions of the Algiers summit should be carried out and those of the foreign ministers ratified. Jordan's role was over in the Ramadan war. Jordan should return to the East Bank and leave Palestinian affairs to the Palestinians.[135]

Saddam Husayn's position. The Iraqi vice-president participated in the summit after Iraq had boycotted the Algiers summit. His position was important insofar as he did not rule out a solution to the conflict through the political process. In principle he accepted the "phased strategy", but disagreed about how to implement it. He rejected political activity based on Resolutions 242 and 338 or on "recognition of the Zionist entity and the occupation of Arab land prior to 5 June 1967". He agreed to "the liberation of the territories occupied after 5 June 1967 and the securing of the rights of the Palestinian people to self-determination and to setting up national rule in the liberated part of their territory, as a first stage", but on condition that this "should not lead to giving up, officially or practically, the historic rights of the Arab nation to the entire Palestinian land". [136]

In this situation, *Sadat* became the central figure in the efforts to find a way out of the tangle. A "five-man committee" was set up with Sadat, Asad, Hasan, Husayn and Arafat as members. The problem was what should be done until the establishment of "Palestinian national rule". They believed that the question of responsibility for the West Bank should not be left open, since a vacuum would mean "consolidation of the occupation". The PLO rejected Egypt's suggestion that Jordan, with full Arab backing, negotiate Israel's withdrawal from the West Bank and hand it over to the Palestinians and the PLO. Instead they proposed that the Egyptian war minister, Ahmad Isma'il, "as commander-in-chief of the confrontation armies", undertake the role of negotiating on the Jordanian front. Saudi Arabia and Morocco made other proposals which were not supported by either side, among them: a referendum among the inhabitants of the West Bank after negotiations by Jordan for its "liberation"; an authorization for Jordan to sign a disengagement agreement with Israel in exchange for her agreement to accept the PLO position; introducing international forces after Israel's withdrawal and holding a referendum under international supervision, or handing the West Bank over to Arab League control until a decision on its future had been reached. In view of the prevailing stalemate, the "five-man committee" had no alternative but to recommend the approval of the recommendations of the foreign ministers. Husayn kept his promise and joined the consensus, which turned into a binding resolution for all the Arab League states. [137]

Summit Resolutions

The resolutions were "top secret", but because of their importance the Palestinian articles were publicized at the end of the summit. On 29 November 1977 Syria published the full text of the secret resolutions in order (it claimed) "to confirm their authenticity after the Egyptian propaganda campaign had tried to distort them in order to justify Sadat's visit to Israel". The summit's resolutions reaffirmed the "interim aim" as set out in the Algiers summit, adding that the "joint Arab action" would be based, among other things, on "rejection of any attempt to achieve partial political settlements, due to the unified and pan-Arab nature of the problem". On the issue of the Palestinian Entity, the summit decided: (1) "To reaffirm the right of the Palestinian people to return to their homeland and to self-determination." (2) "To reaffirm their right to set up an independent national rule, led by the PLO – the sole legitimate representative of the Palestinian people, on any part of the liberated Palestinian territory." "The Arab states will assist this rule when it is established, in any area and at any level." (3) "To help the PLO fulfil its responsibility at the national and international levels." (4) "To call upon Jordan, Syria, Egypt and the PLO to set up a formula for organizing relationships between them in view of these resolutions and in order to carry them out." (5) "All the Arab states should commit themselves to maintaining the Palestinian national unity, and refrain from interfering in the internal affairs of Palestinian activity."[138]

Analysing a declaration of an Arab summit is not different, in principle, from analysing a declaration of any international forum in the Western world, but it requires special emphasis on a number of elements. One is the gap between the letter of the declaration and the intentions behind it or the real thoughts of the decision makers. Here one must note how each party to the declaration interprets its articles, including the problematic ones. What is the practical outcome of such resolutions, and is their implementation at all feasible? Arab resolutions are not considered "sacred words" or "laws" in the Arab world. They are usually implemented as long as there is willingness to do so among the signatories. Egypt had the political might to breach the summit's resolutions, just as it was able to dictate its policy to Arab summits (except for the fifth summit) ever since this institution had been set up through Nasir's initiative in early 1964. In this respect, the resolutions of Arab summits were Egyptian resolutions.

Hence, the problem facing the Arab world after the Rabat summit was how to implement its resolutions. These resolutions were aimed at strengthening Arab solidarity on the basis of a consensus, but after a while became themselves the cause of considerable division. Sadat dodged them in order to maintain the political momentum; his minister of information described them as an "organizational and procedural step towards a solution which would fulfil the strategic aims of the Arab nation". Sadat did not attach to the Rabat resolutions the same importance that Syria and the PLO did; he interpreted them quite liberally in a way that would enable him to reach a further "military agreement" with Israel (which he achieved in September 1975). He assessed, correctly, that strict adherence to the letter of the resolutions would mean a prolonged stalemate in the political process (considering, of course, Israel's fundamental position) and a return to the state of "neither peace nor war". Therefore it is not surprising that in November 1980 he was quoted by Anis Mansur, a journalist close to him, as saying that "the rift in the Arab nation had in fact started in the Rabat summit".[139]

Syria, on the other hand, regarded the resolutions as an achievement in maintaining the "unity of the problem", and limiting Egypt's freedom to pursue a separate or partial political settlement in Sinai, although Syria had no objection to a further "military agreement" there. Syria tried to achieve "an interim agreement" in the Golan but was aware that this was difficult, if not impossible, as long as it required a political agreement – that is, parallel progress on the Palestinian issue. From then on, this was the focus of the "Syrian problem".

Husayn's signing of the Rabat resolutions was, without exaggeration, a historic decision. In certain respects, the circumstances of his decision in Rabat were similar to those of the first summit, which paved the way for the establishment of the PLO. In Rabat (October 1974), the circle which began with his first mistake in Cairo (January 1964) was completed. Both were watershed decisions in the struggle between the Jordanian entity and the Palestinian Entity. Ironically, in both cases Husayn personally contributed to a process whose consequences were the exact opposite of what he had intended. Relying on the Israeli card, Husayn believed that he could cope with the implementation of the Rabat resolutions. He assumed that no settlement on the West Bank could be achieved without him, and therefore he could, in the meantime, erode the status of the PLO. However, exactly as with his decision in the first summit, reality again proved at odds with his personal expectations. Faced with an Arab consensus in the summit, Husayn was again forced to opt for the lesser of two evils: on the one hand isolation, and on the other becoming a "nationalist king". Faced with Arab pressure and the fact that Sadat and Faysal did not stand by him, Husayn had no alternative but to join the Arab consensus. His consent to the resolution suited a group of Jordanian politicians who objected to Jordanian involvement in the West Bank, advocating seclusion in the East Bank. Husayn realized that the summit would in any event endorse the recommendations of the foreign ministers, and that his threats to "resign" from the political process did not impress anyone. In exchange for this step, Husayn enjoyed the longest period of freedom to manoeuvre in the Arab arena since 1952. At this point he could not have made any further concessions, except for relinquishing his rule over the East Bank.

Later, Kissinger regretted not having sought more vigorously a settlement on the Jordanian front before Rabat. In his view, had Israel submitted concrete proposals for a settlement, it would have been possible to block the PLO's path. In his meeting with the Israeli ministerial team (24 May 1975), Husayn argued that had Israel agreed to a disengagement of forces, the Rabat resolutions would have been prevented.[140] Could they both have been right? The answer is no. The Rabat resolutions relating to the PLO were firmly established in the Algiers summit, and again in the tripartite declaration in September 1974. It is safe to assume that a disengagement agreement would, at best, have postponed the final decision (among other reasons, by postponing the convening of the Arab summit) but not prevented it. A disengagement agreement would have sharpened the Jordan–PLO struggle, resulting in enhanced Arab support for the PLO.

The Rabat summit defined the tenets of the "Palestinian national rights", that is, the territorial and national (ruling) elements of the Palestinian Entity or, in practice, the future "Palestinian state". The summit strengthened the linkage between the territorial and national elements of the Palestinian issue with respect to the solution of the West Bank problem. The PLO became the only recognized Palestinian establishment in the Arab arena, without rival in the Palestinian arena. From this position a formal Arab commitment emerged to make the PLO a party to the political process in a solution of the conflict, a status later recognized by UN resolutions (3236, 22 November 1974; 3237, 21 November 1974; 3375–3376, 10 November 1975). The Rabat summit's ratification of the PLO "phased programme" reduced the differences on the West Bank between the nationalists and those who advocated an independent Palestinian Entity. The Rabat resolutions intensified the allegiance to the PLO of the traditional leadership, including those who were considered pro-Jordanian. To a certain extent it is true that the extreme nationalist PLO moved towards the moderates in the Palestinian public who called for the establishment of an independent Palestinian Entity in the territories, but with one major difference: the latter regarded it as a basis for a peace settlement with Israel. As a result some (and later, almost all) moderates began to regard the PLO as the sole representative of the Palestinians. This development, on the one hand, prepared the ground for a clear, declared consensus among all the West Bank leaders, adhering to the Rabat resolutions, and on the other hand reduced their freedom to deal with the Israeli administration. In the view of the local leadership, little was left of Jordan's stand on determining the future of the West Bank, and this was only a result of agreement with the PLO rather than an independent position. For the traditional as well as the nationalist leadership, the decisive stand became that of the PLO.

Conclusion

Fifteen years after Egypt's 1959 initiative and ten years after the establishment of the PLO, the new Palestinian national movement scored its most impressive achievement in the Arab world, and subsequently in the international arena. Nasir's main objective in reviving the Palestinian Entity was almost entirely achieved: the transformation of the Palestinians into a major party in the Arab–Israel conflict, and the setting up of a Palestinian establishment as an expression of the Palestinian Entity to represent the Palestinians. The ideas of Nasir, Qasim and Sadat on a "Palestinian state" on the West Bank and the Gaza Strip, and of the Fatah founders in their early days regarding "national rule in the Arab parts of Filastin", became an interim goal of both Arab strategy and the PLO.

These achievements were the result of: (1) the change in the Middle East political map following the Egyptian Revolution of 1952, which inspired the rise of the nationalist regimes, the rise of Nasirism and later the Ba'th that replaced the traditional regimes (in Egypt, Syria, Iraq and Libya); (2) the transformation of the Arab–Israel conflict into the focus of Arab nationalism; (3) the Palestinian national awakening, which manifested itself in the fidai organizations which took over the Palestinian establishments and epitomized the rise of a new political generation that had been raised in an ambience of radical political movements (Nasirism, the Ba'th and the Arab Nationalists). Only the irony of Middle East politics, keeping in mind the nature of the Palestinian national movement, could account for the fact that this movement had developed out of Arab military defeats (and one strategic victory), the failure of Arab unity and solidarity, as well as the military defeats of the Palestinian movement itself in the armed confrontations both with Arab states (Jordan and Lebanon) and with Israel that culminated in June 1982. Paradoxically, or perhaps even characteristically, these setbacks heightened the Palestinians' sense of identity and increased the determination of the Palestinian establishment and the fidai organizations to work for their aims in their own way. The Palestinian issue became the focal point of the

Arab–Israel conflict (except for Iraq, which placed equal if not more emphasis on its conflict with Iran). Simultaneously, the Palestinian movement became increasingly dependent on the Arab world. Although in Arab summits from January 1964 onwards there were disagreements on the Arab–Israel conflict, there was a general pan-Arab consensus regarding the Palestinian Entity.

The Palestinian national movement became the most militant and radical political movement – except for militant Islamic fundamentalism – in the Arab world, and is likely to remain so for a long time. As such, it replaced bankrupt Arab radical movements. It clashed with almost all the confrontation states, contributed to the decline which had led to the Six Day War and brought about the civil wars in Jordan and, to a large extent, in Lebanon. The Palestinian movement matured within a closed circle full of contradictions which, however, stimulated its development. It oscillated between its pan-Arab character (*qawmi*) and "Palestinization" (*wataniyya*); between Arab unity and Arab division; between, on the one hand, aspiring to independence in decision making and, on the other, depending on Arab support and guardianship; between fidai action and the need to take into account the territorial sovereignty of Arab states. It had to choose between solving the conflict by political process or continuing the "armed struggle"; between progressive, militant and "poor" states, on the one hand, and conservative, monarchic and rich ones, on the other.

The Palestinian establishment encompassed the entire political spectrum of the Arab world. In its official stands, however, the PLO usually maintained a consensus, and Fatah made every effort to reach general agreement on important issues. Nonetheless there were arguments about setting up an "interim aim" and its relation to the strategic aim, and on whether to give priority to "toppling the Jordanian regime", to "liquidation of the state of Israel", or to retain both options. At its inception, Fatah adopted two slogans: "The liberation of Filastin is the way to Arab unity", and "The campaign for Filastin is the solution for the painful contradictions that exist in the Arab homeland." Neither slogan stood up to the test of events. The struggle for the "liberation of Filastin" deepened the division in the Arab world. Throughout this period the Palestinian Resistance was as much, and probably more, an Arab problem than an Israeli one. There were more Palestinian casualties in the confrontations with Arab states than in the armed struggle with Israel. When the "armed struggle" did not achieve the flamboyant initial goals of the organizations, they became increasingly dependent on the Arab states for achieving their political aims; PLO reliance on a pan-Arab consensus brought it into line with this consensus, thereby changing its "interim aims" and mode of operation.

Egypt remained remarkably consistent in its adherence to the aim of a Palestinian Entity and its components – that is, a Palestinian state in the West Bank and Gaza as part of a comprehensive solution to the conflict – attempting throughout the period to moderate the PLO and bring it into the political process. One cannot conceive of the achievements of the Palestinians regarding the Palestinian Entity and in the Arab and international arenas without the relentless efforts of Nasir, later Sadat, and now of Mubarak. This Egyptian position has become a "historic position". Unlike Syria, Egypt strove for an "independent" Palestinian Entity that would not be associated with any Arab state, which was why the Fatah/PLO leaders and Egypt saw eye to eye over the "interim aim". To the extent that the PLO depended on the Arab states, it became apparent that only Egypt could help it achieve its "interim aim" of a Palestinian state in the West Bank and Gaza. Fatah/PLO is still fully aware of this crucial fact, which is why it cannot do without Egypt's good services in this area. Their separate ways must merge if this goal is to be achieved.

Syria, or the Syrian Ba'th, did not take any initiative regarding the Palestinian Entity; it lagged behind Egypt and the PLO on this issue. For the Ba'th under Asad, the Palestinian Entity was not (as it was for Egypt) an aim in itself, but rather a problem that could be considered after the "liberation". However, since the aims and components of the Palestinian Entity had been set up, Syria was forced to adopt a position on it as part of the Ba'th ideological outlook, namely, that the Entity would be part of "greater Syria", the Arab power centre of the Fertile Crescent. The result was Syria's active involvement within the Palestinian establishment. (Egypt, for its part, avoided such involvement.) Syria advocated "an independent Palestinian state" linked to Jordan ("tight federal" link or "attached to Jordan"), or "linked in a confederation with the confrontation states" (i.e., Jordan and Syria) whose centre would be in Damascus. For Asad's regime, the PR became the expression of the Syrian "struggle" ideology after the bankruptcy of the Ba'th slogan of "unity, liberty, socialism". With the Ba'th regime viewing the PR as an extension of the "armed struggle" and Filastin as part of "greater Syria", the PR became a "Syrian" political factor which was obliged to align both its policy and activity with that of the regime. In contrast to Egypt's approach, Syria strove to make the

PLO more militant and to prevent an erosion of the PLO's tactical position. This Syrian concept conflicted with the PLO position on "Independent Palestinian decision making". When the PR seemed reluctant to comply it was seen as in "opposition" to the Syrian regime, a state of affairs Syria could not tolerate. Conflict between them thus became inevitable with Syria trying to protect its essential security and national interests; no wonder, therefore, that in a serious crisis such as in Lebanon in 1976, the regime considered changing the PLO leadership as if it were a Syrian organization. Syria made every effort to alter the political framework of the PLO and especially Arafat's leadership and radically to change its *modus operandi*. But this goal was not feasible as long as Fatah was the dominant factor in the Palestinian establishment. Fatah/PLO was aware that relying on Syria to achieve its "interim aim" would mean an impasse.

Since the establishment of the Hashemite Kingdom of Jordan (April 1950), the Palestinian issue has been central to Jordan's domestic, foreign and inter-Arab policy. For Husayn this issue was and still is "fateful" for Jordan; as such it has been the decisive factor in Jordan's national security. The struggle for survival between the Jordanian entity and the Palestinian Entity left its mark on Jordan, the Palestinians and the PLO, and the Arab arena. In this struggle Jordan held no sway over Arab moves regarding the Palestinian Entity. Husayn was forced to commit himself to the Arab consensus in the first summit and in the Rabat summit. He had no control over developments in this issue and time was not on his side. He conducted "delaying operations" which obviously could not lead to progress, but only to his withdrawal from one defensive line to another. Husayn was partially successful in his attempt to slow down processes and postpone Arab decisions, but he could not ultimately prevent them. His political initiatives on the West Bank backfired because they were anachronistic. He had no choice but to swim upstream; from his point of view there was no room for compromise.

Despite his moderation and his aspiration for a peace agreement with Israel, Husayn was aware that he was unable to reach a separate agreement with Israel that was not congruent with the Arab consensus or at least with the Egyptian position. Dependent on developments in the Arab arena, Husayn could not and did not conduct a long-term policy; his major goal was to maintain his rule. Therefore his policy in the Arab arena was full of zig-zags (though when he decided he did so sharply). When he concluded that there was no short-term prospect of regaining the West Bank on his terms, and that his rule was threatened, Husayn had to resolve the struggle with the PR; at a later stage he formally gave up the West Bank and his representation of the Palestinians for the same reason. His regime proved remarkably viable in spite of plots to remove it and in spite of the fact that central Arab states (Egypt, Syria, Iraq and even Tunisia) had doubts at one point or another about its right to exist.

Until the Rabat resolutions Husayn maintained his basic position on the independent Palestinian Entity and on the representation of the PLO, in spite of his awareness of Arab and Palestinian political developments in this area. He regarded this consistent position as a "front-line defence" to protect the hinterland on the East Bank. Yet when he did make a concession, he gave up (at least formally) everything except his rule over the East Bank. And it hardly seems that the "Palestinization" process, that is, the strengthening of Palestinian identity among West Bank residents as well as among *Israeli* Arabs in general, and the recognition of the PLO's representative status, would leave the East Bank Palestinians immune. In fact, this appears to be the greatest danger to the regime's future stability, one that will no doubt guide Husayn's steps. This process has currently been slowed down by the "lull" in his struggle with the PLO in the wake of his Rabat concessions and the consequent improvement of his status in the Arab arena.

Following the Rabat resolutions and developments regarding the Palestinian issue in the Arab, Palestinian and international arenas – namely, recognition of the PLO and of the right to establish an independent Palestinian state in the West Bank and Gaza – Husayn has rather limited options.

Owing to Jordan's basic political limitations, Husayn was often obliged to choose not the best option but the "lesser of two evils" in his efforts to preserve his rule. Ironically, the options he chose eventually proved to be the best ones. Today, more than ever, Husayn is aware that the prospects of returning the West Bank to his kingdom in the framework of the UAK plan are very remote. Even if it were possible, it would mean the transformation of Jordan into a binational state with a Palestinian majority of two-thirds – or, possibly, into a Palestinian state. It is very doubtful that he could "handle" this population now as successfully as he did until the Six Day War. His grip on the West Bank is now slight and his influence has become marginal now that a new generation has arisen whose deep hostility towards the Jordanian regime, and political affinity with the PLO, is beyond any doubt. Before any attempt to return the

West Bank to Jordan, Husayn would surely ask himself whether such a step would be advisable in light of the unprecedentedly lengthy period of stability, internal calm and freedom to assert himself in the Arab arena he has enjoyed since 1971. This is most likely what was behind his adherence to the Rabat resolutions and also why he coordinated his policy on the Palestinian issue (representation) with that of the PLO.

A neighbouring independent Palestinian Entity (rule or state) would, however, pose a threat to Husayn's regime. At best, it would pose a dilemma for the East Bank Palestinians as to their political and national loyalties, and would give rise to nationalist feelings against the regime.

Husayn's intensive involvement in the Palestinian issue has been aimed at influencing the outcome in order to prevent developments which would aggravate Jordan's vulnerability. Jordan's severing of ties from the Palestinian cause was temporary, never permanent. Indeed, had Jordan dissociated itself from the Palestinian cause after the Rabat summit, it could have slowed down the political process which aimed (*inter alia* in the Arab view) at the establishment of a Palestinian state – this is in light of Israel's attitude towards the PLO and the Palestinian issue in general. And yet Husayn was well aware that a sharp break with the West Bank would create a legal vacuum there that would benefit and eventually strengthen Israel's hold on it, and that this would bring about an Arab–Palestinian front against Jordan. Therefore it is crucial to Husayn that the Palestinian struggle be conducted outside the East Bank – namely, on the West Bank and Gaza Strip. This is to prevent any possibility that Jordan would become the "substitute homeland" (*al-watan al-badil*) for the Palestinians.

It is notable that the PLO needs the services of Jordan, whether as a base for political and military activity or as an intermediary with the US, as long as it is not acceptable to the US as a negotiating partner. But, until the establishment of "Palestinian national rule", Husayn exploits to the full the Israeli card and the Arab and PLO fear of a political and legal vacuum in the West Bank should Husayn sever all links with its inhabitants. In Fatah/PLO's view, such a severance would mean placing the burden of responsibility for West Bank inhabitants on their organization, which is not in any position to carry this responsibility as long as the West Bank remains under Israeli control.

Imbued with consciousness of the Hashemite dynasty's traditional role and its past relations with Filastin and Jerusalem, as well as with his unique Arab nationalism, Husayn was not able to sign a separate peace agreement with Israel. On the basis of his talks with Israeli leaders, he concluded that there was no prospect that Israel would accept his conditions for such agreement, namely "land for peace" (including minor changes in the 1967 borders) and the return of East Jerusalem. Even during his "alliance" period with Nasir, Husayn did not dare to negotiate an agreement with Israel without first coordinating with Nasir and trying to gain his consent. Husayn was frank with the Israeli leaders whom he met during 1968–1970 and later. As in the cases of Nasir and Sadat, there was a striking similarity between Husayn's declared policy and the one he evinced in diplomatic channels, including talks with Israelis, talks which were aimed mainly at getting the Israelis to be more flexible with regard to the territorial issue and also (after 1974) the issue of Palestinian representation.

Towards the end of this period the Arabs and Palestinians agreed that the PLO was the sole representative of the Palestinians. Further, the PLO establishment became so synonymous with the Palestinian national issue that it took on the characteristics of a "myth". Support for the PLO as sole representative of the Palestinians became an expression of commitment to this issue and to the national aspirations of the Palestinian people, including "liberation from Israeli occupation". The representative composition of the PLO was not the criterion for its representative status; the problem of the Palestinian establishment's composition would no doubt arise if (or when) "Palestinian national rule", or any other Palestinian establishment such as a government-in-exile, were set up. Power struggles would then emerge between the various organizations or political groups, as well as between the "outside" and "inside" leadership.

Political issues rather than family-clan considerations became the dominant factor in the West Bank. The latter, as a political factor in Palestinian society, were slowly disappearing with the rise of a younger, nationalistic generation which "revolted" against Palestinian conservatism and traditional leadership. Besides the strengthening of its Palestinian identity, Palestinian society had been undergoing an intensive process of politicization and Palestinization of almost all spheres of social and cultural life. It was against this background that the West Bank became the PLO leaders' focus of attention. Their goal was the political "conquest" of the West Bank. But the PLO leadership was faced with problems between itself and the West Bank and Gaza leadership concerning the day-to-day policies to be pursued. The PLO recognized, in attempting to dictate its policies to the West Bank leadership, that this leadership was subject to pressures from both the IMG and the day-to-day needs of the inhabitants. It turned out that even the nationalist leadership, when eventually elected (1976), was liable, under local pressure and considerations, to take a stand different from that of the PLO.

Being the popular base of the Palestinian national movement, the West Bank and the Gaza Strip have also become the focus for political activities of all the elements involved in the issue of the Palestinian Entity and the future of the West Bank and Gaza – namely, the PLO, Israel, Jordan and indirectly the Arab states. Thus the struggle for the soul of the West Bank Palestinians has intensified, lending importance to the local political leadership.

The confrontation within the PLO will continue to be between Fatah and the radical or rejectionist camp, since Fatah pursues a pragmatic policy, even considering joining the political process under certain conditions. However, despite the radicals' reservations, Fatah will no doubt continue to lead the PLO in the foreseeable future. Certainly at this stage there does not seem to be an alternative to the PLO. No Palestinian body which might be established outside it could challenge its dominant position among the Palestinian population or in the Arab arena.

For the Palestinians, the PLO "became the sole framework which endows them with political identity, and within it they became a people which has national rights; without the PLO they are merely a group of people who have, at most, civil rights".[1]

The two-sided struggle between the Palestinian and the Jordanian entities now became triangular, with Israel representing the third side. Although Jordan has resigned as a direct party in this struggle, albeit unwillingly, it retains links with it. Nonetheless, at present the struggle over the Palestinian Entity is essentially one between the PLO (together with the Arab states) and Israel. As such, it is restricted to *land*, that is, to the West Bank and the Gaza Strip. But this represents only an "interim aim" for the PLO, whose strategic aim, as defined in its Covenant, is a "democratic secular state over the entire land of Filastin", or, in other words, the liquidation of the state of Israel. Any progress towards solving the land problem would require a fundamental change in the PLO's strategic aims in the direction of the Egyptian/Jordanian position.

Arafat is aware that any let-up in efforts to resolve the Palestinian issue will have negative effects. This realization, together with the facts of: (1) the peace accord between Egypt and Israel; (2) Egyptian and Jordanian efforts to advance the political process towards solving this issue; (3) the Arab and international pressure on the PLO to change its attitudes; and (4) Israel's attitude towards and strengthening of its hold on the West Bank – all these will eventually force the PLO to move closer to the Egyptian/Jordanian position in order to maintain momentum. For political developments regarding the Palestinian issue, in particular Husayn's experience, have proved that any attempt to separate the territorial problem of the West Bank from the Palestinian national problem must be doomed to failure.

Since October 1974, the fundamental dilemma of the Arab world and the PLO has been how to implement the Rabat resolutions. Deepening Arab commitment to the Palestinian issue and the Palestinian people, fuelled by developments in the Arab–Israel conflict and protracted crises within the Palestinian national movement, has ensnared the Arab world in the greatest dilemma in its recent history. Only the establishment of an independent Palestinian national rule will free the Arab states from this intricate situation. Its establishment would represent a high degree of nationalist achievement for the contemporary Arab world.

Epilogue

THE PALESTINIAN NATIONAL MOVEMENT BETWEEN THE
RABAT RESOLUTIONS AND THE OSLO AGREEMENT
OCTOBER 1974 – SEPTEMBER 1993

The political processes and developments which the Palestinian national movement underwent after the Rabat–Arab summit Resolutions (October 1974) are in fact those outlined in the conclusion to this volume (pages 316–24). The Rabat Resolutions closed the circle opened by Nasir in 1959 to make the Palestinians a separate, recognized party to the Arab–Israeli conflict, and to place the Palestinian issue at the core of this conflict. One may discern the following major political processes during the period under survey:

1. Egypt, of all the Arab states, continued to be the most involved in the Palestinian national issue and had the greatest impact on the process of solving it by peaceful means. Thus, its influence was paramount on the decision-making in the PLO/Fatah institutions. The Peace Accords between Egypt and Israel (March 1979) were an indispensable step and vital impetus toward achieving the Oslo Agreement. In fact, the Oslo Agreement complemented the Camp David Accords. It was not coincidental that Sadat, as President of Egypt, was the only Arab leader to lay down the principles of a practical and feasible solution to the Palestinian issue – principles which served as the basis of the Camp David Autonomy Plan, the guide-lines for convening the Madrid Conference (1991) and, most important of all, the Oslo Agreement (September 1993). There is no doubt that in the course of time Sadat's ideas worked their way into the minds of Arafat and other Fatah leaders. Indeed, Fatah leaders were fully conscious of both the developments in the peace process, and the fact that the Camp David Agreement would "eventually force the PLO to move closer to the Egyptian–Jordanian position ..." (see page 324 of this volume) in order to achieve their national aims. Moreover, the Oslo Agreement vindicated the assessment that "any progress towards solving the land problem would require a fundamental change in the PLO's strategic aims in the direction of the Egyptian–Jordanian position" (page 323).

2. The changes that took place during this period in the PLO/Fatah attitudes towards a political solution of the Palestianian national issue. The Oslo Agreement between the PLO and Israel was the climax of these changes which had begun with the approval (June 1974) of the "phased programme" by the 12th Palestinian National Congress (PNC) (see pages 245–95). The "phased programme" gave the PLO the go-ahead to participate in the political process. The aim was to bring about a change in the US and Israel's basic attitude toward the PLO. Another important development in the PLO/Fatah strategy was the 19th PNC decision (November 1988) which approved the principle of two states in Palestine and recognized Resolution 242. A further milestone was Arafat's declaration in Geneva (14 December 1988) which paved the way for the US Administration's official dialogue with the PLO, and later for PLO participation in the Madrid Conference as a party to the joint Jordanian–Palestinian delegation. This led to the signing of the Oslo Agreement, a volte-face of both the PLO's and Israel's basic attitudes towards each other.

3. The PLO's status as the sole legitimate representative of the Palestinians strengthened in both the Arab world and international arenas. The PLO establishment had remarkably survived the severe crises and set-backs during this period, namely: the Lebanese civil war (1975–76); the Syrian military incursion into Lebanon (1976); Sadat's peace initiative (November 1977) along with its manifold repercussions; Israel's invasion of Lebanon (June 1982); and Arafat's expulsion from Damascus (June 1983) and Lebanon (December 1983). Paradoxically, as happened after the crisis in Jordan in 1970–71, both Arab support to the PLO strengthened (the Algiers Arab Summit in 1988), and Palestinian national consciousness and identity heightened.

4. The West Bank and Gaza Strip became, increasingly, "the popular base of the Palestinian national movement, and the focus for political activity of all the elements involved in the Palestinian entity and the future of the West Bank and the Gaza Strip" (page 332). Radicalization of political activity in the territories intensified and was accompanied by a deterioration in security conditions, which brought about stricter measures against the PLO supporters and local leadership by the right-wing Likud government headed by Menachem Begin which had come to power in November 1977.

The Intifada was the inevitable consequence of the deep

political and social changes that had occurred in the territories since the occupation in June 1967 as described in this book. The "inside" (*al-dakhil*) political leadership in the West Bank and the Gaza Strip gradually gained prominence in the decision-making at the expense of the "outside" (*al-kharij*) Palestinian establishment.

5. The process of exempting Jordan from any official responsibility to direct negotiations on the West Bank's future intensified following the Rabat Resolutions. In fact, Jordan gradually ceased to play a key role in solving Palestinian national and territorial issues. The Arab Summit (June 1988) added another layer to the Rabat Resolutions by affirming "the right of the Palestinian people to establish its state on its national land".[1] The "Jordanian option", as envisaged by Israel, ended with the approval of the Rabat Resolutions.

The Intifada proved to Husayn that his influence on West Bank politics was almost nil. Jordan's legal and administrative disengagement from the West Bank, declared by Husayn on 31 July 1988, was Jordan's last vestige of official connection with it. The "Palestinian Party" of the joint Jordanian–Palestinian delegation to the Madrid International Conference, and to the following bilateral negotiations with Israel in Washington, behaved as an "independent delegation", receiving directives from Arafat in Tunis. Israel conducted the peace negotiations in Washington directly with the "Palestinian Party". The Oslo Agreement was eventually reached by dealing secretly with the PLO/Fatah delegation.

THE PLO CRISES 1975–83

The above developments took place against the backdrop of two traumatic events experienced by the Palestinians in Lebanon which had become the PLO's "safe-base" since the liquidation of their strongholds in Jordan in 1971. The first event, the Lebanese civil war, erupted in April 1975, with a massive Syrian military intervention in 1976. The second was the Israeli armed incursion into Lebanon in June 1982, which resulted in a resumption of the Syrian military confrontation with Fatah forces. Both events led to a defeat of the PLO/Fatah and a diminishing of Arafat's personal status. Sadat's peace initiative in November 1977 and the peace in March 1979 also dealt heavy blows to the PLO/Fatah political and military struggle against Israel. Thus, during the years 1975–83, the PLO/Fatah, and, above all, the Palestinian inhabitants in Lebanon endured their longest crisis since 1964. The PLO suffered an acute trial of leadership which threatened Arafat's position as head of the PLO and Fatah.

The Crisis in Lebanon

The Lebanese civil war broke out in April 1975 and had far-reaching implications on the Palestinians, on the PLO's as well as Arafat's status, and especially on PLO/Fatah relations with Syria. During the first stage of the war, which lasted until late 1975, the Palestinian organizations refrained from any involvement in the fighting between Muslims and Christians. In the second stage, however, which lasted until the middle of June 1976, Palestinian organizations, and especially Fatah, became active belligerents alongside the Muslim Left headed by Walid Junblat. They called for the Lebanese government's downfall and the installation of a revolutionary one in its place. Syria responded with unrelenting military pressure, deploying commando units in major cities. This culminated in the third, decisive stage of the war, from June 1976 to October 1976.[2]

In early June 1976 Syria launched a two-pronged attack westward into Beirut and southwards towards Jezin and from there to Sidon. The aim was to impose a Syrian-sponsored settlement by continuous pressure in the Biqa', Beirut, and Tripoli areas. On 28 September, a "mountain attack" was initiated that lasted until 17 October and led to the Palestinian organizations' capitulation and the termination of the civil war. Under Syrian dominance, the Shtura Agreement was jointly signed by the Lebanese government and the PLO on 25 July 1977.[3] This agreement dealt with the implementation of the Cairo Agreement (31 November 1969) along with its appendices. The Cairo Agreement defined the basis for the Palestinian presence in Lebanon, the relations between the government and the army with the fidai organizations and the conditions of their activities in Lebanon, within the refugee camps, and, in particular, along the Lebanon–Israel border.[4] Under the Shtura Agreement, the PLO organizations were committed to evacuate their forward bases in Southern Lebanon along the Israeli border, to remove all heavy weapons from refugee camps, and to allow Lebanese army units entry into the camps. However, the organizations did not comply with their side of the deal, refusing, in particular, to withdraw from the area adjacent to the Israeli border.

A change in Syrian–PLO relations occurred in the wake of Sadat's peace initiative in November 1977. The Syrians now eagerly wanted to create a joint Arab front with the PLO in order to thwart the initiative. Thus the Lebanese crisis was pushed aside, and Syria suspended her efforts to impose the Shtura Agreement and temporarily came to terms with the PLO/Fatah. This resulted in the Palestinian organizations winning a five-year respite from Syrian pressure – a period which they utilized to bolster their strongholds and spheres of influence in Southern Lebanon. On 6 June 1982 the Lebanese crisis was abruptly restarted in the wake of the Israel Defense Force's (IDF) invasion.

The Israeli Invasion

Eleven years after the liquidation of their bases in Jordan in July 1971, the Palestinian organizations were again defeated militarily; this time by Israel (and shortly afterwards by Syria) during the "Operation Peace for Galilee" which developed into the "War in Lebanon". The ceasefire with Syria was signed on 11 June 1982. It was followed by the IDF's siege of Beirut which lasted three months, during which time Israel demanded that all Palestinian *fidayyun* vacate the city. On 21 August, the first Palestinian fighters left Beirut, followed by Arafat himself who sailed for Tunis on 30 August. There, he established a new headquarters. Against the background of Syrian attempts to undermine Arafat's leadership in the PLO and Fatah, the deterioration of PLO–Syrian relations becomes clear. One year after the Israeli invasion of Lebanon, Syria officially ordered Arafat to leave Damascus (24 June 1983) and forbade Abu Jihad (Khalid al-Wazir) to enter Syria. Arafat was thus humiliatingly expelled from Syria.[5]

Shortly after, the Syrians resumed their efforts to banish the Fatah organization and its supporters from all of Lebanon. Meanwhile, Arafat returned to Lebanon to take command of his forces now concentrated in Tripoli after pulling out from the Biqa', Shtura, and Ba'albek areas. The Syrians also succeeded in ousting Arafat's fighters from the al-Badawi and Nahr al-Barid refugee camps, forcing them into the Tripoli area. On 24 November 1983 a ceasefire was reached in Tripoli through Arab mediation, and Arafat and his men left the city by sea one month later. Arafat's first stop, and not accidentally, was Egypt. There, on 22 December, he met President Mubarak in Alexandria.

The PLO, and the Fatah in particular, were going through a crisis no less severe than that of 1972. Again, the PLO leaders asked themselves whither the Palestinian national movement and the PLO? The repercussions of the Lebanese War had changed their *modus operandi*. Their main difficulty was the geographical dispersion of the PLO's forces and administrative agencies through-out the Arab world, thousands of kilometres distant from the theatre of operations (the occupied territories). Tunis now became the nerve-centre and staging-area of Fatah and the PLO.

Sadat's Peace Initiative and its Aftermath

Between 1975 and 1977 Sadat persisted in his endeavours to convene the Geneva Conference. He argued that "the PLO must take part in the conference with a stand equal to that of the other participants". His dilemma was how to reconcile the Rabat Resolutions with Israel's negative attitude towards the PLO. In a bold attempt to overcome the impasse he suggested to King Husayn, at a meeting in January 1977, the idea of a joint Jordanian–Palestinian delegation to the Geneva Conference. It seems that the plan under consideration called for PLO representatives to be party to the Jordanian delegation. At any rate, Husayn rejected the proposal. Meanwhile, in his talks with the PLO representatives, Sadat tried to induce some sense of moderation into their position in order to smooth the way for their participation in the Geneva Conference; again his efforts were rebuffed. He was also unsuccessful (April 1977) in attempting to forge a dialogue between the US and the PLO.[6]

The Geneva Conference was frozen in political deadlock and never convened. Sadat decided to enter into a separate peace agreement with Israel. Egypt's main guide-lines in its strategy *vis-à-vis* the Palestinian question had been laid down by Sadat after the Yom Kippur War, and had not changed even after his November 1977 initiative and visit to Jerusalem. However, the means for attaining his objectives were modified after he signed the peace treaty with Israel. In his Knesset speech (20 November 1977) he set forth the guide-lines for a comprehensive settlement of the Arab–Israeli conflict, including the Palestinian issue. "There can be no peace without the Palestinians. It is no use to refrain from recognizing the Palestinian people and their right to statehood and their right of return." Sadat listed the points on which the peace agreement should be based:

I. Complete (Israeli) withdrawal from the Arab lands occupied in 1967 (including East Jerusalem).
II. Realization of the basic rights of the Palestinian people: self-determination and establishment of their own state.
III. The right of all states in the region to live in peace within secure borders.

IV. Commitment of all states in the area to administer their relations in accordance with the objectives and principles of the UN Charter.

V. Termination of the state of war that exists in the region.

He reiterated that "the direct attitude towards the Palestinian problem and the only language with a view to achieving a just and lasting peace lie in the establishment of their state".[7]

The principles outlined in the Camp David Accords concerning the future of the West Bank and the Gaza Strip stated *inter alia* that:

> Egypt and Israel agree that in order to ensure a peaceful and orderly transfer of authority ... there should be transitional arrangements for the West Bank and Gaza for a period not exceeding five years. In order to provide full autonomy to the inhabitants under these agreements, the Israeli military government and its civilian administration will be withdrawn as soon as a self-governing authority has been freely elected by the inhabitants of these areas to replace the existing military government. ... The parties will negotiate an agreement which will define the powers and responsibilities of the self-governing authority to be exercised in the West Bank and Gaza. When the self-governing authority (Administrative Council) in the West Bank and Gaza is established and inaugurated, the transitional period of five years will begin. ... The solution from the negotiations must also recognize the legitimate right of the Palestinian people and their just requirements. In this way the Palestinians will participate in the determination of their own future.[8]

Sadat was forced to compromise on the tactical steps to attain his objectives. Egypt sought to implement the principles regarding a solution of the Palestinian problem (the establishment of a Palestinian state in the West Bank and the Gaza Strip with a land corridor linking the two areas) by means of a broad interpretation of the notion of "the self-governing authority in the West Bank and Gaza", as stipulated in the Camp David Accords. And, indeed, at the conclusion of the Begin–Sadat meeting of November 1977 in Isma'iliya, Sadat declared: "The Egyptian position is that a Palestinian state should be established in the West Bank and the Gaza Strip."[9]

This proposed autonomy (or, in general terms, "the Palestinian problem", as the Egyptians saw it) had become a central issue in the relations between Egypt and Israel since the signing of the peace treaty in March 1979. At a later stage it created an obstacle in the process of normalization between the two countries. For Sadat, and later Mubarak, adherence to the implementation of the autonomy provisions became proof of their pan-Arab nationalist (*qawmi*) approach to solving the conflict.

There was an enormous gap between Egypt's and Israel's views on autonomy. Begin's basic view was that "A Palestinian state will not be set up under any condition. ... It is not accidental that the elected council will be called an administrative council, and only administrative." Israel's official attitude was "full autonomy for the inhabitants but not for the territory", and they emphasized the administrative nature of the self-governing authority. Moreover, the source of authority of the autonomous administration should be the IDF.[10]

Well aware of Begin's attitude towards autonomy, Sadat announced an unmistakenly contradictory position: sovereignty over the West Bank and Gaza belonged to the Palestinian people. Egypt emphasized that the autonomy "will apply to people and to territory", in contrast to Israel which stated that it would apply to people only. Sadat interpreted the notion of "legitimate rights" in the broadest possible manner when he wrote to Prime Minister Begin in August 1980: "What are these rights if they do not include the basic right to self-determination?" In Sadat's view, self-determination meant the establishment of a Palestinian state.[11]

It was expected that Sadat's move, which was a violation of the Rabat Resolutions, would create a deep rift between Egypt and the PLO, and indeed most of the Arab world. It is worth noting that notwithstanding Sadat's initiative, Arafat would have agreed to participate in the political process, had it been his decision, on condition that its aim were to establish an independent Palestinian state. The peace agreement was dubbed "treason". PLO policy was aimed at obstructing the autonomy plan and preventing the Camp David Accords from becoming a master-blueprint for resolving the Palestinian issue. The Israeli "Gaza first" option was also rejected by the PLO. The PFLP asserted that violence would be used against anyone in the territories who showed a readiness to co-operate with the autonomy plan.[12] On the other hand, Egypt called upon the PLO in August 1979 to express its willingness to recognize Israel in exchange for Israeli recognition of the Palestinian right to self-determination. Sadat criticized Arafat's leadership, accusing him of hypocrisy and deceit. He cast doubt on the PLO's legitimacy as the true representative of the Palestinians.[13] In further action,

Egypt closed down the "Voice of Palestine" broadcasts over Radio Cairo, and PLO and Fatah representatives in Cairo were expelled from Egypt. Despite these moves, low-profile contacts between Egyptian and Fatah leadership continued at various levels, while publicly Sadat remained adamant on his position regarding the PLO. During 1981 the PLO/Fatah rejected Egypt's attempts at re-establishing a formal dialogue.

Sadat's assassination on 6 October 1981 was welcomed by all PLO factions. They stuck to their position that unless Egypt's policy was changed and the Camp David Accords annulled, the PLO would remain opposed to any Arab reacceptance of Egypt. PLO media emphasized that the initial decision to sever relations with Egypt was not because of Sinai, but rather the "principle of relations with Israel and the deviation from Arab consensus".[14]

The Israeli invasion of Lebanon and its aftermath was a turning-point in the Egyptian–PLO relationship. The PLO, or more precisely, the Fatah leaders, were only too ready to take political advantage of Egypt's goodwill and Mubarak's offer of assistance. Fatah leaders were assured of Egypt's desire to welcome Arafat at any time. The deterioration of Egyptian–Israeli relations due to the Israeli invasion facilitated this PLO policy switch towards Mubarak, and direct and public contact was resumed after the outbreak of the war. Egypt's decision to recall her ambassador from Tel Aviv after the Sabra-Shatila massacre was praised by Arafat. Beginning in late April 1983, the Egyptian media resumed a positive stance towards the PLO, reporting *inter alia* on the renewal of talks with PLO and Fatah representatives.

President Mubarak, following his meeting with Arafat on 22 December 1983, took a further step forward in improving the official Egyptian position towards the PLO. The contacts between Egyptian officials and Fatah leaders became more frequent, during which the Egyptians reported on their discussions with Washington and Western European countries on the Palestinian issue. The Fatah permanent office in Cairo renewed its intensive contacts with the Egyptian authorities. Mubarak reiterated the notion of reciprocal recognition between the PLO and Israel. His assessment was that this recognition would remove all the restrictions which the American administration had placed on the opening of an official dialogue with the PLO. Moreover, in his dispatch to the Secretary-General of the UN (2 May 1984), the Egyptian foreign minister called for the establishment of an "independent state in Palestine" for the Palestinian people, and "the convening of a peace conference under the auspices of the UN, in which the PLO, Israel, Egypt, Jordan, Syria and Lebanon would participate".[15]

Between October 1982 and April 1983, Husayn and Arafat kept up a continuing dialogue. Egypt argued that Arafat should be realistic and reach an agreement with Husayn so as to enable the US to speed up the peace process. Predictably, Egypt expressed great disappointment in the wake of the dialogue's demise in April 1983. Mubarak advised the PLO to overcome its internal problems, reach an understanding with the Jordanian king, and "get the land back before it [was] too late". Egypt repeated its fundamental belief that the PLO should recognize Israel and UN Resolutions 242 and 338, as this would force the US into recognizing the PLO. In his address before the UN General Assembly in September 1982, Mubarak announced that "the Israelis and the Palestinians must make sacrifices for the sake of the great historical conciliation".[16]

Although the Arafat–Mubarak meeting on 22 December 1983 took place in the wake of the Syrian move to liquidate Fatah's strongholds in Lebanon and to undermine Arafat's leadership in the Fatah and PLO, it should be seen against the background of Arafat's basic assessment, derived from years of experience, that Egypt alone, its peace treaty with Israel notwithstanding, was capable of serving as the PLO's Arab sponsor in any political solution to the Palestinian problem. Arafat's assumption was that the political ramifications from his meeting with Mubarak would spur the resumption of diplomatic activity on the Palestinian question while side-stepping the Lebanon crisis, and at the same time permit him to retain his basic stand towards Israel.

Arafat was well aware of the impact his meeting with Mubarak would have in the Arab arena. He consciously paved the way for the Arab world's return to Egypt's fold. Khalid al-Hasan, one of the founders of Fatah, described in May 1984 the importance of Egypt's position and support:

> The absence of Egypt from the Arab arena destroyed the Arab standing. It has been proved that there is no substitute for her leadership [of the Arab world]. The Arab [summit] decision lacks the dynamics of influence in the international arena. The [PLO's] own interest requires that Egypt return to the arena. We need Egypt and Egypt needs us.[17]

It was not unexpected that from the early 1980s, and in particular since his evacuation from Tripoli in December 1983, Arafat had been coming around slowly but steadily to the conclusion that, in order to reach a realistic *modus vivendi* with Israel, the PLO would have to move closer to the Egyptian position and recognize Israel and Security Council Resolution 242.

THE PLO–JORDANIAN AGREEMENT (11 FEBRUARY 1985)
AND ITS AFTERMATH

The Reagan initiative and the Fez Arab Summit decisions (September 1982) were the background to and stimulus for the opening of a political dialogue between the PLO and Jordan, which aimed at finding a formula for co-operation for advancing the political process in solving the Palestine issue. The dialogue began following Husayn's declaration (20 September 1982) that "the time has come to start a dialogue with the PLO, the sole legitimate representative of the Palestinian people, which would create a kind of confederative unity between the Palestinian and Jordanian entities".[18] Between October 1982 and April 1983, an intensive series of talks were held between Arafat and King Husayn. But on 10 April 1983 Jordan revealed that from her point of view the attempt to achieve a *modus operandi* for joint political action with the PLO had failed.[19] Yet the dialogue resumed after Husayn's speech at the first session of the 17th Palestinian National Council (PNC) in Amman on 22 November 1984. In his speech, Husayn outlined the general guide-lines which would constitute the framework of a joint initiative with the PLO:

> 1) Security Council Resolution 242 is the basis for a just and peaceful settlement. The principle of territory for peace is the landmark which should guide us in any initiative we present to the world.

> 2) The international conference would be held under the auspices of the UN and would be attended by the permanent members of the Security Council and by all the parties involved in the conflict. The PLO would attend on an equal footing with the other parties.

> 3) Organizing the Jordanian–Palestinian relationship is a basic responsibility of the Jordanian and Palestinian people.[20]

Eventually an agreement was hammered out by Husayn and Arafat in Amman on 11 February 1985 called the "Jordanian–Palestinian Joint Action Plan". The accord comprised the following principles:

1) Land in exchange for peace as cited in the UN resolutions, including the Security Council resolutions.

2) The Palestinian people's right to self-determination. The Palestinians will exercise their inalienable right to self-determination when the Jordanians and Palestinians manage to achieve this within the framework of Arab confederation (*ittihad konfidrali 'arabi*) that is intended to be established between the two states of Jordan and Filastin.

3) Solving the Palestinian refugee problem in accordance with the UN resolutions.

4) Solving all aspects of the Palestinian question.

5) Based on this, peace negotiations should be held within the framework of an international conference to be attended by the five UN Security Council permanent member-states and all parties to the conflict, including the PLO, the sole legitimate representative of the Palestinian people, within a joint delegation.

In his letter to Husayn, after the signing of the agreement, Arafat added clarification to article five saying that his preferred choice was "a joint Arab delegation according to Fez resolutions, whereas the Jordanians preferred a joint Jordanian–Palestinian delegation, but they did not object to an Arab delegation". Husayn consented and added this clarification to the official text of the agreement.[21]

Khalid al-Hasan (a Fatah leader) elucidated Fatah's motives behind the agreement: to prevent any possible Jordanian representation of the Palestinian cause, or the signing of a separate agreement on the Palestinian issue, given Israel's negative attitude towards the PLO. The aim of this move was to pressure the US "into accepting the idea of an international conference with the participation of the PLO as the sole legitimate representative of the Palestinian people in an equal status to the other participants".[22]

Talks between Jordan and the US Administration, designed to implement the Amman agreement of February 1985 when Jordan had served as a mediator between the US and the PLO, commenced in March 1985. They centred around two interlocking issues: the first dealt with Palestinian representation either at peace talks or in an international conference; the second issue addressed the PLO's recognition or acceptance of Resolutions 242 and 338. In late

March 1985, the Jordanian government suggested to the US Administration that a dialogue should be opened with a joint Jordanian–Palestinian delegation.[23] In early April 1985, the US expressed its consent in principle, provided that the Palestinian associates were not members of the PLO or of any fidai organizations, and that the number should not exceed four – two from the territories and two from "outside" the territories. The PLO transmitted to Jordan, and Jordan relayed to the US Administration, a list of seven members (including two from the territories) all of whom were from the PNC. Only two of the seven were acceptable to Israel (and thus to the US).

In order to bypass this complicated issue and make some progress in the negotiations, Jordan advised the US to discuss the convening of an international peace conference with the participation of the PLO. Following talks between the US and King Husayn on one side, and between Husayn and Arafat on the other, the Administration summed up its attitude in a letter dispatched to the King of Jordan on 5 January 1986. The US stated that "when it is clearly on the public record that the PLO has accepted Resolutions 242 and 338, and is prepared to negotiate peace with Israel, and renounced terrorism, then the United States would accept the fact that an invitation will be issued to the PLO to attend an international conference". According to Husayn, "the Palestinian leadership surprised us by refusing to accept Security Council Resolution 242 within the context". He explained that "Arafat had expressed his acceptance of 242 during our meeting in August 1985".[24]

The PLO stuck to its position that acceptance of Resolutions 242 and 338 would have to be conditional on "US agreement to the legitimate rights of the Palestinian people including their right to self-determination within the context of a confederation between Jordan and Filastin as stated in the February Accord". Husayn told the Palestinian leadership that self-determination was a matter between Jordan and the Palestinians to discuss while they worked out their confederation, arguing that the first priority was to get back the land. But the Palestinians remained firm in their position. The US reaction was a rejection, on 27 January 1986, of the PLO's stance, maintaining that self-determination could be one of the issues raised by the PLO at the international conference, and that "the United States supports the legitimate rights of the Palestinian people as stated in the Reagan peace initiative" (1 February 1986). Khalil al-Wazir and Hani al-Hasan informed Husayn that the PLO had "finally and totally" rejected Resolutions 242 and 338.[25]

Although it seemed that the talks had reached an impasse, the US made another attempt on the evening of 5 February 1986, presenting Husayn with another offer which contained "US approval for the convening of an international conference on the basis of Resolutions 242 and 338, including the realization of the legitimate rights of the Palestinian people". The same evening Arafat handed Husayn three proposals which, according to the King, "were three differently worded texts, which were the same in substance, reaffirming the same PLO position which we had heard from the start of this round of meetings". All three proposals called for an international conference at which "the PLO would participate on an equal footing within a joint Jordanian–Palestinian delegation". The conference would be held "on the basis of securing the legitimate rights of the Palestinian people, including the right to self-determination within a Jordanian–Palestinian confederation, as stipulated in the Jordanian–Palestinian accord signed in February 1985". Resolutions 242 and 338 were specifically mentioned in the proposals as a basis for the conference, but along with the other UN resolutions that were "pertinent to the Palestinian question". The PLO reaffirmed its "condemnation and rejection of terrorism as endorsed in the Cairo Declaration of November 1985".[26] It should be emphasized, however, that the PLO has always interpretated this November declaration to mean that the armed struggle in Israel, the West Bank and the Gaza Strip would continue.

On 6 February 1986 Arafat met the Jordanian Prime Minister Zayd al-Rifa'i and informed him "that despite the positive development in the American position, recognition of the legitimate rights of the Palestinian people did not encompass the right to self-determination, which the PLO insisted upon, and to which the US must give its prior approval".[27] The US Administration, apparently still believing it could salvage something from the Husayn–Arafat talks, attempted to soften to some degree the PLO's rejection of Resolution 242 when the State Department's spokesman stated on 10 February that:

> The Palestinian problem is more than a refugee problem. Beyond that, there should be no confusion between Resolution 242 and the legitimate rights of the Palestinian people, they deal with different issues and are in fact complementary. ... As a separate but related matter, negotiations regarding the final status of the West Bank and Gaza, in addition to resolving the location of the boundaries and the nature of the

security arrangements, must also recognize the legitimate rights of the Palestinian people. The full manner in which those rights will be exercised will become clear as the process of negotiations proceeds.[28]

As a response to this announcement Faruq al-Qaddumi, a Fatah leader, declared on 12 February that the statement contained "nothing new and did not reflect any change in the known US position". Arafat stated in Cairo that the announcement was merely a repetition of the Reagan Plan.[29] Once again, for Husayn, "another chapter came to an end in the search for peace. Another extremely important and significant round of Jordanian–Palestinian action was terminated ... that would have led to the participation of the PLO in an international conference."[30]

Husayn's statement of 19 February, cancelling the political co-ordination with the PLO leadership, expressed his frustration and disappointment: "We are unable to continue co-ordinating politically with the PLO leadership until such time as their word becomes their bond, characterized by commitment, credibility, and constancy."[31]

On 7 March 1986, in response to Husayn's 19 February speech, the PLO Executive Committee, together with the Fatah Central Committee, declared *inter alia* that:

1) The basic definition of the right of the Palestinian people to choose their representatives must be stressed. No one else is entitled to argue or debate this question.

2) The PLO has reiterated its public stand toward Resolution 242, which it rejected from the beginning because it ignored the core issues of the Palestinian problem: land, people, and the right to have representation.

3) With regard to what had been said about the PLO's direction and credibility and the allegation that it accepted Resolutions 242 and 338 in August 1985, it should be noted that the resolutions of the emergency Arab summit in Casablanca, which was held at that time, affirmed the need to adhere to the Fez summit resolutions and regarded these resolutions as the basis of the Arab and Palestinian–Jordanian moves. They also affirmed the Palestinian people's inalienable rights, thereby contradicting that allegation.

4) How can the PLO be held responsible for the retreat while

the PLO has never accepted Resolution 242 without its being linked to all other UN resolutions and the right to self-determination.[32]

THE "OUTSIDE" AND THE "INSIDE":
DIVISION, CONCILIATION AND ESCALATION

*The Outside (*al-kharij*): Division and Conciliation*

The consensus achieved by the organizations at the 12th PNC over the "phased programme" did not last long. Disputes flared up over the interpretation of its articles and especially those concerning preconditions for PLO participation in the peace process. The PFLP announced (July–August 1974) that it would withdraw from the PLO the moment the PLO participated in the Geneva Conference. In the PFLP's opinion, Palestinian national rule could only be established through armed struggle, which formed the base for the political struggle. At the end of September 1974, the PFLP declared its withdrawal from the PLO Executive Committee.[33] The Arab Liberation Front (ALF), the PFLP-GC (Jibril organization), and the Palestinian Popular Struggle Front (PPSF) all followed the PFLP attitude and together they established "The Rejection Front".

Opposition to Sadat's initiative brought about a closing of the ranks and a unity of purpose among the organizations. The 14th PNC met in Damascus, 15–22 January 1979, with all the Palestinian organizations participating. Its decisions were characterized by the PLO's insistence "to continue escalation of the armed struggle, as well as all manner of political and popular struggle, especially in the occupied lands". The PNC rejected the Camp David autonomy plan and called for its demise.[34] When the 17th PNC convened in Amman (22–29 November 1984), it was against the background of Arafat's expulsion from Tripoli and his meeting with Mubarak in Alexandria, which had been heavily criticized by the Rejection Front organizations and by some of the Fatah leaders including Abu Iyad. In the face of the PFLP's and PDFLP's sharp criticism of his policy and leadership, Arafat decided to convene the PNC in order to reaffirm his status in the PLO. Although these two rejectionist organizations had also been setting preconditions for their participation in the PNC, Arafat did not succumb. The PFLP, PDFLP, and the PLF (which constituted the Democratic Pact organizations), the Communist Party and the pro-Syrian "National

Front Organizations", which were established in May of 1984 and included: the Fatah Rebels, Jibril organization (PFLP-GC), the Syrian Sai'qa organization, and the Palestinian Popular Struggle Front (PPSF), all boycotted the PNC convention. Arafat never-theless succeeded in gathering the required number of members to consitute a quorum for a legitimate session.[35]

The 17th PNC met under the slogan "Support for the Legitimate, Free and Independent Palestinian Decision", and reiterated its former resolutions regarding Resolution 242 and the rejection of the Camp David autonomy plan. But the most important outcome was the vote of confidence for Arafat's leadership of the PLO and chairmanship of the PLO Executive Committee.[36]

The 18th PNC assembled in Algiers, 20–26 April 1987, under the shadow of Husayn's termination of political co-ordination. The PFLP and other radical organizations participated in the 18th PNC, having returned to the fold after Arafat rescinded the Amman Agreement of February 1985 (a precondition for their rejoining the PNC). In mid-April 1986, the PLO Executive Com-mittee decided to repeal the agreement on the ground that it "ceased to be practical", and it repeated the sentiment that "the relationship with Jordan would be based on a confederation between two independent states". The PNC authorized the EC "to define the bases for Palestinian–Egyptian relations according to the PNC's and Arab summit's resolutions".[37] Arafat took advantage of this prerogative to strengthen PLO–Egyptian relations, and on 29 November 1987 the PLO office in Cairo reopened.

*The "Inside" (*al-dakhil*) Escalation*

The municipal elections held in the West Bank on 12 December 1976 proved a political turning-point in the territories. In contrast to the elections of 1972 (see pages 250–6) the PLO supported and even encouraged the inhabitants to vote and submit candidates. The most significant result was the election of a large number (40 per cent) of nationalist candidates who were members and activists in the Ba'th and Communist Parties, the Arab Nationalist Movement, and members of the Palestinian National Front (PNF) (pages 264–6). Also conspicuous was the large number of highly educated candidates elected. The campaign and its results were indicative of the consensus existing among the West Bank inhabi-tants towards the PLO, who were seen as the sole legitimate representative of the Palestinian people. It was only logical that the elected members of the municipalities would pursue the PLO policy *vis-à-vis* the Israeli government and the political process towards solving the Palestinian national issue.

Thus, the setting up of a newly elected official leadership and the strengthening of Palestinian national identity – pledging allegiance to the PLO – combined to bring about a radicalization in the West Bank leadership's attitude towards the Israeli government. On the other hand, the Likud government headed by Menachem Begin, which had been swept into power in the 1977 general elections, appointed Arik Sharon as Defense Minister, and was trying its utmost to block the PLO's growing influence in the territories. This intricate situation of prolonged confrontation between the Israeli government and the local people, on one hand, and with the Palestinian leaders, on the other, was leading inevitably, it appears, to the explosion of the Intifada. The acting body of local leadership in the forefront of the struggle against the Israeli government in this period was "the National Guidance Committee" (NGC) which had been established in October 1978 at a gathering of prominent leaders. Throughout all its activities the NGC emphasized its affiliation to the PLO and its role as the PLO's political arm.[38]

The shock the Palestinians had suffered as a result of the war in Lebanon caused a lapse in the security situation and paradoxically a heightened sense of Palestinian solidarity and identity. The local newspapers described the Palestinians' situation in Lebanon as similar to "the 1948 catastrophe" and "the 1970 massacre", and the withdrawal from Beirut was portrayed as "the Palestinian Dunkirk".[39] Thus, in the wake of the Lebanon War, the level of activities against the Israeli government decreased, and during 1983 and 1984 the number of hostile incidents against Israelis was comparable to that of the previous year, due to limitations imposed on leading activists in the NGC. But during 1985 a deterioration in security set in. Sabotage and violent actions against civilian and military targets increased, and although the number of riots was reduced, a new phenomenon was seen emerging in the Gaza Strip and the West Bank: Islamic fundamentalist groups. These organizations called for the wholesale annihilation of the state of Israel, and the establishment of an Islamic state in its place. There was an increase in violence during 1987 that included hostilities against Israeli soldiers and civilians, as well as so-called "Arab collaborators". Following this escalation the Israeli government reacted by tightening security measures, extending punishments to include expulsions, detention of agitators and political activists, and dismantling of the NGC.

THE PALESTINIANS BETWEEN THE INTIFADA AND THE OSLO AGREEMENT (DECEMBER 1987–SEPTEMBER 1993)

Four important events in 1988 contributed to the process which led to Israeli–PLO reciprocal recognition and the signing of the Oslo Agreement.

1. The Intifada

Although the Intifada broke out on 9 December 1987, its methods and goals were only crystallized during the following year. It was an expected and inevitable consequence of the deep political and social processes at work in the territories since their occupation in June 1967. The Intifada was the culmination of these processes, and not the start of something new. This author wrote, in August 1985, that "The 'generation of the occupation' [in the territories], which had grown up under the impact of the Palestinian national awakening, will lead the struggle against the Israeli government. The scope of this struggle will intensify in the coming years."[40] Indeed, the Intifada did revolutionize its features, intensity and scope dynamically in response to the IDF's and the Israeli government's reactions. But the change also came about as a consequence of the Palestinians' conduct in the territories and the extent of their popular support and involvement, as well as the PLO directives coming from Tunis. It is worth noting that the Intifada was a surprise not only to the Israeli government but also to the PLO leadership.

The Intifada leadership, namely the "Unified National Command", presented itself, in leaflets distributed in the territories, as the PLO's arm, even though it often behaved independently. The Intifada leaders were not blind to the fact that by themselves they could neither bring the occupation to a conclusion nor establish a state of their own. Short-term aims would be the intensification of diplomatic activities and the convening of an international (or regional) peace conference, and they eventually succeeded in these aims. The goal of establishing a state was, of course, the final objective of the whole Palestinian struggle. The leaflets also mentioned the long-range tasks of the national movement as determined in the PNC's resolutions, namely, "achieving national rights, first and foremost the right of return, self-determination, and the establishment of an independent state under PLO leadership". In its message to the Extraordinary Arab Summit in Baghdad, 7 June 1988, the Unified National Command pledged, *inter alia*, to realize the following aims:

1) To pave the way to end the occupation and achieve our people's freedom and independence.
2) The withdrawal of the Zionist army from the cities, villages and camps.
3) Foiling ... the autonomy plan, Camp David, and Shultz' initiative.
4) Convene an international conference ... to be attended by the permanent Security Council members as well an independent PLO on equal footing with all the other parties.
5) Establishing an independent national state under the PLO, its sole, legitimate representative.[41]

2. Jordan's Disengagement from the West Bank

The Intifada proved to Husayn what had been in fact the reality for many years: that his grip on the West Bank was practically non-existent. Husayn justifiably believed that the Intifada could spread to the Palestinian sector of his country, which constituted no less than half of the population, and could thus jeopardize his stable regime. Despite his open threat to disengage from the West Bank if the PLO's proposals were affirmed, the Algiers Arab summit (June 1988) approved "the Palestinian people's right to establish its state on its national land, with Jerusalem as its capital".[42] Thus, in contrast to Husayn's attitude,[43] the summit approved the principle of establishing a Palestinian state in the West Bank and the Gaza Strip.

In his 31 July 1988 speech, Husayn announced the official disengagement of Jordan's administrative and legal ties to the West Bank.[44] In answer to the question of why the decision was made on that specific day and not after the Rabat or Fez Arab summits, for example, King Husayn replied:

> We also need to recall the factors that led to the debates over slogans and objectives which the PLO raised and worked to gain both Arab and international support for the establishment of an independent Palestinian state – this meant that in addition to the PLO's ambition to embody the Palestinian identity on Palestinian national soil, also included was the separation of the West Bank from the Hashemite Kingdom of Jordan. Jordan is not Palestine, and the independent Palestinian state will be established on the occupied Palestinian land after its liberation. There the Palestinian identity will be embodied, and there the Palestinian struggle will come to fruition ...[45]

The legal and administrative ties were the last vestige of Jordan's connections with the West Bank. On 7 August 1988 the King stated that "Jordan has no sovereignty over the West Bank which belongs to the Palestinians in the occupied territories".[46]

Already, on 28 July 1988, the Jordanian government cancelled its five-year development plan (1986–90) for the occupied territories. Two days later the Jordanian Parliament, comprised of representatives from both banks (of the Jordan river), dissolved. Husayn's speech (31 July 1988) was followed by a series of steps designed to implement the official disengagement. On 4 August the government voted to retire almost all Jordanian civil servants employed in the West Bank. The decision affected 18,000 government-employed workers in various departments and institutions. However, the decision did not apply to the employees of the Ministry of *Awqaf* (religious endowment) and Religious Affairs, including the Islamic Religious Court system. They were exempted because, according to the government statement, they embodied "the Islamic Cultural presence in the occupied territories".[47] The Jordanian Minister of *Awqaf* stated (September 1988) that his office continued to spend four million Jordanian Dinar on religious institutions and mosques in the West Bank. This included the upkeep of 750 mosques (the most important of these being the al-Aqsa mosque in Jerusalem), and the payments of salaries to about 3,500 workers in the Ministry (1,800 in the *Awqaf*, 200 in religious courts, 420 teachers, and the rest functionaries in various Islamic institutions).[48]

It seems that Husayn came to the realization that what remained of his connection to the territories had become more of a burden than an advantage. His dilemma lay in deciding which measure to take to strengthen the regime's Jordanian entity, so as to prevent the Palestinian sector from becoming a menace, while at the same time not arousing criticism and antagonism from the PLO and the Arab world. Husayn surmised that the complete "transfer" of official rule over the West Bank and the PLO, in accordance with the Arab summit's resolutions, would be regarded by the Arab world as a nationalist step and, more importantly, it would bestow legitimacy on Husayn's moves to consolidate his regime. It seems that with this new strategy Husayn had chosen the "Jordanian option" rather than the Palestinian one. (This new strategy would eventually bring the King, together with Yitzhak Rabin, to Washington, on 25 July 1994, for the signing of the peace declaration.)

3. The 19th PNC Resolutions: The Change in Strategy

The convening of the 19th PNC in November 1988 had become imperative for Arafat to determine the future strategy of the PLO in the light of recent developments: the flare up of the Intifada and its repercussions; Jordan's disengagement from the West Bank; and the swirl of events in the political process. The PNC's aim was "to move the Intifada from the stone-throwing phase, to the stage of political initiative whereby the Palestinian leadership should adopt creative and innovative tactics by injecting the political process with a new impetus in order to reach the international conference".[49]

Debate in the PNC revolved around the notion of accepting "realistic resolutions" which, according to Fatah's leaders, would pave the way for a political solution to the Palestinian issue. The question remained, though, how to engender a change in the US Administration's attitude towards opening a dialogue with, and the recognition of, the PLO as a partner in negotiations. At the same time, the Fatah leadership was playing the "Intifada card" for all it was worth to gain ground in the international arena. The immediate task thrust upon the PLO was to find a practical answer to the Jordanian "disengagement strategy" by assuming responsibility over the territories. Under these circumstances, the Fatah leaders realized that they had to make profound and dramatic changes in their strategy. Accordingly, on 15 November 1988, the PNC ratified two documents: "The Declaration of Independence" (of the Filastin state) and "The Political Statement".

A. *The Declaration of Independence:*
The PNC declared "the independence of Filastin" and the establishment of "the Filastin state on our land, with Jerusalem as its capital", resting its legal basis on the 1947 UN Partition Resolution:

> Despite the historical injustice inflicted on the Palestinian Arab people resulting in their dispersion and depriving them of their right to self-determination, following upon UN General Assembly Resolution 181 (1947), which partitioned Palestine into two states, one Arab, one Jewish, yet this resolution still provides those conditions for international legitimacy (*al-shar'iyya al-duwaliyya*) that ensure the right of the Palestinian Arab people to sovereignty and national independence ... The PNC ... in the name of the Palestinian Arab people, hereby proclaims the establishment of the state

of Filastin on our national territory with its capital Jerusalem. The state of Filastin is the country of Palestinians wherever they may be.[50]

For the first time, the PLO officially recognized the existence of two states on Palestine Mandate territory – Israel and Filastin – although without specifying their borders. This PNC resolution actually contradicted Article 19 of the 1968 Palestinian National Charter (*al-Mithaq al-Watani al Filastini*) which stated that:

> The partition of Palestine in 1947 and the establishment of the State of Israel are entirely illegal, regardless of the passage of time, because they were contrary to the will of the Palestinian people and to their natural right in their homeland.[51]

B. *The Political Statement:*

1. The necessity of convening an effective international conference on the issue of the Middle East and its core the Palestinian question under the auspices of the United Nations with the participation of the permanent members of the Security Council and all parties to the conflict in the region, including the PLO, the sole legitimate representative of the Palestinian people, which is to be present on equal footing. The international peace conference will be convened on the basis of UN Security Council Resolutions 242 and 338, and the attainment of the legitimate national rights of the Palestinian people, foremost among them the right to self-determination and in accordance with the relevant UN resolutions pertaining to the Palestinian issue.

2. The withdrawal of Israel from all Palestinian and Arab territories occupied in 1967, including Arab Jerusalem.

3. Endeavouring to place the occupied Palestinian territories, including Arab Jerusalem, under the auspices of the UN for a limited period.

4. The settlement of the Palestinian refugee issue in accordance with the relevant UN resolutions.

5. The Security Council is to formulate and guarantee arrangements for security and peace among all states in the region, including the state of Filastin.

6. The PNC reaffirms its previous resolutions on the unique relationship between the Jordanian and Palestinian peoples,

and affirms that the future relationship between the two states of Jordan and Filastin should be based on a confederation resulting from the free and voluntary choice of two fraternal peoples.

7. The PNC also reiterates its rejection of terrorism in all its forms, including state terrorism, and affirms its commitment to previous resolutions on this subject, and the resolution of the 1988 Arab Summit in Algiers, as well as that contained in the Cairo Declaration (7 November 1985) in this respect.[52]

Unlike its former references to 242 which contained reservations, the 19th PNC accepted the Resolution, but not as wholeheartedly as the US demanded. Abu Iyad admitted that the additional condition stemmed from the strong rejection of the Resolution by some of the organizations, foremost among them the PFLP and its leader George Habash.[53]

Regarding terrorism, there was no mollification of the PLO attitude which distinguished, according to Arafat's declaration on 7 November 1985, between "internal" hostilities (inside Israel and the territories), considered legitimate, and "external" actions (Israeli targets abroad). Internal actions were depicted as part of "a war for independence and a repudiation of the occupation".

It is worth noting that the term "armed struggle" was not mentioned in the PNC's resolutions. Instead, the Intifada itself was presented as the embodiment of the struggle against Israeli occupation.

The PNC's resolutions were an indispensable move towards any progress and Palestinian success in the international sphere, and eventually they led to the Oslo Agreement.

4. The Dialogue Between the USA and the PLO

The decision on the part of the US to open an official dialogue with the PLO on 14 December 1988 was a quantum leap for the organization's status in the international arena, and in the political process. This change came about as a result of intensive mediation and unrelenting pressure on Arafat by Sweden and Egypt, in close co-ordination with the Americans, to consent to the US Administration's conditions for opening an official dialogue, that is, to accept clearly and unequivocally Resolutions 242 and 338, recognizing Israel's right to exist and condemning terrorism. Arafat decided to cross the Rubicon, justifying his move by citing the 19th

PNC resolutions. In a press conference, held in Geneva on 14 December, he declared:

> Our statehood provides salvation for the Palestinians and peace to both the Palestinians and Israelis. Self-determination means survival for the Palestinians and our survival does not destroy the existence of Israel as their rulers claim. Yesterday in my speech (at the UN General Assembly) I made reference to Resolution 181 as the basis for Palestinian independence. I also referred to our acceptance of Resolutions 242 and 338 as the basis of negotiations with Israel within the framework of an international conference. In my speech yesterday it was also clear that we mean the right of all parties concerned in the Middle East conflict to exist in peace and security. ... This includes the states of Palestine, Israel, and other neighbours, according to Resolutions 242 and 338. As for terrorism ... I repeat for the record that we totally and absolutely renounce all its forms, including individual, group, and state terrorism.[54]

The US Administration concluded that by these words Arafat had fulfilled their preconditions for opening an official dialogue with the PLO. In a press conference held only hours after Arafat's declaration, George Shultz, the American Secretary of State, officially announced the opening of a dialogue with the PLO: "Arafat's statement was an unambiguous acceptance of American conditions." He added that the initiation of a dialogue did not "imply an acceptance or recognition by the United States of an independent Palestinian state".[55] This launched the official dialogue between members of the PLO Executive Committee, headed by Yasir Abd Rabu, and Robert Pelletreau, the American Ambassador in Tunis, two days later on 16 December 1988. In its first phase the dialogue was planned by the US Administration as both a clarification of the PLO's position on the recognition of Israel and cessation of terror, and as a point of departure for pressing Israel to change her attitude towards the PLO. The US would then serve as a mediator between the two parties, and try to bring about a direct dialogue between them at a later stage.

Looked at from a wider view, the significant turn in US policy meant the recognition of the Palestinians' right to self-determination. It was a conspicuous achievement for the PLO, and the result of its determined and protracted efforts, with Egyptian and Jordanian assistance, during the last decade.

Thus, the dialogue set the stage for the entrance of the Palestinian delegation, as a contingent of the Jordanian, to the Madrid
Conference in 1991. The dialogue, however, was postponed in the
wake of a terrorist attack on a Tel Aviv beach-front in 1990, carried
out by the Abu al-Abbas organization, a member of the PNC and
the PLO-Executive Committee. Arafat refrained from condemning
the attack or punishing Abu al-Abbas by removing him from the
EC. (He eventually left the EC in October 1991.) Nevertheless,
the American–PLO dialogue continued through indirect channels,
namely the leadership in the territories who represented the PLO
and co-ordinated their activities with the organization. It would
take over two years before the direct dialogue officially resumed,
following the Oslo Agreement, signed in Washington between
Arafat and Rabin on 13 September 1993.

The issue of the Palestinian representation in the political process
was resolved at the Madrid Conference. The Palestinian delegates
were appointed by Arafat, receiving directives straight from him,
and although they were part of the Jordanian delegation, they
functioned separately and independently. For the first time in the
Arab–Israeli conflict, "independent" Palestinian representatives
took part as a major party, with almost-equal status, in a conference
that included Israel, Syria, Jordan and Lebanon. Indeed, the
Palestinian delegation conducted separate negotiations with the
Israelis concerning the future of the territories. Later, both sides
would hold direct talks in Washington on the Palestinian issue.

The participation of a Palestinian delegation at an international
peace conference, dealing, *inter alia*, with the specific Palestinian
national problem, was the fulfilment of Nasir's vision in 1959. He
initiated the revival of the Palestinian Entity in order to turn the
Palestinians into a separate factor in the Arab–Israeli conflict,
"and the Palestinian issue from one of refugees" and borders into a
national issue of "a people that has a homeland" who thus had the
right to self-determination.

CONCLUSION

There is no doubt that the Oslo Agreement and the establishment
of autonomy in the Gaza Strip and Jericho (and in all of the West
Bank at a later stage) are decisive steps towards the Palestinian
people's self-determination and the eventual setting up of the
Filastin state. This agreement has been the result of inevitable
changes that have occurred in the strategies of both Israel and the

PLO as they realized that there was no choice other than mutual recognition, with the PLO accepted as the sole representative of the Palestinian people's national aspirations. Against the background surveyed in this volume, the PLO's accomplishment should be viewed as the achievement not only of the Palestinian national movement, but also of pan-Arab nationalism (*qawmi*).

Ironically, the peace agreement between Egypt and Israel paved the way for the Oslo Agreement, even though Sadat deviated from the Arab consensus confirmed at the Rabat Arab summit (October 1974). The Camp David Automony Plan, which the PLO overtly rejected, set the actual guide-lines for the Oslo Agreement which itself cleared the way for the Jordan–Israel peace agreement, and opened most of the Arab world to Israel. Husayn, who always acquiesced to the Arab consensus embodied in the Arab summits' resolutions (1964, 1974, 1988), could not allow himself to sign a peace agreement with Israel until the Palestinian national issue had been solved. Nevertheless, as he had so often reiterated, the Palestinian issue remained "fateful" for Jordan; and as such it has long been and will continue to be a decisive factor in Jordan's national security.

President Asad was surprised by the Oslo Agreement and the Agreement of Principles between Jordan and Israel. He strongly criticized both their timing and tenets. Both agreements wiped his cards off the table in negotiations with Israel. Whereas the Oslo Agreement deprived Syria of her position as patron of the Palestinian issue, a status Asad had vaunted since his rise to power, the peace agreement with Jordan weakened and even invalidated his claim for a comprehensive settlement of the Arab–Israeli conflict. It seems that, notwithstanding a strategic change and entering into direct peace negotiations with Israel, he still has difficulty digesting the historical impact of a possible Syrian brokered peace agreement (accompanied by a similar agreement signed by Lebanon) that would signal a formal termination of the Arab–Israeli conflict. For this reason, apparently, he is endeavouring his utmost to make sure that his peace agreement with Israel will go down in the conflict's history as the best one from the Arab perspective, with conditions far exceeding those of the others, and Egypt's in particular.

The Oslo Agreement was first and foremost a Fatah achievement under the leadership of Arafat, who, together with the other founders, Abu Jihad, Abu Iyad, Abu Yusuf, Kamal Udwan, Abu al-Sa'id (Khalid al-Hasan), Abu Lutuf, and Abu Mazin, has led the

PLO since the 1960s. Fatah continued to be the "backbone" of the PLO and the leading organization of the Palestinian national movement. Abu Iyad's statement in March 1975 that "the decision of Fatah is the Palestinian decision" (page 161) vindicated itself again during the period under survey. The creation of a strong opposition to Fatah within the PLO, with the massive support of Syria, failed to shake the PLO's status and Arafat's leadership. There existed no viable alternative to either.

Fatah has been leading the PLO and the Palestinian national movement throughout the crises and achievements that have been surveyed in this book. Fatah also waged the campaign for changes in the PLO's strategy and political attitude in 1974 and 1988, and for the PLO's participation in the Madrid Conference (1991), and above all for working out the Oslo Agreement. The Declaration of Principles between Israel and the PLO endowed the 12th PNC resolutions with a better historical perspective and dimension than before, and the basic significance given to these resolutions during the previous two decades had remained valid. Arafat reiterated these resolutions in order to legitimize the Agreement. He argued, and rightly so, that the Oslo Agreement was, in fact, the implementation of the 12th PNC decisions. Thus, the resolutions of the 12th PNC may be seen, retrospectively, as the start of a process which led to the 19th PNC decisions of November 1988, culminating in the signing of the agreement between the PLO and Israel in 1993.

The Oslo Agreement was also the achievement of the Intifada, and the local leaders of the territories. The Intifada years left their impact on both the Palestinians and the Israelis. The contribution of the local leadership in endorsing the 19th PNC resolutions and the PLO participation in the Madrid Conference was highly significant. These leaders were dramatically elevated to the forefront of Palestinian politics, and their status was strengthened following the establishment of the Palestinian National Authority in the Gaza Strip and Jericho. The Intifada was the decisive impetus that precipitated the process which brought about Israel's recognition of the PLO as representative of the Palestinian people. This was a *de facto* recognition of the Palestinian people's right to self-determination and to independent national government.

The Intifada signalled and embodied the Palestinian "social revolution". Today, we are facing a society in transition: from one that has lived under occupation for almost 30 years and was led by militant organizations, into a society being ruled, overnight as it were, by a Palestinian civil autonomous government. Arafat, in his new role as head of the Palestinian National Authority, is confronted with two basic interlocking problems. The first is the need to enforce his authority on the Palestinian population and establish law and order. The second is the appearance of Islamic fundamentalist organizations (Hamas and al-Jihad al-Islami) that are opposed not only to the Oslo Agreement but also to the existence of Israel.

Comparing the composition of the current leadership of the Fatah/PLO with that of 1974, the picture seems less promising for Arafat. Today, he is surrounded mostly by so-called leaders who have emerged from the second echelon of Fatah leadership, except for Abu Mazin and Faruq al-Qaddumi. Qaddumi (Abu Lutuf), who is not the most charismatic figure, opposed the Oslo Agreement and remained in Tunis. In 1974 the Fatah/PLO leadership comprised, besides Arafat, two charismatic personalities, namely, Abu Iyad (Salah Khalaf) and Abu Jihad (Khalil al-Wazir). Indeed, in 1974 Abu Iyad successfully led the campaign to convince the Palestinians of the need to change the PLO strategy. It is the present lack of strong and charismatic Fatah leadership that might explain the difficulties confronting Arafat in trying to win the PLO institutions' endorsement of the accord with Israel, and gaining acceptance from Palestinian public opinion. Although it would be reasonable to describe the status of Arafat's leadership as weaker now than in 1974, he still retains power and authority in the eyes of the Palestinians as the symbol of the Palestinian revolution and the veteran leader of the Fatah/PLO and the Palestinian national movement. There is no alternative to his leadership of the Palestinian National Authority, nor substitute for his dominating presence in the quest for attaining a permanent agreement with Israel. Arafat will be recorded in the history of the Palestinian national movement as the right person, in the right role, at the right time.

March 1995

Notes

CHAPTER ONE

1. Isa al-Shu'aybi, *al-Kiyaniyya al-Filastiniyya 1947–1977*, Beirut, 1979, p. 88; Adli Hashad, *Sha'b Filastin fi Tariq al-Awda*, Cairo, 1964, p. 104; Ahmad al-Shuqayri, *Min al-Qumma ila al-Hazima*, Beirut, 1971, p. 57; also *al-Ahram*, 6.4.59.
2 Muhammad Hasanayn Haykal (Haykal), *al-Ahram*, 20.12.58; Jamal Abd al-Nasir (Nasir), *al-Ahram*, 24.12.58.
3. This term was used by Butrus Ghali, *Dirasat fi al-Diblumasiyya al-Arabiyya*, Cairo, 1973, p. 233; and by M.H. Kerr, *The Arab Cold War*, third edition, London, 1971.
4. Michel Aflaq, lecture before Ba'th members in Paris, 21.6.64, Nidal Hizb al-Ba'th, *Bayanat Qiyadatihi al-Qawmiyya 1963–1966*, Beirut, October 1971, pp. 147–148.
5. For the meaning of these slogans see Nasir, *Filastin Min Aqwal al-Ra'is*, Cairo, n.d., speeches during the period December 1953 – June 1964 (*Aqwal*), pp. 39, 42, 145–147, *al-Ahram*, 23.2.62; Haykal, *al-Ahram*, 10.3.61, 29.12.61, 9.3.62, 28.8.64.
6. See also UAR Memorandum to the Arab League Secretary-General, *al-Ahram*, 5.1.60; Nasir's assessment during UAR government's discussion on the Jordan River problem in Haykal, *al-Ahram*, 18.5.62; also Haykal, *al-Ahram*, 4.1.63.
7. See Nasir, *Aqwal*, pp. 64, 90.
8. See Nasir, *al-Ahram*, 18.4.59, 21.2.60, 4.3.61, *Aqwal*, pp. 65, 67, 76; Haykal, *al-Ahram*, 10.3.61.
9. Nasir in Haykal, *al-Ahram*, 18.5.62, quoting from the UAR Government Protocol; Josef Abu Khatir (then Lebanese ambassador in Cairo), *Liqa' at Ma'a Jamal Abd al-Nasir*, Beirut, 1971, pp. 101–102, quoting Nasir in meeting with him on 17.9.62.
10. *Ruz al-Yusuf*, 15.12.63; Nasir, *al-Ahram*, 24.12.61, 27.6.62, 23.7.63, 28.8.63; Haykal, *al-Ahram*, 7.9.62, went too far in writing "we do not want war as an adventure; the war ought to be well planned".
11. Nasir, *al-Ahram*, 26.4.60, 19.10.60, 1.6.65, *Aqwal*, p. 82, 21.3.60.
12. On 14 February 1959, the Egyptian newspaper *al-Ahram*, probably as a result of instructions from high quarters, began a campaign which continued for some weeks which cautioned against "the great danger threatening Arab nationalism", in the shape of three million Jews from the Eastern Bloc immigrating to Israel. The UAR succeeded in drawing the whole Arab world into this campaign including the Arab media and the Arab League Institutions. *Al-Ahram*, 15.2.59–10.3.59; Nasir, *al-Ahram*, 22.2.59; for further Arab references to this subject see Egypt: *al-Musawwar*, 20.2.59; *Ruz al-Yusuf*, 23.2.59; *al-Akhbar*, 21.2.59; *al-Ahram*, 20.5.59; *Akhir Sa'a*, 11.3.59; Syria: *al-Nasr*, Damascus, 5.3.59; Jordan: *al-Jihad*, 16.2.59, 22.2.59; *Filastin*, Amman, 18.2.59, 21.2.59; *al-Difa'*, 19.2.59; Lebanon: *al-Jarida*, 17.2.59, 19.2.59, 22.2.59; *al-Hayat*, 24.2.59; Iraq: *Baghdad Radio*, (R) commentaries, 17.2.59, 18.2.59.
13. See *Proposals for the Continuation of United Nations Assistance to Palestinian*

Refugees, document submitted by the secretary-general, 14th Session, A/4121, 15 June 1959.

14. Nasir even went so far as to connect Israel's attempts to break the blockade of the Suez Canal by sending a Danish ship, the Inga Toft, to the "wave of expected Jewish immigration to Israel". He presented these attempts as "a new measure in the final process of eliminating the Palestinian problem". See Nasir's assessment of the situation presented to Haykal, *al-Ahram*, 30.6.59; Haykal, *al-Ahram*, 21.9.62, published the text of President Kennedy's despatch (11.5.61) and Nasir's reply (18.8.61); see also Nasir, *al-Ahram*, 14.7.60, *Aqwal*, pp. 46, 50; UAR FM's speech at the ALC, *al-Ahram*, 27.8.60.

15. See Nasir, *al-Ahram*, 19.10.60, 4.3.61, 27.6.62 (speech before the members of the Legisiative Council of the Gaza Strip), 24.12.62, 14,24.12.63, *Aqwal*, p. 136; Haykal, *al-Ahram*, 27.1.61 (quoting Nasir), 16.11.62.

16. On the development of the ANM and its connections with Egypt see Walid Kazziha, *Revolutionary Transformation in the Arab World*, London, 1975; on the Palestinians' activities in pan-Arab movements and pro-Nasirist parties see Hani al-Hasan (a Fatah leader), Fatah Bayna al-Nazariyya wa al-Tatbiq, *Shuun Filastiniyya* (Shuun), No. 7, March 1972, pp. 9–21; Fatah, Dirasat wa-Tajarib Thawriyya, No. 1, *Min Muntalaqat al-'Amal al-Fidai*, August 1967, pp. 38–39; Adnan Badr, Sab' Sanawat lil-Jabha al-Sha'biyya li-Tahrir Filastin, *al-Hadaf*, Beirut, 14.12.74.

17. Haykal, *al-Ahram*, 17.8.62; Khayri Hammad, *al-Ahram*, 2.3.63, 3.3.63, two articles entitled Filastin wa Qadiyyat al-Wahda.

18. *Damascus R.*, 25.6.60, the resolutions of the National Union Congress of the Syrian Region; on the Egyptian concept see *al-Musawwar*, 10.7.59; *Akhbar al-Yawm*, 31.12.60; *al-Akhbar*, 14.8.59; *al-Ahram*, 13.8.59, 27.8.59, 14.2.60, 15.12.60; *Ruz al-Yusuf*, 5.9.60; *al-Wahda*, Damascus, 20.5.59; *al-Siyasa*, Beirut, 17.4.62; *al-Sayyad*, Beirut, 27.4.61.

19. *Al-Jarida al-Rasmiyya*, Law No. 255, 1955, al-Qanun al-Asasi li al-Mantiqa al-Waqi'a Tahta Raqabat al-Quwwat al-Misriyya; also *al-Ahram*, 6.9.60; the Gaza Strip was subordinated to the War Ministry as an occupied area; although the governor of the Gaza Strip was called the administrative governor, he was always a senior army officer who was nominated by the president, so that he was in fact a military governor.

20. Al-Nizam al-Dusturi li-Qita' Ghazza, *al-Jarida al-Rasmiyya*, No. 75, 29.3.62; *al-Ahram*, 6.9.60, 10.3.62; *Akhir Sa'a*, 23.5.62; *al-Sha'b*, Cairo, 17.2.59; *al-Hayat*, 18.2.59.

21. The idea of the PLF had already been mentioned in the pro-Egyptian newspapers in Lebanon in November 1961; see, for example, *Kul Shay*, Beirut, 11.11.61; on the development of this project and contact with Palestinians in other Arab states see *al-Akhbar*, 5.11.62, 15.5.63; *al-Jumhuriyya*, Cairo, 5.11.62, 7.12.62; *Nidal al-Awda*, Gaza, October 1962; *Ruz al-Yusuf*, 5.11.62, 12.8.63; *al-Sayyad*, 16.8.62; *al-Hawadith*, 29.11.62; *Sawt al-Uruba*, Beirut, 4.8.62.

22. See Nasir, *al-Ahram*, 26.4.60; Abd al-Hamid al-Sarraj, then head of the Executive Council of the Syrian Region, *Baghdad R.*, 11.7.61; resolutions of the General Congress of the National Union, *al-Ahram*, 17.7.60; also *al-Ahram*, 24.1.62.

23. For details on the Palestinian units which existed in the Gaza Strip after the 1956 war see *Middle East Record*, Shiloah Research Centre, Tel Aviv (MER), Vol. 1, 1960, p. 138.

24. General Agrudi, *al-Quwwat al-Musallaha*, Cairo, 1.10.61; *Nida al-Awda*, Gaza, May 1961; *al-Akhbar*, 12.3.61; *al-Ahram*, 24.7.60, described their appearance in the parade as "the vanguards of the Palestinian army".

25. See Nasir, *al-Ahram*, 5.8.59; Haykal, *al-Ahram*, 14.8.60, 10.2.61, 3.5.61, 31.3.61 (text of Nasir's letter to Husayn dated 13.3.61), 3.5.63, 27.9.63 (report on his meeting with Husayn in Paris); see also *al-Ahram*, 17.12.62, quoting official sources in Cairo; *al-Jarida*, 18.10.60, an article by Tawfiq al-Maqdisi, analysing

Nasir's speeches; *Akhbar al-Yawm*, 27.4.63, an article by Mustafa Amin in which he emphasized "the belief that the way to Filastin will shortly pass through Amman".

26. *Akhir Sa'a*, 23.5.62; *al-Hayat*, 7.6.64 reported in an article by "an Arab veteran politician" that "in discussions which took place two years ago between high-level Arab and international officials a solution to the Palestinian problem was suggested"; the idea was "to overthrow the Jordanian regime and establish a Palestinian Arab Republic on the two Banks".

27. See Haykal, *al-Ahram*, 14.8.60; Nahid Munir al-Rayis, *Kalima fi al-Kiyan al-Filastini*, Cairo, January 1962, p. 58; resolutions of the General Congress of the National Union, *al-Ahram*, 17.7.60; al-Nizam al-Dusturi, *op. cit.*, article, 2; *Cairo R.*, commentary, 3.6.60; *Sawt al-Arab R.*, commentary, 17.6.60.

28. See Jordanian secret and top-secret records of the General Investigations, General Security and Military Intelligence Departments in Israel State Archives, Section 114, Jerusalem (hereafter SA JISM), reports from Nablus district commander (DC) to Nablus area commander (AC), 380/3 dated 2.4.60, 19.4.60, 24.4.60, 666/3 19.4.60, letter from head of General Security Department (GSD) to Nablus DC, 795/9, 7.1.61.

29. See *al-Ahram*, 4.4.59, text of secret military agreement between Iraq and UAR dated 10.11.58, and text of top-secret letter dated 1.12.58 which was sent by the First Army Commander (the Syrian army) to the C-in-C Iraqi army; *al-Ahram*, 10.3.60; Mustafa Amin, *Akhbar al-Yawm*, 19.5.62; *al-Difa'*, 17.1.60; *al-Jihad*, 18.1.60; *Hawl al-Alam*, Amman, 18.2.60 in the letter of credentials of the new Consul of the UAR (January 1960). In the old city of Jerusalem, Egypt stated that the Consul was being appointed the "General Consul of all the territories located west of the Jordan River" being "a part of Filastin which was conquered by the Jordanian Army". Jordan reacted strongly: on 16.1.60 the credentials of the UAR Consul General in the Old City of Jerusalem were rejected by the Jordanian government on the grounds that they infringed its sovereignty.

30. *Al-Zaman*, Baghdad, 16.12.59.

31. Qasim, *Baghdad Radio* (Bag. R.), 14.7.59, 17.1.60, 23.3.60, 14.7.60, *Iraq News Agency* (INA), 28.5.60, 2.8.60, *al-Nahar*, 3.10.61; Hashim Jawwad, FM, *INA*, 23.8.60; also Abu Khatir, *op. cit.*, p. 229, reporting on meeting with Qasim on 16.7.59; Tawfiq al-Maqdisi, *al-Jarida*, 30.11.60, 1,2,3.12.60, four articles on Iraq based on talks with Iraqi leaders.

32. Maqdisi, *op. cit.*, quoting minister of guidance on Iraq's policy in the Arab arena; Qasim, *al-Nahar*, 3.10.61, *al-Ayyam*, Khartoum, 9.4.60, *Bag. R.*, 22.3.59, 7.1.60, 23.6.60, 2.2.61, *INA*, 15.8.60.

33. Abu Khatir, *op. cit.*, pp. 227–229, reporting on meeting with Qasim 16.7.59; Qasim, *al-Thawra*, Baghdad, 17.8.61, *al-Bilad*, Baghdad, 8.11.59, *Bag. R.*, 18.12.59, 16.5.60, 29.7.60, 10.12.62; Qasim participated in the 1948 war as a battalion commander.

34. Qasim, *Bag. R.*, 18.12.59, 14.7.60, 15.10.60, 2.11.61, 20.3.62, 27.6.62, *al-Thawra*, 21.11.61; Jawwad, *al-Jarida*, 23.1.62; Abu Khatir, *op. cit.*, p. 229; for details on his military and financial aid to the FLN see Qasim, *Bag. R.*, 28.10.59, 23.11.59, 7.3.60, 21.11.61, *al-Thawra*, 21.11.60.

35. On the UAR propaganda campaign against Qasim see MER, 1960, pp. 144–147.

36. Nidal al-Ba'th, *al-Qiyada al-Qawmiyya 1955-1961*, Vol. 4, Beirut, 1964, p. 113.

37. Qasim, *Bag. R.*, 25.6.61.

38. Qasim, *Bag. R.*, 23.11.59.

39. *Bag. R.*, 16.3.62, joint communiqué published at the end of a meeting between al-Qudsi, president of Syria, and Qasim which took place in Rutba, 14.3.62.

40. Qasim, *Bag. R.*, 15.12.59, 18.12.59, 29.7.60, 2.2.61, *al-Thawra*, 7.5.62; Jawwad, *al-Jarida*, 20.8.60.

41. Qasim, *al-Thawra*, 6.9.60, 9.4.62, 7.5.62, 13.5.62, *al-Zaman*, 20.5.62, 12.8.62, *Iraq Times*, 17.8.60, *Bag. R.*, 28.12.59, 13.1.60, 16.5.60, 14.7.60, 11.8.60, 6.9.60,

2.2.61, 2.11.61; Jawwad, *al-Jarida*, 20.8.60, 23.1.62; MER, 1960, p. 135.

42. Qasim, *Bag. R.*, 15,18,21.12.59, 7,13.1.60, 5.4.60, 16.5.60, 16.5.62, *al-Thawra*, 8.4.62, *al-Zaman*, 20.5.62; Jawwad, *al-Jarida*, 20.8.60.

43. Qasim, *Bag. R.*, 28.3.60.

44. *Al-Waqai' al-Iraqiyya*, 29.8.60, pp. 14–15.

45. See Qasim, *al-Ayyam*, Khartoum, 5.4.60, *Bag. R.*, 16.5.60; Shuqayri, *op. cit.*, pp. 69–72; Isam Sakhnini, al-Filastiniyyun fi al-Iraq, *Shuun*, No. 13, September 1972, pp. 90–116; also *al-Zaman*, 17.4.60, 6.12.62; *al-Bilad*, 17.4.60; *al-Akhbar*, Baghdad, 6.4.60; *al-Thawra*, 19.2.62, 13.5.62.

46. Qasim, *Bag. R.*, 28.10.59, 21.12.59, 2.1.60, 7.1.60, *al-Akhbar*, 17.12.59; also *Bag. R.*, commentaries, 20.1.60, 2.3.60.

47. Qasim, *Bag. R.*, 15.10.60; Maqdisi, *op. cit.; al-Jarida*, 14,15.10.60.

48. Qasim, *al-Zaman*, 12.8.60, *Bag. R.*, 2.1.60.

49. On 6.5.62 *al-Thawra* editorial called upon the Mufti to convene a General Palestinian Congress which would represent all the Palestinian national groups in the Arab states. This Congress would become a popular base for the establishment of the Palestinian National Liberation Front. The editorial proposed that from this Front would arise the Provisional Government for Filastin, which should undertake the administration of the Gaza Strip and the West Bank of Jordan.

50. This section is based on the Ba'th documents including internal secret leaflets. These documents were incorporated in three series of books:

a. The old series entitled *Nidal al-Ba'th:* I. Vol. 4, *al-Qiyada al-Qawmiyya 1955–1961*, Beirut, 1964 (hereafter Nidal I); II. Vol. 7, *al-Qutr al-Iraqi 1958–1963*, second edition, Beirut, February 1972 (Nidal II); III. Vol. 8, *al-Qutr al-Lubnani 1951–1961*, Beirut, March 1972 (Nidal III).

b. The new series entitled *Nidal Hizb al-Ba'th al-Arabi al-Ishtiraki: IV. Abr Bayanat Qiyadatihi al-Qawmiyya 1955–1962*, second edition, Beirut, 1971 (Nidal IV); V. *Abr Mutamaratihi al-Qawmiyya 1947–1964*, Beirut, June 1971 (Nidal V); VI. *Abr Mutamaratihi al-Qawmiyya al-Mutamar al-Thamin*, Beirut, April 1972 (Nidal VI); VII. *Abr Bayanat Qiyadatihi al-Qawmiyya 1963–1966*, Beirut, October 1971 (Nidal VII).

c. The series *al-Ba'th wa-Qadiyyat Filastin: VIII. Vol. 3*, 1955–1959, Beirut, 1974 (Ba'th-Filastin Vol. 3); IX. Vol. 4, 1959–1964, Beirut, 1974 (Ba'th-Filastin Vol. 4); X. Vol. 5, 1964–1967, Beirut, May 1975 (Ba'th-Filastin Vol. 5).

51. Haykal, *al-Ahram*, 20.10.61.

52. *Nidal VII*, Aflaq's lecture, 1.7.63, pp. 50–51.

53. *Nidal V*, Aflaq's speech before the 6th NC, October 1963, p. 257, Recommendations of the 4th NC, August 1960, pp. 96–97, Report of the 7th NC, February 1964, pp. 260–263.

54. *Nidal VII*, Aflaq in his discussions with party members in Paris, 21.6.64, pp. 149–151, internal secret circular entitled On the Crisis of the Party and the Regime, 26.12.64, pp. 183–188; *Nidal V*, Report on the 7th NC, February 1964, pp. 254–261.

55. *Nidal VI*, internal report entitled Filastin Problem, submitted by Filastin Branch of the Ba'th party in Lebanon to the 8th NC, April 1965, p. 139, the Recommendations of the Congress on the Filastin Problem, p. 148; also *Ba'th-Filastin*, Vol. 5, pp. 62–80.

56. *Nidal V*, editor's introduction to the Report on the 7th NC, p. 254.

57. *Nidal I*, pp. 121–122; *al-Sahafa*, Beirut, 16.2.60.

58. *Nidal III*, secret internal circular entitled The Report on the 4th Regional Congress, distributed by the party in Lebanon, December 1959, pp. 209–210. The Lebanese Branch gave special attention to the Palestinian problem during 1959, more than any other branch of the party; see, for example, its declaration, *al-Sahafa*, 15.5.59.

59. *Nidal II*, Resolutions and Recommendations of the Iraqi Regional Congress, August 1960, submitted to the 4th NC, pp. 80–82.

60. *Nidal I*, pp. 259–263; *Nidal IV*, pp. 121–124; also *al-Sahafa*, 9.1.60, which attacked Qasim's plan describing it as a "transparent tactic to mislead Arab public opinion and an attempt to get Iraq out of its stifling isolation".

61. *Nidal III*, pp. 175–177.

62. *Nidal I*, pp. 192–193 (resolutions of the 4th NC), 228–238, memorandum submitted to the Arab FMs Conference held in Baghdad 31.1.61; it included a section entitled The Problem of the Political Entity for the Palestinian People; see also *al-Ishtiraki* (organ of the party), 11.3.61, an article entitled The Palestinian Liberation Front is the Road to Return (to Filastin).

63. *Nidal II*, pp. 84–85, declaration dated 20.9.60.

64. See Husayn, *Amman R.*, 17.2.60; Wasfi al-Tall, PM, *Amman R.*, 2.7.62; Musa Nasir, FM, *Ruz al-Yusuf*, 5.9.60; *Amman R.*, commentaries, 17.2.60, 26.10.61; see also SA JISM, secret *Weekly Political Reports* (WPR) written by Nablus AC, Tulkarm AC, and Jenin AC, 646/1 21.12.59, 380/3 MNN/20/15 11.1.60, 18.3.60, 24.4.60, 666/3 21.3.60, 666/4 17.2.60. These reports and those of other area and district commanders generally expressed the regime's policy towards the Palestinian Entity. It seems that area commanders, who relied on the reports of the junior investigations officers, expressed the regime's attitudes as if they were the people's. Most likely the people, in their talks with government personnel, simply mouthed the regime's point of view in order to please their audience. In these documents there is a clear parallel between the WPR and the regime's claims concerning the Palestinian Entity; therefore, one should review these documents with reservations.

65. For information during the years 1959–1962 see for example SA JISM, 121/–SA JISM, MQ/20/11/1, the year 1963, SA JISM unclassified file No. 20/11, entitled Control over Dangerous Elements (hereafter UN/20/11), MQ/20/4/.

66. For details on plots against the regime in 1958–1960, the assassination of Majali, the trial of the culprits and the execution, see MER, 1960, pp. 326–330.

67. Possibly following unreliable information from their agents in Syria. For confirmation for this assessment see *Amman R.*, commentary, 3.9.60, which called on the Syrian people to revolt against the UAR rulers, also MER, 1960, p. 152.

68. See *al-Ahram*, 18.9.60; *Amman R.*, 4.10.60, the text of the Egyptian protest against these concentrations and the Jordanian reply; *Sawt al-Arab R.*, 17.9.60 broadcast news referring to President Eisenhower's intervention; *Amman R.*, commentary, 26.9.60, denied the Egyptian claim that Britain and the USA warned Jordan not to attack Syria.

69. SA JISM, 121/–/10 23.1.62, 121/–/22 13.2.62, 121/–/33 20.3.62, MQ/20/4/3169 26.4.63, MQ/21/45 5605 21.5.61, MQ/21/45/5763 26.10.61, MQ/21/45/330 14.1.62, MQ/1/25/876 27.1.62, MQ/20/41/3169 26.4.63.

70. A similar demand came from the Western powers.

71. See JISM, UN/20/11. During 1963 information flowed increasingly to the GSD and the Intelligence Department concerning preparations by the Egyptians for sabotage activities in Jordan and plans to assassinate the Jordanian leaders including King Husayn. On calling to eliminate the regime see Haykal, *al-Ahram*, 20.4.63; *Cairo R.*, commentary, 1.11.63; *Ruz al-Yusuf*, 15.12.63, article by Ahmad Sa'id.

72. See SA JISM, 380/MN/20/15/7984 28.4.60., 121/–/59 17.9.60, 121/1/57 30.1.61, 121/–/245 10.10.61, 121/–/22 13.2.62 (list of Egyptian intelligence agents and previously Syrian intelligence agents or fidaiyyun), UN/20/11/84 22.9.63 (summary of Egyptian intelligence activities in Lebanon), 14 14.1.63, 30 2.2.63, 59 13.3.63, 136 27.11.63, 8 12.1.64.

73. See reports from Nablus DC to the head of the General Intelligence Department (GID), SA JISM, 755/5 4.3.59, 646/9 4.9.59; also SA JISM, 121/–/207 26.12.60, 518/8 covers the period 9.7.57–4.7.60.

74. Abu Khatir, *op. cit.*, p. 197, cable to Foreign Ministry dated 12.5.61.

75. *Ibid.*, p. 90, report on meeting with Nasir 3.5.61; for details on Jordan's initiative

see *Filastin*, Amman, 7.6.59, 1.7.59, 3.7.59, 2.10.59; *Hawl al-Alam*, 2.7.59; *al-Bilad*, Amman, 19.7.59; *al-Jihad*, 16.9.59, 26.10.59, 22.2.60, 4.4.61; *Ruz al-Yusuf*, 14.9.59; *al-Hayat*, 10.6.61.

76. Haykal, *al-Ahram*, 3.3.61, 11.5.61, published the text of the letters; Abu Khatir, *op. cit.*, p. 197, quoting Nasir in meeting with him on 12.5.61, also cites the Soviet ambassador in Cairo who said that Britain urged Husayn to take this step "in order to paralyse Cairo's activities".

77. An indication of the fact that the exchange of letters was also designed to fulfil internal needs (it succeeded beyond all expectations) was the enthusiastic reactions to the exchanges of the letters in the streets of Jordan. This public fervour reached dangerous proportions when Nasir's photographs appeared for the first time since 1957 in the newspapers, on calendars and in cafés.

78. Husayn in a military camp, *Amman R.*, 13.3.60.

79. See Husayn, *Amman R.*, 16.3.60; Majali, *Amman R.*, 23.8.59, 12.1.60, 10.3.60, 12.1.61, *al-Jihad*, 14, 16.9.59; Wasfi al-Tall, *Amman R.*, 2.7.62; *Filastin*, Amman, editorial, 14.1.60.

80. See Husayn, *al-Difa'*, 23.2.60, 13, 17.3.60, 13.1.63, *Amman R.*, 19.1.60, 1.3.60, 21.10.60; Majali, *al-Jihad*, 16.9.59, *Amman R.*, 22.12.59, *al-Sayyad*, 3.3.60.

81. Husayn, *Amman R.*, 19, 20.1.60, 13.3.60; Majali, *al-Difa'*, 24.3.60, *al-Jihad*, 14, 16.9.59; *Filastin*, 23.12.59, 13.1.60; Tall, *Filastin*, 3.7.62; Musa Nasir, *al-Difa'*, 11.1.61; Abdulla Zurayqat, head of the Jordanian delegation to the ALC, *Amman R.*, 22.9.63.

82. For reactions to this plan in the West Bank see SA JISM, Nablus AC WPR, 380/3/MNN/20/15; he emphasized that the inhabitants were expecting "the declaration of the Palestinian–Jordanian Kingdom".

83. See *al-Jumhuriyya*, 10.11.60; *Middle East News Agency*, Cairo (MENA), 21.1.61; *al-Nasr*, Damascus, 23.1.61; *Ruz al-Yusuf*, 5.8.61.

84. *Al-Jihad*, 3.7.62, *Filastin*, 4.7.62, 5.7.62, *al-Manar*, 6.7.62, 8.7.62, 9.7.62; see also Husayn's letter to the 12th Arab Student Congress in the USA, 25.8.63, *Jordanian Official Brochure*.

85. On Shuqayri's visit, his speeches, his discussions with the local politicians, the latter's activities and the reactions of the people see reports of Nablus DC to the heads of the GSD and GID, SA JISM, 380/7 29.4.62, 3.5.62, reports of Nablus AC to Nablus DC, 646/7 7.5.62, 380/7, 28, 29, 30.4.62, also reports of Jenin AC to Nablus DC 380/7 28.4.62; on Jordanian activities see *Filastin*, 22.5.62, 3.7.62, 29.12.62; *al-Jihad*, 28.5.62, 21.10.62; *al-Difa'*, 29.4.62; *al-Manar*, 26.4.62; *al-Hayat*, 29.5.62; *al-Jarida*, 25.7.62.

86. See *al-Thawra*, Baghdad, 26.4.62; *al-Sayyad*, 19.4.62; *Kul Shay*, 5.5.62; *al-Jumhuriyya*, Cairo, 5.5.62; *al-Hawadith*, 11.5.62.

87. See SA JISM, 380/3 MNN/1/30/9 1.1.60, MNN/30/15/1708, 21.3.60, MKH/20/3/B/1854, 6.4.60, 11/2/2/72, 12.4.60 (letter from governor of Hebron to the interior minister), M/2/43, 3.7.61; see also *Filastin*, 13.8.59, 28.4.63; *al-Jihad*, 16.2.60; *al-Difa'*, 18.1.61; *al-Manar*, 30.8.60.

88. SA JISM, 666/4/23–260, 2, 7, 9.3.60, 121/–/ 36 5.5.60, 226–227 3.10.61, 666/3, 21, 25.3.60, 28.4.60, 380/3 11.1.60 14.2.60, 11.4.60, 24.4.60, 646/1 28.12.59, 646/5 21.1.60, 380/7 13.3.62, 646/7 12.3.63, 8.4.61; 380/5 2.7.60.

89. Muhammad Amin al-Husayni, *Haqaiq An Qadiyyat Filastin*, third edition, Cairo, 1977, pp. 235–238; see also *Filastin*, organ of the AHC, No. 42–43, August–September 1964, p. 21, No. 36, February 1964, p. 23.

90. On the Egyptian campaign see *Ruz al-Yusuf*, 6, 20, 27.7.59, 3, 10, 17.8.59; see also *al-Nasr*, Damascus, 21.7.59; *al-Nahar*, 22.7.59; *al-Wahda*, Damascus, 21.7.59; on his settlement in Lebanon see *al-'Amal*, 14.8.59; also *al-Jarida*, 21.8.59, which stated that the Mufti "lives in a different world. He demands to follow his old political line, which he himself conceived and which resulted in the loss of Filastin and the humiliation of the Arabs".

91. See SA JISM, 692/6 23.12.59, 121/– 16, 18.1.60, 666/4 17.2.60, 667/1, 6, 18.6.61,

692/6 21.10.62; on the renewing of the Egyptian campaign see pro-Egyptian Lebanese newspapers *al-Hawadith*, 22.1.60, 23.6.61, 8.9.61, 30.11.62; *al-Kifah*, Beirut, 15.1.60, which called on the Mufti to quit the political scene; *Sawt al-Uruba*, Beirut, 29.11.62; *Kul Shay*, 4.3.61; see also *Ruz al-Yusuf*, 19.12.60, 11.6.62; *al-Jumhuriyya*, 9.10.63, an article by Nasir al-Din al-Nashashibi who called upon the Mufti to abandon the political arena.

92. See SA JISM, 380/3 21.3.60, 666/3 21.3.60, 646/2 25.8.59, 121/1 24.9.60, 1.5.62, 692/6 18.10.62.

93. *Al-Zaman*, Baghdad, 4.5.62, 8.5.62; *al-Thawra*, Baghdad 24.4.62, 18.4.62, 6.5.62, 7.5.62, 14.5.62; *al-Hawadith*, 21.6.63; *Bag. R.*, 15.2.63, statement by official spokesman referring to the Iraqi attitude towards the AHC.

94. Majali, *Amman R.*, 12.1.60; *Filastin*, 13.8.59, cable from Senator Rashad al-Khatib and from House of Deputies member Isma il-Hijazi to the Palestine Experts Committee; SA JISM, file MQ/20/1/HA entitled The Arab Higher Committee covers the year 1962, 121/–/ 20.1.60, 21.9.60, 10.12.60, 30.4.61, 12.6.62, MQQ/20/1/3306 20.6.63.

95. See, for example, *al-Hayat*, September 1960, August 1961, March 1962, December 1963.

96. See *Filastin*, No. 36, February 1963, pp. 22–23; *al-Hayat*, 11.9.62.

97. Ghali, *op. cit.*, pp. 230–231.

98. Nasir's letter to President Shihab, *al-Ahram*, 9.9.62; Nasir, *al-Ahram*, 1.6.65; Abu Khatir, *op. cit.*, p. 101, report on meeting with Nasir 17.9.62; Haykal, *al-Ahram*, 10.2.61, 9.2.62, 17.8.62, 31.8.62; Nasir's Charter for National Action, *al-Ahram*, 21.5.62.

99. Majali, *Amman R.*, 23.3.60, Egypt accompanied this debate with acute propa-ganda campaign against Jordan; *al-Ahram*, 10.3.60 claimed that "Husayn wants to annihilate the Palestinian Entity and annex the West Bank, which is part of Filastin, to Jordan".

100. Hashad, *op. cit.*, pp. 105–106; JISM, unclassified Shuqayri's report entitled al-Kiyan al-Filastini Appendix No. 3, which he submitted to the second Arab summit, September 1964, p. 9 (hereafter Shuqayri's R.).

101. For the text of the resolutions see Hashad, *op. cit.*, p. 106; Shu'aybi, op. cit., p. 89.

102. Jordan FM stated that "this resolution suited the Jordanian point of view, that is, the integration of the Palestinian Entity issue in the general planning, and transferring all the subject to one experts committee. This is what we initially have asked for", *Filastin*, 11.1.61; also Zurayqat, *Amman R.*, 22.9.63.

103. See JISM, *Shuqayri's R.*, p. 12; Shu'aybi, *op. cit.*, p. 90; Hassuna, *Akhir Sa'a*, 17.5.61; Musa Nasir, *Filastin*, 11.1.61; Rafiq al-Husayni, Jordan's representative on the Palestinian Experts Committee, *Amman R.*, 7.6.61.

104. See JISM, *Shuqayri's R.*, pp. 13–14; Hashad, pp. 107–108; also *al-Ahram*, 1, 2, 6, 7.6.61.

105. *Shuqayri's R.*, pp. 15–16; Shuqayri, *al-Ahram*, 14.9.63; *al-Ahram*, 11.9.63; *al-Jamahir*, Baghdad, 1.9.63, 11.9.63; *al-Hayat*, 11.9.63; Naji Alush, *al-Masira Ila Filastin*, Beirut, 1964, p. 123, claims that the Iraqi proposal was an "improvisation of the Iraqi FM Talib Shabib".

106. JISM, *Shuqayri's R.*, pp. 10–11, 17.

107. Salah Khalaf (Abu Iyyad), *Filastini Bila Hawiyya*, Kuwait, n.d. (Filastini), pp. 61, 70.

108. Ghassan Kanafani, *Filastin*, supplement to *al-Muharrir*, Beirut, 30.12.65.

109. See SA JISM, file 20/1/JF, 1962–63 entitled Jabhat Tahrir Filastin, JF/1 entitled The Palestinian Front 1963 and MN 130/15 No. 4, Political Reports 1961, M/2/2 entitled Political Affairs 1962–1963; also QM/20/15, No. 4 17772 6.7.61; MN/20/15, 10.7.61; Subhi Muhammad Yasin, *Nazariyyat al-'Amal li-Istirdad Filastin*, Cairo, 1964; also *al-Hawadith*, 17.2.61, 10.8.62; *al-Sayyad*, 3.5.62; *Kul Shay*, 10.11.61; *al-Anwar*, Beirut, 20.5.62; *al-Hayat*, 18.12.62, 5.9.63; *al-Nahar*, 21.8.63.

110. See *al-Ayyam*, Damascus, 6.9.60; *al-Akhbar*, Baghdad, 14.5.61; *Akhbar al-Yawm*, 28.7.62; al-Watan, Kuwait, 25.2.63; *al-Zaman*, Baghdad, 31.5.60; *al-Tali'a*, Baghdad, 16.5.63; *al-Siyasa*, 11.7.63.
111. *Filastinuna*, Beirut, No. 11, November 1960, p. 3.

CHAPTER TWO

1. Shuqayri, *Min al-Qumma*, p. 50; Hassuna, secretary-general of the Arab League (AL), *al-Jumhuriyya*, 6.2.64.
2. Hassuna, *Ruz al-Yusuf*, 24.8.64.
3. Shuqayri, *Min al-Qumma*, pp. 105, 135–138, 216; JISM, *Shuqayri's R.*, p. 6.
4. Haykal, *al-Ahram*, 15.10.70.
5. *Al-Jumhuriyya*, Cairo, 19.1.64.
6. Nasir in Ahmad al-Shuqayri, *Ala Tariq al-Hazima*, Beirut, 15.6.72, p. 97.
7. Abu Khatir, *op. cit.*, p. 115.
8. Nasir, *Cairo R.*, 22.2.66, 15.6.66, 22, 26.7.66; Haykal, *al-Ahram*, 5, 18.8.66; Abu Khatir, *op. cit.*, p. 178.
9. Haykal, *al-Ahram*, 15.9.64.
10. On Nasir's strategy see Nasir, *Cairo R.*, 31.5.65, 22.7.65, 30.8.65, *al-Ahram*, 20.11.65; Husayn, *Amman R.*, 12.3.67; Shuqayri, *Min al-Qumma*, pp. 143–144; *Ala Tariq*, reports by the C-in-C UAC to the second and the third Arab summits, pp. 262–269; Haykal, *al-Ahram*, 15.9.64; also *Al-Ahram*, 5.6.65; *al-Hayat*, 10.9.64; *al-Jarida*, 10.9.64.
11. Nasir, *Aqwal*, pp. 139–142.
12. See Shuqayri, *Min al-Qumma*, pp. 19–23, 72–90, 94–95; *al-Hayat*, 16.10.63.
13. Shuqayri, *ibid.*, p. 127; for different versions regarding his appointment see Alush, *op. cit.*, p. 188; Isam Sakhnini, al-Kiyan al-Filastini 1964–1974, *Shuun*, No. 41–42, February 1975, pp. 46–72.
14. See Shuqayri in Abu Khatir, *op. cit.*, p. 143; Shuqayri, *Min al-Qumma*, pp. 20–23, 76–77, 184, *Ala-Tariq*, pp. 3, 76–77, 104; see also *Filastin*, Amman, 2.11.63; *al-Manar*, 17.10.63; *al-Jihad*, 15.10.63; *al-Hayat*, 13.10.63.
15. See Shuqayri, *Min al-Qumma*, pp. 62, 272; JISM, *Shuqayri's R.*, p. 2; *al-Akhbar*, Cairo, 9.10.63.
16. Shuqayri, *Min al-Qumma*, p. 183.
17. *Ibid.*, pp. 61–62; see also Husayn's statement "We [he and Shuqayri] discussed all the surveys on the Palestinian Entity", *al-Jihad*, 13.2.64.
18. Relying on this principle, he called on Palestinian organizations to join the PLO and to work within under his leadership in the framework of "national unity" – in other words, to disband. See PLO, the *Palestinian National Covenant* (the Covenant) and the *Constitution*, official brochure, n.d.; JISM, *Shuqayri's R.; Shuqayri, al-Difa'*, 21.2.64, *Min al-Qumma*, pp. 83–84, *Cairo R.*, 14.2.64.
19. The geographical division was as follows: Amman, 72 representatives; Zarqa, 10; Irbid, 8; Karak, 4; Aqaba, 1; the Karama refugee camp, 1; al-Aghwar, 1; Auja, 1; Jerusalem, 21; Jericho, 11; Bethlehem, 7; Ramalla, 19; Hebron, 18; Nablus, 21; Jenin, 11; Tulkarem, 10; the diaspora, 2; women's organizations, 10; workers and trade unions, 11; the Preparatory Committee, 8; daily newspapers, 5; municipalities, 5; Syria, 24 (2 were absent); Lebanon, 22 (3 were absent); Qatar and Doha, 7; Libya, 8; Algeria, 9; Gaza Strip, 47; Kuwait, 20; Iraq, 3. In the same report the members of the EC were divided as follows: Jordan, 7; Gaza Strip, 4; Syria, 1; Lebanon, 1; Kuwait, 1. JISM, *Shuqayri's R.*, pp. 47–55, 107.
20. Shuqayri, *Min al-Qumma*, p. 134, *Cairo R.*, 14.2.64; *al-Hayat*, 28.3.64.
21. Among the "Jordanian" representatives were: 25 members of municipalities in the West Bank; 39 members of the House of Deputies and Senators; 16 were past members of the Jordanian House of Deputies; 6 clergymen, including 2

Christians. For reactions to these dual loyalties, see SA JISM, MN/1/25/21, 2.9.64.

22. Among them were 11 members of the Supreme Executive Council (25 members) of the Palestinian National Union appointed by the governor of the Gaza Strip in May 1962; 6 (out of 10) members of the Legislative Council of the Gaza Strip; 9 members of the regional committees of the PNU in the Gaza Strip. *Al-Waqai' al-Filastiniyya*, special edition, Gaza, 30.5.62, pp. 737–741.

23. *Al-Difa'*, 6.5.64; *Kul Shay*, 30.5.64.

24. See *al-Hayat*, 11.8.64; *al-Usbu' al-Arabi*, 17.8.64; *al-Hawadith*, 12.6.64; *al-Ahram*, 7.9.64; *Akhbar al-Yawm*, 25.7.64; *al-Jihad*, 17.9.64; SA JISM, 666/1/74 22.7.64, 666/1/83 18.8.64, MN 20/15/5200 19.8.64, MN/1/25/20 31.8.64; Shuqayri, *Min al-Qumma*, pp. 110–113.

25. See Shuqayri, *Min al-Qumma*, pp. 104, 116, 128–129; JISM, *Shuqayri's R.*, p. 5; *al-Jumhuriyya*, 16.9.64.

26. See Shuqayri, *Min al-Qumma*, pp. 37–38, 44–47.

27. *Al-Jumhuriyya*, 10, 21.1.64, 29.5.64, 16.9.64; also Abd al-Rahman Yusuf, *Mutamar al-Qumma al-Arabi*, brochure No. 8 in the series Nidaluna, Armed Forces HQ, Cairo, March 1964; *Cairo R.*, commentaries, 17, 21, 23, 25.1.64, 28–30.5.64.

28. In September 1964 Hikmat al-Masri and Walid al-Shak'a, two leaders of Nablus, travelled to Beirut to meet the Egyptian ambassador there. It is reasonable to assume that the purpose of the meeting was to discuss Shuqayri's plan. In March 1964 Hikmat al-Masri and Qadri Tuqan went to Cairo for the same purpose. SA JISM, 666/1/2 29.1.64, 666/1/12 26.2.64, 666/1/23–25 17–24. 3.64.

29. Sources close to Husayn leaked to the Jordanian press Nasir's compliments to Husayn to improve his nationalist image among the Palestinians in the West Bank; see *al-Jihad*, 15.1.65; *al-Manar*, 15.1.64.

30. See Husayn, *al-Jihad*, 13.2.64; Shuqayri, *op. cit.*, pp. 46, 50; Tall, *al-Jihad*, 5.7.66, *al-Difa'*, 17.7.66.

31. Shuqayri, *ibid.*, p. 94; *al-Hawadith*, 5.6.64; *Kul Shay*, 23.5.64; SA JISM, 681/5, ANM, *Adwa' Ala al-Mutamar al-Qawmi al-Filastini*, Jordan, June 1964. The ANM claimed that as a result of adding the members of the House of Deputies and of the Senate, the numbers of the PNC increased from 200, as originally planned, to 381; PLO, *Constitution*, Articles 13, 30, 31; PLO, *al-Mutamar al-Filastini al-Awwal*, June 1964.

32. Shafiq al-Hut's report on the PNC, *al-Hawadith*, 5.6.64.

33. See PLO, the *Covenant*, the *Constitution*, n.d.

34. See Shuqayri, *ibid.*, p. 95; JISM, *Shuqayri's R.*, pp. 60–61, 92–93; *al-Manar*, 29.5.64; *Filastin*, Amman, 30.5.64; Hut's report, *al-Hawadith*, 5.6.64, *al-Jarida*, 30.5.64; SA JISM, 681/5 ANM, *Adwa'*.

35. See SA JISM, MN/1/25, Alia Brigade commander's *"Operation Order"*, 27.5.64, A1/20/801, Alia brigade commander's *"Security Order"* No. 2, 25.5.64, memorandum from the minister of interior to the governor of Jerusalem district, 27.5.64, A1/59/A/89 memorandum from C-in-C's assistant for operation to the minister of defence, 26.5.64, D1/25/2177, general security director's *"Security Order"*, No. 1, addressed to the army and the police commanders, 24.5.64, MN1/25/Q/2534 letter from Nablus DC to Nablus AC 27.5.64, 666/5 daily reports from Nablus AC to Nablus DC 28.5–30.5.64; also *al-Hawadith*, 5.6.64; *al-Jarida*, 30.5.64.

36. See *Nidal VII*, pp. 63–66, 127–129; *Ba'th-Filastin*, Vol. 5, pp. 8–9, 70–73; Abd al-Wahab al-Kayyali, *al-Qadiyya al-Filastiniyya, Ara wa-Mawaqif 1964–1966*, Beirut, December 1973, pp. 21–27, 222; Amin al-Hafiz, *Damascus (Dam.) R.*, 8.3.64; *Dam. R.*, commentaries, 27.2.64, 30.3.64, 28.5.64, 16–18.6.64; *al-Ba'th*, 8, 29.5.64, 2.6.64; *al-Jarida*, 7.6.64, statement by Syrian minister of information.

37. *Nidal VII*, pp. 140–144; *al-Ba'th*, 24, 25, 29.5.64.

38. Abu Iyad, Memoirs, *al-Watan*, Kuwait, 9.10.78, *Filastini*, pp. 77–79; on Shuqayri's version of these talks see Shuqayri, *Min al-Qumma*, p. 9.

39. See Abu Iyad, *ibid.*; *Fatah, al-Milad wa al-Masira*, pp. 32–33; Fatah, *Mafahim*

Asasiyya, for members only, August 1972, p. 2; *al-Thawra*, Fatah Lebanon branch organ for members only, No. 21, October 1976; Kamal Udwan (one of the founders of Fatah), *Lecture in the first Cadres Course of Fatah*, 16.8.72, brochure for members only.

40. *Filastinuna*, No. 36, April 1964, p. 5; on the call for an "armed Palestinian revolution" see No. 38, July 1964, p. 5, No. 39, September 1964, pp. 28–31.

41. B. al-Kubaisi, *The Arab Nationalists Movement 1951–1971*, doctoral dissertation, the American University, 1971, p. 95.

42. SA JISM, 681/5 ANM, pamphlet "On the Palestinian Entity", April 1964, *Adwa'*, and ANM *Proclamation on 15 May 1964*; also *al-Anwar*, 15.3.64.

43. Kazziha, *op. cit.*, p. 83; in May 1964 this move was endorsed by the ANM Conference.

44. See SA JISM, 681/5 ANM, *op. cit.*; also JISM, MN/20/15/1412 12.3.64, M/2/5/63.

45. Abu Khatir, *op. cit.*, p. 153.

46. See Shuqayri, *Min al-Qumma*, pp. 47, 131–132; SA JISM, 1/25 intelligence reports, report dated 1.9.64, on discussion with a Palestinian who worked for the Saudi Arabian newspaper *Umm al-Qura*; Faysal, *Filastin*, No. 40, 1.6.64; *Ruz al-Yusuf*, 7.9.64, 14.9.64; *al-Ahram*, 11.9.64; *Akhbar al-Yawm*, 30.5.64; *al-Difa'*, 17.6.64; *al-Manar*, 27.5.64; *al-Hayat*, 30.8.64, 2.9.64; *al-Nahar*, 1.9.64.

47. *Filastin*, No. 37, 1.3.64, 38 1.4.64, 40 1.6.64, 41 1.7.64, 44 1.10.64, 46 1.12.64, 47 1.1.65, 52 1.6.65; AHC, *al-Kiyan al-Filastini Bayna al-Madi wa al-Hadir wa al-Mustaqbal*, Beirut, 11.4.64; SA JISM, 666/1/23 17.3.64; *al-Hayat*, 8.1.64, 19.2.64, 3.3.64, 17.7.64, 21.7.64, 26.6.65, 12.3.66; *al-Jarida*, 25.2.64; *al-Safa*, 8.9.64; *al-Ahhad*, Beirut, 14.11.65; *al-Difa'*, 6.2.64; *al-Manar*, 1.5.64, 26.5.64; *al-Jihad*, 14.4.64, Amman *al-Masa*, 31.8.64.

48. SA JISM, M/2/5/63 20.2.64, 12.3.64, MNN/1/25(316) 17.3.64, 666/5 30.5.64, 666/1 29.1.64, 11.2.64, 30.5.64, MN/1/25/9762, 21.10.64; also *al-Hayat*, 31.1.64, 22.2.64; *al-Huriyya*, 10.5.66; *al-Siyasa*, 12.3.64; *al-Safir*, 8.9.64; *al-Difa'*, 6.2.64; *al-Manar*, 1, 26.5.64, 16.10.64.

49. The gunman was a former Syrian officer called Ali Bushnaq; he was detained by the Jordanian police but later released. See *al-Akhbar*, Cairo, 15.6.64; *al-Musawwar*, 5.6.64; for another version of this event see SA JISM, 681/5 ANM, *Adwa'*; on the Mufti's subversive activities see SA JISM, MNN1/25 17.3.64, 1/25 intelligence September 1964, MNN/20/15 3.3.64, 2609 16.5.64, 666/1 20.5.64, 16.6.64.

50. See SA JISM, MNN/20/15/719 11.2.64, 666/5/101–102 30, 31.5.64, 666/1/10 11.2.64, 666/8/49 20.5.64, MNN/1/5/(316) 1500 17.3.64, also *Akhbar al-Usbu'*, 1.2.64, 10.3.67; *al-Difa'*, 5.2.67, 3.3.67; also *al-Manar*, 5.2.67; *al-Hayat*, 2, 4.3.67; *al-'Amal*, 19.6.66; *Filastin*, No. 73, 1.4.67.

51. *Filastin*, No. 38, 1.4.64, 42–43, August–September 1964, 46 1.11.64; *al-Difa'*, 10.8.64; *Ba'th-Filastin*, Vol. 5, pp. 66–67, 79; *Nidal VII*, p. 148.

52. His visit to Jordan was presented as an attempt "to eliminate the problem of Filastin and to cause the fidaiyyun activities to fail". See *al-Jumhuriyya*, Cairo, 15, 16.4.64, 11.10.64, 13, 22.3.67; *Akhir Sa'a*, 24.6.64, 16.11.66; *Ruz al-Yusuf*, 23.3.64, 13.4.64, 31.8.64; *al-Akhbar*, 15.6.64, 26.1.65; *al-Musawwar*, 24.4.64, 5.6.64; *Sawt al-Uruba*, 28.6.66; *Filastin*, Beirut, 9.3.67, 23.3.67, 6.4.67.

53. *Al-Ahrar*, 15.3.64; *al-Muharrir*, 16.3.64; *Filastinuna*, No. 36, April 1964, p. 4.

54. *Al-Hayat*, 23.5.64; *al-Hawadith*, 29.5.64.

55. See SA JISM, MNH/1/2/1063 26.2.64, MN/20/15 January–May 1964, 1/25 intelligence reports, August–September 1964, 666/5 14.1.64, 666/5/35 18.3.64, 666/5/46 30.5.64.

56. Abu Iyad, *Filastini*, pp. 79–81.

57. Fatah published a military announcement on 1.1.65 and its first political announcement on 28.1.65 under the name of Asifa. *Ibid.*; Fatah, *Wathaiq Askariyya*, Vol. 1, 1968 (Wathaiq), p. 9.

58. Husam al-Khatib, *Fi al-Tajriba al-Thawriyya al-Filastiniyya*, Damascus, 1972,

p. 25; Khatib was a member of the PLO EC from 1.9.69 to 13.7.71. On the support of the Palestinians for Fatah see SA JISM, 487/4/8 20.1.65, 487/3/– 8.7.65, 29.7.65, 489/4/– 9.9.65, 13.10.65.

59. Nasir, *Cairo R.*, 23.12.63, 22.2.64, 1.5.64, 1.7.64, *al-Ahram*, 12, 13.3.65, 20.11.65; Haykal, *al-Ahram*, 18.5.62, 25.9.64.

60. See Amir's secret memorandum to Hassuna dated 1.11.64, and secret report by Hassuna to the Heads of Arab Governments Conference (HAGC) held on 1.1.65, *al-Nahar*, 9–10. 1.65; Amir's secret report to the second Arab summit, *al-Jarida*, 8.9.64; Shuqayri, *Ala Tariq*, quoted Amir's C-in-C UAC report to the third Arab summit September 1965, pp. 268–269, also Amir's report to HAGC held in January and May 1965, pp. 266–267, and in *Kul Shay*, 29.5.65, *al-Nahar*, al-Hayat, al-Kifah, 30–31.5.65, 1.6.65, *al-Jarida*, 29.5.65; Shuqayri, *Min al-Qumma*, pp. 143–144; Nasir, quoted in Shuqayri, *Ala Tariq*, p. 43, *al-Ahram*, 1.6.65; Haykal, *al-Ahram*, 15.9.64; *Ba'th Filastin*, Vol. 5, p. 131; also *al-Ahram*, 7.9.64, 5.6.65; *al-Nahar*, 25–26.5.65; *al-Jarida*, 10, 13.9.64; *al-Hayat*, 17.9.64; *al-Yawm*, 22.4.67.

61. See General Mahmud Shit Khattab, *al-Wahda al-Askariyya al-Arabiyya*, Beirut, 1969, pp. 81–96; *al-Ahram*, 27.1.67.

62. Nasir, in Abu Khatir, *op. cit.*, p. 106; see also Abu Khatir's assessment of the UAC, pp. 140–141; on the preconditions for Arab victory in war with Israel see Haykal, *al-Ahram*, 4.9.64, 25.9.64.

63. See Amir's reports to the second and third summits, *op. cit.*

64. Nasir, in Abu Khatir, *op. cit.*, pp. 106–109; Nasir, *al-Nahar*, 8–9.9.64, *al-Hayat*, *al-Jarida*, 8–10.9.64, *al-Ahram*, 1.6.65, *Cairo R.*, 22.7.65; Haykal, *al-Ahram*, 24.1.64; Shuqayri, *Ala Tariq*, pp. 46, 262; also Ahmad Baha al-Din, *Akhbar al-Yawm*, 11.1.64, *al-Musawwar*, 11.6.65; *Kul Shay*, 29.5.65; *al-Ahram*, 5.6.65.

65. Nasir, *al-Ahram*, 1.6.65.

66. This can be seen in the harnessing of the ANM to his policy and in a series of articles (November–December 1964) on his policy by Burhan al-Dajani, who concluded that only Egypt could stand up to Israel and sooner or later solve the problem of Filastin. Burhan al-Dajani (then lecturer in economics at the American University of Beirut), *Filastin*, Beirut, 19.11.64, 13, 17, 31.12.64.

67. See Nasir, *al-Ahram*, 1.6.65, *Cairo R.*, 22.7.64, in Shuqayri, *Ala Tariq*, p. 97; Haykal, *al-Ahram*, 11.9.64, 15, 22, 29.7.66, 5, 12, 18.8.66; Husayn Fahmi, *al-Akhbar*, 6.2.67; Shuqayri, *Min al-Qumma*, p. 143; Maqdisi, *al-Jarida*, 1.6.65.

68. *Al-Anwar*, 3.1.65; *al-Muharrir*, 6.2.65; also Shafiq al-Hut, *Filastin*, Beirut, 30.12.65; Salah al-Shibil (an ANM member), *al-Anwar*, 6.11.65.

69. See memorandum from C-in-C UAC to secretary-general of the AL as quoted by C-in-C Jordanian army in his memorandum to the SG AL, dated 26.11.66, *Amman R.*, 27.11.66; Tall, *al-Hawadith*, 9.12.66; Lebanon PM, *al-Hayat*, 18.6.65, *al-Nahar*, 19.6.65; JISM UC, memorandum from C-o-S Jordanian army to the C-in-C JA dated 24.5.65.

70. Abu Iyad, *Filastini*, p. 81; also unclassified records of the Egyptian General Investigations – Internal Security Department, the Gaza Strip Government (EGI), file entitled Fatah.

71. Nasir, *al-Ahram*, 1.6.65.

72. *Al-Jarida al-Rasmiyya*, Cairo, No. 28, 7.2.65.

73. *Al-Waqai' al-Filastiniyya*, No. 263, p. 2, 15.4.65; see also unclassified PLO, Gaza Office Records (PLO GOR); Shuqayri, *Min al-Qumma*, p. 139; *Akhbar Filastin*, 15.2.65, 15.3.65; *al-Jumhuriyya*, 28.2.65.

74. As early as 28 August 1964 Haykal complained about "the non-appearance of a revolutionary Palestinian leadership", and in November 1965 Shuqayri was accused in the Egyptian press of turning the PLO into "his private property". See Haykal, *al-Ahram*, 28.8.64; Nashashibi, *al-Jumhuriyya*, 25.6.64; *al-Musawwar*, 24.11.65; Shuqayri, *Min al-Qumma*, pp. 268–272.

75. See *al-Jumhuriyya*, 23.6.66; *al-Ahram*, 21.11.66; *Akhbar al-Yawm*, 19.11.66; *al-*

Notes

Notes

Hawadith, 19.8.66, 11, 18.11.66, 2.12.66; *al-Muharrir*, 21.11.66; for reservations about the timing of fidai actions see Kamal Rif'at, *al-Ahram*, 4.8.66; Salah al-Shibil, *al-Muharrir*, 26, 27.7.66; *al-Hawadith*, 2.12.66.

76. Abu Iyad, *Filastini*, pp. 87–88; Fathi al-Dib, ex-intelligence officer, *al-Jumhuriyya*, 4.8.66; EGI, Fatah file.

77. Nasir, *Cairo R.*, 4.2.67, *al-Ahhad*, 12.2.67; the change in Egypt's attitude stood out when *Sawt al-Arab R.*, 22.2.67, was the first to broadcast the Fatah's announcements of 22.2.67, and of 1.3.67; *Cairo R.* broadcast also on 20.2.67 the announcement of the Abtal al-Awda; Sabri al-Khuli, *Ruz al-Yusuf*, 20.2.67; also Shibil, *al-Muharrir*, 6.2.67; *al-Nahar*, 10.1.67, letter to the editor by a Palestinian from the Gaza Strip.

78. *Nidal VII*, pp. 145–146.

79. See *Nidal VII*, secret circulars and National Command proclamations, pp. 173–190, Aflaq, 191–212, 283–307, Munif al-Razzaz, 307–310.

80. *Ba'th Filastin*, Vol. 5, pp. 48–51, 77, 100, 106–117, 136.

81. *Ibid.*, p. 75, The Filastin Problem, report submitted by "the Filastin Branch" of the Ba'th party in Lebanon to the 8th NC, April 1965; Ministry of Information, *al-Manhaj al-Marhali*, approved by the Regional Congress June 1965, Damascus, 22 July 1965, pp. 14–20.

82. Amin al-Hafiz, *Amman al-Masa*, 8.6.65; Razzaz, *Amman al-Masa*, 8.6.65; *al-Ba'th*, 18.5.65; *al-Thawra*, 5.9.65; *Dam. R.*, commentary, 3.6.65.

83. *Ba'th-Filastin*, Vol. 5, pp. 73–80, 140–141; SA JISM, 686/59/-*Sawt al-Jamahir* (organ of the Ba'th in Jordan), No. 22, 28.12.65; Kayyali, *op. cit.*, pp. 150–152, 181–185, 214–218, 238–242.

84. *Ba'th-Filastin*, Vol. 5, pp. 145–155; Kayyali, *ibid.*, pp. 243–252; *al-Ba'th*, 3.11.65; *al-Ahrar*, Beirut, 12, 13.10.65, 20.2.66.

85. *Dam. R.*, 21.1.65, was the first to broadcast the extended announcement of *al-Asifa*; also *Dam. R.*, 5.5.65, 30.5.65, 6.9.65; *al-Ba'th*, 27.8.65, 17.9.65, 26.9.65, 1.11.65; Kayyali *op. cit.*, pp. 174–180, 194–197.

86. See *Ba'th-Filastin*, Vol. 5, pp. 67–80; Abu Iyad, *Filastini*, pp. 84–86; *al-Awda* (organ of the Palestinian Students' Union in West Germany; in fact it expressed Fatah's attitudes), No. 3, October 1965; *Fatah*, internal circular, for members of Fatah in West Germany, June 1966.

87. On the Popular Liberation War see *Bayan al-Qiyada al-Qutriyya*, Damascus, 8.10.66; *al-Tali'a*, Damascus, 16.2.67, 16.3.67; Atasi, *Dam. R.*, 7, 17.4.66, 22.5.66, 15.6.66, 11.7.66, 2.11.66, 7.12.66, 16.12.66, 22.2.67, 11.4.67; Suwaydani, *al-Munadil*, January 1967, *al-Musawwar*, 28.4.67, *Dam. R.*, 22.5.66, 21.11.66; Assad, *Dam. R.*, 12.5.66, 24.5.66; Zu'ayyin, *Dam. R.*, 10, 16.7.66, 11.10.66; Jadid, *al-Ba'th*, 26.11.66, *Dam. R.*, 23.8.66; Makhus, *Ruz al-Yusuf*, 19.9.66; *al-Ba'th*, 13.3.66; *al-Thawra*, 25.11.66.

88. *Ba'th-Filastin*, Vol. 5, pp. 175–194; Kayyali, *op. cit.*, pp. 325–333; *al-Jumhuriyya*, Cairo, 6.12.66.

89. An agreement was reached on cooperation between the Palestinian Organization of the Ba'th and Fatah, according to which the Palestinian Ba'th would undertake reconnaissance and intelligence inside Israel, and would transfer arms, explosives and money to the Palestinian Ba'th in Jordan. Fatah, internal circular, *op. cit.*; Abu Iyad, *Filastini*, pp. 84–86; *al-Ba'th*, 13.5.66; *Kifah al-Amal al-Ishtiraki*, 17.7.66; JISM UC, Tulkarem and Jerusalem Areas Police Records, files entitled Control of Suspicious and Dangerous Persons, 1.1.67–24.5.67, 20.5.66–22.5.67, respectively; *al-Muharrir*, 14.5.66.

90. See Shuqayri, *Min al-Qumma*, pp. 69, 104, 281–282, *Ala Tariq*, pp. 102, 105, 163, 201–202, *al-Ahram*, 12.2.67, *Ruz al-Yusuf*, 4.7.66, *PLO R.*, 1.7.65, 18.7.66, 10.9.66; Shafiq al-Hut, *al-Hawadith*, 2.12.66; *PLO GOR*, circular by the director of Moral Guidance Department, December 1966.

91. On Shuqayri's demands see Shuqayri, *Ala Tariq*, pp. 90–92, *Min al-Qumma*. p. 281; Shuqayri, *PLO R.*, 8.12.65, 22.12.65, 21.2.66 (PLO memorandum defining

the PLO spheres of activities in Jordan), *al-Ahram*, 9.10.65, *al-Jumhuriyya*, 13.12.65, *Akhir Sa'a*, 5.1.66, *al-Muharrir*, 16.12.65; see also *al-Jarida*, 25.1.66; *Filastin*, Beirut, 26.12.65, 5.5.66; *al-Hawadith*, 1.7.66; Jordan Foreign Ministry proclamation, official brochure, *Mawqif al-Urdun Min Matalib Rais Munazamat al-Tahrir al-Filastiniyya*, 6.12.65 (J. Mawqif).

92. Wasfi al-Tall, *al-Difa'*, 17.7.66.
93. On Jordan's conception, see Tall, *al-Difa'*, 17.7.66, *Filastin*, Amman, 21.2.65; Husayn, *Ruz al-Yusuf*, 21.9.64, *Amman R.*, 29.3.66, in Shuqayri, *Min al-Qumma*, p. 282; Husayn's letter to Nasir dated 14.7.66, in *Ala Tariq*, p. 214; *J. Mawqif; al-Urdun wa Qadiyyat Filastin*, Husayn's speech on 5.1.66, official brochure; also JISM UC, Wasfi al-Tall's top-secret memorandum to the ministers, the C-in-C and the C-o-S armed forces, governors, the head of GI and the head of GS, dated 5.3.66, entitled PLO (Tall's memorandum).
94. Indeed, the dismantling of the National Guard allowed Husayn in 1965 to initiate his plan for the doubling of the Jordanian army, as approved by the UAC, through the formation within five years of five infantry-brigade groups and a number of armoured battalions. As a result, personnel strength of the army in 1967 was (according to Husayn) more than 55,000 soldiers. Husayn, *Amman R.*, 4.10.65, 5.1.66, 14.6.66 (speech in Ajlun), 5.1.67, *al-Jihad*, 28.7.66, *al-Nahar*, 17.9.65; *J. Mawqif;* Tall, *al-Jihad*, 5.7.66, *al-Ahhad*, 28.11.65; also *al-Hayat*, 8.9.65.
95. Training of the residents of the front-line villages was done on a voluntary basis. But the villagers' response was very low, and the "operation" failed, just as the authorities had predicted and hoped. However, Jordan could claim to Shuqayri that she had distributed arms to the villages and so no longer needed the arms Shuqayri was offering for this purpose. See Tall, *Amman R.*, 6.6.65; *J. Mawqif;* SA JISM, 487/3/23 16.6.65, 489/4/–17.10.65, 666/8/36 23.6.66, 666/8/46 20.8.66; JISM UC, Hittin Brigade, file entitled Defence of the Front-Line Cities and Villages, 11.6.65, Alia Brigade, file entitled Jordan's Defence Plan, 12.12.65.
96. *J. Mawqif;* Shuqayri, *PLO R.*, 8.12.65.
97. See Tall, *al-Difa'*, 17.7.66; Shuqayri, *Min al-Qumma*, p. 140; PLO GOR, Political Department file, the third Arab summit decisions concerning the Palestinian Entity and the PLA, Filastin Department, UAR Foreign Ministry.
98. See *al-Jihad*, 20.6.65; *Filastin*, Amman, 19.6.65, 30.7.65; *al-Manar*, 7.7.65; *al-Difa'*, 7.7.65; *Akhbar al-Usbu'*, 10.7.65; *al-Huriyya*, 16.8.65; Shuqayri, *PLO R.*, 6.8.65; on the PLA attitudes see *al-Huriyya*, 30.8.65; *al-Manar*, 1.12.66.
99. See Shuqayri, *Ala Tariq*, pp. 98–108, 114; *al-Jihad*, 26, 27, 31.10.65; *al-Manar*, 26.10.65; *al-Hayat*, 27.10.65; on Jordan propaganda attacks see *Filastin*, 26.12.65; *al-Manar*, 26.12.65; *al-Jihad*, 26.12.65; *al-Difa'*, 28.12.65; see also Shuqayri, *Kalimat Ala Tariq al-Tahrir 1965*, Gaza, 11.1.1966, pp. 100–141.
100. For text of the agreement see *PLO R.*, 8.1.66; *al-Hayat*, 5.1.66; also *al-Ahram*, 31.1.66; *al-Akhbar*, 4.1.66.
101. For text of the agreement see *PLO R.*, 10.1.66; also *Amman R.*, 10.1.66; *J. Mawqif*.
102. *Filastin*, Amman, 22.4.66; on the law of the Liberation Tax see SA JISM, 487/3/– 14.7.65. See also PLO GOR, report of the PLO EC to the 3rd PNC.
103. Tall's memorandum, 5.3.66.
104. See *al-Hayat*, 14, 15.4.65; *al-Difa'*, 8.5.66, 6, 7, 8.7.66; *al-Manar*, 10, 12, 14, 15.7.66; *al-Muharrir*, 14.4.66, 25, 28.6.66; *al-Nida*, Beirut, 28.6.66; *Sawt al-Uruba*, 23.10.66.
105. Jordan made a mistake in preventing many Jordanian–Palestinian delegates from participating in the PNC. This made it easier for Shuqayri to co-opt representatives of Palestinian organizations and thus turn the gathering into an anti-Jordanian demonstration. Husayn, *Amman R.*, 14.6.66; Shuqayri, *Ala Tariq*, p. 206; JISM UC, intelligence report on the 3rd PNC.
106. Husayn, *Amman R.*, 14.6.66; Husayn's letter to Nasir (14.7.66) in Shuqayri, *Ala Tariq*, pp. 213–214.

107. Husayn, *Amman R.*, 14.6.66; first attack on Nasir published in *al-Manar*, 1, 2.5.66; Nasir, *Cairo R.*, 22.2.66, 1.5.66; on 23.2.67 Jordan announced that she had recalled her ambassador in Cairo after Nasir's virulent attack on Jordan in his speech on 22.2.67.
108. See Fatah, internal circular, *op. cit.*; JISM UC, intelligence report on the PLO expected increased activities, 17.5.66, report on the 3rd PNC; SA JISM, MKH/10/ 7/1/79 19.3.66; also PLO, *al-Dawra al-Thalitha li al-Majlis al-Watani al-Filastini 20–24.5.66;* *al-Muharrir*, 14, 16, 17, 20.5.66.
109. On the instigations see *PLO R.*, 25.11.66, 1, 8, 31.1.67; *Sawt al-Arab R.*, 2, 3.1.67; *Cairo R.*, 27.11.66, 2, 13.12.66; *Dam. R.*, 27.11.66, 13.12.66; *al-Ahram*, 27.11.66, 2.12.66; *al-Jumhuriyya*, 17.11.66, 5, 26.12.66; *al-Ba'th*, 17.12.66; the Jordanian ambassador in Beirut, *al-Anwar*, 29.11.66; the minister of the interior, *Amman R.*, 26.11.66.
110. On Egypt's policy see Haykal, *al-Ahram*, 18.11.66, 29.12.66; *al-Jumhuriyya*, 17, 19, 23.11.66; *al-Akhbar*, 23.11.66, 6.12.66; *al-Ahram*, 19.11.66; *Akhbar al-Yawm*, 19.11.66; *Sawt al-Arab R.*, commentaries by Ahmad Sa'id, 26, 30.11.66, 1.12.66; see also pro-Egyptian newspapers, *al-Hawadith*, 18, 25.11.66, 16.12.66; *al-Yawm*, 16.11.66; *Sawt al-Urub*, 18.11.66.
111. *Al-Manar*, 3.2.67.
112. See SA JISM, 666/1/2 29.1.64, MN/1/25/78 9.12.64, 489/4 29.12.65.
113. See SA JISM, 1/25 intelligence report 13.8.64, 666/1/12 26.2.64, MN/1/25/46 15.10.64, 489/4 3, 20, 24, 29.10.65, 666/8 29.11.66, 487/3 7.7.65; also *al-Nahar*, 16.12.66; *al-Anwar*, 16.12.66; *al-Liwa*, 9.12.66.
114. See *al-Ahram*, 10.1.66; *al-Muharrir*, 7.1.66; *PLO R.*, 29.12.65; SA JISM, 489/4 19.12.65.
115. See *al-Jumhuriyya*, Cairo, 6.12.66; *al-Muharrir*, 27.12.66; *PLO R.*, 5.12.66; JISM UC, telegram from the head of the GS to the head of the Hebron District Police.
116. Fatah, internal circular, *op. cit.*; SA JISM, 489/4 7.10.65, 22.12.65; JISM UC, files entitled Dangerous and Suspicious Persons, of the Tulkarem Area Police, 1.1.67– 24.5.67, Jerusalem Area Police 20.5.66–22.5.67, Hebron District Police 1.2.66– 22.12.66, *al-Muharrir*, 14, 16, 17, 20.5.66.
117. See SA JISM, 489/4 23.11.65, 22, 29.12.65, 666/1/117 2.9.64, QQ/20/25/6044 31.8.64, QQ/20/15/6878 12.8.64, QR/20/15/9549 14.10.64, 666/8 23.6.66, 19.8.66, 29.11.66, MKH/10/7/1/220 29.4.67, 221 6.5.67; JISM UC WPR file, Jenin District Police, 8.2.66–17.10.66, Military Censorship file, West Front HQ 19.3.66, Unions and Clubs file Nablus Intelligence, June 1965 – April 1966; *al-Akhbar*, 22.6.66; *PLO R.*, 5.1.67.
118. Tall, *al-Ahhad*, Beirut, 28.11.65; *al-Manar*, 30.11.65, omitted the paragraph regarding Fatah in order not to encourage Fatah members or the support of the Palestinians in Jordan for Fatah; SA JISM, DM/70/240 27.6.65.
119. On Jordanian policy towards Fatah see Husayn, *Amman R.*, 4.10.65, 25.5.66, 2.12.66; Tall, *Amman R.*, 21.11.66; *al-Ahrar*, 5.10.65; *al-Muharrir*, 24.10.66, 7.11.66; *al-Hawadith*, 18.11.66, 6.1.67; *Sawt al-Uruba*. 19.1.67; *al-Huriyya*, 23.1.67; *al-Manar*, 10.2.67; also SA JISM, 288/1/24 27.3.65, 730/6 11.5.65, A2/31/ 26, A2/24/A/12, 26.4.67; JISM UC, Fatah file, Jenin District Police, 7.5.66– 28.5.66, memorandum from C-o-S JA to the commanders of the army, 24.5.65.
120. Shuqayri, *al-Hayat*, 14.7.66.
121. See *al-Hayat*, 3.1.65; Shuqayri, *Akhbar Filastin*, 15.3.65, *al-Ahhad*, 13.6.65, *al-Kifah*, 9.6.65, *al-Ahram*, 22.7.65; Shafiq al-Hut, *Filastin*, 30.12.65, *al-Sayyad*, 3.6.65.
122. *Al-Awda*, No. 3, October 1965; Shuqayri, *al-Ahhad*, 15.8.65, *al-Masa*, 11.6.65, *Bag. R.*, 15.7.65; see also *al-Hayat*, 28.5.65, 8.2.66; *al-Kifah*, 16.6.65, *al-Ittihad al-Lubnani*, 21.6.65, *al-Musawwar*, 9.7.65.
123. See Fatah, series Dirasat wa-Tajarib Thawriyya, No. 9, *Wahdat al-Thawra al-Filastiniyya*, n.d., pp. 43–47; Fatah, *Mawaqif wa-Muntalaqat Thawriyya*, n.d.; Fatah, *Wathaiq*, pp. 20–53; *al-Ahhad*, 6, 20.6.65; *al-Thawra*, 15.3.66; *Filastin*,

Beirut, 24.3.66; *al-Awda*, No. 3, October 1965.

124. Shuqayri, *Min al-Qumma*, p. 62; Shuqayri, *al-Anwar*, 13.2.67.

125. See PLO GOR, reports of the PLO EC submitted to the 2nd and the 3rd PNC.

126. PLO, *al-Majlis al-Watani, al-Dawra al-Thaniya*, 31.5.65–4.6.65.

127. See SA JISM, 487/4/19 10.2.65, 487/4/30 25.2.65, 487/4/51 1.4.65, 666/12/13 9.2.65, 488/1 1–23.3.65, 489/4 22.9.65, 16.11.65; PLO GOR, EC report to the 3rd PNC.

128. PLO GOR, *ibid.*, files No. 22, 27 entitled Da'irat al-Tanzim al-Sha'bi, protocol of discussions of the Political Bureau of the PLO Gaza Strip, 5–6.12.64; *Akhbar Filastin*, 15.3.65.

129. PLO GOR, *ibid.*; *al-Muharrir*, 3, 5.1.66; *Filastin*, Beirut, 30.12.65; *al-Ahrar*, 18.6.66; *al-Nahar*, 9.1.66; *al-Anwar*, 6.1.66; *al-Ahram*, 23, 24.12.65; *al-Jumhuriyya*, Cairo, 3.1.66; *al-Ba'th*, 17.2.66; *al-Thawra*, 6.1.66.

130. PLO GOR, EC report to the 3rd PNC; PLO, *al-Dawra al-Thaniya*; JISM UC, Hebron District Police, PWR file, 1.2.66–25.12.66; PLO, Kuwait office, *Information Bulletin*, No. 14, 28.11.65; Shuqayri, *Ala Tariq*, p. 206; *Akhbar Filastin*, 8.11.65, 11.4.66, 25.4.66; *al-Ahram*, 2.4.66; *al-Thawra*, 24.11.65; *al-Anwar*, 20.7.65; *Filastin*, Amman, 26, 29.3.66; *al-Jihad*, 24, 27.3.66, 5.4.66; *al-Manar*, 22, 27.3.66, *al-Difa'*, 24.5.66, *al-Ahhad*, 17.4.66; *al-Muharrir*, 9.4.66.

131. PLO GOR, EC report, military memorandum submitted by Shuqayri to the second Arab summit, UAR armed forces HQ, Organization Order, No. 27, 31.12.66, Shuqayri's report to the third summit, 11.9.65; Shuqayri, *Min al-Qumma*, pp. 116, 126–129, 137–141, 147–168, 192–193, 287–291, *Ala Tariq*, pp. 91–93, *Cairo R.*, 15.9.64, *al-Jihad*, 30.9.64, 6.1.65, *Akhir Sa'a*, 20.1.65, *Ruz al-Yusuf*, 15.2.65, *al-Jumhuriyya*, 7.10.65, *al-Hayat*, 8.9.65, *Sawt al-Uruba*, 1.7.64, *al-Hawadith*, 17.1.66; see also *al-Jumhuriyya*, 28.10.64, 17.10.65, 25.5.66; *al-Akhbar*, 27.5.66; *Filastin*, Amman, 12.9.64; *al-Manar*, 22.9.65; *al-Ahram*, 11.9.65; *al-Hawadith*, 23.9.66; on PLA in the Gaza Strip see *Akhbar Filastin*, 23.11.64, 4.10.65; *al-Huriyya*, 26.9.66; Syria, see Shuqayri, *al-Jihad*, 7.6.66, *al-Thawra*, 16.12.65; Amin al-Hafiz, *Dam. R.*, 13.1.65, 3.5.65; *al-Muharrir*, 17.12.65; Lebanon, see *al-Jihad*, 28.6.65; Iraq, see Arif, *Akhbar Filastin*, 28.12.64; *al-Jihad*, 3.10.64; *al-Anwar*, 26.11.64.

132. See Shuqayri, *al-Jarida*, 11.6.65, *al-Hayat*, 2, 9.9.65; *al-Hayat* (supported financially by Saudi Arabia and Jordan; gave special emphasis to the opposition in the PLO), 7, 9, 26, 31.8.65, 2, 4, 9.9.65; *al-Jihad*, 9.8.65; *Filastin*, Beirut, 11.7.65; *al-Ahrar*, 30.6.65, 22.12.65; *al-Nahar*, 1.6.66; *al-Kifah*, 2.9.65; *al-Huriyya*, 30.8.65, 6.6.66; *al-Ba'th*, 19, 21, 22, 24.12.65; *al-Anwar*, 13.5.67; *al-Jumhuriyya*, 7.7.65; *Ruz al-Yusuf*, 30.5.66; *Kul Shay*, 4.6.66. On reactions to these activities among the Palestinians see SA JISM, 487/4 5, 6.5.65, 22, 28.4.65, 489/4 1.9.65, 13.10.65, 487/3/4–29 13.3–7.7.65.

133. *Al-Jihad*, 21.6.65; SA JISM, 487/3/16 3.6.65; PLO, *al-Dawra al-Thaniya*, p. 66.

134. See *al-Thawara*, Damascus, 8.2.66; *al-Anwar*, 6.2.66; *al-Hayat*, 8, 12, 16.2.66; *al-Huriyya*, 21.2.66; *al-Jumhuriyya*, Cairo, 19.2.66; *Filastin*, Beirut, 24.3.66, 7, 21.4.66, 5.5.66, 29.12.66; Shuqayri, *PLO R.*, 21.5.66; PLO GOR, the 3rd PNC file.

135. See JISM UC, *Special report on the 3rd PNC*, file of Nablus D. intelligence officer; *al-Ahram*, 16.7.66; PLO, *al-Dawra al-Thalitha*, pp. 64–66.

136. See Daud Awda (PLO representative in Baghdad), *al-Thawra al-Arabiyya*, Baghdad, 15.5.66; Shuqayri, *al-Huriyya*, 5.9.66, 21.11.66, *al-Muharrir*, 21.11.66, *PLO R.*, 27.11.66, 11.12.66, 21.1.67, 2.2.67, 10.2.67.

137. On Abtal al-Awda see *PLO R.*, 23.1.67, 24.1.67; *al-Muharrir*, 18.1.67; on the Abd al-Qadir al-Husayni Unit see Shuqayri, *PLO R.*, 27.11.66; *PLO R.*, 3.2.67; see also *al-Muharrir*, 28.10.66; *Kul Shay*, 5.11.66.

138. *Al-Hawadith*, 28.4.67; Fatah, internal circular, *op. cit.*; *al-Awda*, June 1966.

139. See Shuqayri, *PLO R.*, 27.12.66, 10, 19.2.67, *al-Akhbar*, 29.12.66, *al-Jumhuriyya*, Baghdad, 8.1.67, *al-Anwar*, 13.2.67; see also *Akhbar Filastin*, 2.1.67, 23.1.67;

Akhir Sa'a, 18.1.67; *al-Nahar*, 29.12.66; *al-Hawadith*, 16.2.66; for positive reactions see *al-Jumhuriyya*, 28.12.66; *al-Muharrir*, 29.12.66.

140. Shafiq al-Hut, *al-Filastini Bayna al-Tih wa al-Dawla*, Beirut, May 1977, pp. 64–66, *al-Hayat*, 16.2.67, *al-Hawadith*, 3.2.67, 16.2.67, *al-Anwar*, 15.2.67, *Beirut al-Masa*, 17.2.67 (on 17.2.67 an attempt on Hut's life was made in Beirut). Wajih al-Madani, *al-Anwar*, 13.2.67; also *Filastin*, 29.12.66; *al-Hawadith*, 16.2.67; *al-Anwar*, 13.5.67; *al-Huriyya*, 20.2.67.

141. *PLO R.*, 26.2.67; Shuqayri, *PLO R.*, 31.1.67 (statement after he met Nasir), *al-Hawadith*, 12.5.67; *al-Anwar*, 13.5.67.

142. Hut, *al-Muharrir*, 25.9.67; Kanafani, *al-Anwar*, 23.8.67; see also *al-Usbu' al-Arabi*, 27.11.67; *al-Huriyya*, 11.12.67; *al-Hawadith*, 8.9.67; *al-Anwar*, 23.8.67, 7.9.67; *al-Jarida*, 4.9.67; *al-Ahram*, 5.8.67, 2.9.67; *al-Hayat*, 30.9.67; Jordanian Ministry of Information, *Mutamar al-Qumma al-Arabi al-Rabi'*, Amman, September 1967.

143. Shuqayri, *PLO R.*, 1.8.67, 14, 19, 31.10.67, *al-Hawadith*, 8.9.67, 13.10.67; *PLO R.*, 17.7.67, PLO EC proclamation; *al-Nahar*, 3.9.67; *al-Hayat*, 3.9.67.

144. Shuqayri, *PLO R.*, 9, 14, 19, 27.10.67, 4, 9, 11, 16, 19, 25.11.67, 9, 19.12.67, *Bag. R.*, 21.11.67; *al-Muharrir*, 8.12.67; *al-Anwar*, 3.12.67.

145. See *al-Huriyya*, 11.12.67; *al-Hayat*, 14.12.67; *al-Yawm*, 3, 14.11.67; *al-Risala*, Kuwait, No. 305, December 1967; Shuqayri, *al-Hawadith*, 13.10.67; Fatah, *Wathaiq*, pp. 343–344; on the Fatah propaganda campaign see *al-Yawm*, 3.10.67; *al-Hayat*, 5.10.67.

146. *Al-Huriyya*, 27.12.67; *al-Anwar*, 19, 22, 24.12.67; *al-Nahar*, 20, 22.12.67; *al-Muharrir*, 19.12.67; *al-Ahram*, 19.12.67.

147. *Al-Hayat*, 20.12.67; *al-Ahram*, 21, 25, 26.12.67; *al-Jarida*, 23.12.67; *PLO R.*, 24, 25.12.67.

148. *Al-Huriyya*, 16.5.66, an article by an Arab historian.

149. Avi Shay, *op. cit.*, Part II.

CHAPTER THREE

1. Haykal, *Middle East News Agency* (MENA), 6.8.70; see also Haykal, *al-Ahram*, 18.1.68; Asad, *al-Anwar*, 15.11.70; Atasi, *Dam. R.*, 5.6.68; Husayn al-Awdat, head of Syrian Arab News Agency (SANA), *al-Thawra*, Damascus, 30.12.69.

2. Nasir, *Cairo R.*, 13.3.68; Abd al-Majid Farid (head of Nasir's Arab Affairs Bureau and secretary-general of the President's Office until the death of Nasir), *Min Mahadir Ijtima'at Abd al-Nasir al-Arabiyya wa al-Duwaliyya 1967–1970*, Beirut, 1979, p. 190; Haykal, *MENA*, 5.1.70.

3. Haykal, *MENA*, 6.8.70.

4. See Nasir, in Farid , *op. cit.*, pp. 49, 99–101, 131, 249; Haykal, *al-Ahram*, 26.2.71, quoting Nasir in his discussion with leaders of Fatah; Haykal, *al-Tariq ila Ramadan*, Beirut, 1975, p. 54; Shafiq al-Hut, citing text of Khartoum resolutions, *Shuun*, No. 109, December 1980, p. 21; Mahmud Riyad, *al-Ahram*, 28.9.69; Shuqayri, *al-Hazima al-Kubra*, Part II, Beirut, 1973 (al-Hazima), pp. 170–227; also *al-Ahram*, 2.9.67.

5. See Nasir, *al-Ahram*, 13.3.68, 11, 16.4.68, 24.7.68 in Farid, *op. cit.*, pp. 80, 190; Haykal, *MENA*, 9.1.70, *al-Tariq*, p. 77.

6. The Rabat summit was described by Haykal as "a meeting between presidents and kings whom the hand of chance had brought to Rabat". See Nasir in Farid, *op. cit.*, pp. 195–196; Haykal, *al-Ahram*, 4.1.70, 19.6.70, *MENA*, 5.1.70, 29.10.70, *al-Anwar*, 24.10.71, *al-Tariq*, pp. 74–77; Faysal, *MENA*, 10.4.68, *al-Siyasa*, 20.9.68, *al-Hayat*, 21.9.68; Saqqaf, Saudi FM, *al-Bilad*, Jedda, 19.11.69, *al-Hayat*, 7.12.69; also *al-Nahar*, 7, 12, 18.11.69; *al-Ahram*, 11.11.69; Jordanian Ministry of

Information, *Mutamar al-Qumma al-Khamis*, Amman, January 1970.

7. Haykal, *MENA*, 9.5.69, 24.12.70; Nasir, *al-Ahram*, 12.6.70.
8. Abu Lutuf (Faruq al-Qaddumi), *Lecture in Fatah's Course for Its Cadres*, 15.8.72, unpublished pamphlet (Lecture), *Akhir Sa'a*, 16.12.70; see also Abu Mahir, *Lecture in Fatah's Course for Its Cadres*, 22.8.70, unpublished pamphlet (Lecture); Arafat, *al-Usbu' al-Arabi*, 23.11.70; Qaddumi, *Fatah*, Damascus, 2.10.70.
9. See Nasir, in Farid, *ibid.*, pp. 79–80 (in Arab Steadfastness Conference, 18.7.67), 90–108 (in Khartoum summit), 109–114, 169 (government meetings (GM) on 18.2.68, 7.4.68, 31.8.69), 114–116 (meeting of the Supreme Executive Committee – Arab Socialist Union (SEC–ASU), 28.10.68), 134–137 (in his meeting with Arif, 10.2.68), in Shuqayri, *al-Hazima*, pp. 181–182, 204, 214–218, in Haykal, *al-Tariq*, pp. 58, 150, *al-Ahram*, 26.2.71; also Nasir, *Cairo R.*, 5.9.67, 29.4.69, 13.5.69, 8, 15.2.70, *al-Ahram*, 4.3.68, 24.7.68, 17.9.68, 21.1.69, 2.2.69, 2.5.69, 2.5.70, *al-Anwar*, 17.4.70.
10. Nasir, in Farid, *ibid.*, pp. 92–99 (Khartoum summit), 117–120 (SEC–ASU, 4, 12.11.68), 110–111, 123, 162, 165 (in government meetings, 7.4.68, 29.12.68, 18.2.69, 8.6.69), also pp. 163, 181–184 (Confrontation States Conference), 269, *Cairo R.*, 24.3.70, *al-Ahram*, 24.11.67, 21.1.69; also Haykal, *al-Tariq*, pp. 55–56.
11. Nasir, in Farid, *ibid.*, pp. 91–92, 100, 118 (SEC–ASU, 12.11.68), 124 (GM, 29.12.68), 248 (meeting with Husayn, 21.8.70), 268; also Nasir, *Cairo R.*, 5, 25.4.68, 21.4.69, 23.7.69, *al-Ahram*, 24.11.67, 5, 13.3.68, 24.7.68, 2.5.69, 7.11.69; Haykal, *al-Ahram*, 18.1.68.
12. Nasir, *al-Ahram*, 2.2.69; Nasir's memorandum to Husayn dated 21.9.70 in Haykal, *al-Ahram*, 25.12.70; Haykal, *al-Ahram*, 18.1.68, 3.1.69; *al-Shabab al-Arabi*, Cairo, 7.9.70; *al-Quwwat al-Musallaha*, Cairo, 10.3.71.
13. Nasir, in Farid, *op. cit.*, pp. 153, 162, 168 (GM, 7.4.68, February 1969), 131 (meeting with Tito, 5.2.68), 136 (meeting with Arif, 10.2.68), 269 (meeting with Nyerere, 18.1.69); Nasir, *al-Ahram*, 24.11.67, 13.3.68, *Cairo R.*, 30.3.68; Haykal, *al-Tariq*, pp. 53–57, *MENA*, 26.4.68.
14. Nasir, in Farid, *ibid.*, pp. 113, 115, 152–154 (GMs 7.4.68, 5.5.68); Nasir, *Cairo R.*, 10, 15, 18.4.68; Haykal, *al-Tariq*, pp. 49, 62–64.
15. On 26 October 1968, the Egyptian army again opened heavy artillery fire. The IDF raid on Naj Hamadi on 31 October/1 November 1968 put a stop to the gunfire until the beginning of March 1969, when Egypt renewed her activities in the Canal Zone and Sinai. Nasir, in Farid, *ibid.*, pp. 120–121, 157 (SEC–ASU, 4, 12.11.68, 30.12.68), 155, 162 (GMs, 31.10.68, February 1969); Nasir, *Cairo R.*, 14.9.68, 23, 25.7.69, *al-Ahram*, 3.12.68, 21.1.69, 2.2.69, 2.5.69; on the Arab Sinai Organization see *al-Ahram*, 16, 17, 18.12.68, 24.5.69; *Akhir Sa'a*, 8.6.69.
16. Muhammad Fawzi, the Minister of War, commented that the purpose of these measures was *inter alia* "an intensification of the bloody clashes". On 23 July 1969 Nasir confirmed that "we are engaged in a protracted campaign ... for the attrition of the enemy" and that "the policy of all Arab states should be one of attrition". See Nasir, in Farid, *ibid.*, pp. 163, 181–182, 187; Nasir, *Cairo R.*, 23, 25.7.69, *al-Ahram*, 2.5.69; see also *Harb Ramadan*, written by the senior officers, Liwa Hasan al-Badri, Liwa Taha al-Majdub and Amid Diya al-Din Zuhdi, Cairo, 1974, p. 18, who divided this period into three stages: (1) al-Sumud, June 1967–August 1968; (2) al-Difa' al-Nashit, September 1968–February 1969; (3) al-Istinzaf, March 1969–August 1970; Lieutenant-Colonel Yona, "Nasir's Struggle Policy" (Hebrew), *Ma'rakhot*, Tel Aviv, No. 223, June 1972, pp. 30–41.
17. For text of Rogers' letter see Farid, *ibid.*, pp. 220–224; on Nasir's attitude, considerations and policy see Farid, *ibid.*, pp. 224–238; Haykal, *al-Tariq*, pp. 82, 89–94; Haykal, *MENA*, 30.7.70, 3.12.70; top-secret memorandum from Fawzi, the Egyptian minister of war to Hammad Shihab, the Iraqi defence minister, dated 25.8.70, in Haykal, *al-Ahram*, 18.12.70; text of the cease-fire/standstill agreement, see Dan Hofstadter, ed., *Egypt and Nasser*, Vol. 3, 1967–72, New York, 1973, pp. 235–238.

18. See Haykal, *al-Tariq*, pp. 54, 58, 60–63, *MENA*, 3.12.70, 10.12.70, *al-Ahram*, 18.12.70 (Fawzi's memorandum); Nasir, in Farid, *ibid.*, pp. 137 (discussion with Arif, 10.12.68), 149, 168 (GMs, 18.2.68, 10.8.68), 175–176 (meeting with Atasi, 31.9.69), 140, 248 (meetings with Husayn, 6.4.68, 21.8.70); Fawzi, in Farid, *ibid.*, p. 147 (GM, February 1968); Sadat, *al-Akhbar*, Cairo, 29.12.69; see also *al-Nahar*, 16.3.68, 19.11.69; *al-Ahram*, 24.8.70; *Ruz al-Yusuf*, 22.12.69; *al-Thawra*, Baghdad, 17, 19.4.70, 20.12.70; *al-Muharrir*, 27.5.68; *al-Anwar*, 21.6.68; MER, 1968, pp. 162–164.
19. See Farid, *ibid.*, pp. 179–182, 212–213; Haykal, *al-Tariq*, p. 71; Haykal, *MENA*, 20.10.70, 3, 10, 20.12.70, *al-Ahram*, 18.12.70, Fawzi's memorandum to Shihab dated 25.8.70; *al-Thawra*, Baghdad, 9.8.70, Iraqi plan for establishing Supreme Military Command agreed upon with Qadhafi in his visit to Iraq, dated 4.6.70, an Egyptian version of this plan published in *al-Ahram*, 7.8.70; *al-Thawra*, Baghdad, 20.12.70, Shihab's memorandum to Fawzi, dated 16.8.70, a response to Fawzi's memorandum of 9.8.70; see also Tikriti, *MENA*, 2.9.70; Bakr, *INA*, 20.7.70; Saddam Husayn, *al-Thawra*, Baghdad, 13.5.70; *Mahdi Ammash*, Iraqi vice-president, *al-Thawra*, Baghdad, 12.5.70; Sadat, *Cairo R.*, 28.2.71, 7.7.71; Husayn, *al-Ahram*, 18.3.69; *al-Nahar*, 19.11.69; *al-Ahram*, 18.1.71; *Sawt al-Uruba*, 3.9.70; *al-Muharrir*, 30, 31.7.70; on Iraq's attitude see also *al-Thawra*, Baghdad, 20.8.70, 17.12.70.
20. Nasir, in Farid, *ibid.*, pp. 113, 123, 154, in Haykal, *al-Ahram*, 26.2.71, *Cairo R.*, 10.4.68, *al-Shabab al-Arabi*, 7.9.70; Abu Iyad, *Filastini*, p. 112; Haykal, *al-Tariq*, p. 64, *al-Ahram*, 19.1.68, 16.8.68, 3, 19.1.69, *al-Anwar*, 24.10.71, *MENA*, 9.5.69, 6.8.70, 24.12.70; for reactions to Haykal's articles see *Fatah* (organ of Fatah), 9.8.70, 10.8.70; *al-Hayat*, 18.5.69; *Amman al-Masa*, 19.8.68; see also Lutfi al-Khuli, *al-Tali'a*, September 1968, October 1968, May 1969; Ahmad Baha al-Din, *al-Thawra*, Baghdad, 24.4.68; *al-Ahram*, 12.4.68, 26.5.68, 5.2.69; *al-Akhbar*, 12.4.68; *al-Jumhuriyya*, Cairo, 4.2.69; *Ruz al-Yusuf*, 20.5.68; *al-Musawwar*, 3.1.69.
21. Thus Haykal in May 1969 was able to state that: "Fatah, which is the biggest and strongest of all the organizations...is an organization which in practical and historical terms is better fitted than any other for this important role." Nasir, in Farid, *ibid.*, p. 191 (meeting with Faysal, 18.12.69), *al-Ahram*, 12.6.70, 24.7.70; Abu Iyad, *ibid.*, pp. 108–110; Haykal, *al-Tariq*, pp. 62–65, *al-Ahram*, 16.8.68, *MENA*, 9.5.69, 20.8.70, 24.12.70, 22.7.71, *al-Nahar*, 2.8.70.
22. Nasir, *Cairo R.*, 21.4.69, *MENA*, 13.5.69, 18.2.70, *Le Monde*, 19.2.70, *al-Ahram*, 21.1.69, 2.2.69, 2.11.69, 24.7.70; Haykal, *MENA*, 24.8.70; Lutfi al-Khuli, *al-Ahram*, 12.6.68; *Sawt al-Arab*, commentary, 17.6.70.
23. Nasir, *al-Ahram*, 24.7.68, *MENA*, 18.2.70; Haykal, *MENA*, 9.5.69; Khuli, *al-Ahram*, 12.6.68.
24. Nasir in Abu Iyad, *op. cit.*, p. 135, *al-Ahram*, 5.3.68; Haykal, *MENA*, 9.5.69, 22.7.71, *al-Nahar*, 13.10.70; *al-Jumhuriyya*, 17.11.68, conclusions of a research directed by Dr Mahmud Yunis; Hamdi Fuad, *al-Harb al-Diblomasiyya Bayna Misr wa Israil*, Beirut, 1976, p. 413.
25. Ahmad Baha al-Din, *Iqtirah Dawlat Filastin*, Beirut, January 1968, pp. 11–23, 67–84, 169–181; also *al-Musawwar*, 13, 27.10.67, 3, 17.11.67; Shafiq al-Hut, Walid al-Khalidi, Ghassan Kanafani, *al-Musawwar*, 20.10.67; Butrus Awda, *al-Musawwar*, 27.10.67; Burhan al-Dajani, Mazin al-Bandak, *al-Musawwar*, 3.11.67; Yusuf al-Siba'i, *Akhir Sa'a*, 8.11.67; Subhi Yasin, Mustafa al-Husayni, Anis Sayigh, Klofis Maqsud in Baha al-Din, *ibid.*, pp. 39–44, 143–150, 87–92, 55–64, respectively; for more reactions see *al-Jumhuriyya*, 22.10.67; *al-Musawwar*, 27.10.67; *Akhir Sa'a*, 8.11.67; *al-Anwar*, 28.11.67; *Amman al-Masa*, 6.11.67; it is noteworthy that *al-Musawwar* of 10.11.67 was censored by Jordanian authorities before being distributed in Jordan. Another expression of Egypt's attitude was the appeal launched by the pro-Egyptian Lebanese weekly *al-Sayyad* on 18 August 1969, and directed at the organizations of the PR calling on them to consider the

founding of a "Palestinian state" in the Gaza Strip and the West Bank "so as to ensure their rule of the territories after the elimination of the traces of aggression".

26. Nasir, *al-Ahram*, 2.2.69, *Cairo R.*, 10.4.68, in Farid, *op. cit.*, pp. 268–269; Abu Iyad, *Filastini*, p. 110; Haykal, *MENA*, 5.1.70, 21.8.70, 24.12.70.

27. Haykal, *al-Tariq*, pp. 65–66, 79–80, *MENA*, 8.10.70; Farid, *ibid.*, p. 154 (Nasir in GM, 28.10.68); *al-Sayyad*, 8.1.70; *al-Yawm*, Beirut, 5.7.68; MER, 1968, pp. 25–26; *Pravda, MENA*, 10.7.68 (joint communiqué following Nasir's visit to USSR); *Moscow R.*, commentaries, 1.1.69, 28.2.69, *Tass*, 28.2.69; see also *al-Nahar*, 19.7.68; *Filastin al-Thawra*, 29.12.74, p. 106; Rif'at Awda, *Filastin al-Thawra*, No. 124, December 1974.

28. Nasir, *Cairo R.*, 29.4.68, 9.12.68, *al-Ahram*, 24.7.68, 5.12.68, 7.11.69, 12.6.70, *MENA*, 25.3.70, 19.9.70, *al-Shabab al-Arabi*, 7.9.70; Haykal, *MENA*, 24.12.70 (Nasir's message to Husayn, 21.9.70); Farid, *ibid.*, p. 154; also *al-Ahram*, 13.11.70, report of the Central Committee of the ASU.

29. Haykal, *MENA*, 24.12.70, *al-Anwar*, 24.10.71; also *Akhir Sa'a*, 23.10.68; *al-Ahram*, 26.5.68, 4.6.70; Sidqi al-Dajani, *al-Jumhuriyya*, 2.7.69; a full citation of the huge list of articles and commentaries in the Egyptian media on behalf of the PR in this period would be superfluous.

30. See Haykal, *al-Ahram*, 16.8.68, *MENA*, 9.5.69, 24.12.70, *al-Nahar*, 2.8.70; Nasir, *Cairo R.*, 18, 29.4.68, *al-Ahram*, 16.8.68; MER, 1968, p. 215; also *al-Musawwar*, 3.1.68, 24.5.68; *al-Akhbar*, 18.1.68, 18.4.68, 1.1.70; *al-Jumhuriyya*, 9.5.68; *al-Tali'a*, January 1968; *Ruz al-Yusuf*, 29.4.68, 6.5.68 (article by Khayri Hammad), 20.5.68 (Mustafa al-Husayni); *al-Ahram*, 15, 16.3.68, 5.2.69, 1.1.70; *Akhir Sa'a*, 22.5.68; on Arafat see *al-Musawwar*, 24.5.68; *Akhir Sa'a*, 24.4.68; *al-Ahram*, 5.2.69; *Ruz al-Yusuf*, 16.11.70.

31. On the military aid to the PFLP see Kazziha, *op. cit.*, pp. 84–85, 99–104; Kubaisi, *op. cit.*, pp. 98–100; *al-Ahhad*, Beirut, 23.3.69; *al-Yawm*, Beirut, 12.6.68; *Ruz al-Yusuf*, 15.4.68; on the aid to the APO see *al-Shabab al-Arabi*, 1.12.69; *al-Jumhuriyya*, 6.11.69; on the aid to Fatah see Haykal, *al-Tariq*, pp. 65–66, *al-Ahram*, 23.8.70, *MENA*, 21.8.70; Abu Iyad, *op. cit.*, p. 110; see also *al-Jumhuriyya*, 4.11.68; *al-Akhbar*, 12.4.68; *al-Ahram*, 23.8.70; *Akhir Sa'a*, 4.9.68; *Jerusalem Post*, 7, 15.1.68; *Ha'aretz*, Tel Aviv, 8.1.68; MER, 1968, p. 363.

32. Abu Mahir, Abu Lutuf, Kamal Udwan, *Lectures; Fatah*, *MENA*, 2.10.70; Shafiq al-Hut, *al-Muharrir*, 3.10.70.

33. See Abu Iyad, *op. cit.*, pp. 120, 134; Kamal Udwan, *Lecture; Abu Lutuf*, Abu Mahir, *Lectures; Nasir*, in Farid, *op. cit.*, p. 250; Haykal, *al-Nahar*, 2.8.70, *al-Ahram*, 25.12.70; Khalil Hindi, *al-Muqawama al-Filastiniyya wa al-Nizam al-Urduni*, Beirut, September 1971, pp. 96–105; Munir Shafiq, *Shuun*, No. 9, May 1972, special supplement; Arafat, *Sawt al-Asifa*, 25.7.70, *al-Hayat*, 1.8.70; Habash, *MENA*, 26.7.70; *al-Sharara* (organ of the PDFLP), 15.8.70, 29.8.70; PDFLP spokesman, *MENA*, 24.7.70; Central Committee–PLO announcement, *MENA*, 26.7.70; *Sawt al-Asifa*, 24, 25.7.70; *Fatah*, 24, 28.7.70, 9, 12, 23, 27.8.70; *al-Nahar*, 25.7.70, 13.8.70 (EC–PLO announcement), 11.8.70; *INA*, 10, 14.8.70; *al-Anwar*, 12.8.70.

34. Haykal, *al-Ahram*, 14.8.70, 25.12.70, *al-Nahar*, 2.8.70, *MENA*, 23.8.70; Nasir, in Farid, *ibid.*, pp. 226–227 (SEC–ASU, 18.7.70), 250 (meeting with Husayn, 21.8.70); Arafat's report to the PNC, *MENA*, 28.8.70; *al-Ahram*, 24.8.70; *al-Akhbar*, 23.8.70; *Ruz al-Yusuf*, 24.8.70; *al-Shabab al-Arabi*, 7.9.70; *Kul Shay*, 8.8.70.

35. Munir Shafiq, *op. cit.*; Hindi, *op. cit.*, pp. 104–105; resolutions of the emergency session of the PNC (27, 28.8.70), *Fatah*, 29.8.70; *al-Ahram*, 28, 29.8.70; Arafat, *MENA*, 26.8.70, 29.8.70; Egyptian envoy to the PNC, *MENA*, 28.8.70; see also *Fatah*, 27.8.70; *al-Nahar*, 27.8.70; *al-Muharrir*, 27.8.70; *al-Anwar*, 27.8.70; *Akhir Sa'a*, 2.9.70.

36. *Al-Ba'th*, Damascus, 17.9.67, statement issued by an emergency session of the 9th National Congress (NC); see also *al-Ba'th*, 6.6.68, statement by the National

Command.

37. Asad, *al-Anwar*, 15, 17.11.70, speech in the 4th Extraordinary Regional Congress (RC), March 1969; *al-Nahar*, 23.3.69.

38. See *al-Hayat*, 13, 26, 29.10.68, 2, 3, 8, 23, 28.3.69, 18.10.70, 14, 15.11.70; *al-Anwar*, 20.10.68, 26.10.68, 31.10.68; *al-Hawadith*, 1.11.68; *al-Nahar*, 26.10.68, 2, 5, 24.3.69, 18, 19.10.70; *al-Jadid*, 15.11.68; *al-Huriyya*, 23.12.68; *al-Sayyad*, 26.12.68; *al-Jarida*, 8.11.68, 3.3.69; Asad, *al-Anwar*, 15, 17.11.70; *al-Nahar*, 23.3.69; *Dam. R.*, 5.4.69, statement by the new Regional Command; Atasi, *Dam. R.*, 23.4.69; *al-Raya*, Beirut, organ of Jadid wing, 14.11.70, 24.5.71, 5.6.71, 12, 19.7.71.

39. See Mustafa Tlas, *al-Kifah al-Musallah*, Damascus, n.d., pp. 224–227; al-Talai', *Nahwa Fahm Ilmi li-Mahiyyat al-Thawra*, n.d., pp. 44–51; Zuhayr Muhsin, *al-Thawra al-Filastiniyya Bayna al-Hadir wa al-Mustaqbal*, Damascus, May 1973 (al-Hadir), p. 69; Ghazi Khorshid, *Dalil Harakat al-Muqawama al-Filastiniyya*, Beirut, 1971 (Dalil), pp. 87–89; Sami al-Attari, *Shuun*, No. 7, March 1972, pp. 27–36; see also Husayn al-Awdat, *al-Thawra*, Damascus, 30.12.69; Abu Fida, deputy commander of Sa'iqa, *al-Muharrir*, 18.11.69; *al-Ahhad*, Beirut, 3.8.69; *al-Ba'th*, 23.1.69; *Nidal al-Fallahin*, 5.7.67.

40. Atasi, *Dam. R.*, 25, 29.11.67, *al-Thawra*, 22.4.68, *al-Ba'th*, Damascus, 17.4.69, *SANA*, 7.3.68, 5.5.69; Zu'ayyin, *SANA*, 1.5.68; Makhus, *Dam. R.*, 7, 20.5.68, *SANA*, 1.5.68, *al-Thawra*, 30.12.69; *al-Ba'th*, 18.9.67, announcement by the NC; *Dam. R.*, 5.6.68, statement by the National Command; *al-Ba'th*, 6.6.69, statement by the Regional Command; *al-Ba'th*, 9.12.68, resolutions of the 10th NC; *al-Thawra*, 9.1.70, statement by the National Command on the 5th Arab summit; Rabah al-Tawil, *SANA*, 24.12.69, *Dam. R.*, 1.1.70; Muhsin, *al-Hadir*, p. 25; see also *al-Thawra*, 28.11.68, interview with commander in Sa'iqa; Amir Khalaf, *al-Ba'th*, 4.10.67; *al-Ba'th*, 3.11.70.

41. Atasi, *al-Ba'th*, 30.11.67, 17.4.69; Zu'ayyin, *SANA*, 1.5.68; *al-Thawra*, 9.1.70, statement by the National Command; *al-Ba'th*, 18.9.67, declaration of the 9th NC; *Dam. R.*, 5.6.68, National Command's statement; *Dam. R.*, 8.12.68, communiqué issued by Malik al-Amin, member of the National Command, summing up the 10th NC; also *al-Ba'th*, 4.10.67, 3.1.69; *al-Thawra*, 30.12.69; *al-Nahar*, 26.3.69; see also series of articles by Husayn al-Awdat in *al-Thawra*, 25, 27, 28.12.69.

42. Abu Iyad, *al-Ray al-Amm*, Kuwait, 29.12.75; Abu Lutuf, *Lecture*; see also *al-Anwar*, 15.10.68, official of Fatah.

43. Atasi, *al-Thawra*, 22.4.68; Zu'ayyin, *SANA*, 1.5.68; Tawil, *Dam. R.*, 1.1.70; *Dam. R.*, 5.6.68, *al-Thawra*, 9.1.70, National Command's statements; *al-Ba'th*, 9.12.68, 10th NC resolutions; Sa'iqa, *Nahwa Fahm*, pp. 25–26; see also *al-Ba'th*, 24.12.69, 24.2.70, 30.8.70; *Dam. R.*, commentaries, 20.12.69, 12.2.70, 30.8.70.

44. Talai' Harb al-Tahrir, al-Qutr al-Lubnani, *Nashra Tathqifiyya II*, Qadaya Asasiyya Yatrahuha Tatawwur al-Amal al-Fidai, n.d. (internal circular); see also Muhsin, *op. cit.*, pp. 33–37; Talai', *Nahwa Fahm*, pp. 45–50; for criticism of fidai activities see *al-Thawra*, 2.9.69; Hisham Dajani, *Jaysh al-Sha'b*, Damascus, 15.10.68.

45. See interviews with senior commanders in Sa'iqa, including Abu Nidal in *al-Ba'th*, 27.12.68, *al-Muharrir*, 18.11.69, 2, 27.12.69, *Dam. R.*, 12.12.68, 27.12.68, *al-Anwar*, 30.11.69; Muhsin, secretary-general of Sa'iqa, *al-Muharrir*, 6.7.71; Attari, *op. cit.*; see also *al-Thawra*, 2.10.68, 28.12.68; *al-Anwar*, 22.11.70; Salim al-Lawzi, *al-Hawadith*, 13.3.70; *al-Hawadith*, 3.10.69; *al-Nahar Arab Report*, Vol. 5, No. 13, 1.4.74; Khorshid, *Dalil*, pp. 85–87.

46. Muhsin, *al-Muharrir*, 6.7.71; Attari, *op. cit.*; *al-Jarida*, 15.4.70; *al-Hayat*, 3.10.68; *Kul Shay*, 17.8.68.

47. Al-Talai', al-Qutr al-Lubnani, *Nashra Tanzimiyya III*, al-Qiyada al-Tanfidhiyya, n.d. (internal circular); Muhsin, *al-Hadir*, pp. 60–62, 99–100; Sa'iqa, *Special Document*, in Khorshid, *op. cit.*, pp. 94–100; Attari, *op. cit.*; Sa'iqa, *Bayan Siyasi*

Hawla al-Majlis al-Watani, February 1969; *Dam. R.*, 12.7.68, Sa'iqa's declaration prior to 4th PNC; *al-Ba'th*, 17.2.69, political statement by Sa'iqa; Mahmud al-Mu'ayta, *al-Yawm*, 10.3.70; see also *al-Ahhad*, 3.8.69; *al-Sayyad*, 12.3.70; *Dam. R.*, *Sawt Filastin Corner*, 6, 13.6.68, 14.8.68, 27.12.68; *al-Thawra*, 11.10.68; *al-Anwar*, 22.11.70.

48. See Muhsin, *ibid.*, pp. 29–31; Attari, *ibid.; Sa'iqa*, Special Document, *ibid.*; interviews with Sa'iqa's senior commanders, *al-Muharrir*, 18.11.69; *Dam. R.*, *Sawt Filastin*, 2.12.69.

49. See *Sawt Filastin*, organ of the PLA, Nos. 5, 6, August 1968, No. 12, January 1969; Abu Iyad, *Shuun*, No. 5, November 1971, pp. 40–42; Budayri, *Sawt Filastin*, No. 13, February 1969, p. 5, *al-Qabas*, Kuwait, 12.7.77, *MENA*, 19.4.72; Jabi, *al-Yawm*, 6.11.68; Haddad, *al-Yawm*, 11.12.68; Usama al-Naqib, member of the EC–PLO, *al-Jumhuriyya*, Cairo, 28.8.68; Khorshid, *op. cit.*, pp. 97–98, 101; *al-Hadaf*, 6.1.79; *al-Nahar*, 10.8.68, 13.9.68, 11.11.68; *al-Hayat*, 6.8.68, 11, 13.8.69; *al-Anwar*, 3, 10.8.68; *al-Huriyya*, 26.8.68.

50. See Sa'iqa, *al-Talai' fi Masiratiha*, Vol. 1, n.d.; Fatah, *Wathaiq*, pp. 184, 195; on support by Syrian media see, for example, *Dam. R.*, commentaries, 8.11.68, 21.1.70, 19.3.70, 12, 18, 19.6.70, 29, 30, 31.8.70, 10, 26.9.70; *al-Ba'th*, 23.1.69, 31.10.69, 29.3.70, 19.6.70, 1, 11, 17.9.70, 12, 29.10.70; *al-Thawra*, 16.2.68, 13.6.70, 18.9.70.

51. See Amin al-A'war, *al-Muharrir*, 15.11.67; *al-'Amal*, Tunis, 19.4.68; *Kul Shay*, 17.8.68, 26.9.68; letter to the editor from Qatar quoting speech by a leader of Fatah in a meeting of Palestinians there, *al-Hawadith*, 6.6.69; *al-Huriyya*, 15.4.68; *al-Hayat*, 6.10.68; Syrian minister of information, Habib Haddad, *MENA*, 10.8.68; Syrian FM, *Dam. R.*, 26.9.67; it is noteworthy that the first time *Dam. R.* reported any Fatah military communiqué was on 8.11.67; IDF spokesman's announcements (*IDFS*).

52. See Sa'iqa, al-Talai' fi Masiratiha, *op. cit.*; Fatah military communiqués, *Sawt al-Asifa*, 20.8.69, 1, 2, 3.9.69; MER, 1969–70, pp. 193–196, 203; *IDFS*.

53. See Tawil, *Dam. R.*, 1.1.70; *Dam. R.*, 9.8.70, joint communiqué of Fatah, Sa'iqa and PFLP–GC; also *Sawt al-Asifa*, 31.3.70; *Dam. R.*, commentary, 17.6.70; *al-Ba'th*, 24.2.70, 10.3.70; MER, 1969–70, pp. 197–206; *IDFS*.

54. On the regime's measures see *al-Huriyya*, 15.7.68, 12.8.68, 16.9.68, 21.10.68; *Kul Shay*, 17.8.68; *al-Jumhuriyya*, Beirut, 16.7.68; *al-Hayat*, 6.10.68; Hani al-Hasan, a Fatah leader, in Adnam Badr, *al-Hadaf*, 14.12.74; SG of the Arab Liberation Front, *al-Ahrar*, Beirut, 3.4.70; *Dam. R.*, 11.8.68, Sawt al-Asifa, 13.8.68, Fatah's spokesman; on the arrest of PFLP leaders see Kazziha, *op. cit.*, p. 99; *al-Jarida*, 16.3.68; *al-Huriyya*, 19.2.68, 25.3.68, 15.4.68, 5.8.68, 16.9.68; *al-Hawadith*, 29.3.68; *al-Nahar*, 12.4.68; *Sawt al-Uruba*, 17.4.68; *al-Muharrir*, 12.4.68; *al-Anwar*, 21.4.68, 7, 9.11.68; *al-Yawm*, 23.4.68; *al-Jumhuriyya*, Beirut, 7.8.68; *al-Ray al-Amm*, Kuwait, 16.4.68.

55. *Al-Jarida*, 15.4.78; see also *al-Hayat*, 1.2.71; on the measures against the ALF see ALF, *al-Mutamar al-Suhufi*, 31.8.69; *al-Sayyad*, 31.7.69; *al-Hayat*, 22, 24.7.69.

56. This section is mainly based on the following Iraqi Ba'th and ALF documents: I. al-Qiyada al-Qawmiyya, *al-Taqrir al-Siyasi*, al-Mutamar al-Qawmi al-Ashir, Baghdad, 1–10.3.70 (Taqrir); II. ALF, *al-Mutamar al-Suhufi*, 30.8.69 (Mutamar); III. ALF, *al-Bayan al-Siyasi*, second edition, September 1976 (Bayan); IV. ALF, *Ma Hiya Jabhat al-Tahrir al-Arabiyya*, n.d. (Ma Hiya); V. ALF, *al-Amal al-Fidai wa Tahaddiyat al-wad' al-Lubnani*, March 1970 (Amal); VI. ALF, *Ahadith wa Mawaqif*, n.d. (Ahadith); VII. ALF, *Tatawwur al-Ilaqa Bayna al-Muqawama wa al-Anzima*, n.d. (Tatawwur); VIII. ALF, *al-Tariq al-Qawmi li-Tahrir Filastin*, Beirut, April 1970 (Tariq); IX. ALF, *al-Tajriba al-Qawmiyya fi al-Amal al-Fidai*, second edition, September 1976 (Tajriba); X. ALF, *Hawla al-Wahda al-Wataniyya al-Filastiniyya*, n.d. (Wahda).

57. See *Taqrir*, pp. 69, 77, 82; Iraqi Ba'th National Command secret circular dated 26.7.70, in Haykal, *MENA*, 10.12.70; SG ALF, *al-Ahrar*, 3.4.70.

58. See *Taqrir*, pp. 38–39, 76–78, 84–87, 112–113; *Bayan*, pp. 10–11; *Tariq*, pp. 21–22; *Ahadith*, pp. 10–11 (Jalal Sharif's lecture); *Ma Hiya*, pp. 1–6; also Abd al-Wahab al-Kayyali, *Shuun*, No. 7, March 1972, pp. 37–49; *al-Huriyya*, 17.2.69; Kayyali, *al-Muqawama al-Filastiniyya wa al-Nidal al-Arabi 1969–1973*, Beirut, December 1973, pp. 25–39; Munif al-Razzaz, *al-Sabil ila Tahrir Filastin*, Beirut, February 1971, pp. 53–55; *al-Thair al-Arabi*, No. 19, 31.1.81, p. 33; *INA*, 22.10.69, statement by the Revolutionary Command Council (RCC); *al-Ahrar*, 17.4.70, political declaration of the Iraqi Ba'th 10th NC.
59. See *Wahda*, pp. 27–31; *Tatawwur*, pp. 7–11; Kayyali, *Shuun, op. cit.;* *al-Thair al-Arabi*, No. 7, 13.9.69, pp. 1–3; Khorshid, *op. cit.*, pp. 175–177; *al-Ahrar*, 26.9.69, ALF report on the 6th PNC.
60. See *Ma Hiya*, p. 1; *Tariq*, pp. 7–16, 109–132, 145–150; *Mutamar; Tajriba*, pp. 8–13; Michel Aflaq, in *Taqrir*, pp. 97–103, 112–120; Kayyali, *ibid.*, SG ALF, *al-Thawra*, Baghdad, 1.9.69; Shibli al-Aythami, deputy SG Iraqi Ba'th party, *al-Sayyad*, 22.5.69; also *al-Muharrir*, 24.8.70.
61. Kayyali, *ibid.;* *Wahda*, pp. 11–24.
62. *Wahda*, pp. 12–19, 32–37; *Mutamar*, pp. 4–5; *al-Thair al-Arabi*, No. 23, 15.4.70; Khorshid, *op. cit.*, pp. 178–179; *al-Ahrar*, 1.5.70, memorandum of the ALF to the PLO United Command; *INA*, 9.5.70, announcement by the ALF; SG ALF, *al-Ahrar*, 3.4.70, 26.6.70; *PLO R.*, 12.7.69, statement by PLO spokesman on the ALF's joining the PASC.
63. *Wahda*, pp. 19–20, 29, 37–40, 62–83; *al-Ahrar*, 1.5.70.
64. See *al-Thawra*, Baghdad, 27.1.68, 31.8.69; *al-Yawm*, 12.6.68; MER, 1968, p. 379.
65. See Kayyali, *op. cit.;* *Wahda*, p. 50; *al-Huriyya*, 30.9.68, 15.3.71; Haykal, *MENA*, 9.5.69; Saddam Husayn, *al-Kifah*, 25.3.71; Aythami, *al-Ahhad*, 3.4.71; Ali Ghannam, member of the Iraqi Ba'th National Command, *INA*, 13.8.71; see also *al-Thawra*, Baghdad, 7.12.69; *Alif Ba*, Baghdad, 12.11.69; *Kul Shay*, 3.4.71; *al-Kifah*, 15.9.70, 18.6.71; *INA*, 9, 12.8.71; on visits of PFLP, PDFLP delegations to Iraq, *Bag. R.*, 4, 23.3.71.
66. On the Ba'th attitude to a possible Palestinian state see Kayyali, al-Muqawama al-Filastiniyya, *op. cit.*, pp. 55–70; *Wahda*, p. 70; *Tariq*, pp. 109–114; *Tajriba*, p. 47; *al-Thawra*, Baghdad, 15.10.70; *INA*, 4.12.70; *al-Kifah*, 24.10.70; see also *al-Ahram*, 27.9.70.
67. See *Wahda*, pp. 72–73, 77, 86; *Ahadith*, pp. 18–22; *Tajriba*, pp. 46–47; *Tariq*, pp. 111–132; Kayyali, *ibid.*, pp. 55–70; Kayyali, *Shuun, op. cit.*
68. Haykal, *MENA*, 9.5.69; Abu Lutuf, *Lecture;* *al-Huriyya*, Beirut, 21.4.69; *al-Nida*, Beirut, 17.4.69; *MENA*, 17.4.69; *al-Muharrir*, 24.8.70; *al-Sayyad*, 17.4.69; *al-Risala*, Kuwait, 11.5.59; Nayif Hawatma, *al-Muqawama al-Filastiniyya fi Waqi'iha al-Rahin*, Beirut, September 1969, pp. 146–147; also Iraqi information minister, *al-Jumhuriyya*, Baghdad, 27.5.69.
69. Isam Sakhnini, al-Filastiniyyun fi al-Iraq, *Shuun*, No. 13, September 1972, p. 112; *Taqrir*, pp. 119–121; *al-Huriyya*, 21.6.71; *al-Muharrir*, 16.10.71; *al-Hayat*, 8.12.69, interview with officer in the ALF.
70. See Husayn, *al-Dustur*, 11.8.67, *al-Jarida*, 22.8.67, *Der Spiegel*, 4.9.67; Husayn and Nasir, in Farid, *op. cit.*, pp. 89–103 (Khartoum summit); Shuqayri, Dhikrayat An Mutamar al-Qumma fi al-Khartoum, *Shuun*, No. 4, September 1971, pp. 90–99, *al-Hazima*, pp. 199–222.
71. See Farid, *ibid.*, pp. 137–143, 176–178 (meetings between Husayn and Nasir, 6.4.68, 31.8.69), 92, 97, 150, 154; see also *Amman R.*, 31.3.71, Husayn's Memorandum to the Heads of Arab States, dated 25.11.70; on the secret meetings between Husayn and Israeli leaders see Moshe Zak, articles entitled On the Meetings with Husayn, *Ma'ariv*, Tel-Aviv, 31.3.80, 6.4.80; Haykal, *Tariq*, p. 59.
72. See Husayn, *al-Nahar*, 1.3.69, 3.4.70, *al-Dustur*, 12.10.69; *al-Muharrir*, 12.4.69, *NYT*, 18.4.69; *Time*, 18.4.69; Nasir, in Farid, *ibid.*, pp. 137–142, meeting with Husayn, 6.4.68.
73. Husayn, *Amman R.*, 4.9.67, 8.9.67, 16.2.68, 10, 24.7.68, 13.9.68 (message to

Talhuni), 7.10.68, 19.12.68, 31.3.71 (Husayn's memorandum, dated 25.11.70), 3.4.71, 1.12.71, *al-Jarida*, 22.8.67, *al-Dustur*, 11.8.67, 1.8.69, *al-Nahar*, 20.4.69, 23.11.70, *MENA*, 20.3.68, 18.3.69 (*al-Ahram); Sa'd Jum'a, Amman R.*, 5.7.67, 10.9.67; Talhuni, *Jordanian News Agency* (JNA), 24.7.68; *Amman R.*, 18.11.67, government statement in the House of Deputies; see also *al-Wathaiq al-Urduniyya*, Ministry of Information, Amman, 16.10.73 (Wathaiq Urduniyya), pp. 223–226, 241, 281–286, 292; *Kalimat al-Husayn*, June 1967–June 1968, Ministry of Information, Amman, n.d., second edition, pp. 10–19.

74. Husayn, *Observer*, 15.12.68, *al-Dustur*, 1.8.69, *Amman R.*, 8.1.71, 26.2.71, 1.12.71, *MENA*, 5.8.69, *al-Nahar*, 1.3.69, 20.4.69; *Amman R.*, 15.12.68, communiqué by official source in the Royal Court; *Ha'aretz*, 16.12.68; Anwar al-Khatib, *al-Quds*, Jerusalem, 16.3.72.

75. Unpublished notes on ideology and strategy, written in a school exercise book, probably by one of Fatah's leaders, presumably in the late 'fifties or early 'sixties; Naji Alus, *al-Masira*, pp. 221–224.

76. See Abu-Mazin, *Lecture*, in Fatah's course for its cadres, 11.8.72 (Lecture); Abu-Salih, *Lecture*, in Fatah's course for its cadres, 19.8.72 (Lecture); Abu Lutuf, *Lecture*; Hani al-Hasan, *Shuun*, No. 8, April 1972, p. 43, *al-Ray al-Amm*, Kuwait, 19.4.70; *al-Thawra al-Filastiniyya*, article entitled "al-Qa'ida al-Amina aw al-Istishhad", No. 25, April 1970, presumably written by Hani al-Hasan; Fatah, *Kifahuna al-Musallah Bayna al-Nazariyya wa al-Tatbiq*, June 1970; Fatah, *al-Thawra al-Filastiniyya al-Musallaha*, internal pamphlet, No. 106, pp. 16–17; Habash, *Shuun*, No. 4, September 1971, p. 291; Hawatma, *Shuun*, No. 5, November 1971, p. 49; Fatah, *al-Thawra al-Arabiyya wa al-Thawra al-Filastiniyya*, n.d., pp. 12–13; Muhsin, *op. cit.*, p. 100; *IDFS*.

77. Fatah, al-Thawra al-Arabiyya, *ibid.*, pp. 12–15; Fatah, *Muhadarat Harakiyya*, No. 4, internal pamphlet, n.d., p. 4; Fatah, Dirasat wa Tajarib Thawriyya, No. 1, *Min Muntalaqat al-Amal al-Fidai*, August 1967, pp. 55–56, No. 11, *Hadhihi Thawratina*, p. 8; PLO, *al-Majlis al-Watani al-Filastini fi al-Qahira* 10–17.7.1968 (the 4th PNC), p. 21.

78. Nasir, in Farid, *op. cit.*, p. 238; Abu Lutuf, *Lecture*; Abu Jihad and Abu al-Abd, *Lectures*, in Fatah's course for its cadres, 18.8.72, 22.8.72 (Lecture); Hawatma, *al-Muqawama*, *op. cit.*, pp. 98, 130–131, *Shuun*, No. 5, November 1971, p. 52; Khatib, *op. cit.*, p. 83; Bilal al-Hasan, Ahdath Aylul, *Shuun*, No. 1, pp. 39–55; Bilal al-Hasan and Munir Shafiq, *Shuun*, No. 9, May 1972, special supplement; Hindi, *op. cit.*, pp. 53–55; *Shuun*, No. 4, September 1971, Khalid al-Hasan, pp. 279, 290, Habash, pp. 291–299; see also *al-Hayat*, 1.8.70; *al-Muharrir*, 18.6.70. One of the major lessons noted after September 1970 by the organizations' leaders and Palestinian researchers was the claim that "the Palestinian Resistance movement had swallowed up the Jordanian national movement, wiped out its existence and become a substitute for it". The claim, however, was unfounded. No "Jordanian national movement" had existed in Jordan.

79. Shuqayri, al-Hazima, *op. cit.*, pp. 203–204; Husayn, in Farid, *op. cit.*, pp. 138–143, meeting with Nasir, 6.4.68; Husayn, *al-Dustur*, 5.9.67, 3.10.67, *Amman R.*, 16.2.68, 28.2.68, 8.3.68, 18.3.68, *al-'Amal*, Tunis, 28.2.68, *al-Hayat*, 21.2.68, *al-Anwar*, 14.1.68; Sa'd Jum'a, *Amman R.*, 26.9.67; Talhuni, *al-Ahram*, 15.1.68, *al-Dustur*, 20.2.68, on his attitude see also *Amman al-Masa*, 26.2.68; Salah Abu Zayd, *Le Monde*, 20.9.67; Hasan al-Kaid, *Amman R.*, 17.2.68; see also *al-Dustur*, 20, 25.2.68; *al-Difa'*, 20.2.68; *Amman R.*, commentary, 20.2.68; *MENA*, 21.2.68; *Wathaiq Urduniyya*, pp. 44–52, 64–69; *al-Ahram*, 21.2.68; on the PR attitude see Hindi, *op. cit.*, pp. 33–37; announcement by Fatah, *Bag. R.*, 19.2.68; Abu Jihad, *Lecture*.

80. Farid, *ibid.*, pp. 137–143, meeting between Husayn and Nasir, 6.4.68; Husayn, *al-Dustur*, 24.3.68, 10.7.68, 14.9.68, 20.12.68, *al-Jumhuriyya*, Cairo, 7.4.68, *JNA*, 13.9.68, letter to Talhuni, *JNA*, 31.10.68, interview with minister of information, *Wathaiq Urduniyya*, pp. 152–156; Talhuni, *al-Muharrir*, 29.3.68, *al-Anwar*,

9.5.68, *al-Ahram*, 26.10.68; Salah Abu Zayd, *JNA*, 30.5.68.
81. See *al-Dustur*, 7.8.68, 3.8.68, 11.9.68; *Amman al-Masa*, 12.8.68; *al-Difa'*, 26.9.68; also Hindi, *op. cit.*, pp. 38–39; MER, 1968, pp. 598–601.
82. For background see MER, 1968, pp. 374–378, 592–593; see also *al-Difa'*, 25, 26.6.68; *al-Jumhuriyya*, Cairo, 4.11.68; Hindi, *op. cit.*, p. 39; Major-General Bar-Lev, *Ma'ariv*, 20.3.81.
83. See Husayn, *Amman R.*, 4.11.68, 6.11.68; Talhuni, *al-Ahram*, 26.10.68; announcements by the minister and the ministry of interior, *Amman R.*, 4.11.68, 6.11.68; fidai organizations announcements, *Amman R.*, 4.11.68, 6.11.68, *Sawt al-Asifa*, 13, 15.10.68; *Wathaiq Urduniyya*, pp. 352–404; Hindi, *op. cit.*, pp. 41–52; MER, 1968, pp. 592–597; *IDFS*; for the text of the 16.11.68 agreement see *MENA*, 16.11.68.
84. See Husayn, *al-Dustur*, 29, 30.4.69, 26.5.69, 1.8.69, 2.11.69, *MENA*, 13.3.69, 5.8.69, *al-Jarida*, 28.8.69, *al-Ahram*, 17.3.69, *Ruz al-Yusuf*, 10.3.69, *British Television*, 14.1.69; *Thalathat Khitabat lil-Husayn*, in 1969, Ministry of Information, Amman, February 1970; Tahjuni, *Amman R.*, 7.12.68; Husayn and Rifa'i, *MENA*, 5, 6.8.69; Rifa'i, *al-Hawadith*, 16.5.69; Talhuni, Tuqan, Rifa'i, *al-Hawadith*, *al-Akhbar*, Cairo, *MENA*, 5.8.69; Nasir, in Farid, *op. cit.*, pp. 175, 177 (meeting with Husayn, in 31.8.69); Nasir Bin Jamil, *al-Anwar*, 27.7.69; see also *Amman al-Masa*, 2, 9.6.69, 13.10.69; *al-Dustur*, 22.5.69, 2.6.69, 1.1.70; *IDFS*.
85. See Husayn, *al-Dustur*, 29.4.69, 2.11.69, *NYT*, 11.4.69; for announcements by the Ministry of Interior see *Amman R.*, 6, 7.10.69, *al-Nahar*, 7.10.69; Minister of Interior, *UPI*, 7.10.69; see also *al-Nahar*, 24.5.69; *al-Nahar* and *al-Anwar*, 20–24.7.69; PLO spokesman, *MENA*, 2.5.69; *Sawt al-Asifa*, 19.10.69; *al-Huriyya*, 7.7.69; *al-Muharrir*, 21.10.69; *al-Hayat*, 13.8.69; *al-Dustur*, *al-Difa'*, 1.7.69 (the office of C-in-C had been abolished on 9.10.67).
86. The twelve-point communiqué had actually been planned in January after the Rabat summit, but implementation was postponed until after the king's return from the second Confrontation States Conference in Cairo (7–8 February 1970). See *al-Dustur*, Amman, 11.2.70 (twelve points); Abu Lutuf, Abu Jihad, *Lectures*; Abu Iyad, *Shuun*, No. 5, November 1971, pp. 29–46; Khalid al-Hasan, *Shuun*, *op. cit.*, Husam al-Khatib, *Shuun*, No. 4, September 1971, pp. 5–30; Hindi, *op. cit.*, pp. 53–64; Mashhur Haditha, *Ruz al-Yusuf*, 29.6.70.
87. See *al-Nahar*, 12–20.2.70; *al-Anwar*, 14.2.70; *al-Muharrir*, 11.2.70; *al-Hadaf*, 14.2.70; *al-Ahram*, 12, 20.2.70; *al-Dustur*, 13, 15, 22, 24.2.70, 18.4.70; Moshe Zak, *Ma'ariv*, 31.3.80; Husayn, *al-Dustur*, 15.2.70, 16.4.70; Hindi, *ibid.*
88. See Husayn, *al-Nahar*, 12, 15, 18.6.70, *Amman R.*, 17.6.70; Arafat, *al-Muharrir*, 15.6.70, *al-Nahar*, 25.6.70; Habash, *al-Nahar*, 18.6.70; Abu Nidal (PFLP), *al-Muharrir*, 19.6.70; Hawatma, *al-Huriyya*, 22.6.70; Jami'ani (Sa'iqa), Zayd Haydar (ALF), *al-Nahar*, 19.6.70; Hindi, *ibid.*, pp. 65–90; also see *al-Nahar*, 8, 10–15, 17.6.70; *Amman al-Masa*, 8.6.70; *Fatah*, 26.6.70.
89. See Husayn, *al-Anwar*, 5.8.70, *al-Difa'*, 30.8.70; text of the 10.7.70 agreement see Hindi, *ibid.*, pp. 408–410; see also *al-Nahar*, 27, 29, 30.6.70, 7, 8, 17.7.70; *al-Dustur*, 28.6.70, 2, 5.7.70; Hindi, *ibid.*, pp. 91–95, 102.
90. See Husayn, *Amman R.*, 27.6.70; *al-Ahram*, 24.8.70; *al-Dustur*, 6.8.70, letter from Jordanian FM, dated 5.8.70, to Rogers; *al-Dustur*, 27.7.70, Husayn's message to Nasir; Haykal, *MENA*, 17.12.70; *al-Aqsa*, 25.6.70, 5, 26.8.70, 16.9.70; Abbas Murad, *al-Dawr al-Siyasi lil-Jaysh al-Urduni*, 1921–1973, Beirut, December 1973, pp. 129–130; Hindi, *Shuun*, No. 4, September 1971, pp. 31–54; also Hindi, *ibid.*, pp. 109–131, 140; PFLP, *al-Sharara*, no. 8, February 1972, pp. 21–26, *Azmat al-Muqawama*, cited by Adil Amin in *Shuun*, No. 9, May 1972, special supplement, p. 74 (Azma); Abu Iyad, *Filastini*, p. 130; *MENA*, 10.8.70, announcement by CC PLO; *al-Jarida*, 1.5.70, 10.7.70; *al-Ahrar*, 26.6.70; *Fatah*, 19.9.70; *al-Nahar*, 20, 23, 24.6.70; *al-Hawadith*, 11.7.70.
91. On Tall's concept see *al-Jadid*, Beirut, 16.8.68 (memorandum summarized his discussion with Husayn), *al-Hayat*, 10.4.68; Wasfi al-Tall, *Kitabat fi al-Qadaya al-*

Arabiyya, Amman, 1980, pp. 64–74, 79–100, 232–240, 245–252, 414–432; *Wathaiq Urduniyya, op. cit.*, pp. 251–258; also *al-Nahar*, 2.3.69.

92. See Farid, *op. cit.*, pp. 247–251; *al-Ahram*, 24.8.70; Nasir's message to Husayn dated 21.9.70, in Haykal, *al-Ahram*, 25.12.70; Haykal, *al-Tariq*, p. 93, *MENA*, 22.7.71; another version see PDFLP, *al-Sharara*, 1.9.70.

93. Hawatma, al-Muqawama, *op. cit.*, pp. 98–99, 146; PDFLP, The Political Bureau Report to the Constituent Conference of the PDFLP, 21.8.70, Chapter 1, quoted by Bilal al-Hasan, *Shuun*, No. 1, March 1971; PDFLP, *al-Sharara*, No. 7, May 1970, No. 8, 15.8.70, No. 12, 29.8.70, *Mashru' Barnamij Jabha Wataniyya Filastiniyya Muwahhada*, 1.9.69, p. 33.

94. Alush, *Dirasat Arabiyya*, Beirut, No. 4, February 1971, pp. 9–16, *Nahwa Thawra Filastiniyya Jadida*, Beirut, November 1972 (Nahwa), pp. 43–44; Hani al-Hasan, *al-Siyasa*, Kuwait, 14.4.70, *al-Thawra al-Filastiniyya*, No. 26, May 1970, pp. 2–19 (presumably written by him), *Shuun*, No. 8, April 1972, pp. 41–57; Arafat, *INA*, 28.12.70; *al-Mujahid*, Algiers, 23.1.72; Kamal Udwan, *Lecture*; Abu Hatim, *Lecture*, in Fatah's course for its cadres, 20.8.72 (Lecture); Munir Shafiq, *Shuun*, No. 9, *op. cit.*; Abu Iyad, *op. cit.*, p. 132.

95. See PDFLP, *Hamlat Aylul wa al-Muqawama al-Filastiniyya*, Beirut, 1971, pp. 42–43; PFLP, *Azma*; Abu Himam (Haytham al-Ayyubi), *al-Muqawama Askariyyan*, Beirut, May 1970, pp. 37–38; Abu Iyad, *al-Anwar*, 13.1.71, *Filastini*, pp. 136–137; Arafat, *INA*, 28.12.70, *al-Anwar*, 1.1.71; Alush, *Nahwa*, pp. 49–50; *Fatah*, 29.8.70, resolutions of the PNC; *Fatah*, 10.9.70, *MENA*, 10.9.70, CC announcement; Ghazi al-Khalili, Durus Mustafada Min Tajribat al-Muqawama fi al-Urdun, *Shuun*, No. 55, March 1976.

96. On Iraqi promises see Bakr, *al-Ahrar*, 17.7.70; Hardan Tikriti, vice-president, *MENA*, 2.9.70; minister of information, *al-Jumhuriyya*, Baghdad, 27.5.69; Shihab, minister of defence, *Bag. R.*, 12.9.70; statement by the RCC, *INA*, 22.10.69; an official source in the RCC, *INA*, 22.10.69, *Bag. R.*, 11.2.70; Iraq's memorandum to the Jordanian government, *Bag. R.*, 1.9.70, *Amman R.*, 2.9.70; see also *Fatah*, 19.8.70; *Akhbar al-Yawm*, 20.8.70; for Iraqi pretexts see statements by the RCC, *al-Thawra*, Baghdad, 28.9.70, *Bag. R.*, 26.10.70; Iraqi ambassador in Beirut, *al-Hawadith*, 27.8.71; al-Ba'th, *al-Taqrir al-Siyasi of the 8th RC*, January 1974, Baghdad, pp. 181–188; also Abu Nidal, Fatah's representative in Baghdad, *INA*, 21.9.70.

97. Haykal, *MENA*, 15.10.70; Hindi, *op. cit.*; *al-Nahar*, 22.9.70; *al-Raya*, organ of Jadid wing, Beirut, 17.7.72.

98. Farid, *op. cit.*, pp. 252–259; Haykal, *al-Tariq*, pp. 94–98, *MENA*, 22.9.70, 15.10.70, 24.12.70; Abu Iyad, *Filastini*, pp. 134–136, 147; Shafiq al-Hut, *Bayna al-Tih*, pp. 82–83; see also *al-Ahram*, 18, 21, 23, 25, 27.9.70; *al-Nahar*, 20, 23, 25, 28.9.70.

99. For texts of Cairo Agreement and Amman Agreement see Hindi, *op. cit.*, pp. 435–447; Shuqayri, *Inni Attahim*, Beirut, 1973, pp. 191–199; on Palestinian interpretations see Isam al-Salih, *Shuun*, No. 23, July 1973, p. 78; Isa al-Shu'aybi, *Shuun*, No. 41–42, January–February 1975, p. 215.

100. Husayn, *Amman R.*, 23.9.70, 3.4.71, 17.7.71; *al-Jarida*, 30.4.71; Wasfi al-Tall, *Amman R.*, 29.3.71, 13.4.71, *MENA*, 13.5.71, 19.7.71, *al-Bilad*, Jedda, 22.12.70; see also *al-Ray*, Amman, 30.7.71, 8.9.71, 22.11.71.

101. These detailed instructions and the banning of all the organizations' and the PLO's activities were handed down as an order to all government levels, including the security and intelligence services. Husayn, *al-Nahar*, 18.7.71, 26.10.71, *al-Siyasa*, Kuwait, 6.2.72, *Amman R.*, 3.4.71; Tall, *MENA*, 19.7.71, *al-Jumhuriyya*, Cairo, 21.7.71; *Le Monde*, 6.4.71; *al-Sayyad*, 18.11.71 (Jordanian work-paper); *Amman R.*, 16.8.71 (Jordanian work-paper submitted to Saudi-Arabian FM); Nuhad Nusayba, *al-Nahar*, 27.12.72; Abu Iyad, *Sawt al-Asifa*, 29.4.71; *INA*, 13.10.70, 31.10.71, official sources in Fatah; also *al-Nahar*, 19.7.71, 26.10.71; *al-Hayat*, 2.8.71, 1.11.71; Alush, *Shuun*, No. 5, November 1971, pp. 205–207; on the PLA

see *al-Ahhad*, 12.9.71, *al-Ray*, Amman, 26.9.71, 17.10.71.

102. Husayn, *al-Dustur*, 13.12.70, *al-Nahar*, 30.7.70, 11.8.71, *al-Hawadith*, 26.11.71, *al-Hayat*, 21.12.71, *al-Siyasa*, 5.2.72; *al-Dustur*, 10.12.70, response of Senate and House of Deputies to Crown speech; *al-Ray*, Amman, 30.7.71, statement by House of Deputies to heads of all Arab states; *al-Dustur*, 25.2.71, resolution of House of Deputies stating that "The House represents the Jordanian people on the two Banks"; Alush, Man Yumathil al-Sha'b al-Filastini, *Shuun*, No. 6, pp. 213–214; see also articles and commentaries, *al-Ray*, 5.8.71, 8, 22, 28.10.71, 15, 17, 22.11.71.

103. See Khatib, *Shuun*, No. 7, March 1972, p. 24; Abu Mazin, Abu Hatim, Abu Lutuf, Abu Salih, Abu Jihad, Kamal Udwan, *Lecture(s)*; Arafat, *al-Ahram*, 31.7.71; Abu Iyad, *al-Liwa*, 5.3.72; Saqqaf, *al-Anwar*, 13.9.71; PDFLP, Hawla, *op. cit.*, pp. 64–65.

104. See Abu Lutuf, *Lecture*; Arafat, *Al-Ahram*, 31.1.71, 16.4.71, *al-Sayyad*, 8.4.71, *MENA*, 17.4.71; Abu Iyad, *Sawt al-Asifa*, 28, 29.4.71, 22.7.71, *al-Ahram*, 9.4.71, *MENA*, 16.5.71; Ibrahim Bakr, *al-Ahram*, 9.4.71; see also *Sawt al-Asifa from Algiers*, 12.3.71, 2.4.71; *Sawt al-Asifa*, commentary, 1.7.71; *Ila al-Amam*, organ of PFLP–GC, May 1971 editions; Alush, *Shuun*, No. 3, July 1971, pp. 150–152; on the mediation by Egypt and Saudi Arabia see Bilal al-Hasan, *Shuun*, No. 4, September 1971, pp. 167–171, No. 5, November 1971, pp. 194–199, No. 6, January 1972, pp. 193–197; Alush, *Shuun*, No. 5, November 1971, pp. 203–209; Khalili, Qabla al-Khuruj Min al-Urdun, *Shuun*, No. 58, June 1976.

105. See Abu Iyad, *Sawt al-Asifa*, 22.7.71 (this was the first time that a leader of Fatah publicly confirmed the existence of the clandestine organization in Jordan), *Filastini*, p. 155; Bilal al-Hasan, *Shuun*, No. 3, July 1971, pp. 144–145; *Sawt al-Asifa*, 17.5.71, 30.6.71, confirmed indirectly; *Amman R.*, 21.6.71; on PFLP–GC see also *al-Nahar*, 17.5.71; *al-Ray*, Amman, 2.6.71.

106. Fatah, *Barnamij al-Amal al-Siyasi wa al-Tanzimi lil-Thawra al-Filastiniyya*, approved by the 8th PNC, 28.2.–5.3.71; *Fatah*, 15.7.71, announcement by the 9th PNC, 13.7.71; Arafat, *al-Ahram*, 7.7.71, *al-Mujahid*, Algiers, 23.1.72; Abu Lutuf, *Lecture*.

107. See Hawatma, *al-Sayyad*, 8.4.71; PDFLP, *al-Khatt al-Siyasi al-Amm*, approved by the 1st General National Congress, October 1971 (al-Khatt), third internal edition, 1972, pp. 53–55; Habash, *Shuun*, No. 4, December 1971, pp. 291–296; PFLP, *al-Taqrir al-Siyasi*, approved by PFLP 3rd National Congress, March 1972, first edition, May 1972 (al-Taqrir), pp. 101–102, 171–184.

108. See Abu Iyad, *Filastini*, pp. 155–173, *Libyan News Agency (LNA)*, 26.7.71, *Jeune Afrique*, 19.10.71, *Fatah*, 29.7.71, *Sawt al-Asifa*, 22.7.71, *al-Muharrir*, 20.11.74; Abu Jihad, Kamal Udwan, Abu Hatim, Abu Mazin, Abu Mahir, *Lecture(s)*; Khatib, *op. cit.*, p. 106; Alush, Dirasat, *op. cit.*, p. 136; Khalid al-Hasan, *Shuun*, No. 5, pp. 201–202, No. 6, pp. 197–198; on the sabotage actions see official source in the Jordanian Interior Ministry, *Amman R.*, 22, 26.9.71, 3, 4, 17, 24, 26.10.71; *Fatah*, 30.7.71, 10, 20, 17.10.71, 3, 10.11.71; *Sawt al-Asifa*, 18.9.71; see also *al-Sayyad*, 12.9.71; *Fatah*, 27.7.71; *al-Nahar*, 30.11.71, 1.12.71; *Sawt al-Asifa*, 24.7.71, PLO memorandum to the heads of Arab states; see also confessions by Abu Daud, a leader of Fatah, in Jordanian intelligence interrogations, in *al-Dustur*, Amman, 25.3.71, also in *al-Nahar*, 1.4.73; Fatah (presumably, Abu Nidal's faction), *Mawaqif Harakiyya*, No. 6, 1974, pp. 174–175.

109. Text of the PLO memorandum, *Fatah*, 23.7.70, Abu Iyad, *LNA*, 26.7.71, *MENA*, 24.7.71; see also *Fatah*, 15.7.71, announcement by the 9th PNC, 13.7.71; Bilal al-Hasan, *Shuun*, No. 4, pp. 174–175, No. 5, 177–197, No. 6, pp. 194–196; Fatah, *al-Nizam al-Dakhili*, approved by the Fatah 3rd Congress, 1971.

110. Haykal, *MENA*, 3.12.71.

111. Arafat, *MENA*, 20.1.70; see also Ahmad al-Yamani (Abu Mahir), *al-Hadaf*, 27.1.79; PFLP political statement, *al-Hadaf*, 13.1.79; Samir Ghosha, *al-Watan al-Arabi*, Paris, 11.1.79; political report submitted to the PFLP–GC 3rd Congress,

held in April 1971, *Ila al-Amam*, 30.4.71; see also Kanafani, *al-Anwar*, 5, 12, 26.5.68.

112. See Nazih Qarra, *Ta'lim al-Filastiniyyin*, Beirut, 1975, p. 55; Shihada Yusuf, *al-Waqi' al-Filastini wa al-Haraka al-Naqabiyya*, Beirut, September 1973, pp. 54–61; Anis al-Qasim, *Min al-Tih ila al-Quds*, Tripoli, Libya, 1965, p. 33; Halim Barakat, al-Ightirab wa al-Thawra fi al-Hayat al-Arabiyya, *Mawaqif*, Beirut, No. 5, July–August 1969, pp. 18–44; Abu Iyad, *al-Tali'a*, June 1969; *al-Sayyad*, 14.10.71; *al-Hawadith*, 30.1.70.

113. See Arafat, *Ruz al-Yusuf*, 10.2.69; Abu Iyad, *Shuun*, No. 5, p. 30; Khalid al-Hasan, *Shuun*, No. 4, pp. 280–281; Khatib, *Shuun*, No. 4, p. 28; Habash, *al-Ahhad*, 10.10.69, 23.5.70, *Shuun*, No. 4, p. 293; Fatah, *al-Nizam al-Dakhili*, 1973, Article 10; Dr Fathi Musa, *al-Ba'th*, 12.3.70; *MENA*, 9.2.69, Fatah official statement; *SANA*, 22.7.71, Fatah plan for national unity submitted to the 8th PNC; *al-Hadaf*, 13.3.71, PFLP answers to CC PLO questions; *al-Hadaf*, 27.2.71, PFLP unity programme submitted to the 8th PNC; *al-Huriyya*, 12.7.71, PDFLP unity plan submitted to the 9th PNC; *al-Hawadith*, 5.3.71, scientists' study; PFLP–GC, *al-Mithaq*, January 1969; PFLP–GC, Talal Naji, *Mawaqif Thabita*, 16.11.77, pp. 71–75.

114. See Fatah, Dirasat wa Tajarib Thwariyya, No. 11, *Hadhihi Thawratina*, October 1968, p. 14; Fatah, *al-Nizam al-Dakhili*, 1973; Fatah, *Mafahim Asasiyya*, August 1972 (Mafahim), pp. 14–16; Fatah, *al-Thawra*, Nashra Tanzimiyya, for Fatah members in Lebanon, No. 21, October 1976; Fatah, Maktab al-Ta'bia wa al-Tanzin, *Muhadarat Harakiyya*, internal pamphlets, n.d., Nos. 4, 7, 12, 13, 14; Fatah, *Kibar Ulama al-Islam*, n.d.; Fatah, *Statement Concerning the PLO*, n.d., published also by *MENA*, 6.2.69; Fatah's letter to Arab Students' Congress held in Amman, 31.7.69, *al-Thawra al-Filastiniyya*, No. 8, August 1969; Lecture by Abu Iyad in AUB, 28.11.69, *al-Wathaiq al-Filastiniyya al-Arabiyya*, Vol. 5, 1969, Beirut, pp. 485–491; *al-Masira*, August–September 1971, pp. 3–11.

115. See PFLP, *al-Muqawama wa Mu'dalatiha*, Kitab al-Hadaf, No. 5, Beirut, n.d.; PFLP, *Internal circular*, distributed in the Gaza Strip, dated 20.10.68; PFLP, *al-Istratijiyya al-Siyasiyya wa al-Tanzimiyya*, approved by the February 1969 Congress (Istratijiyya); PFLP, Abu Himam, *al-Fikr al-Askari*, Kitab al-Hadaf, No. 1, Beirut, November 1970, pp. 9–95, 141–177 (Ala Tariq); PFLP, *al-Amaliyyat al-Kharijiyya*, Kitab al-Hadaf, No. 2, Beirut, n.d.; *Tariq al-Thawra*, No. 1, June 1970, pp. 2–16, No. 2, April 1971, pp. 52–81; see also *al-Hadaf*, 26.7.69, 2, 9, 16, 23.8.69; PFLP, *al-Silah al-Nazari fi Ma'rakat al-Tahrir*, n.d., pp. 19–32.

116. See Hawatma, *al-Tali'a*, Cairo, November 1969, pp. 85–106, *Shuun*, No. 5, November 1971, pp. 47–78; *al-Huriyya*, 19.2.79; *Amman al-Masa*, 9.6.69, al-Muqawama, *op. cit.*; PDFLP, *Hawla Azmat al-Muqawama al-Filastiniyya*, Beirut, November 1969; PDFLP, *Hawla al-Afwiyya wa al-Nazariyya fi al-'Amal al-Fidai*, n.d., pp. 90–115; PDFLP, *Malamih Tatawwur al-Nidal al-Filastini*, n.d. (Malamih), pp. 61–71; *al-Taqrir al-Siyasi al-Asasi*, August 1968, pp. 49–64.

117. On Qadhafi's attitude see *al-Hayat*, 11.6.70; *al-Thawra*, Libya, 29.6.70; *al-Sha'b*, Libya, 7.4.70; Arafat, *LNA*, 31.12.69, *al-Raid*, Libya, 31.12.69, *MENA*, 1.1.70; Abu Iyad, *al-Jumhuriyya*, Cairo, 15.12.69; Qadhafi, *Al-Anwar*, 19.4.70, *al-Nahar*, 16.11.71; Farid, *op. cit.*, p. 210, meeting with Nasir, 10.6.70; Haykal, *al-Tariq*, pp. 95–96; on Saudi Arabia's attitude see *al-Hayat*, 3, 4, 13.6.69, 25.12.69, 13.3.70, 14.3.70; *al-Bilad*, Jedda, 7.12.67, 1, 2.6.69; Alush, *Shuun*, No. 5, November 1971, pp. 204–205; Abu Hisham, Fatah's representative in Saudi Arabia, *al-Hawadith*, 23.3.73; on the Algerian attitude see Boumedienne, *al-Sha'b*, Algiers, 11.4.69, 26.12.69; Kanafani, *al-Anwar*, 12.5.68; see also Hamid abu Sitta, *al-Anwar*, 2.6.70; Abu Iyad, *Shuun*, No. 5, November 1971, p. 30; Khalid al-Hasan, *Shuun*, No. 4, September 1971, p. 282.

118. See Yahya Hammuda, *Akhir Sa'a*, 17.1.68, *PLO R.*, 8.1.68, 22.1.68, *MENA*, 23.4.68, *al-Ahram*, 19.1.68; announcements by the EC, *PLO R.*, 14.1.68, 11.2.68, 23.2.68, 4.3.68, 1.5.68; see also, *Ila al-Amam*, 14.1.68; *al-Hayat*, 17.3.68; *al-*

Nahar, 7.3.68; *al-Huriyya*, 16.6.68; *al-Anwar*, 16.6.68.

119. See PFLP, memorandum from Political Bureau to the EC PLO, n.d., published also in *al-Anwar*, and *Sawt al-Uruba*, 9.1.68; PFLP, *Istratijiyya*, pp. 99–100; PFLP, *al-Bayan al-Siyasi*, December 1967, published also in *al-Anwar*, *al-Huriyya*, 11.12.67; Salah Shibl, *al-Hawadith*, 12.1.68.

120. Fatah, *Mafahim*, p. 21; Abu Iyad, *Filastini*, pp. 112–113; Mahmud Abbas (a leader of Fatah) and Khalid al-Fahum, quoted in Faysal Hurani, *al-Fikr al-Siyasi al-Filastini*, 1964–1974, Beirut, 1980, p. 135; *al-Thawra al-Filastiniyya*, January 1970, p. 13; MER, 1968, pp. 422–426; see also *Ruz al-Yusuf*, 22.1.68, 5.2.68; *al-Akhbar*, 18.1.68; *al-Ahram*, 6.1.68; *al-Nahar*, 22.1.68; *al-Huriyya*, 8.4.68; *al-Ba'th*, Damascus, 19.1.68.

121. See Hurani, *op. cit.*, p. 135; Abu Iyad, *ibid.*, p. 113; Ibrahim Bakr, *al-Liwa*, Beirut, 26.7.68; *al-Huriyya*, 10.6.68; *Ruz al-Yusuf*, 3.6.68, 15.7.68; *Akhir Sa'a*, 5.6.68, 24.7.68; *al-Anwar*, 13, 16.6.68; *al-Hawadith*, 21.6.68; *al-Muharir*, 6.7.68; PLO, *The 4th PNC; MER*, 1968, pp. 426–427.

122. PLO, *The 4th PNC*, pp. 19–29, 76–84; Salih Sariyya, lecturer in psychology and sociology at Baghdad University, also Dr Wadi' Haddad (PFLP), both members of the PNC, *Akhir Sa'a*, 17.7.68; *Sawt al-Asifa* broadcast the text of Fatah's letter to the 2nd PNC, 6–10.7.68; Fatah's announcements, *Sawt al-Asifa*, 14–16, 18.7.68, *al-Jumhuriyya*, Baghdad, 20, 21.7.68, *al-Muharrir*, 5.8.68; *Sawt al-Asifa*, 19.7.68, Fatah's leader speech in the PNC; also *al-Musawwar*, 19.7.68; *al-Huriyya*, 15.7.68; *al-Hawadith*, 12.7.68; *al-Nahar*, 19.7.68.

123. See Fatah, *Statement Concerning the PLO*, n.d., published also in *MENA*, 6.2.69; Abu Iyad, *al-Tali'a*, Cairo, June 1969; Abu Mahir, *Lecture*; Fatah, *Mafahim*, pp. 23–24; *al-Thawra al-Filastiniyya*, No. 18, August 1969, pp. 12–18 (Fatah's letter to Arab Students Congress held in Amman), 31.7.69, No. 19, September 1969, p. 61, No. 22, January 1970, pp. 4–14, 34–35; Arafat, *MENA*, 20.1.70; Khalid al-Hasan, *Ruz al-Yusuf*, 22.12.69; see also *al-Ba'th*, Damascus, 2.10.68; *al-Hawadith*, 4.7.68, commander in Fatah, quoted by Nashat al-Taghlibi; *al-Nahar*, 31.5.70; *Sawt al-Asifa*, commentaries, 15, 31.12.69; *PLO R.*, commentary, 15.12.69.

124. PFLP, *Bayan Siyasi Hamm*, 29.8.69; PFLP, *Bayan*, 30.5.70, pamphlet; PFLP, *al-Kadihun wa al-Thawra al-Filastiniyya*, n.d.; PFLP, *Limadha*, pamphlet, n.d.; PFLP, *al-Thawra wa al-Ummal*, Amman, 10.5.70 (Habash's speech, 1.5.70); PFLP, *Hawla Qadaya al-Thawra*, Amman, 15.7.70 (Habash's speech, 5.5.70); PFLP, *Ala Tariq*, pp. 46–53, 181–216; PFLP, *al-Taqrir*, pp. 99–101; PFLP, *al-Fikr*, pp. 50–51; Adnan Badr, *al-Hadaf*, 14.12.74; *al-Hadaf*, 27.2.71, 10.7.71, statements by the PFLP; PFLP, *Tudih Mawqifaha*, pamphlet, 1.9.69; *Shuun*, No. 4, September 1971, pp. 172–173, memorandum from PFLP to 9th PNC; *al-Ahhad*, 27.7.69, answers from PFLP to al-Ahhad's questions; see also *al-Hadaf*, 13.3.71; *al-Anwar*, 20.12.68; *al-Nahar*, 1.6.70; *INA*, 7.7.71, PFLP spokesman.

125. See Hawatma, *al-Muqawama*, pp. 41–53, 129–143; Hawatma, *al-Tali'a*, Cairo, November 1969, pp. 85–106; *al-Anwar*, 14.9.69, *Amman al-Masa*, 9.6.69, *Shuun*, No. 5, November 1971, pp. 47–78; PDFLP, *Memorandum submitted to the 7th PNC*; PDFLP, *Waqi' Harakat al-Muqawama al-Filastiniyya*, and PDFLP, *Mashru' Barnamij Jabha Wataniyya Filastiniyya Muwahhada*, both submitted to the 6th PNC, 1.9.69; see also *al-Ahhad*, 27.7.69, answers from the PDFLP to al-Ahhad's questions; *al-Huriyya*, 2, 7.7.71, statements by PDFLP.

126. Basim Sirhan, Shuhada al-Thawra al-Filastiniyya, *Shuun*, No. 9, May 1972, pp. 78–84. In addition 4.2% had academic degrees, 17.1% had had secondary-school education, 34% elementary education and 5% were illiterate.

127. See Abu Iyad, *MENA*, 11.5.70; Salah al-Dabbagh, *al-Muharrir*, 13.3.69; Ibrahim Bakr, *al-Huriyya*, 3.3.69; PDFLP, *Malamih*, p. 66; on exaggeration see *al-Thawra al-Filastiniyya*, No. 17, July 1969, p. 25; *al-Hawadith*, 5.6.70; *Kul Shay*, 29.3.69 (quoting a leader of a fidai organization); *al-Nahar*, 28.7.70; *al-Nahar*, 1.6.70, report of the EC to the 7th PNC; *al-Hawadith*, 11.4.69, 5.6.70; *al-Usbu' al-Arabi*, 23.9.68; *Ila al-Amam*, 24.7.70, letter from PFLP–GC to spokesman of PASC; on

public opinion poll see *al-Yawm*, Beirut, 7.6.69.
128. See Abu Iyad, *al-Nahar*, 27.3.75, *al-Sayyad*, 14.7.71, *al-Musawwar*, 16.7.71; Kanafani, *al-Anwar*, 5.5.68; Qadhafi, *al-Nahar*, 16.11.71; see also *al-Hadaf*, 6.3.71; Khalil al-Wazir (Abu Jihad), *al-Nahar al-Duwali wa al-Arabi*, Paris, 25.12.78; Hani al-Hasan, in lecture at the AUB, *al-Hayat*, *al-Nahar*, 2.12.69; Sirhan, *op. cit.*; see also *al-Nahar*, 18.1.70; *al-Hayat*, 19.12.71, Fatah won in the council elections of the Union of Palestinian Students in Lebanon.
129. See letter by Salih al-Barghuthi of Qatar, member of PNC, to *al-Hawadith*, 9.4.71; Abu Musa, a leader of Sa'iqa, *Fatah*, Amman, 12.7.70; Muhsin, *al-Nahar*, 10.9.73; see also *al-Nahar*, 3.6.70.
130. See *al-Ahram*, 1.2.69; *al-Huriyya*, 13.1.69, 10.2.69; *MENA*, 1, 3.2.69; *al-Musawwar*, 7.2.69; *PLO R.*, 3.2.69; *al-Thawra al-Filastiniyya*, No. 18, August 1969, p. 18, No. 22, January 1970, p. 13.
131. See *al-Jarida*, 3, 5.9.69; *al-Anwar*, 5.9.69; *al-Usbu' al-Arabi*, 8.9.69; *al-Nahar*, 5, 7.9.69; *MENA*, 2, 6.9.69; *PLO R.*, 2.9.69; interestingly, Rashid Hamid, in his book *Muqarrarat al-Majlis al-Watani al-Filastini 1964–1974*, Beirut, August 1975, p. 31, added the number of absent members of the PFLP to the number of those included in the independents' category.
132. See *al-Anwar*, 3.6.70; *al-Hawadith*, 5.6.70; *al-Nahar*, 1.6.70; *MENA*, 31.5.70, 1.6.70; *SANA*, 4.6.70.
133. See *al-Hayat*, 7.3.71; *al-Dustur*, Amman, 3.3.71; *MENA*, 6.3.71, report by the editor for Arab affairs.
134. See *al-Hayat*, 24.6.71; *MENA*, 21.6.71; *Fatah*, 9.7.71; *SANA*, 30.6.71; *al-Ahram*, 23.6.71, 9, 10.7.71; *Akhir Sa'a*, 30.6.71; *al-Sayyad*, 10.6.71, 1.7.71, article by Talal Salman; Bilal al-Hasan, *Shuun*, No. 4, September 1971, pp. 172, 174–176.
135. Hindi, *op. cit.*, p. 105; Adnan Badr, *al-Hadaf*, 15.6.70; *MENA*, 2.3.71, report by al-Sayyad correspondent in Cairo; Fuad Matar, *al-Nahar*, 7.3.71; Khatib, *op. cit.*, pp. 66–67; Abu Iyad, *al-Sayyad*, 14.7.71; Ibrahim Salama, *al-Hawadith*, 12.3.71; Salih Barghuthi, *al-Hawadith*, 9.4.71; Munir Shafiq, *Hawla al-Wahda al-Wataniyya al-Filastiniyya*, 12.3.76, pp. 10–11, *Shuun*, No. 41/42, January/February 1975, pp. 86–94; see also *al-Hawadith*, 5.6.70; *al-Nahar*, 1.3.71.
136. Adnan Badr, *al-Hadaf*, 15.6.70; see also PFLP, *al-Taqrir*, pp. 49–51.
137. See *al-Huriyya*, 1, 15.3.71; Fuad Matar, *al-Nahar*, 1.6.70; *al-Nahar*, 19.2.71; *al-Kifah*, Beirut, 19.2.71; *MENA*, 20.2.71, memorandum submitted by Yahya C-in-C PLA to CC-PLO; *MENA*, 17.6.71, spokesman of the PLA; *MENA*, 24.6.71, PLA HQ – statement; *al-Hawadith*, 5.6.70, 12.3.71; *al-Sayyad*, 28.5.70; Talal Salman, *al-Sayyad*, 1.7.71; *Kul Shay*, 26.6.71; *al-Ahram*, 11.7.71; *Sawt Filastin*, organ of the PLA, February 1969, p. 5; Yahya, *Sawt Filastin*, No. 28, May 1970; PLFS, *al-Thawri*, Maqalat Fikriyya, Siyasiyya, Tanzimiyya, 10.2.1970.
138. On their memorandum to the 7th PNC see *al-Nahar*, 3.6.70, *al-Hawadith*, 5.6.70, *al-Anwar*, 30.5.70; statement in the 8th PNC, *al-Hadaf*, 6.3.71; see also *al-Sayyad*, 2.3.71; *MENA*, 2.3.71; on their activities in the 9th PNC see *al-Sayyad*, 14.7.71; Bilal al-Hasan, *Shuun*, No. 4, September 1971, p. 172; *al-Nahar*, 7.7.71; on Shuqayri's activities see *Kul Shay*, 26.12.71; *al-Nahar*, 12.12.71; *Sawt al-Asifa*, 8.12.71; PFLP, Qiyadat al-Ard al-Muhtalla, *Ta'mim Hawla al-Wad' fi Qita' Ghaza*, 26.10.71, internal circular; *al-Hadaf*, 5.2.72; see also *Ruz al-Yusuf*, 16.11.70; Mustafa al-Husayni, *Ruz al-Yusuf*, 1.3.71.
139. Shafiq, *op. cit.*, p. 14; Abu Iyad, *al-Tali'a*, Cairo, June 1969, pp. 51–87; Kanafani, *al-Anwar*, 6.4.69; ALF, *Wahda*, p. 32; PFLP–GC, political communiqué, the first half of October 1969; Khatib, *op. cit.*, pp. 66–67; Bakr, *Sawt Filastin*, May 1970; Arafat, *al-Jumhuriyya*, Cairo, 6.1.70, *al-Ahram*, 10.2.70; Fatah, *1969 Yearbook*, pp. 171–172; Habash, *al-Ahhad*, 17.1.71; also *Ruz al-Yusuf*, 11.5.70; *al-Hayat*, 19.12.69; *al-Nahar*, 6.8.69; *Amman al-Masa*, 20.10.69.
140. See Khatib, *op. cit.*, pp. 68–70; *al-Sayyad*, 19.3.70, attitudes of Fatah, PFLP, PDFLP, PFLP–GC, ALF, Sa'iqa; *Reuter*, 21.2.70, interview with Habash; Hawatma, *al-Ahhad*, 15.3.70; Bakr, *Sawt Filastin*, May 1970; Hut, *Sawt Filastin*,

April 1970; Arafat, *Kul Shay*, 28.2.70; see also *al-Akhbar*, Beirut, 22.2.70; *al-Ahram*, 15.2.70; *al-Thawra al-Filastiniyya*, March 1970, April 1970; *MENA*, 22.2.70.

141. For text of joint communiqué, 6.5.70, and resolutions of 7th PNC see Khatib, *op. cit.*, pp. 172–177, also see 71–78; Abu Iyad, *Fatah*, 29.7.71; Yahya, *al-Sayyad*, 1.7.71; Arafat, *al-Nahar*, 3.6.70; Khalid al-Hasan, *MENA*, 13.9.70; *al-Hayat*, 17.6.70; *al-Nahar*, 3.6.70 (attitudes of Fatah and PFLP); *INA*, 11.9.70; *MENA*, 13.9.70; *Fatah*, 13.9.70.

142. This section is based *inter alia* on my interviews with politicians and leaders of the West Bank; the discussion in this section is restricted to developments on the West Bank, which are, much more than those on the Gaza Strip, a key to understanding the developments of Palestinian Entity.

143. Except the mayors of Ramalla and al-Bira.

144. Among the MC members were the governor of Jerusalem, Anwar al-Khatib; the mayor of Jerusalem, Ruhi al-Khatib; the chairman of the Jerusalem Chamber of Commerce, Ali Taziz; and senators/cabinet ministers who had been PLO activists of the Shuqayri era. See Petition to the Military Governor of the West Bank dated 24.7.67, *The Resistance of the Western Bank of Jordan to Israeli Occupation 1967*, the Institute for Palestine Studies, Beirut, 1967, pp. 11–14; also Abu Mayzar, *Shuun*, No. 32, April 1974, pp. 42–43.

145. The National Charter was signed by 142 prominent persons from all towns of the West Bank, including Jerusalem, representing the entire political spectrum of the West Bank. Exceptions were three men who advocated the founding of an independent Palestinian Entity on the West Bank. These were Ja'bari, Aziz Shahada and Taji al-Faruqi. For text of the National Charter see *al-Anwar*, 4.10.67; for complete text see *al-Hayat*, 6.10.67, also in Mahdi Abd al-Hadi, *al-Masa'la al-Filastiniyya 1934–1974*, Beirut, July 1975, pp. 351–355; see also statements by the political leaders, dated 15.5.68, in *Wathaiq Urduniyya*, pp. 171–172.

146. On its activities see *Bayan ila al-Muwatinin fi al-Diffa al-Gharbiyya*, Da'wa ila al-Idrab on 19.9.67; *al-Watan*, organ of the Communist party in the West Bank (first issue November 1967), No. 18, January 1969; *Jerusalem Post* (JP), 3.6.68; *al-Dustur*, 2.6.68; *al-Ba'th*, 19.9.67; MER, 1968, p. 565.

147. See *al-Watan*, No. 15, September 1968; *al-Anwar*, 2.2.69; *JP*, 7.1.69, 7.5.69, 10.6.69, 30.9.69; *Lamerhav*, Tel-Aviv, 6.1.69, 12.2.69; *Ma'ariv*, 2.3.69, 7, 9.7.69; *al-Quds* (East Jerusalem), 7.1.69, 10.6.69.

148. On the establishment of the PIC and its activities see *al-Quds*, 1.8.69, 26.9.69, 10, 11.3.70, 8, 26, 28.4.70, 5, 6.5.70, 18.10.70; *al-Anba*, Jerusalem, 1.8.69, 10, 11.3.70, 28.4.70, 4.5.70, 18.10.70; *Davar*, Tel-Aviv, 13.7.70.

149. See *al-Quds*, 7.10.69; *JP*, 12.8.69, 7.10.69; *al-Ahram*, 7.9.69; MER, 1968, p. 454, 1969–70, pp. 362–363.

150. See *Ha'aretz*, 10.12.68, 2, 4, 6, 13.3.69; *al-Anba*, 2.7.70; *JP*, 19.3.69, 4.5.69, 9.6.69, 4.9.69; *Ma'ariv*, 25.10.68, 2, 4, 6.3.69, 10.6.69, 22.1.70; *al-Anwar*, 2.2.69; MER, 1968, pp. 450–452, 1969–70, pp. 358–361.

151. See Brigadier-General Gazit, Coordinator of Activities in the Territories, *Ha'aretz*, 30.6.69; Dayan, defence minister, *Ha'aretz*, 17.12.69; *Ha'aretz*, 22.6.69, 17.12.69, 18.5.81; *al-Anba*, 3, 5.8.69, 5.10.69; *Ma'ariv*, 23.6.69; *al-Quds*, 5.10.69; IDFS.

152. *Al-Tali'a*, Cairo, March 1974, Hiwar Ma'a al-Jabha al-Wataniyya fi al-Ard al-Muhtalla; for warning against collaboration and threats against would-be collaborators see *Sawt al-Asifa*, 24, 25.5.68, 28.6.68, 30.9.68, 27.8.69, 7.7.71; *MENA*, 19, 21.7.69, 24.8.70; *PLO R.*, 2, 14.8.69; also reported in *al-Akhbar*, Cairo, 27.11.67; *al-Liwa*, Beirut, 17.11.67; *Lamerhav*, 6.7.69; *Yedi'ot Aharonot*, Tel Aviv, 23.4.70; on the warnings against candidates and their refusal see *Sawt al-Asifa*, 2, 4, 6.2.70; *al-Quds*, 5, 8.2.70; *al-Anba*, 8.2.70.

153. See Anwar Nusayba, *al-Anba*, 21.8.70, *al-Quds*, 1.5.70, 30.7.70, *Ma'ariv*, 23.10.70, *JP*, 28.8.70, 28.7.71; Rashid al-Nimr, *al-Quds*, 15.12.70 (on his return

from Cairo); Anwar al-Khatib, *al-Quds*, 13.5.70; Abd al-Razaq al-Jarrar, *al-Quds*, 17.5.70; Qadri Tuqan, *al-Quds*, 8.12.70, *Ma'ariv*, 7.8.70, *al-Jadid*, Beirut, 23.3.68; Hikmat al-Masri, *al-Quds*, 20.1.69, 20.2.69, 4.5.71, *al-Anba*, 8.10.70, *Lamerhav*, 7.1.69, *Ha'aretz*, 8.1.69; Dr Hamdi al-Taji al-Faruqi, *al-Quds*, 11.9.70; see also Nasir, in Farid, *op. cit.*, pp. 119, 154; Hadi, *op. cit.*, pp. 348–349; for cases of incitement of West Bank inhabitants by Egyptian media see especially *Cairo R.* and *Sawt al-Arab*, 18, 19, 23, 25, 26, 28.10.68; see also Nasir, *al-Ahram*, 5.12.68; on reactions in West Bank to Nasir's death see *al-Quds*, 29, 30.9.70, 1, 5, 18, 20, 21, 25, 27.10.70; *al-Anba*, 4–6, 12, 15, 18, 27.10.70; see also *al-Akhbar*, 16.10.70.

154. See Qadri Tuqan, *al-Quds*, 8.12.70; Anwar Nusayba, *JP*, 28.7.71; Hamdi Kan'an, Walid Shak'a, *al-Quds*, 27.9.70; mayors of Jenin, Araba, Tubas and Ya'bid, *al-Quds*, 8.4.71; for more reactions to the September massacre see *al-Quds*, 20, 25, 27–29.9.70, 4, 10, 15, 27.4.71; *al-Anba*, 27–29.9.70, 31.12.70, 20, 22.4.71; *al-Bashir*, Bethlehem, articles by Ibrahim Handal, 9.1.71, 10.4.71, Adnan al-Samman, 10.1.71.

155. Hilmi Hanun, *al-Anba*, 29.11.68; Qadri Tuqan, *al-Jadid*, 22.3.68; Hamdi Kan'an, *al-Nahar*, 1.12.68, *JP*, 5.12.68, *Lamerhav*, 8.12.68, 13.1.69, *al-Hayat*, 24.12.68, *al-Quds*, 2, 6.1.69, *al-Anba*, 5.11.71; see also *al-Difa'*, *al-Dustur*, 4.1.69; *Ma'ariv*, 10.6.69, 11.12.70; Anwar Nusayba, *al-Anba*, 21.8.70; Taji Faruqi, *The New Middle East*, No. 10, July 1969, pp. 13–15; also *al-Dustur*, 11.9.68.

156. For text of Shahada's plan and minutes of his meeting, accompanied by Kan'an, with Dayan on 16.4.68 see Hadi, *op. cit.*, pp. 333–343; also Shahada, *al-Quds*, 13.6.69, 30.3.70, 24–26.11.70, *Davar*, 17.1.69; Aziz Shahada, "Freedom from Outside Influences", *New Outlook*, Vol. 12, No. 9, November–December 1969, pp. 41–43; see also *al-Hadaf*, 11.10.69, 1.11.69, 29.8.70; reports on threats, *JP*, 17.4.70, *Ha'aretz*, 26.4.70.

157. For text of his plan see leaflet entitled *al-Dawla al-Filastiniyya al-Muqtaraha*, n.d.; also in Hadi, *ibid.*, pp. 325–332; Faruqi, *al-Quds*, 24.7.69, 14.5.70 (response to Eban's proposal), 11.9.70, 4.3.71, *al-Anba*, 29.5.70; Faruqi, "What Palestinians Want", *The New Middle East*, No. 10, July 1969, pp. 13–15; see also *al- Anwar*, 30.12.67; *al-Hadaf*, 29.8.70.

158. Ja'bari, *al-Quds*, 16, 26.4.70, 17, 20.12.70, 6.5.73, *al-Anba*, 4, 12.2.70, 8.5.70, 31.1.71, 17.6.71, 6.12.71, 29.7.73, *al-Sha'b*, Jerusalem (East), 6.6.73, *JP*, 23.9.71, *Yedi'ot Aharonot*, 6.5.73; for threats against him see *Sawt al-Asifa*, 24, 26.3.70, *Dam. R.*, 2.8.69, also reported in *JP*, 17.4.70; see also *Amman R.*, 8.9.67.

159. See, for example, Abu al-Zuluf, editorials, *al-Quds*, 8, 16.1.69, 27.8.70, 31.12.70, 22.2.71, 4.6.71; Abu Shalbaya, *al-Quds*, 17.8.69, 23.12.69, 12.8.70, 9.12.70, 10.2.71; Bitar, *al-Quds*, 19.3.70, 27.10.70, 12.2.71, 21.3.71; Adnan al-Samman, *al-Quds*, 7, 19.8.70; Ibrahim Handal, *al-Quds*, 28.8.70, 11.10.70; Abu Marwan (Yusuf al-Najjar), *al-Quds*, 23.1.70, 18.2.71, 4.6.71; Dr Amin Maghagh, *al-Quds*, 27.8.70; Abd al-Halim Mustafa, *al-Quds*, 30.12.70; see also *al-Usbu' al-Arabi*, *al-Quds*, 24.11.69.

160. On Israeli proposals and activities see Moshe Sasson, *Lamerhav*, 8.5.68, *Hatzofe*, Tel Aviv, 25.7.69; Dayan, *Ha'aretz*, 26.5.68, 3.6.69, *al-Anba*, 4.10.70, *al-Quds*, 4.10.70; Eban, *al-Anba*, 6.2.70; see also *al-Quds*, 30.4.70, 25.6.70, 14.7.70; *al-Ittihad*, organ of the Israeli Communist party, Haifa, 16.7.68; *Ha'aretz*, 21.4.68, 12.9.69; *JP*, 25.1.68, 23.1.69, 14.10.69; *al-Akhbar*, Cairo, 19.7.68; *al-Difa'*, 12.8.68, 23.9.68; *al-Dustur*, 25.7.68; on reactions of local political leaders see Anwar al-Khatib, *al-Quds*, 13.5.70; Kan'an *al-Nahar*, 1.12.68, *al-Quds*, 30.12.68, 7.12.70, *al-Usbu' al-Arabi*, 11.10.71; Qadri Tuqan, *al-Usbu' al-Arabi*, 15.2.71; Anwar Nusayba, *al-Anba*, 21.8.70, *al-Bashir*, 12.2.72; Hikmat al-Masri, *al-Quds*, 4.5.71; Walid al-Shak'a, *al-Anwar*, 4.6.69; Ja'bari, *al-Quds*, 17.12.70; Rashid al-Nimr, *al-Quds*, 15.12.70; see also Dr Abd al-Razaq al-Jarrar, *al-Quds*, 17.5.70; *Wathaiq Urduniyya*, pp. 171–172, communiqué by local leaders dated 15.5.68.

161. For threats by fidai organizations see *PLO R.*, 3, 12.11.67, 24.5.69, 9, 16.6.69,

14.8.69, 17.2.70, 10, 17, 31.3.70; *Sawt al-Asifa*, 13.9.68, 4.3.69, 15, 16.6.69, 17,
19.8.70, 5.5.71; *Fatah*, 2, 26.11.70; *al-Hadaf*, 31.7.71; Arafat, *al-Musawwar*,
13.11.70; Abu Iyad, *Filastini*, pp. 219–220; Abu Iyad, quoted by Isa al-Shu'aybi,
al-Kiyaniyya al-Filastiniyya, *op. cit.*, p. 158; also *al-Hawadith*, 4.9.70; *MENA*,
Fatah, 24.8.70, resolution by the CC PLO; *MENA*, 21.2.71, CC PLO statement
emphasizing sole representation by PLO.
162. See PLO, *The 4th PNC*, pp. 39–40; Munir Shafiq, "Limadha Yarfud al-
Filastiniyyun Mashru' al-Dawla al-Filastiniyya", *Shuun*, No. 7, March 1972, pp.
65–73; Nabil Sha'ath, "Filastin al-Ghad", *Shuun*, No. 2, May 1971, pp. 5–23; Abu
Lutuf, *Dirasat Arabiyya*, February 1971, pp. 2–8; Kamal Udwan, *Lecture*; Hindi,
op. cit., p. 215; Muhsin, *op. cit.*, pp. 69–70; Zuhayr Muhsin, *al-Thawra al-
Filastiniyya Bayna al-Fikr wa al-Mumarasa*, Damascus, August 1972, pp. 29–40
(al-Fikr); *al-Talai'*, Damascus, 20.3.72; Abu Iyad, *al-Hayat*, 4.1.71; Kanafani,
"Shabah al-Dawla al-Filastiniyya", *al-Hadaf*, 6.3.71; Yusuf al-Najjar (Abu
Yusuf), a leader of Fatah, *al-Jadid*, 3.1.71; Hisham Sharabi, Walid al-Khalidi,
Yusuf Sayigh in *al-Sayyad*, 25.2.71 and *al-Anwar*, 18.2.71; Fatah, *Qarar Majlis al-
Amn wa Mashru' Rojers*, September 1970; Fatah, Maktab al-Ta'bia wa al-
Tanzim, Lubnan, *al-Dawla al-Filastiniyya*, 10.12.70, pamphlet for members
only; Khalid al-Hasan and Arafat, *al-Thawra al-Filastiniyya*, January 1971;
Arafat, *MENA*, 14.11.70; see also *al-Thawra al-Filastiniyya*, July 1969.
163. Hamdi Kan'an, leaflet entitled *Bayan wa Haqiqa ila al-Sha'b al-Urduni*, dated
30.12.68 (published also in *al-Quds*, 2.11.69); Kan'an, *al-Quds*, 2.1.69, 12.2.69,
12.3.69, 27.9.70, 22.10.70, 7.12.70, 1.8.71, *al-Anba*, 5.11.71; on his resignation
see *al-Quds*, 13.9.68, *Lamerhav*, 13, 15.9.68; *Ha'aretz*, 21.2.69; on his dispute
with Talhuni see also *al-Watan*, No. 18, January 1969; *al-Quds*, 22.10.70; *al-Difa'*,
26.12.68, 3, 4.1.69; *al-Dustur*, 4.1.69; for criticism of the traditional leadership see
Walid Istitya, *al-Quds*, 17.9.70; Samir Abd al-Hadi, *al-Quds*, 10.10.70; Ahmad al-
Bahash, *al-Quds*, 18.11.70; Sani al-Bitar, *al-Quds*, 21.3.71.
164. Abu Lutuf, *Lecture; Abd al-Karim Abu al-Nasr*, *al-Nahar*, weekly supplement,
31.12.67; also *al-Huriyya*, 19.5.69.
165. Nasir, in Farid, *op. cit.*, p. 260; Husayn, *al-Nahar*, 24.8.71, *NYT*, 12.12.71.
166. Kamal Udwan, *Lecture*.
167. Khalid al-Hasan, *Shuun*, No. 4, September 1971, pp. 279–290.

CHAPTER FOUR

1. Sadat's speeches and interviews are quoted from three volumes of books entitled
Majmu'at Khutab wa Ahadith al-Ra'is Anwar al-Sadat, Ministry of Information,
Cairo, n.d., Vol. 1 containing speeches during the period September 1970 –
December 1971, Vol. 2 January–December 1972, Vol. 3 January–December 1973
(Khutab); I shall note only the dates of speeches, other sources are the Egyptian
newspaper *al-Ahram* of the day following the delivery of the speech, as well
as *Cairo Radio* of the day of the speech; see *Khutab*, 16.2.72, 1.5.72, 15.10.72,
28.12.72, 26.3.73, 1, 27.5.73, 23.7.73; see also Haykal, *MENA*, 1.7.72; Qudus,
Akhbar al-Yawm, 23.9.72.
2. See Sadat, *Khutab*, 10.6.71, 7.7.71, 16.9.71, 23.7.72, 15.10.72, 28.12.72; Anwar
al-Sadat, *al-Bahth An al-Dhat*, Cairo, April 1978 (al-Bahth), p. 634, see also p.
288; Sadat, *al-Sayyad*, 29.9.72, speech to Arab foreign ministers; Haykal, *MENA*,
26.11.71; Fuad Matar, *al-Nahar*, 22.12.72. (Matar was, during this period, *al-
Nahar* correspondent in Cairo. He was very close to highly placed sources,
including both civilian and military leaders of the regime. In particular he was a
close friend of Haykal. His information invariably proved to be accurate. The
regime frequently used him as a channel for "leaking" information, especially
concerning preparations for the War and relations between Egypt, Jordan and the

PLO.)
3. Sadat, *Khutab*, 14.5.71, 23.7.71, 30.8.71, 16.2.72, 1.9.72, 1.5.73, 23.7.73; Haykal, *al-Anwar*, 24.10.71; Asad, *Dam. R.*, 8.3.72; Mahmud al-Ayyubi, PM, *Dam. R.*, 18.2.73.
4. Sadat, *Khutab*, 17.4.71, 16.2.72, 1, 14.5.72, 15.10.72, 23.7.73; on Sadat's efforts to gain the support of the ASU institutions and the People's Assembly for the proposed constitution of the Federation of Arab Republics, see Fuad Matar, *Ayna Asbaha Abd al-Nasir fi Jumhuriyyat al-Sadat*, Beirut, July 1972; also Haykal, *MENA*, 19.8.71, *al-Anwar*, 24.10.71.
5. PFLP, the Central Command (CCD), *Ta'mim Dakhili No. 4*, concerning the meeting of the CCD, 25.11.72 (Ta'mim No. 4); Political Programme, the 10th PNC, Hamid, *op. cit.*, pp. 198–208; Sabri Abu al-Majd, *al-Musawwar*, 8.9.72; Mrs Golda Meir, PM, *Davar*, Tel Aviv, 13.4.73, *Yedi'ot Aharonot*, Tel Aviv, 15.4.73 (Protocol Discussion of the Labour Party's Bureau), *Ma'ariv*, Tel Aviv, 8.9.72, *Ha'aretz*, 1, 25.3.71, 29.9.72; *Bammahane*, Tel Aviv, 2.5.73.
6. Sadat, *Khutab*, 15.4.72, *Cairo R.*, 4.9.75, 3.2.76, 14.3.76, *MENA*, 10.12.75, 20.7.76, *al-Ahram*, 30.3.75, 15.7.75, 9.9.75, *Ruz al-Yusuf*, 24.3.75, *Akhbar al-Yawm*, 12.4.75, *al-Hawadith*, *MENA*, 3.2.76, *al-Nahar*, 17.1.75.
7. Sadat, *Khutab*, 4, 14.2.71, 4.3.71, 7, 17.4.71, 6.2.71, 6.2.72, 30.3.72, 26.3.73.
8. See Sadat, *Khutab*, 4, 28.2.71, 7.3.71, 1, 20.5.71, 22.6.71, 23.7.71, 16.9.71, 11.11.71, 13.1.72, 28.2.72, 23.7.72, 28.9.72, 26.3.73, 23.7.73, *al-Ahram*, 16.2.71, *al-Bahth*, pp. 370–372; Haykal, *MENA*, 29.4.71, 13.5.71, 24.6.71, 5, 26.11.71; Hasan al-Zayyat, FM, *Akhir Sa'a*, 28.11.72; Sa'd al-Din al-Shadhli, *Harb October*, Paris, 1980, cites Sadat in two meetings: the Supreme Council of the Armed Forces (SCAF) 24.10.72, p. 125, and of officers of the General Staff, 11.5.71, pp. 95–96; Hamdi Fuad, *op. cit.*, pp. 189–190, cites Sadat in his meeting with Donald Bergus, the American representative in Cairo, on 30.3.71; Moshe Zak, *Ma'ariv*, 19.10.81; Y. Rabin, *Pinkas Sherut* (Hebrew), Vol. 2, Tel Aviv, September 1979, pp. 327–336.
9. John N. Moore, ed., *The Arab–Israeli Conflict*, Vol. 3, Documents, Princeton, New Jersey, 1974, pp. 1104–1108, Jarring's *Aide Mémoire* to Egypt and Israel, February 8, 1971, and Egypt's reply, February 15, 1971; Sadat, *Khutab*, 4, 14, 28.2.71, 20, 26.5.71, 11.11.71, 27.5.73, *al-Ahram*, 7.12.79; *al-Nahar*, 2.8.72; Lutfi al-Khuli, series of articles on Sadat's political doctrine, *al-Ahram*, 11.6.75, 9, 16.7.75, 6, 13, 20.8.75.
10. Haykal explained the meaning of "the year of decision" as "a year of decision making, and not a year of carrying out" the decision regarding war or peace. See Matar, *op. cit.*; Sadat, *al-Bahth*, pp. 308–309, 381, *Khutab*, 22.6.71, 12, 30.8.71, 16.9.71, 13, 25, 30.1.72; Matar, *al-Nahar*, 6.11.71, 1.3.72; Haykal, *al-Tariq*, pp. 141–142, *al-Nahar*, 17.9.71, *MENA*, 29.4.71, 12.8.71, 5, 26.11.71; Musa Sabri, *Wathaiq Harb October*, 3rd edition, Cairo, 1975, pp. 213–232, Shadhli, *op. cit.*, pp. 93–102, Sadat in his meeting with officers of the General Staff, 4.11.71; Sayyid Mar'i, *Awraq Siyasiyya*, Vol. 3, Ma'a al-Ra'is Anwar al-Sadat, Cairo, January 1979, pp. 308, 660, 705.
11. See Sadat, *al-Bahth*, Tawjih Siyasi wa Askari (political and military) from the president to the minister of war and commander-in-chief of armed forces, dated 1.10.73, pp. 436–443, Tawjih Istratiji to the minister of war and commander-in-chief dated 5.10.73, p. 444, also pp. 329–300, 321, 331, *Khutab*, 26.3.73, *MENA*, 2.4.73, *al-Akhbar*, 3.10.74, *al-Jumhuriyya*, 23.10.75, *Cairo R.*, 28.9.74, *Ruz al-Yusuf*, 23.9.74, 13.1.75, *al-Usbu' al-Arabi*, 8.10.74, *al-Hawadith*, 25.4.74; Shadhli, *op. cit.*, cites Sadat in meetings of the SCAF, 3.6.71, p. 99, 24.10.72, pp. 123–129, also pp. 23–26; Shadhli, *al-Anwar*, 16.11.72; Badri, *op. cit.*, pp. 18–23, 32–35; Musa Sabri, *op. cit.*, pp. 213–232, 269–287; H. Kissinger, *Years of Upheaval*, London, 1982, pp. 210–216, 223–227; Rabin, *op. cit.*, pp. 382–385; *al-Hawadith*, 16.8.74; Ahmad Isma'il, minister of war, *al-Nahar*, 7.10.74 (interview with Matar), *al-Anwar*, 18.11.73 (interview with Haykal); General Gamasi, *al-*

Hawadith, London, 17.11.78; Haykal, *al-Tariq*, pp. 164–165, cites Sadat in meeting of the National Security Council 24.10.72, *al-Anwar*, 22.4.72, *MENA*, 20.8.71; Matar, *al-Nahar*, 1.11.72, 22.12.72, 11.6.73; Abu Iyad, *Filastini*, pp. 195–198; on the economic preparations see Mahmud Fawzi, vice-president, *MENA*, 11.1.73; Aziz Sidqi, PM, *Cairo R.*, 12.12.72, 19.1.73, *MENA*, 11.2.73; Lieutenant-Colonel Avi Shay, Towards the Yom Kippur War, Aims of the War and the Plan of the Attack (Hebrew), *Ma'rakhot*, Tel Aviv, No. 250, July 1976, pp. 15–38.

12. On Sadat's attitude see Sadat, *Khutab*, 10.1.71, 1.5.71, 23.7.71, 30.8.71; Haykal, *MENA*, 29.7.71, 5.8.71, *al-Anwar*, 24.10.71; Matar, *al-Nahar*, 20.1.73; on Husayn's attitude see Order of the Day (Secret) from Husayn – The Supreme Commander of the Armed Forces to the Officers of the Armed Forces, of the General Security and of the General Intelligence 13.5.73, in *L'Orient – Le Jour*, Beirut, 31.5.73 (Order), *Amman R.*, 3.2.73; *al-Sabah*, Amman, 24.9.73; *Amman R.*, commentaries, 29.2.72, 15.11.72, 11.12.72, 29.1.73; *al-Ray*, Amman, 28.2.72, 16.11.72, 20.4.73; *Akhbar al-Yawm*, 15.9.73; *al-Akhbar*, 1.6.73; *al-Ahram*, 4.6.73, 15.8.73; *al-Hawadith*, 17.3.72, 18.12.72; *al-Hayat*, 17.9.73; *al-Anwar*, 16.11.72.

13. See Shadhli, *Harb*, pp. 198–202; Sadat, *Khutab*, 23.7.71, 17.4.72, 1.5.73; Sa'id Abd al-Baqi, Iraqi FM, *al-Hawadith*, Salim al-Lawzi, 22.12.72; Matar, *al-Nahar*, 5.5.72; Saddam Husayn, *Akhir Sa'a*, 16.8.72, *INA*, 19.7.73, *al-Jumhuriyya*, Baghdad, 1.1.72.

14. See Shadhli, *op. cit.*, pp. 183–213; secret protocol of ALC discussions, September 1972 in *al-Sayyad*, 21.9.72; protocol of sessions of the Arab FMs, *al-Anwar*, 16.11.72; PLO memorandum to the ADC, *al-Ray al-Amm*, Kuwait, 16.11.72; Syrian proposals to the FMs' Conference, *Kul Shay*, 25.11.72; Mahmud Zakariyya Isma'il, Syrian Assistant FM, *Dam. R.*, 1.12.72; Husayn, *al-Siyasa*, Kuwait, 3.12.73; Zayd Rifa'i, *Amman R.*, 12.5.74; also *Kul Shay*, 28.4.73; *al-Hayat*, 11, 12.9.72; *al-Usbu' al-Arabi*, 13.11.72; *al-Nahar*, 17.11.72; *al-Hawadith*, Salim al-Lawzi, 22.12.72; *al-Jumhur*, Beirut, 23.11.72; *al-Siyasa*, Kuwait, 5.2.73; *Ruz al-Yusuf*, 11, 18.9.72, 25.12.72, 29.1.73; *al-Jumhuriyya*, 19.11.72; *al-Musawwar*, 24.12.72; *al-Ahram*, 22, 29.1.73.

15. Sadat's lack of confidence in Husayn was already evident during the 1950s, when Sadat was editor of *al-Jumhuriyya*. See Sadat, *al-Jumhuriyya*, 2, 5.8.57 in Karam Shalabi, *al-Sadat wa Thawrat 23 Yulyu – 1948–1959*, Cairo, 1977, pp. 218–219; Sadat, *Khutab*, 12.11.70, 10.1.71, 28.3.71, 1.5.71, 7, 23.7.71; Hafiz Isma'il, *MENA*, 31.3.71; Haykal, *MENA*, 22.7.71; Qudus, *Akhbar al-Yawm*, 3.4.71; *al-Ahram*, 22.2.71, 29.8.71; on the attitudes of the media see *al-Musawwar*, 11.6.71; *al-Ahram*, 19.12.70, 10.1.71, 13, 14.2.71, 30, 31.3.71, 1, 8, 9, 17.4.71, 17.5.71; *al-Akhbar*, 10.1.71, 31.3.71, *Cairo R.*, commentaries, 12.12.70, 1.1.71, 12.2.71, 2.4.71; *Sawt al-Arab R.*, commentaries, 9.1.71, 1, 6, 10.4.71.

16. Sadat, *Khutab*, 23.7.71 (for assessment of this speech see *MENA*, 24.7.71), 30.8.71; Hatim, minister of information, *Cairo R.*, 20.7.71; Tripoli (Libya) summit declaration, *al-Nahar*, 1.8.71; Marsi Matruh Conference declaration (14–17.7.71, Sadat, Qadhafi and representatives of Syria and Sudan), *al-Nahar*, *al-Ahram*, 18.7.71; Tahsin Bashir, Egyptian official spokesman, *Cairo R.*, 14.7.71, *Fatah*, 15.7.71; Qadhafi, *al-Ahram*, 3.8.71; *Kul Shay*, 9.10.71; on the Egyptian support to the PR see Haykal, *MENA*, 22.7.71; resolutions of the ASU National Congress, *Cairo R.*, 26.7.71; *Akhbar al-Yawm*, 29.11.71; *al-Ahram*, 15.7.71, 29.8.71, 18.12.71; *al-Akhbar*, 15.7.71; *Cairo R.*, commentaries, 20, 21.7.71; *Sawt al-Arab*, commentaries, 22.7.71.

17. Ahmad Baha al-Din argued that Husayn "does not in fact grant [the Palestinians] the right to self-determination in the conventional sense ... he grants them ... a large municipal council". Sadat, *Khutab*, 30.3.72, 6, 17.4.72, 1.5.72, 17.8.72, 18.9.72, 15.10.72; Haykal, *MENA*, 17.3.72, *al-Anwar*, 22.4.72; *al-Nahar*, 19.3.72, declaration by the presidents of the Federation of Arab Republics; Murad

Ghalib, FM, *al-Anwar*, 31.3.72; Kissinger, *op. cit.*, pp. 215–216; on the media campaign see Ahmad Baha al-Din, *al-Ahram*, 19, 26.3.72; *al-Ahram*, 17, 19.3.72, 7, 9.4.72, 2.8.72; Qudus, *MENA*, 14.10.72; *Ruz al-Yusuf*, 21.2.72, 20.3.72 (Ibrahim Izzat); *al-Musawwar*, 24, 31.3.72; *al-Akhbar*, 16, 17.3.72, 22.7.72; *al-Jumhuriyya*, 20.3.72, 25.8.72, 19.12.72; *Akhbar al-Yawm*, 9.4.72; *Cairo R.*, commentaries, 16, 19.3.72, 7, 9.4.72; *Sawt al-Arab*, commentaries, 19, 27.3.72, 2, 7, 8, 9.4.72, 24.8.72.

18. Sadat, *Khutab*, 27.5.73, 28.9.73, *al-Bayraq*, Beirut, 8.1.73; Husayn, *Akhbar al-Yawm*, 15.9.73; Lawzi, PM, *al-Nahar*, 22.3.73; Matar, *al-Nahar*, 7.12.72, 20.1.73, 11, 21, 26, 27.6.73, 7.8.73, 18.9.73; *al-Nahar*, Abu Jawda, 12.9.73, Abu al-Nasr, 19.9.73; *al-Nahar*, 17.11.73, 17.9.73; *al-Ahram*, 2, 28.2.73, 4, 25.6.73, 15.8.73, 20.9.73; *al-Akhbar*, 1.6.73; *Akhbar al-Yawm*, 15.9.73; *Sawt al-Arab*, commentaries, 11, 21.9.73; *al-Sayyad*, 20.9.73; *al-Anwar*, 17.11.72; *al-Usbu' al-Arabi*, 13.11.72.

19. Sadat, *Khutab*, 15.1.71, 4, 14, 28.2.71, 26.5.71, 10.6.71; on his support for Fatah see Sadat, *Khutab*, 23.7.71, 25.1.72, 16.2.72; *al-Ahram*, 21.2.72, 10.6.73; Abu Iyad, *Filastini*, pp. 195–198; on his opposition to the radical organizations see Sadat, *Khutab*, 23.7.71; PFLP, *al-Munadil al-Thawri*, internal pamphlet No. 6, July 1973, pp. 96–98; PFLP, the CCD, *Ta'mim Dakhili*, No. 6, on the meeting of the CCD, 1.1.73 (Ta'mim No. 6); on criticism see Faysal Hurani, *Ruz al-Yusuf*, 6.12.71; Muhammad al-Sha'ir, *Ruz al-Yusuf*, 19.7.71; also *Ruz al-Yusuf*, 13.9.71.

20. See Sadat, *Khutab*, 6.4.72, 15.10.72; on the organizations' attitudes see Fatah, Maktab al-Ta'bia wa al-Tanzim, Lebanon Region, *News bulletin No. 1008/B*, limited internal circular, 24.4.72; Abu Iyad, *al-Balagh*, Beirut, 24.12.73; PFLP, *al-Badil al-Thawri li-Mashru' al-Dawla al-Filastiniyya* (Badil), April 1974, pp. 17–18; PDFLP, *al-Munadil*, internal pamphlet No. 3, May 1972 (al-Munadil).

21. Sadat, *Khutab*, 28.9.72, 15.10.72, 27.5.73, *al-Hawadith*, 6.10.72; Isma'il Fahmi, FM, *al-Nahar*, 7.1.74; Qudus, *Akhbar al-Yawm*, 1.7.72, 9.9.72; Baha al-Din, *al-Ahram*, 2.7.72; *Akhbar al-Yawm*, 7.8.71; *al-Ahram*, editorials, 29.9.72, 6.10.72; *Cairo R.*, commentaries, 30.9.72, 2, 4, 10.10.72; Abu Iyad, *Filastini*, pp. 195–197; PDFLP, *al-Munadil; al-Hadaf*, 6.1.73, protocol of discussions between PLO information delegation visiting USSR, and representatives of journalists' union of Leningrad.

22. See Sadat, *Khutab*, 28.2.71; Mahmud Riyad, FM, *West German Television*, 25.3.71; Dr Hasan al-Zayyat, *MENA*, 6.6.73, 15.6.73 (speech in the Security Council), 17.6.73 (W.Berlin Radio), 19.6.73 (Danish television), 23.6.73 (press conference), *al-Nahar*, 16.6.73, *Akhbar al-Yawm*, 10, 30.6.73, *al-Ahram*, 11.8.73; see also *al-Ahram*, 10.6.73; *Sawt al-Arab*, 6, 8.6.73; *al-Nahar*, 12.6.72, 28.7.73; Habib Bourguiba, *al-Akhbar*, 4.9.73; *al-Nahar*, 7.6.73.

23. See Arafat, *Ila al-Amam*, Beirut, 29.6.73, *al-Ray al-Amm*, Kuwait, 13.7.73, *al-Muharrir*, 17.7.73; Abu Iyad, *Kul Shay*, 30.6.73; Habash, *al-Hadaf*, 14.7.73; Nabil Sha'ath, *Shuun*, No. 23, July 1973, pp. 4–11; Isam Sakhnini, *Shuun*, No. 24, August 1973, pp. 224–229; Naji Alush, *Shuun*, No. 23, July 1973, pp. 227–228; *Fatah R.*, Dar'a, commentaries, 9, 20, 21, 22, 26.6.73.

24. Sadat, *Khutab*, 28.2.71, 15.10.72, 9.1.73, 23.7.73; on the massive support of the Egyptian media see as examples: Haykal, *MENA*, 22, 29.7.71; *Ruz al-Yusuf*, 10.1.72, 28.2.72, 2.4.73; *al-Jumhuriyya*, 23.10.71, 8.1.72, 1.3.72, 1.7.72, 16, 17.8.72, 1, 6.9.72, 2.1.73, 12.3.73; *al-Ahram*, 14, 28.2.71, 3, 31.3.71, 17.4.71, 27.6.71, 9, 10, 12, 15.7.71, 29.8.71, 15.9.71, 21.10.71, 22.1.72, 22.2.72, 6.3.72, 6, 7, 8.4.72, 31.5.72, 1.6.72, 11.12.72, 11.1.73, 10.3.73; *al-Akhbar*, 31.3.71, 7, 10, 15.7.71, 9.11.71, 12.1.72, 7.4.72, 2.7.72, 7.9.72; *Sawt al-Arab*, commentaries, 30, 31.3.71, 24.10.71, 8.1.72, 3.4.72, 3.7.72, 30.10.72, 5.11.72, 8.1.73; on the propaganda directed to the West Bank and Gaza Strip see Sadat, *Khutab*, 6.4.71, 28.9.71, 1.5.73; Murad Ghalib, *al-Anwar*, 31.3.72; Ahmad Baha al-Din, *al-Ahram*, 16, 23.1.72, 27.8.72.

25. Sadat, *Khutab*, 28.2.71, 7, 23.7.71, 6.4.72, 14, 27.5.73, 23.7.73, *al-Sayyad*,

28.9.72; on the discussions and resolutions of the inter-Arab forums at the end of 1972 and beginning of 1973, see Note 14 and also Bilal al-Hasan, *Shuun*, No. 17, January 1973, p. 28, *Shuun*, No. 19, March 1973, pp. 182–184.

26. Yusuf al-Najjar argued that "the fidaiyyun do not undertake to coordinate their activities with the UAC or to contact it as long as war has not been decided upon". Information leaked by Egypt, including even the content of private talks with Fatah leaders, to the effect that its closer links with Jordan were part of its war preparations, was in vain. See PLO Planning Center (PCR), *Taqrir Siyasi Khass*, On the General Arab Situation and the Tasks of the Resistance Movement, No. 25, limited circulation, 22.8.72 (Taqrir No. 25); PLO–PCR, *Taqrir Khass*, On the Arab and International Situation and Its Relation to the PR, No. 34, limited circulation, 11.1.73 (Taqrir No. 34); Fatah, Maktab al-Ta'bia wa al-Tanzim, Lebanon Region, *News bulletin No. 1012/B*, internal circular, 8.8.72; PFLP, the CCD, *Ta'mim Dakhili No. 2*, concerning the meeting of the CCD, 18.11.72 (Ta'mim No. 2); PDFLP, *al-Munadil; Yusuf al-Najjar (Abu Yusuf)*, a leader of Fatah, *al-Nahar*, 30.1.73 (speech in ADC 28.1.73); Abu Iyad, Abu Yusuf, *al-Nahar*, 1.2.73; Abu Iyad, *Fatah R.*, Cairo, 21.3.73; Abu Mahir, *Lecture*; Kamal Udwan, *Lecture*; Matar, *al-Nahar*, 11.6.73; *Ruz al-Yusuf*, 22.1.73; for criticism of the Arab attitude see EC PLO declaration 20.9.73, *al-Nahar*, 23.9.73.

27. A leader of Fatah cited by Zuhayr Muhsin, *al-Watan*, Kuwait, 26.4.77; Kamal Udwan, *Lecture*; Abu Jihad, *Lecture*; Hawatma, *Didd al-Ghazu al-Suri*, 1.10.76, p. 80, Asad, *Dam. R.*, 9.12.70, 9.6.73.

28. Arafat, cited by *al-Nahar*, 19.1.73; Abu Iyad, *Filastin al-Thawra*, 23.5.76, *al-Nahar*, 23.6.75; Abu Jihad, *Lecture*; Kamal Udwan, *Lecture*; Husam al-Khatib, *Shuun*, No. 21, May 1973, pp. 51–57; Franjiyya, quoted by Salim al-Lawzi, *al-Hawadith*, 11.5.73; EC PLO, *Political Report to the 11th PNC*, 6.1.73; PLO–PCR, *Taqrir No. 34; Fatah*, Maktab al-Ta'bia wa al-Tanzim, Lebanon Region, *News bulletin No. 1011/B*, limited internal circular, 30.6.72; *Ila al-Amam*, memorandum prepared for submission to the 11th PNC by PFLP–GC; PFLP–GC, Ahmad Jibril, *al-Waqi' al-Rahin wa al-Khuruj min-Ma'zaq*, n.d.

29. PLO–PCR, *Taqrir No. 34; Fatah*, internal political report on May 1973 crisis between the PR and Lebanese authorities, published by *al-Nahar*, 12.6.73; Abu Jihad, *Lecture*.

30. Ghalib al-Kayali, parts from his book on Asad the Leader published in *Tishrin*, Damascus, 8, 10.1.78; Asad, *al-Thawra*, 17.1.71, *MENA*, 16.3.71, *Dam. R.*, 5.12.70, 22.2.71, 7.12.71, *al-Nahar*, 17.3.71; the Ba'th National Command declaration, *SANA*, 15.11.71; Regional Command declarations, *al-Ba'th*, 22, 23.2.71, 16.11.71; Khlayfawi, PM, *Dam. R.*, 17.5.71; Zuhayr Muhsin, *al-Thawra al-Filastiniyya Bayna al-Fikr wa al-Mumarasa*, Damascus, August 1972 (al-Fikr), pp. 9–13; Khlayfawi, PM, *al-Thawra*, 17.4.71.

31. Asad, *al-Ba'th*, 7.1.71, 24.6.71, *Kul Shay*, 25.11.72, *al-Nahar*, 17.3.71, *al-Anwar*, 17.11.70, 27.5.71, 10.8.72; Zuhayr Muhsin, *Ila al-Amam*, 17.8.73; declaration by the Ba'th 12th National Congress, *al-Ba'th*, 5.8.75; Khaddam, *al-Muharrir*, 2.3.71.

32. Asad, *al-Anwar*, 17.11.70, 27.5.71, 10.8.72, *al-Ba'th*, 10.12.70, 21.2.71, *al-Thawra*, 8.4.73, *Dam. R.*, 22.2.71, 8.3.72, 10.12.73, *al-Nahar*, 17.3.71; Khaddam, FM, *al-Ray al-Amm*, 13.12.71, *Ruz al-Yusuf*, 22.11.71; Mahmud al-Ayyubi, PM, *al-Ahram*, 3.8.73; Kayali, *op. cit.*; declaration by the Ba'th 12th National Congress, *al-Ba'th*, 5.8.75; Ayyubi, *al-Thawra*, 18.2.71; declarations by the National Command, *al-Thawra*, 8.9.71; *al-Ba'th*, 16.11.71; declaration by the Regional Command, *al-Ba'th*, 8.3.72; Zuhayr Muhsin, *Bayna al-Hadir wa al-Mustaqbal*, Damascus, May 1973 (al-Hadir), p. 64.

33. Asad, *MENA*, 16.3.71, *al-Nahar*, 17.3.71, *al-Anwar*, 17.11.70, 27.5.71, 10.8.72, *al-Thawra*, 9.3.72, *al-Ba'th*, 24.6.71; Khaddam, *Ruz al-Yusuf*, 22.11.71, *al-Anwar*, 16.11.72, *al-Ray al-Amm*, Kuwait, 28.5.71; Mustafa Tlas, extracts from his book on the Arab–Israel conflict, *al-Nahar*, 27.2.74; Mahmud al-Ayyubi, PM,

al-Ba'th, 19.2.73.

34. Kayali, *op. cit.*; Asad, *al-Ba'th*, 2.4.71, *Dam. R.*, 9.12.70, 22.2.71, 8.3.72, 18.2.73, 9.6.73, *MENA*, 16.3.71, *al-Nahar*, 17.3.71; declarations by the Ba'th National and Regional Commands, *Dam. R.*, *al-Ba'th*, 16.11.71; Khlayfawi, PM, *Dam. R.*, 17.5.71; Ayyubi, PM, *al-Ahram*, 3.8.73; Khaddam, *al-Muharrir*, 2.3.71; *Dam. R.*, commentaries, 14.7.71, 27.9.72.

35. No wonder, therefore, that the Fertile Crescent and "greater Syria" plans were viewed positively by the regime as "step[s] towards Arab unity ... in spite of their imperialistic source". Kayali, *op. cit.*; Asad, *Dam. R.*, 8.3.74, 8.3.75, *al-Thawra*, 9.3.74, *al-Ray al-Amm*, Kuwait, 13.12.81, *al-Hawadith*, 26.6.75; Zuhayr Muhsin, *al-Nahar*, 10.9.73; Mustafa Sa'd al-Din, military commander of Sa'iqa, *al-Talai' wa al-Jamahir*, Beirut, December 1971; Kamal Junbalat, *Hadhihi Wasiyyati*, June 1978, pp. 98, 101–102, 105, written against the background of the Syrian invasion of Lebanon 1976, thus strongly anti-Syrian; Hawatma, *op. cit.*, p. 7; Fatah, Lebanon Region, *al-Thawra*, Organizational Bulletin, for members only, No. 24, 2.11.76.

36. Asad, *al-Anwar*, 27.5.71, *Dam. R.*, 25.2.75, 8, 20.3.75, *SANA*, 26.2.73, *al-Ray al-Amm*, Kuwait, 13.12.81; declaration by the National Command, *al-Ba'th*, 16.11.71; Zuhayr Muhsin, *al-Fikr*, pp. 97–103, *al-Talai' wa al-Jamahir*, June 1972; Junbalat, *op. cit.*, pp. 21–22, 102, 105; *Dam. R.*, commentary, 19.9.73; Fatah, *al-Thawra*, No. 23, 20.11.76.

37. See Muhsin, *al-Nahar*, 10.9.73, *al-Hadir*, p. 149; Zuhayr Muhsin, *Ahadith: al-Nidal al-Watani al-Filastini fi Muwajahat al-Tahaddiyat al-jadida*, January 1974 (Ahadith), p. 7.

38. Asad, *al-Hawadith*, 26.6.75; Khaddam, *Sawt al-Uruba*, Beirut, 23.9.71, *Ruz al-Yusuf*, 22.11.71; Muhsin, *al-Nahar*, 10.9.73.

39. For Syrian support of the PR during its crisis in Jordan see Asad, *Dam. R.*, 22.2.71, *al-Anwar*, 27.5.71; Khaddam, *op. cit.*; statement by the Regional Command, *Dam. R.*, 15.11.71; Syrian official spokesman, *al-Ba'th*, 21.7.71, 13.8.71; declaration by the National Command, *al-Thawra*, 8.9.71; also *al-Ba'th*, 11.1.71, 29, 31.3.71, 11.4.71, 28.6.71, 19, 20.7.71, 13.8.71; *al-Thawra*, 9, 12.1.71, 31.3.71, 21, 22.7.71; *Dam. R.*, commentaries, 10.1.71, 29, 31.3.71, 1, 6, 8.9.4.71, 22, 29.7.71, 10, 11, 13.8.71, 23.10.71; for Syrian criticism of the PR see Muhsin, *al-Fikr*, pp. 13, 18–21, 41–47, *al-Hadir*, pp. 48–53, 61–66; Hanna Bat-hish, Sa'iqa leader, *al-Talai' wa al-Jamahir*, December 1971; also *al-Nahar*, 5.6.71, 18.7.71.

40. See statement by the National Command on Husayn's plan, *al-Ba'th*, 19.3.72; Asad, *al-Thawra*, 8.4.72; Muhsin, *al-Fikr*, pp. 63–76, *al-Hadir*, 79–89; *al-Thawra*, 16.3.72; *al-Ba'th*, 16.3.72; *Dam R.*, commentaries, 16.3.72, 17, 18, 28.3.72, 3.4.72, 16.8.72; *al-Hadaf*, 22.4.72.

41. See Asad, *Dam. R.*, 18.2.73, 9.6.73; Husayn, *al-Siyasa*, Kuwait, 31.2.73; Z. Rifa'i, *Amman R.*, 12.5.74; Muhsin, *al-Hadir*, p. 122, *al-Nahar*, 10.9.73, *MENA*, 1.10.73; *MENA*, quoting al-Talai', 2.10.72, 16.8.72, 16.8.73, 20.9.73; Matar, *al-Nahar*, 7.12.72, 26, 27.6.73, 7.8.73; *al-Nahar*, 12.9.73 (Abu al-Nasr), 17.9.73; *al-Hayat*, 2.12.72; *al-Sayyad*, 20.9.73; *al-Hawadith*, 11.5.73; for Syrian support see *al-Ba'th*, 3.12.72, 1.5.73; *al-Thawra*, 12.12.72; *Jaysh al-Sha'b*, Damascus, 12.6.73; political statement by the United Palestinian Organization of the Ba'th Regional Command, *Dam. R.*, 15.5.73; *Dam. R.*, commentaries, 6.8.73, 6, 18.9.73; *Dam. R.*, *Sawt Filastin corner*, 26.3.73, 7, 19.9.73; on the PR attitude see EC PLO statement, *Fatah R.*, Cairo, 22.9.73; *Fatah R.*, Cairo, 12.7.73, 22.9.73; *Fatah R.*, Dar'a, 1, 5.9.73.

42. See *MENA*, 23.11.70; Muhsin, *al-Muharrir*, 6.7.71.

43. See Muhsin, *al-Fikr*, pp. 77–95, *al-Hadir*, pp. 75–89, 99–101, 128–129, 141–143.

44. See Muhsin, *al-Fikr*, pp. 77–95, *al-Hadir*, pp. 75–76, *al-Nahar*, 10.9.73; Sami al-Attari, chairman of the National Fidai Action Bureau and secretary of the Sa'iqa Command, *Dam. R.*, 19.1.73, *Akhir Sa'a*, 12.4.72; Sa'iqa memorandum to the 11th PNC concerning national unity, *Dam. R.*, *Sawt Filastin corner*, 7.1.73; al-

Ba'th, National Command, Sami al-Attari, *press conference*, 7.6.76, internal circular; *Sawt al-Tali'a*, internal bulletin of the United Palestinian Organization of the Ba'th Regional Command, No. 19, n.d. (June 1976?); Hanna Bat-hish, *al-Talai' wa al-Jamahir*, June 1972.

45. Muhsin, *al-Fikr*, pp. 29–40, 49–61, 67–70, *al-Hadir*, 43–47, 69–72, *al-Nahar*, 10.9.72; Sa'iqa memorandum to the 11th PNC, *Dam. R.*, *Sawt Filastin corner*, 7.1.73; on the media campaign see *Dam. R.*, commentaries, 5.1.72, 12.2.72, 15.3.72, 16.8.72; *al-Ba'th*, 17.3.72, 6.9.72; *al-Thawra*, 18.3.72.

46. See Muhsin, *al-Hadir*, pp. 72–75, 89, 135–151; Attari, *al-Muharrir*, 28.3.72; *al-Ba'th*, 17.3.72; *al-Thawra*, 30.9.72.

47. See Asad, *al-Thawra*, 27.11.70, 10.12.70, 12.1.71, 19.10.71, 9.3.72, *al-Ba'th*, 21.2.71, 9.3.71, *al-Nahar*, 17.3.71, *al-Anwar*, 27.5.71, 10.8.72, *Dam. R.*, 9.6.73; Abu Iyad, *al-Ray al-Amm*, 29.12.75; Abu Mazin, *Lecture*; PDFLP, *al-Munadil*; Khaddam, *al-Ba'th*, 23.12.71, *al-Ray al-Amm*, Kuwait, 13.12.71, *Sawt al-Uruba*, 23.9.71; declaration by the 5th Regional Congress, *al-Thawra*, 19.5.71; declaration by the 11th National Congress, *al-Thawra*, 8.9.71; *Dam. R.*, *Sawt Filastin corner*, 19.9.73; on the reorganization of the information system see *Dam. R.*, *Sawt Filastin Corner*, 1.1.73.

48. See Asad, *SANA*, 20.7.76, *al-Anwar*, 27.5.71, 10.8.72, *al-Nahar*, 17.3.71; the *IDF spokesman's* announcements during this period; Abu Iyad, *Fatah R.*, Cairo, 21.1.73; PFLP, CCD, *Ta'mim Dakhili* No. 5, concerning the meeting of the CCD, 12.12.72; military announcements by PFLP–GC on its actions in the Golan Heights, *MENA*, 14, 27.11.71; *Ila al-Amam*, 2, 3.73; *Dam. R.*, commentary, 26.11.72; *al-Ba'th*, 1.10.72, 17.11.72.

49. See Junbalat, *op. cit.*, p. 105; Ayyubi, PM, *Dam. R.*, 18.2.73; Khaddam, *loc. cit.*; Muhsin, *al-Fikr*, pp. 97–103; Attari, *Shuun*, No. 7, March 1972, p. 36, *Dam. R.*, 19.1.73; *MENA*, al-Talai', 24.1.71; *Fatah*, Damascus, 15.3.72; *Fatah R.*, Dar'a, 10.1.72; Bilal al-Hasan, *Shuun*, No. 10, June 1972, p. 260; *al-Nahar*, 8.9.73; also *al-Ba'th*, 8, 22.1.71, 20.6.71, 1.5.73; *al-Thawra*, 4.1.73, 29.4.73; for criticisms of "actions abroad" see *Dam. R.*, *Sawt Filastin corner*, 18, 19, 20, 21, 24, 25, 26, 27.3.73, 1.4.73, 7, 8.9.73; see also Muhsin, *al-Yawm*, 6.8.73; *Dam. R.*, commentary, 6.8.73; *al-Hayat*, 15.9.73, quoting al-Talai'.

50. See Abu Jihad, *Lecture*; Abu Iyad, *Filastini*, p. 154, *Fatah R.*, Cairo, 21.1.73; Arafat, *al-Mujahid*, Algiers, 23.1.72, *al-Muharrir*, 27.4.72, *al-Hawadith*, 12.1.73, 27.4.73; Muhsin, *al-Hayat*, 6.7.71; Abu Hisham, Fatah leader, *MENA*, 5.8.71 (*Beirut*, Beirut, 4.8.71); Bilal al-Hasan, *Shuun*, No. 4, September 1971, p. 171; Mazin al-Bandak, series of articles, *al-Qabas*, Kuwait, 1–6.7.76; *al-Huriyya*, 12.7.71; *Kul Shay*, 10.7.71; *Ila al-Amam*, 2.3.73.

51. Husayn, *Order*, Amman R., 1.11.72; Mraywud al-Tall, *Ma'ariv*, Tel Aviv, 30.1.72; *al-Ahram*, 28.1.72, 15.8.73; Hasan, *Le Monde*, Amman R., 9.6.76; for the emphasis on sovereignty, stability, security and order see Husayn, *al-Ray*, 4.6.72; *al-Dustur*, 22.8.72; Lawzi, PM, *al-Dustur*, 15.9.72; Zayd al-Rifa'i, PM, *al-Dustur*, 10.6.73.

52. Husayn, *Order*, Amman R., 1.11.72, 3.2.73, *al-Nahar*, 15.8.72, *Le Monde*, 27.10.72; *Washington Evening Star News*, 7.2.73, *Ma'ariv*, Tel Aviv, 28.1.72; for examples of Jordan's propaganda against Egypt see *al-Ray*, 25.7.71, 2.8.71, 7, 13, 16.4.72; *al-Dustur*, 1.3.72, 3.4.72; *Amman R.*, commentaries, 24.7.71, 10.4.72, 14.5.72.

53. Husayn, *Order*, Amman R., 1.9.71, 3.2.73, 3.4.73, *al-Nahar*, 24.8.71, *al-Usbu' al-Arabi*, 5.12.72, *al-Siyasa*, Kuwait, 5.2.72, *Ma'ariv*, 28.1.72, *NBC Television*, 21.1.73, *CBS Television*, 19.11.71, *US News and World Report*, 8.1.73, *NYT*, 12.12.71; *The Times*, 3.2.73; also Husayn's interviews to Western media quoted by *al-Nahar*, 21.11.71, 18.4.72, *al-Muharrir*, 7.6.72; see also *al-Ray*, Amman, 3.9.71; *Amman R.*, commentary, 4.9.71.

54. See Husayn, *al-Dustur*, 11.10.72, 2.11.72, 9.2.73, *Amman R.*, 3, 9.2.73, *al-Nahar*, 24.8.71, 15.8.72, *al-Siyasa*, 5.2.72, *al-Usbu' al-Arabi*, 5.12.72, *Le Monde*, 4.11.72,

The Times, 3.2.72, *CBS–TV*, "Face the Nation", 11.2.73, *NYT*, 2.4.72, *Washington Evening Star News*, 7.2.72, *BBC Television*, Panorama, 30.10.72, *International Herald Tribune*, 17.4.72, *US News and World Report*, 8.1.73, *NBC Television*, 21.1.73, *Ma'ariv*, 28.1.72; also interviews to Western media quoted by *al-Muharrir*, 26.11.71, 7.6.72, *al-Nahar*, 29.1.73; Salah, FM, *al-Ray*, 5.6.72; Rifa'i, PM, *al-Dustur*, 10.6.73; Abu Awda, *al-Anba*, 6.10.72; Moshe Zak, *Ma'ariv*, 6.4.80; Dan Margalit, *Ha'aretz*, 15.2.72, 15.9.72; also *Ha'aretz*, 27.8.72; *NYT*, 26.8.72; *al-Ray*, 14.6.63.

55. Husayn, *Order*, *Amman R.*, 3.2.73, *al-Ray*, 28.9.73 (*al-Bayraq*, Beirut), *al-Siyasa*, 5.2.72; Mustafa Dudin, general secretary of the Arab National Union, *Amman R.*, 12.6.72; on Jordanian attitude to PLA and Abu Hani Group see Nuhad Nusayba, *al-Nahar*, 27.12.72, 28.1.73; *Ila al-Amam*, 22.12.72; *al-Jumhuriyya*, 19.12.72, WAFA, 17.12.72; on the regime's attitude towards and propaganda against the fidai organizations see Husayn, *Akhbar al-Yawm*, 15.9.73, *al-Nahar*, 4.4.72; Lawzi, PM, *al-Nahar*, 22.3.73; Salah Abu Zayd, *al-Ahram*, 30.1.73; *al-Ray*, Amman, 21.2.72, 2.7.72; *al-Aqsa*, 7.6.72.

56. See Husayn, *al-Dustur*, 16, 24.3.72, 11.10.72, 2.11.72, *al-Nahar*, 4.4.72; Sa'd Jum'a, *al-Ray*, 22.3.72; Rashad al-Khatib, Fayiz Jabir, *al-Aqsa*, 19.4.72; Abd al-Hadi, *op. cit.*, pp. 410–415; see also *al-Hayat*, 22, 23.3.72; *al-Sabah*, Amman, 24.4.72; *al-Ray*, 22.3.72, 28.9.73; *al-Urdun*, 16.3.72; *al-Dustur*, Amman, 16.3.72; *al-Sayyad*, 30.3.72.

57. Husayn, *Amman R.*, 15, 23.3.72, 16.8.72, 1.11.72, *al-Ray*, 28.9.73 (al-Bayraq), *al-Nahar*, 24.8.72, *Beirut*, 2.7.72, *The Times*, 3.7.73; Lawzi, PM, *al-Dustur*, 6.9.72; speeches of members of House of Deputies, *Amman R.*, 11.6.73; *Amman R.*, commentaries, 14, 16.8.72; *al-Urdun*, 16.8.72; *al-Ray*, 5.9.72, 23.10.72; Rashad al-Shawwa, *Amman R.*, 1, 4–7.7.72, 16, 17.8.72, *al-Dustur*, Amman, 16.8.72.

58. See Abd al-Hadi, *op. cit.*, pp. 412–415; resolutions of the Arab National Union (Jordanian), *Amman R.*, 11.4.72; *al-Ray*, 2.4.72; *Amman R.*, commentary, 10.4.72; INA, 11.4.72; MENA, INA, 2, 3.4.72; *Fatah R.*, Cairo, 8.4.72; *al-Ahram*, 7.4.72; *al-Sayyad*, 30.3.72; *al-Hawadith*, 24.3.72.

59. Husayn, *Amman R.*, 10.10.72; *al-Ray*, 29.9.73, 14, 15.6.73; *al-Aqsa*, 20.6.73.

60. Bourguiba in Abd al-Hadi, *op. cit.*, pp. 242–264, *al-Nahar*, 6.7.73, *Newsweek*, 16.7.73; Husayn, *Amman R.*, 19.7.73, *al-Nahar*, 28.7.73; Zayd Rifa'i, PM, *al-Hayat*, 19.7.73, *al-Ray al-Amm*, Kuwait, 26.7.73; Jordanian memorandum to President Bourguiba, *al-Dustur*, 12.7.73; also *Akhbar al-Usbu'*, Amman, 20.7.73; *al-Ray*, 8.7.73; *Amman R.*, commentaries, 20.7.73; *al-Hawadith*, 17.8.73.

61. See Kamal Udwan, Abu Mazin, Abu Mahir, *Lecture(s)*; PDFLP, *al-Khatt*, pp. 53–55; PFLP, *al-Taqrir*, pp. 172–173, 189–190.

62. Abu Mahir, *Lecture*; PFLP, *al-Taqrir*, p. 172; PLO EC, *Political Programme*, submitted to 11th PNC, 6.1.73.

63. PDFLP, *al-Khatt*, pp. 45, 54–83.

64. PFLP, *al-Taqrir*, pp. 98, 171–182, 192–193, *al-Munadil al-Thawri*, No. 6, pp. 40, 128–129.

65. See Abu Iyad, *Fatah. R.*, Cairo, 21.1.73, *Filastin al-Thawra*, 28.4.73; declaration by Fatah's Revolutionary Council, 17.3.72, *Fatah*, Damascus, 22.3.72; PLO Planning Center, *Taqrir Siyasi Khass 'An Mashru' Jabhat al-Tahrir al-Wataniyya al-Filastiniyya al-Urduniyya*, No. 15, not for publication, 23.3.72; Political Programmes and declarations of the 10th PNC and of the 11th PNC in Hamid, *op. cit.*, pp. 195–245; for the propaganda campaign against Jordan see *Fatah R.*, Cairo, 19.3.72; *Fatah R.*, Dar'a, 5.6.72, 19.11.72, 25, 29.12.72, 18, 21.2.73, 5.3.73; *Filastin al-Thawra*, 10.1.73.

66. See Abu al-Walid (Sa'd Sail), *Lecture*; PFLP, *Ta'mim No. 5*; PFLP, *al-Taqrir*, pp. 183–184; on Hindawi affair see Husayn, MENA, *al-Nahar*, 27.11.72; *al-Jarida*, 28.11.72; *al-Nahar*, 26.11.72; *al-Hayat*, 25.11.72; on the exaggeration of the affair by the organizations see Abbas Murad, *op. cit.*, p. 148; Bilal al-Hasan, *Shuun*, No. 17, January 1973, pp. 198–199; *al-Yawm*, 9.12.72; on Abu Daud affair see Abu

Iyad, *Filastini*, pp. 161–165; *al-Nahar*, 16.2.72; Abu Daud recording of his confession during interrogations by the General Security, *Amman R.*, 19.2.72, 24.3.72; also his interview to *al-Nahar*, 1.4.73; Ma'an Abu Nuwwar, minister of information, *Amman R.*, 23.3.73; *Fatah R.*, Cairo, 17.2.73, 6.3.73; *Fatah R.*, Dar'a, 7, 15.3.73; also *Kul Shay*, 3.3.73.

67. See Abu Jihad, *Lecture*; PFLP, *Ta'mim Dakhili*, 31.5.72; Bilal al-Hasan, *Shuun*, No. 7, March 1972, pp. 238–239, *Shuun*, No. 10, June 1972, pp. 258–259; Fatah military spokesman, *MENA*, 1.4.72; interview with the so-called leader of the Jordanian National Front, *al-Siyasa*, Beirut, 27.5.72; official document of Fatah dated 6.10.72 signed by Abu Mahir, deputy general commander for administrative affairs, published in *al-Ray*, 18.10.72; for official Jordanian announcements on sabotage actions see *Amman R.*, 10.5.72, 15.12.72; see also *al-Ray*, 2, 18.10.72; *al-Siyasa*, Beirut, 7.10.72; INA, 24.2.73; *Fatah R.*, Dar'a, 24.2.72; *al-Hayat*, 1.4.72; *al-Nahar*, 19.4.72.

68. PLO–PCR, *Taqrir Khass*, No. 15, 23.3.72; A.M., Nahwa Jabhat Tahrir Wataniyya Filastiniyya Urduniyya, research by PLO-PCR, *Shuun*, No. 9, May 1972, pp. 38–43; PFLP, *al-Taqrir*, pp. 174, 189–196, *al-Munadil al-Thawri*, No. 6, pp. 128–129; PDFLP, *al-Khatt*, pp. 53–55; PDFLP, The National Action Programme, Political Bureau, Summer 1973 in *Barnamij al-Amal al-Watani al-Dimoqrati fi al-Urdun*, Beirut, August 1975 (Barnamij), pp. 57–60; the Political Programme, the 10th PNC, in Hamid, *op. cit.*, pp. 198–220; EC PLO, *The Political Programme, The Political Report*, both submitted to the 11th PNC, 6.1.73; Abu al-Walid, *Lecture*.

69. See Khalid al-Hasan (head of the Political Department EC PLO), Mudhakkara Tahliliyya Hawla Mashru' al-Malik Husayn, *Shuun*, No. 8, April 1972, pp. 258–266, *al-Ahram*, 17.3.72; EC PLO, *loc. cit.*; Fatah's Revolutionary Council declaration, *Fatah*, 22.3.72; the Political Programme, the 10th PNC, Hamid, *loc. cit.*; EC PLO announcement, 16.3.72, and other reactions by the organizations in Bilal al-Hasan, *Shuun*, No. 9, May 1972, pp. 247–253; PDFLP, *loc. cit.*; PFLP, *al-Taqrir*, pp. 189–190; PLO–PCR, *Taqrir No. 34*; Arafat, *al-Musawwar*, 31.3.72; Abu Mahir, *Lecture*; Naji Alush, *Ruz al-Yusuf*, 20.3.72, *Shuun*, No. 9, May 1972, pp. 237–239; Khalid al-Fahum, *Cairo R.*, 6.4.72; Najib al-Ahmad, *MENA*, 15.3.72; *al-Yawm*, 31.3.72; *Fatah*, Damascus, 15.3.72; *Fatah R.*, Cairo, 5.2.73; *Fatah R.*, Dar'a, 23.3.72, 5.2.73.

70. Isam Sakhnini (senior researcher in PLO's Palestine Research Centre), Muhawala Ula fi Utruhat Sharq al-Urdun al-Filastiniyya, *Shuun*, No. 49, September 1975, pp. 22–26, al-Kiyan al-Filastini 1964–1974, *Shuun*, No. 41/42, January/February 1975, pp. 46–72.

71. PLO–PCR, *Taqrir Siyasi*, No. 25, 22.8.72; Kamal Udwan, Tahlil al-Mawqif al-Siyasi, *Shuun*, No. 11, July 1972, pp. 274–281; PFLP, *al-Munadil al-Thawri*, No. 4, p. 10; Fatah, internal political report on crisis in Lebanon, May 1973, *al-Nahar*, 12.6.73; Isam Sakhnini, *Shuun*, No. 24, August 1973, pp. 227–228, *Shuun*, No. 25, September 1973, p. 214; Nabil Sha'ath, *Shuun*, No. 9, May 1972, p. 205; *Ila al-Amam*, 15.12.72, 26.1.73; Abu Mahir, Abu Salih, *Lectures*; Arafat, Kamal Nasir, *Akhir Sa'a*, 10.1.73; Abu Iyad, *Fatah R.*, Cairo, 21.1.73; Habash, *al-Nahar*, 13.8.73; *al-Nahar*, 5.5.73 (agreement between the PR and the Lebanese army); announcements by IDF spokesman.

72. See Khalid al-Hasan, *al-Ray al-Amm*, Kuwait, 29.1.73, *al-Sayyad*, 1.3.73; Abu Jihad, *Lecture*; Kamal Udwan, *Lecture*, *al-Ahram*, 21.4.72; Bilal al-Hasan, *Shuun*, No. 16, December 1972, pp. 223–224; PFLP, *Ta'mim*, No. 5; PDFLP, *al-Munadil; Ila al-Amam*, 26.1.73; *al-Hayat*, *al-Anwar*, *al-Jarida*, 20.10.72; *al-Nahar*, 19, 20.10.72, 24.1.73; *al-Hawadith*, 14.4.72 (by Lawzi), 12.1.73; *al-Sayyad*, 18.1.73; *Kul Shay*, 3.2.73.

73. See Naji Alush, *Shuun*, No. 8, April 1972, pp. 224–228; Habash, PFLP, *Bulletin No. 2*, April 1972; Abu Shihab (leader of the PRFLP), *al-Anwar*, 14.3.72; *al-Hadaf*, 25.3.72, 1.4.72; *MENA*, 7, 11.3.72; *al-Muharrir*, *al-Nahar*, 8.3.72; *al-*

Hayat, 9.3.72; *al-Yawm*, 9.3.72, authoritative source in the PFLP.

74. Hani al-Hasan, *Lecture*, in Fatah's Course for its cadres, 23.8.72; Abu Mazin, Kamal Udwan, *Lecture(s)*; Abu Iyad, *Fatah R.*, Cairo, 21.1.73; Abu Iyad, Abu Yusuf, *al-Nahar*, 1.2.73; Abu Adnan, PDFLP leader, *al-Siyasa*, Kuwait, 17.6.73; Arafat, *al-Nahar*, 2.7.72; *al-Hadaf*, 13.1.73, protocol discussions of PLO information delegation with the Russian Committee for Afro-Asian Solidarity in Moscow; the Political Programme, the 11th PNC, Hamid, *op. cit.*, pp. 225–237.

75. PFLP, *al-Taqrir*, pp. 99–104, *Ta'mim No. 5*, *al-Munadil al-Thawri*, internal pamphlet No. 4, August 1972, pp. 13–15, *Ta'mim Dakhili*, 31.5.72; Habash, *al-Nahar*, 18.3.73; *al-Yawm*, 10.5.72, the PFLP's answers to the newspaper's questions; *al-Yawm*, 30.3.73, PFLP responsible source.

76. PDFLP, text of the plan for national unity, *al-Nahar*, *al-Anwar*, 5.4.72; PDFLP, *al-Munadil*; PDFLP, *Ta'mim Sari'*, No. 2, to all active members and candidates on the questions of national unity and a United National Front, 21.5.72 (Ta'mim No. 2); Hawatma, *Kul Shay*, 3.6.72.

77. ALF, *Wahda*, memoranda submitted to the PPC, 6.4.72, and the 11th PNC, 6.1.73, pp. 97–108.

78. PLO–PCR, text of plan for national unity, *MENA*, 7.4.72; Fatah, Maktab al-Ta'bia wa al-Tanzim, *Mashru' al-Barnamij li-Tawhid Fasail al-Thawra al-Filastiniyya*, submitted by the EC to the PPC, 6–9.4.72; Nabil Sha'ath, Special Report on the PPC, *Shuun*, No. 9, May 1972, pp. 205–215; Bilal al-Hasan, *Shuun*, No. 10, June 1972, pp. 256–259; PFLP, *Ta'mim*, No. 5, al-Munadil al-Thawri, No. 4, August 1972, pp. 13–15; PDFLP, *Ta'mim*, No. 2, *al-Munadil; declaration by the 10th PNC, Fatah*, 13.4.72; statement by Fatah Central committee, *Fatah R.*, Cairo, 2.4.72; Arafat, *Akhir Sa'a*, 12.4.72, *Fatah R.*, Cairo, 27.8.72, *MENA*, 6.4.72; Abu Iyad, Kamal Udwan, Arafat, quoted by Salim al-Lawzi, *al-Hawadith*, 14.4.72; Abu Jihad, *Lecture*; *MENA*, 12.4.72, Talal Salman report to *al-Anwar*.

79. EC PLO, *Report*, by the National Unity Committee submitted to the 11th PNC, 6.1.73; PFLP, *Ta'mim*, 31.5.72, *Ta'mim No. 6.*, 1.1.73, PFLP, *al-Munadil al-Thawri*, No. 4, August 1972, pp. 13–15; PDFLP, *Ta'mim No. 2*, 21.5.72; Fatah, Lebanon Region, internal *News bulletin No. 1010/B*, 25.5.72; Sa'id Hamud, General Notes on 11th PNC, *Shuun*, No. 18, February 1973, pp. 188–190; Bilal al-Hasan, report on the 11th PNC, *Shuun*, No. 18, February 1973, pp. 184–187; Arafat, *MENA*, 6.1.73, *Ruz al-Yusuf*, 15.1.73, *Fatah R.*, Dar'a, 3.2.73; Muhammad Sabih, secretary of the 11th PNC, *MENA*, 15.1.73; see also *al-Sayyad*, 18, 25.1.73; *Ila al-Amam*, 12.1.73; *Kul Shay*, 13, 20.1.73; *al-Usbu' al-Arabi*, 15.1.73; *al-Anwar*, 8, 13, 26.1.73.

80. See Ahmad al-Yamani (Abu Mahir), PFLP leader, *al-Yawm*, 28.3.73, *al-Hadaf*, 7.4.73; *al-Yawm*, 30.3.73, PFLP responsible source; PFLP, *al-Munadil al-Thawri*, No. 6, July 1973, pp. 96–105; Abu Iyad, Habash, *al-Nahar*, 18.3.73; Zuhayr Muhsin, *al-Nahar*, 10.9.73.

81. Nabil Sha'ath, Special Report on the PPC, *loc. cit.*; PDFLP, *al-Munadil; al-Anba*, Jerusalem, 2.4.72; *al-Quds*, Jerusalem-East, 14.3.72; *al-Ray*, Amman, 2.4.72; *INA*, 1, 3.4.72; *al-Ahram*, 2.4.72; *Fatah*, 5.4.72.

82. Sha'ath also proposed that the PNC be expanded through representation of the Palestinian masses by means of trade unions and workers associations, democratic representation of the militia and of the Palestinian concentrations in countries where it was possible to conduct open activity and also by increased representation of research and planning institutes connected with the PLO. PDFLP, *al-Munadil*; Nabil Sha'ath, *loc. cit.*; Clovis Maqsud, *al-Ahram*, 12.4.72; Arafat, *MENA*, 12.4.72, Talal Salman's report to *al-Anwar; Salah Khalaf*, *MENA*, 10.4.72; *al-Hawadith*, Salim al-Lawzi, 14.4.72; also *al-Nahar*, 24.1.73; *MENA*, 11.4.72; *Kul Shay*, 13.1.73, 3.2.73.

83. See PFLP, *Ta'mim No. 5; declaration by the 11th PNC*, *al-Anwar*, 13.1.73; Hammid, *op. cit.*, p. 38, mentions that the 11th PNC had 180 members; Bilal al-Hasan, *Shuun*, No. 18, February 1973, pp. 184–187 (also mentions that the PNC

had 180 members); Sami al-Attari, *Dam. R.*, 19.1.73; also *INA*, 7.1.73; *MENA*, 7, 12.1.73; *al-Usbu' al-Arabi*, 15.1.73; *Kul Shay*, 3.2.73; *Ila al-Amam*, 26.1.73.

84. See Musbah al-Budayri, chief-of-staff PLA, *al-Qabas*, Kuwait, 12.7.77; *MENA*, 19.4.72, quoting Budayri; Kamal Udwan, *Lecture*; Abu Iyad, *Shuun*, No. 5, November 1971, pp. 29–46; *Ila al-Amam*, quoting Abu Iyad, 26.1.73; Abu Jihad, *Lecture*; Nuhad Nusayba, *al-Nahar*, 21.12.72, 28.1.73; Zuhayr Muhsin, *al-Nahar*, 10.9.72; Attari, *Dam. R.*, 19.1.73; Bilal al-Hasan, *loc. cit.*, *Shuun*, No. 11, July 1972, p. 228; EC PLO, *Report*, by the National Unity Committee, submitted to the 11th PNC, 6.1.73; PFLP, *Ta'mim No. 6*, 1.1.73; *Sawt Filastin*, organ of the PLA, January, February, April, May, June 1972, July, August 1973; *al-Sayyad*, citing Arafat, 18.1.73; *al-Hawadith*, citing Arafat, 12.1.73; *Kul Shay*, 13.1.73; *al-Nahar*, 9.1.73; *al-Hayat*, 23.4.72; *al-Dustur*, Amman, 16.6.72.

85. PDFLP, *al-Munadil; al-Hadaf*, 6.1.73, Protocol of discussions between PLO information delegation visiting USSR and members of the Journalists' Union in Leningrad; Arafat, *al-Difa'*, 26.12.69, *Moroccan News Agency*, 24.11.69, *Beirut R.*, 15.6.71, *Akhir Sa'a*, 25.3.70; Abu Iyad, *Fatah R.*, Cairo, 3.6.71, *al-Yawm*, 25.3.72; Abu Mazin, *Lecture*; Khalid al-Hasan, *al-Musawwar*, 9.7.71, interview to *Reuter*, 10.10.72; Kamal Nasir, *MENA (al-Nahar)*, 29.9.72, 2.10.72, *al-Akhbar*, 17.10.72; Fahum, *MENA*, 25.3.72, *Fatah R.*, Cairo, 7.10.72; Attari, *al-Muharrir*, 28.3.72; PLO–PCR, *Taqrir Siyasi*, No. 15, 23.3.72; Hawatma, *Kul Shay*, 14.7.73; *Shuun*, No. 15, November 1972, Bilal al-Hasan, pp. 219–220, Naji Alush, p. 226; announcements by Fatah, *al-Hayat*, 21.3.72, 3.10.72; *MENA*, 27.5.71, quoting Fatah circles; *MENA*, 18.3.72, Fatah reliable sources; *Fatah R.*, Dar'a, 29.9.72; *PLO R.*, commentary, 28.6.69; *al-Usbu' al-Arabi*, 10.4.72; *Ila al-Amam*, 13.10.70; *al-Nahar*, 30.9.72, 2.10.72; *al-Muharrir*, 29.9.72; *al-Quds*, 19.3.72; PFLP–GC, Abu al-Abbas, *Muhimmatina fi al-Marhala al-Rahina*, n.d., pp. 8–12.

86. PDFLP, *Barnamij*, pp. 37–60, 68–77; PDFLP, al-Khatt al-Amm lil-Barnamij al-Marhali fi al-Manatiq al-Muhtalla wa al-Urdun, resolutions of the fourth session of the PDFLP Central Committee, August 1973, in *al-Wad' fi al-Manatiq al-Muhtalla wa Muhimmat al-Thawra*, Beirut, August 1975 (al-Wad'), pp. 7–9, 120–124; PDFLP, *al-Wad' al-Rahin fi al-Manatiq al-Muhtalla wa Muhimmatina*, n.d., pp. 38–39; Hawatma, *al-Huriyya*, 20.8.73, 19.2.79, *al-Nahar*, 17.8.73.

87. This section is based *inter alia* on my discussions with politicians and leaders of the West Bank.

88. On the views of *al-Sha'b* see, for example, editorials written mostly by Abu Ghassan (Ali al-Khatib) under the title "Good Morning", *al-Sha'b*, 14, 15, 16, 17, 23, 24, 27.8.72, 23.10.72, 7, 8.1.73, 29.6.73, 12, 17, 19, 20, 26.7.73; on *al-Fajr*'s views see editorials and articles in *al-Fajr*, 12.5.72, 9, 23.6.72, 9, 23.9.72, 7.10.72, 4, 11.11.72, 1, 16, 30.12.72, 17, 20.2.73, 10, 17.3.73, 4.4.73, 14.7.73, 4.8.73.

89. The Jordanian Municipal Law, see *al-Jarida al-Rasmiyya*, No. 1, 125, Law No. 29, 1.5.55; for the views of the PLO and organizations see Arafat, *MENA*, 24.3.72; Abu Lutuf, *Lecture*; Kamal Udwan, *Lecture*; PFLP, *al-Taqrir*, pp. 155–164; PLO–PCR, *Taqrir Khass*, No. 15, 23.3.72; Kamal Nasir, *al-Hayat*, 30.12.71, *al-Usbu' al-Arabi*, Beirut, 21.2.72, *Fatah R.*, Cairo, 26.11.71, 26.12.71; *al-Hadaf*, 14.4.73; *MENA*, 10.2.72, EC PLO declaration; *MENA*, 13.2.72, on the resolutions of the EC; see also *al-Watan*, organ of the Jordanian Communist Party in the West Bank; *leaflets*, distributed in the West Bank and signed by the Popular Resistance Front in the West Bank, mid-January 1972, early March 1972, late March 1972; *al-Kifah*, 24.12.71; *al-Quds*, 11, 22.2.72, 1.3.72; *al-Sha'b*, 3.6.73; for incitements against the municipal elections and candidates see Arafat, *al-Mujahid*, Algiers, 23.1.72, *al-Quds*, 1.3.72, *MENA*, 22.3.72; Kamal Nasir, *al-Usbu' al-Arabi*, 24, 26.1.72, 5, 15.2.72, 22, 23, 26.3.72; *Fatah R.*, Dar'a, 26, 28.3.72; *Fatah*, Damascus, 26.1.72, 22.3.72, 5.4.72; *al-Hadaf*, 12.12.72, 18.3.72.

90. On the municipal elections see Shabtai Teveth, series of articles under the title "The West Bank after Five Years", including reliable details on the municipal

elections, *Ha'aretz*, 8, 15, 22.9.72; also *Ha'aretz*, *Ma'ariv*, 29.3.72; *Ha'aretz*, 31.3.72; *al-Hawadith*, 14.4.72; *al-Sabah*, Amman, 27.3.72; *al-Fajr*, 12.5.72; for the attitudes and assessments of the IMG, see Brigadier-General Raphael Vardi, commander, Judea and Samaria Region 1967–1973, *Ha'aretz*, 11, 12, 13, 15.4.82; Colonel David Farhi, adviser on Arab affairs of the Judea and Samaria Command, *Ma'rakhot*, No. 231, July 1973, pp. 9–14; for analysis of the election results by Israeli researchers see Shaul Mish'al, Judea and Samaria: Anatomy of the Municipal Elections, *Hamizrah Hehadash (Hebrew)*, Vols. 1–2, 1974, pp. 63–67; Dr Michael Yizhar, Political Aspects of the Municipal Elections (Hebrew), *Medina ve Mimshal*, Jerusalem, Vol. 4, 1974; for Jordan's policy see Husayn, *Amman R.*, 23.3.72; government statement, *al-Dustur*, 9.12.71; Ya'qub Abu Ghosh, minister of interior, *Amman R.*, 11.12.71; *al-Dustur*, Amman, 27.11.71, 1.2.72, 1.4.72; *al-Urdun*, 9.12.71; *al-Aqsa*, 16.3.72; *Amman al-Masa*, 11.12.71, 15.1.72; *Amman R.*, 16.12.71; *Fatah R.*, Cairo, 8.7.72.

91. See Kamal Udwan, Abu Lutuf, Abu Mahir, *Lecture(s)*; declaration by the PPC, 10.4.72, *Fatah*, 12.4.72; *al-Quds*, 3.5.72.

92. On the local leaders' attitude towards the self-administration proposals see Ma'zuz al-Masri, *al-Quds*, 26.9.73, *al-Fajr*, 22.9.73; Hilmi Hanun, Elyas Frayj, *al-Fajr*, 29.9.73; also Arabi Awad, *Shuun*, No. 32, April 1974, pp. 38–42; for the campaign against the traditional leadership see Abu Ghassan, *al-Sha'b*, 23.8.72, 11, 12.2.73, 3, 28.5.73, 16.6.73, 12.7.73, 10, 21.9.73; *al-Fajr*, 10.3.73, 27.7.73.

93. See "A Well-Known Palestinian Politician", *al-Quds*, 16, 19, 26.3.72; *al-Quds*, 10, 26.4.72, 9, 10.5.72; *al-Bashir*, 22.4.72; *al-Fajr*, 23.9.72; Abd al-Hafiz Muharib, *Shuun*, No. 9, May 1972, pp. 266–267, responses by Ma'zuz al-Masri, Anwar Nusayba, Hamdi Kan'an and Ja'bari.

94. See *al-Sha'b*, 6.3.72, 9, 14, 16.5.73; *al-Quds*, 6, 8.3.73, 9.5.73; also *al-Sha'b*, *al-Quds*, *al-Fajr*, 12–30.4.73.

95. Among the most prominent signatories of the second memorandum were Hilmi al-Muhtasib, Anwar al-Khatib, Yusuf al-Najjar, Karim Khalaf, Abd al-Jawwad Salih, Dr Alfred Tubasi, Hikmat and Ma'zuz al-Masri, the pharmacist Hilmi Shakhashir, Andalib al-Amad, Dr Hatim Abu Ghazala, Dr Walid Qamhawi, Elyas Frayj, Hikmat al-Hamuri, Mustafa Milhim and Dr Haydar Abd al-Shafi. Text of the memorandum to the chairman of the Security Council, *al-Sha'b*, 23.7.73; another memorandum to the chairman of the Security Council, signed by representatives of trade unions and popular organizations, *al-Quds*, 24.7.73; petition to the secretary-general UN 30.8.73; see also Hawatma, *al-Nahar*, 17.8.73.

96. For views of supporters of an independent Palestinian Entity see, as examples, Abu Shalbaya, *al-Anba*, 15.2.72, 12.4.72, 16.8.72, 27.6.73, 20.7.73, 1, 3, 5.8.73, *al-Bashir*, 19.2.72; Faruqi, *al-Bashir*, 18.3.72; also *al-Bashir*, 18.3.72; *al-Anba*, 12.2.73; for opposition to Nusayba's mediation see telegram to PM Golda Meir, 15.2.72, signed, *inter alia*, by Abu Shalbaya, Ibrahim D'aybis, Jamil Hamad, Rizq Safur, Aziz Shahada and Ahmad Barham; also *al-Quds*, 11, 28.2.73, 14.3.73; on *al-Quds*'s views see editorials of *al-Quds*, 19, 20.3.72, 24, 25, 27.8.72, 8, 9, 23.10.72, 13.11.72, 21.1.73, 9, 21, 24.6.73, 8, 11, 19, 26, 31.7.73.

97. Ja'bari, *al-Anba*, 19, 23.3.72, 17.6.73, 29.7.73, 7.8.73, *al-Quds*, 30.4.72; Abu Shalbaya, *al-Anba*, 3.8.73.

98. On Fatah's assessment see Abu Lutuf, Abu Mahir, Abu al-Walid, Abu Jihad, Abu Salih, *Lecture(s)*; PLO–PCR, *Taqrir*, No. 25, 22.8.72; No. 34, 15.12.72; Fatah, Asifa HQ, *Ta'mim Dakhili*, No. 3, 4.4.73; on the PFLP assessment see PFLP, the Occupied Territory Command (OTC), *al-Barnamij al-Siyasi wa al-Askari fi al-Ard al-Muhtalla*, September 1972; PFLP, *al-Taqrir*, pp. 145–171; PFLP, *Ta'mim No. 5*, 12.12.72; PFLP, *al-Munadil al-Thawri*, No. 4, August 1972, p. 10, No. 6, July 1973, p. 125; Abu Himam (Haytham al-Ayyubi, PFLP Military Arm leader), *al-Hadaf*, 31.7.71; PFLP, internal pamphlet, *al-Amal fi al-Ard al-Muhtalla*, 4.9.71.

99. See *IDF* announcements, *Ha'aretz* and *Ma'ariv* during this period; *Ha'aretz*, 18.5.81; see also Habash, *al-Nahar*, 11.7.73, 13.8.73, *al-Yawm*, 11.7.73, *Fatah R.*, Cairo, 12.3.73, *News Agencies*, 17.3.73; Abu Iyad, Abu Yusuf, *al-Nahar*, 1.2.73; *Fatah R.*, Dar'a, 20.8.73; Arafat, *MENA*, 6.1.73, 16.9.73, *Ruz al-Yusuf*, 15.1.73; Karim Khalaf, *al-Bashir*, 12.5.73.

100. On the PLO's and organizations' policy see declaration by the 10th PNC and the 11th PNC, Hamid, *op. cit.*, pp. 220–245; Kamal Udwan, Abu Lutuf, *Lecture(s)*; Abu Iyad, *Fatah R.*, Cairo, 21.1.73; Fatah Lebanon Region, internal *News bulletin No. 1010/B*, 25.5.72, *No. 1011*, 30.6.72; Habash, *al-Nahar*, 11.7.73, 5.8.73; Hawatma, *al-Nahar*, 17.8.73, *Kul Shay*, 14.7.73; PFLP, OTC, *op. cit*; *Fatah R.*, Cairo, 21, 30.8.72; *Fatah R.*, Dar'a, 20.10.72; for threats against Shawwa see *Fatah R.*, Cairo, 20, 21, 26, 30.7.72, 21.8.72, 21.9.72, 28.10.72, 28.1.73, 12, 14, 20, 28.2.73, 1.3.73, 3.8.73; *Fatah R.*, Dar'a, 23.10.72, 14.2.73; for threats against Ja'bari see *Fatah R.*, Cairo, 4.9.72; *Fatah R.*, Dar'a, 27.9.72, 20.10.72, 31.12.72.

101. See *Barnamij al-Jabha al-Wataniyya al-Filastiniyya fi al-Ard al-Muhtalla*, August 1973, pamphlet, 15.9.73; *al-Watan*, early April 1972, end September 1972, mid-September 1973; leaflets signed by the Palestinian Resistance Front – West Bank, early April 1973, early November 1973; resolutions of the EC PLO regarding the PNF, *MENA*, 6.9.72; resolutions of the 11th PNC, Hamid, *op. cit.*, p. 236; statement by the EC, *Fatah R.*, Cairo, 22.9.73; *The Political Report*, submitted by the EC to the 11th PNC 6.1.73; Arabi Awad, secretary of the Commanding Committee of the JCP, *al-Tali'a*, Cairo, March 1974, pp. 71–73, *Shuun*, No. 32, April 1974, pp. 38–42, *al-Nahar*, 30.5.74; *Summary of the Political Report*, Palestinian Communist Party – West Bank Command, late August 1979, p. 63; *al-Safir*, Beirut, 28, 29, 31.8.81, symposium of representatives of Fatah, PFLP, PDFLP, Sa'iqa, Palestinian Communist Party – West Bank; PFLP, *al-Taqrir*, pp. 155–164; PFLP, *al-Munadil al-Thawri*, No. 6, July 1973, p. 124; Ahmad al-Yamani, *al-Yawm*, 28.3.73; *al-Hadaf*, 30.9.73; PFLP, *Ta'mim*, No. 5, 12.12.72, No. 6, 1.1.73; Maluh, member of the PFLP Political Bureau, *al-Hadaf*, 22.9.79; PLO–PCR, *Taqrir*, No. 15; PDFLP, resolutions of the fourth session of the Central Committee, August 1973, *al-Wad'*, p. 123; *al-Quds*, 18.1.73.

102. See Sadat, *Cairo R.*, 20.1.74, 1.5.74, 1.6.74, 14.3.76, *al-Ahram*, 7.6.74, 7.9.74, 19.5.75, *al-Jumhuriyya*, 15, 17.5.75, *MENA*, 3.2.75, *al-Bayraq*, Beirut, 9.1.75, *al-Siyasa*, *al-Ahram*, 9.9.75, *al-Sayyad*, 22.8.74; Qudus, *Akhbar al-Yawm*, 26.1.74, 23.2.74.

103. For the text of the Algiers summit top-secret resolutions see *al-Nahar*, 4.12.73; the summit declaration, Mahmud Riyad, SG AL, *MENA*, 28.11.73, *Algiers R.*, 28.11.73; Fuad Naffa', Lebanese FM, *Beirut R.*, 1, 5.12.73; Sa'd al-Sabah, Kuwait defence minister, *Beirut R.*, 20.11.73, *SANA*, 1.12.73; Sayyid Mar'i, chief assistant of President Sadat, *al-Ahram*, 30.11.73; Faysal, *MENA*, 28.11.73; Franjiyya, *Beirut R.*, 7.12.73; on Egypt's attitude see Sadat, *Cairo R.*, 16.10.73, *al-Hayat*, 28.11.73, *MENA*, 27, 28.11.73; the Egyptian press, 21–29.11.73; on Syria's see Asad, *MENA*, 28, 29.11.73; *al-Thawra*, 29.11.73; Abd al-Ghani al-Rafi'i, assistant Syrian FM, *Dam. R.*, 22.11.73; *Dam. R.*, commentaries, 21, 25, 26, 27, 29.11.73; on Algeria's see Huwari Boumedienne, *MENA*, 28.11.73, 2–3.12.73, *Kuwait R.*, 1.12.73, *al-Jumhuriyya*, 4.12.73; on Tunisia's see Habib Bourguiba, *al-Ahram*, *MENA*, 2.12.73; Muhammad al-Masmudi, FM, *al-Hayat*, 24.11.73; on Iraq's see Murtada Abd al-Baqi, FM, *al-Diyar*, Beirut, 17.11.73; *al-Thawra*, Baghdad, 21.11.73; *al-Jumhuriyya*, Baghdad, 27, 28.11.73; also Hawatma, *al-Muhimmat al-Rahina lil-Thawra al-Filastiniyya*, January 1974 (Muhimmat), pp. 56–57; Zuhayr Muhsin, *al-Anwar*, 3.12.73; Arafat, *MENA*, 24.11.73; Qaddumi, *Fatah R.*, Cairo, 28.11.73; also *Ruz al-Yusuf*, 3.12.73; *Akhir Sa'a*, 5.12.73; *al-Sayyad*, 29.11.73, 6.12.73; *al-Anwar*, 1.12.73.

104. See Husayn, *L'Orient–Le Jour*, 11.12.73, *Amman R.*, 6.12.73, *al-Siyasa*, Kuwait, 3.12.73, *al-Dustur*, Amman, 2.12.73, *al-Anwar*, 5.11.73; Bahjat al-Talhuni, *Amman R.*, 26, 27, 28.11.73; Zayd al-Rifa'i, *al-Anwar*, 6.11.73, *Amman R.*,

12.5.74; Jordanian top-secret memorandum to the superpowers entitled Jordan's Policy Concerning the Arab–Israel Problem, *al-Nahar*, 5.12.73; *al-Ray*, 27.11.73; *Amman R.*, commentaries, 27.11.73, 7.12.73; Lieutenant-Colonel David, The Jordanian Army in the Yom Kippur War (Hebrew), *Ma'rakhot*, Tel Aviv, No. 266, October–November 1978, pp. 28–36; also see *al-Hayat*, 25.11.73; *al-Ahram*, 24.11.73; *al-Sayyad*, 25.10.73, 6.12.73; *al-Muharrir*, 10.12.73.

105. See Sadat, *Cairo R.*, 31.10.73, 23.7.74, 23.10.74, 29.3.75, 4.9.75, *MENA*, 20.1.74, 24.2.74, 17.3.74, 13.4.74, 1, 26.6.74, 7, 22.9.74, *al-Ahram*, 30.3.75, *al-Hawadith*, 26.4.74, 31.3.75, 3.2.76, *al-Sayyad*, 26.6.74, 22.8.74, *al-Anwar*, 6.2.74, *al-Usbu' al-Arabi*, 8.10.74; Isma'il Fahmi, FM, *MENA*, 13.10.74, 24.3.75, *al-Ahram*, 31.5.74, *al-Hawadith*, 13.9.74; also Ahmad Baha al-Din, *al-Ahram*, 2.11.74; *MENA*, 24.7.74, announcement by the ASU.

106. Sadat, *Cairo R.*, 30.10.74, *MENA*, 30.3.74, 24.10.74, 19.1.75, 25.8.76, *al-Anwar*, 22.6.75, *al-Hawadith*, 21.3.75, *al-Siyasa*, 13.8.76, *Observer*, 24.10.74, *NBC Television*, 5.11.75; Fahmi, *al-Ahram*, 31.5.74, *al-Musawwar*, 22.11.74, *Cairo R.*, 13.12.74, *MENA*, 1.10.74.

107. See Sadat, *MENA*, 23.1.74, 24.2.74, 18, 30.3.74, 22.6.74, 6.9.74, 9.10.74, *Cairo R.*, 14.4.75, *al-Siyasa* (*MENA*), 11.4.75, *al-Nahar*, 14.4.75, *al-Anwar* (*MENA*), 10.1.75; Fahmi, *al-Jumhuriyya*, 1.8.74, *MENA*, 13.10.74, *al-Hawadith*, 13.9.74; Kissinger, *op. cit.*, pp. 956, 1033, 1075–1076, 1089.

108. See Asad, *Dam. R.*, 25.2.75, 5.3.75, 26.6.75, *al-Ba'th*, 4.6.74, 17.9.74, 19.12.74, *al-Thawra*, 16.10.73, 9.3.74, 3.6.74, *al-Ray al-Amm*, Kuwait, 18.10.75, *al-Ahram*, 6.7.74; Khaddam, *al-Sayyad*, 24.1.74, *al-Ray al-Amm*, Kuwait, 5.2.74, *Lecture*, 23.1.78, Ba'th party internal circular, March 1978; Zuhayr Muhsin, *al-Talai' wa al-Jamahir*, 3.11.73, *al-Hayat*, 1.2.74, *Ahadith*, p. 12; George Sadqani, minister of information, *al-Sayyad*, 14.2.74; Ahmad Iskandar, minister of information, *SANA*, 14.5.75; Official Spokesman, *al-Thawra*, 19, 21.12.73; declarations by the National Command, *al-Thawra*, 16.11.73, *al-Ba'th*, 5.8.75; declarations by the Ba'th Regional Command, *al-Ba'th*, 21.6.74, 21.4.75; Bassam al-Asali, *al-Ba'th*, 16.10.75; declaration by the Ba'th 5th NC, *al-Ba'th*, 31.5.74; also *al-Hayat*, 25.10.73.

109. See Asad, *Dam. R.*, 8.3.75, 25.2.75, 20.3.75, *SANA*, 26.2.75, *al-Ahram*, 6.7.74, *al-Hawadith*, 26.6.75; Muhsin, *Ahadith*, pp. 5–13, 22–30, *al-Talai'*, 25.12.73, *al-Balagh*, Beirut, 31.12.73, *al-Sayyad*, 1.1.74, *Shuun*, No. 30, February 1974, pp. 42–48; declaration by the Ba'th National Command, *al-Ba'th*, 4.9.75.

110. See Husayn, *Amman R.*, 1, 6.12.73, 10.2.74, 1.5.74, 8.8.74, *al-Dustur*, 23.11.73, 2.12.73, 2, 13.5.74, 18.6.74, 29.10.74, *al-Hawadith*, 4.1.74, *al-Siyasa*, Kuwait (*Amman R.*), 3.12.74, *al-Anwar*, 5.11.73, 23.6.74, *al-Hayat*, 29.8.74, *L'Orient – Le Jour*, 11.12.73; Rifa'i, *al-Dustur*, 22.12.73, 13.5.74, 2.9.74, *al-Anwar*, 6.11.73, 25.6.74, *al-Hawadith*, 30.11.73; Talhuni, *Amman R.*, 27, 28.11.73; top-secret Jordanian memorandum to the superpowers, *al-Nahar*, 5.12.73; see also *al-Dustur*, Amman, 29.11.73, 9.12.73 (the Senate response to Husayn's speech), *al-Ray*, 27.11.73; *Ruz al-Yusuf*, 3.12.73; *al-Jumhur*, Beirut, 6.12.73.

111. See Husayn, *Amman R.*, 8, 29.8.74, *al-Dustur*, 2.12.73, 2.5.74, 18.6.74, 29.10.74, *al-Anwar*, 6.11.73, 23.6.74, *al-Hayat*, 29.8.74; Rifa'i, *al-Dustur*, 22.12.73, 13.5.74, 2.9.74, *al-Anwar*, 25.6.74; Kissinger, *op. cit.*, pp. 786–787, 846–848, 976–978, 1037–1039, 1138–1139; Moshe Zak, *Ma'ariv*, 31.3.80, 6.4.80, 10.9.82; Mati Golan, *Ha'aretz*, 3.9.82; Rabin, *Kol Israel*, Jerusalem broadcasting, 16.4.80.

112. See Sadat, *Cairo R.*, 31.10.73, *MENA*, 23.1.74, 29.3.74 *al-Ahram*, al-Anwar, 18.5.75, in Anis Mansur, *October*, Cairo, 30.11.80, *al-Ahram*, 2.6.74, *Observer*, 6.10.74, *al-Nahar*, 14.4.74; Fahmi, *al-Ahram*, 31.5.74, 11.6.74, *al-Akhbar*, 18.6.74; Baha al-Din, *al-Ahram*, 31.5.74, 7, 8.6.74; Kissinger, *op. cit.*, p. 1037; also see Abu Iyad, *Filastini*, pp. 205–210, *al-Nahar*, 12.2.74, *al-Dustur*, Beirut, 19.11.73; Arafat, *al-Ahram*, 28.11.73, 18.1.74, 17.5.74, *al-Sayyad*, 8.11.73; Fatah's spokesman, *Fatah R.*, Cairo, 4.11.73; on the talks between Fatah's and Egypt's leaders see also *al-Ahram*, 26.3.74, 7.4.74, 2, 18.5.74; *Akhbar al-Yawm*,

2.2.74; *al-Musawwar*, 21.12.73, 18.1.74; *Ruz al-Yusuf*, 3.6.74; *al-Jumhuriyya*, 6.6.74; *al-Nahar*, 7.1.74, 23.5.74 (Fuad Matar).

113. See PLO, *The Covenant*; Abu Iyad, *al-Balagh*, Beirut, 24.11.73, in Shafiq al-Hut, *Bayna al-Tih*, pp. 135–140, *INA*, 9.12.73, *al-Yawm*, 24.12.73; Arafat, *MENA* (*al-Muharrir*), 31.10.73, *al-Sayyad*, 8.11.73, *al-Dustur*, Beirut, 19.11.73, *INA* (*MENA*), 10.12.73; Shafiq al-Hut, Itlala Ala Tahaddiyyat Marhala Jadida, *Shuun*, No. 28, December 1973, pp. 118–126; Sakhnini, *Shuun*, No. 28, December 1973, pp. 178–182.

114. See Abu Iyad, *Filastini*, pp. 219–222; *Filastinuna*, No. 11, November 1960, p. 3; *al-Nahar*, 28.12.73, the CC PLO resolutions.

115. See Abu Iyad (Salah Khalaf), *Filastini*, pp. 200–225, Afkar Jadida Amam Marhala Ghamida, *Shuun*, No. 29, January 1974, pp. 5–10, *al-Balagh*, 24.12.73, *Fatah R.*, Cairo, 28.11.73, 28.3.74, 8.6.74, *Fatah R.*, San'a, 6.3.74, *Libya R.*, 14.3.74, *al-Nahar*, 12.12.73, 1.1.74, *INA*, 9.12.73, 15.3.74, *Filastin al-Thawra*, 21.8.74, *Shuun*, No. 30, February 1974, pp. 24–27, 53–56; Arafat, *Fatah R.*, Cairo, 30.1.74, 26.3.74, 31.5.74, *Fatah R.*, San'a, 24.1.74, *Filastin al-Thawra*, 29.1.74, 27.2.74, *MENA*, 12.1.74 (*al-Diyar*), 5.3.74, *al-Ahram*, 28.11.73, 22.3.74, *INA*, 7.4.74; Faruq al-Qaddumi, al-Nidal al-Siyasi al-Filastini, *Shuun*, No. 39, November 1974, pp. 6–10, *Fatah R.*, Cairo, 18.2.74; Khalid al-Hasan, *al-Jumhuriyya*, Cairo, 17.6.74; Munir Shafiq, *al-Yawm*, 10.1.74; Sakhnini, Mukawwanat al-Qarar fi al-Majlis al-Watani al-Filastini, *Shuun*, No. 35, July 1974 (Mukawwanat), pp. 4–11, *Shuun*, No. 28, December 1973, pp. 178–182, No. 29, January 1974, pp. 175–177; Rabin, *Pinqas*, pp. 424–425; see also Hawatma, *INA*, 23.11.73; *al-Nahar*, 25.11.73, 26.1.74; *al-Anwar*, 4.12.73, 25.1.74 (Fahmi–Gromyko joint communiqué); PLO–Soviet communiqué, *Tass*, 26.11.73; also *Filastin al-Thawra*, 9.1.74; *al-Muharrir*, 31.10.73.

116. See Hawatma, *Muhimmat*, pp. 45–60, 64–72, *al-'Amal Ba'da Harb Tishrin*, April 1974, *al-Hukuma al-Thawriyya al-Muwaqqata*, 1.12.74, *al-Huriyya*, 17.12.73, *al-Nahar*, 7.12.73, 22.3.74, *MENA*, 7.12.73, 25.2.74, *INA*, 16.5.74, *Shuun*, No. 30, February 1974, pp. 7–11, 31–42; Abd Rabbu (a PDFLP leader), *al-Nahar*, 15.12.73; PDFLP, *al-Wad'*, pp. 125–132 (declaration by the CC PDFLP, November 1973); declarations by the PDFLP, *al-Huriyya*, 28.1.74, *INA*, 16.5.74; see also *al-Yawm*, 22.1.74; *al-Nahar*, 10.12.73, 18.5.74; *al-Anwar*, 18, 19.5.74.

117. PFLP, *Badil*, pp. 36–99; PFLP's announcements, *al-Hadaf*, 26.1.74, 28.9.74; Habash, *al-Hadaf*, 22.12.73, 5, 17.1.74, 16.2.74, *INA*, 19, 24.2.74, 10.10.74, *Bag. R.*, 27.2.74, *al-Bayraq*, Beirut, 4.2.75, *al-Dustur*, Beirut, 20.1.75, *al-Nahar*, 18.12.73, *Ila al-Amam*, 17.1.75, *Shuun*, No. 30, February 1974, pp. 15–24, 48–53; Abu Ali Mustafa (a PFLP leader), *al-Hadaf*, 4.4.81; Ahmad al-Yamani, *al-Nahar*, 29.5.74; Salah Salah (a PFLP leader), *INA*, 3.11.73, *al-Yawm*, 27.3.74; Abu al-Tib, *MENA*, 4.6.74; Bassam Abu Sharif, PFLP spokesman, *INA*, 31.10.73.

118. For the working papers see *al-Nahar*, 13, 17.2.74, 10.5.74; *al-Yawm*, 11.5.74; *Filastin al-Thawra*, 19.2.74; Abu Iyad, *Libya R.*, 14.3.74; Sakhnini, *Shuun*, No. 32, April 1974, pp. 178–180; Muhsin, *MENA*, 23.2.74, *al-Nahar*, 13.2.74; on the discussions between the organizations see *Kul Shay*, 4.5.74; *al-Yawm*, 25.5.74; *al-Nahar*, 9.5.74; *al-Hayat*, 10.5.74; Qaddumi, *MENA*, 20.5.74, *Fatah R.*, Cairo, 23.5.74; also see the EC PLO Political Report submitted to the 12th PNC session, *INA*, 2.6.74.

119. The eight expelled National Palestinian Front leaders who joined the PNC were: Abd al-Jawwad Salih, Abd al-Muhsin Abu Mayzar, Jiriyis Qawas, Damin Husayn Awda, Husayn al-Jaghub, Dr Walid Qamhawi, Dr Shakir Abu Hajla and Arabi Awwad. See PLO, *al-Barnamij al-Siyasi al-Marhali, al-Bayan al-Siyasi*, the 12th PNC session; Hamid, *op. cit.*, pp. 247–252; also *Filastin al-Thawra*, 12.6.74; for details of the discussion between Sadat and the EC PLO members, *MENA* (*al-Ahram*), 11.6.74; on the debates of the 12th PNC see Abu Iyad, *Fatah R.*, Cairo, 8.6.74; Arafat, *al-Musawwar*, 7.6.74, *MENA*, 5.6.74; Sami al Attari, Sa'id Hamami, Abu Iyad, Khalid al-Hasan, Zuhayr Muhsin, Shafiq al-Hut, Sidqi al-

Dajani, Khalid al-Fahum, Fayiz Sayigh, Hawatma, *MENA*, 30.5.74, 1, 2, 4, 5, 9.6.74, *MENA* (*al-Anwar*) 3, 8.6.74, *MENA* (*al-Sayyad*) 13.6.74, *al-Ahram*, 1.6.74, *al-Musawwar*, 7.6.74, *al-Huriyya*, 10, 17.6.74, *al-Jumhur*, Beirut, 13.6.74; also *Filastin al-Thawra*, 12.6.74; *Kul Shay*, 15.6.74; see also Bassam Abu Sharif, *INA*, 19.6.74; *Bag. R.*, 9.6.74, the ALF and PFLP reservations; for analysis of the "ten points" by Palestinian writers see Faysal Hurani, *op. cit.*, pp. 207–221; Sakhnini, *Mukawwanat*.

120. The two "concessions" were expressed in Husayn's strategic speech on 1 May 1974, when he talked about division of roles between Jordan and the PLO in the Conference and Jordan's recognition of the PLO as the "legitimate representative" of the Palestinians. For text of Sadat–Husayn joint communiqué see *al-Dustur*, Amman, 7.4.74; see also Sadat, *MENA*, 13.4.74, 22.6.74; Fahmi, *al-Akhbar*, 18.6.74; Husayn, *al-Dustur*, 2.5.74; Rifa'i, *al-Dustur*, 13.5.74; Fuwaz Abu al-Ghanam, Jordanian ambassador in Cairo, *al-Musawwar*, 17.5.74; Rifa'i, Qaddumi, Khalid al-Hasan, quoted in *al-Musawwar*, 8.3.74; Sadat's discussion with the EC PLO members, *MENA* (*al-Ahram*), 11.6.74; Mustafa al-Husayni, *Ruz al-Yusuf*, 17.6.74; Muhammad Sayyid Ahmad, *al-Ahram*, 17.7.74; Baha al-Din, *al-Ahram*, 14.7.74; see also *al-Ahram*, *al-Jumhuriyya*, *al-Akhbar*, *Sawt al-Arab*, commentaries, 7.4.74.

121. For text of Alexandria Communiqué see *al-Ahram*, 19.7.74; see also Kamal Abu al-Majd, Egyptian minister of information, *MENA*, 17.7.74; *al-Ahram*, 17.7.74; *al-Jumhuriyya*, 19.7.74; *al-Dustur*, *al-Ray*, Amman, 19.7.74; Anis Mansur, *October*, Cairo, 30.11.80; Rabin, *op. cit.*, pp. 432–442.

122. On the PLO's and organizations' reactions see *Filastin al-Thawra*, 31.7.74 (announcement by the EC PLO); Sakhnini, *Shuun*, No. 37, September 1974, pp. 182–186; for Syria's reaction see Khaddam, *al-Anwar*, 27.7.74; Hanna Bat-hish, *al-Muharrir*, 22.7.74; announcement by Sa'iqa; *Dam. R.*, 22.7.74; Muhsin, *al-Nahar*, 18.8.74.

123. See Sadat, *MENA*, 14, 25, 28.8.74, 6.9.74, 9.10.74, 8.10.74 (*al-Usbu' al-Arabi*), *Cairo R.*, 28.9.74, *al-Ahram*, 24.7.74, *al-Hawadith*, 20.7.74, *Observer*, 6.10.74, *Christian Science Monitor*, 27.10.74; Fahmi, *MENA*, 25.7.74, 1.8.74 (*al-Jumhuriyya*), 8.8.74 (in Paris), 15.8.74, 16.8.74 (NBC), 13.10.74, *al-Ahram*, 19.7.74, 5.8.74, *al-Hawadith*, 13.9.74; Abu al-Majd, *MENA*, 25.7.74, 1.8.74; see also *al-Jumhuriyya*, *al-Ahram*, *al-Akhbar*, 19.7.74; *al-Ahram*, 26.7.74; *al-Musawwar*, 12.9.74; *Cairo R.*, commentary, 19.7.74; *Sawt al-Arab*, Filastin corner, commentary, 12.8.74; *al-Nahar*, 21.7.74, citing reliable sources; *al-Nahar*, 1.9.74, quoting Palestinian sources; Abu Iyad, *MENA*, 21.8.74; Arafat, *SANA*, 19.8.74; *Amman R.*, 20.7.74, Rifa'i's message to Riyad, SG AL; *al-Dustur*, Amman, 26.7.74, Jordanian spokesman; also *al-Ray*, 8.8.74.

124. See Sadat in Anis Mansur, *October*, 30.11.80; Kissinger, *op. cit.*, pp. 1138, 1140–1141; Mahmud Riyad, *Mudhakkarat 1948–1978*, al-Bahth An al-Salam wa al-Sira' fi al-Sharq al-Awsat, Beirut, 1981, p. 512, Rabin, *op. cit.*, pp. 432–448; Moshe Zak, *Ma'ariv*, 6.4.80; *al-Ahram*, 16, 18.8.74; *al-Nahar*, 3.11.74; on the Egyptian official invitation for the tripartite conference see *MENA*, 26, 27.8.74 (meeting of Fahmi with Sa'id Kamal, deputy head of the PLO Political Department); *Akhbar al-Yawm*, 24.8.74; see also Khaddam, *MENA*, 24.8.74; Abu Iyad, *MENA*, 21.8.74; *al-Nahar*, 25.8.74.

125. On the discussions and resolutions of the ALC see *MENA*, 1, 2.9.74; Mahmud Riyad, SG AL, *INA*, 31.8.74; Fahmi, *MENA*, 4.9.74; Qaddumi, *MENA*, 1.9.74; Arafat, *al-Nahar*, 4.9.74; Isam Sakhnini, *Shuun*, No. 38, October 1974, pp. 191–192; see also *al-Nahar*, 3.9.74 (Abu al-Nasr); *al-Ahram*, 5.9.74; *Sawt al-Arab*, commentary, 2.9.74.

126. For text of the tripartite declaration see *MENA*, 21.9.74.

127. On the Jordanian reactions see *al-Ray*, 23, 24.9.74; *al-Dustur*, 24, 25.9.74; *Amman R.*, commentary, 23.9.74; also see *Amman R.*, 22.9.74, Jordanian communiqué on Khaddam's visit to Jordan; Khaddam, *Amman R.*, 22.9.74; Rifa'i

quoted by *MENA* (*al-Sayyad*), 2.10.74; *MENA* (*al-Bayraq*), 1.10.74.
128. See Husayn, *al-Dustur*, 29.10.74; Husayn–Ford joint communiqué, *al-Dustur*, 19.8.74; Kissinger, *op. cit.*, pp. 1140–1141; Rabin, *op. cit.*, pp. 432–448, *Kol Israel*, Jerusalem broadcasting, 16.4.80; Moshe Zak, *Ma'ariv*, 6.4.80; Mati Golan, *Ha'aretz*, 3.9.82; also Sadat, *Cairo R.*, 28.9.75, in Anis Mansur, *October*, 30.11.80.
129. On the working papers see *MENA*, 23, 24, 25.10.74; *al-Safir*, Beirut, 23.10.74; see also Fahmi, *MENA*, 22.10.74; Rifa'i, *Amman R.*, 25.10.74; Salim al-Lawzi, then press counsellor of the Umani delegation to the summit, *al-Hawadith*, 1.11.74; Sa'id Kamal, PLO delegation spokesman, *Moroccan News Agency*, 25.10.74; Qaddumi, *MENA*, 22.10.74, *Libya R.*, 24.10.74; Abu Mayzar, *MENA*, 25.10.74; Ahmad al-Araqi, Moroccan FM, *MENA*, 22.10.74; see also *al-Usbu' al-Arabi*, 4.11.74; *al-Ray*, Amman, 26, 27.10.74; *al-Hayat*, 24.10.74, quoting Qaddumi, Rifa'i and Abu Mayzar.
130. See Sadat, *Cairo R.*, 30.10.74, 28.9.75; Fahmi, *MENA*, *al-Hayat*, 24.10.74; Hamdi Fuad, *op. cit.*, pp. 242–243; Riyad, *op. cit.*, p. 497; Lawzi, *loc. cit*; Abu al-Majd, *MENA*, 28, 29.10.74; King Hasan, *MENA*, 30.10.74; Baha al-Din, *al-Ahram*, 24.10.74, 2.11.74; also *al-Ahram*, 26.10.74; *al-Nahar*, 3.11.74.
131. See Asad, *al-Ba'th*, 30.10.74, *Dam. R.*, 8.3.75, 26.6.75 (*al-Hawadith*), in Anis Mansur, *October*, 30.11.80; Khaddam in Lawzi, *loc. cit.*, *Tishrin*, 21.10.75; Riyad, *op. cit.*, pp. 496–497; *al-Ba'th*, 1.2.77 (an article published in *al-Munadil*, internal circular of the Syrian Ba'th); Abd al-Rahim Ghanim, *al-Munadil*, internal circular, August or September 1975; Rabin, *Pinqas*, pp. 444–446; also *al-Thawra*, *al-Ba'th*, 27.10.74; *al-Nahar*, 22.10.74, Abu Jawda.
132. See Husayn, *al-Dustur*, 29.10.74, in Sadat, *Cairo R.*, 28.9.75, *al-Hawadith*, 31.6.75, in Anis Mansur, *October*, 30.11.74, in Lawzi, *loc. cit*; Riyad, *op. cit.*, pp. 493–495; Rifa'i, *MENA*, 27, 29.10.74, in Lawzi, *loc. cit*; also see Rabin, *loc. cit*; Sadat, *Observer*, 6.10.74, *MENA* (*al-Usbu' al-Arabi*), 8.10.74; *al-Dustur*, Amman, 26.10.74.
133. See Arafat, *MENA*, 30.10.74; Arafat, Qaddumi, Abu Mayzar, in Lawzi, *loc. cit*; Abu Iyad, *Filastini*, pp. 227–237, *al-Muharrir*, 20.12.74; Abd Rabbu, an EC PLO member, *MENA*, 27, 28.10.74; *al-Nahar*, 3.11.74.
134. Lawzi, *al-Hawadith*, 1.11.74.
135. See Boumedienne, *MENA*, 27.10.74, *Sawt al-Arab*, 28.10.74, *al-Musawwar*, 30.10.74, in Lawzi, *loc. cit.*
136. Saddam Husayn, *INA*, 27, 28.10.74; Iraqi official spokesman summing up Saddam Husayn's speech at the summit on 28.10.74, *INA*, 30.10.74; also Hasan al-Bakr, *INA*, 17.7.75.
137. See Abu al-Majd, *MENA*, 28.10.74; Lawzi, *loc. cit*; *al-Nahar*, 3.11.74; *al-Ahram*, 28.10.74; *INA*, *Beirut R.*, 24.10.74, citing Sadat.
138. Text of the Rabat summit top-secret resolutions, *al-Safir*, 30.11.77; also see King Husayn, *Moroccan News Agency*, 31.10.74; the Iraqi delegation registered its objections to articles 1–3.
139. See Sadat in Anis Mansur, *October*, 30.11.80; Abu al-Majd, *MENA*, 29.10.74.
140. See Kissinger, *op. cit.*, pp. 1138–1139, 1141; Moshe Zak, *Ma'ariv*, 6.4.80; Mati Golan, *Ha'aretz*, 3.9.82.

CONCLUSION

1. Dr Saib Ariqat (al-Najah University, Nablus), *al-Quds*, 6.12.85.

EPILOGUE

1. On the Algiers Arab summit's decisions, see *Shuun Filastiniyya*, No. 184, July 1988, pp. 122–123.

2. On the development of Syrian relations with the PLO and Fatah, the Syrian invasion of Lebanon, and the stages of Palestinian involvement in the civil war, see Reuven Avi-Ran, *The Syrian–Palestinian Conflict in Lebanon: Syrian Nationalism vis-à-vis Palestinian Particularism*, Dayan Center, Tel-Aviv University, May 1988 (Hebrew); Reuven Avi-Ran, *Syrian Involvement in Lebanon 1975–1985*, Tel-Aviv, 1986, pp. 27–61; Itamar Rabinovich, *The War for Lebanon 1970–1983*, London, 1984.

3. Loc. cit., see also Itamar Rabinovich and Hana Zemer, *War and Crisis in Lebanon* (Hebrew), Tel-Aviv, 1982, pp. 232–238.

4. For the text of the Cairo Agreement 1969, see *al-Nahar*, 20.4.70.

5. See Rashid Khalidi, *Under Siege: PLO Decision Making during the War 1982*, New York, 1986; see also Avi-Ran, *Syrian Involvement*, pp. 179–186; see also Damascus Radio, 24.6.83.

6. See Sadat, *al-Ahram*, 5.1.75; *MENA*, 13.1.75, 26.2.76, 12.3.77, 24.7.77; *Cairo Radio*, 17.2.77; *The Sunday Telegraph*, 16.1.77; Ashraf Gurbal, *Radio Cairo*, 19.5.77.

7. Sadat, *Ha'aretz*, 21.11.77.

8. See *Middle East Contemporary Survey (MECS)*, The Shiloah Center, Tel-Aviv University, New York and London, Vol. II, 1977–1978, pp. 149–154.

9. Sadat, *New York Times*, 6.7.78; *MECS*, loc. cit.

10. See Begin, *Ma'ariv*, Tel-Aviv, 1.10.78; *Yedi'ot Aharonot*, 2.2.79; *MECS*, Vol. III, pp. 78–79, 170–171.

11. On the Egyptian attitude regarding the autonomy and the Palestinian state, see Mustafa Khalil, PM, *al-Junhuriya*, 18.2.80, 3.7.80; Butrus Ghali, *al-Ahram*, 3.10.79; *Akhbar al-Yawm*, 5.1.80, 26.7.80; Sadat, *Ma'ariv*, 21.3.80; *MECS*, Vol. IV, 1979–1980, pp. 117–132; see also Moshe Gammer, ed., *The Autonomy Negotiations* (April 1979–October 1980), Main Documents, Shiloah Center, March 1981 (Hebrew).

12. For details on the PLO and the Palestinian organizations' attitude see Abu Iyad, *Financial Times*, 3.10.78; *al-Sharq al-Awsat* (London), 25.5.79; *L'Humanite*, Paris, 18.6.79; Arafat, *Sawt Filastin Radio*, 19.8.78; Faruq al-Qaddumi, *Monday Morning*, 21.1.80; see also, *Sawt Filastin Radio* (Lebanon), 19.11.77, 15.12.77, 19.9.78 (the EC announcement); *al-Siyasa*, Kuwait, 5.10.78, 11.6.79; *al-Hadaf*, Beirut, 22.9.79.

13. See Sadat, *al-Akhbar*, 11.9.79, 1.10.79; *October*, Cairo, 7.10.79; *al-Jumhuriya*, 8.6.80; *Washington Post*, 3.4.80.

14. Qaddumi, *al-Mustaqbal*, 17.10.81; *Sawt Filastin*, 26.10.81, 8.5.82.

15. *Davar*, Tel-Aviv, 3.5.84; Usama al-Baz, *Davar*, 14.5.84.

16. Mubarak, *Cairo Radio*, 28.9.82, 23–25.9.82, 12.12.82, 23–25.4.83; Butrus Ghali, *al-Akhbar*, 17.5.83; *MECS*, Vol. VII, 1982–1983, pp. 159–161.

17. Khalid al-Hasan, *al-Hawadith*, 25.5.84.

18. Husayn, *al-Safir*, Beirut, 21.9.82, *Shuun Filastiniyya*, No. 132–133, November–December 1982, p. 134.

19. For the Jordanian announcement see *Amman Radio*, 10.4.83; see also, *al-Nahar al-Arabi wa al-Duwali*, 2.5.83; *al-Watan*, Beirut, 25.4.83.

20. Husayn, *Amman Radio*, 22.11.84, 19.2.86.

21. For the text of the agreement see Khalid al-Hasan, *al-Ittifaq al-Urduni al-Filastini lil Taharuk al-Mushtarak (The Jordanian–Palestinian Agreement for a Joint Action)*, Amman, 11.2.85, Jerusalem, 1985, pp. 158–159.

22. Khalid al-Hasan, ibid., p. 154.

23. Husayn, *Amman Radio*, 19.2.86. In his speech the King surveyed the details given in this part concerning the dialogue that included his attitude, Arafat's and the American Administration's attitudes; for the English text see, *Journal of Palestine Studies (JPS)*, No. 60, Summer 1986, pp. 206–241 (hereafter Husayn's speech).

24. Husayn's speech.

25. *Sawt Filastin*, Baghdad, 2.2.86; *MECS*, 1980, p. 169.

26. For the wording of the PLO's three proposals see, *JPS*, No. 60, Summer 1986, pp. 241–243.
27. Husayn's speech.
28. *Jerusalem Post*, 11.2.86; *MECS*, 1986, pp. 171–172.
29. *Jerusalem Post*, 16.2.86; *Cairo Radio*, 14.2.86; *MENA*, 15.2.86; *MECS*, 1986, p. 172.
30. Husayn's speech.
31. Ibid.
32. *JPS*, No. 60, Summer 1986, pp. 232–241.
33. See Allain Gresh, *The PLO, the Struggle Within*, London 1988, pp. 185–186.
34. For the 14th PNC meeting, its decisions and its political statement see, *Shuun Filastiniyya*, February–March 1979, pp. 262–265.
35. See *Shuun Filastiniyya*, No. 142–143, January–February 1985, pp. 136–138.
36. Ibid.; also, *Shuun Filastiniyya*, No. 140–141, November–December 1984, pp. 146–174.
37. See *Shuun Filastiniyya*, No. 170–171, May–June 1987, pp. 166–170.
38. See *al-Sha'b*, East Jerusalem, 2, 3.10.78.
39. See *al-Fajr*, East Jerusalem, 20.6.82, 1.7.82, 9.9.82; *al-Sha'b*, 28.6.82; *al-Tali'a*, East Jerusalem, 1.7.82; *al-Quds*, 25.8.82.
40. Moshe Shemesh, *Ha'aretz*, 6.8.85.
41. *JPS*, No. 69, Autumn 1988, pp. 271–272.
42. For the text of the Algiers summit's resolutions see, *Shuun Filastiniyya*, No. 184, July 1988, pp. 122–124.
43. On Jordan's attitude see, *Shuun Filastiniyya*, ibid., pp. 109–124; Husayn, *al-Qabas*, Kuwait, 9.6.88; *al-Dustur*, Amman, 1.8.88; *al-Nahar*, 8.6.88; *al-Mustaqbal*, Paris, 18.6.88.
44. Husayn's speech see, *al-Dustur*, Amman, 1.8.88.
45. Loc. cit.
46. King Husayn in a press conference (7.8.88), *JPS*, No. 69, Autumn 1988, pp. 290–300.
47. On the Jordanian steps, see Hani al-Khasawna, Information Minister, Interview (3.8.88), *JPS*, No. 69, Autumn 1988, p. 285; see also, *Shuun Filastiniyya*, No. 185, August 1988, p. 138; No. 186, September 1988, pp. 103–104; also, *MECS*, 1988, pp. 591–593.
48. Loc. cit.
49. See Abu Iyad, *al-Tadamun*, London, 28.11.88; *al-Anba*, London, 30.11.88.
50. For the text of the "Declaration of Independence" see, *Shuun Filastiniyya*, No. 188, November 1988, pp. 3–5; for English version see, *MECS*, 1988, pp. 260–261; *JPS*, No. 70, Winter 1989, pp. 213–216.
51. PLO (an official brochure), the 4th PNC, 10–17 July 1968 (Arabic).
52. For the Arabic text of the "Political Statement" see, *Shuun Filastiniyya*, No. 188, November 1988, pp. 6–12; for the English version see *MECS*, ibid., pp. 262–265; *JPS*, ibid., pp. 216–223.
53. Abu Iyad, *Shuun Filastiniyya*, No. 189, December 1988, pp. 123–131.
54. For the text of Arafat's statement see, *MECS*, 1988, pp. 221–272; for the Arabic version see, *Shuun Filastiniyya*, No. 190, January 1989, pp. 141–145.
55. For Schultz's statement see, *MECS*, 1988, p. 28.

Bibliography

The Bibliography lists only those sources which are directly cited in the text. Unpublished sources are marked "UP". State media are included under *Media*, even where generally regarded as expressing only government policies. Official organs of the Palestinian organizations are, however, classified under *Palestinian Organizations*.

PRIMARY SOURCES

A. ARCHIVES

Israel State Archives, Jerusalem, Section 114, Jordanian Records of the General Investigations, General Security and Military Intelligence Departments. (UP)
Records of the Egyptian General Investigations – Internal Security Department, the Gaza Strip Government, 1965–1966. (UP)

B. BOOKS AND ARTICLES

Abd al-Hadi, Mahdi, *al-Masala al-Filastiniyya 1934–1974* (Beirut, July 1975).
Abu Khatir, Josef, *Liqaat Ma'a Jamal Abd al-Nasir* (Beirut, 1971).
al-Badri, Hasan, Taha al-Majdhub and Diya al-Din Zuhdi, *Harb Ramadan* (Cairo, 1974).
Baha al-Din, Ahmad, *Iqtirah Dawlat Filastin* (Beirut, January 1968).
Farid, Abd al-Majid, *Min Mahadir Ijtima'at Abd al-Nasir al-Arabiyya wa al-Duwaliyya* (Beirut, 1979).
Fuad, Hamdi, *al-Harb al-Diblomasiyya Bayna Misr wa Israil* (Beirut, 1976).
Hamid, Rashid, *Muqarrarat al-Majlis al-Watani al-Filastini 1964–1974* (Beirut, August 1975).
Haykal, Muhammad Hasanyan, *"Bisaraha"*, weekly articles in *al-Ahram*, 1959–1971.
al-Tariq Ila Ramadan (Beirut, 1975).
Hofstadter, Dan (ed.), *Egypt and Nasser*, Vol. 3, 1967–72 (New York, 1973).
al-Husayni, Muhammad Amin, *Haqaiq An Qadiyyat Filastin,* 3rd edition (Cairo, 1977).
Junbalat, Kamal, *Hadhihi Wasiyyati* (June 1978).
Kissinger, H., *Years of Upheaval* (London, 1982).

al-Lajna al-Arabiyya al-Uliya, *al-Kiyan al-Filastini Bayna al-Madi wa al-Mustaqbal* (Beirut, 11.4.64).

Mar'i, Sayyid, *Awraq Siyasiyya,* Vol. 3, Ma'a al-Ra'is Anwar al-Sadat (Cairo, January 1979).

Matar, Fuad, *Ayna Asbaha Abd al-Nasir fi Jumhuriyyat al-Sadat* (Beirut, July 1972).

Moore, John N. (ed.), *The Arab Israeli Conflict,* Vol. 3, Documents (Princeton, New Jersey, 1974).

Rabin, Y., *Pinkas Sherut* (Hebrew), Vol. 2 (Tel Aviv, September 1979).

Riyad, Mahmud, *Mudhakkarat 1948–1978, al-Bahth an al-Salam wa al-Sira' fi al-Sharq al-Awsat* (Beirut, 1981).

Sabri, Musa, *Wathaiq Harb October,* 3rd edition (Cairo, 1975).

al-Sadat, Anwar, *al-Bahth An al-Dhat* (Cairo, April 1978).

al-Shadhli, Sa'd al-Din, *Harb October* (Paris, 1980).

Shiloah Research Centre, *Middle East Record,* Vol. 1 1960, Vol. 2 1961, Vol. 3 1967, Vol. 4 1968, Vol. 5 1969–1970 (Tel Aviv University).

al-Shuqayri, Ahmad, *Ala Tariq al-Hazima* (Beirut, 15.6.72).

Dhikrayat An Mutamar al-Qumma fi al-Khartoum, *Shuun Filastiniyya,* No. 4, September 1971.

al-Hazima al-Kubra, Part 2 (Beirut, 1973).

Inni attahim (Beirut, 1973).

Kalimat Ala Tariq al-Tahrir 1965 (Gaza, n.d.).

Min al-Qumma ila al-Hazima (Beirut, 1971).

al-Tall, Wasfi, *Kitabat fi al-Qadaya al-Arabiyya* (Amman, 1980).

Tlas, Mustafa, *al-Kifah al-Musallah* (Damascus, n.d.)

Al-Wathaiq al-Arabiyya, Vols. 1–13, 1964–1975 (American University of Beirut).

Al-Wathaiq al-Filastiniyya, Vols. 1–7, 1965–1971 (Institute for Palestine Studies, Beirut).

C. OFFICIAL DOCUMENTS

1. Egypt

Abd al-Nasir, Jamal, *Filastin Min Aqwal al-Ra'is* (Cairo, n.d.).

al-Nizan al-Dusturi li-Qita' Ghazza, *al-Jarida al-Rasmiyya,* No. 75, 29.3.62.

al-Qanun al-Asasi lil-Mantiqa al-Waqi'a Tahta Raqabat al-Quwwat al-Misriyya, *al-Jarida al-Rasmiyya,* Law No. 255, 1955.

al-Sadat, Anwar, *Majmu'at Khutab wa Ahadith al-Ra'is Anwar al-Sadat,* Ministry of Information, 3 vols. (Cairo, n.d.).

al-Waqai' al-Filastiniyya (Gaza).

2. Iraq

(a) Ba'th

al-Ba'th, al-Qiyada al-Qawmiyya, al-Taqrir al-Siyasi, al-Mutamar al-Qawmi al-Ashir, Baghdad, 1–10.3.70.

al-Qutr al-Iraqi, *al-Taqrir al-Siyasi al-Sadir An al-Mutamar al-Qutri* al-Thamin, January 1974, Baghdad, 8–12.1.74.

al-Kayyali, Abd al-Wahab, *al-Muqawama al-Filastiniyya wa al-Nidal al-Arabi 1969–1973* (Beirut, December 1973).

al-Qadiyya al-Filastiniyya, Ara wa Mawaqif 1964–1966 (Beirut, December 1973).

Shuun Filastiniyya, No. 7, March 1973, pp. 37–49.

al-Razzaz, Munif, *al-Sabil ila Tahrir Filastin* (Beirut, February 1971).

al-Waqai' al-Iraqiyya.

(b) *Arab Liberation Front*

ALF, *Ahadith wa Mawaqif* (n.d.).

al-Amal al-Fidai wa Tahaddiyat al-Wad' al-Lubnani (March 1970).

al-Bayan al-Siyasi, second edition (September 1976).

Hawla al-Wahda al-Wataniyya al-Filastiniyya (n.d.)

Ma Hiya Jabhat al-Tahrir al-Arabiyya (n.d.).

al-Mutamar al-Suhufi, 30.8.69.

al-Tajruba al-Qawmiyya fi al-Amal al-Fidai, 2nd edition (September 1976).

al-Tariq al-Qawmi li-Tahrir Filastin (Beirut, April 1970).

Tatawwur al-Ilaqa Bayna al-Muqawama wa al-Anzima (n.d.).

al-Thair al-Arabi.

3. Jordan

Husayn, *Kalimat al-Husayn June 1967 – June 1968*, 2nd edition, Ministry of Information (Amman, n.d.).

Letter to the 12th Arab Students' Congress in the USA, 25.8.63, Ministry of Information (Amman).

Thalathat Khtabat lil-Husayn fi 1969, Ministry of Information (Amman, February 1970).

al-Urdun wa Qadiyyat Filastin, speech on 5.1.66, official brochure, Ministry of Information (Amman).

Ministry of Foreign Affairs, *Mawqif al-Urdun Min Matalib Ra'is Munazzamat al-Tahrir al-Filastiniyya* (6.12.65).

al-Urdun wa al-Qadiyya al-Filastiniyya wa al-Ilaqat al-Arabiyya (Amman, 1964).

Ministry of Information, *Mutamar al-Qumma al-Arabi al-Rabi'* (Amman, September 1967).

Mutamar al-Qumma al-Arabi al-Khamis fi al-Rabat wa Mutamar al-Qumma li-Duwal al-Muwajaha fi al-Qahira (Amman, January 1970).

al-Wathaiq al-Urduniyya 1968 (Amman, 16.10.73).

Qanun al-Baladiyyat, *al-Jarida al-Rasmiyya lil-Mamlaka al-Urduniyya al-Hashimiyya*, No. 125, Law No. 29, 1.5.55.

4. Syria

(a) *Ba'th*

al-Ba'th wa Qadiyyat Filastin, Vol. 3, 1955–1959 (Beirut, 1974).
Vol. 4, 1959–1964 (Beirut, 1974).
Vol. 5, 1964–1967 (Beirut, May 1975).
Ministry of Information, *al-Manhaj al-Marhali li-Thawrat al-Thamin min Adhar*, approved by the Extraordinary Regional Congress, June 1965 (Damascus, 22.7.65).
al-Munadil – internal circular.
Nidal al-Ba'th, old series, Vol. 4, *al-Qiyada al-Qawmiyya 1955–1961* (Beirut, 1964).
Vol. 7, *al-Qutr al-Iraqi 1958–1963*, 2nd edition (Beirut, February 1972).
Vol. 8, *al-Qutr al-Lubnani 1951–1961* (Beirut, March 1972).
Nidal Hizb al-Ba'th al-Arabi al-Ishtiraki, new series, *Abr Bayanat Qiyadatihi al-Qawmiyya 1955–1962*, 2nd edition (Beirut, 1971).
Abr Bayanat Qiyadatihi al-Qawmiyya 1963–1966 (Beirut, October 1971).
Abr Mutamaratihi al-Qawmiyya 1947–1964 (Beirut, June 1971).
Abr Mutamaratihi al-Qawmiyya, al-Mutamar al-Thamin (Beirut, April 1972).

(b) *Sa'iqa*

al-Attari, Sami, *Press Conference 7.6.76*, the Ba'th National Command, internal circular.
Shuun Filastiniyya, No. 7, March 1972, pp. 27–36.
Muhsin, Zuhayr, *Ahadith al-Nidal al-Watani al-Filastini fi Muwajahat al-Tahaddiyat al-Jadida* (January 1974).
al-Thawra al-Filastiniyya Bayna al-Fikr wa al-Mumarasa (Damascus, August 1972).
al-Thawra al-Filastiniyya Bayna al-Hadir wa al-Mustaqbal (Damascus, May 1973).
Shuun Filastiniyya, No. 30, February 1974, pp. 11–14, 42–48.
Sa'iqa, *Bayan Siyasi Hawla al-Majlis al-Watani* (February 1969).
Sawt al-Tali'a, bulletin of the United Palestinian Organization of the Ba'th Regional Command, No. 19, n.d.
al-Talai' fi Masiratiha al-Nidaliyya, Vol. 1 (n.d.).
al-Talai', *Nahwa Fahm Ilmi li-Mahiyyat al-Thawra* (n.d.).
al-Talai' (Damascus weekly).
al-Talai' wa al-Jamahir (Beirut, monthly).
Talai' Harb al-Tahrir, al-Qutr al-Lubnani, *Nashra Tathqifiyya 2, Qadaya Asasiyya Yatrahuha Tatawwur al-Amal al-Fidai*, internal circular (n.d.). (UP)
Nashra Tanzimiyya 3, al-Qiyada al-Tanfidhiyya, internal circular (n.d.). (UP)

D. PALESTINIAN ORGANIZATIONS

1. *Arab Liberation Front (see Iraq)*
2. *Fatah*

(a) *Official Documents*

Fatah, *Barnamij al-Amal al-Siyasi wa al-Tanzimi lil-Thawra al-Filastiniyya*, approved by the 8th PNC, 28.2.–5.3.71.

Bayan Siyasi, 10.12.76 (leaflet).

al-Dawla al-Filastiniyya, 10.12.70, pamphlet for members only. (UP)

Dirasat Thawriyya, No. 1 (n.d.).

Dirasat Thawriyya No. 4, *al-Nizam al-Urduni wa al-Dawr al-Impiriyali al-Manut Bihi* (presumably by Abu Nidal faction) (n.d.).

Dirasat wa Tajarib Thawriya:

No. 1, *Min Muntalaqat al-Amal al-Fidai* (August 1967).

No. 9, *Wahdat al-Thawra al-Filastiniyya* (n.d.).

No. 10, *Mawaqif wa Muntalaqat Thawriyya* (n.d.).

No. 11, *Hadhihi Thawratina* (October 1968).

Kibar Ulama al-Islam (n.d.).

Kifahuna al-Musallah Bayna al-Nazariyya wa al-Tatbiq (June 1970). (UP)

al-Kitab al-Sanawi 1968 (Beirut 1969), 1969 (Beirut 1970).

Mafahim Asasiyya (August 1972). (UP).

al-Maktab al-Amm, Maktab al-Ta'bia wa al-Tanzim, Dawrat al-Kawadir al-Ula, 14–24.8.72, *Lectures* (UP), by:

Abu al-Abd, 18.8.72

Abu Hatim, 20.8.72

Abu Jihad, Abu Mahir and Abu al-Walid, 22.8.72

Abu Lutuf, 15.8.72

Abu Mazin, Abu Salih, 15.8.72

Abu Salih, 19.8.72

Hani al-Hasan, 23.8.72

Kamal Udwan, 16.8.72

Maktab al-Ta'bia wa al-Tanzim, *Muhadarat Harakiyya*, internal pamphlets Nos. 4, 7, 12, 13, 14 (n.d.). (UP)

Maktab al-Ta'bia wa al-Tanzim, Lebanon Region, *News bulletin No. 1008/B*, 29.4.72, limited internal circular. (UP)

News bulletin No. 1010/B, 25.5.72, limited internal circular. (UP)

News bulletin No. 1011/B, 30.6.72, limited internal circular. (UP)

News bulletin No. 1012/B, 8.8.72, limited internal circular. (UP)

Maktab al-Ta'bia wa al-Tanzim, *Mashru' al-Barnamij li-Tawhid Fasail al-Thawra al-Filastiniyya*, submitted by the EC to the PPC, 6–9.4.74. (UP)

Mawaqif Harakiyya, No. 6 (presumably Abu Nidal's faction) (1974).

al-Milad wa al-Masira (n.d.).

al-Mudhakkara al-Marfu'a ila Ra'is wa A'da al-Majlis al-Watani al-Filastini fi al-Qahira fi Dawratihi al-Thaniya (28.5.65).

Muhadarat Harakiyya, No. 4, internal pamphlet (n.d.). (UP)

al-Nizam al-Dakhili, approved by the Fatah 3rd Congress (1971).

Notes on Ideology and Strategy: probably by one of Fatah's leaders, presumably in late fifties or early sixties. (UP)

Qarar Majlis al-Amn wa Mashru' Rogers (September 1970).

Ta'mim Dakhili No. 3 (4.4.73), al-Asifa HQ. (UP)

al-Thawra, Nashra Tanzimiyya, Lebanon Region, for members only.

al-Thawra al-Arabiyya wa al-Thawra al-Filastiniyya (n.d.). (UP)

al-Thawra al-Filastiniyya al-Musallaha wa Marahil Tatawwuriha, internal pamphlet No. 106 (n.d.). (UP)

Wathaiq Askariyya, Vol. 1 (1968).

(b) *Books and Articles*

al-Hasan, Hani, Fatah Bayna al-Nazariyya wa al-Tatbiq, *Shuun Filastiniyya*, No. 7, March 1972.

al-Qa'ida al-Amina wa al-Istishhad, *al-Thawra al-Filastiniyya*, No. 25, April 1970.

Waqfa Inda al-Dhikra li-Ma'rakat al-Karama, *Shuun Filastiniyya*, No. 8, April 1972.

al-Hasan, Khalid, *Shuun Filastiniyya*, No. 4, September 1971, pp. 279–290.

Mudhakkara Tahliliyya Hawla Mashru' al-Malik Husayn, *Shuun Filastiniyya*, No. 8, April 1972.

Khalaf, Salah (Abu Iyad), *Filastini Bila Hawiyya* (Kuwait, n.d.).

Shuun Filastiniyya, No. 5, November 1971, pp. 29–46.

Afkar Wadiha Amam Marhala Ghamida, *Shuun Filastiniyya*, No. 29, January 1974.

Shuun Filastiniyya, No. 30, February 1974, pp. 24–27, 53–56.

al-Qaddumi, Faruq, al-Nidal al-Siyasi al-Filastini, *Shuun Filastiniyya*, No. 39, November 1974.

al-Thawra al-Filastiniyya wa Mushkilatiha, *Dirasat Arabiyya*, Beirut, February 1971.

Udwan, Kamal, Akhir Hadith, *Shuun Filastiniyya*, No. 21, May 1973, pp. 28–38.

Fatah: al-Milad wa al-Masira, *Shuun Filastiniyya*, No. 17, January 1973, pp. 45–57.

Tahlil al-Mawaqif al-Siyasi, *Shuun Filastiniyya*, No. 11, July 1972.

(c) *Organs*

al-Awda, organ of the General Union of Palestinian Students in West Germany and Austria, Frankfurt (1965–1966).

Fatah, weekly.

Fatah, Internal Circular for members of Fatah in West Germany, 1966.

Filastinuna.
al-Masira.
al-Thawra al-Filastiniyya.

(d) *Radio Stations*

Sawt al-Asifa (Fatah Radio), Cairo, Dar'a, San'a, Algiers.

3. *The Popular Democratic Front for the Liberation of Palestine*

(a) *Official Documents*

PDFLP, *Adwa Min Fikr al-Jabha al-Dimoqratiyya ... Hawla al-Muhimmat al-Rahina lil-Thawra al-Filastiniyya* (al-Dar al-Bayda, n.d.) (October 1973?).
   Barnamij al-Amal al-Watani al-Dimoqrati fi al-Urdun (Beirut, August 1975).
   Hamlat Aylul wa al-Muqawama al-Filastiniyya (Beirut, 1971).
   Hawla al-Afwiyya wa al-Nazariyya fi al-Amal al-Fidai (n.d.).
   Hawla Azmat al-Muqawama al-Filastiniyya (Beirut, November 1969).
   al-Khatt al-Siyasi al-Amm fi al-Marhala al-Rahina, al-Mawdu'at al-Siyasiyya, approved by the 1st National Congress October 1971, 3rd internal edition (1972).
   Malamih Tatawwur al-Nidal al-Filastini (n.d.).
   Mashru' Barnamij Jabha Wataniyya Filastiniyya Muwahhada, submitted to the 6th PNC (1.9.69).
   Memorandum, submitted to the 7th PNC, pamphlet.
   Ta'mim Sari', No. 2, to all active members and candidates on the questions of national unity and a United National Front (21.5.72). (UP)
   al-Taqrir al-Siyasi al-Asasi lil-Jabha al-Sha'biyya li-Tahrir Filastin (August 1968).
   al-Wad' fi al-Manatiq al-Muhtalla wa Muhimmat al-Thawra (Beirut, August 1975).
   al-Wad' al-Rahin fi al-Manatiq al-Muhtalla wa Muhimmatina (n.d.).
   Waqi' Harakat al-Muqawama al-Filastiniyya, submitted to the 6th PNC (1.9.69).

(b) *Books and Articles*

Hawatma, Nayif, *al-Amal Ba'da Harb Tishrin* (April 1974).
   Didd al-Ghazu al-Suri (1.10.76).
   al-Hukuma al-Thawriyya al-Muwaqqata (1.12.74).
   al-Muhimmat al-Rahina lil-Thawra al-Filastiniyya (January 1974).
   al-Muqawama al-Filastiniyya fi Waqi'iha al-Rahin (Beirut, September 1969).
   Shuun Filastiniyya, No. 5, November 1971, pp. 47–78.
   Shuun Filastiniyya, No. 30, February 1974, pp. 7–11, 31–42.

(c) *Organs*

al-Huriyya.
al-Munadil (internal pamphlets). (UP)
al-Sharara.

4. *The Popular Front for the Liberation of Palestine*

(a) *Official Documents*

PFLP, *Ala Tariq al-Thawra al-Filastiniyya* (Beirut, November 1970).
   Qiyadat al-Ard al-Muhtalla, *al-Amal fi al-Ard al-Muhtalla*, internal
      pamphlet (4.9.71). (UP)
   al-Amaliyyat al-Kharijiyya, Kitab al-Hadaf, No. 2 (Beirut, n.d.).
   al-Badil al-Thawri li-Mashru' al-Dawla al-Filastiniyya al-Tasfuwi (April
      1974).
   *Qiyadat al-Ard al-Muhtalla, al-Barnamij al-Siyasi wa al-Askari fi al-Ard
      al-Muhtalla*, internal pamphlet (September 1972). (UP)
   al-Bayan al-Siyasi (December 1967).
   Bayan Siyasi Hamm, pamphlet (29.8.69).
   Bulletin No. 2 (April 1972).
   al-Fikr al-Askari, Kitab al-Hadaf, No. 1 (Beirut, n.d.).
   Hawla Qadaya al-Thawra (Amman, 15.7.70).
   Internal circular distributed in Gaza Strip (20.10.68). (UP)
   al-Istratijiyya al-Siyasiyya wa al-Tanzimiyya, approved by the PFLP
      Congress (February 1969).
   al-Kadihun wa al-Thawra al-Filastiniyya (n.d.).
   *Limadha Darabat al-Jabha al-Sha'biyya ... didd al-Muassasat al-
      Israiliyya ...* (n.d.).
   *Limadha Tashtarik al-Jabha al-Sha'biyya ... fi al-Majlis al-Watani al-
      Sabi' wa bi-Shakl Ramzi?* (30.5.70).
   Muhimmat al-Marhala al-Jadida, al-Taqrir al-Siyasi, approved by PFLP
      3rd National Congress March 1972, 1st edition (May 1972).
   al-Munadil al-Thawri, No. 4, August 1972, No. 6, July 1973, internal
      pamphlets.
   al-Muqawama wa Mu'dalatiha, Kitab al-Hadaf, No. 5 (Beirut, n.d.).
   al-Nizam al-Dakhili, approved by the PFLP 3rd National Congress
      (March 1972).
   al-Silah al-Nazari fi Ma'rakat al-Tahrir (n.d.).
   al-Qiyada al-Markaziyya (the Central Command), *Ta'mim Dakhili*,
      31.5.72. (UP)
   Ta'mim Dakhili No. 2, concerning the meeting of the Central Command
      (18.11.72). (UP)
   Ta'mim Dakhili No. 4, concerning the meeting of the Central Command
      (25.11.72). (UP)
   Ta'mim Dakhili No. 5, concerning the meeting of the Central Command
      (12.12.72). (UP)

Ta'mim Dakhili No. 6, on the meeting of the Central Command (1.1.73). (UP)

Qiyadat al-Ard al-Muhtalla, *Ta'mim Hawla al-Wad' fi Qita' Ghaza,* internal circular (26.10.71). (UP)

al-Thawra wa al-Ummal (Amman, 10.5.70).

Tudih Mawqifuha Min al-Ishtirak fi al-Majlis al-Watani wa al-Lajna al-Tanfidhiyya wa Qiyadat al-Kifah al-Musallah (1.9.69).

(b) *Books and Articles*

Abu Himam (Haytham al-Ayyubi), *al-Muqawama Askariyyan* (Beirut, May 1970).

Badr, Adnan, Sab' Sanawat lil-Jabha al-Sha'biyya li-Tahrir Filastin, *al-Hadaf,* Beirut, 14.12.74.

Special Supplement, *Shuun Filastiniyya,* No. 9, May 1972.

Habash, George, *Shuun Filastiniyya,* No. 4 September 1971, pp. 291–299.

Shuun Filastiniyya, No. 30, February 1974, pp. 15–24, 48–53.

Kanafani, Ghassan, Shabah al-Dawla al-Filastiniyya, *al-Hadaf,* 6.3.71.

Shuun Filastiniyya, No. 2, May 1971, pp. 57–74.

(c) *Organs*

al-Hadaf.

Tariq al-Thawra, No. 1, June 1970, No. 2, April 1971.

5. *The Popular Front for the Liberation of Palestine – General Command*

(a) *Official Document*

PFLP–GC, *al-Mithaq* (January 1969).

(b) *Books*

Abu al-Abbas, *Muhimmatina fi al-Marhala al-Rahina* (n.d.).

Jibril, Ahmad, *al-Waqi' al-Rahin wa al-Khuruj min al-Mazaq* (n.d.).

Talal, Naji, *Mawaqif Thabita* (16.11.77).

(c) *Organ*

Ila al-Amam.

6. *Palestine Liberation Army*

(a) *Organs*

Sawt Filastin.

al-Thawri.

al-Thawri, pamphlet (10.2.70).

7. *Palestine Liberation Organization*

(a) *Official Documents*

PLO, *al-Barnamij al-Siyasi al-Marhali, al-Bayan al-Siyasi al-Dawra al-Thaniya Ashar*, Cairo, 1–8.6.74.
al-Dawra al-Thalitha lil-Majlis al-Watani al-Filastini, 20–24.5.66.
Gaza Office Records. (UP)
Kuwait Office, *Information Bulletins.*
al-Majlis al-Watani al-Dawra al-Thaniya, 31.5–4.6.65.
al-Majlis al-Watani fi al-Qahira, the 4th PNC, 10–17.7.68.
al-Mithaq al-Qawmi al-Filastini, al-Nizam al-Asasi (n.d.).
al-Mutamar al-Filastini al-Awwal, Cairo 28.5–2.6.64.
PLO EC, *The Political Programme, The Political Report* (Arabic), submitted to the 11th PNC (6.1.73).
Report by the National Unity Committee (Arabic), submitted to the 11th PNC (6.1.73).
PLO Planning Center, *Nahwa Jabhat Tahrir Wataniyya Filastiniyya Urduniyya*, research prepared by the PLO–PCR, *Shuun Filastiniyya*, No. 9, May 1972.
Taqrir Siyasi Khass No. 15, An Mashru' Jabhat al-Tahrir al-Wataniyya al-Filastiniyya al-Urduniyya, not for publication (23.3.72). (UP)
Taqrir Siyasi Khass No. 25, On the General Situation and Tasks of the Resistance Movement, limited circulation (22.8.72). (UP)
Taqrir Khass No. 34, On the Arab and International Situation and Its Relation to the Palestinian Resistance, limited circulation (11.1.73). (UP)

(b) *Organs*

Akhbar Filastin.
Filastin al-Thawra.
Shuun Filastiniyya (PLO, Palestine Research Centre).

(c) *Radio Station*

PLO Radio (Cairo Radio).

8. *Sa'iqa (see Syria)*

E. THE WEST BANK

Barnamij al-Jabha al-Wataniyya al-Filastiniyya fi al-Ard al-Muhtalla August 1973, pamphlet (15.9.73).
al-Faruqi, Hamdi Taji, al-Dawla al-Filastiniyya al-Muqtaraha, pamphlet (n.d.).

What Palestinians Want, *The New Middle East*, London, No. 10, July 1969.

Hiwar Ma'a al-Jabha al-Wataniyya fi al-Ard al-Muhtalla, *al-Tali'a*, Cairo, March 1974.

The Institute for Palestine Studies, *The Resistance of the West Bank of Jordan to Israeli Occupation, 1967* (Beirut, 1967).

Wathaiq Muqawamat al-Difa al-Gharbiyya lil-Urdun lil-Ihtilal al-Israili 1967 (Beirut, 1967).

Jabhat al-Muqawama al-Filastiniyya, *Leaflets*, early April 1973, early November 1973.

Jabhat al-Muqawama al-Sha'biyya, *Leaflets*, mid-January 1972, early March 1972, late March 1972.

Kan'an, Hamdi, *Bayan wa Haqiqa ila al-Sha'b al-Urduni*, leaflet, 30.12.68.

al-Lajna al-Ulya lil-Tawjih al-Watani, *Bayan ila al-Muwatinin fi al-Difa al-Gharbiyya, Da'wa ila al-Idrab fi 19.9.1967* (leaflet).

Palestinian Communist Party, West Bank Command, *Summary of the Political Report* (Arabic) (August 1979).

Shahada, Aziz, Freedom from Outside Influences, *New Outlook*, Vol. 12, No. 9, November–December 1969.

F. MEDIA

1. *News Agencies*

Egypt: Middle East News Agency (Cairo)
Iraq: Iraqi News Agency
Jordan: Jordanian News Agency
Libya: Arab Revolution News Agency (Tripoli–Libya)
Morocco: Moroccan News Agency
PLO: Palestinian News Agency (WAFA)
Syria: Syrian Arab News Agency

2. *Radio*

Egypt: Cairo, Sawt al-Arab
Iraq: Baghdad
Israel: Voice of Israel – Jerusalem
Jordan: Amman
Lebanon: Beirut
Libya: Tripoli
Syria: Damascus and Sawt Filastin

3. *The Press and Television*

(a) *Arab States*

Algeria:	al-Mujahid	al-Sha'b
Egypt:	al-Ahram	Nidal al-Awda
	al-Akhbar	October
	Akhbar al-Yawm	al-Quwwat al-Musallaha
	Akhir Sa'a	Ruz al-Yusuf
	al-Jumhuriyya	al-Sha'b
	al-Musawwar	al-Shabab al-Arabi
		al-Tali'a
Iraq:	al-Akhbar	al-Mustaqbal
	al-Bilad	al-Tali'a
	Iraq Times	al-Thawra
	al-Jamahir	al-Thawra al-Arabiyya
	al-Jumhuriyya	al-Zaman
Jordan:	Amman al-Masa	Hawl al-Alam
	al-Aqsa	al-Jihad
	al-Bilad	al-Manar
	al-Difa'	al-Ray
	al-Dustur	al-Sabah
	Filastin	
Kuwait:	al-Ray al-Amm	al-Qabas
	al-Risala	al-Watan
	al-Siyasa	
Lebanon:	al-Ahhad	Kul Shay
	al-Ahrar	al-Liwa
	al-'Amal	L'Orient Le-Jour
	al-Anwar	al-Muharrir
	al-Balagh	al-Nahar
	Beirut al-Masa	al-Nahar Arab Report
	Filastin (AHC)	al-Raya
	Filastin (al-Muharrir)	al-Safir
	al-Hawadith	al-Sahafa
	al-Hayat	al-Sayyad
	al-Jadid	al-Siyasa
	al-Jarida	al-Usbu' al-Arabi
	al-Jumhur	al-Yawm
	al-Kifah	
Libya:	al-Haqiqa	al-Sha'b
	al-Raid	al-Thawra
Saudi Arabia:	al-Bilad	

Sudan: al-Ayyam

Syria: al-Ayyam   Nidal al-Fallahin
                  al-Ba'th   al-Thawra
                  Jaysh al-Sha'b   Tishrin
                  Kifah al-Amal al-Ishtiraki   al-Wahda
                  al-Nasr   al-Wahda al-Arabiyya

(b) *Israel and the West Bank*

Press: al-Anba   Jerusalem Post
                  al-Bashir (Bethlehem)   Lamerhav
                  Bammahane   Ma'ariv
                  Davar   Ma'rakhot
                  al-Fajr   al-Quds
                  Ha'aretz   al-Sha'b
                  Hatzofe   al-Watan (Clandestine
                  al-Ittihad   organ of the Communist
                                                         Party of the West Bank)
                                                     Yedi'ot Aharonot

Israel Defence Forces: announcements and communiqués, 1959–1974.

(c) *France*

Press: International Herald   Le Monde
                      Tribune   al-Nahar al-Duwali al-Arabi
                  al-Watan al-Arabi

(d) *Great Britain*

Press: The New Middle East   The Times
                  The Observer

Television: BBC

(e) *USA*

Press: Christian Science Monitor   Time
                  Newsweek   U.S. News and World
                  New York Times   Report
                                                     Washington Evening Star

Television: CBS   NBC

SECONDARY SOURCES

A. BOOKS

Alush, Naji, *al-Masira ila Filastin* (Beirut, 1964).
Nahwa Thawra Filastiniyya Jadida (Beirut, November 1972).
Ghali, Butrus, *Dirasat fi al-Diblomasiyya al-Arabiyya* (Cairo, 1973).
Hashad, Adli, *Sha'b Filastin fi Tariq al-Awda* (Cairo, 1964).
Hindi, Khalil, *al-Muqawama al-Filastiniyya wa al-Nizam al-Urduni* (Beirut, September 1971).
Hurani, Faysal, *al-Fikr al-Siyasi al-Filastini 1964–1974* (Beirut, 1980).
al-Hut, Shafiq, *al-Filastini Bayna al-Tih wa al-Dawla* (Beirut, May 1977).
Kazziha, Walid, *Revolutionary Transformation in the Arab World* (London, 1975).
Kerr, M.H., *The Arab Cold War*, 3rd edition (London, 1971).
al-Khatib, Husam, *Fi al-Tajriba al-Thawriyya al-Filastiniyya* (Damascus, 1972).
Khattab, Mahmud Shit, *Al-Wahda al-Askariyya al-Arabiyya* (Beirut, 1969).
Khorshid, Ghazi, *Dalil Harakat al-Muqawama al-Filastiniyya* (Beirut, 1971).
al-Kubaisi, B., "The Arab Nationalists Movement 1951–1971", doctoral dissertation, American University, Washington, D.C. (1971).
Murad, Abbas, *al-Dawr al-Siyasi lil-Jaysh al-Urduni 1921–1973* (Beirut, December 1973).
Proposals for the Continuation of United Nations Assistance to Palestinian Refugees, Document submitted by the secretary-general, 14th session, A/4121, 15 June 1959.
Qarra, Nazih, *Ta'lim al-Filastiniyyin* (Beirut, 1975).
al-Qasim, Anis, *Min al-Tih ila al-Quds* (Tripoli, Libya, 1965).
al-Rayis, Nahid Munir, *Kalima fi al-Kiyan al-Filastini* (Cairo, January 1962).
Shafiq, Munir, *Hawla al-Wahda al-Wataniyya al-Filastiniyya* (12.3.76).
Shalabi, Karim, *al-Sadat wa Thawrat 23 Yulyu 1948 – 1959* (Cairo, 1977).
Shihada, Yusuf, *al-Waqi' al-Filastini wa al-Haraka al-Niqabiyya* (Beirut, September 1973).
al-Shu'aybi, Isa, *al-Kiyaniyya al-Filastiniyya 1947–1977* (Beirut, 1979).
Yasin, Subhi Muhammad, *Nazariyyat al-Amal li-Istirdad Filastin* (Cairo, 1964).
Yusuf, Abd al-Rahman, *Mutamar al-Qumma al-Arabi*, Brochure No. 8 in the series Nidaluna, Armed Forces HQ (Cairo, March 1964).

B. ARTICLES

Alush, Naji, Man Yumathil al-Sha'b al-Filastini, *Shuun Filastiniyya*, No. 6, January 1972.

Nahwa Istratijiyya Jadida lil-Thawra al-Filastiniyya, *Dirasat Arabiyya*, Beirut, February 1971.

Amin, Adil, Special Supplement, *Shuun Filastiniyya*, No. 9, May 1972.

Barakat, Halim, al-Ightirab wa al-Thawra fi al-Hayat al-Arabiyya, *Mawaqif*, Beirut, No. 5, July–August 1969.

David, Lieutenant-Colonel, The Jordan Army in the Yom Kippur War (Hebrew), *Ma'rakhot*, Tel Aviv, No. 266, October–November 1978.

Farhi, David, Political Attitudes in Judea and Samaria (Hebrew), *Ma'rakhot*, No. 231, July 1973.

Hammad, Khayri, Filastin wa Qadiyyat al-Wahda, *al-Ahram*, 2,3.3.63.

Hamud, Sa'id, al-Majalis al-Wataniyya al-Filastiniyya wa al-Wahda al-Wataniyya, *Shuun Filastiniyya*, No. 18, February 1973, pp. 73–90.

Mulahadat Amma Hawla al-Majlis al-Watani 6–12.1.73, *Shuun Filastiniyya*, No. 18, February 1973, pp. 188–190.

al-Hasan, Bilal, Ahdath Aylul wa Masuliyyat al-Nizam al-Urduni, *Shuun Filastiniyya*, No. 1, March 1971.

Special Supplement, *Shuun Filastiniyya*, No. 9, May 1972.

Hindi, Khalil, al-Ta'bia al-Urduniyya Didd al-Muqawama al-Filastiniyya Qabl Hajmat September 1970, *Shuun Filastiniyya*, No. 4, September 1971.

al-Hut, Shafiq, Itlala Ala Tahaddiyat Marhala Jadida, *Shuun Filastiniyya*, No. 28, December 1973.

Nahwa Istratijiyya Jadida, *Shuun Filastiniyya*, No. 109, December 1980.

al-Khatib, Husam, al-Thawra al-Filastiniyya: Ila Ayn? *Shuun Filastiniyya*, No. 4, September 1971.

Hudud Muqfala wa Jusur Maftuha, *Shuun Filastiniyya*, No. 21, May 1973.

al-Khalili, Ghazi, Durus Mustafada Min Tajribat al-Muqawama fi al-Urdun, *Shuun Filastiniyya*, No. 55, March 1976.

Qabla al-Khuruj min al-Urdun Waqai' wa Ahdath, *Shuun Filastiniyya*, No. 58, June 1976.

Mish'al, Shaul, Judea and Samaria: Anatomy of the Municipal Elections (Hebrew), *Hamizrah Hehadash*, Jerusalem, Vol. 1–2, 1974.

al-Muqawama al-Filastiniyya fi Wad'iha al-Rahin, Bilal al-Hasan, Shafiq al-Hut, Ghassan Kanafani, Nabil Sha'ath, *Shuun Filastiniyya*, No. 2, May 1971.

Sakhnini, Isam, al-Filastiniyyun fi al-Iraq, *Shuun Filastiniyya*, No. 13, September 1972.

al-Kiyan al-Filastini 1964–1974, *Shuun Filastiniyya*, No. 41–42, January–February 1975.

Mukawwanat al-Qarar fi al-Majlis al-Watani al-Filastini, *Shuun Filas-*

tiniyya, No. 35, July 1974.

Muhawala Ula fi Utruhat Sharq al-Urdun al-Filastiniyya, *Shuun Filastiniyya*, No. 49, September 1975.

al-Salih, Isam, Siyasat al-Malik Husayn al-Filastiniyya, *Shuun Filastiniyya*, No. 23, July 1973.

Sha'ath, Nabil, Filastin al-Ghad, *Shuun Filastiniyya*, No. 2, May 1971.

Taqrir Khass, on the Palestinian Popular Congress, *Shuun Filastiniyya*, No. 9, May 1972.

al-Thawra al-Filastiniyya wa al-Taswiya al-Siyasiyya, *Shuun Filastiniyya*, No. 23, July 1973, pp. 4–11.

Shafiq, Munir, Limadha Yarfud al-Filastiniyyun Mashru' al-Dawla al-Filastiniyya, *Shuun Filastiniyya*, No. 7, March 1972.

Hawla al-Wahda al-Wataniyya al-Filastiniyya, *Shuun Filastiniyya*, No. 41–42, January–February 1975.

Ma'rakat al-Karama, *Shuun Filastiniyya*, No. 19, March 1973.

Special Supplement, *Shuun Filastiniyya*, No. 9, May 1972.

Shay, Avi, The Egyptian Army 1956–1967 (Hebrew). Part I, *Ma'rakhot*, Tel Aviv, No. 227, January 1973, Part II, *Ma'rakhot*, No. 228, March 1973.

Towards the Yom Kippur War: Aims of the War and the Plan of the Attack (Hebrew), *Ma'rakhot*, Tel Aviv, No. 250, July 1976.

al-Shu'aybi, Isa, Ashr Sanawat min al-Sira' Bayna al-Hikm al-Urduni wa Munazzamat al-Tahrir al-Filastiniyya, *Shuun Filastiniyya*, No. 41–42, January–February 1975.

Sirhan, Basim, Shuhada al-Thawra al-Filastiniyya, *Shuun Filastiniyya*, No. 9, May 1972.

Teveth, Shabtai, The West Bank after Five Years (Hebrew), *Ha'aretz*, 8,15,22.9.72.

Vardi, Raphael, The Policy towards the West Bank: Past and Present (Hebrew), *Ha'aretz*, 11,12,13,15.4.82.

Yizhar, Michael, Political Aspects of the Municipal Elections (Hebrew), *Medina ve-Mimshal*, Jerusalem, Vol. 4, 1974.

Yona, Lieutenant-Colonel, Nasir's Struggle Policy (Hebrew), *Ma'rakhot*, Tel Aviv, No. 223, June 1972.

Zak, Moshe, On the Meetings with Husayn (Hebrew), *Ma'ariv*, Tel Aviv, 31.3.80, 6.4.80.

Index